P9-DDI-704

OUTSTANDING STATEMENTS ON AUDITING STANDARDS

SAS No.	Title	AU Section
60	Communication of Internal Control Related Matters Noted in an Audit	325
61	Communication with Audit Committees	380
62	Special Reports	623
64	Omnibus Statement on Auditing Standards – 1990	341; 508; 543
65	The Auditor's Consideration of the Internal Audit Function in an Audit of Financial Statements	322
67	The Confirmation Process	330
69	The Meaning of *Present Fairly in Conformity with Generally Accepted Accounting Principles* in the Independent Auditor's Report	411
70	Reports on the Processing of Transactions by Service Organizations	324
71	Interim Financial Information	722
72	Letters for Underwriters and Certain Other Requesting Parties	634
73	Using the Work of a Specialist	336
74	Compliance Auditing Considerations in Audits of Governmental Entities and Recipients of Governmental Financial Assistance	801
75	Engagements to Apply Agreed-Upon Procedures to Specified Elements, Accounts, or Items of a Financial Statement	622
76	Amendments to Statement on Auditing Standards No. 72, *Letters for Underwriters and Certain Other Requesting Parties*	634; AT 300
77	Amendments to Statements on Auditing Standards No. 22, *Planning and Supervision*, No. 59, *The Auditor's Consideration of an Entity's Ability to Continue as a Going Concern*, and No. 62, *Special Reports*	311; 341; 544; 623
78	Consideration of Internal Control in a Financial Statement Audit: An Amendment to Statement on Auditing Standards No. 55	110; 319; 324; 325
79	Amendment to Statement on Auditing Standards No. 58, *Reports on Audited Financial Statements*	508
80	Amendment to Statement on Auditing Standards No. 31, *Evidential Matter*	326
81	Auditing Investments	332
82	Consideration of Fraud in a Financial Statement Audit	110; 230; 312; 316
83	Establishing an Understanding with the Client	310
84	Communications between Predecessor and Successor Auditors	315
85	Management Representations	333
86	Amendment to Statement on Auditing Standards No. 72, *Letters to Underwriters and Certain Other Parties*	634
87	Restricting the Use of the Auditor's Report	532

AUDITING & ASSURANCE SERVICES

A SYSTEMATIC APPROACH

AUDITING & ASSURANCE SERVICES

A SYSTEMATIC APPROACH

Second Edition

William F. Messier, Jr.
Deloitte & Touche Professor
School of Accountancy
Georgia State University

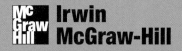

Boston   Burr Ridge, IL   Dubuque, IA   Madison, WI   New York   San Francisco   St. Louis   Bangkok   Bogotá
Caracas   Lisbon   London   Madrid   Mexico City   Milan   New Delhi   Seoul   Singapore   Sydney   Taipei   Toronto

McGraw-Hill Higher Education ⚡

*A Division of The **McGraw-Hill** Companies*

AUDITING AND ASSURANCE SERVICES: A SYSTEMATIC APPROACH

Copyright © 2000, 1997 by The McGraw-Hill Companies, Inc. All rights reserved. Printed in the United States of America. Except as permitted under the United States Copyright Act of 1976, no part of this publication may be reproduced or distributed in any form or by any means, or stored in a data base or retrieval system, without the prior written permission of the publisher.

This book is printed on acid-free paper.

domestic   1 2 3 4 5 6 7 8 9 0 DOW/DOW 9 0 9 8 7 6 5 4 3 2 1 0 9
international   1 2 3 4 5 6 7 8 9 0 DOW/DOW 9 0 9 8 7 6 5 4 3 2 1 0 9

ISBN 0-07-290828-9

Vice president/Editor-in-chief: *Michael W. Junior*
Publisher: *Jeffrey J. Shelstad*
Developmental editor: *Tracey Klein Douglas*
Senior marketing manager: *Rhonda Seelinger*
Project manager: *Amy Hill*
Senior production supervisor: *Lori Koetters*
Freelance design coordinator: *Laurie J. Entringer*
Supplement coordinator: *Rose M. Range*
Compositor: *Shepherd Incorporated*
Typeface: *10/12 New Aster*
Printer: *R. R. Donnelley & Sons Company*

Library of Congress Cataloging-in-Publication Data
Messier, William F.
     Auditing: a systematic approach / William F. Messier, Jr. — 2nd ed.
        p.   cm.
     Includes index.
     ISBN 0–07–290828–9
     1. Auditing.   I. Title.
HF5667.M46   1999
657'.45—dc21   98–49843

INTERNATIONAL EDITION   ISBN 0-07-116970-9

Copyright © 2000. Exclusive rights by The McGraw-Hill Companies, Inc. for manufacture and export.
This book cannot be re-exported from the country to which it is consigned by McGraw-Hill.
The International Edition is not available in North America.

http://www.mhhe.com

This book is dedicated to my wife, Teddie

and my children, Stacy and Mark

for their support, encouragement, and love.

About the Author

Professor William F. Messier, Jr., is the Deloitte & Touche Professor at the School of Accountancy, Georgia State University. He holds a Professor II position at the Institute for Accounting and Auditing, Norwegian School of Economics and Business Administration, and he is a visiting professor at SDA Bocconi in Milan, Italy. Professor Messier has a BBA from Siena College, an MS from Clarkson University, and an MBA and DBA from Indiana University. He is a CPA in Florida and has taught at the Universities of Florida and Michigan.

Professor Messier has served as the Chairperson of the Auditing Section of the American Accounting Association and as co-editor of the *Journal of Accounting Literature.* He currently serves on the AICPA's International Auditing Standards Subcommittee. Professor Messier has authored or coauthored over 45 articles in accounting, decision science, and computer science journals.

Contents in Brief

CONTENTS

14   Auditing Selected Asset Accounts: Prepaid Expenses and Property, Plant, and Equipment   511

Preface

In recent years, tremendous changes have affected the practice of public accounting. Changes in technology, including the extraordinary growth of electronic commerce, have increased the speed with which information is transmitted within and between entities. This has allowed corporations to more easily expand their activities globally. Two other issues have more directly affected the public accounting profession. First, there has been a growing demand by various groups for auditors to assume more responsibility as part of their role in society. The profession has responded to this challenge by issuing an auditing standard that has increased the auditor's responsibility to detect fraud. Second, there is a growing emphasis for auditors to provide assurance services, including assurance on information system reliability, electronic commerce, and health care performance measurement. These types of services build on the auditor's traditional attributes of competence, objectivity, and independence. Although these new services are likely to be a major source of revenues for public accounting firms, it must be remembered that financial statement audits still represent a major, ongoing source of revenues for public accounting firms, and many of our students will continue to be heavily involved in financial statement audits. Such changes and events represent challenges for auditors; they also offer significant opportunities for auditors to contribute to the effective and efficient flow of information and capital in our society.

The changes impacting the profession require that students thoroughly understand the audit process, broadly defined to include assurance services. I believe that this is best accomplished by having students understand the basic concepts that underlie the audit process and how to apply those concepts to various audit and assurance services. The second edition of *Auditing and Assurance Services: A Systematic Approach* contains a number of significant changes and revisions that respond to this changing environment. First, Chapter 1 contains a more detailed overview of the relationship between assurance, attestation, and auditing services, while Chapter 21 covers assurance and attestation engagements. Second, Chapter 3 has been revised to include a much broader view of the auditor's risk assessment process consistent with current practice. The chapter includes detailed discussion of client business risk. Third, the book includes a new case for a mail-order retailer, EarthWear Clothiers, that is used throughout the book to demonstrate important concepts. There are Internet home pages for EarthWear and its auditors. EarthWear's home page has assurance provided through a CPA *WebTrust*^{SM} engagement. Last, the book has a new design format, more extensive learning objectives, and Internet problems.

As the title indicates, the book takes a *systematic approach* to the audit process by first introducing the three basic concepts that underlie the audit process: *materiality, audit risk,* and *evidence.* These concepts are then applied to each major accounting cycle and related account balances using a risk-based approach. For example, each accounting cycle chapter starts with an overview of the information system followed by a discussion of inherent risk factors that are relevant for the cycle and account balances. The assessment of control risk is then described, followed by discussion of the nature, timing, and extent of evidence necessary to reach the appropriate level of detection risk.

In covering these important concepts and their applications, the book focuses on the decision-making processes followed by auditors. Much of auditing practice involves the use of auditor judgment. If a student understands these basic concepts and how to apply them on an audit engagement, he or she will know how to practice in today's dynamic audit environment.

The book can be used in a one-semester or one-quarter introductory auditing or assurance services course, or in a two-course sequence at the undergraduate and graduate levels. It can also be used in introductory professional development courses for CPAs, internal auditors, and government auditors.

Organization

Auditing and Assurance Services: A Systematic Approach is divided into eight parts:

Part	Description	Chapters
I	Introduction to Auditing and Assurance Services	1–2
II	Basic Auditing Concepts: Materiality, Audit Risk, and Evidence	3–4
III	Planning the Audit and Understanding Internal Control	5–7
IV	Statistical Tools for Auditing	8–9
V	Auditing Accounting Applications and Related Accounts	10–16
VI	Completing the Audit and Reporting Responsibilities	17–18
VII	Professional Responsibilities	19–20
VIII	Assurance, Attestation, and Other Forms of Services	21

Part I: Introduction to Auditing and Assurance Services

This part of the textbook introduces auditing, attestation, and assurance services. Chapter 1 covers auditing by discussing the demand for auditing services; the relationship between auditing, attestation, and assurance services; the types of audit engagements and types of auditors; the public accounting profession; issues faced by the profession; organizations that impact the profession; and auditing standards. Chapter 1 also describes EarthWear Clothiers, a fictitious company based on a real-world entity. This case is used throughout the text to demonstrate important concepts. EarthWear and its auditors have home pages that can be used for various case assignments. Chapter 2 provides a unique overview of financial statement audits. It presents the management assertions contained in financial statements and their relationship to audit objectives, the auditor's responsibility for errors and fraud, and the auditor as a business and industry expert; and it covers the three fundamental concepts that underlie the audit process: materiality, audit risk, and evidence. The chapter also includes a brief overview of sampling, ethics and independence, and audit reporting.

Part II: Basic Auditing Concepts: Materiality, Audit Risk, and Evidence

Part II provides detailed coverage of the three basic concepts that underlie the audit process. Chapter 3 discusses materiality and audit risk and their role in the auditor's decision-making process. The audit risk model is also presented in this chapter, including a discussion of client business risk. Chapter 4 provides detailed coverage of the concepts related to evidential matter, including the various types of audit evidence used by auditors and the basics of working paper documentation.

Part III: Planning the Audit and Understanding Internal Control

Part III is devoted to audit planning and understanding internal control. Chapter 5 outlines an organized approach to audit planning and describes the different types of audit tests, with detailed coverage of analytical procedures. Chapter 6 covers the auditor's consideration of internal control when planning and performing an audit, including the basic framework for assessing control risk. Chapter 7 extends the coverage of internal control to include the effect of information technology on the audit and discusses the tools available to the auditor for auditing in an information technology environment.

Part IV: Statistical Tools for Auditing

This part of the book presents the application of statistical and nonstatistical sampling techniques to auditing. Chapter 8 contains an overview of the types of audit sampling, the requirements of auditing standards, and the use of attribute sampling as applied to tests of controls. Chapter 9 applies statistical sampling to testing account balances and focuses on the use of monetary-unit sampling. Classical variable sampling techniques are covered in the appendix to Chapter 9.

Part V: Auditing Accounting Applications and Related Accounts

Part V describes the application of internal control concepts and evidence-gathering procedures to various accounting cycles. Chapters 10–16 discuss inherent risk considerations, the assessment of control risk, and substantive testing for each accounting cycle and its related account balances.

Part VI: Completing the Audit and Reporting Responsibilities

Part VI focuses on the steps followed at the end of the audit and provides expanded coverage of audit reporting. Chapter 17 discusses contingent liabilities, commitments, and subsequent events, and also describes the final evidential evaluation process followed by the auditor. Chapter 18 presents the details of audit reporting and covers a number of special reporting issues.

**Part VII:
Professional
Responsibilities**

Part VII is devoted to the auditor's professional responsibilities. Chapter 19 reviews the Code of Professional Conduct and quality control standards. Chapter 20 discusses the legal environment that confronts the auditing profession.

**Part VIII:
Assurance,
Attestation, and
Other Forms
of Services**

Part VIII covers assurance services, including the demand for such services. It also presents detailed examples of two assurance services. Chapter 21 introduces the attestation standards, describes two attestation services, and discusses accounting and review services.

Distinguishing Features of This Text

Auditing and Assurance Services: A Systematic Approach has a number of important features:

- The text takes a systematic approach to the audit process by building on the basic concepts of materiality, audit risk, and evidential matter.
- The text follows a risk-based approach to auditing with materiality and audit risk presented in a manner that is consistent with auditing standards and current practice.
- A cycles approach is followed, with the components of the audit risk model addressed in each cycle chapter.
- The discussion of internal control in each accounting cycle assumes some level of computerization. As a result, the effect of computer processing on the audit is introduced immediately after, and as an extension of, the consideration of internal control. The use of IT audit techniques is presented as a part of the discussion of auditing each accounting cycle and account balance.
- An overview of sampling is presented at the beginning of Chapter 8 to give the student a frame of reference for studying statistical and nonstatistical sampling techniques. The two chapters on sampling also present the use of microcomputer software for statistical sampling applications.
- The end-of-chapter materials contain review questions, multiple-choice questions from CPA examinations, and problems. The review questions allow students to quickly test their knowledge of the learning objectives for each chapter. The multiple-choice questions provide a sound basis for testing the chapter material included on the CPA examination. The problems are drawn from the CPA and CIA examinations and from problems developed by the author.
- Most chapters also contain Internet assignments and discussion cases. The Internet assignments involve solving problems related to the EarthWear case and gathering various types of accounting and

industry information. Many of the discussion cases were developed from real-world examples and require the student to research the answers using various information sources.
- The text can easily incorporate the use of the Simulated Case for Audit Decision Making (SCAD).

Integrated Case

The book contains a new integrated case company, EarthWear, which is introduced in Chapter 1. This case is based on a real-world company and is used to demonstrate important auditing concepts throughout the book. A home page for the company contains extensive information on EarthWear, and a home page for the company's auditors contains extensive audit-related information. These pages can be accessed from *www.mhhe.com/earthwear* and *www.mhhe.com/willisandadams*. There are also numerous problems and Internet assignments related to EarthWear throughout the text. The Calabro Paging Services case that was included in the first edition has been shortened and included as a discussion problem in Chapter 3. It is also used in various chapters to demonstrate important concepts with an alternative industry. A number of problems in the book are based on the Calabro case.

Supplements

- The **Instructor's Manual** (0-07-290830-0) includes the author's suggestions on an approach to teaching the material in each chapter, an outline of the topics, and other instructional aids.
- **Ready Shows** (0-07-233236-0) PowerPoint® slides are available for each chapter. This allows the instructor to use the PowerPoint® presentation in the classroom or use the slides as overheads.
- The **Solutions Manual** (0-07-290829-7) contains thorough, up-to-date solutions to the book's end-of-chapter materials.
- The **Test Bank** (0-07-290831-9) includes additional multiple-choice questions adapted from professional examinations. All test questions are available in a computerized format, **Computest** (0-07-231745-0). Professors may use this software to create, edit, and print a variety of tests. All of the instructor supplements are available on an **Instructor's CD-ROM** (0-07-231747-7).
- **Ready Notes** (0-07-290832-7), a new supplement for students, contains PowerPoint® screen printouts to facilitate note-taking during a PowerPoint® presentation.
- *Communication for Accountants: Effective Strategies for Students and Professionals* (0-07-038390-1), authored by Maurice Hirsch of Southern Illinois University–Carbondale and Susan Gabriel and Rob Anderson, both of St. Louis University, is a brief and inexpensive handbook that addresses the need for accountants to communicate effectively through both writing and speaking.

```
┌──────────────────────────────────────────────────────────────────────────┐
│ □                                                                      ▣▤ │
│  ◄      ►      ✖      C      ⌂      ◎      ◔      ✳      A      A      ▤    │
│ Back  Forward  Stop  Refresh  Home  Search  Mail  Favorites Larger Smaller Preferences   e │
│ Address: ▼  http://www.mhhe.com/messier                                    │
├──────────────────────────────────────────────────────────────────────────┤
│                         EARTHWEAR CLOTHIERS                                 │
│                       Consolidated Balance Sheet                           │
│                          December 31, 2000                                 │
│                            (In thousands)                                  │
│                                                                            │
│                               Assets                                       │
│  ──────────────────────────────────────────────────────────────────────   │
│  Cash and cash equivalents                                    $   41,772   │
│  Receivables                                                       3,933   │
│  Inventory                                                        64,100   │
│                                                                            │
└──────────────────────────────────────────────────────────────────────────┘
```

- The **Web site (www.mhhe.com/messier)** serves as an extension of the text, and from it students and instructors can access regularly undated materials that include applications of auditing practices, a link to the EarthWear annual report, downloadable supplements, and links to industry sites and information sources.

Acknowledgments and Development Focus

I would like to acknowledge the American Institute of Certified Public Accountants for permission to quote from auditing standards, the Code of Professional Conduct, the Uniform CPA Examination, and the *Journal of Accountancy.* I would also like to thank Bill Kinney and the PricewaterhouseCoopers LLP Foundation for granting permission to use selected case materials, and for providing permission to use PW STAT in Chapters 8 and 9.

We have received extensive feedback from users and nonusers of the first edition. Our market research included surveys and reviews, and the valuable suggestions provided by that process helped us develop and enhance the product. Thank you to the following colleagues for the invaluable advice:

Reviewers:

Ron Abrahams, *University of Northern Iowa*
Pervaiz Alam, *Kent State University*
Elizabeth Dreike Almer, *University of Miami*
Barbara Apostolou, *Louisiana State University*
Stephen Casper, *Northern Illinois University*
Jan Colbert, *Western Kentucky University*
James Crockett, *University of Southern Mississippi*
William Dilla, *University of Missouri—St. Louis*
William Felix, *University of Arizona*
Stephen Goldberg, *Grand Valley State University*
James Hansen, *North Dakota State University*
Ko-Cheng Hsu, *University of South Alabama*
Raymond Johnson, *Portland State University*
Charles Klemstine, *University of Michigan*
W. Robert Knechel, *University of Florida*
Joseph Larkin, *St Joseph's University*
Malcolm Lathan, *University of Virginia*
Mark Linville, *Washington State University*
Charles Malone, *North Carolina A&T University*
Theodore Mock, *University of Southern California*
Katherine Moffeit, *Southwest Texas State University*
Donald McConnell, *University of Texas at Arlington*
James Mutchler, *Pennsylvania State University*
Frederick Neumann, *University of Illinois*
David Plumlee, *University of Kansas*
Lawrence Ponemon, *State University of New York at Binghamton*
Robert Ramsay, *University of Kentucky*
James Rebele, *Lehigh University*
Alan Reinstein, *Wayne State University*
John Rigsby, *Mississippi State University*
Richard Rogers, *Indiana University at Indianapolis*
Michael Ruble, *Western Washington University*
Eric Spires, *Ohio State University*
Mark Taylor, *University of Nebraska at Lincoln*
Scott Whisenant, *Georgetown University*

Survey Respondents:

Marvin Albin, *University of Southern Mississippi*
Jack Armitage, *University of Nebraska at Omaha*
Vicky Arnold, *University of Massachusetts—Dartmouth*
Jane Baird, *Mankato State University*
Nancy Baldiga, *College of the Holy Cross*
Peter Battelle, *University of Vermont*
Douglas Beets, *Wake Forest University*
Frank Buckless, *North Carolina State University*
Homer Burkett, *University of Mississippi*
Freddie Choo, *San Francisco State University*
Raymond Clay, *University of North Texas*
Paul Clikeman, *University of Richmond*
Gary Colbert, *University of Colorado at Denver*
Janet Colbert, *Western Kentucky University*
William Coyle, *Babson College*
Jefferson Davis, *Clarkson University*
William Dent, *University of Texas at Dallas*
Todd DeZoort, *University of South Carolina*
David Donnelly, *Kansas State University*
Martha Doran, *San Diego State University*
William Felix, *University of Arizona*
Timothy Fogarty, *Case Western Reserve University*
Karl Fraedrich, *University of Wisconsin—Whitewater*
Lori Fuller, *University of Delaware*
Lyal Gustafson, *University of Wisconsin—Whitewater*
James Hansen, *North Dakota State University*
Robert Harrington, *Fort Lewis College*
Don Herrmann, *Oregon State University*
Doris Holt, *George Mason University*
Stanley Jenne, *University of Montana*
Mark Kaiser, *Plattsburgh State University*
Joyce Kilpatrick, *Austin Peay State University*
Marilyn Kintzele, *Indiana University at Kokomo*
Konrad Kubin, *Virginia Polytechnic Institute and State University*

Joshua Livnat, *New York University*
Jordan Lowe, *University of Nevada Las Vegas*
Frank Marino, *Assumption College*
Alan Mayper, *University of North Texas*
John McEldowney, *University of North Florida*
Robert Moffie, *North Carolina Central University*
William Nealon, *Union College*
Edwin Nelson, *University of New Hampshire*
Jack Paul, *Lehigh University*
Ceil Pillsbury, *University of Wisconsin—Milwaukee*
Steven Platau, *University of Tampa*
Alan Reinstein, *Wayne State University*
Cynthia Rooney, *Xavier University*
Cindy Seipel, *New Mexico State University*
Ira Solomon, *University of Illinois*
Linda Specht, *Trinity University*
Victor Stanton, *California State University—Hayward*
William Thomas, *Baylor University*
Forrest Thompson, *Florida A&M University*
Richard Turpen, *University of Alabama at Birmingham*
John Wermert, *Drake University*
Tommy Wooten, *Belmont University*
Gregory Yost, *University of West Florida*
Douglas Ziegenfuss, *Old Dominion University*

A special thanks to Steven Mintz, California State University—San Bernardino, for his comments on the Code of Professional Conduct and Zoe-Vonna Palmrose, University of Southern California, for her helpful comments on legal liability.

I also want to thank the editorial staff at Irwin/McGraw-Hill—Jeff Shelstad, Tracey Douglas, Rhonda Seelinger, Amy Hill, Lori Koetters, Laurie Entringer, and Rose Range—for their assistance and guidance in the production of this book.

William F. Messier, Jr.

AUDITING & ASSURANCE SERVICES

SERVICES   A SYSTEMATIC APPROACH

INTRODUCTION TO AUDITING AND ASSURANCE SERVICES

Chapter 1

An Introduction to Auditing and Assurance Services

LEARNING OBJECTIVES

Upon completion of this chapter you will

[1] Understand why there is a demand for auditing.

[2] Understand the relationships among auditing, attestation, and assurance services.

[3] Know the different types of audits.

[4] Know the different types of auditors.

[5] Understand the public accounting profession.

[6] Identify the organizations that affect financial statement audits.

[7] Know generally accepted auditing standards and their relationship to Statements on Auditing Standards.

RELEVANT ACCOUNTING AND AUDITING PRONOUNCEMENTS

SAS No. 1, "Responsibilities and Functions of the Independent Auditor" (AU 110)

SAS No. 1, "Generally Accepted Auditing Standards" (AU 150)

SSAE No. 1, "Attestation Standards" (AT 100)

Reliable information is necessary if managers, investors, creditors, and regulatory agencies are to make informed decisions about resource allocation. Auditing plays an important role in this process by providing objective and independent reports on the reliability of information. The following examples present situations where auditing enters into economic transactions and increases the reliability and credibility of an entity's financial statements:

Jay Johnstone is the owner of a small auto parts distributor. His one-store operation has been very profitable. He financed his current store mainly from personal savings and some borrowings from his family. Mr. Johnstone would like to expand his operations by opening two stores in nearby towns. Mr. Johnstone approached his local bank to request the necessary financing. He provided the loan officer with a set of financial statements that he prepared with the assistance of his bookkeeper. The loan officer informed Mr. Johnstone that because of the amount of the requested financing and his lack of prior credit with the bank, he would have to have his company's financial statements audited by an independent public accountant. Based on the

company's financial performance and prospects and the credibility added by the auditor's report, the bank granted the loan.

Sara Thompson, a local community activist, has been operating a not-for-profit center that provides assistance to abused women and their children. She has financed most of her operations from private contributions. Ms. Thompson has applied to the state Health and Human Services Department requesting a large grant to expand her two shelters to accommodate more women. In completing the grant application, Ms. Thompson discovered that the state's laws for government grants require that recipients have their financial statements audited prior to the final granting of funds. Ms. Thompson hired a CPA to audit the center's financial statements. Based on the center's activities, the intended use of the funds, and the auditor's report, the grant was approved.

Conway Computer Company has been a successful wholesaler of computer peripheral products such as disk drives and tape backup systems. The company was started by George and Jimmy Steinbuker five years ago. Two years ago, a venture capital firm provided needed capital for expansion by acquiring 40 percent of the company. Conway Computer has been very successful, with revenues and profits increasing by 25 percent in each of the last two years. The Steinbuker brothers and the venture capital firm are considering taking the company public through a stock sale. They have contacted a number of underwriters about the public offering. The underwriters have informed the company that the company's financial statements will need to be audited by a major public accounting firm before a registration statement can be filed with the Securities and Exchange Commission. The company hired a major public accounting firm. Subsequently, the company successfully sold stock to the public.

These situations show the importance of auditing to both private and public enterprise. By adding the audit function to each situation, the users of the financial statements have reasonable assurance that the financial statements do not contain material misstatements or omissions.

Auditors can also provide valuable assurance in other types of situations. Consider the following example:

EarthWear Clothiers has been a successful mail-order retailer of high-quality clothing for outdoor sports. The company is interested in developing sales through an Internet site. Marketing research indicated that consumers were reluctant to provide credit card information over the Internet because of security concerns. EarthWear discussed this issue with its public accounting firm, Willis & Adams. Willis & Adams accountants were aware that a new service, called CPA *WebTrust,* had been developed by the American Institute of Certified Public Accountants (AICPA). The *WebTrust* seal of assurance indicates to potential customers that a CPA has evaluated the Web site's business practices and controls to determine whether they conform to *WebTrust* Principles and Criteria for Business-to-Consumer Electronic Commerce. These principles and criteria relate mainly to business practices, transaction integrity, and information protection. Willis & Adams conducted a *WebTrust* assurance engagement for EarthWear and issued an unqualified report. The *WebTrust* symbol was then added to EarthWear's Web site.

Services like *WebTrust* build on the auditor's historical approach to audits by going beyond standard reporting on financial statements to provide assurance on information that is not only reliable, but relevant and timely.

This is both an interesting and a challenging time to be studying auditing. Numerous forces are affecting the auditing profession. An audit of financial statements increases the reliability of information for users, reduces the cost of capital for entities, and generates a stable source of revenues for public accounting firms. However, critics have charged that the cur-

rent audit has failed to meet user expectations regarding (1) the detection of fraud, (2) treatment of financial distress and going concern issues, and (3) treatment of risks, uncertainties, and estimates. The auditing profession has responded to these criticisms by issuing standards and guidance that address each of these issues.

In recent years, auditors have been asked to expand their services into areas beyond the traditional audit of financial statements. These areas include services such as examination of forecasts and projections, reporting on internal control, and compliance with statutory, regulatory, and contractual requirements. Additionally, auditors have created new services that provide assurance on business risk assessment, business performance measurement, health care performance measurement, and elder care. Such services are valuable to users because auditors can report *independently* and *objectively* on various types of activities and events. These types of engagements create opportunities for auditors to expand their services into new areas.

Information technology is also affecting auditing. New technologies are altering the way information is acquired, stored, processed, and disseminated. Business entities can conduct transactions with suppliers and customers electronically using electronic data interchange (EDI), and consumers can purchase products and services over the Internet. Many companies (such as Intel and Microsoft) place their annual reports and other financial information on their home pages. Additionally, new sources of information that are useful in evaluating the financial position and performance of an entity are available electronically. This information can be accessed on a more timely basis than the information contained in an entity's annual report. The Elliott Committee has suggested that, in the future, auditing will move from a "one size fits all" report prepared on annual financial statements to continuous assurance on a set of real-time financial and nonfinancial information.[1] Such changes will provide the auditing profession with opportunities to offer services (such as *WebTrust*) related to information systems reliability and electronic commerce.

Most readers of an introductory auditing text have little understanding of what an audit entails. This chapter starts by analyzing why there is a demand for auditing and discussing auditing, attestation, and assurance services. Next, the types of audits and auditors are presented. The remainder of this chapter provides information on the public accounting profession and the major organizations that affect the activities of independent auditors.

---

[1]See the Special Committee on Assurance Services Report on the Future of the Financial Statement Audit (http:// aicpa.org/assurance/scas/comstud/futfinst/index.htm) for a detailed discussion of the changing audit paradigm.

The Demand for Auditing[2]

[LO 1]   An important question a student might ask is "Why do entities request an audit?" The answer to this question can be found in the economic relationships both within an entity, and between the entity and other parties that have a vested interest in the entity. A historic relationship exists between accounting and auditing in entities. For example, evidence shows that some forms of accounting and auditing existed in early Greece in approximately 500 BC.[3] Until the late 18th and early 19th centuries most organizations were relatively small and were owned and operated as sole proprietorships or partnerships. However, the birth of modern accounting and auditing occurred during the industrial revolution, when corporations needed to raise capital to finance expansion.[4] Corporations issued stocks and bonds to the public and borrowed funds from financial institutions. Thus, the growth of the modern corporation led to the presence of absentee owners (stockholders) and the use of professional managers who ran the corporation on a day-to-day basis. In this setting, the managers served as *agents* for the stockholders (referred to as *principals*) and fulfilled a *stewardship* function by managing the corporation's assets.

Accounting and auditing play an important role in this principal–agent relationship. First, the agency relationship between an owner and manager produces a natural *conflict of interest* because of the information asymmetry that exists between the manager and the absentee owner. *Information asymmetry* means that the manager generally has more information about the "true" financial position and results of operations of the entity than the absentee owner does. If both parties seek to maximize their own self-interest, it is likely that the manager will not act in the best interest of the owner. For example, the manager may spend entity funds to provide excessive personal benefits or manipulate the reported earnings in order to earn a larger bonus. The owner can protect himself or herself against such activities by adjusting the manager's compensation by the amount of such perquisites that the owner expects the manager to consume. In an attempt to compensate for this possibility, the manager may agree to some type of monitoring provisions in his or her employment contract. For example, the two parties may agree that the manager will periodically report on how well he or she has managed the owner's assets. The reporting of this financial information to the owner generally follows some agreed-upon accounting principles.

However, because the manager is responsible for reporting and the absentee owner cannot observe the manager's actions, the manager may manipulate the reports. The owner is price-protected against this possibility by again assuming that the manager will manipulate the reports to his or

---

[2]See G. L. Sundem, R. E. Dukes, and J. A. Elliott, *The Value of Information and Audits* (New York: Coopers & Lybrand, 1996), for a more detailed discussion of the demand for accounting information and auditing.

[3]G. J. Costouros, "Auditing in the Athenian State of the Golden Age (500–300 BC)," *The Accounting Historian Journal* (Spring 1978), pp. 41–50.

[4]See M. Chatfield, *A History of Accounting Thought* (Hinsdale, IL.: Dryden Press, 1974), for a discussion of the historical development of accounting and auditing.

her benefit and by adjusting the manager's compensation accordingly. It is at this point that the demand for auditing arises. If the manager is honest and the cost of an audit does not exceed the amount by which the owner may adjust the manager's compensation, it is in the manager's self-interest to hire an auditor to monitor his or her activities. The auditor's role is determining whether the reports prepared by the manager conform to the contract's provisions. Thus, the auditor's verification of the financial information adds credibility to the report. While auditing is one possible form of additional monitoring, the extensive presence of auditing in such contracts suggests that auditing is a cost-effective monitoring device. Figure 1–1 provides an overview of this agency relationship.

These same ideas apply to other relationships that involve the entity. Debtholders have similar concerns about management when lending money to the entity. For example, how can a debtholder prevent management from taking the borrowed funds and using them for its own purposes? One way is to place restrictive covenants in the debt agreement that must be complied with by the entity and its management. Many times, such debt agreements require a separate audit opinion that reports on the entity's compliance with the debt covenants.

Similar economic relationships exist within the entity between the employer and employees. Employers use various forms of auditing to monitor the activities of their employees. For example, an employee may be given a

FIGURE 1–1

Overview of the Agency Relationship Leading to the Demand for Auditing

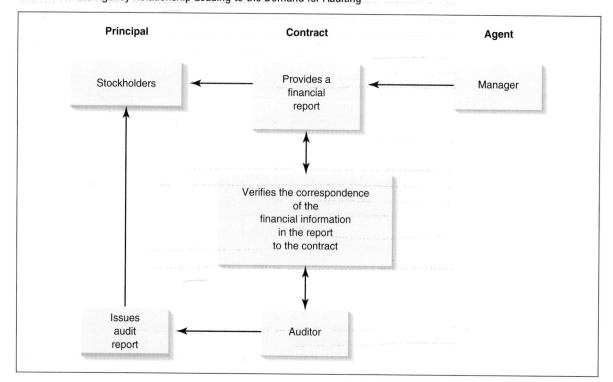

budget to limit or control his or her actions. Periodically, this employee is required to report how actual results compare to budgeted results. The employer can use such reports to monitor the employee's actions to ensure that the employee is conforming to expected behavior.

This characterization of the demand for auditing may seem quite simplistic given current audit practice. However, such a characterization does realistically portray the initial development of auditing. While some have argued that the demand for auditing resulted from regulations such as the Securities Act of 1933 and Securities Exchange Act of 1934, the empirical evidence does not support this view. One research study showed that in 1926, 82 percent of the companies on the New York Stock Exchange were audited by independent auditors.[5] Additional evidence for the demand for auditing is also provided by the fact that many private companies and municipalities, which are not subject to the securities acts, contract for audit services nonetheless.

The purpose of this section was to demonstrate that there is a demand for auditing services in a free market. While regulations such as the securities acts account for some demand, they cannot account for all of it. Auditing is demanded because it plays a valuable role in monitoring the contractual relationships between the entity and its stockholders, managers, employees, and debtholders.

Auditing, Attestation, and Assurance Services

[LO 2] While the historical demand for auditing services developed from contractual relationships between shareholders and managers, recent changes in the business environment have resulted in requests for auditors to provide services beyond traditional financial statement audits. Figure 1–2 shows the relationship among auditing, attestation, and assurance services. Auditing services are a subset of attestation services, which, in turn, are a subset of assurance services. The remainder of this section discusses each of these forms of services in more detail.

Auditing

The Committee on Basic Auditing Concepts has provided the following general definition of auditing:

> **Auditing** is a systematic process of objectively obtaining and evaluating evidence regarding assertions about economic actions and events to ascertain the degree of correspondence between those assertions and established criteria and communicating the results to interested users.[6]

A number of phrases in this definition require additional explanation. The phrase *systematic process* implies that there should be a well-planned approach for conducting an audit. This plan involves *objectively obtaining*

---

[5]G. J. Benston, "The Value of the SEC's Accounting Disclosure Requirements," *The Accounting Review* (July 1969), pp. 515–532.

[6]American Accounting Association, Committee on Basic Auditing Concepts, "A Statement of Basic Auditing Concepts" (Sarasota, FL: AAA, 1973).

The Relationship among Auditing, Attestation, and Assurance Services

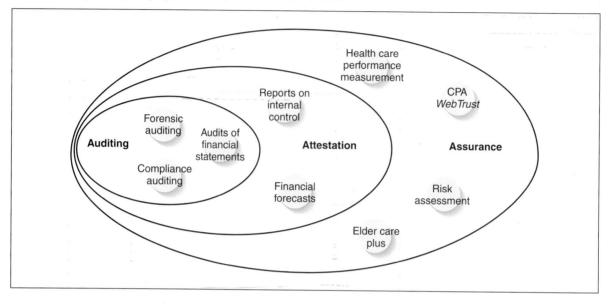

and evaluating evidence. Two activities are involved here. The auditor must *objectively search for* and *evaluate* the relevance and validity of evidence. While the type, quantity, and reliability of evidence may vary between audits, this process of gathering and evaluating evidence makes up most of the auditor's activities on an audit.

The evidence gathered by the auditor must relate to *assertions about economic actions and events.* For example, financial statements prepared by management contain numerous assertions. If the balance sheet contains an amount of $10 million for property, plant, and equipment, management is asserting that the company owns the assets, that it uses them in the production of goods and services, and that this amount represents their undepreciated historical cost. The auditor compares the evidence gathered to assertions about economic activity in order to assess *the degree of correspondence between those assertions and established criteria.* While numerous sets of criteria are available for measuring the degree of correspondence, generally accepted accounting principles (GAAP) are normally used for preparing financial statements.

The last important phrase, *communicating the results to interested users,* is concerned with the type of report the auditor provides to the intended users. The type of communication will vary depending on the type and purpose of the audit. In the case of financial statement audits, very specific types of reports communicate the auditor's findings. For other types of audits, the content and form of the reports vary with the circumstances. The intended users may include stockholders, debtholders, employees, suppliers, government agencies, stock exchanges, and other groups.

Figure 1–3 graphically presents a simplified overview of the audit function for a financial statement audit. The auditor gathers evidence about

FIGURE 1–3

An Overview of the Audit
Function for a Financial
Statement Audit

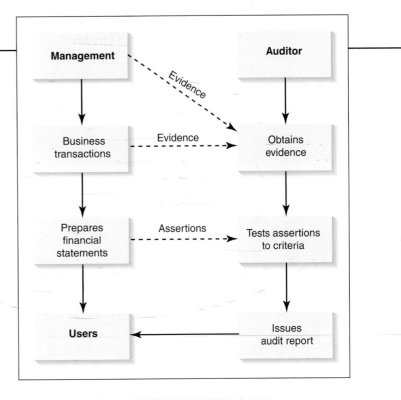

the business transactions that have occurred (economic activity and events) and about management (the preparer of the report). The auditor uses this evidence to compare the assertions contained in the financial statements to the criteria chosen by the user. The auditor's report communicates to the user the degree of correspondence between the assertions and the criteria. Compliance auditing, performance auditing, and forensic auditing (discussed later in this chapter) follow a similar process of comparing evidence against criteria (such as rules or procedures) and issuing a report on their correspondence.

Attestation

The definition of auditing provided previously was intentionally broad so that it would encompass many types of activities that may be referred to as *auditing.* Many times, the term *attestation* is used to describe the same activities as auditing. At a very general level, these terms are interchangeable because they encompass the evaluation of reliable evidence to ascertain the degree of correspondence between some assertion and some measurable criteria, and the issuance of a report indicating the degree of correspondence. Attestation standards provide the following definition for attestation:

> **Attestation** occurs when a practitioner is engaged to issue or does issue a written communication that expresses a conclusion about the reliability of a written assertion that is the responsibility of another party.

Very specific auditing standards, referred to as *generally accepted auditing standards* (GAAS), are provided for conducting financial statement audits. The profession has been asked to provide services beyond the traditional financial statement audit. In many instances, auditors found it difficult to provide such services because they were prohibited by auditing standards. The profession responded by issuing a separate set of attestation standards that are broader in scope and allow auditors to meet the demands of society. Some examples of engagements that fall under the attestation standards include

- Future-oriented financial information.
- Management's discussions and analysis.
- The description and effectiveness of internal control systems.
- Compliance with statutory, regulatory, or contractual obligations.

Chapter 21 provides detailed coverage of attestation standards and attestation engagements.

Assurance

Auditing and attestation are concerned mainly with the reliability of financial information and the credibility added by the auditor's independence and competence. The accounting profession through the work of the Special Committee on Assurance Services[7] (referred to as the "Elliott Committee"), has extended the auditing and attestation functions to include what is referred to as *assurance services*. The Special Committee on Assurance Services has defined assurance services as follows:

> **Assurance services** are independent professional services that improve the quality of information, or its context, for decision makers.

Extending auditors' activities to assurance services allows the auditor to report not only on the reliability and credibility of information but also on the *relevance* and *timeliness* of that information. Some examples of assurance services include the following:

- *Risk assessment*—assurance that the entity's profile of business risks is comprehensive and evaluation of whether the entity has appropriate systems in place to effectively manage those risks.
- *Information system reliability*—assurance that an entity's internal information systems provide reliable information for operating and financial decisions.
- *Electronic commerce*—assurance that systems and tools used in electronic commerce provide appropriate data integrity, security, privacy, and reliability.
- *Health care performance measurement*—assurance about the effectiveness of health care services provided by HMOs, hospitals, doctors, and other providers.

Chapter 21 provides extended coverage of assurance services.

---

[7] See the AICPA's home page (www.aicpa.org) for the Report of the Special Committee on Assurance Services and information on assurance services currently being offered by the AICPA.

TABLE 1–1	Relationships among the Auditing, Attestation, and Assurance Services

Service	Characteristics of Information Reported on	Definition of Service
Auditing	Reliability Credibility	A written report on an examination of financial statements for a client.
Attestation	Reliability Credibility	The expression of a conclusion about the reliability of a written assertion of another party.
Assurance	Reliability Credibility Relevance Timeliness	Professional services that improve the quality of information, or its context, for decision makers.

Table 1–1 shows the relationship among auditing, attestation, and assurance services. Note that the definitions included in Table 1–1 progress from very specific for auditing services to very general for assurance services. This text focuses on one type of auditing, financial statement audits, because it represents the major service offered by public accounting firms. However, in many instances, the approach, methods, and techniques used for financial statement audits also apply to attestation and assurance service engagements.

Types of Audits

[LO 3]   While there are many types of audits based on the definition previously provided, generally they are discussed under four types: *financial statement audits, compliance audits, operational audits,* and *forensic audits.* Each of these types of audits is discussed briefly. Excellent textbooks and articles are available that provide detailed coverage of compliance, operational, and forensic audits.[8]

Financial Statement Audits

A financial statement audit determines whether the overall financial statements present fairly in accordance with specified criteria. This type of audit usually covers the basic set of financial statements (balance sheet, income statement, statement of stockholders' equity, and a statement of cash flows), and *generally accepted accounting principles* (GAAP) serve as the criteria. However, certain financial statement audits may entail the use of other

---

[8]For example, see R. L. Ratliff, W. A. Wallace, J. K. Loebbecke, and W. G. McFarland, *Internal Auditing: Principles and Techniques,* 2nd ed. (Altamonte Springs, FL: The Institute of Internal Auditors, 1996); D. Galloway, *Internal Auditing: A Guide for the New Auditor* (Altamonte Springs, FL: The Institute of Internal Auditors, 1996); or J. T. Wells, *Fraud Examination: Investigative and Audit Procedures* (New York: Quorum Press, 1992).

criteria, such as cash basis or income tax basis. For example, many real estate partnerships prepare financial statements using an income tax basis.

Compliance Audits

A compliance audit determines the extent to which rules, policies, laws, covenants, or governmental regulations are followed by the entity being audited. For example, a company may have auditors determine whether corporate rules and policies are being followed by departments within the organization. The corporate rules and policies serve as the criteria for measuring the departments' compliance. Another example is examination of tax returns of individuals and companies by the Internal Revenue Service for compliance with the tax laws. In this example, the Internal Revenue Code provides the criteria for measuring compliance. Another example is the Single Audit Act of 1984, which requires state and local governments that receive total federal assistance equal to or greater than $300,000 in a fiscal year to have an audit performed in accordance with the act. Such audits examine whether the entity receiving federal assistance is in compliance with applicable laws or regulations.

Operational Audits

An operational audit involves a systematic review of an organization's activities, or a part of them, in relation to the *efficient* and *effective* use of resources. The purpose of an operational audit is to assess performance, identify areas for improvement, and develop recommendations. Sometimes this type of audit is referred to as a *performance audit* or *management audit*. Operational audits are generally more difficult to conduct than financial statement audits or compliance audits because it can be very difficult to identify objective, measurable criteria that can be used to assess effectiveness and efficiency.

Operational auditing has increased in importance in recent years, and it is likely that this trend will continue. With entities restructuring and downsizing, most facets of the entity are being evaluated. For example, the General Accounting Office (GAO) conducts operational audits of government programs. A recent GAO audit evaluated the effectiveness and efficiency of the Food and Drug Administration's procedures for introducing new drugs to the market. An example from the private sector would be when an entity employs auditors to assess the efficiency and effectiveness of the entity's use of computer resources.

Forensic Audits

A forensic audit's purpose is the detection or deterrence of a wide variety of fraudulent activities. The use of auditors to conduct forensic audits has grown significantly, especially where the fraud involves financial issues. Some examples where a forensic audit might be conducted include

- Business or employee fraud.[9]
- Criminal investigations.

---

[9] See J. T. Wells, *Occupational Fraud and Abuse* (Austin, TX: Obsidian, 1997), for an excellent discussion of various types of business fraud.

- Shareholder and partnership disputes.
- Business economic losses.
- Matrimonial disputes.

For example, in a business fraud engagement, an audit might involve tracing funds or asset identification and recovery. An employee fraud investigation might involve the existence, nature, extent, and identification of the perpetrator of asset misappropriation. A forensic audit can also be conducted to trace and locate assets in a divorce proceeding.

Types of Auditors

[LO 4] There are a number of different types of auditors; however, they can be classified under four headings: *external auditors, internal auditors, government auditors,* and *forensic auditors*. Each type of auditor will be discussed briefly. One important requirement of each type of auditor is independence, in some manner, from the entity being audited.

External Auditors

External auditors are often referred to as *independent auditors* or *certified public accountants* (CPAs). Such auditors are called "external" because they are not employed by the entity being audited. In this textbook, the terms external auditor, independent auditor, and CPA will be used interchangeably. External auditors audit financial statements for publicly traded and private companies, partnerships, municipalities, individuals, and other types of entities. They may also conduct compliance, operational, and forensic audits for such entities. An external auditor may practice as a sole proprietor or as a member of a CPA firm.

The CPA certificate is regulated by state law through licensing departments in each state. The requirements for becoming a CPA vary among the states, with most states requiring a four-year college degree with selected courses in business and accounting. In addition, many states require some type of professional experience before the CPA certificate is granted. All states require that an individual pass the uniform CPA examination monitored by the American Institute of Certified Public Accountants (AICPA). The AICPA has passed a resolution that those individuals applying for membership who first become eligible to take the CPA examination after the year 2000 must obtain 150 semester credit hours of education at an accredited college or university, including a bachelor's degree or its equivalent. More than 50 percent of the states have passed the 150-hour requirement.

Professional standards require that external auditors maintain their objectivity and independence when providing auditing or other attestation services for clients. Later in the text, independence and objectivity will be discussed in depth.

Internal Auditors

Auditors employed by individual companies, partnerships, government agencies, individuals, and other entities are called internal auditors. In major corporations, internal audit staffs may be very large, and the director of internal auditing is usually a major job title within the entity.

The Institute of Internal Auditors (IIA) has developed a set of standards that should be followed by internal auditors and has established a certification program. An individual meeting the certification requirements set up by the IIA, which include passing a uniform written examination, can become a certified internal auditor.[10] Many internal auditors also have a CPA certificate.

Like external auditors, internal auditors must be objective and independent. To help ensure the objectivity and independence of internal auditors, the IIA suggests that the director of internal auditing report directly to either the board of directors or the audit committee of the board or have free access to the board. If the internal auditors report to the chief financial officer or a similar financial officer within the organization, a conflict of interest may arise. Internal auditors may not be objective and independent when evaluating certain organizational functions.

Internal auditors can be involved in all four types of audits. Their primary activities are to conduct compliance and operational audits within their organizations. However, internal auditors may conduct forensic audits within the entity if necessary. Additionally, they may assist the external auditors with the annual financial statement audit.

Government Auditors

Government auditors are employed by federal, state, and local agencies. At the federal level, two agencies use auditors extensively: the General Accounting Office (GAO) and the Internal Revenue Service (IRS). The GAO is under the direction of the comptroller general of the United States and is responsible to Congress. It assists Congress in carrying out its constitutional responsibilities regarding the expenditure of public funds. GAO auditors conduct audits of activities, financial transactions, and accounts of the federal government. They also assist Congress by performing special audits, surveys, and investigations. The majority of the audits conducted by GAO auditors are compliance and operational audits. The fact that they report directly to Congress provides the GAO with an organizational arrangement that ensures the objectivity and independence needed to audit government activities.

The IRS is part of the US Treasury Department. The main activity of IRS auditors is examining and auditing the books and records of individuals and other organizations to determine their federal tax liability. IRS audits are typically compliance audits.

Two other federal agencies that conduct audits are the Army Audit Agency and the Federal Bureau of Investigation (FBI). FBI auditors, for example, frequently audit fraud in government agencies and organizations subject to federal laws.

Last, most state and local governments have auditing agencies that perform functions similar to GAO and IRS auditors.

---

[10] See the IIA's home page (www.theiia.org) for more information on the IIA and the certified internal auditor program.

Forensic Auditors

Forensic auditors are employed by corporations, government agencies, public accounting firms, and consulting and investigative services firms. They are trained in detecting, investigating, and deterring fraud and white-collar crime. Some examples of situations where forensic auditors have been involved include

- Analyzing financial transactions involving unauthorized transfers of cash between companies.
- Reconstructing incomplete accounting records to settle an insurance claim over inventory valuation.
- Proving money-laundering activities by reconstructing cash transactions.
- Embezzlement investigation and documentation, and negotiation of insurance settlements.

The Association of Certified Fraud Examiners offers a certification program for individuals to become Certified Fraud Examiners (CFE). An individual interested in becoming a CFE must pass the Uniform CFE Examination, which covers four areas: (1) fraudulent financial transactions, (2) legal elements of fraud, (3) fraud investigation, and (4) criminology and ethics. CFEs are required to follow the association's Code of Professional Ethics and meet certain continuing education requirements.[11]

The Public Accounting Profession

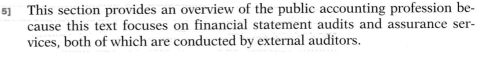 **[LO 5]** This section provides an overview of the public accounting profession because this text focuses on financial statement audits and assurance services, both of which are conducted by external auditors.

Issues Currently Affecting the Profession

The public accounting profession is currently confronting a number of important issues. This section briefly discusses five of these issues. The reader is encouraged to examine the references cited for further details.

An Expectation Gap   For some time there has been a growing recognition that differences exist between the public's expectations of the role and responsibilities of auditors and the auditor's role and responsibilities as set forth in professional auditing standards. The first explicit recognition of this problem can be found in the charge to the Commission on Auditors' Responsibilities, which was to "consider whether a gap may exist between what the public expects or needs and what auditors can and should reasonably expect to accomplish."[12] In 1988 the public accounting profession

---

[11]See the Association of Certified Fraud Examiners home page (www.acfe.org) for more information on the association and the CFE program.

[12]American Institute of Certified Public Accountants, *The Commission on Auditors' Responsibilities: Report, Conclusions, and Recommendations* (New York: AICPA, 1978).

responded to the expectation gap by issuing nine auditing standards.[13] However, there are still lingering complaints that auditors are not meeting the public's expectations. For example, many users believe that auditors are responsible for detecting *all* types of fraud and misstatements, while auditing standards state that an auditor cannot obtain *absolute* assurance that material misstatements in the financial statements will be detected.

Litigation   Recent years have seen an increase in litigation against auditors. For example, members of the largest public accounting firms issued a Statement of Position entitled "The Liability Crisis in the United States: Impact on the Accounting Profession,"[14] which spells out the extent of the problem, its potential effect on firms and the profession, and some proposed solutions. One reason for such lawsuits is that auditors are perceived as having "deep pockets," and injured parties hope to recover some or all of their losses from the auditors. The Statement of Position indicates the impact of litigation on the profession. For example, litigation-related costs represent 9 percent of the largest six public accounting firms' audit revenues in the United States, and the estimated damage claims against the entire accounting profession are estimated to be approximately $30 billion. Additionally, the seventh largest public accounting firm (Laventhol & Horwath) entered bankruptcy in 1990 with legal liabilities cited as one of the reasons for the firm's failure.[15]

The public accounting profession is attempting to resolve the litigation problem through tort reform. Congress passed the Private Securities Litigation Reform Act of 1995, which limits the financial liability of accountants for lawsuits under the federal securities acts. Litigation at the state level, however, still can be substantial.

Expanded Services   The introduction to this chapter discussed the growing demand for auditors to expand their services beyond the traditional financial statement audit. One service involves forensic auditing. While the objective of a financial statement audit is to provide an opinion on the fairness of the financial statements, auditors are also being asked to provide services that are designed to prevent and detect fraud. Such engagements may involve the auditor conducting an investigation after a fraud has been uncovered and attempting to determine the cause of the fraud and/or the extent of the loss.

---

[13]The reader is referred to American Institute of Certified Public Accountants, *Implementing the Expectation Gap Standards* (New York: AICPA, 1989), which reprints seven articles that describe the new auditing standards.

[14]Arthur Andersen & Co., Coopers & Lybrand, Deloitte & Touche, Ernst & Young, KPMG Peat Marwick, and Price Waterhouse, "The Liability Crisis in the United States: Impact on the Accounting Profession, A Statement of Position" (August 6, 1992).

[15]See L. Berton, "Laventhol & Horwath Beset by Litigation, Runs into Hard Times," *The Wall Street Journal* (May 17, 1990); P. Pae, "Laventhol Says It Plans to File for Chapter 11," *The Wall Street Journal* (November 20, 1990); and P. Pae, "Laventhol Bankruptcy Filing Indicates Liabilities May Be as Much as $2 Billion," *The Wall Street Journal* (November 23, 1990), for a discussion of the Laventhol & Horwath bankruptcy.

Another example of users requesting expanded services is reported by the AICPA Special Committee on Financial Reporting.[16] Its report indicates that users think that, in addition to reporting on the financial statements, auditors should provide additional *qualitative* commentary on the quality of a company's earnings. This might include commentary on the entity's accounting and reporting practices in relation to alternative accounting methods, reasonableness of estimates used in the financial statements, and information on risks associated with realizing recorded assets. Users also believe that there is an increased need for external auditors to focus on internal controls within the entity.

The AICPA has taken an active approach on the future of the profession through its CPA Vision Project.[17] The CPA Vision Project is a unique effort to redefine the CPA's role in an era marked by intense competition and significant changes in information technology. The Vision Project is (1) building an awareness of future opportunities and challenges for the profession, (2) leading the profession as it navigates the changing demands of the marketplace, and (3) leveraging the CPA's core competencies and values. The CPA Vision Project home page (www.cpavision.org) contains additional information on the initiatives that will lead the profession as it looks to the next 10–15 years.

Globalization   More and more business entities are involved with either the manufacture or distribution of products around the world. One public accounting firm[18] has noted the following about the global business environment:

> In today's world, distance is no longer a barrier to market entry, technologies are rapidly replicated by competitors, and information and communications technologies are shaping a new economic order. To manage their business risks effectively, organizations must now view their playing field as the whole global economy (pp. 26–27).

This firm also stated that

> Today's global economy and the business organizations operating within it, however, have become so complex and interdependent that new approaches to auditing must be developed (p. 1).

The public accounting profession is being affected by the globalization of business. While most of the major public accounting firms have international operations, the need to deliver many different services worldwide to clients has led to mergers among the major firms. Smaller firms have found it necessary to establish international affiliations or associations in order to service their clients' foreign operations. Issues have also been

---

[16]American Institute of Certified Public Accountants, Special Committee on Financial Reporting, *The Information Needs of Investors and Creditors* (New York: AICPA, 1994).

[17]See "The Vision Process," *Journal of Accountancy* (December 1998), pp. 24–73 and the CPA Vision Web site (www.cpavision.org) for more information.

[18]T. B. Bell, F. O. Marrs, I. Solomon, and H. Thomas, *Auditing Organizations Through a Strategic-Systems Lens: The KPMG Business Measurement Process* (New York: KPMG Peat Marwick LLP, 1997).

EXHIBIT 1–1

Big 6 to Merge to Big 5

The merger of Coopers & Lybrand with Price Waterhouse, and the proposed merger of Ernst & Young and KPMG Peat Marwick, appear to have been driven by increasing client demand for global professional services and industry expertise. Corporate clients are interested in "one-stop shopping" for professional services. As clients expand into new markets they expect their accounting firms to have the necessary talent and resources to provide the specialized expertise they need. This is particularly important as companies move into emerging markets such as China, Southeast Asia, the former Soviet Union, and Eastern Europe.

The merger also provides important synergies in the firms' industry and consulting practices. For example, Coopers & Lybrand has a strong practice in telecommunications that fits well with Price Waterhouse's entertainment and media practice. Additionally, the merged firms' consulting practices will be strengthened and better able to compete with Andersen Consulting.

Sources: R. Bonte-Friedheim, S. Murray, E. MacDonald, J. Lublin, and A. C. Copetas, "Consulting Industry Heats Up in Merger of Two Top Players," *The Wall Street Journal—Europe* (September 19–20, 1997); E. MacDonald, "Ernst & Young to Merge with KPMG," *The Wall Street Journal* (October 20, 1997); B. C. Inman, Letter to Accounting Faculty, Coopers & Lybrand (October 20, 1997).

raised about the diversity of accounting and auditing standards between countries. To deal with this problem, there is a strong movement to establish international accounting and auditing standards.[19]

Mergers   The last decade has witnessed a number of mergers among public accounting firms. Among the major firms, the Big 8 became the Big 5. In 1989 Deloitte, Haskins & Sells merged with another Big 8 firm, Touche Ross. This was followed in 1992 by the merger of Ernst & Whinney and Arthur Young & Co., resulting in the Big 6.[20] In 1998 Coopers & Lybrand and Price Waterhouse merged to form PricewaterhouseCoopers. Additionally, two other mergers were discussed: Ernst & Young and KPMG Peat Marwick, and Deloitte & Touche and Arthur Andersen & Co. Similar mergers have occurred among smaller firms. These mergers have been brought about by increased competition for clients, expected efficiencies of scale, and a need to service the international activities of clients (see Exhibit 1–1).

Public Accounting Firms

Public accounting firms are organized as proprietorships, general or limited liability partnerships, or corporations. Typically, local public accounting firms are organized as proprietorships, general partnerships, or corporations. Regional, national, and international firms are normally

---

[19]See R. S. Roussey, "Developing International Accounting and Auditing Standards for World Markets," *Journal of International Accounting, Auditing and Taxation* 1, no. 1 (1992), pp. 1–11.

[20]See C. W. Wootton, S. D. Tonge, and C. M. Wolk, "From the 'Big 8' to the 'Big 6' Accounting Firms," *The Ohio CPA Journal* (Spring 1990), pp. 19–23, for a discussion of the effect of mergers among the major public accounting firms.

structured as general or limited liability partnerships. Structuring public accounting firms as proprietorships and partnerships offers additional protection for users of their services because such organizational structures, unlike a corporation, do not provide limited liability for the owners or partners. Thus, users can seek recourse not only against the CPA firm's assets but also against the personal assets of individual partners. This lends additional credibility to the services provided to the public because the individual CPAs are willing to risk the loss of their personal wealth.

With the increase in litigation against CPAs in recent years, public accounting firms are organizing as corporations when possible. However, because corporations are incorporated by individual states, it is not currently possible for regional, national, or international firms to structure themselves using the corporate form. The large national and international firms have restructured themselves as limited liability partnerships (LLPs). An LLP is generally governed by the laws applicable to general partnerships. This organizational structure offers accounting firms the ability to preserve the partnership structure, culture, and taxation but provides more personal protection against lawsuits. Under an LLP, partners are not personally responsible for firm liabilities arising from other partners' and most employees' negligent acts.[21] However, the assets of the partnership are available for settlements of lawsuits resulting from other partners' or employees' acts.

Public accounting firms can be categorized by size. For example, there are the Big 5 public accounting firms: Arthur Andersen & Co. LLP, Deloitte & Touche LLP, Ernst & Young LLP, KPMG Peat Marwick LLP, and PricewaterhouseCoopers LLP. These large international organizations have annual revenues ranging from $8 billion to $19 billion. As a group, the Big 5 audit 90 percent of publicly traded companies in the United States with annual sales greater than $1 million. This includes most of the largest and most prominent public companies in the United States, including the following categories:

- 494 of *Fortune* magazine's 500 industrial corporations.
- 97 of *Fortune* magazine's 100 fastest-growing companies.
- 99 of *Fortune*'s 100 largest commercial banks.
- 92 of the top 100 defense contractors.
- 195 of the 200 largest insurance companies.[22]

Following the Big 5 in size are several national firms with international affiliations. These include Grant Thornton, McGladrey & Pullen, and BDO Seidman. The annual revenues for these firms range from $180 million to $300 million. These firms compete with the Big 5 and provide basically the same services. Last, there are regional and local CPA firms that have one or

---

[21]The reader is referred to G. Simonetti, Jr., and A. R. Andrews, "Limiting Accountants' Personal Liability Won't Solve the Country's Liability Crisis!" *Journal of Accountancy* (April 1994), pp. 46–54, for an excellent discussion of organizational reform of CPA firm structure.

[22]Arthur Andersen & Co. et al., "The Liability Crisis in the United States: Impact on the Accounting Profession, A Statement of Position." Also see C. W. Wootton, S. D. Tonge, and C. M. Wold, "Pre and Post Big 8 Mergers: Comparisons of Auditor Concentration," *Accounting Horizons* (September 1994), pp. 58–74.

TABLE 1–2	Selected Duties of Audit Team Members

Audit Team Member	Selected Duties
Partner	• Reaching agreement with the client on the scope of the service to be provided. • Ensuring that the audit is properly planned. • Ensuring that the audit team has the required skills and experience. • Supervising the audit team and reviewing the working papers. • Signing the audit report.
Manager	• Ensuring that the audit is properly planned, including scheduling of staff. • Supervising the preparation and approving the audit program. • Reviewing the working papers, financial statements, and audit report.
Senior/Auditor-in-charge	• Assisting in the development of the audit plan. • Preparing budgets. • Assigning audit tasks to staff and directing the day-to-day performance of the audit. • Supervising and reviewing the work of the staff.
Staff	• Performing the audit procedures assigned to them. • Preparing adequate and appropriate working papers. • Informing the senior about any auditing or accounting problems encountered.

a few offices. These CPA firms provide audit, tax, and accounting services, generally to smaller organizations.

Audits are usually conducted by teams of auditors. The typical audit team is composed of, in order of authority, a partner, a manager, a senior, and staff members. Staff members are typically responsible for conducting portions of the audit work assigned to them by the senior. The senior or in-charge auditor participates in the planning, conduct, and supervision of the audit work. The senior also reviews the staff members' work prior to reviews by the manager and partner. In addition to reviewing the staff and senior's work, the manager and partner have various administrative responsibilities related to the audit engagement, such as scheduling the engagement and billing the client. The partner has the final authority and decision-making responsibility for accounting and auditing matters, including the issuance of the audit report. Table 1–2 summarizes the duties performed by each member of the audit team.

Types of Services

In addition to auditing and assurance services, public accounting firms perform three broad categories of services.

Tax Services   Clients of public accounting firms are required to pay various types of federal, state, and local taxes. Public accounting firms have tax departments that assist clients with preparing and filing tax returns, provide advice on tax and estate planning, and provide representation on tax issues before the Internal Revenue Service or tax courts.

FIGURE 1–4

Practice Mix of Services by Major International Public Accounting Firms

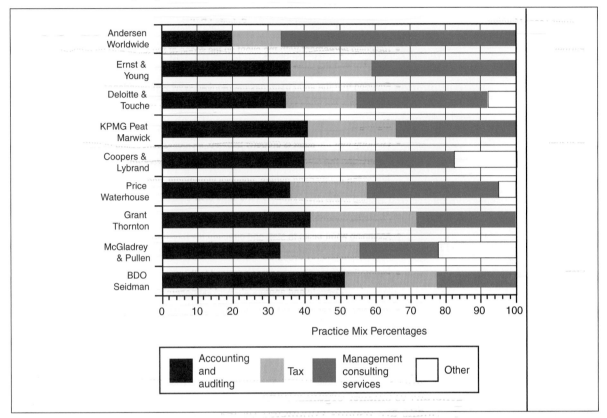

Source: Public Accounting Report's Annual Survey of National Accounting Firms—1998, (*Public Accounting Report* EXTRA, Special Supplement, February 28, 1998, p. S–2). Reprinted by special permission of Public Accounting Report. Copyright 1998 by Strafford Publications, Inc., Postal Drawer 13729, Atlanta, GA 30324-0729. 404/881-1141.

Management Advisory Services   Management advisory services (MAS) are consulting activities that may involve providing advice and assistance concerning an entity's organization, personnel, finances, operations, systems, or other activities. Many public accounting firms have separate groups within the firm that perform such services. Additionally, the MAS department may be divided further into areas of specialization such as small-business consulting, management information systems development, litigation support services, and actuarial/pension services. Because of the diverse nature of the services performed, the MAS department may be composed of CPAs and of other business experts as well. In recent years, consulting services of public accounting firms have grown tremendously. For example, KPMG Peat Marwick reported that revenues from consulting services rose from 18 percent in 1993 to 34 percent in 1997.[23] Figure 1–4 presents the practice mix of the major international firms.

---

[23]KPMG Peat Marwick, *Annual Report 1997* (New York: KPMG Peat Marwick, 1997).

Accounting and Review Services   Public accounting firms perform a number of accounting services for clients. These services may include bookkeeping, payroll processing, and preparing financial statements. When accounting services for financial statements are provided for nonpublic companies, either a compilation or a review is performed. These forms of services provide less assurance on the correspondence between assertions and established criteria than a financial statement audit does. A *compilation* presents financial statement information that is the representation of management, and the compilation report issued by the CPA does not provide any assurance on the compiled financial statements. A *review*, on the other hand, provides limited assurance that no material modifications are necessary in order for the financial statements to conform to established criteria. In contrast, an audit provides reasonable assurance that the financial statements conform to established criteria. Accounting services are discussed in more detail in Chapter 21.

Organizations That Affect Financial Statement Audits

[LO 6]   A number of organizations affect the practice of auditing by independent auditors. Figure 1-5 provides a graphic representation of the relationship of these organizations to the independent audit. The following subsections discuss the activities of six of these organizations.

American Institute of Certified Public Accountants (AICPA)

The AICPA performs a number of functions that directly bear on the activities of member CPAs. The most important of these functions is the promulgation of rules and standards that guide audit practice and related services. Table 1–3 lists the types of rules and standards issued by various boards and committees within the AICPA.

- **Bylaws.** The bylaws establish the rules and regulations that govern the activities of the AICPA. The bylaws include issues such as

TABLE 1–3	Rules and Standards Issued by the AICPA

- Bylaws
- Code of Professional Conduct
- Statements on Auditing Standards
- Statements on Standards for Accounting and Review Services
- Statements on Standards for Attestation Engagements
- Statements on Quality Control Standards
- Standards for Performing and Reporting on Peer Reviews
- Statements on Standards for Consulting Services
- Statements on Responsibilities in Tax Practice

admission, retention, and termination of membership; organization; financial management; and other activities.

- ***Code of Professional Conduct.*** The code was adopted by the membership of the AICPA to guide all members in the performance of their professional responsibilities. It is composed of two major sections: "Principles" and "Rules of Conduct." The code also contains interpretations and rulings by the Professional Ethics Division on specific ethical situations. The principles provide the framework for the rules, and the rules govern an AICPA member's performance. For example, Rule 101 states that a member in public practice shall be independent in the performance of professional services as required by bodies of the AICPA. Changes to the Code of Professional Conduct are voted on by the membership of the AICPA. The code is covered in detail in Chapter 19.

FIGURE 1–5

Organizations Affecting the Financial Statement Audit

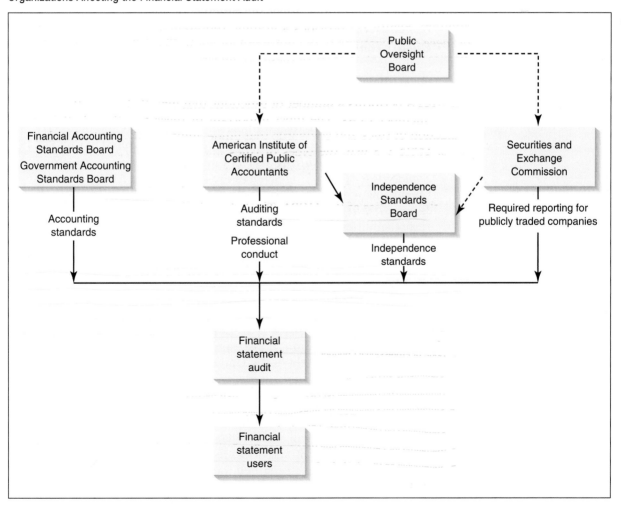

- *Auditing standards.* The Auditing Standards Board (ASB) is responsible for establishing generally accepted auditing standards and issuing pronouncements on auditing matters. These are called *Statements on Auditing Standards* (SAS) and are discussed later in this chapter. The SAS provide the framework for conducting financial statement audits.

- *Compilation and review standards.* The AICPA's Accounting and Review Services Committee is responsible for issuing pronouncements related to the conduct of compilations and reviews. These standards are referred to as *Statements on Standards for Accounting and Review Services.*

- *Attestation standards.* In response to user demand for accountants to provide services beyond audits of historical financial statements, the AICPA has authorized the ASB, the Accounting and Review Services Committee, and the Management Advisory Services Executive Committee to issue *Statements on Standards for Attestation Engagements.* For example, attestation standards currently cover services such as examining financial forecasts and reporting on an entity's internal control over financial reporting to determine their correspondence to measurable criteria. Attestation standards and related services are covered in Chapter 21.

- *Quality control standards.* CPA firms should maintain a system of quality control that ensures that a firm's practice meets professional standards. In order for a firm to designate itself a member of the AICPA, the firm must join the AICPA Division for CPA Firms. Members of the AICPA Division for CPA Firms must adhere to the quality control standards promulgated by the AICPA and undergo a peer review every three years. Quality control is covered in Chapter 19.

- *Standards for consulting services and tax practice.* *Statements on Standards for Consulting Services* are issued by the AICPA's Management Advisory Services Executive Committee. *Statements on Responsibilities in Tax Practice* emphasize the practitioner's responsibilities when involved with tax engagements.

In addition to its standard-setting role, the AICPA supports accounting and auditing research, produces a number of important publications, and provides a wide range of continuing education programs. For example, the AICPA publishes the *Journal of Accountancy, The Tax Advisor,* Auditing Research Monographs, Auditing Practice Releases, and Industry Audit and Accounting Guides. The AICPA is responsible for preparing and grading the uniform CPA examination. It also sponsors continuing education seminars and workshops throughout the United States and publishes numerous continuing education self-study guides.

Public Oversight Board

The Public Oversight Board (POB) is an autonomous board that monitors and reports on the system of self-regulation developed by the AICPA and, on the basis of its oversight activities, recommends improvement when it observes an opportunity to strengthen the system of self-regulation. Its five members represent a broad spectrum of business, professional, regulatory, and legislative experience. To ensure its independence and objectivity, the POB appoints its own members, chairperson, and staff and establishes its own compensation and operating procedures. The POB's two main functions are (1) overseeing the operation of the AICPA's peer review activities and (2) overseeing the Quality Control Inquiry Committee's inquiries into alleged audit failures.[24] Oversight by the POB makes the AICPA's self-regulatory system both more effective and more credible.

Financial Accounting Standards Board

The Financial Accounting Standards Board (FASB) is a privately funded body whose mission is to establish standards for financial accounting and reporting. Students should be familiar with the operations of the FASB from their financial accounting classes. The Statements of Financial Accounting Standards (SFAS) and interpretations issued by the FASB are recognized as GAAP in the rules of the Code of Professional Conduct. The FASB follows a *due process* procedure when a new standard is being considered. This process allows all interested parties to provide input into the FASB's decision-making process.

An important group within the FASB is the Emerging Issues Task Force (EITF). The EITF was established by the FASB to meet accountants' needs for timely guidance on accounting practices and methods and to limit the number of issues requiring formal pronouncements from the FASB.[25] The EITF is composed of 15 members, including senior technical partners from the major CPA firms, senior partners from smaller firms, financial executives, and other representatives of business. The chief accountant of the SEC also plays a major role in the activities of the EITF. The EITF issues consensus opinions when no more than two members object to a suggested accounting approach.

Government Accounting Standards Board

The Government Accounting Standards Board (GASB) was formed in 1984 to address the reporting issues of state and local government entities. The operations of the GASB are similar to those of the FASB. The GASB issues *Statements of Governmental Accounting Standards*, which establish accounting principles for the government sector.

Securities and Exchange Commission

The Securities and Exchange Commission (SEC) is a government agency that administers the Securities Act of 1933 and the Securities Exchange Act of 1934. The Securities Act of 1933 regulates disclosure of material information in a registration statement for an initial public offering of securities. *S forms*, which are used for issuing the securities, contain the audited financial statements of the registrant. The Securities Exchange Act of 1934 regulates ongoing reporting by companies whose securities are listed and traded

---

[24]See Public Oversight Board, *A Special Report: What Is QCIC? What Is Peer Review? What Is the POB? What Is Self-Regulation?* (New York: POB, 1994), for more information on the operations of the POB.

[25]See W. S. Upton, Jr., and D. K. Scott, "What You Should Know About the EITF," *Journal of Accountancy* (June 1988), pp. 56–62, for more details on the operations of the EITF.

on a stock exchange or who possess assets greater than $1 million and equity securities held by 500 or more persons. The most common documents encountered by auditors under the Securities Exchange Act of 1934 are the *10K, 10Q,* and *8K.* The 10K and 10Q are, respectively, the annual and quarterly reports, which include the financial statements that are filed with the SEC by a publicly traded entity. An 8K is filed whenever a significant event occurs that may be of interest to investors (such as sale of a division).

The Securities Exchange Act of 1934 gives the SEC the power to establish accounting standards. Historically, the SEC has allowed private-sector standard-setting bodies such as the FASB and GASB to establish such standards. The SEC, however, has considerable influence in setting accounting and auditing standards. The FASB, GASB, and ASB work closely with the SEC when formulating accounting and auditing standards.

Independence Standards Board[26]

The Independence Standards Board (ISB) was established in May 1997 with the mission of developing "a conceptual framework for independence applicable to audits of public entities which will serve as the foundation for the development of principle-based independence standards." The ISB came about through the joint efforts of the AICPA and SEC, and it will be part of the SEC Practice Section of the AICPA. The ISB was created in response to a rapidly changing and complex business environment in which SEC registrants and their auditors many times operate under regulations and rules that do not provide adequate guidance for assessing independence. Most large public accounting firms have evolved into multidisciplinary professional service firms that offer both audit and nonaudit services to their clients (see Figure 1–4). Tremendous changes in technology have created an increasing number of business relationships between professional service firms and other entities. Such relationships seek to respond to the demands of a competitive global marketplace.

The ISB will establish core principles of independence, promulgate guidelines on how those principles should be applied, identify appropriate types of safeguards, and require public accounting firms to draft independence codes implementing the system, subject to ISB review. The principal advantage of such independence codes is that they will allow public accounting firms to design an independence system that reflects the firm's culture, organizational structure, quality controls, and personnel policies. A firm's code would be available to the public and periodically reviewed by a committee of the ISB.

Generally Accepted Auditing Standards

[LO 7]   Auditing standards are measures of the quality of the auditor's performance. The AICPA first issued the 10 generally accepted auditing standards (GAAS) in 1947 and has periodically modified them to meet changes

---

[26] AICPA, *Serving the Public Interest: A New Conceptual Framework for Auditor Independence* (New York: October 20, 1997). The document is available from the AICPA's home page. The ISB's home page (www.cpaindependence.org) contains detailed information on the ISB's activities.

TABLE 1–4	Generally Accepted Auditing Standards

General Standards:

1. The audit is to be performed by a person or persons having adequate technical training and proficiency as an auditor.

2. In all matters relating to the assignment, an independence in mental attitude is to be maintained by the auditor or auditors.

3. Due professional care is to be exercised in the planning and performance of the audit and the preparation of the report.

Standards of Field Work:

1. The work is to be adequately planned and assistants, if any, are to be properly supervised.

2. A sufficient understanding of the internal control is to be obtained to plan the audit and to determine the nature, timing, and extent of tests to be performed.

3. Sufficient, competent evidential matter is to be obtained through inspection, observation, inquiries, and confirmations to afford a reasonable basis for an opinion regarding the financial statements under audit.

Standards of Reporting:

1. The report shall state whether the financial statements are presented in accordance with generally accepted accounting principles.

2. The report shall identify those circumstances in which such principles have not been consistently observed in the current period in relation to the preceding period.

3. Informative disclosures in the financial statements are to be regarded as reasonably adequate unless otherwise stated in the report.

4. The report shall contain either an expression of opinion regarding the financial statements, taken as a whole, or an assertion to the effect that an opinion cannot be expressed. When an overall opinion cannot be expressed, the reasons therefore should be stated. In all cases where an auditor's name is associated with financial statements, the report should contain a clear-cut indication of the character of the auditor's work, if any, and the degree of responsibility the auditor is taking.

in the auditor's environment. The GAAS are composed of three categories of standards: *general standards, standards of field work,* and *standards of reporting.* Table 1–4 contains the 10 GAAS.

General Standards

The three general standards are concerned with the auditor's qualifications and the quality of his or her work. The first general standard recognizes that an individual must have adequate training and proficiency as an auditor. This is gained through formal education, continuing education programs, and experience. It should be recognized that this training is ongoing with a requirement on the part of the auditor to stay up-to-date with current accounting and auditing pronouncements. Auditors should also be aware of developments in the business world that may affect the auditing profession.

The second general standard requires that the auditor always maintain an attitude of independence on an engagement. Independence precludes relationships that may impair the auditor's objectivity. A distinction is often made between *independence in fact* and *independence in appearance.* An auditor must not only be independent in fact but also avoid actions that may appear to affect independence. If an auditor is perceived as not being independent, users may lose confidence in the auditor's ability to report truthfully on financial statements. For example, an auditor might have a financial interest in an auditee but still conduct the audit in an objective manner.

Third parties, however, may assume that the auditor was not independent because the financial interest could have prevented the auditor from maintaining objectivity during the audit. Public confidence is impaired if an auditor is found to lack independence. The Code of Professional Conduct identifies actions, such as financial or managerial interests in clients, that are believed to impair the auditor's appearance of independence.

Due professional care is the focus of the third general standard. In simple terms, due care means that the auditor plans and performs his or her duties with a degree of skill commonly possessed by others in the profession. The third general standard imposes an obligation on the members of the audit team to observe the standards of field work and reporting, and to perform the work at the same level as any other professional auditor who offers such services to clients.

Standards of Field Work

The standards of field work relate to the actual conduct of the audit. These three standards provide the conceptual background for the audit process. The first standard of field work deals with planning and supervision. Proper planning can lead to a more effective audit that is more likely to detect material misstatements if they exist. Proper planning also assists in completing the engagement in a reasonable amount of time. Additionally, this standard requires that assistants on the engagement be properly supervised.

The second standard of field work requires that the auditor gain sufficient understanding of the auditee's internal control to plan an audit. Internal control is a process, effected by an entity's board of directors, management, and other personnel, that is designed to provide reasonable assurance regarding the achievement of the following objectives: (1) reliability of financial reporting, (2) compliance with applicable laws and regulations, and (3) effectiveness and efficiency of operations. The degree to which the auditor relies on the auditee's internal control directly affects the nature, timing, and extent of the work performed by the independent auditor.

Sufficient, competent evidence is the focus of the third field-work standard. Most of the auditor's work involves the search for and evaluation of evidence to support management's assertions in the financial statements. The auditor uses various audit procedures to gather this evidence. For example, if the balance sheet shows an amount for accounts receivable of $1.5 million, management asserts that this amount is the net realizable value, or the amount expected to be collected from customers, for those receivables. The auditor can send confirmations to customers and examine subsequent payments by customers as audit procedures to gather sufficient competent evidence on the proper value of accounts receivable.

Standards of Reporting

The four standards of reporting require that the auditor consider each of the following issues before rendering an audit report: (1) the financial statements are presented in accordance with generally accepted accounting principles, (2) those principles are consistently applied, (3) all informative disclosures have been made, and (4) what degree of responsibility the auditor is taking and the character of the auditor's work.

Statements on Auditing Standards

Statements on Auditing Standards (SAS) are issued by the Auditing Standards Board and are considered interpretations of GAAS. The SAS receive their authority from Rule 202 of the Code of Professional Conduct. The GAAS and the SAS are considered to be *minimum standards* of performance for auditors. (When "GAAS" is used in this text, it generally refers to the 10 GAAS and the SAS.)

Unlike accounting pronouncements, which usually provide very specific rules, the SAS tend to be general and typically provide only guidance to the auditor. The auditor must then apply sound *professional judgment* given the particular circumstances of the engagement in conducting an audit. The auditor never has sufficient evidence to "guarantee" that the financial statements do not contain material misstatements. Rather, the auditor uses his or her knowledge of the client's business and industry, the quality and integrity of management, and audit evidence to make inferences about the fair presentation of the financial statements.

SAS are classified by two numbering categories: SAS and AU numbers. The SAS numbering applies to the order in which the standards are issued by the ASB. The AU numbering follows an AICPA codification scheme that classifies a standard by its relationship to the following categories, with the numbers in parentheses representing the section:

Introduction (100)

The General Standards (200)

The Standards of Field Work (300)

The First, Second, and Third Standards of Reporting (400)

The Fourth Standard of Reporting (500)

Other Types of Reports (600)

Special Topics (700)

Compliance Auditing (800)

Special Reports of the Committee on Auditing Procedures (900)

For example, SAS No. 58, "Reports on Audited Financial Statements," is also classified under section number AU 508 in the AICPA codification.

Auditing standards are measures of the quality of the auditor's performance. Audit procedures relate to acts that are performed by the auditor while trying to gather evidence, and refer specifically to the methods or techniques used in the conduct of the audit. Presentations in the remainder of the text are guided by auditing standards.

REVIEW QUESTIONS

[LO 1,2] 1-1 The Committee on Basic Auditing Concepts has provided a widely cited definition of auditing. What does the phrase *systematic process* mean in this definition?

[1,2,3] 1-2 List sets of established criteria other than GAAP that can be used to measure economic actions and events.

[1,2,3] 1-3 What is meant by the statement "The agency relationship between absentee owners and managers produces a natural conflict of interest"?

[1] 1-4 Discuss what leads to the demand for auditing services in a free-market economy. What evidence suggests that auditing would be demanded even if it were not required by government regulation?

[2] 1-5 Define auditing, attestation, and assurance services.

[3] 1-6 Define the four general types of audits.

[3] 1-7 Give three examples each of compliance, operational, and forensic audits.

[4] 1-8 List the various types of auditors.

[4] 1-9 What policy suggested by the Institute of Internal Auditors is intended to ensure that internal auditors are objective and independent?

[3,4] 1-10 What types of audits are typically conducted by GAO and IRS auditors?

[3] 1-11 What forms of organizations can be used by public accounting firms? What is a limited liability partnership?

[2,5] 1-12 What types of services are commonly offered by public accounting firms?

[6] 1-13 How do the actions of the FASB and GASB affect the public accounting profession? What is the function of the EITF?

[6] 1-14 What are some of the common documents encountered by auditors that are required by the Securities Exchange Act of 1934? What is the purpose of each of these documents?

[6] 1-15 What is the mission of the ISB? What is the principal advantage of the ISB allowing public accounting firms to draft their own independence codes?

[7] 1-16 List the three categories of GAAS.

[7] 1-17 Why is independence such an important standard for auditors? How does independence relate to the agency relationship between owners and managers?

[7] 1-18 Discuss why the GAAS and the SAS are considered minimum standards of performance for auditors.

[7] 1-19 Distinguish between auditing standards and audit procedures.

MULTIPLE-CHOICE QUESTIONS FROM CPA EXAMINATIONS

[1,2,5] 1-20 Independent auditing can best be described as
a. A branch of accounting.
b. A discipline that attests to the results of accounting and other functional operations and data.

c. A professional activity that measures and communicates financial and business data. *what management does in preparing f/s*

d. A regulatory function that prevents the issuance of improper financial information. *no* *not always*

[1,2,3]   1-21   An independent audit aids in the communication of economic data because the audit

a. Confirms the accuracy of management's financial representations. *not 100%*

(b.) Lends credibility to the financial statements.

c. Guarantees that financial data are fairly presented. *no*

d. Assures the readers of financial statements that any fraudulent activity has been corrected. *no*

[1,2,5]   1-22   Which of the following best describes the reason why an independent auditor reports on financial statements?

a. Management fraud may exist, and it is more likely to be detected by independent auditors. *not necessarily*

(b.) Different interests may exist between the company preparing the statements and the persons using the statements. *agency theory*

c. A misstatement of account balances may exist, and it is generally corrected as a result of the independent auditor's work. *no - only if material*

d. A poorly designed internal control system may exist.

[3]   1-23   Operational auditing is oriented primarily toward

(a.) Future improvements to accomplish the goals of management.

b. The accuracy of data reflected in management's financial records.

c. Verification that a company's financial statements are fairly *f/s* presented.

d. Past protection provided by existing internal control.

[3]   1-24   A typical objective of an operational audit is to determine whether an entity's

a. Internal control is adequately operating as designed. *attestation*

b. Operational information is in accordance with generally accepted governmental auditing standards. *No*

c. Financial statements present fairly the results of operations. *f/s*

(d.) Specific operating units are functioning efficiently and effectively.

[6]   1-25   The Securities and Exchange Commission has authority to

a. Prescribe specific auditing procedures to detect fraud concerning inventories and accounts receivable of companies engaged in interstate commerce.

b. Deny lack of privity as a defense in third-party actions for gross negligence against the auditors of public companies.

(c.) Determine accounting principles for the purpose of financial reporting by companies offering securities to the public.

d. Require a change of auditors of governmental entities after a given period of years as a means of ensuring auditor independence.

[6]   1-26   The authoritative body designated to promulgate standards concerning an accountant's association with unaudited financial statements of an entity that is *not* required to file financial statements with an agency regulating the issuance of the entity's securities is the

a. Financial Accounting Standards Board.

b. General Accounting Office.

(c.) Accounting and Review Services Committee.

d. Auditing Standards Board.

[7]   1-27   Which of the following best describes what is meant by the term *generally accepted auditing standards*?
    a. Procedures to be used to gather evidence to support financial statements. *tests*
    (b) Measures of the quality of the auditor's performance.
    c. Pronouncements issued by the Auditing Standards Board. *SAS*
    d. Rules acknowledged by the accounting profession because of their universal application.

[7]   1-28   The third general standard states that due care is to be exercised in the performance of an examination. This standard means that a CPA who undertakes an engagement assumes a duty to perform each audit
    (a) As a professional possessing the degree of skill commonly possessed by others in the field.
    b. In conformity with generally accepted accounting principles.
    c. With reasonable diligence and without fault or error.
    d. To the satisfaction of governmental agencies and investors who rely upon the audit. *no – exp. app*

[7]   1-29   As guidance for measuring the quality of the performance of an auditor, the auditor should refer to
    a. Statements of the Financial Accounting Standards Board.
    (b) Generally accepted auditing standards.
    c. Interpretations of the Statements on Auditing Standards.
    d. Statements on Quality Control Standards.

[7]   1-30   Which of the following is *not* required by the generally accepted auditing standard that states that due professional care is to be exercised in the performance of the examination?
    a. Observance of the standards of field work and reporting.
    b. Critical review of the audit work performed at every level of supervision.
    c. The degree of skill commonly possessed by others in the profession.
    (d) Responsibility for losses because of errors of judgment.

[7]   1-31   The fourth standard of reporting requires the auditor's report to contain either an expression of opinion regarding the financial statements taken as a whole or an assertion to the effect that an opinion cannot be expressed. The objective of the fourth standard is to prevent
    (a) Misinterpretations regarding the degree of responsibility the auditor is assuming.
    b. An auditor from reporting on one basic financial statement and *not* the others.
    c. An auditor from expressing different opinions on each of the basic financial statements.
    d. Restrictions on the scope of the examination, whether imposed by the client or by an inability to obtain evidence.

[7]   1-32   The third standard of field work states that sufficient competent evidential matter is to be obtained through inspection, observation, inquiries, and confirmations to afford a reasonable basis for an opinion regarding the financial statements under audit. The

substantive evidential matter required by this standard may be obtained, in part, through
a. Flowcharting the internal control system.
b. Properly planning the audit engagement.
c. Analytical procedures.
d. Auditor working papers.

[7] 1-33 To exercise due professional care, an auditor should
a. Attain the proper balance of professional experience and formal education.
b. Design the audit to detect all instances of illegal acts.
c. Critically review the judgment exercised by those assisting in the audit.
d. Examine all available corroborating evidence supporting management's assertions.

[7] 1-34 What is the general character of the three generally accepted auditing standards classified as standards of field work?
a. The competence, independence, and professional care of persons performing the audit.
b. Criteria for the content of the auditor's report on financial statements and related footnote disclosures.
c. Criteria for audit planning and evidence gathering.
d. The need to maintain an independence of mental attitude in all matters relating to the audit.

PROBLEMS

[1,2,3] 1-35 Felix Potvine, the sole owner of a small hardware business, has been told that the business should have financial statements reported on by an independent CPA. Potvine, having some bookkeeping experience, has personally prepared the company's financial statements and does not understand why such statements should be examined by a CPA. Potvine discussed the matter with Steve Barber, a CPA, and asked Barber to explain why an audit is considered important.

Required:
a. Describe the objectives of an independent audit.
b. Identify five ways in which an independent audit may be beneficial to Potvine.

(AICPA, adapted)

[1,2] 1-36 Greenbloom Garden Centers is a small, privately held corporation that has two stores in Orlando, Florida. The Greenbloom family owns 100 percent of the company's stock, and family members manage the operations. Sales at the company's stores have been growing rapidly, and there appears to be a market for the company's sales concept—providing bulk garden equipment and supplies at low prices. The controller prepares the company's financial statements, which are not audited. The company has no debt but is considering expanding to other cities in Florida. Such expansion

may require long-term borrowings and is likely to reduce the family's day-to-day control of the operations. The family does not intend to sell stock in the company.

Required:

Discuss the factors that may make an audit necessary for the company.

[3,4]   1-37   Audits can be categorized into four types: (1) financial statement audits, (2) compliance audits, (3) operational audits, and (4) forensic audits.

Required:

For each of the following descriptions, indicate which type of audit (financial statement audit, compliance audit, operational audit, or forensic audit) best characterizes the nature of the audit being conducted. Also indicate which type of auditor (external auditor, internal auditor, government auditor, or forensic auditor) is likely to perform the audit engagement.

a. Evaluate the policies and procedures of the Food and Drug Administration in terms of bringing new drugs to the market.

b. Determine the fair presentation of Ajax Chemical's balance sheet, income statement, and statement of cash flows.

c. Review the payment procedures of the Accounts Payable Department for a large manufacturer.

d. Examine the financial records of a division of a corporation to determine if any accounting irregularities have occurred.

e. Evaluate the feasibility of forecasted rental income for a planned low-income public housing project.

f. Evaluate a company's Computer Services Department in terms of the efficient and effective use of corporate resources.

g. Audit the partnership tax return of a real estate development company.

h. Investigate the possibility of payroll fraud in a labor union pension fund.

[7]   1-38   Dale Boucher, the owner of a small electronics firm, asked Sally Jones, CPA, to conduct an audit of the company's records. Boucher told Jones that the audit was to be completed in time to submit audited financial statements to a bank as part of a loan application. Jones immediately accepted the engagement and agreed to provide an auditor's report within one month. Boucher agreed to pay Jones her normal audit fee plus a percentage of the loan if it was granted.

Jones hired two recent accounting graduates to conduct the audit and spent several hours telling them exactly what to do. She told the new hires not to spend time reviewing the internal control but instead to concentrate on proving the mathematical accuracy of the general and subsidiary ledgers and summarizing the data in the accounting records that supported Boucher's financial statements. The new hires followed Jones's instructions, and after two weeks gave Jones the financial statements excluding footnotes. Jones reviewed the statements and prepared an unqualified auditor's report. The report, however, did not refer to generally accepted accounting principles. Additionally, no audit procedures were conducted to verify the year-to-year application of such principles.

Required:
Briefly describe each of the generally accepted auditing standards and indicate how the action(s) of Jones resulted in a failure to comply with *each* generally accepted auditing standard.

(AICPA, adapted)

[7] 1-39 Terri Harrison, CPA, has discussed various reporting considerations with three of her audit clients. The three clients presented the following situations and asked how they would affect the audit report.

a. A client has changed its depreciation method on its machinery from straight-line to double declining balance. Both Harrison and the client agree that the new depreciation method better reflects the usage of the machinery in the manufacturing process. The client agrees with Harrison that the change is material but claims that it needs disclosure only in the "Summary of Significant Accounting Policies" footnote to the financial statements, not in Harrison's report.

b. A client has a loan agreement that restricts the amount of cash dividends that can be paid and requires the maintenance of a particular current ratio. The client is in compliance with the terms of the agreement, and it is not likely that there will be a violation in the foreseeable future. The client believes there is no need to mention the restriction in the financial statements because such mention might mislead the readers.

c. During the year, a client correctly accounted for the acquisition of a majority-owned domestic subsidiary but did not properly present the minority interest in retained earnings or net income of the subsidiary in the consolidated financial statements. The client agrees with Harrison that the minority interest presented in the consolidated financial statements is materially misstated but takes the position that the minority shareholders of the subsidiary should look to that subsidiary's financial statements for information concerning their interest therein.

Required:
Each of the situations presented relates to one of the four generally accepted auditing standards of reporting. Identify and describe the applicable generally accepted auditing standard (GAAS) of reporting in each situation and discuss how the particular client situation relates to the standard.

(AICPA, adapted)

[1,2] 1-40 You recently attended your five-year college reunion. At the main reception, you encountered an old friend, Lee Beagle, who recently graduated from law school and is now practicing with a large law firm in town. When you told him that you were a CPA and employed by a regional CPA firm, he made the following statement and snickered. "You know, if the Securities Acts had not been

passed by Congress in the 1930s, no one would be interested in having an audit performed. You auditors are just creatures of regulations." Since you did not wish to cause a scene at the reunion, you let his comment pass. You and Lee agreed to have lunch the following week to talk over old times. However, you were still upset over Lee's comment.

Required:

In preparation for your luncheon with Lee, draft a memo that highlights your thoughts about why auditors are not "creatures of regulations." Cite any relevant evidence of a demand for auditing services in your memo.

DISCUSSION CASES

[1,2,5,6]   1-41   In 1993 the Public Oversight Board (POB) published a report, *In the Public Interest: Issues Confronting the Accounting Profession,*[27] that expressed concern about the independence and objectivity of the auditing profession. In early 1994 the chief accountant of the Securities and Exchange Commission (SEC) delivered a speech that criticized independent auditors for "not standing up to their clients on financial accounting and reporting issues when their clients take a position that is, at best, not supported in the accounting literature or, at worst, contrary to existing accounting pronouncements." In response to this criticism, the POB appointed an advisory panel to determine whether the SEC Practice Section of the AICPA's Division for CPA Firms, the accounting profession, or the SEC should take steps to assure the independence, integrity, and objectivity of auditors.

Following are two of the recommendations made by the advisory panel:[28]

- Developing positions for submission to the FASB and the SEC is part of an accounting firm's public responsibility. Therefore, it is essential that the firm's internal organization and processes for developing those positions be insulated from undue pressure from or on behalf of clients. In addition, communications about firm positions on FASB proposals must be done in a judicious, professional way that does not appear to curry favor with clients or appear to be part of an organized campaign.

- Public accounting firms should adopt mechanisms to ensure that (1) their national technical offices are independent of practice partners who feel the direct pressure from client companies and (2) the standard to which the national technical office personnel should be held in advising engagement partners is not just "what

---

[27]Public Oversight Board, *In the Public Interest: Issues Confronting the Accounting Profession* (New York: POB, 1993).

[28]Public Oversight Board, *Strengthening the Professionalism of the Independent Auditor: A Report to the Public Oversight Board of the SEC Practice Section, AICPA, from the Advisory Panel on Independence* (New York: POB, 1994).

In March 1993 the company launched operations in the United Kingdom by opening a telephone order and distribution center outside of London and mailing its first UK catalog. EarthWear now maintains four stores in the United Kingdom and, during 2000, mailed six issues of its pound-denominated catalog.

In June 1995 EarthWear opened two stores in Germany and mailed its first German-language, deutsche mark-denominated catalog. During 2000 the company mailed six issues of this catalog. The company's telephone center, administrative functions, and distribution center are located in Mannheim.

In the spring of 1997 the company launched operations in Japan, and in 2000 the company mailed six issues of its Japanese-language, yen-denominated catalog. The company's telephone center and administrative functions operate from its Tokyo offices. The distribution center is located in Fujieda.

Customer Database

A principal factor in the company's success has been the development of its own list of active customers. At the end of 2000 the company's mailing list consisted of about 19.7 million persons, approximately 6.8 million of whom were viewed as customers because they had made at least one purchase from the company within the last 24 months. The company routinely updates and refines the database before mailing catalogs to monitor customer interest as reflected in criteria such as the recency, frequency, dollar amount, and product type of purchases.

EarthWear believes that its customer database has desirable demographic characteristics and is well suited to the products offered in the company's catalogs. A survey conducted by the company in the United States during 1998 indicated that approximately 49 percent of its customers were in the 35–54 age group and had median incomes of $55,000.

The company advertises nationally to build the company's reputation and to attract new customers. In 2000 this advertising campaign appeared in about 35 national magazines, as well as on national television. In addition, the company advertises in approximately 75 national, regional, and local publications in Canada, the United Kingdom, Germany, and Japan. EarthWear has recently begun advertising on a number of Internet search engines and Web sites.

Product Development

EarthWear concentrates on clothing and other products that are aimed at customers interested in outdoor activities. The company products are styled and quality crafted to meet the changing tastes of the company's customers rather than to mimic the changing fads of the fashion world. At the same time, the company seeks to maintain customer interest by developing new products, improving existing core products, and reinforcing its value positioning.

The company continues to incorporate innovations in fabric, construction, and detail that add value and excitement and differentiate EarthWear from the competition. In order to ensure that products are manufactured to the company's quality standards at reasonable prices, product managers, designers, and quality assurance specialists develop the company's own products.

3

EarthWear deals directly with its suppliers and seeks to avoid intermediaries. All goods are produced by independent manufacturers except for most of its soft luggage, which is assembled at the company's facilities. During 2000 the company purchased merchandise from more than 200 domestic and foreign manufacturers. However, no single manufacturer accounted for more than 10 percent of company purchases in each of the last three years. In 2000 nearly 40 percent of the company's merchandise was imported. The remaining 60 percent was purchased through US suppliers, who may source portions of their production through programs in Central America. The company will continue to take advantage of worldwide sourcing without sacrificing customer service or quality standards.

Order Entry, Fulfillment, and Delivery

EarthWear has toll-free telephone numbers that customers can call 24 hours a day, seven days a week (except Christmas Day) to place orders or to request a catalog. Approximately 90 percent of catalog orders are placed by telephone. Telephone calls are answered by the company's well-trained sales representatives, who utilize on-line computer terminals to enter customer orders and to retrieve information about product characteristics and availability. The company's three US telephone centers are located in Boise, Idaho; Reston, Virginia; and Canton, Ohio. International telephone centers are located in London, England; Tokyo, Japan; and Mannheim, Germany.

The company's order entry and fulfillment system permits shipment of in-stock orders on the following day, but orders requiring monogramming or inseaming typically require one or two extra days. The company's sales representatives enter orders into an on-line order entry and inventory control system. Customers using the company's Internet site see color photos of the products, their availability, and prices. When ordering a product over the Internet, the customer completes a computer screen that requests information on product code, size, color, and so on. When the customer finishes shopping for products, he or she enters delivery and credit card information into a computer-based form. EarthWear provides assurance through CPA WebTrust℠ that the Web site has been evaluated and tested to meet WebTrust℠ principles and criteria. This assurance service is provided by the company's independent auditors, Willis & Adams, LLP.

Computer batch processing of orders is performed each night, at which time shipping tickets are printed with bar codes for optical scanning. Inventory is picked based on the location of individual products rather than orders, followed by computerized sorting and transporting of goods to multiple packing stations and shipping zones. The computerized inventory control system also handles the receipt of shipments from manufacturers, permitting faster access to newly arrived merchandise, as well as the handling of customer return items.

Orders are generally shipped by United Parcel Service (UPS) at various tiered rates that depend on the total dollar value of each customer's order. Other expedited delivery services are available at additional charge. The company utilizes two-day UPS service at standard rates, enhancing its customer service.

Merchandise Liquidation

Liquidations (sales of overstock and end-of-season merchandise at reduced prices) were approximately 9 percent, 11 percent, and 10 percent of net sales in 2000, 1999, and 1998, respectively. Most liquidation sales were made through catalogs and other print media. The balance was sold principally through the company's outlet retail stores.

Competition

The company's principal competitors are retail stores, including specialty shops, department stores, and other catalog companies. Direct competitors include Eddie Bauer, Land's End, L. L. Bean, Patagonia, and Timberland. The company may also face increased competition from other retailers as the number of television shopping channels and the variety of merchandise offered over the Internet increase. The apparel retail business in general is intensely competitive. EarthWear competes principally on the basis of merchandise value (quality and price), its established customer list, and customer service, including fast order fulfillment and its unqualified guarantee.

EarthWear is one of the leading catalog companies in the United States. The company attributes the growth in the catalog industry to many factors, including customer convenience, widespread use of credit cards, the use of toll-free telephone lines, customers having less time to shop in stores, and purchasing of products over the Internet. At the same time, the catalog business is subject to uncertainties in the economy, which result in fluctuating levels of overall consumer spending. Due to the lead times required for catalog production and distribution, catalog retailers may not be able to respond as quickly as traditional retailers in an environment of rapidly changing prices.

 ## Trademarks

The company uses the trademarks of "EarthWear" and "EWC" on products and catalogs.

Seasonality of Business

The company's business is highly seasonal. Historically, a disproportionate amount of the company's net sales and most of its profits have been realized during the fourth quarter. If the company's sales were materially different from seasonal norms during the fourth quarter, the company's annual operating results could be materially affected. Accordingly, results for the individual quarters do not necessarily indicate results to be expected for the entire year.

Employees

The company believes that its skilled and dedicated workforce is one of its key resources. Employees are not covered by collective bargaining agreements, and the company considers its employee relations to be excellent. As a result of the highly seasonal nature of the company's business, the size of the company's workforce varies, ranging from approximately 3,500 to 5,300 individuals in 2000. During the peak winter season of 2000, approximately 2,700 of the company's 5,300 employees were temporary employees.

Executive Officers of the Company

James G. Williams, 60, is chairman of the board and former chief executive officer. Mr. Williams was one of the two original founders of EarthWear. He stepped down as chief executive officer in December 1998.

Calvin J. Rogers, 52, is president and chief executive officer of the company. Mr. Rogers was one of the two original founders of the company. He assumed his present position in December 1998.

Dominique DeSantiago, 51, is executive vice president and chief operating officer. Mr. DeSantiago joined the company as chief operating officer in June 1991. He was promoted to vice president in October 1994. Mr. DeSantiago was previously employed by Eddie Bauer in various capacities.

Linda S. McDaniel, 40, is senior vice president of sales. She joined the company in July 1996. Ms. McDaniel served as divisional vice president, merchandising, with Patagonia between 1986 and 1990. Ms. McDaniel was the president and chief executive officer for Mountain Goat Sports from 1990 until 1996. She has been serving as a director of the company since November 1997.

James C. ("JC") Watts, 40, is senior vice president and chief financial officer. Mr. Watts joined the company in May 1996, assuming his current position. He was previously employed by Federated Department Stores.

Mary Ellen Tornesello, 42, is senior vice president of operations. Ms. Tornesello joined the company in 1994 as operations manager. She served as vice president of operations from 1995 until 1997, at which time she assumed her present position.

Market Information

The common stock of the company is listed and traded on NASDAQ under the symbol EWCC. The high and low prices of the company's common stock for 2000 were $31 1/4 and $22 7/8 per share. The closing price of the company's stock on December 31, 2000, was $27 7/8 per share.

Shareholders

As of December 31, 2000, the number of shareholders of record of common stock of the company was 2,236. This number excludes shareholders whose stock is held in nominee or street name by brokers.

Independent Auditors

The company has been audited by Willis & Adams since incorporation in 1975.

Consolidated Financial Statements

	For the period ended December 31		
	2000	1999	1998
Net sales	$ 503,434	$ 464,197	$ 446,448
Cost of sales	274,126	264,608	257,069
Gross profit	229,308	199,589	189,379
Selling, general, and administrative expenses	190,976	176,618	160,882
Charges from sale of subsidiary	630	847	1,575
Income from operations	37,702	22,124	26,922
Other income (expense):			
Interest expense	(230)	(1,247)	(796)
Interest income	517	114	138
Other	224	1,925	585
Total other income (expense), net	511	792	(73)
Income before income taxes	38,213	22,916	26,849
Income tax provision	15,284	9,166	10,605
Net income	$ 22,929	$ 13,750	$ 16,244
Net income per share	$ 1.57	$ 0.90	$ 1.03

EARTHWEAR CLOTHIERS
Consolidated Balance Sheets
(In thousands)

	December 31	
Assets	**2000**	**1999**
Current assets:		
Cash and cash equivalents	$ 41,772	$ 7,729
Receivables	3,933	3,629
Inventory	64,100	74,167
Prepaid advertising	4,980	7,121
Other prepaid expenses	2,448	2,383
Deferred income tax benefits	5,185	4,911
Total current assets	122,418	99,940
Property, plant, and equipment, at cost:		
Land and buildings	32,562	32,512
Fixtures and equipment	44,389	37,746
Leasehold improvements	1,931	1,310
Construction in progress	602	—
Total property, plant, and equipment	79,484	71,568
Less accumulated depreciation and amortization	32,826	27,025
Property, plant, and equipment, net	46,658	44,543
Intangibles, net	1,045	1,090
Total assets	$ 170,121	$ 145,573
Liabilities and stockholders' equity		
Current liabilities:		
Lines of credit	$ 5,038	$ 4,194
Accounts payable	34,463	28,071
Reserve for returns	2,333	2,050
Accrued liabilities	12,663	10,688
Accrued profit sharing	1,322	667
Income taxes payable	9,686	5,965
Total current liabilities	65,505	51,635
Deferred income taxes	3,914	3,245
Long-term liabilities	297	157
Stockholders' equity:		
Common stock, 18,145 shares issued	181	181
Donated capital	3,780	3,780
Additional paid-in capital	11,844	11,774
Deferred compensation	(617)	(537)
Currency translation adjustments	170	162
Retained earnings	139,978	117,049
Treasury stock, 3,500 and 2,952 shares at cost, respectively	(54,931)	(41,873)
Total stockholders' equity	100,405	90,536
Total liabilities and stockholders' equity	$ 170,121	$ 145,573

EARTHWEAR CLOTHIERS
Consolidated Statements of Cash Flows
(In thousands)

	For the period ended December 31		
	2000	1999	1998
Cash flows from operating activities:			
Net income	$ 22,929	$ 13,750	$ 16,244
Adjustments to reconcile net income to net cash flows from operating activities:			
Depreciation and amortization	6,101	5,605	4,640
Deferred compensation expense	143	102	261
Deferred income taxes	447	(301)	(1,190)
Loss on disposal of fixed assets	146	695	405
Changes in assets and liabilities excluding the effects of acquisitions and divestitures:			
Receivables	(304)	(2,200)	(119)
Inventory	10,067	640	(7,449)
Prepaid advertising	2,141	(3,743)	(261)
Other prepaid expenses	(65)	(725)	530
Accounts payable	6,392	4,328	(942)
Reserve for returns	283	(205)	497
Accrued liabilities	1,975	(994)	3,829
Accrued profit sharing	655	(88)	(269)
Income taxes payable	3,721	1,745	(752)
Other	176	17	80
Net cash flows from operating activities	54,807	18,624	15,503
Cash flows from investing activities:			
Cash paid for capital additions and businesses acquired	(8,316)	(6,257)	(14,446)
Proceeds from divestiture	—	749	—
Net cash flows used for investing activities	(8,316)	(5,508)	(14,446)
Cash flows from financing activities:			
Proceeds from short-term borrowings	844	801	3,393
Payment of long-term debt	—	(18)	(18)
Purchases of treasury stock	(13,564)	(9,000)	(12,591)
Issuances of treasury stock	272	386	890
Net cash flows used for financing activities	(12,448)	(7,831)	(8,326)
Net increase (decrease) in cash and cash equivalents	34,043	5,285	(7,269)
Beginning cash and cash equivalents	7,729	2,442	9,706
Ending cash and cash equivalents	$ 41,772	$ 7,727	$ 2,437
Supplemental cash flow disclosures:			
Interest paid	$ 230	$ 1,247	$ 796
Income taxes paid	11,367	7,603	12,418

	For the period ended December 31		
	2000	1999	1998
Common stock			
Beginning balance	$ 181	$ 181	$ 90.5
Two-for-one stock split	—	—	90.5
Ending balance	$ 181	$ 181	$ 181
Donated capital balance	$ 3,780	$ 3,780	$ 3,780
Additional paid-in capital			
Beginning balance	$ 11,774	$ 11,618	$ 11,200
Tax benefit of stock options exercised	70	156	509
Two-for-one stock split	—	—	(90)
Ending balance	$ 11,844	$ 11,774	$ 11,619
Deferred compensation			
Beginning balance	$ (537)	$ (639)	$ (900)
Issuance of treasury stock	(223)	—	—
Amortization of deferred compensation	143	102	261
Ending balance	$ (617)	$ (537)	$ (639)
Foreign currency translation			
Beginning balance	$ 162	$ 128	$ 111
Adjustment for the year	8	34	17
Ending balance	$ 170	$ 162	$ 128
Retained earnings			
Beginning balance	$117,049	$103,299	$ 87,057
Net income	22,929	13,750	16,243
Issuance of treasury stock	—	—	(1)
Ending balance	$ 139,978	$117,049	$ 103,299
Treasury stock			
Beginning balance	$ (41,873)	$ (33,259)	$ (21,559)
Purchase of treasury stock	(13,564)	(9,000)	(12,591)
Issuance of treasury stock	506	386	891
Ending balance	$ (54,931)	$ (41,873)	$ (33,259)
Total stockholders' equity	$ 100,405	$ 90,536	$ 85,109

EARTHWEAR CLOTHIERS
Five-Year Consolidated Financial Summary (unaudited)
(In thousands, except per share data)

	For the period ended December 31				
	2000	1999	1998	1997	1996
Income statement data:					
Net sales	$503,434	$464,197	$446,448	$391,489	$330,130
Pretax income	38,212	22,916	26,849	31,442	24,315
Percent to net sales	7.6%	4.9%	6.0%	8.0%	7.4%
Net income	22,929	13,750	16,243	19,678	15,075
Per share of common stock:					
Net income per share	$ 1.57	$ 0.90	$ 1.03	$ 1.22	$ 0.93
Cash dividends per share	—	—	—	$ 0.10	$ 0.10
Common shares outstanding	14,599	15,147	15,672	16,160	16,225
Balance sheet data:					
Current assets	$ 122,418	$ 99,940	$ 89,176	$ 86,524	$ 61,889
Current liabilities	65,505	51,635	46,223	40,972	30,292
Property, plant, equipment, and intangibles, net	46,658	44,543	41,750	36,699	33,422
Total assets	170,121	145,573	133,925	123,224	95,311
Noncurrent liabilities	4,211	3,402	2,595	2,473	2,295
Shareholders' investment	100,405	90,536	85,109	79,778	62,725
Other data:					
Net working capital	$ 56,913	$ 48,305	$ 42,953	$ 45,552	$ 31,597
Capital expenditures	8,316	6,257	14,446	7,631	4,484
Depreciation and amortization expense	6,101	5,605	4,640	3,729	3,555
Return on average shareholders' investment	24%	16%	20%	28%	25%
Return on average assets	15%	10%	13%	18%	16%

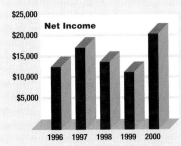

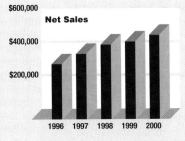

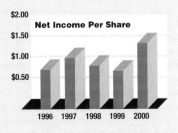

Note A: Summary of Significant Accounting Policies

Nature of Business   EarthWear markets high-quality clothing for outdoor sports, casual clothing, accessories, shoes, and soft luggage. The company sells its products primarily in the United States; other markets include Canada, Europe, and Japan.

Principles of Consolidation   The consolidated statements include the accounts of the company and its subsidiaries after elimination of intercompany accounts and transactions.

Notes to the Consolidated Financial Statements

Inventory   Inventory is stated at the last-in, first-out (LIFO) cost, which is lower than market. If the first-in, first-out method of accounting for inventory had been used, inventory would have been approximately $14.4 million and $10.1 million higher than reported at December 31, 2000 and 1999, respectively.

Advertising   The company expenses the costs of advertising for magazines, television, radio, and other media the first time the advertising takes place, except for direct-response advertising, which is capitalized and amortized over its expected period of future benefits. Direct-response advertising consists primarily of catalog production and mailing costs, which are generally amortized within three months from the date catalogs are mailed.

Depreciation   Depreciation expense is calculated using the straight-line method over the estimated useful lives of the assets, which are 20 to 30 years for buildings and land improvements and 5 to 10 years for leasehold improvements and furniture, fixtures, equipment, and software. The company allocates one-half year of depreciation to the year of addition or retirement.

Intangibles   Intangible assets consist primarily of goodwill, which is amortized over 40 years on a straight-line basis. Other intangibles are amortized over five years.

Reserve for Losses on Customer Returns   At the time of sale, the company provides a reserve equal to the gross profit on projected merchandise returns, based on prior returns experience.

Foreign Currency and Transactions   Financial statements of the foreign subsidiaries are translated into US dollars in accordance with Statement of Financial Accounting Standards No. 52. Translation adjustments are accumulated in a separate component of stockholders' equity.

Note B: Stockholders' Equity

Common Stock   The company currently is authorized to issue 70 million shares of $0.01 par value common stock.

Treasury Stock The company's board of directors has authorized the purchase of a total of 5.5 million shares of the company's common stock. A total of 3.5 million and 2.95 million had been purchased as of December 31, 2000 and 1999, respectively.

Stock Awards and Grants The company has a restricted stock award plan. Under the provisions of the plan, a committee of the company's board may award shares of the company's common stock to its officers and key employees. Such shares vest over a 10-year period on a straight-line basis.

The granting of these awards has been recorded as deferred compensation based on the fair market value of the shares at the date of the grant. Compensation expense under these plans is recorded as shares vest.

Stock Options The company has 1.1 million shares of common stock that may be issued pursuant to the exercise of options granted under the company's stock option plan. Options are granted at the discretion of a committee of the company's board of directors to officers and key employees of the company. No option may have an exercise price less than the fair market value per share of the common stock at the date of the grant.

Note C: Lines of Credit

The company has unsecured domestic lines of credit with various US banks totaling $50 million. There were no amounts outstanding at December 31, 2000 and 1999. In addition, the company has unsecured lines of credit with foreign banks totaling the equivalent of $20 million for its wholly owned subsidiaries. At December 31, 2000, $5.0 million was outstanding at interest rates averaging 3.7 percent, compared with $4.2 million at December 31, 1999.

Note D: Long-Term Debt

There was no long-term debt at December 31, 2000 and 1999.

Note E: Leases

The company leases store and office space and equipment under various lease arrangements. The leases are accounted for as operating leases.

Note F: Retirement Plans

The company has a retirement plan that covers most regular employees and provides for annual contributions at the discretion of the board of directors. Included in the plan is a 401(k) feature that allows employees to make contributions.

Management's Discussion and Analysis: Results of Operations for 2000 Compared to 1999

The year ended December 31, 2000, was a year of marked improvement. Sales began to improve strongly in the last part of the third quarter. Gross margins improved throughout the year, as did the performance of the catalogs and Internet sales, resulting in a 67 percent increase in net income for the year.

Management's Discussion and Analysis

Net Sales Grew by 8.5 Percent   Net sales for the year totaled $503 million, compared with $464 million in 1999. The sales increase in 2000 came mainly from growth in our specialty and international business, Internet sales, and our core catalog sales. This growth was primarily due to improvements in overall catalog productivity (sales per page) and the results of stronger creative presentations and more compelling products. Internet sales also increased.

Inventory Declined by 13.5 Percent   Our inventory balance at the end of the year 2000 was $64.1 million, down 13.5 percent from the 1999 ending inventory of $74.2 million. Because of strong sales in the third quarter of 2000, we entered the holiday season with lower inventory levels and were unable to fill orders at our usual seasonal rate in the fourth quarter.

Gross Profit Margin Improved   Gross profit increased by approximately 15 percent in 2000, and, as a percentage of net sales, gross profit rose to 45.5 percent in 2000, compared to 43 percent in 1999. Our gross margin improvement was primarily due to lower costs associated with liquidating overstocked product, as well as lower merchandise costs from improvements in sourcing and a greater proportion of sales in higher-margin businesses.

Selling, General, and Administrative Expenses   Selling, general, and administrative (SG&A) expenses rose 8.1 percent in 2000, but they declined slightly as a percentage of net sales in 2000 (37.9 percent) compared with 1999 (38 percent). Increased productivity of the catalogs, as well as a larger number of orders and higher average order volume, benefited our SG&A expenses. This was mostly offset by increased bonus and profit-sharing expenses associated with our improved profitability.

Utilization of Credit Lines Decreased   Because of lower inventory levels throughout the year, borrowings under our short-term lines of credit decreased, reducing interest expense by $1 million from 1999. With more cash to invest, our interest income increased to $.5 million in 2000 from $.1 million in 1999. Our lines of credit peaked at $12 million in October 2000 compared with a peak of $47 million in 1999. At December 31, 2000, we had short-term debt outstanding for foreign subsidiaries of $5 million and no long-term debt.

Responsibility for the Consolidated Financial Statements

The management of EarthWear Clothiers and its subsidiaries has the responsibility for preparing the accompanying financial statements and for their integrity and objectivity. The statements were prepared in accordance with generally accepted accounting principles applied on a consistent basis. The consolidated financial statements include amounts that are based on management's best estimates and judgments. Management also prepared the other information in the annual report and is responsible for its accuracy and consistency with the consolidated financial statements.

Management's Report on Financial Statements

The company's consolidated financial statements have been audited by Willis & Adams, independent certified public accountants. Management has made available to Willis & Adams all the company's financial records and related data, as well as the minutes of shareholders' and directors' meetings. Furthermore, management believes that all representations made to Willis & Adams during the audit were valid and appropriate.

Management of the company has established and maintains a system of internal control that provides appropriate division of responsibility, reasonable assurance as to the integrity and reliability of the consolidated financial statements, the protection of assets from unauthorized use or disposition, the prevention and detection of fraudulent financial reporting, and the maintenance of an active program of internal audits. Management believes that, as of December 31, 2000, the company's system of internal control is adequate to accomplish the objectives discussed herein.

Two directors of the company, not members of management, serve as the audit committee of the board of directors and are the principal means through which the board supervises the performance of the financial reporting duties of management. The audit committee meets with management, the internal audit staff, and the company's independent auditors to review the results of the audits of the company and to discuss plans for future audits. At these meetings, the audit committee also meets privately with the internal audit staff and the independent auditors to ensure its free access to them.

Calvin J. Rogers
President and Chief
Executive Officer

James C. Watts
Senior Vice President and
Chief Financial Officer

Independent Auditors' Report

To the Stockholders
EarthWear Clothiers, Inc.

We have audited the consolidated balance sheets of EarthWear Clothiers as of December 31, 2000 and 1999, and the related consolidated statements of operations, stockholders' equity, and cash flows for the years then ended. These financial statements are the responsibility of the company's management. Our responsibility is to express an opinion on these financial statements based on our audits.

We conducted our audits in accordance with generally accepted auditing standards. Those standards require that we plan and perform the audit to obtain reasonable assurance about whether the financial statements are free of material misstatement. An audit includes examining, on a test basis, evidence supporting the amounts and disclosures in the financial statements. An audit also includes assessing the accounting principles used and significant estimates made by management, as well as evaluating the overall financial statement presentation. We believe that our audits provide a reasonable basis for our opinion.

In our opinion, the consolidated financial statements referred to above present fairly, in all material respects, the financial position of EarthWear Clothiers as of December 31, 2000 and 1999, and the results of its operations and its cash flows for the years then ended in conformity with generally accepted accounting principles.

Willis & Adams

Willis & Adams, CPAs
February 15, 2001

An Overview of Financial Statement Auditing

LEARNING OBJECTIVES

Upon completion of this chapter you will

[1] Understand generally accepted accounting principles as audit criteria and learn the GAAP hierarchy.

[2] Understand the relationships among financial statements, management assertions, and audit objectives.

[3] Know the auditor's responsibility for errors, fraud, and illegal acts.

[4] Understand the importance of ethics and independence to the audit function.

[5] Understand why the auditor must be a business and industry expert.

[6] Develop a preliminary understanding of how the concepts of materiality, audit risk, and evidence apply to the audit process.

[7] Understand why auditors use sampling techniques to audit.

[8] Learn the major phases of the audit process.

[9] Know the basic elements of audit reporting.

RELEVANT ACCOUNTING AND AUDITING PRONOUNCEMENTS

FASB Statement of Financial Accounting Concepts No. 2, "Qualitative Characteristics of Accounting Information" (CON2)

SAS No. 22, "Planning and Supervision" (AU 311)

SAS No. 31, "Evidential Matter" (AU 326)

SAS No. 47, "Audit Risk and Materiality in Conducting an Audit" (AU 312)

SAS No. 55, "Consideration of Internal Control in a Financial Statement Audit" (AU 319)

SAS No. 58, "Reports on Audited Financial Statements" (AU 508)

SAS No. 69, "The Meaning of *Present Fairly in Conformity with Generally Accepted Accounting Principles* in the Independent Auditor's Report" (AU 411)

SAS No. 78, "Consideration of Internal Control in a Financial Statement Audit: An Amendment to SAS No. 55" (AU 319)

SAS No. 80, "Amendment to Statement on Auditing Standards No. 31, *Evidential Matter*" (AU 326)

SAS No. 82, "Consideration of Fraud in a Financial Statement Audit" (AU 316)

SAS No. 83, "Establishing an Understanding with the Client" (AU 310)

SAS No. 84, "Communications between Predecessor and Successor Auditors" (AU 315)

This chapter provides an overview of a financial statement audit. For those readers who have relatively little knowledge about the conduct of an audit engagement, this overview is intended to introduce the important concepts and material presented in subsequent chapters. References to chapters where the concepts and material are covered in more depth are provided throughout this chapter.

The chapter covers the following topics:

- Generally accepted accounting principles as an audit criterion.
- Management assertions and audit objectives.
- The auditor's responsibility for errors, fraud, and illegal acts.
- Ethics and independence.
- The auditor as a business and industry specialist.
- Three fundamental concepts in conducting an audit.
- Sampling: inferences based on limited observations.

The last two sections of the chapter present an overview of the audit process and an introduction to audit reporting. 🌎

Generally Accepted Accounting Principles as an Audit Criterion

[LO 1]   The demand for auditing arises from the potential conflict of interest that exists between owners (stockholders) and managers. The contractual arrangement between these parties normally requires that management issue a set of financial statements that purports to show the financial position and results of operations of the entity. In order to properly evaluate the financial statements, the parties to the contract must agree on a benchmark or criterion to measure performance. Without an agreed-upon criterion, it is impossible to measure the fair presentation of the financial statements.

Generally accepted accounting principles (GAAP) have, over time, become the primary criteria used to prepare financial statements. As the term implies, these principles are generally accepted by the diverse users of financial statements. The authority for using GAAP as the benchmark comes from generally accepted auditing standards (GAAS). The first standard of reporting requires that the auditor's report indicate whether the financial statements are presented in accordance with GAAP. The auditor's standard audit report states that "the financial statements . . . present fairly . . . in conformity with generally accepted accounting principles." In making this statement in the audit report, the auditor judges whether (1) the accounting principles have general acceptance, (2) the accounting principles are appropriate in the circumstances, (3) the financial statements, including the footnotes, contain adequate disclosure, (4) the information in the financial statements is classified and summarized in a reasonable manner, and (5) the financial statements reflect the underlying transactions and events in a manner that presents the financial position, results of operations, and cash flows stated within a range of acceptable limits (AU 411.04).

In SAS No. 69 (AU 411), the Auditing Standards Board created a hierarchy for the sources of established accounting principles. Table 2–1 presents the GAAP hierarchy. Note that the hierarchy distinguishes between nongovernmental entities and state and local governments. If a conflict arises between the sources shown in Table 2–1, the auditor should follow the treatment specified in the higher category. However, in judging the proper accounting treatment for a transaction or event, the auditor should always consider whether the substance of the transaction differs from its

TABLE 2–1	Summary of the GAAP Hierarchy

Nongovernmental Entities	State and Local Governments
Established Accounting Principles	
FASB Statements and Interpretations, APB Opinions, and AICPA Accounting Research Bulletins	GASB Statements and Interpretations, plus AICPA and FASB pronouncements if made applicable to state and local governments by a GASB Statement or Interpretation
FASB Technical Bulletins, AICPA Industry Audit and Accounting Guides, and AICPA Statements of Position	GASB Technical Bulletins, and the following pronouncements if specifically made applicable to state and local governments by the AICPA: AICPA Industry Audit and Accounting Guides and AICPA Statements of Position
Consensus positions of the FASB Emerging Issues Task Force and AICPA Practice Bulletins	Consensus positions of the GASB Emerging Issues Task Force and AICPA Practice Bulletins if specifically made applicable to state and local governments by the AICPA
AICPA accounting interpretations, "Qs and As" published by the FASB staff, as well as industry practices widely recognized and prevalent	"Qs and As" published by the GASB staff, as well as industry practices widely recognized and prevalent
Other Accounting Literature	
Other accounting literature, including FASB Concepts Statements; APB Statements; AICPA Issues Papers; International Accounting Standards Committee Statements; GASB Statements, Interpretations, and Technical Bulletins; pronouncements of other professional associations or regulatory agencies; AICPA *Technical Practice Aids;* and accounting textbooks, handbooks, and articles	Other accounting literature, including GASB Concepts Statements; pronouncements in categories (a) through (d) of the hierarchy for nongovernmental entities when not specifically made applicable to state and local governments; APB Statements; FASB Concepts Statements; AICPA Issues Papers; International Accounting Standards Committee Statements; pronouncements of other professional associations or regulatory agencies; AICPA *Technical Practice Aids;* and accounting textbooks, handbooks, and articles

Source: SAS No. 69, "The Meaning of *Present Fairly in Conformity with Generally Accepted Accounting Principles* in the Independent Auditor's Report" (AU 411).

form. Transactions should be recorded to reflect their economic substance. For example, if a company enters into a lease transaction in which the substance of the transaction is the purchase of the asset with debt, the transaction should be recorded as a capital lease rather than an operating lease.

It is important to consider how GAAP and GAAS are related in the audit function. Figure 1–3 in Chapter 1 presented an overview of the audit function for a financial statement audit. Management and their accountants record business transactions through the entity's accounting system in accordance with GAAP. Therefore, the financial statements that are prepared based on the entity's operations should also be in accordance with GAAP. GAAS, on the other hand, guide the auditor on how to gather evidence to test management's assertions to determine if they are in accordance with GAAP. If the auditor has gathered sufficient evidence to provide reasonable assurance that the financial statements present fairly in accordance with GAAP, an unqualified report can be issued.

TABLE 2–2	Summary of Management Assertions
• *Existence or occurrence*	The assets and liabilities *exist,* and the recorded transactions have *occurred.*
• *Completeness*	The accounts and transactions that should be included are included; thus, the financial statements are *complete.*
• *Rights and obligations*	The assets are *rights* of the entity, and the liabilities are its *obligations.*
• *Valuation or allocation*	Assets, liabilities, equity, revenues, and expenses are appropriately *valued* and are *allocated* to the proper accounting period.
• *Presentation and disclosure*	Amounts shown in the financial statements are properly *presented* and *disclosed.*

Financial Statements, Management Assertions, and Audit Objectives

[LO 2]   Financial statements issued by management contain assertions about the components of those financial statements (refer to Figure 1–3). For example, when the financial statements contain a line item that inventory is $2,500,000, management asserts among other things that inventory *exists,* that the entity *owns* the inventory, and that it is properly *valued.* Similarly, if the financial statements contain a line item that states accounts payable are $750,000, management asserts among other things that the accounts payable are *obligations* of the entity and the amount for accounts payable contains all such obligations (an assertion as to *completeness*).

Auditing standards (AU 326) classify management assertions into five categories:

- Existence or occurrence
- Completeness
- Rights and obligations
- Valuation or allocation
- Presentation and disclosure

Table 2–2 summarizes and explains management assertions.

The independent auditor's work consists of searching for and evaluating evidence concerning assertions. Operationally, this is accomplished by developing audit objectives that relate to management's assertions. In the previous example, management asserted that accounts payable of $750,000 were complete (all accounts payable were included). The completeness assertion can be divided into two audit objectives: *completeness* and *cutoff.* By disaggregating the assertions into more specific audit objectives, the auditor is better able to design audit procedures for obtaining sufficient competent evidence to test management assertions. In our example, the audit objective for completeness is tested to determine if all accounts payable were included in the account, while the audit objective for cutoff tests whether all accounts payable were recorded in the proper accounting period. One audit procedure that would provide evidence about the completeness objective would be a search for unrecorded liabilities. One step in this search would be to examine vendor bills recorded in the period after year-end to

FIGURE 2–1

The Relationships among
Management's Assertions,
Audit Objectives, Audit
Procedures, and Audit
Evidence

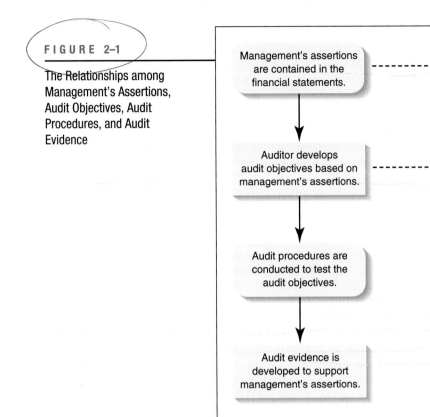

Management's assertions
are contained in the
financial statements.

Existence and occurrence
Completeness
Rights and obligations
Valuation or allocation
Presentation and disclosure

Auditor develops
audit objectives based on
management's assertions.

Validity
Completeness
Cutoff
Ownership
Accuracy
Valuation
Classification
Disclosure

Audit procedures are
conducted to test the
audit objectives.

Audit evidence is
developed to support
management's assertions.

determine if those liabilities relate to the current period. Once the auditor
has sufficient evidence that the audit objective is met, he or she has reasonable assurance that the assertion is appropriate.

Figure 2–1 graphically represents the relationships among management assertions, audit objectives, audit procedures, and audit evidence.
Chapter 4 contains detailed coverage of these relationships.

The Auditor's Responsibility for Errors, Fraud, and Illegal Acts

[LO 3]   The financial statements are the responsibility of management, while the
auditor's responsibility is to express an opinion on the financial statements. Many readers of financial statements believe that auditors have a
responsibility to detect *all* errors, fraud, and illegal acts. Auditing standards (AU 110.02) provide the following responsibility for auditors:

> The auditor has a responsibility to plan and perform the audit to obtain rea-
> sonable assurance about whether the financial statements are free of material
> misstatement, whether caused by error or fraud. Because of the nature of
> audit evidence and the characteristics of fraud, the auditor is able to obtain
> reasonable, but not absolute, assurance that material misstatements are de-
> tected. The auditor has no responsibility to plan and perform the audit to ob-
> tain reasonable assurance that misstatements, whether caused by errors or
> fraud, that are not material to the financial statements are detected.

The auditor's responsibility to detect misstatements resulting from illegal acts is the same as that for error or fraud. Thus, the auditor provides only *reasonable* assurance that the financial statements are free of *material* misstatements caused by errors, fraud, and illegal acts. It is therefore possible that an auditor could conduct an audit in accordance with GAAS and issue an unqualified opinion, and the financial statements might still contain material misstatements.

The third general auditing standard (see Table 1–4) requires that the auditor exercise due professional care in the planning and performance of the audit. Due professional care requires that the auditor exercise *professional skepticism,* which is an attitude that includes a questioning mind and a critical assessment of audit evidence. The auditor should not assume that management is either honest or dishonest. Professional skepticism requires that the auditor *objectively* evaluate audit evidence. If the auditor suspected that there might be a material misstatement due to fraud, the auditor would be more sensitive to the selection and type of evidence examined. More information on the auditor's responsibility for errors, fraud, and illegal acts is contained in Chapters 3 and 5.

Ethics and Independence

[LO 4]   Ethical behavior and independence on the part of an auditor are vital to the audit function. As discussed in Chapter 1, the demand for auditing arose from the need for a competent, independent person to monitor the contractual arrangements between the principal and agent. If an auditor is neither competent nor independent, the parties to the contract will place little or no value on the service provided.

Ethics refers to a system or code of conduct based on moral duties and obligations that indicates how we should behave. *Professionalism* refers to the conduct, aims, or qualities that characterize or mark a profession or professional person.[1] All professions operate under some type of code of ethics or code of conduct. Professions establish such codes to demonstrate to the users of their services that members of the profession follow standards of behavior. The AICPA has the 10 GAAS and a Code of Professional Conduct that establish acceptable behavior for auditors. For example, the first general standard requires that an audit be performed by a person or persons having adequate technical training and proficiency as an auditor, while the second general standard requires that auditors maintain an independent attitude when conducting an audit engagement. The Code of Professional Conduct contains principles, rules of conduct, and interpretations of the rules that clarify the intent of the 10 GAAS. Chapter 19 contains a detailed discussion of the Code of Professional Conduct. A major portion of the code identifies actions that may impair auditors' independence. For example, auditors are not allowed to have financial or managerial interests in their clients (see Exhibit 2–1).

---

[1]S. M. Mintz, *Cases in Accounting Ethics and Professionalism,* 3rd ed. (New York: McGraw-Hill, 1997).

EXHIBIT 2–1

AICPA Bans Borrowing by Members from Financial Institutions They Audit

In November 1991 the AICPA revised its independence rules for loans from financial institution clients. The former ethics rules permitted accountants to take several types of loans from audit clients: home mortgages, loans that are not material to the borrower's net worth, and certain other secured loans. The new rules permit only the following types of loans: (1) automobile loans and leases collateralized by the automobile, (2) loans fully collateralized by the surrender value of a life insurance policy, (3) loans fully collateralized by cash deposits at the same financial institution, and (4) credit cards and cash where the aggregate outstanding balance is reduced to $5,000 or less by the payment due date. Such loans must be kept current as to all terms.

The new rules appear to have been in reaction to an SEC lawsuit against Ernst & Young for its audits of First RepublicBank Corp. The SEC accused the firm of violating federal securities laws by failing to report the existence of loans that jeopardized the firm's independence. At the time of the audits, Ernst & Young partners had $21.8 million in loans from the bank. Ernst & Young claimed that the loans in question met the former standards for auditor independence.

Sources: G. Brooks, "CPA Body Bans Borrowing by Members from Financial Institutions They Audit," *The International Bank Accountant* (June 21, 1991); K. G. Salwen, "Ernst & Young Faces Lawsuit from the SEC," *The Wall Street Journal* (June 14, 1991).

In today's audit environment, auditors are faced with situations that may test their ethical behavior and independence. For example, competition among public accounting firms for audit clients has led to heavily discounted audit fees (referred to as *low-balling*). Low-balling involves intentionally underbidding for the engagement not only in order to obtain the audit, but also with the hope of entering into lucrative management consulting services. In such situations, the auditor may decrease the time allocated to the audit and the extent of audit procedures. This may compromise the auditor's integrity, objectivity, and independence. Auditors may also have their independence tested when a client engages in *opinion shopping*—that is, when a client seeks the views of other CPAs who will agree with the client's desired accounting treatment. The client may attempt to force the auditor to go along with the desired accounting treatment by threatening to change auditors.

The point of this section is to emphasize the importance of ethical behavior and independence on the part of auditors. Independence is the hallmark of the auditing profession. If auditors do not demonstrate to users that they perform audit services in an ethical and independent manner, the service will lose its value and the demand for auditing will decline.

The Auditor as a Business and Industry Expert

[LO 5]   The auditor must have extensive knowledge about the nature of the client's business and industry in order to determine whether financial statement assertions are valid. The auditor must understand the strategic business risks faced by the client in addition to understanding the risks that affect the traditional processing and recording of transactions. Bell, Marrs,

Solomon, and Thomas[2] have defined client business risk as "the risk that an entity's business objectives will not be attained as a result of the external and internal factors, pressures, and forces brought to bear on the entity and, ultimately, the risk associated with the entity's survival and profitability" (p. 15). They have also made the following observations concerning the need to evaluate a client's business risk:

> As the global economy, the business organizations operating within it, and organizations' business strategies become increasingly complex and interdependent, we believe more attention should be paid to the development of auditing methods and procedures that focus on assertions at the entity level–methods and procedures that promise greater power to detect material misstatements as they allow the auditor to ground key judgments in a more critical and holistic understanding of the client's systems dynamics (p. 12).
>
> In today's world, distance is no longer a barrier to market entry, technologies are rapidly replicated by competitors, and information and communications technologies are shaping a new economic order. To manage their business risks effectively, organizations must now view their playing field as the whole global economy (p. 27).

Consideration of an entity's business risks requires that the auditor know the client's business strategy and how it plans to respond to, or control, changes in its business environment. Numerous rapid or momentous changes have significantly affected an industry or an entity within that industry. For example, the sale of books over the Internet by Amazon.com through a "virtual" bookstore significantly affected the retail book industry. Traditional bookstores (like Barnes & Noble) had to respond to this new competitor or lose sales and customers. Similarly, rapid and significant technological changes in telecommunications and in computers and peripheral equipment increase the business risks for entities that operate in those industries. Lastly, deregulation in banking and utilities has significantly increased the risks for entities that operate in those industries.

This focus on the client's business risks leads to a more strategic and systematic approach to the audit. The auditor uses knowledge of the client's business and industry to develop a more efficient and effective audit. The auditor places less emphasis on routine transactions that are likely to be tightly controlled through the client's internal control system. Instead, the focus shifts to identifying nonroutine transactions, accounting estimates, and valuation issues that are much more likely to lead to misstatements in the financial statements. A detailed discussion of the auditor's understanding and evaluation of client business risk is contained in Chapter 3.

Three Fundamental Concepts in Conducting an Audit

[LO 6]   A financial statement audit requires an understanding of three fundamental concepts: *materiality, audit risk,* and *evidence*. The auditor's judgment of materiality and audit risk establishes the type and amount of the audit

---

[2]T. B. Bell, F. O. Marrs, I. Solomon, and H. Thomas, *Auditing Organizations Through a Strategic-Systems Lens: The KPMG Business Measurement Process* (New York: KPMG Peat Marwick LLP, 1997).

work to be performed (referred to as the *scope* of the audit). In establishing the scope of the audit, the auditor must make decisions about the nature, extent, and timing of evidence to be gathered. This section briefly discusses each of these concepts. The next two chapters cover these concepts in greater depth.

Materiality

The auditor's consideration of materiality is a matter of *professional judgment* and is affected by what the auditor perceives as the view of a reasonable person who is relying on the financial statements. There are no formal standards or guidelines for making this judgment. The Financial Accounting Standards Board has provided the following definition of materiality:

> **Materiality** is the magnitude of an omission or misstatement of accounting information that, in the light of surrounding circumstances, makes it probable that the judgment of a reasonable person relying on the information would have been changed or influenced by the omission or misstatement.[3]

The focus of this definition is on the users of the financial statements. In planning the engagement, the auditor assesses the magnitude of a misstatement that may affect the users' decisions. This is sometimes referred to as *accounting materiality*. The auditor uses accounting materiality as a starting point for determining an amount that will be used for establishing the preliminary judgment about materiality. This assessment is sometimes referred to as *auditing materiality*. Auditing materiality is generally assessed to be less than accounting materiality because the auditor needs to allow for the difficulty in assessing what is material to the diverse groups of financial statement users. When "materiality" is used in the remainder of this text, it refers to auditing materiality.

The earlier example of an inventory balance of $2,500,000 is used to demonstrate this approach. Suppose the auditor assesses that the inventory component of the financial statements can be misstated by $50,000 before users' decisions will be affected. The $50,000 is accounting materiality. The auditor may set auditing materiality at a lower amount, say $40,000, to provide for any uncertainty that may be present in his or her assessment of accounting materiality. The $40,000 is used by the auditor to *design* the planned audit work. This amount would also be used to *evaluate* the auditor's findings. By establishing an auditing materiality level such as $40,000, the auditor is focusing on *material misstatements*, where a misstatement is the difference between what management asserts is the balance and the balance based on the auditor's findings.

As we shall see later in this chapter, the wording of the auditor's standard audit report includes the phrase "the financial statements present fairly *in all material respects.*" This is the manner in which the auditor communicates the notion of materiality to the users of the auditor's report. Further, there is no guarantee that the auditor will uncover *all* material misstatements. The auditor can only provide reasonable assurance

---

[3]Financial Accounting Standards Board, Statement of Financial Accounting Concepts No. 2, "Qualitative Characteristics of Accounting Information" (CON2). This definition is also included in SAS No. 47, "Audit Risk and Materiality in the Conduct of an Audit" (AU 312.10).

that all material misstatements are detected. The notion of *reasonable assurance* leads to the second concept.

Audit Risk

The second major concept involved in auditing is *audit risk*.

> **Audit risk** is the risk that the auditor may unknowingly fail to appropriately modify his or her opinion on financial statements that are materially misstated.[4]

As mentioned previously, an audit does not guarantee or provide absolute assurance that all misstatements will be detected. The auditor's standard report states that the audit provides only reasonable assurance that the financial statements do not contain material misstatements. The term *reasonable assurance* implies some risk that a material misstatement could be present in the financial statements and the auditor will fail to detect it. In conducting an audit, the auditor decides what level of audit risk he or she is willing to accept and plans the audit to achieve that level of audit risk. The auditor controls the level of audit risk by the effectiveness and extent of the audit work conducted. The more effective and extensive the audit work, the less the risk that the misstatement will go undetected and the auditor will issue an inappropriate report. However, as discussed previously, an auditor could conduct an audit in accordance with GAAS and issue an unqualified opinion, and the financial statements might still contain material misstatements.

Evidence

Most of the auditor's work in arriving at an opinion on the financial statements consists of obtaining and evaluating evidence. Evidential matter supporting the financial statements consists of the underlying accounting data and all corroborating information available to the auditor.[5]

In designing an audit program to obtain evidence about management's assertions contained in the financial statements, the auditor develops specific audit objectives that relate to each management assertion (see Figure 2–1). The audit objectives, in conjunction with the assessment of materiality and audit risk, are used by the auditor to determine the type, amount, and timing of evidence to be gathered. Because the audit objectives are derived from management's assertions, once the auditor has obtained sufficient competent evidence that the audit objectives are met, reasonable assurance is provided that the financial statements are fairly presented.

In searching for and evaluating evidence, the auditor is concerned with the relevance and reliability of the evidence. *Relevance* refers to whether the evidence relates to the specific audit objective being tested. If the auditor relies on evidence that relates to a different audit objective from the one being tested, an incorrect conclusion may be reached about a management assertion. For example, suppose the auditor wants to test whether

---

[4]SAS No. 47, "Audit Risk and Materiality in Conducting an Audit" (AU 312.02).
[5]SAS No. 31, "Evidential Matter" (AU 326.15).

the client owns certain property. If the auditor physically examines the property, this would not be relevant evidence. It is possible, for example, that the client is leasing the property the auditor examined.

Reliability refers to the diagnosticity of the evidence. In other words, can a particular type of evidence be relied upon to signal the true state of the assertion or audit objective? Suppose an auditor has the choice of gathering evidence from an independent, competent source *outside* the client or from a source *inside* the client. For example, evidence provided by an attorney on the outcome of a lawsuit against the client would be considered more reliable than the controller's assessment of the outcome. In this instance, the external source, the attorney, would be chosen because evidence from the outside source would be viewed as independent and thus more reliable.

The auditor seldom has convincing evidence about the true state of an audit objective and, therefore, the related management assertion. In most situations, the auditor obtains only enough evidence to be persuaded that the audit objective is fairly stated. The nature of the evidence obtained by the auditor seldom provides absolute assurance about an audit objective because the types of evidence have different degrees of reliability. Additionally, for many parts of an audit, the auditor examines only a sample of the transactions processed during the period. Thus, as explained in the next section, the auditor reaches a conclusion based on a subset of the evidence available.

Sampling: Inferences Based on Limited Observations

[LO 7]   The reader might ask why the auditor uses concepts such as materiality and audit risk to set the scope of an audit. Why not test all transactions that occurred during the period? The main reason is the cost and feasibility of such an audit. In a small business, the auditor might be able to examine all transactions that occurred during the period and still issue the audit report in a reasonable amount of time after year-end. However, it is unlikely that the owner of the business could afford to pay for such an extensive audit. For a large organization, the sheer volume of transactions prevents the auditor from examining every transaction. Thus, there is a trade-off between the exactness or precision of the audit and its cost.

To deal with this problem, the auditor uses (1) his or her knowledge about the transactions and/or (2) a sampling approach to examine the transactions. Many times the auditor is aware of items in an account balance that are likely to contain misstatements based on factors such as previous audits of the client or knowledge of the industry. For example, the auditor's prior knowledge may indicate that transactions with certain types of customers or large dollar transactions are likely to contain misstatements. The auditor can use this knowledge to select those transactions for examination. When the auditor has no special knowledge about which transactions may be misstated, he or she uses sampling procedures that increase the likelihood of obtaining a sample *representative* of the population of transactions. In such cases, the auditor is using the laws of probability to identify transactions that are misstated.

The size of a sample is a function of materiality and acceptable audit risk. There is an *inverse* relationship between sample size and either materiality or acceptable audit risk. For example, if an auditor assesses materiality to be a small amount for a given level of audit risk, a larger sample will be needed than if materiality was a larger amount. This occurs because the auditor must gather more evidence (a larger sample) to support a lower level of materiality. Similarly, as the amount of audit risk the auditor is willing to accept decreases for a given materiality amount, the sample size necessary to test the audit objective becomes greater. This occurs because the auditor must gather more evidence in order to reduce the amount of uncertainty or risk associated with the test.

Overview of the Audit Process

[LO 8]   This section discusses the major phases of a financial statement audit. The presentation provides the reader with an overall picture of the steps necessary to complete an audit engagement. While these steps are presented as separate phases, on many engagements some of these steps may be conducted concurrently. Note also that there is important feedback among the various phases about the results of the audit work conducted. For example, when testing an accounts receivable balance, the auditor sets the scope of the tests based on the assessment of the internal controls over the revenue cycle. If the auditor detects more misstatements than expected when auditing the accounts receivable account, it may provide evidence that the internal controls in the revenue cycle are not operating as effectively as originally assessed. In this case, the auditor should revise the internal control assessment for the revenue cycle and adjust other planned audit tests that may be affected by the revenue cycle.

The phases of the audit are shown in Figure 2–2. The first phase, client acceptance and retention, is discussed in detail in this section. Subsequent chapters in this book cover the other phases in more detail.

Client Acceptance and Retention

The Statements on Quality Control Standards require that public accounting firms establish policies and procedures for deciding whether to accept new clients or retain current clients. The purpose of such policies is to minimize the likelihood that an auditor will be associated with clients who lack integrity. If an auditor is associated with a client who lacks integrity, material misstatements may exist and not be detected by the auditor (see Exhibit 2–2). This can lead to lawsuits brought by users of the financial statements.[6] In discussing this issue, a distinction is made between evaluating a prospective client and continuing a current client. In the case of a continuing client, the auditor has more firsthand knowledge about the entity's operations and management's integrity.

---

[6]See Z. Palmrose, "Litigation and Independent Auditors: The Role of Business Failure and Management Fraud," *Auditing: A Journal of Practice & Theory* (Spring 1987), pp. 90–103, for a discussion of the impact of management fraud on litigation against auditors.

FIGURE 2–2

Overview of the Major
Phases in an Audit

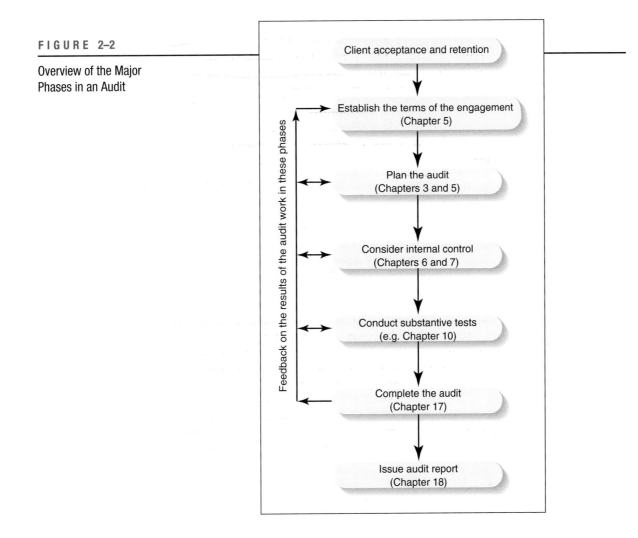

Prospective Client Acceptance   Public accounting firms should investigate a prospective client prior to accepting an engagement.[7] Table 2–3 lists procedures that a firm might conduct to evaluate a prospective client. Performance of such procedures would normally be documented in a memo or by completion of a client acceptance questionnaire or checklist.

When the prospective client has previously been audited, SAS No. 84, "Communications between Predecessor and Successor Auditors" (AU 315), requires that the successor auditor make certain inquiries of the predecessor auditor before accepting the engagement. The successor auditor should request permission of the prospective client before contacting the predecessor auditor. Because the Code of Professional Conduct does not allow an auditor to disclose confidential client information without the

---

[7]See H. F. Huss and F. A. Jacobs, "Risk Containment: Exploring Auditor Decisions in the Engagement Process," *Auditing: A Journal of Practice and Theory* (Fall 1991), pp. 16–32, for a description of the client acceptance process of the Big 5 firms.

| EXHIBIT 2–2 | **President of Phar-Mor Indicted for Fraud and Embezzlement** |

Phar-Mor operated drugstores that attracted customers based on low prices made possible by bulk purchases. Phar-Mor grew rapidly, with more than 300 stores and $3 billion in annual sales in 1992. On August 3, 1992, Phar-Mor issued a press release stating that a scheme had been uncovered and the financial results had been overstated by $350 million (subsequently increased to over $500 million). It appears that a number of factors led the officers and employees of Phar-Mor to participate in the fraud. In particular, the president had pledged his Phar-Mor stock as collateral for a number of personal loans, and a drop in stock price would have led to personal bankruptcy. He was also an autocratic leader who surrounded himself with people whom he could influence.

The officers and employees used various schemes to conceal the fact that Phar-Mor's financial results had deteriorated significantly. Some of the major means used to perpetrate the fraud included improper recognition of income on multiyear contracts with vendors, inventory manipulations, and manipulation of rebates from vendors.

In February 1993 the president of Phar-Mor was indicted on charges of fraud and embezzlement. The auditors of Phar-Mor, Coopers & Lybrand, were sued by investors and creditors for losses incurred.

Source: See Chapter 20, appendix, for a more detailed summary of this case. G. Stern, "Grand Jury Indicts Monus on Charges of Fraud, Embezzlement at Phar-Mor," *The Wall Street Journal* (February 1, 1993).

| TABLE 2–3 | **Procedures for Evaluating a Prospective Client** |

1. Obtain and review available financial information (annual reports, interim financial statements, income tax returns, etc.).
2. Inquire of third parties about any information concerning the integrity of the prospective client and its management. (Such inquiries should be directed to the prospective client's bankers and attorneys, credit agencies, and other members of the business community who may have such knowledge.)
3. Communicate with the predecessor auditor as required by SAS No. 84 (AU 315) about whether there were any disagreements about accounting principles, audit procedures, or similar significant matters.
4. Consider whether the prospective client has any circumstances that will require special attention or that may represent unusual business or audit risks, such as litigation or going-concern problems.
5. Determine if the firm is independent of the client and able to provide the desired service.
6. Determine if the firm has the necessary technical skills and knowledge of the industry to complete the engagement.
7. Determine if acceptance of the client would violate any applicable regulatory agency requirements or the Code of Professional Conduct.

client's consent, the prospective client must authorize the predecessor auditor to respond to the successor's requests for information. The successor auditor's communications with the predecessor auditor should include questions related to the integrity of management; disagreements with management over accounting and auditing issues; communications with audit committees or an equivalent group regarding fraud, illegal acts, and internal-control-related matters; and the predecessor's understanding of the reason for the change in auditors. Such inquiries of the predecessor auditor may help the successor auditor determine whether to accept the engagement. The predecessor auditor should respond fully to the successor's requests unless an unusual circumstance (such as a lawsuit) exists. If the predecessor's response is limited, the successor auditor must be informed that the response is limited.

In the unusual case where the prospective client refuses to permit the predecessor to respond, the successor auditor should have reservations about accepting the client. Such a situation should raise serious questions about management's motivations and integrity.

After accepting the engagement, the successor auditor may need information on beginning balances and consistent application of GAAP in order to issue an unqualified report. The successor auditor should request that the client authorize the predecessor auditor to permit a review of his or her working papers. In most instances, the predecessor auditor will allow the successor auditor to make copies of any working papers of continuing interest (for example, details of selected balance sheet accounts).

If the client has not previously been audited, the public accounting firm should complete all the procedures listed in Table 2–3, except for the communication with the predecessor auditor. The auditor should review the prospective client's financial information and carefully assess management integrity by communicating with the entity's bankers and attorneys, as well as other members of the business community. In some cases, the public accounting firm may hire an investigative agency to check on management's background.

Continuing Client Retention   Public accounting firms need to evaluate periodically whether to retain their current clients. This evaluation may take place at or near the completion of an audit or when some significant event occurs. Conflicts over accounting and auditing issues or disputes over fees may lead a public accounting firm to disassociate itself from a client.

Establish the Terms of the Engagement

The auditor should establish an understanding with the client regarding the services to be performed. For small, privately held entities, the auditor normally negotiates directly with the owner-manager. For larger private or public entities, the auditor will normally be appointed by a vote of the stockholders after recommendation by the audit committee of the board of directors. In all cases, an engagement letter should document the terms agreed to by the auditor and client. Such terms would include, for example, the responsibilities of each party, the assistance to be provided by client personnel and internal auditors, and the expected audit fees. Chapter 5 provides an example of an engagement letter and discusses the audit committee and internal auditors.

Plan the Audit

Proper planning of an audit is important to ensure that the audit is conducted in an effective and efficient manner. The steps taken during this phase include (1) gaining knowledge of the client's business and industry so that the auditor understands events, transactions, and practices that may affect the financial statements and (2) conducting preliminary analytical procedures (such as ratio analysis) to identify specific transactions or account balances that should receive special attention because they may contain material misstatements. In many instances, audit planning will include a preliminary consideration of the client's internal control system. Based on this initial work, an overall audit strategy is developed. This includes the preliminary assessment of materiality and audit risk, as well as an audit plan involving the types of audit procedures to be performed and the amount of evidence to be gathered. The audit plan serves as a starting point for the engagement, but adjustments may be required as the audit progresses. Chapters 3 and 5 cover the issues that are involved in this phase of the audit.

Consider Internal Control

Internal control is a process effected by an entity's board of directors, management, and other personnel that is designed to provide reasonable assurance regarding the achievement of objectives in the following categories: (1) effectiveness and efficiency of operations, (2) reliability of financial reporting, and (3) compliance with applicable laws and regulations (AU 319). The auditor must sufficiently understand the client's internal controls in order to determine which controls exist within the entity. The auditor then evaluates the internal controls in order to assess the risk that they will not prevent or detect a material misstatement in the financial statements. This risk (referred to as *control risk*) directly impacts the scope of the auditor's work. When the auditor assesses control risk at less than the maximum, the internal controls should be tested. The auditor's tests are intended to ensure that the internal controls are operating in the manner intended and therefore are effective in preventing or detecting misstatements. The evidence gathered from testing the internal controls is used to arrive at a final assessment on the level of control risk. When control risk is assessed low, based on tests of the internal controls (referred to as *tests of controls*), less audit work is required to audit the account balances (referred to as *substantive tests*) because the auditor has evidence that the accounting systems are generating materially accurate financial information. Conversely, if control risk is high, the auditor has to conduct more extensive audit work in the account balances because the evidence about internal controls suggests that material misstatements could occur because controls do not exist or are not operating effectively. Chapter 6 provides detailed coverage of internal control in a financial statement audit. Later chapters apply this process to various accounting cycles; for example, see Chapter 10.

Conduct Substantive Tests

In this phase, the auditor conducts more analytical procedures and examines the details of the account balances. For example, the auditor may calculate an estimate of interest expense by multiplying total debt by the average interest rate on the entity's debt. This estimate of interest expense can be compared to interest expense reported in the general ledger for reasonableness. The purpose of such analytical procedures is to determine whether the accounts contain a material misstatement. The auditor will examine other account balances by testing the detailed transactions that make up the balance. For example, the auditor can examine the vendors' bills for newly acquired equipment that is included in the machinery and equipment account to ensure that the equipment is recorded at its acquisition cost. On most engagements, this phase comprises most of the time spent on the audit. A number of chapters in this textbook discuss substantive tests performed on the various accounts included in the financial statements.

Complete the Audit

After the auditor has completed testing the account balances, the sufficiency of the evidence gathered needs to be evaluated. The auditor must have sufficient competent evidence in order to reach a conclusion on the fairness of the financial statements. In this phase, the auditor also assesses the possibility of contingent liabilities, such as lawsuits, and searches for any events subsequent to the balance sheet date that may impact the financial statements. Chapter 17 covers each of these issues in detail.

Issue the Report

The final phase in the audit process is choosing the appropriate audit report to issue. When the auditor has gathered sufficient competent evidence and complied with GAAS, and the financial statements conform to GAAP, the auditor can issue a standard unqualified audit report. When sufficient evidence is not gathered or the financial statements are not in accordance with GAAP, the auditor will issue a different type of report. The remainder of this chapter presents coverage of the auditor's standard unqualified audit report and an overview of the exceptions to the unqualified report. Audit reporting is covered early in the text so that the reader has a better understanding of how the results of the evidence-gathering process affect the auditor's choice of audit reports. Chapter 18 provides detailed coverage of audit reporting.

Audit Reporting

[LO 9] The auditor's report is the main product or output of the audit. This report communicates the auditor's findings to the users of the financial statements. It is the culmination of a process of collecting and evaluating sufficient competent evidence concerning the fair presentation of management's assertions in the financial statements. The audit report adds value to the financial statements because of the auditor's objective and independent opinion on the fairness of the financial statements. SAS No. 58, "Reports on Audited Financial Statements" (AU 508), provides authoritative guidance on audit reporting. Figure 2–3 provides an overview of audit reporting.

The Auditor's Standard Unqualified Audit Report

The most common type of audit report issued is the standard unqualified audit report because management's assertions about the entity's financial statements are usually found to conform to generally accepted accounting principles. Such a conclusion can be expressed only when the audit was performed in accordance with generally accepted auditing standards. Exhibit 2–3 presents an audit report issued on Intel Corporation. This report covers financial statements that include balance sheets for two years and statements of income, stockholders' equity, and cash flows for three years.

Overview of Audit Reporting

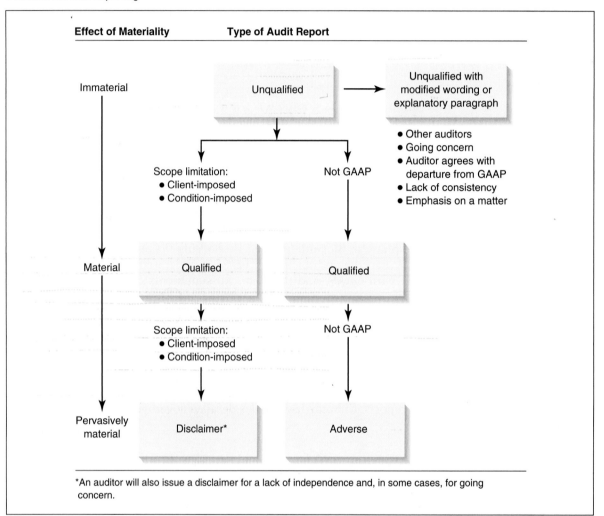

*An auditor will also issue a disclaimer for a lack of independence and, in some cases, for going concern.

This is the standard type of report issued for publicly traded companies. The auditor's standard unqualified audit report can also cover a single year. The Intel report contains a number of important elements.

Title   Auditing standards require that the report be titled and include the word *independent* so that it is clear to the user that the financial statements have been audited by an individual or firm that has an objective perspective about the entity. An example of an acceptable title is "Independent Auditor's Report" or "Report of Independent Auditor."

Addressee   The audit report is addressed to the individual or group that engaged the auditor. In the normal situation, the report is addressed to the entity, its board of directors, and/or the entity's stockholders.

EXHIBIT 2–3 ✕

	The Auditor's Standard Unqualified Audit Report— Comparative Financial Statements
Title:	Report of Ernst & Young LLP, Independent Auditors
Addressee:	The Board of Directors and Stockholders, Intel Corporation
Introductory paragraph:	We have audited the accompanying consolidated balance sheets of Intel Corporation as of December 27, 1997 and December 28, 1996, and the related consolidated statements of income, stockholders' equity, and cash flows for each of the three years in the period ended December 27, 1997. These financial statements are the responsibility of the Company's management. Our responsibility is to express an opinion on these financial statements based on our audits.
Scope paragraph:	We conducted our audits in accordance with generally accepted auditing standards. Those standards require that we plan and perform the audit to obtain reasonable assurance about whether the financial statements are free of material misstatement. An audit includes examining, on a test basis, evidence supporting the amounts and disclosures in the financial statements. An audit also includes assessing the accounting principles used and significant estimates made by management, as well as evaluating the overall financial statement presentation. We believe that our audits provide a reasonable basis for our opinion.
Opinion paragraph:	In our opinion, the consolidated financial statements referred to above present fairly, in all material respects, the consolidated financial position of Intel Corporation at December 27, 1997 and December 28, 1996, and the consolidated results of its operations and its cash flows for each of the three years in the period ended December 27, 1997, in conformity with generally accepted accounting principles.
Name of the auditor:	*Ernst & Young LLP*
Date of report:	San Jose, California January 12, 1998

Introductory Paragraph   The introductory paragraph contains three important facts. First, it states that an audit was conducted and indicates which financial statements are covered by the audit report. Second, it contains a statement that the financial statements are the responsibility of management. Third, it identifies the auditor's responsibility—to express an opinion on the financial statements.

Scope Paragraph   The second, or scope, paragraph communicates to the users, in very general terms, what an audit entails. In addition to indicating that the audit was conducted in accordance with generally accepted auditing standards, it emphasizes the fact that the audit provides only *reasonable assurance* that the financial statements contain no material misstatements. The scope paragraph also discloses that an audit involves examining evidence on a test basis, an assessment of accounting principles used and significant estimates, and an overall evaluation of financial statement presentation. The overall evaluation is in terms of the agreed-upon criteria. In Exhibit 2–3, GAAP are the criteria used for the fairness of the financial statements.

Opinion Paragraph   The third paragraph contains the auditor's opinion concerning the fairness of the financial statements based on the audit evidence. Two important phrases contained in this paragraph require further explanation. First, the phrase "present fairly . . . in conformity with generally accepted accounting principles" is the wording used by the auditor to comply with the first standard of reporting. Second, the opinion paragraph also contains the phrase "in all material respects." As mentioned earlier, this phrase is included in the report to stress the concept of materiality.

Name of the Auditor   This is the manual or printed signature of the CPA firm.

Date of Report   Generally, the auditor's report is dated as of the date on which the auditor has completed all significant auditing procedures. The audit report date indicates to the user the last day of the auditor's responsibility for the review of significant events that have occurred after the date of the financial statements.

In the remaining sections, departures from an unqualified audit report and other types of audit reports are covered briefly so that the reader will understand the auditor's reporting options when a standard unqualified report is not appropriate. Chapter 18 provides detailed coverage, including examples of the other types of reports.

Departures from an Unqualified Audit Report

There are three basic reasons why an auditor may be unable to express an unqualified opinion (see Figure 2–3):

1. **Scope limitation.** A scope limitation results from a lack of evidence such as an inability to conduct an audit procedure considered necessary. For example, if the client had an equity investment in a foreign affiliate and the auditor is unable to obtain audited financial statements for the affiliate, the auditor does not have sufficient competent evidence to determine the amount of equity income or the reported amount of the investment account.

2. **A departure from GAAP.** The financial statements are prepared using an accounting principle that is not in conformity with GAAP. For example, if the client does not include overhead costs in inventory, the inventory account is valued using an accounting principle that is not in accordance with GAAP.

3. **The auditor is not independent.** The auditor must be independent of the entity being audited in order to comply with the second general standard and the Code of Professional Conduct. For example, if an auditor had a material financial interest in or performed managerial functions for the entity, he or she would not be independent of the entity.

Other Types of Audit Reports

The auditor can assume different degrees of responsibility for the financial statements. In a sense, auditing standards provide for a graded set of audit reports. There are three types of audit reports other than unqualified:

1. *Qualified.* The auditor's opinion is qualified for either a scope limitation or a departure from GAAP with material consequences, but the *overall* financial statements present fairly. With a qualified report, the opinion paragraph is modified by the words "except for."

2. *Disclaimer.* When issuing a disclaimer, the auditor states that he or she cannot give an opinion on the financial statements because of a lack of sufficient competent evidence to form an opinion on the overall financial statements or because of a lack of independence. In this case, the scope limitation is so significant that the overall financial statements may not be fairly presented.

3. *Adverse.* The auditor's opinion states that the financial statements do not present fairly in conformity with GAAP because the departure affects the overall financial statements. In this case, the departure from GAAP is so significant that the overall financial statements may not be fairly presented.

The choice of which audit report to issue depends on the condition and the materiality of the departure (see Figure 2–3).

REVIEW QUESTIONS

[LO 1] **2-1** The independent auditor normally uses GAAP as a benchmark to measure management's reporting of economic activity and events. The auditor's report states that "the financial statements . . . present fairly . . . in conformity with generally accepted accounting principles." In making this statement, what judgments does the auditor make concerning GAAP?

[1] **2-2** Auditing standards state that "present fairly" should be applied within the framework of GAAP. List the hierarchy of sources of established accounting principles. Give an example of each.

[2] **2-3** How do management assertions relate to the financial statements? To audit objectives?

[3] **2-4** What are the auditor's responsibilities for errors and fraud? For illegal acts?

[3] **2-5** Describe what is meant by the statement that "due care requires that the auditor exercise professional skepticism."

[4] **2-6** Why are ethical behavior and independence so vital to the audit function?

[5,6] **2-7** What is meant by *client business risk,* and why is it important for the auditor to properly assess this risk?

[6] **2-8** Define *materiality.* How is this concept reflected in the auditor's report?

[6] **2-9** Define *audit risk.* How is this concept reflected in the auditor's report?

[6] **2-10** Describe what is meant by the *relevance* and *reliability* of audit evidence.

[7]   2-11   Briefly describe why on most audit engagements an auditor tests only a sample of transactions that occurred.

[8]   2-12   What is the purpose of establishing quality control policies for new client acceptance?

[8]   2-13   What types of inquiries about a prospective client should an auditor make to third parties?

[8]   2-14   Who is responsible for initiating the communication between the predecessor and successor auditors? What type of information should be requested from the predecessor auditor?

[9]   2-15   What is the purpose of the fourth standard of reporting?

[9]   2-16   Identify the elements of the auditor's standard unqualified report.

[9]   2-17   What three important facts are contained in the introductory paragraph of the standard unqualified audit report?

[9]   2-18   What is the significance of the audit report date?

[9]   2-19   Identify the conditions that result in a departure from an unqualified audit report.

MULTIPLE-CHOICE QUESTIONS FROM CPA EXAMINATIONS

[1]   2-20   Several sources of GAAP consulted by an auditor conflict as to the application of an accounting principle. Which of the following should the auditor consider the most authoritative?
a. FASB Technical Bulletins.
b. AICPA Interpretations of Rules of Conduct.
c. FASB Statements of Financial Accounting Concepts.
d. AICPA Technical Practice Aids.

[5,8] 2-21   Prior to beginning the field work on a new audit engagement in which a CPA does *not* possess expertise in the industry in which the client operates, the CPA should
a. Reduce audit risk by lowering the preliminary levels of materiality.
b. Design special substantive tests to compensate for the lack of industry expertise.
c. Engage financial experts who are familiar with the nature of the industry.
d. Obtain a knowledge of matters that relate to the nature of the entity's business.

[8]   2-22   Before accepting an audit engagement, a successor auditor should make specific inquiries of the predecessor auditor regarding the predecessor's
a. Awareness of the consistency in the application of generally accepted accounting principles between periods.
b. Evaluation of all matters of continuing accounting significance.
c. Opinion of any subsequent events occurring since the predecessor's audit report was issued.
d. Understanding as to the reasons for the change of auditors.

[3,6] 2-23   Which of the following, if material, would be fraud?
a. Mistakes in the application of accounting principles.
b. Clerical mistakes in the accounting data underlying the financial statements.

    c. Misappropriation of an asset or groups of assets.

    d. Misinterpretations of facts that existed when the financial statements were prepared.

[3,6]　2-24　Under Statements on Auditing Standards, which of the following would be classified as an error?

    a. Misappropriation of assets for the benefit of management.

    b. Misinterpretation by management of facts that existed when the financial statements were prepared.

    c. Preparation of records by employees to cover a fraudulent scheme.

    d. Intentional omission of the recording of a transaction to benefit a third party.

[9]　2-25　The auditor's report should be dated as of the date on which the

    a. Report is delivered to the client.

    b. Field work is completed.

    c. Fiscal period under audit ends.

    d. Review of the working papers is completed.

[9]　2-26　An auditor's responsibility to express an opinion on the financial statements is

    a. Implicitly represented in the auditor's standard report.

    b. Explicitly represented in the opening paragraph of the auditor's standard report.

    c. Explicitly represented in the scope paragraph of the auditor's standard report.

    d. Explicitly represented in the opinion paragraph of the auditor's standard report.

[1,9]　2-27　For an entity's financial statements to be presented fairly in conformity with generally accepted accounting principles, the principles selected should

    a. Be applied on a basis consistent with those followed in the prior year.

    b. Be approved by the Auditing Standards Board or the appropriate industry subcommittee.

    c. Reflect transactions in a manner that presents the financial statements within a range of acceptable limits.

    d. Match the principles used by most other entities within the entity's particular industry.

[9]　2-28　An auditor may *not* issue a qualified opinion when

    a. A scope limitation prevents the auditor from completing an important audit procedure.

    b. The auditor's report refers to the work of a specialist.

    c. An accounting principle at variance with generally accepted accounting principles is used.

    d. The auditor lacks independence with respect to the audited entity.

[1,9]　2-29　The management of Hill Company has decided not to account for a material transaction in accordance with the provisions of an FASB Standard. In setting forth its reasons in a note to the financial statements, management has clearly demonstrated that due to unusual circumstances the financial statements presented in

accordance with the FASB Standard would be misleading. The auditor's report should include a separate explanatory paragraph and contain a(n)

a. Qualified opinion.
b. Disclaimer.
c. Adverse opinion.
d. Unqualified opinion.

PROBLEMS

[6]   2-30 Sheri Shannon was recently hired by the CPA firm of Honson & Hansen. Within two weeks, Sheri was sent to the first-year staff training course. The instructor asked her to prepare answers for the following questions:

a. How is evidential matter defined?
b. How does evidence relate to assertions or audit objectives, and to the audit report?
c. What characteristics of evidence should an auditor be concerned with when searching for and evaluating evidence?

[6,8] 2-31 John Josephs, an audit manager for Tip, Acanoe, & Tylerto, was asked to speak at a dinner meeting of the local Small Business Administration Association. The president of the association has suggested that he talk about the various phases of the audit process. John has asked you, his trusted assistant, to prepare an outline for his speech. He suggests that you answer the following:

a. List and describe the various phases of an audit.
b. Describe how the results of work completed in certain phases provide feedback to earlier completed phases. Give an example.
c. One of the phases involves understanding an entity's internal control. Why might the members of the association be particularly interested in the work conducted by auditors in this phase of the audit?

[9]   2-32 The auditor's standard report consists of an "introductory" paragraph describing the financial statements and management and auditor responsibilities; a "scope" paragraph describing the nature of the examination; and an "opinion" paragraph expressing the auditor's opinion. In some circumstances the auditor's standard report is modified by adding one or more separate explanatory paragraphs and/or modifying the wording of one or more of the paragraphs included in the report.

For this question, assume the auditor is independent and has expressed an unqualified opinion on the prior year's financial statements. For the current year, only single-year (not comparative) statements are presented.

Required:

Identify the circumstances necessitating modification of the auditor's standard report. For each circumstance, indicate the type of opinion that would be appropriate. Organize the answer as indicated in the following example:

Circumstances	Types of Opinion
1. The financial statements are materially affected by a departure from generally accepted accounting principles.	1. The auditor should express a qualified opinion or an adverse opinion.

[9] (2-33) The following auditors' report was drafted by Moore, a staff accountant of Tyler & Tyler, CPAs, at the completion of the audit of the financial statements of Park Publishing Company, Inc., for the year ended September 30, 2000. The report was submitted to the engagement partner, who reviewed the audit working papers and properly concluded that an unqualified opinion should be issued. In drafting the report, Moore knew that the financial statements for the year ended September 30, 1999, were to be presented for comparative purposes. Tyler & Tyler previously audited these statements and expressed an unqualified opinion.

Auditor's Report

To the Board of Directors of Park Publishing Company, Inc.:

We have audited the accompanying balance sheets of Park Publishing Company, Inc., as of September 30, 2000 and 1999, and the related statements of income and cash flows for the years ended then. These financial statements are the responsibility of the company's management.

We conducted our audits in accordance with generally accepted auditing standards. Those standards require that we plan and perform the audit to obtain reasonable assurance about whether the financial statements are fairly presented. An audit includes examining, on a test basis, evidence supporting the amounts and disclosures in the financial statements. An audit also includes assessing significant estimates made by management, as well as evaluating the overall financial statement presentation. We believe that our audits provide a basis for determining whether any material modifications should be made to the accompanying financial statements.

In our opinion, the financial statements referred to above present fairly, in all material respects, the financial position of Park Publishing Company, Inc., as of September 30, 2000, and the results of its operations and its cash flows for the year then ended in conformity with generally accepted accounting principles.

Tyler & Tyler, CPAs
November 5, 2000

Required:

Identify the deficiencies in the auditors' report as drafted by Moore. Group the deficiencies by paragraph and in the order in which the deficiencies appear. Do *not* redraft the report.

(AICPA, adapted)

DISCUSSION CASE

[1]   2-34   BioPharm, Inc., is a biotechnology company that is solely involved in research and development of antibodies for various diseases. Once an antibody has been developed, BioPharm contracts with

large pharmaceutical companies to manufacture and distribute the antibodies. BioPharm's licensing agreements provide that the company will receive royalties based on a percentage of product sales.

Your firm has audited BioPharm since it went public five years ago. Johan Splice, the company's controller, has contacted you about accounting for a transaction under which the company would sell to Big Drugs, Inc., the right to receive a portion of the future royalties on its new antibody. Big Drugs provided BioPharm with R&D financing two years ago. Under the agreement, Big Drugs would pay BioPharm $3 million in 2000 and another $2.5 million in 2001 for the right to receive 5 percent of the royalties received by BioPharm on sales of the antibody during 2002 to 2007. The agreement also specifies that if the cumulative payments exceed $25 million, the royalty rate will drop from 5 percent to 1 percent.

BioPharm projects that Big Drugs will earn a 28 percent return on its investment. The agreement does not require BioPharm to guarantee any royalties, and, if the new antibody is replaced by a better treatment before 2002, Big Drugs will receive no payments. The agreement is noncancelable, there is no minimum guaranteed amount, and Big Drugs has no recourse against BioPharm.

BioPharm's only requirement under the agreement is to defend the related patents against infringements.

Required:

a. How should BioPharm account for the proceeds of this transaction in 1999? Provide the relevant accounting pronouncements to support your answer.

b. Assume that your answer to (a) indicated conflicting outcomes between the various accounting pronouncements. Following the GAAP hierarchy, which pronouncement should be followed?

INTERNET ASSIGNMENTS

2-35   Visit EarthWear Clothiers' home page (www.mhhe.com/earthwear) and become familiar with the type of information contained there.

2-36   Willis & Adams are the auditors of EarthWear. Visit Willis & Adams' home page (www.mhhe.com/willisandadams) and become familiar with the information contained there.

2-37   Use one of the Internet search engines to do the following:

a. Visit Intel's (www.intel.com) and Microsoft's (www.microsoft.com) home pages and review their financial statements, including their auditors' reports.

b. Search the Web for the home page of a non-US company and review its financial statements, including its auditor's report. For example, BMW's home page (www.bmw.com) allows a visitor to download the financial statement as a .pdf file. The auditor's report on BMW's financial statements is based on German auditing standards.

c. Compare the standard US audit report with the audit report for the non–US company. Note that in some cases, non–US-based companies' reports use a US audit report (for example, Daimler-Chrysler's home page: www.daimlerchrysler.de).

Part II

BASIC AUDITING CONCEPTS: MATERIALITY, AUDIT RISK, AND EVIDENCE

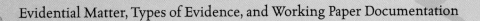

Chapter 3

Materiality and Audit Risk

LEARNING OBJECTIVES

Upon completion of this chapter you will

[1] Understand the concept of materiality.

[2] Identify the steps to applying materiality in an audit.

[3] Apply the materiality steps to a detailed example (EarthWear).

[4] Understand the concepts of audit risk and auditor business risk.

[5] Learn the form and components of the audit risk model.

[6] Understand how to use the audit risk model.

[7] Identify the factors that determine the auditor's assessment of client business risk.

[8] Identify the factors that determine the auditor's assessment of the risk of material misstatement.

[9] Learn the limitations of the audit risk model.

RELEVANT ACCOUNTING AND AUDITING PRONOUNCEMENTS

FASB Statement of Financial Accounting Concepts No. 2, "Qualitative Characteristics of Accounting Information" (CON2)

SAS No. 22, "Planning and Supervision" (AU 311)

SAS No. 39, "Audit Sampling" (AU 350)

SAS No. 47, "Audit Risk and Materiality in Conducting an Audit" (AU 312)

SAS No. 54, "Illegal Acts" (AU 317)

SAS No. 82, "Consideration of Fraud in a Financial Statement Audit" (AU 316)

Chapter 2 briefly discussed three fundamental concepts that underlie the conduct of a financial statement audit. This chapter provides detailed coverage of two of those concepts: *materiality* and *audit risk*. SAS No. 47, "Audit Risk and Materiality in Conducting an Audit" (AU 312), provides the auditor with professional guidance in considering materiality and audit risk when planning and performing an audit in accordance with GAAS.

The wording of the auditor's report recognizes both of these concepts. First, the scope paragraph states that the auditor obtains "reasonable assurance" that the financial statements are free of material misstatements. *Reasonable assurance* informs the reader that there is some level of risk that the audit did not detect *all* material misstatements. Second, the opinion paragraph states that the financial statements present fairly, "in all material respects." This phrase communicates to third parties that the audit report is limited to *material* information. Financial statements are materially misstated when they contain errors or fraud that cause them not to present fairly in conformity with GAAP.

Materiality and audit risk significantly impact the auditor's evidence decisions. The auditor considers both concepts in planning the nature, extent, and timing of audit procedures and in evaluating the results of those procedures. The auditor must also recognize that there is an inverse relationship between both materiality and audit risk, and the amount of audit evidence. For example, if the auditor establishes a small amount for materiality for a particular client given a specified level of audit risk, more audit evidence has to be gathered in order to provide reasonable assurance that the financial statements are free of material misstatement than if a large amount is established for materiality. Similarly, if the auditor establishes a low level for audit risk for a particular client given a specified level of materiality, the scope of the audit will be greater than if the auditor has established a high level for audit risk. The important point is that both materiality and audit risk affect the *scope* of the audit.

This chapter discusses materiality and then audit risk. The appendix contains an alternative approach for allocating materiality to account balances. 🌏

Materiality

[LO 1]   The auditor's consideration of materiality on an audit is a matter of *professional judgment*. As discussed in Chapter 2, materiality is assessed in terms of the potential effect of a misstatement on decisions made by a reasonable user of the financial statements. This focus arises from the FASB's Statement of Financial Accounting Concepts No. 2, "Qualitative Characteristics of Accounting Information," which provides the following definition:

> **Materiality** is the magnitude of an omission or misstatement of accounting information that, in the light of surrounding circumstances, makes it probable that the judgment of a reasonable person relying on the information would have been changed or influenced by the omission or misstatement.

Simply stated, materiality is an account or fact that would affect decisions made by users relying on the financial statements. This perspective requires that the auditor assess the amount of misstatement that could affect a reasonable user's decisions.

Professional standards provide little specific guidance on how to assess what is material to a reasonable user. As a result, auditing firms and the AICPA have developed policies and procedures to assist auditors in establishing materiality. The following sections present an approach to assessing materiality. The presentation is based on the general approach provided by auditing standards and to some extent on the more specific policies and procedures suggested by the AICPA.[1] While the policies and procedures of individual CPA firms may differ in some respects, the approach presented here provides the reader with a basic framework for understanding the consideration of materiality in an audit.

In establishing materiality for an audit, the auditor should consider both quantitative and qualitative aspects of the engagement. Although materiality may be planned and implemented using a quantitative approach, the qualitative aspects of misstatements of small amounts may also materially affect the users of financial statements. For example, a client may illegally pay a commissioned agent to secure a sales contract. While the amount of the illegal payment may be immaterial to the financial statements, the disclosure of the illegal act may result in loss of the contract and substantial penalties that may be material. The next section presents an approach to applying materiality, which is then followed by a detailed example.

Steps in Applying Materiality

[LO 2]   Figure 3–1 presents the three major steps in the application of materiality to an audit. Steps 1 and 2 are normally performed early in the engagement as part of planning the audit (see Figure 2–2 in Chapter 2). Step 3 is performed when the auditor evaluates the evidence at the completion of the audit to determine if it supports the fair presentation of the financial statements (again, refer to Figure 2–2).

---

[1]American Institute of Certified Public Accountants, Auditing Practice Release, *Audit Sampling* (New York: AICPA, 1999). Also see G. R. Zuber, R. K. Elliott, W. R. Kinney, Jr., and J. J. Leisenring, "Using Materiality in Audit Planning," *Journal of Accountancy* (March 1983), pp. 42–55.

FIGURE 3–1

Steps in Applying Materiality
on an Audit

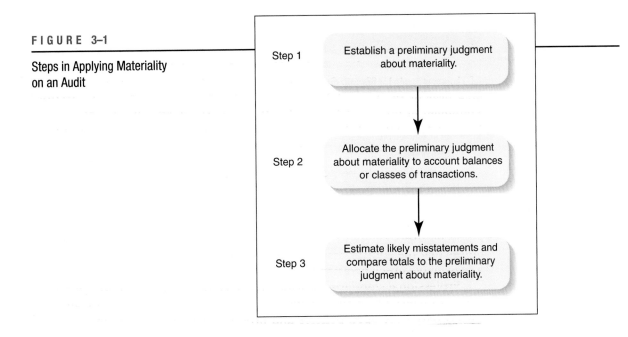

Step 1	Establish a preliminary judgment about materiality.
Step 2	Allocate the preliminary judgment about materiality to account balances or classes of transactions.
Step 3	Estimate likely misstatements and compare totals to the preliminary judgment about materiality.

Step 1: Establish a Preliminary Judgment about Materiality

SAS No. 22, "Planning and Supervision" (AU 311), requires that the auditor establish a preliminary judgment about materiality as part of planning the audit. While auditing standards do not require that the auditor quantify and document this judgment, the author believes that such an approach offers benefits to CPA firms and their personnel. By quantifying materiality, the audit team is better able to plan the scope of the audit and evaluate the results of the audit tests.

The preliminary judgment about materiality is the maximum amount by which the auditor believes the financial statements could be misstated and still *not* affect the decisions of reasonable users. Materiality, however, is a relative, not an absolute, concept. For example, $5,000 might be considered highly material for a small sole proprietorship, but this amount would clearly be immaterial for a large multinational corporation. Thus, the relative size of the company being audited affects the preliminary judgment about materiality.

In specifying materiality, an auditor should establish a base (or bases) that, when multiplied by a percentage factor, determines the initial quantitative judgment about materiality. The resulting materiality amount can then be adjusted for any qualitative factors that may be relevant to the engagement. Table 3–1 lists some common bases used and qualitative factors considered by auditors.

Total assets, total revenues, and some form of net income are frequently used by auditors when establishing materiality. An advantage of using total assets or total revenues is that for many companies these factors are more stable from year to year than net income before taxes. Difficulties also arise in using net income as a base when the entity is close to

TABLE 3–1	Common Bases and Qualitative Factors for Establishing Materiality

Common Bases for Establishing Materiality:
- Total assets.
- Total revenues.
- Net income before taxes.
- Gross profit.
- Average of three years' net income before taxes.

Selected Qualitative Factors for Assessing Materiality:
- Fraud or illegal acts.
- Small amounts that might violate covenants in a contract.
- Amounts that might affect the trend in earnings.

breaking even or experiencing a loss. For example, suppose that an entity has net income before taxes of $3,000,000 one year and the auditor decides that 5 percent of that amount ($150,000) would be material. The scope of the audit in that year would be based on a preliminary judgment about materiality of $150,000. Suppose, in the following year, the entity's net income before taxes falls to $250,000 due to a temporary decrease in sales prices for its products. If the auditor uses the 5 percent factor, the preliminary judgment about materiality would be $12,500 ($250,000 × .05), and a much more extensive audit would be required.

Current accounting and auditing standards do *not* provide any specific materiality guidelines for a number of reasons. First, it is difficult, if not impossible, to assess what is material to the diverse groups of users (such as investors, creditors, employees, and government agencies) that rely on financial statements. Second, auditors are unable to agree among themselves on what is material. Finally, some auditors seem reluctant to quantify materiality due to litigation. As a result, some CPA firms provide general guidelines that allow their auditors considerable leeway in establishing materiality, while other firms provide detailed quantitative guidelines. Exhibit 3–1 provides an example of a materiality worksheet that can be used for establishing a preliminary judgment about materiality. This worksheet is adopted from the materiality worksheet included in the AICPA audit practice release.[2]

This worksheet has two bases: total assets and total revenues. The auditor first enters the larger of total assets or total revenues as the base amount. The base amount is then multiplied by the appropriate percentage factor from the materiality multiplier table, and a fixed amount is added to that result. The materiality multiplier table contains a set of percentages that decrease as the size of the entity increases. This calculation

---

[2]AICPA, Auditing Practice Release, *Audit Sampling* (New York: AICPA, 1999).

EXHIBIT 3–1

Worksheet for Calculating the Preliminary Judgment about Materiality (Planning Materiality)

Client: _____

Balance sheet date: _____

Identify base amount:
   Base amount: $_____ (the greater of total assets or total revenues)

Calculating planning materiality:

   _____ × _____ + _____ = _____
   (Base amount)   (Planning materiality)

Use the following table to determine the percentage and additional amount to be used to calculate planning materiality.

Materiality Multiplier Table*

Amount			
Over	But Not Over	Times	Plus
$ 0	$ 30 thousand	.054	0
30 thousand	100 thousand	.029	750
100 thousand	300 thousand	.018	1,850
300 thousand	1 million	.0125	3,500
1 million	3 million	.0083	7,700
3 million	10 million	.006	14,600
10 million	30 million	.004	34,600
30 million	100 million	.00272	73,000
100 million	300 million	.0019	155,000
300 million	1 billion	.00125	350,000
1 billion	3 billion	.00087	730,000
3 billion	10 billion	.00058	1,600,000
10 billion	30 billion	.0004	3,400,000
30 billion		.00027	7,300,000

*The amounts used in this table are taken from Appendix D of the AICPA's Auditing Practice Release, *Audit Sampling* (New York: AICPA, 1999).

results in the initial quantitative estimate of planning materiality. This amount may then be increased or decreased based on qualitative factors that are relevant to the audit. For example, planning materiality may be increased based on favorable qualitative factors, such as past audit history (few misstatements in prior years, no illegal acts, no violations of debt covenants), strong financial condition, or sound economic conditions in the entity's industry. Conversely, unfavorable qualitative factors, such as numerous misstatements in prior years, depressed industry conditions, or possible violations of debt covenants, may result in a decrease in planning materiality.

Step 2: Allocate the Preliminary Judgment about Materiality to Account Balances or Classes of Transactions

Step 2 involves allocating the preliminary judgment about materiality, as determined in Step 1, to the account balances or classes of transactions. An *account balance* represents an individual line item on the financial statements, such as accounts receivable or inventory. A *class of transactions* refers to a type of transaction processed by the client's accounting system, such as revenue or purchase transactions. The purpose of allocating a portion of the preliminary judgment about materiality is to plan the scope of audit procedures for the individual account balance or class of transactions. For example, if a small amount of materiality were allocated to a specific account, such as accounts receivable, more evidence would be gathered than if a larger amount of materiality were allocated.

Because of the many factors involved, there is no required or optimal method for allocating materiality to an account balance or class of transactions. The process can be done judgmentally or using some formal quantitative approach. Once the preliminary judgment about materiality is allocated to an account, it is referred to as *tolerable misstatement* (AU 350). In allocating materiality, the auditor should consider the following factors:

- The magnitude of the account relative to the financial statements.
- The expectation of error.
- The relative cost to audit the account balance or class of transactions.

For example, the larger an account balance, the greater the amount of materiality that can be allocated to it. It seems reasonable to assume that a $25,000,000 account balance can contain a larger misstatement than a $3,000,000 account balance and still not affect a user's judgments. Similarly, if the auditor expects little or no misstatement in an account, a larger amount of materiality can be allocated to the account. Because the auditor's expectation of error is low, the scope for auditing the account can be reduced. Finally, if an account balance is very expensive to audit, the auditor may allocate more materiality to the account. Because the auditor wants to conduct a cost-effective audit, the allocation of a greater amount of materiality to an account balance that is expensive to audit results in less audit work for that particular account. However, the auditor must be careful not to allow such cost considerations to affect his or her ability to detect material misstatements.

Step 3: Estimate Likely Misstatements and Compare Totals to the Preliminary Judgment about Materiality

Step 3 is completed near the end of the audit, when the auditor evaluates all the evidence that has been gathered. Based on the results of the audit procedures conducted, the auditor aggregates misstatements from each account or class of transactions. The aggregate amount includes known misstatements and projections based on the sample data collected. It should also include consideration of the effect of likely misstatements carried forward from the prior period. The auditor compares this aggregate misstatement (referred to as *likely misstatement*) to the preliminary judgment about materiality established in Step 1. If the auditor's judgment about materiality at the planning stage (Step 1) was based on the same information available at the evaluation stage (Step 3), materiality for planning and evaluation would be the same. However, the auditor may identify factors or items during the course of the audit that cause a revision to the preliminary judgment about materiality. Thus, the preliminary judgment about materiality may differ from the materiality judgment used in evaluating the audit findings. When this occurs, the auditor should carefully document the reasons for revising the preliminary judgment about materiality.

When the likely misstatements are less than the preliminary judgment about materiality, the auditor can conclude that the financial statements are fairly presented. Conversely, when the likely misstatements are greater than the planned judgment about materiality, the auditor should request that the client adjust the financial statements. If the client refuses to adjust the financial statements for the likely misstatements, the auditor should issue a qualified or adverse opinion because the financial statements do not present fairly in conformity with GAAP.

An Example

🖋 **[LO 3]**

In this example, the three steps for applying materiality are discussed. Exhibit 3–2 contains aggregated financial information for EarthWear Clothiers for the year ended December 31, 2000. This financial information is taken from the case illustration included in Chapter 1 and serves as the basis for the example.

Step 1: Determine the Preliminary Judgment about Materiality

The materiality worksheet shown in Exhibit 3–1 is used to estimate the preliminary judgment about materiality for EarthWear Clothiers. (Exhibit 3–3 presents the calculations using this materiality worksheet.) Because EarthWear's total revenues are larger than its total assets, the $503,434,000 of revenues is used for the base amount. Using the materiality multiplier table in Exhibit 3–3, the $503,434,000 is multiplied by .00125 and $350,000 is added to that amount, resulting in a preliminary judgment of materiality of $980,000 (rounded). To determine the final amount for materiality, the auditor should consider whether any qualitative factors are relevant for the engagement (see Table 3–1). In our example, assume that the auditor has determined that none of the qualitative factors are relevant and that the $980,000 will be used for the preliminary judgment about materiality. This is the amount that is allocated to the specific accounts or classes of transactions in Step 2.

Step 2: Allocate the Preliminary Judgment of Materiality

Public accounting firms use a number of different approaches to accomplish this step. For simplicity, materiality is allocated only to the balance sheet accounts in this example. On many engagements, the auditor may allocate materiality to selected income statement accounts and tests of certain classes of transactions (such as purchasing and cash disbursements).

This chapter presents two approaches for allocating materiality to accounts. The first approach is based on the auditor's judgment after

EXHIBIT 3–2

Financial Information for Estimating Materiality

EARTHWEAR CLOTHIERS
Consolidated Balance Sheet
December 31, 2000
(In thousands)

Assets

Cash and cash equivalents	$ 41,772
Receivables	3,933
Inventory	64,100
Prepaid advertising	4,980
Other prepaid expenses	2,448
Deferred income tax benefits	5,185
Property, plant, and equipment, net	46,658
Intangibles, net	1,045
Total assets	$ 170,121

Liabilities and Shareholders' Investment

Lines of credit	$ 5,038
Accounts payable	34,463
Reserve for returns	2,333
Accrued liabilities	12,663
Accrued profit sharing	1,322
Income taxes payable	9,686
Deferred income taxes	3,914
Long-term liabilities	297
Common stock and paid-in capital	12,025
Donated capital	3,780
Less: Deferred compensation	(617)
Currency translation adjustments	170
Retained earnings	139,978
Less: Treasury stock	(54,931)
Total liabilities and shareholders' investment	$ 170,121
Net sales	$ 503,434
Net income before taxes	$ 38,213

EXHIBIT 3–3

Address: ▼ | http://www.mhhe.com/messier

Worksheet for Calculating the Preliminary Judgment about Materiality (Planning Materiality)

Client: *EarthWear Clothiers*

Balance sheet date: *December 31, 2000*

Identify base amount:
  Base amount: $503,434,000 (the greater of total assets or total revenues)

Calculating planning materiality:
  $503,434,000 × .00125 + 350,000 = $980,000 (rounded)
  (Base amount)   (Planning materiality)

Use the following table to determine the percentage and additional amount to be used to calculate planning materiality.

Materiality Multiplier Table*

Amount		Times	Plus
Over	But Not Over		
$ 0	$ 30 thousand	.054	0
30 thousand	100 thousand	.029	750
100 thousand	300 thousand	.018	1,850
300 thousand	1 million	.0125	3,500
1 million	3 million	.0083	7,700
3 million	10 million	.006	14,600
10 million	30 million	.004	34,600
30 million	100 million	.00272	73,000
100 million	300 million	.0019	155,000
300 million	1 billion	.00125	350,000
1 billion	3 billion	.00087	730,000
3 billion	10 billion	.00058	1,600,000
10 billion	30 billion	.0004	3,400,000
30 billion		.00027	7,300,000

*The amounts used in this table are taken from Appendix D of the AICPA's Auditing Practice Release, *Audit Sampling* (New York: AICPA, 1999).

---

considering the magnitude of the accounts, the expectation of errors, and relative audit costs. The other approach, which is included in the appendix, uses a quantitative method based on the relative magnitude of the financial statement accounts for allocation purposes. As the reader will see, the two approaches result in different allocations to individual accounts.

For example, the quantitative approach shown in the appendix allocates amounts to accounts that are greater in total than the preliminary judgment about materiality. This, in turn, may result in different levels of audit effort for individual accounts. Some CPA firms apply an arbitrary percentage (usually between 50 percent and 75 percent) of the preliminary judgment about materiality to *each* account in order to determine tolerable misstatement. Like the quantitative method, this approach allocates a total amount that is greater than the preliminary judgment about materiality.

In allocating materiality to the balance sheet accounts in EarthWear's financial statements, assume that intangibles, lines of credit, long-term liabilities, deferred income tax accounts, and shareholders' investment accounts will be audited 100 percent. Such an assumption is justified because intangibles, lines of credit, long-term liabilities, and shareholders' investment accounts are generally composed of few transactions that are easy to verify, and deferred taxes is a computed balance that either is prepared by the auditor for the client or can be recalculated by the auditor. Because 100 percent of these accounts are audited, there is no need to allocate materiality to them. Additionally, no allocation is needed for retained earnings because it represents a residual amount. Exhibit 3–4 presents the results of this allocation scheme.

In the example, the auditor initially allocated the preliminary judgment about materiality ($980,000) to EarthWear's balance sheet accounts using the relative dollar magnitude of the accounts (see Exhibit 3–4). The allocation is made by dividing each balance sheet amount by the total of all balance sheet accounts to which materiality is to be allocated and then multiplying this percentage by $980,000. In our example, the sum of all balance sheet accounts to which materiality is to be allocated amounts to $214,672,000 (see Exhibit 3–4). Thus, the allocation of the preliminary judgment about materiality to inventory (rounded to the nearest $1,000) is determined as follows:

$$\$293,000 = \frac{64,100,000}{214,672,000} \times \$980,000$$

The auditor can judgmentally adjust this initial allocation to take into account the factors discussed previously. For example, because a large portion of property, plant, and equipment and other assets is composed of amounts that were audited in prior years, these accounts can be audited at a tighter tolerance by allocating a smaller amount of materiality to these accounts. Thus, the initial allocation of $213,000 was reduced to $150,000 for property, plant, and equipment. The amount of tolerable misstatement allocated to accounts receivable was increased from $18,000 to $45,000 because the entity has strong control procedures and most sales are paid with cash or credit cards. Similarly, the $157,000 originally allocated to accounts payable was increased to $200,000 because of strong control procedures in the purchasing cycle. The presence of strong control procedures reduces the likelihood that misstatements will occur. Tolerable misstatement for inventory was decreased from $293,000 to $250,000 because of obsolescence (net realizable value). Other minor changes are made to other accounts. In auditing Earthwear, the auditor uses the tolerable misstatement allocated to the balance sheet accounts to set the scope of audit testing for each account.

EXHIBIT 3–4

Allocation of the Preliminary Judgment about Materiality

EARTHWEAR CLOTHIERS
December 31, 2000
(In thousands)

	Balance Sheet Amount	Materiality Allocation Based on Relative Size	Tolerable Misstatement
Cash and cash equivalents	$ 41,772*	$ 191	$ 191
Receivables	3,933*	18	45
Inventory	64,100*	293	250
Prepaid advertising	4,980*	23	23
Other prepaid expenses	2,448*	11	11
Deferred income tax benefits	5,185	†	†
Property, plant, and equipment, net	46,658*	213	150
Intangibles, net	1,045	†	†
Total	$ 170,121		
Lines of credit	$ 5,038	†	†
Accounts payable	34,463*	$ 157	$ 200
Reserve for returns	2,333*	10	25
Accrued liabilities	12,663*	58	60
Accrued profit sharing	1,322*	6	25
Income taxes payable	9,686	†	†
Deferred income taxes	3,914	†	†
Long-term liabilities	297	†	†
Common stock and paid-in capital	12,025	†	†
Donated capital	3,780	†	†
Less: Deferred compensation	(617)	†	†
Currency translation adjustments	170	†	†
Retained earnings	139,978	N/A	N/A
Less: Treasury stock	(54,931)	†	†
Total	$ 170,121	$ 980	$ 980

*The sum of these items is $214,672 (in thousands).
† = Account will be audited 100%; no allocation of tolerable misstatement is necessary.
N/A = Not applicable; retained earnings are a residual.

Step 3: Estimate the Likely Misstatement and Compare to Materiality

The allocated amounts of materiality (tolerable misstatement) are also used for determining the fair presentation of the individual accounts after completion of the audit work. Exhibit 3–5 presents an example of a working paper that can be used to aggregate the effects of misstatements identified during the audit. Assume that during the course of the audit the auditor identified four misstatements. The misstatements are compared to the tolerable misstatement allocated to each account. For example, the first misstatement indicates an error in the accrual of payroll expense and bonuses. The total misstatement of accrued payroll is $36,200. As shown in Exhibit 3–5, $60,000 of materiality was allocated to accrued liabilities. Since the accruals are not misstated by more than $60,000, it is not necessary for the client to make the proposed adjusting entry. The second entry is based on the results of a statistical sampling application for inventory. The statistical results indicated a projected misstatement plus an allowance for sampling risk of $112,500. This overstatement of inventory is less than the tolerable misstatement of $250,000 allocated to inventory. The same analysis can be made for the other two proposed adjusting entries. Before making a final decision, the auditor should consider further possible misstatements that may be due to sampling and misstatements that carry forward from the prior year. If one of the entries were in excess of the tolerable misstatement for an account balance, the client would have to adjust the account balance or the auditor would have to issue a qualified or adverse opinion.

Audit Risk

[LO 4]   Risk is the second fundamental concept that underlies the audit process. The two major types of risk faced by an auditor engaged to audit a set of financial statements are *audit risk* and *auditor business risk*. They are defined as follows:

> **Audit risk** is the risk that the auditor may unknowingly fail to appropriately modify the opinion on financial statements that are materially misstated.
>
> **Auditor business risk** is the auditor's exposure to loss or injury to professional practice from litigation, adverse publicity, or other events arising in connection with financial statements audited and reported on.

In simple terms, audit risk is the risk that an auditor will issue an unqualified opinion on materially misstated financial statements. Audit risk is discussed extensively throughout the remainder of this chapter.

Auditor business risk relates to an auditor's exposure to financial loss and damage to his or her professional reputation. For example, an auditor may conduct an audit in accordance with GAAS and still be sued by the client or a third party. Although the auditor has complied with professional standards and may ultimately win the lawsuit, his or her professional reputation may be damaged in the process by the negative publicity.

Auditor business risk cannot be directly controlled by the auditor, although some control can be exercised through the careful acceptance and retention of clients. Audit risk, on the other hand, can be directly controlled

EXHIBIT 3–5

Example Working Paper for Estimating Likely Misstatements

EARTHWEAR CLOTHIERS
Schedule of Proposed Adjusting Entries
12/31/00

Workpaper Ref.	Proposed Adjusting Entry	Tolerable Misstatement	Assets	Liabilities	Equity	Revenues	Expenses
N10	Payroll expense						12,200
	Bonuses						24,000
	Accrued liabilities	60,000		36,200			
	To accrue payroll through 12/31 and recognize 2000 bonuses.						
F20	Cost of sales	250,000					112,500
	Inventory		(112,500)				
	To adjust ending inventory based on sample results.	250,000					
F22	Inventory	200,000	27,450				
	Accounts payable			27,450			
	To record inventory in transit at 12/31.						
R15	Accounts receivable	45,000	9,850			9,850	
	Sales						
	To record sales cutoff errors at 12/31.						
	Total		(75,200)	63,650		9,850	148,700

Conclusion: Based on the above analysis, the account balances for EarthWear Clothiers are fairly stated in accordance with GAAP.

by the scope of the auditor's test procedures. As the next section demonstrates, the *audit risk model* provides a framework for auditors to follow.

The Audit Risk Model

[LO 5]

Auditing standards state that the auditor should plan the engagement so that audit risk will be at a sufficiently low level before issuing an opinion on the financial statements. However, audit standards do not provide specific guidance on what is an appropriate level of audit risk. The determination of audit risk and the use of the audit risk model involve considerable judgment on the part of the auditor.

The audit risk model can be applied at both the overall financial statement level and the account balance or class of transactions level. When considered at the individual account balance or class of transactions level, audit risk directly assists the auditor in determining the scope of auditing procedures for a particular account balance or class of transactions. In this text, the discussion of the various accounting cycles and their related account balances follows the components of the audit risk model.

The audit risk model, as applied at the *financial statement level,* can be specified as

$$AR = IR \times CR \times DR$$

where

AR = Audit risk (the risk that the auditor may fail to modify the opinion on materially misstated financial statements)

IR = Inherent risk (the susceptibility of an assertion to material misstatements, assuming no related internal controls)

CR = Control risk (the risk that material misstatements that could occur will not be prevented or detected by the internal controls)

DR = Detection risk (the risk that the auditor will not detect a material misstatement that exists in the financial statements)

Detection risk can be decomposed further into analytical procedures risk (*APR*) and substantive tests of details risk (*TDR*) (AU 350.48). *Analytical procedures risk* is the risk that analytical procedures and other relevant substantive tests will fail to detect material misstatements, while *tests of details risk* is the allowable risk for failing to detect a material misstatement that is not detected by internal controls or analytical procedures and other relevant substantive tests. In discussion of the audit risk model in the remainder of this text, detection risk will not be decomposed for ease of presentation.

When audit risk is considered at the *account balance* or *class of transaction level,* it consists of

1. The risk that the balance or class contains a tolerable misstatement that could be material to the financial statements when aggregated with tolerable misstatement in other balances or classes (inherent risk and control risk).

2. The risk that the auditor will not detect the tolerable misstatement (detection risk).

From the auditor's perspective, inherent risk and control risk differ from detection risk in that inherent risk and control risk exist independently of the audit. In other words, the levels of inherent risk and control risk are functions of the client and its environment. The auditor has little control over these risks. Sometimes the combination of inherent risk and control risk is referred to as *auditee risk*. Detection risk, on the other hand, can be controlled by the auditor through the scope of the audit procedures performed. Detection risk has an inverse relationship to inherent risk and control risk. For example, if an entity's inherent risk and control risk are judged to be high, the auditor sets a lower level of detection risk in order to meet the planned level of audit risk. Conversely, if inherent risk and control risk are low, detection risk is set at a higher level.

The auditor's assessment of audit risk and its component risks (*IR, CR,* and *DR*) is a matter of professional judgment. At the completion of the audit, the *actual* level of audit risk is *not* known with certainty by the auditor. If the auditor assesses the *achieved* audit risk as being less than or equal to the *planned* level of audit risk, an unqualified report can be issued. If the assessment of the achieved level of audit risk is greater than the planned level, the auditor should either conduct additional audit work or qualify the audit report.

Inherent Risk (IR)   Inherent risk is the susceptibility of an assertion to material misstatement in the financial statements in the absence of internal controls. Although the audit risk model treats inherent risk as being independent of control risk on most audit engagements, the specific factors that increase or decrease inherent risk may also impact control risk. Thus, in many cases, there is a direct relationship between inherent risk and control risk.

At the beginning of an engagement, the auditor must assess specific factors related to the client that may increase or decrease the likelihood of a material misstatement occurring. Many CPA firms have developed questionnaires, checklists, or computerized decision aids that assist their personnel in making and documenting the assessment of inherent risk.

Control Risk (CR)   Control risk is the risk that material misstatements will not be prevented or detected on a timely basis by an entity's internal control. The auditor may decide to assess control risk at the maximum (100 percent) because he or she believes that the control policies or procedures are not effective and thus cannot be relied upon to produce materially accurate financial information. The auditor may also set control risk at the maximum level in the belief that it is more efficient (that is, less costly) to conduct extensive substantive tests of the account balances than to conduct detailed tests of the internal controls.

If an auditor decides to assess control risk below the maximum, he or she has made a preliminary decision to rely on the control procedures contained in the client's accounting system. Suppose an auditor develops a detailed understanding of the internal controls in a client's revenue cycle. In the preliminary assessment of the client's control risk, the auditor (1) identifies specific internal controls relevant to specific audit assertions or objectives that are likely to prevent or detect material misstatements and (2) tests internal controls to evaluate their ineffectiveness. For example, the entity may have specific policies for granting credit to customers. To test such a policy, the auditor can select a sample of sales invoices and determine whether proper credit was granted to the customers.

SAS No. 55, 78, and 82 note factors that impact the auditor's assessment of control risk. Because of the significance of assessing control risk, Chapter 6 contains a detailed discussion of this topic.

Detection Risk (DR)   Detection risk is the risk that the substantive audit procedures performed will not detect a material misstatement that exists in an account balance or class of transactions. Detection risk is a function of the effectiveness of auditing procedures and their application by the auditor.

Detection risk is composed of two risks or uncertainties. The first risk, referred to as *sampling risk*, relates to the fact that, in many instances, the auditor does not examine 100 percent of the account balance or class of transactions. Because the auditor examines only a subset of the population, the sample drawn may not represent the population, and the auditor may thus draw the wrong conclusion on the fairness of the account balance.

The second risk is called *nonsampling risk* and can occur because the auditor used an inappropriate audit procedure, failed to detect a misstatement when applying an appropriate audit procedure, or misinterpreted an audit result. Nonsampling risk may be present even when the auditor examines 100 percent of the population. Nonsampling risk can, however, be minimized through adequate training, planning, and supervision.

If the auditor encounters evidence during substantive tests that alters the original assessments of inherent risk or control risk, he or she should reevaluate the scope of the audit procedures performed. If such evidence indicates that the assessment of inherent risk or control risk was too low, additional audit work should be performed to maintain the planned level of audit risk.

Use of the Audit Risk Model

[LO 6]

The discussion that follows concerning the audit risk model is limited to its use as an audit planning tool. Three steps are involved in the auditor's use of the audit risk model at the account balance or class of transaction level:

1. Setting a planned level of audit risk.
2. Assessing inherent risk and control risk.
3. Solving the audit risk equation for the appropriate level of detection risk.

In applying the audit risk model in this manner, the auditor determines or assesses each component of the model using either quantitative or qualitative terms. In Step 1, the auditor sets audit risk for each account balance or class of transaction in such a way that, at the completion of the engagement, an opinion can be issued on the financial statements at a low level of audit risk (AU 312.26). Step 2 requires that the auditor assess inherent risk and control risk. In assessing these two components of the model, the auditor should assess client business risk and the risk of material misstatement due to error or fraud. This is accomplished by identifying and evaluating factors that impact client business risk and the risk of material misstatement due to error or fraud. Figure 3–2 shows the relationship of the assessment of client business risk and risk of material misstatement due to error or fraud to the inherent risk and control risk components or

FIGURE 3–2

The Relationship of Client Business Risk and the Risk of Material Misstatement Due to Error or Fraud to the Determination
of Audit Risk.

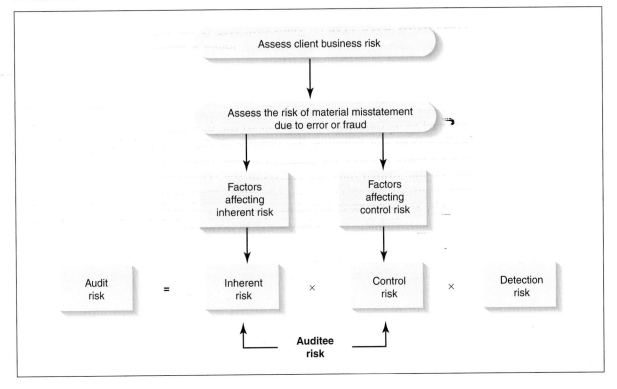

the audit risk model. These assessments are described in detail in the next
two sections of the chapter. In Step 3, the auditor determines the appropriate level of detection risk by solving the audit risk model as follows:

$$AR = IR \times CR \times DR$$

$$DR = \frac{AR}{IR \times CR}$$

In using the audit risk model, the auditor sets audit risk, assesses inherent risk and control risk, and determines detection risk. The auditor
then uses this level of detection risk to design the audit procedures that
will reduce audit risk to an acceptable level. However, it is not appropriate
for an auditor to rely completely on his or her assessments of inherent risk
and control risk to the exclusion of performing substantive tests of account
balances where material misstatements could exist (AU 312.25). Auditing
standards include this caveat because of the imprecision that may occur in
assessing inherent risk and control risk.

Consider the following numerical example:

Suppose that the auditor has determined that the planned audit risk for the
accounts receivable balance can be set at .05 based on the significance of the
account to the financial statements. By establishing such a low level of audit

risk, the auditor is reducing the possibility that the account may contain a material misstatement. Assume further that the auditor assesses inherent risk for accounts receivable to be .80. After evaluating the internal control over the revenue cycle, the auditor assesses control risk to be .60. Substituting the values for *AR*, *IR*, and *CR* into the equation indicates that the auditor should set *DR* at approximately .10 [$DR = .05/(.80 \times .60)$] for testing the accounts receivable balance. Thus, the auditor establishes the scope of the audit for accounts receivable so that there is only a 10 percent chance that a material misstatement, if present, is not detected.

A CPA firm may find it more appropriate to use nonquantitative or qualitative terms to implement the audit risk model. For example, audit risk might be classified into three categories, *very low, low,* and *moderate*. It is not likely that an audit planned in accordance with GAAS would consider a high level of audit risk. The remaining component of the audit risk model may be classified into categories such as *low, moderate,* or *high*. This method of using the model is identical to that followed when using the numerical values. Audit risk would be set using one of the category choices. Similarly, the auditor would assess the appropriate category for inherent risk and control risk. The various combinations of the components would be used to determine the level of detection risk. Following are three examples of the use of a nonquantitative approach to the audit risk model.

Example	AR	IR	CR	DR
1	Very Low	High	High	Low
2	Low	Low	High	Moderate
3	Moderate	High	Low	Moderate

In Example 1, the auditor has determined that a very low level of audit risk is appropriate for this account because of its importance to the financial statement. Assume further that the auditor has assessed inherent risk and control risk as high. A high assessment for these components indicates that there is a high risk that a material misstatement occurred and was not prevented or detected by the internal control system. Given a low level of audit risk and high assessments for inherent and control risk, the auditor would set detection risk as low. A low assessment for detection risk implies that the auditor will conduct a more detailed investigation of this account than if the assessment of detection risk were high.

Assessing Client Business Risk

[LO 7]

In Chapter 2, *client business risk* was defined as the risk that an entity's business objectives will not be attained as a result of the external and internal factors, pressures, and forces brought to bear on the entity and, ultimately, the risk associated with the entity's survival and profitability. In order to properly judge the fair presentation of the financial statements, the auditor needs to understand the entity's business strategy and risks and its ability to respond to changing environmental conditions. The auditor must then determine if those business risks affect audit risk. Figure 3–2 shows how client business risk relates to audit risk. The auditor's assessment of client business risk is part of the assessment of the risk of material misstatement due to error or fraud. In other words, the auditor assesses the specific business

FIGURE 3–3

The Relationship between Client Business Risk and The Global, Local, and Internal Environments

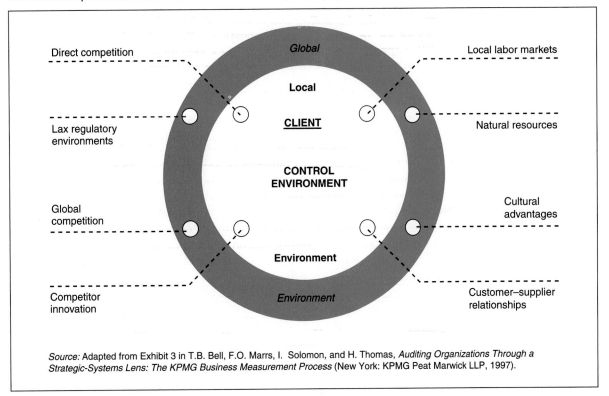

Source: Adapted from Exhibit 3 in T.B. Bell, F.O. Marrs, I. Solomon, and H. Thomas, *Auditing Organizations Through a Strategic-Systems Lens: The KPMG Business Measurement Process* (New York: KPMG Peat Marwick LLP, 1997).

risks that the entity faces in order to determine if they might result in errors or fraud, and ultimately in materially misstated financial statements. A number of the factors that enter into the assessment of client business risk are included in the auditing standards that guide the assessment of material misstatement due to errors or fraud. However, by taking a top-down view of the entity, rather than a bottom-up transaction-based approach, the auditor can use strategic analysis to plan the audit. Figure 3–3 shows some factors that affect the client's internal, local, and global environments. Focusing on client business risk in this manner should lower audit risk.

Assessing client business risk requires that the auditor understand the client's business and industry at two levels. The auditor should first develop a thorough understanding of the industry. This includes knowledge about

- The critical issues facing the industry.
- The significant industry business risks.
- The structure and profitability of the industry.
- The relationship between the industry and the broad economic business environment.

 For example, EarthWear Clothiers operates in the retail clothing industry, selling mainly through mail order. This industry is highly fragmented and subject to stiff competition. Profitability within the industry is highly variable and affected by overall consumer spending. Additionally, for many entities in the industry, sales are seasonal.

The auditor must then understand how the client fits within the industry. This includes developing knowledge about the following:

- The entity's position within the industry in terms of market share, profitability, and so on.
- The entity's plans for increasing or maintaining market share, profitability, and so on.
- Threats to the entity's position in the industry.
- How the entity deals with its customers and competitors.
- How the entity measures and monitors performance.

Again, using EarthWear as an example, the company is well positioned within the retail clothing industry. EarthWear ranks in the top third of the companies operating in the industry in terms of market share and profitability; however, it does have a number of competitors. EarthWear deals with its customers principally on the basis of quality and price, its established customer list and customer service, and its unqualified guarantee.

The auditor uses the industry and client information to identify strategic risks that may impact the audit. Once the risks have been identified, the auditor should determine whether the client has controls in place to monitor those risks and whether to test those controls. The assessment of client business risk is an input into the auditor's assessment of the risk of material misstatement due to errors or fraud. Client business risk affects inherent risk and control risk and the level of the auditor's work through detection risk.

Assessing the Risk of Material Misstatement Due to Error or Fraud[3]

[LO 8]

Auditing standards state that the auditor has a responsibility to plan and perform the audit to obtain reasonable assurance about whether the financial statements are free of material misstatement, whether caused by error or fraud (AU 110.02). *Errors* are unintentional misstatements or omissions of amounts or disclosures and may involve

- Mistakes in gathering or processing data from which financial statements are prepared.
- Unreasonable accounting estimates arising from oversight or misinterpretation of facts.
- Mistakes in the application of accounting principles relating to amount, classification, manner of presentation, or disclosure.

Fraud, from the auditor's perspective, involves intentional misstatements that can be classified into two types: (1) misstatements arising from

---

[3]Further nonauthoritative guidance on applying SAS No. 82 can be found in AICPA, *Considering Fraud in a Financial Statement Audit: Practical Guidance for Applying SAS No. 82* (New York: AICPA, 1997). The AICPA's Internet home page (www.aicpa.org) contains a set of teaching materials and cases for faculty and students on SAS No. 82. The reader is also referred to J. Mancino, "The Auditor and Fraud," *Journal of Accountancy* (April 1997), pp. 32–34, and A. H. Barnett, J. E. Brown, R. Fleming, and W. J. Read, "The CPA as Fraud-Buster," *Journal of Accountancy* (May 1998), pp. 69–73.

fraudulent financial reporting and (2) misstatements arising from misappropriation of assets. Thus, the primary distinction between errors and fraud is whether the misstatement was intentional or unintentional. Unfortunately, it is often difficult to determine intent. For example, suppose the auditor detects a misstatement in an account that requires an estimate, such as bad debt expense; it may be difficult to determine whether the misstatement was intentional.

Misstatements arising from fraudulent financial reporting include misstatements or omissions of amounts or disclosures in financial statements intended to deceive users of the financial statements. Fraudulent financial reporting may involve acts such as the following:

- Manipulation, falsification, or alteration of accounting records or supporting documents from which financial statements are prepared.
- Misrepresentation in, or intentional omission from, the financial statements of events, transactions, or other significant information.
- Intentional misapplication of accounting principles relating to amounts, classification, manner of presentation, or disclosure.

Misstatements arising from misappropriation of assets (sometimes referred to as *defalcation*) involve the theft of an entity's assets where the theft causes the financial statements to be misstated. Examples of misappropriation include

- Embezzling cash receipts.
- Stealing assets.
- Causing the entity to pay for goods or services not received.

Fraudulent financial reporting and misappropriation of assets differ in that fraudulent financial reporting is committed, usually by management, to deceive financial statement users, while misappropriation of assets is committed against an entity, most often by employees. An auditor can obtain only reasonable assurance that material misstatements in the financial statements will be detected because fraudulent activity often involves collusion or falsified documentation and requires professional judgment in the identification and evaluation of risk factors affecting inherent and control risk.

The auditor should specifically assess the risk of material misstatement of the financial statements due to error or fraud and should consider that assessment in designing the audit procedures. In making this assessment, the auditor should consider risk factors that relate to material misstatement of the financial statements. The risk factors described in SAS No. 47 and SAS No. 82 cover a broad range of situations typically faced by auditors, but they are only examples. Their significance will vary in entities of different sizes, with different ownership characteristics, in different industries, or because of other characteristics or circumstances. Accordingly, the auditor should use professional judgment when assessing the significance and relevance of risk factors.

Risk factors that relate to the possible presence of material misstatements in the financial statements can be grouped into three categories:

- Management's characteristics and influence over the control environment.

- Industry conditions.
- Operating characteristics and financial stability.

Risk factors that relate to misappropriation of assets can be grouped into two categories:

- Susceptibility of assets to misappropriation.
- Controls.

These five categories of risk factors will be discussed next.

Management's Characteristics and Influence over the Control Environment
These factors pertain to management's abilities, pressures, style, and attitude relating to internal control and the financial reporting process. Table 3–2 presents examples of such factors. Note that many of these factors impact both inherent risk and control risk.

If management has a strong incentive to meet earnings projections in order to support stock market expectations or to meet compensation arrangements based on recorded performance, it may adopt an aggressive attitude toward financial reporting. This might include premature recognition of income, deferral of expenses, and favorable accounting policies (see Exhibit 3–6). In such circumstances, the auditor should increase the assessment of auditee risk and carefully examine any financial statement accounts or transactions that may involve estimates or subjective judgments by management.

If a single person dominates the entity's operating and financing decisions, there is a higher risk that a material misstatement in the financial statements could occur because these important decisions may not be reviewed, and actions that are not in the best interests of the entity may be taken. Such dominance by one individual may lead to processing accounting transactions that are not consistent with the entity's controls (see Exhibit 3–7). When important operating and financing decisions are reviewed and approved by the entity's board of directors or major committees composed of directors, there is less risk that the financial statements will be materially misstated.

When the auditor observes frequent personnel turnover in important management positions, his or her assessment of the potential for material misstatement should increase because honest individuals are likely to resign their management positions rather than perpetuate some type of fraud. This would be particularly true if the turnover occurred in senior accounting positions. If the auditor notes such turnover among accounting personnel, he or she should increase his or her assessment of auditor risk and increase the scope of the audit.

Additional management characteristics may be important. For example, if management has a poor reputation in the business community, the auditor should assess inherent risk as high. The auditor can obtain information on management's reputation by inquiring at local banks and business organizations such as the Better Business Bureau. Finally, management may also be evasive in responding to the auditor's inquiries, or there may be frequent disputes between the auditor and management. Such situations should lead the auditor to assess auditee risk higher.

TABLE 3–2	Risk Factors Relating to Management's Characteristics and Influence over the Control Environment

- A motivation for management to engage in fraudulent financial reporting. Specific indicators might include
  - A significant portion of management's compensation represented by bonuses, stock options, or other incentives, the value of which is contingent upon the entity achieving unduly aggressive targets for operating results, financial position, or cash flow.
  - An excessive interest by management in maintaining or increasing the entity's stock price or earnings trend through the use of unusually aggressive accounting practices.
  - A practice by management of committing to analysts, creditors, and other third parties to achieve what appear to be unduly aggressive or clearly unrealistic forecasts.
  - An interest by management in pursuing inappropriate means to minimize reported earnings for tax-motivated reasons.
- A failure by management to display and communicate an appropriate attitude regarding internal control and the financial reporting process. Specific indicators might include
  - An ineffective means of communicating and supporting the entity's values or ethics, or communication of inappropriate values or ethics.
  - Domination of management by a single person or small group without compensating controls such as effective oversight by the board of directors or audit committee.
  - Inadequate monitoring of significant controls.
  - Management failing to correct known reportable conditions on a timely basis.
  - Management setting unduly aggressive financial targets and expectations for operating personnel.
  - Management displaying a significant disregard for regulatory authorities.
  - Management continuing to employ an ineffective accounting, information technology, or internal auditing staff.
- Nonfinancial management's excessive participation in, or preoccupation with, the selection of accounting principles or the determination of significant estimates.
- High turnover of senior management, counsel, or board members.
- Strained relationship between management and the current or predecessor auditor. Specific indicators might include
  - Frequent disputes with the current or predecessor auditor on accounting, auditing, or reporting matters.
  - Unreasonable demands on the auditor, including unreasonable time constraints regarding the completion of the audit or the issuance of the auditor's reports.
  - Formal or informal restrictions on the auditor that inappropriately limit his or her access to people or information or his or her ability to communicate effectively with the board of directors or the audit committee.
  - Domineering management behavior in dealing with the auditor, especially involving attempts to influence the scope of the auditor's work.
- Known history of securities law violations or claims against the entity or its senior management alleging fraud or violations of securities laws.

Industry Conditions   These factors relate to the economic and regulatory environment in which the entity operates. Table 3–3 presents examples of these risk factors, which impact the auditor's inherent risk assessment. Industry factors may also interact with some of the operating characteristics and financial stability factors discussed in the next section.

The operating results of entities in certain industries are very sensitive to economic factors. Some examples include the results of financial institutions affected by changes in interest rates, pharmaceutical companies with

EXHIBIT 3-6	**Chambers Development—Aggressive Accounting for Managing Waste**
	Chambers Development, once a waste management star on Wall Street, announced on March 17, 1992, that it would start expensing indirect costs related to developing landfill sites. The change resulted in a $27 million charge that wiped out more than half of 1991 net income. Apparently, this change in accounting came after the company's auditor, Grant Thornton, refused to sign off on Chambers's 1991 report and was fired.
	Chambers followed very aggressive methods in booking expenses associated with developing landfills. Normally, indirect costs for such things as scouting sites and negotiating with municipalities are treated as current expense. Chambers deferred recognizing these items and amortized them over several years. It also stretched the definition of development expenses to cover such items as public relations and legal fees, executives' salaries and travel expenses, and interest expense. A subsequent audit report by Deloitte & Touche states that the company covered its losses by understating expenses.
	More recently, Waste Management took a writedown of $3.54 billion for charges related to accounting methods.
	Sources: "Burying Trash in Big Holes—On the Balance Sheet," *Business Week* (May 11, 1992); R. Khalaf, "Fuzzy Accounting," *Forbes* (June 22, 1992); and G. Stern, "Audit Report Shows How Far Chambers Would Go for Profits," *The Wall Street Journal* (October 21, 1992); J. Bailey, "Waste Management Takes Charges, Write-Downs of $3.54 Billion," *The Wall Street Journal* (February 25, 1998).

EXHIBIT 3-7	**Founder of Crazy Eddie's Embezzled Millions of Dollars**
	Eddie Antar was the founder of and major shareholder in Crazy Eddie's. The company made several public offerings of securities, including the sale of shares held by Eddie Antar and his family. The financial statements gave the impression that Crazy Eddie's was a rapidly growing firm. However, the financial statements were misstated using a number of schemes. Net income and inventory were inflated through improper financial reporting practices. The company also reported higher per store sales figures than actually existed. These actions appear to have been taken by Mr. Antar to support the price of Crazy Eddie's stock. Mr. Antar also approved sales to himself and members of his family of inventory that was later resold to others. When Mr. Antar resigned his position as president, the successor management discovered an estimated inventory shortage of $65 million, and the company's net worth was only $7 million.
	Sources: In re Crazy Eddie Securities Litigation (714 F., Supp. 1285); Berstein v. Crazy Eddie, Inc. (702 F., Supp. 962).

TABLE 3-3   Risk Factors Relating to Industry Conditions

- New accounting, statutory, or regulatory requirements that could impair the financial stability or profitability of the entity.
- High degree of competition or market saturation, accompanied by declining margins.
- Declining industry with increasing business failures and significant declines in customer demand.
- Rapid changes in the industry, such as high vulnerability to rapidly changing technology or rapid product obsolescence.

international operations affected by changes in the exchange rate of the US dollar relative to currencies in countries in which they operate, and defense contractors affected by government spending on defense products. Management personnel coping with the effects of such economic factors may be motivated to misstate financial statements. Inherent risk should therefore be increased for clients that are affected by economic factors such as these.

Other industry-related factors also give the auditor useful information for assessing inherent risk. First, how profitable is this entity relative to other entities in the industry? The answer to this question may provide information on the adequacy and consistency of the entity's earnings, and thus information on management's incentives for manipulating income. Second, what is the rate of change in the industry? Generally, industries that are subject to rapid changes are more likely to have materially misstated financial statements. For example, in the high technology sector, frequent changes may affect the fair market value of products sold. Finally, how healthy is the industry as a whole? If the industry is distressed, the risk of a material misstatement is higher than when the industry is financially sound. In a distressed industry, significant issues concerning valuation on the financial statements may arise. For example, an entity in a distressed industry can experience slow product sales, which may lead to questions about the proper fair market value for inventories. The auditor must be particularly aware of industry-specific information that may increase inherent risk.

Operating Characteristics and Financial Stability   These factors relate to the nature and complexity of the entity and its transactions, the entity's financial condition, and its profitability. Table 3–4 demonstrates factors that affect an entity's operating characteristics and financial stability. Again, most of these factors would impact the auditor's assessment of inherent risk.

The nature of business transactions has changed dramatically in recent years. As the accounting for transactions such as derivatives, leases, and pensions has become more complex, the risk of material misstatement has increased. Similarly, for many clients, the accounting for certain types of transactions may result in disagreement between management and the auditor. Recognition of income on long-term contracts and valuation of assets are just two examples of transactions that may cause disagreement. When complex or contentious accounting issues are present, the auditor should increase inherent risk.

The nature of a client's business may make transactions or account balances difficult to audit. Proper accounting for such accounts or transactions may involve considerable judgment on the part of the client. Two examples of such transactions are the recognition of income on long-term contracts when the percentage of completion method is used and establishing the amount of loan loss reserves for a financial institution. In such cases, the auditor should assess a higher level of inherent risk because of the possibility that such estimates may lead to materially misstated financial statements.

Although a basic assumption in accounting is that an entity will continue as a going concern, operating and financing problems may raise significant doubt about the validity of this assumption for a particular entity. When an entity is identified as having numerous symptoms that indicate it

TABLE 3–4	Risk Factors Relating to Operating Characteristics and Financial Stability

- Inability to generate cash flows from operations while reporting earnings and earnings growth.
- Significant pressure to obtain additional capital necessary to stay competitive considering the financial position of the entity—including need for funds to finance major research and development or capital expenditures.
- Assets, liabilities, revenues, or expenses based on significant estimates that involve unusually subjective judgments or uncertainties, or that are subject to potential significant change in the near term in a manner that may have a financially disruptive effect on the entity—such as ultimate collectibility of receivables, timing of revenue recognition, realizability of financial instruments based on the highly subjective valuation of collateral or difficult-to-assess repayment sources, or significant deferral of costs.
- Significant related-party transactions not in the ordinary course of business or with related entities not audited or audited by another firm.
- Significant, unusual, or highly complex transactions, especially those close to year-end, that pose difficult "substance over form" questions.
- Significant bank accounts or subsidiary or branch operations in tax-haven jurisdictions for which there appears to be no clear business justification.
- Overly complex organizational structure involving numerous or unusual legal entities, managerial lines of authority, or contractual arrangements without apparent business purpose.
- Difficulty in determining the organization or individual(s) that controls the entity.
- Unusually rapid growth or profitability, especially compared with that of other companies in the same industry.
- Especially high vulnerability to changes in interest rates.
- Unusually high dependence on debt or marginal ability to meet debt repayment requirements; debt covenants that are difficult to maintain.
- Unrealistically aggressive sales or profitability incentive programs.
- Threat of imminent bankruptcy or foreclosure, or hostile takeover.
- Adverse consequences on significant pending transactions, such as a business combination or contract award, if poor financial results are reported.
- Poor or deteriorating financial position when management has personally guaranteed significant debt of the entity.

is not a going concern, the auditor should assess a higher risk of material misstatement and therefore increase the assessment of inherent risk.

Studies of audit practice[4] have shown that accounts that were found to be misstated in previous audits are likely to contain similar misstatements in the current year. Thus, when an auditor has encountered material misstatements in prior audits, the auditor should assess inherent risk higher than on audits where few or immaterial misstatements have been found in the past.

Finally, an auditor who is examining the financial statements of a long-standing client will have gained a tremendous amount of experience

---

[4]See, for example, W. R. Kinney, Jr., "The Predictive Power of Limited Information in Preliminary Analytical Review: An Empirical Study," *Journal of Accounting Research* (Suppl. 1979), pp. 148–165; A. Wright and R. H. Ashton, "Identifying Audit Adjustments with Attention-Directing Procedures," *The Accounting Review* (October 1989), pp. 710–28.

TABLE 3–5	Risk Factors Relating to Susceptibility of Assets to Misappropriation

- Large amounts of cash on hand or processed.
- Inventory characteristics, such as small size, high value, or high demand.
- Easily convertible assets, such as bearer bonds, diamonds, or computer chips.
- Fixed asset characteristics, such as small size, marketability, or lack of ownership identification.

TABLE 3–6	Risk Factors Relating to Controls

- Lack of appropriate management oversight (for example, inadequate supervision or monitoring of remote locations).
- Lack of job applicant screening procedures relating to employees with access to assets susceptible to misappropriation.
- Inadequate recordkeeping with respect to assets susceptible to misappropriation.
- Lack of appropriate segregation of duties or independent checks.
- Lack of appropriate system of authorization and approval of transactions (for example, in purchasing).
- Poor physical safeguards over cash, investments, inventory, or fixed assets.
- Lack of timely and appropriate documentation for transactions (for example, credits for merchandise returns).
- Lack of mandatory vacations for employees performing key control functions.

and knowledge about the client and its operations. The auditor on a new engagement lacks this type of information. Thus, in general, the assessment of inherent risk for new clients should be higher than the assessment of inherent risk for continuing clients.

Susceptibility of Assets to Misappropriation   These factors relate to the nature of the entity's assets and the degree to which they are subject to theft. Table 3–5 provides examples of such factors, most of which would impact the auditor's assessment of inherent risk. For example, if the entity processes large amounts of cash, susceptibility to misappropriation is increased. Similarly, if the entity produces small, highly valuable products such as computer chips, such assets may be stolen. When an audit client faces these types of risk factors, the auditor should increase the assessment of inherent risk.

Controls   These risk factors, which involve the lack of controls designed to prevent or detect misappropriation of assets, directly affect the auditor's assessment of control risk. Table 3–6 provides examples of such factors. For example, if the entity does not have adequate management oversight of high-risk areas or has inadequate recordkeeping for assets susceptible to theft, the auditor should increase the control risk assessment. Similarly, if the entity does not adequately segregate duties or use independent checks, collusion can occur and assets can be misappropriated. And if the entity has not installed an appropriate system for authorizing and approving transactions, the entity may pay for goods and services not received.

The Auditor's Response to the Results of the Risk Assessments

Based on assessment of the risk factors that affect client business risk and the risk of material misstatement due to error or fraud, the auditor assesses inherent risk and control risk. As mentioned previously, the auditor then determines the level of detection risk. Next the auditor designs audit procedures to respond to the risk factors identified. If the risk factor assessment indicates that fraud might be present, the auditor might respond as follows:

- Increase professional skepticism by questioning and critically assessing audit evidence.
- Assign more experienced auditors who have the knowledge, skill, and ability commensurate with the increased risk of the engagement.
- Consider management's selection and application of significant accounting policies, particularly those related to recognizing revenue, valuing assets, or capitalizing versus expensing.
- Modify the nature, timing, and extent of audit procedures to obtain more reliable evidence and use increased sample sizes or more extensive analytical procedures.

Evaluation of Audit Test Results

At the completion of the audit, the auditor should consider whether the accumulated results of audit procedures affect the assessments of client business risk and the risk of material misstatement due to error or fraud. When audit test results identify misstatements in the financial statements, the auditor should consider whether such misstatements may indicate fraud.

When the auditor has determined that a misstatement is or may be the result of fraud, but the effect of the misstatement is not material to the financial statements, the auditor should evaluate the implications. If the matter involves higher-level management, it may indicate a more pervasive problem. In such circumstances the auditor should reassess of the risk of material misstatement due to error or fraud and its resulting impact on the audit.

If the auditor has determined that the misstatement is or may be the result of fraud, and either has determined that the effect could be material to the financial statements or has been unable to evaluate whether the effect is material, the auditor should

- Consider the implications for other aspects of the audit.
- Discuss the matter and the approach to further investigation with an appropriate level of management that is at least one level above those involved and with senior management.
- Attempt to obtain sufficient competent evidential matter to determine whether, in fact, material fraud exists, and, if so, its effect.
- If appropriate, suggest that the client consult with legal counsel.

If the results of the audit tests indicate a significant risk of fraud, the auditor should consider withdrawing from the engagement and communicating the reasons for withdrawal to the audit committee or others with equivalent authority and responsibility.

Documentation of the Auditor's Risk Assessment and Response

In planning the audit, the auditor should document in the working papers evidence that the risk of material misstatement due to error or fraud was assessed, including how risk factors were considered. Where risk factors are identified, the documentation should describe (1) the risk factors identified and (2) the auditor's response to those risk factors.

If, during the performance of the audit, fraud risk factors or other conditions are identified that cause the auditor to believe that an additional response is required, such risk factors or other conditions, and any further response that the auditor concluded was appropriate, also should be documented.

Communications about Fraud to Management, the Audit Committee, and Others

Whenever the auditor has found evidence that a fraud may exist, that matter should be brought to the attention of an appropriate level of management. Fraud involving senior management and fraud that causes a material misstatement of the financial statements should be reported directly to the audit committee of the board of directors. (See Chapter 5 for a detailed discussion of the audit committee.) In addition, the auditor should reach an understanding with the audit committee regarding the expected nature and extent of communications about misappropriations perpetrated by lower-level employees.

The disclosure of fraud to parties other than the client's senior management and its audit committee ordinarily is not part of the auditor's responsibility and ordinarily would be precluded by the auditor's ethical or legal obligations of confidentiality. The auditor should recognize, however, that in the following circumstances a duty to disclose outside the entity may exist:

- To comply with certain legal and regulatory requirements.
- To a successor auditor when the successor makes inquiries in accordance with SAS No. 84, "Communications between Predecessor and Successor Auditors."
- In response to a subpoena.
- To a funding agency or other specified agency in accordance with requirements for the audits of entities that receive governmental financial assistance.

Limitations of the Audit Risk Model

[LO 9]

Auditing standards provide for the use of the audit risk model as a way of ensuring that the risk of issuing materially misstated financial statements is kept to an acceptably low level. However, this model has a number of limitations that must be considered by auditors and their firms.[5]

The audit risk model was proposed as a planning tool (AU 311 and AU 312). If an auditor uses the model to *revise* an audit plan or to *evaluate* audit results, the *actual* level of audit risk may be greater than the audit risk indicated by the formula. This may occur because the model assumes that the

---

[5]See B. E. Cushing and J. K. Loebbecke, "Analytical Approaches to Audit Risk: A Survey and Analysis," *Auditing: A Journal of Practice and Theory* (Fall 1983), pp. 23–41; W. R. Kinney, Jr., "A Note on Compounding Probabilities in Auditing," *Auditing: A Journal of Practice and Theory* (Spring 1983), pp. 13–22; and W. R. Kinney, Jr., "Achieved Audit Risk and the Audit Outcome Space," *Auditing: A Journal of Practice and Theory* (Suppl. 1989), pp. 67–84, for more detailed discussions of the limitations of the audit risk model.

components (*IR*, *CR*, and *DR*) are *independent* of one another as indicated by the multiplicative form of the model. However, in practice, the risk of a material misstatement (*IR*) occurring may be a function of the client's internal controls (*CR*). Thus, inherent risk may depend on control risk. In practice, some public accounting firms make a *combined risk assessment* for *IR* and *CR*.

Other limitations may also be present. Because the auditor *assesses* inherent risk and control risk, such assessments may be higher or lower than the *actual* inherent risk and control risk that exist for the client. Such differences can affect the determination of detection risk and the achieved audit risk. The audit risk model also does not consider the possibility of nonsampling risk.

The point of this discussion is to alert the reader to the possible limitations of the audit risk model. The model, however, does serve as an important tool that auditors can use for planning an audit engagement.

APPENDIX:

A Quantitative Approach to Allocating Materiality

In this appendix, a quantitative approach to allocating the preliminary judgment about materiality is presented. One method that has been proposed in the professional literature[6] is referred to as the *relative magnitude method*. The relative magnitude method allocates the preliminary judgment about materiality using the following formula:

$$TM = PJM \times \sqrt{\frac{\text{Book value of account}}{\substack{\text{Total amount of all components} \\ \text{to which materiality is being allocated}}}}$$

where

    TM = Tolerable misstatement for a balance sheet account
    PJM = Preliminary judgment about materiality

The denominator of the term under the radical is the total amount of all components to which materiality is being allocated. For EarthWear this amount is $214,672,000. Exhibit 3–8 presents the allocation of the $980,000 preliminary materiality judgment determined in Exhibit 3–3 using the relative magnitude formula. The amounts shown for tolerable misstatement have been rounded to the nearest $1,000.

For example, the allocation for accounts receivable would be made as follows:

$$\$536,000 = \$980,000 \times \sqrt{\frac{\$64,100,000}{\$214,672,000}}$$

Note that the sum of the amounts allocated ($2,622,000) using this method exceeds the preliminary judgment about materiality. This occurs because the tolerable misstatements are generally nonadditive. To the extent that

---

[6]See G. R. Zuber, R. K. Elliott, W. R. Kinney, Jr., and J. J. Leisearing, "Using Materiality in Audit Planning," *Journal of Accountancy* (March 1983) pp. 42–55.

EXHIBIT 3–8

Allocation of the Preliminary Judgment about Materiality

EARTHWEAR CLOTHIERS
Consolidated Balance Sheet
December 31, 2000
(In thousands)

Address: http://www.mhhe.com/messier

	Balance Sheet Amount	Tolerable Misstatement
Cash and cash equivalents	$ 41,772*	$ 432
Receivables	3,933*	133
Inventory	64,100*	536
Prepaid advertising	4,980*	149
Other prepaid expenses	2,448*	105
Deferred income tax benefits	5,185	†
Property, plant and equipment, net	46,658*	457
Intangibles, net	1,045	†
Total	$ 170,121	
Lines of credit	$ 5,038	†
Accounts payable	34,463*	$ 393
Reserve for returns	2,333*	102
Accrued liabilities	12,663*	238
Accrued profit sharing	1,322*	77
Income tax payable	9,686	†
Deferred income taxes	3,914	†
Long-term liabilities	297	†
Common stock and paid-in-capital	12,025	†
Donated capital	3,780	†
Less: Deferred compensation	(617)	†
Currency translation adjustments	170	†
Retained earnings	139,978	N/A
Less: Treasury stock	(54,931)	†
Total	$ 170,121	$ 2,622

*The sum of these items is $214,672 (in thousands).
† = Account will be audited 100%; no allocation of tolerable misstatement is necessary.
N/A = Not applicable; retained earnings are a residual.

each of the audit tests is independent of the other, this formula will prevent the auditor's risk of rejecting the client's financial statements as not being fairly presented from becoming too great for practical application. After using the relative magnitude formula to determine tolerable misstatement for each account, the auditor may still want to reallocate tolerable misstatement among the accounts, based on judgmental or qualitative factors.

REVIEW QUESTIONS

[handwritten: Some immaterial misstatements may be in f/s]

[LO 1,2] 3-1   The opinion paragraph contains the term *in all material respects.* How should users of the audit report interpret this term?

[handwritten: Consistency within the firm]

[1,2]   3-2   Why is it important for CPA firms to develop policies and procedures for establishing materiality? *because standards provide very little guidance*

[2]   3-3   List and describe the three major steps in applying materiality to an audit. *preliminary, allocate, compare likely to preliminary*

[2,3]   3-4   Materiality is considered a relative rather than an absolute concept. How does the relative size of the entity being audited affect the preliminary judgment about materiality? *larger size → larger materiality*

[2,3]   3-5   Discuss why total assets or revenues might be better bases for determining materiality than net income before taxes. *more stable*

[2,3]   3-6   Give two examples of qualitative factors that might affect the preliminary judgment about materiality. *past history, known violations*

[2,3]   3-7   Discuss the factors that should be considered in allocating materiality to an account balance. *size of A/c, errors expected, cost to audit*

[4]   3-8   Distinguish between audit risk and auditor business risk.

[5]   3-9   Define each of the components in the audit risk model.

[4,5]   3-10   Discuss the relationship between inherent risk and control risk.

[handwritten: auditor control]

[4,5]   3-11   How do inherent risk and control risk differ from detection risk?

[6,7,8]   3-12   How does client business risk relate to the auditor's assessment of the risk of material misstatement due to error or fraud?

[7]   3-13   What type of industry knowledge must the auditor have to assess client business risk?

[6,7,8]   3-14   Distinguish between errors and fraud. Give three examples of each.

[8]   3-15   List the three groups of factors that affect the auditor's assessment of the presence of material misstatements in the financial statements, and give three examples from each group.

[8]   3-16   List the two groups of factors that relate to the misappropriation of assets. Give two examples from each group.

[17]   3-17   Distinguish between sampling and nonsampling risk.

[9]   3-18   What are some limitations of the audit risk model?

[handwritten: assumes independent components, risk assessments may be wrong, does not consider non-sampling risk]

MULTIPLE-CHOICE QUESTIONS FROM CPA EXAMINATIONS

[2,3]   3-19   In considering materiality for planning purposes, an auditor believes that misstatements aggregating $10,000 would have a material

effect on an entity's income statement but that misstatements would have to aggregate $20,000 to materially affect the balance sheet. Ordinarily, it would be appropriate to design auditing procedures that would be expected to detect misstatements that aggregate

a. $10,000.

b. $15,000.

c. $20,000.

d. $30,000.

procedures overlap BS & IS
pick smallest one

[2,6]   3-20   As lower acceptable levels of both audit risk and materiality are established, the auditor should plan more work on individual accounts to

a. Find smaller errors.

b. Find larger errors.

c. Increase the tolerable error in the accounts.

d. Decrease the risk of overreliance.

[1,4]   3-21   Which of the following elements underlies the application of generally accepted auditing standards, particularly the standards of field work and reporting?

a. Internal control.

b. Corroborating evidence.

c. Quality control.

d. Materiality and relative risk.

[5,6]   3-22   As the acceptable level of detection risk increases, an auditor may change the

DR is last
determines
scope
(nature, amount, timing, extent)

a. Assessed level of control risk from below the maximum to the maximum level.

b. Assurance provided by tests of controls by using a larger sample size than planned.

c. Timing of substantive tests from year-end to an interim date.

d. Nature of substantive tests from a less effective to a more effective procedure. *(backwards)*

[5,6]   3-23   On the basis of audit evidence gathered and evaluated, an auditor decides to increase the assessed level of control risk from that originally planned. To achieve an overall audit risk level that is substantially the same as the planned audit risk level, the auditor would

$AR = IR \times CR \times DR$

a. Increase inherent risk. *(don't control)* *CR↑*

b. Increase materiality levels. ✗

c. Decrease substantive testing. ✗

d. Decrease detection risk.

[4]   3-24   The existence of audit risk is recognized by the statement in the auditor's standard report that the auditor

a. Obtains reasonable assurance about whether the financial statements are free of material misstatement.

b. Assesses the accounting principles used and also evaluates the overall financial statement presentation.

c. Realizes that some matters, either individually or in the aggregate, are important while other matters are not important.

d. Is responsible for expressing an opinion on the financial statements, which are the responsibility of management.

[5,6]   3-25   As the acceptable level of detection risk decreases, the assurance directly provided from
a. Substantive tests should increase.
b. Substantive tests should decrease.
c. Tests of controls should increase.
d. Tests of controls should decrease.

[5,6]   3-26   Which of the following audit risk components may be assessed in nonquantitative terms?

	Inherent Risk	Control Risk	Detection Risk
a.	Yes	Yes	No
b.	Yes	No	Yes
c.	No	Yes	Yes
d.	Yes	Yes	Yes

[5,6]   3-27   As the acceptable level of detection risk decreases, an auditor may change the
a. Timing of substantive tests by performing them at an interim date rather than at year-end. ✗
b. Nature of substantive tests from a less effective to a more effective procedure. ✓
c. Timing of tests of controls by performing them at several dates rather than at one time. ✗
d. Assessed level of inherent risk to a higher amount. ✗

[8]   3-28   Which of the following is an example of fraudulent financial reporting?
a. Company management falsifies inventory count tags, thereby overstating ending inventory and understating cost of sales.
b. An employee diverts customer payments to his personal use, concealing his actions by debiting an expense account, thus overstating expenses.
c. An employee steals inventory, and the shrinkage is recorded as a cost of goods sold.
d. An employee borrows small tools from the company and neglects to return them; the cost is reported as a miscellaneous operating expense.

[8]   3-29   Auditing standards (SAS No. 82) require auditors to make certain inquiries of management regarding fraud. Which of the following inquiries is required?
a. Whether management has ever intentionally violated the securities laws.
b. Whether management has any knowledge of fraud that has been perpetrated on or within the entity.
c. Management's attitudes toward regulatory authorities.
d. Management's attitudes toward internal control and the financial reporting process.

[8]   3-30   Which of the following is correct concerning SAS No. 82's requirements concerning auditor communications about fraud?
a. Fraud that involves senior management should be reported directly by the auditor to the audit committee regardless of the amount involved.

b. Fraud with a material effect on the financial statements should be reported directly by the auditor to the Securities and Exchange Commission.

c. Any requirement to disclose fraud outside the entity is the responsibility of management and not that of the auditor.

d. The professional standards provide no requirements related to the communication of fraud, but the auditor should use professional judgment in determining communication responsibilities.

PROBLEMS

[1,2,3]   **3-31**   During the course of an audit engagement an independent auditor seriously considers the concept of materiality. This concept of materiality is inherent in the work of the independent auditor and is important for planning the scope of the audit. The concept of materiality underlies the application of all the generally accepted auditing standards, particularly the standards of field work and reporting.

Required:
a. Briefly describe what is meant by the independent auditor's concept of materiality.
b. What are some common relationships and other considerations used by the auditor in judging materiality?
c. Identify how planning the scope of an audit might be affected by the independent auditor's concept of materiality.

(AICPA, adapted)

[1,2,4,5]   **3-32**   The auditor should consider audit risk and materiality when planning and performing an examination of financial statements in accordance with generally accepted auditing standards. Audit risk and materiality should also be considered together in determining the nature, timing, and extent of auditing procedures and in evaluating the results of those procedures.

Required:
a. 1. Define *audit risk*.
   2. Describe its components of inherent risk, control risk, and detection risk.
   3. Explain how these components are interrelated.
b. 1. Define *materiality*.
   2. Discuss the factors affecting its determination.
   3. Describe the relationship between materiality for planning purposes and materiality for evaluation purposes.

(AICPA, adapted)

[2,3]   **3-33**   Jim Johnson, an audit manager, is planning the audit for Commodore Container Corporation (CCC), a major producer of containerboard and corrugated boxes. At December 31, 2000, CCC's unaudited balances for accounts receivable, inventory, and plant assets (net) are $102.5 million, $65.3 million, and $591 million,

respectively. Total assets amount to $823.9 million. Unaudited net income is $4.5 million on revenues for the year of $778 million. Total current liabilities are $43.6 million, and long-term debt is $670 million.

Required

a. Make a preliminary judgment about materiality for CCC using the worksheet included in Exhibit 3–1.
b. Allocate the preliminary judgment about materiality to the accounts included, using only their relative size.

[4,5,6] 3-34 The CPA firm of Koch & Tabbs uses a quantitative approach to implementing the audit risk model. Calculate detection risk for each of the following hypothetical clients.

Client No.	Audit Risk	Inherent Risk	Control Risk	Detection Risk
1	5%	40%	50%	
2	5%	60%	80%	
3	10%	50%	25%	
4	10%	80%	50%	

[4,5,6] 3-35 The CPA firm of Petersen & Pauley uses a qualitative approach to implementing the audit risk model. Audit risk is categorized using three terms: very low, low, and moderate. Inherent risk and detection risk are categorized using three terms: low, moderate, and high. Control risk is categorized using four terms: very low, low, moderate, and high. Calculate detection risk for each of the following hypothetical clients.

Client No.	Audit Risk	Inherent Risk	Control Risk	Detection Risk
1	Moderate	High	Low	
2	Very low	Low	Very low	
3	Low	Moderate	High	
4	Very low	High	Moderate	

[8] 3-36 Sandy Pitts is auditing Hofmeister Hardware Company, a fast-growing retail hardware chain in the Atlanta area. While Pitts has previously worked on this engagement, this is her first year as the audit manager. As she planned the engagement, Pitts identified a number of risk factors (such as strong interest in maintaining the company's earnings and stock price, unrealistic forecasts, and high dependence on debt financing for expansion) that indicated that fraud might exist.

Required:

a. How should Pitts respond to the possibility of fraud at the planning stage? What is the required documentation for identified risk factors?
b. If Pitts had evidence that suggested that fraud existed, what would be her communication responsibilities to management, the audit committee, and others?

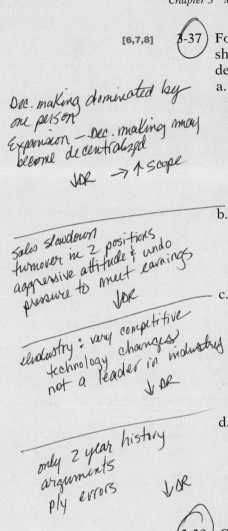

Dec. making dominated by one person
Expansion — Dec. making may become decentralized
↓AR → ↑ Scope

Sales slowdown
turnover in 2 positions
aggressive attitude & undo
pressure to meet earnings
↑AR

Industry: very competitive
technology changes
not a leader in industry
↓AR

only 2 year history
arguments
p/y errors
↑AR

[6,7,8] 3-37 For each of the following situations, explain how inherent risk should be assessed and what effect that assessment will have on detection risk.

a. Johnson, Inc., is a fast-growing trucking company operating in the southeastern part of the United States. The company is publicly held, but Ivan Johnson and his sons control 55 percent of the stock. Mr. Johnson is chairman of the board and CEO. He personally makes all major decisions with little consultation with the board of directors. Most of the directors, however, are either members of the Johnson family or long-standing friends. The board basically rubber-stamps Mr. Johnson's decisions.

b. Close-Moor Stores has experienced slower sales during the last year. There is a new vice president of finance and a new controller. Mr. Musiciak, president of the company, has a reputation for hard-nosed business tactics, and he is always concerned with meeting forecast earnings.

c. MaxiWrite Corporation is one of several companies engaged in the manufacture of high-speed, high-capacity disk drives. The industry is very competitive and subject to quick changes in technology. MaxiWrite's operating results would place the company in the second quartile in terms of profitability and financial position. The company has never been the leader in the industry, with its products typically slightly behind the industry leader's in terms of performance.

d. The First National Bank of Pond City has been your client for the past two years. During that period you have had numerous arguments with the president and the controller over a number of accounting issues. The major issue has related to the bank's reserve for loan losses and the value of collateral. Your prior audits have indicated that a significant adjustment is required each year to the loan loss reserves.

[7,8] 3-38 Green, CPA, is considering audit risk at the financial statement level in planning the audit of National Federal Bank (NFB) Company's financial statements for the year ended December 31, 2000. Audit risk at the financial statement level is influenced by the risk of material misstatements, which may be indicated by a combination of factors related to management, the industry, and the entity. In assessing such factors Green has gathered the following information concerning NFB's environment.

Company Profile

NFB is a federally insured bank that has been consistently more profitable than the industry average by marketing mortgages on properties in a prosperous rural area, which has experienced considerable growth in recent years. NFB packages its mortgages and sells them to large mortgage investment trusts. Despite a recent volatility in interest rates, NFB has been able to continue selling its mortgages as a source of new lendable funds.

NFB's board of directors is controlled by Smith, the majority stockholder, who also acts as the chief executive officer. Management at the bank's branch offices has authority for directing and controlling NFB's operations and is compensated based on branch profitability. The internal auditor reports directly to Harris, a minority shareholder, who also acts as chairman of the board's audit committee.

The accounting department has experienced little turnover in personnel during the five years Green has audited NFB. NFB's formula consistently underestimates the allowance for loan losses, but its controller has always been receptive to Green's suggestions to increase the allowance during each engagement.

Recent Developments

During 2000, NFB opened a branch office in a suburban town 30 miles from its principal place of business. Although this branch is not yet profitable due to competition from several well-established regional banks, management believes that the branch will be profitable by 2002.

Also during 2000, NFB increased the efficiency of its accounting operations by installing a new, sophisticated computer system.

Required:

Based only on the information given, describe the factors that most likely would affect the risk of material misstatements. Indicate whether each factor increases or decreases the risk. Use the following format:

Environmental Factor	Effect on Risk of Material Misstatements
Branch management has authority for directing and controlling operations.	Increase

(AICPA, adapted)

[4,5]   **3-39**   When planning a financial statement audit, a CPA must understand audit risk and its components.

Required:

For each illustration, select the component of audit risk that is most directly illustrated. The components of audit risk may be used once, more than once, or not at all.

Components of Audit Risk:
a. Auditor business risk
b. Control risk
c. Detection risk
d. Inherent risk

Illustration	Component of Audit Risk
1. A client fails to discover employee fraud on a timely basis because bank accounts are not reconciled monthly.	*CR*
2. Cash is more susceptible to theft than an inventory of coal.	*IR*
3. Confirmation of receivables by an auditor fails to detect a material misstatement.	*DR*
4. Disbursements have occurred without proper approval.	*CR*
5. There is inadequate segregation of duties.	*CR*
6. A necessary substantive audit procedure is omitted.	*DR*
7. Notes receivable are susceptible to material misstatement, assuming there are no related internal controls.	*IR*
8. Technological developments make a major product obsolete.	*IR*
9. An auditor complies with GAAS on an audit engagement, but the shareholders sue the auditor for issuing misleading financial statements.	*ABR*
10. XYZ Company, a client, lacks sufficient working capital to continue operations.	*IR*

DISCUSSION CASES

[2,3]   3-40   Richard Yates, CPA, is auditing the Levitan Corporation for the year ended December 31, 2000. In prior years, Levitan's financial statements were audited by another CPA firm. Levitan's unaudited statements at December 31 show the following balances:

LEVITAN CORPORATION
Balance Sheet
December 31, 2000

Assets

Cash	$ 1,750,000
Accounts receivable	2,500,000
Inventory	7,750,000
Property, plant, and equipment, net	15,000,000
Other assets	11,000,000
Total	$38,000,000

Liabilities and Stockholders' Equity

Current portion of long-term debt	$ 1,900,000
Accounts payable	3,000,000
Other current liabilities	4,500,000
Long-term debt	12,000,000
Deferred income taxes	1,000,000
Common stock	1,950,000
Retained earnings	13,650,000
Total	$38,000,000
Revenue	$35,000,000
Net income before taxes	$ 4,500,000

Because Yates has not previously audited Levitan, he decides to audit all of the balance sheet accounts.

Required:

a. Determine the preliminary judgment about materiality for Levitan using the worksheet included in Exhibit 3–1.

b. Allocate the preliminary judgment of materiality to the balance sheet accounts using the relative size of the accounts as the basis for allocation. Consider any accounts that are likely to be audited 100 percent. You know the following about Levitan's accounts: (1) controls over accounts payable are weak, but the account balance is composed of a small number of individual vendor accounts; (2) long-term debt is composed of two privately placed bond issues that are held by four insurance companies; and (3) other assets mainly include goodwill from three acquisitions in prior years.

c. Consider whether any of the amounts allocated in part (b) should be adjusted to reflect the following facts: Of the $15 million of net plant assets, $1.4 million represents current-year additions.

During your review of the prior auditor's working papers, you noted that numerous customer accounts were found to be uncollectible and that Levitan had not provided any allowance for their uncollectibility. The company has very strong controls over inventory due mainly to a sophisticated computerized perpetual inventory system.

The company in the following case will serve as an example throughout the textbook. The company will be used directly in some chapters as an illustration of the material being presented. It will also be utilized in some chapter problem assignments.

General Information: Calabro Paging Services.

Calabro Paging Services is a business services company that uses wireless communications technology to develop solutions for business and organizational problems. The company owns and operates paging systems; manufactures, leases, and sells pagers; and provides commercial paging services in 12 major metropolitan areas in the southeastern part of the United States. The company emphasizes its systems, reliability, solution-oriented marketing, and high level of customer service. The company provides high-quality, low-cost service to the marketplace.

Calabro was founded 15 years ago, when Ronald Calabro purchased a local paging company in Tampa, Florida. The company expanded by building paging systems in major metropolitan areas. Calabro Paging Services went public 10 years ago, and its stock is traded on the NASDAQ stock exchange. Five years ago, the day-to-day operations of the company were turned over to the founder's son, Matthew Calabro, who has served as chief executive officer since that time. Ronald Calabro continues to serve as chairman of the board.

As of 2000, the company has built and still operates 12 paging systems, with the last system constructed in 1995. In recent years the company has focused on internal growth rather than geographic expansion, and its compound annual subscriber growth rate has been 20 percent. The company improved its earnings during this period an used its excess cash provided by operations to reduce its debt burden to approximately $3.5 million at December 31, 2000.

Company Operations

Calabro offers a variety of pagers to its subscribers. Subscribers may lease a pager from the company or purchase a pager and pay only an access fee for the company paging system. Each subscriber enters into a service contract with the company, which provides for the payment of the access fee and the purchase or lease of one or more pagers. The company's contracts with customers with large numbers of pagers are typically for three- to five-year terms, while contracts for smaller quantities are typically for one-year terms with annual renewal. The combined lease and access fee of a single leased pager currently ranges from approximately $5.00 to $40.00 per month, depending upon the type of pager and optional features selected. The company charges a monthly access fee for service to each customer-owned pager. Volume discounts on access fees and lease costs are typically offered to large-unit-volume subscribers. Comparably to prior years, approximately 82 percent of the company's pages in service at December 31, 2000, were leased from the company, and approximately 18 percent were owned by subscribers.

[2,3]   3-41   Don Jones is the senior in charge of the audit of Calabro Paging Services. Jones's firm, Abbott & Johnson, LLP, has audited Calabro for 10 years. Calabro's unaudited statements are shown here for the year ended December 31, 2000.

CALABRO PAGING SERVICES

| | Year Ended December 31, | | | | |
	2000	1999	1998	1996	1995
	(Dollars in thousands, except per share amounts)				
At end of period:					
Pagers in service	145,872	130,400	117,514	98,718	80,364
Operating data:					
Revenues	$20,742	$18,289	$17,465	$15,452	$12,526
Operating income (loss)	2,663	1,801	1,510	762	(452)
Income (loss) before extraordinary item	1,535	1,710	774	210	(500)
Net income (loss)	1,535	1,710	1,279	385	(500)
Net income (loss) per share:					
Before extraordinary item	.38	.42	.19	.05	(.13)
Net income (loss)	.38	.42	.32	.10	(.13)
Balance sheet data:					
Total assets	$29,611	$27,465	$25,934	$23,850	$23,244
Long-term debt, including current maturities	3,890	3,539	4,859	4,599	4,842
Total liabilities	9,564	8,116	8,187	7,631	7,424
Total stockholders' equity	19,851	19,349	17,747	16,219	15,821
Other data:					
Earnings before taxes, other income (expense), depreciation, and amortization	$7,203	$5,776	$5,164	$3,988	$2,316

CALABRO PAGING SERVICES
Consolidated Balance Sheet

Assets

	December 31,	
	2000	**1999**
Current assets:		
Cash and cash equivalents	$ 516,709	$ 128,018
Trade accounts receivable, less allowance for doubtful accounts of $135,300 and $110,800 as of December 31, 2000 and 1999, respectively	3,582,600	3,389,775
Inventories	864,963	820,048
Other current assets	2,074,265	1,782,123
	$ 7,038,537	$ 6,119,964
Property, plant, and equipment:		
Land	2,383,800	2,043,222
Buildings	7,154,400	6,129,670
Pagers	19,207,010	17,000,432
Communications equipment	9,737,543	8,799,951
Office equipment	1,347,489	1,269,904
	$39,830,242	$35,243,179
Less accumulated depreciation	(19,645,924)	(16,138,402)
	$20,184,318	$19,104,777
Other assets, net of accumulated amortization of $1,935,600 and $1,427,800 as of December 31, 2000 and 1999, respectively	2,388,415	2,240,735
Total	$29,611,270	$27,465,476

Liabilities and Stockholders' Equity

	2000	1999
Current liabilities:		
Accounts payable	$ 621,390	$ 664,128
Other accrued expenses and liabilities	5,052,073	3,913,809
Current maturities of long-term obligations and capital lease obligations	424,061	398,864
	$ 6,097,524	$ 4,976,801
Long-term debt, less current maturities	3,466,346	3,139,673
Deferred tax liability	196,785	—
Commitments		
Stockholders' equity:		
Common stock, $0.01 par value, 10,000,000 authorized, 4,182,800 and 4,116,200 issued	41,828	41,162
Additional paid-in capital	19,903,523	19,769,264
Retained earnings (deficit)	1,090,185	(235,420)
Less treasury stock at cost	(1,184,921)	(226,004)
	$19,850,615	$19,349,002
Total	$29,611,270	$27,465,476

CALABRO PAGING SERVICES
Consolidated Statement of Operations

	Year Ended December 31,	
	2000	**1999**
Revenues:		
Pager lease and access fees	$18,753,376	$16,434,978
Pager and paging equipment sales	1,989,024	1,854,421
	$20,742,400	$18,289,399
Cost of sales and services:		
Pager lease and access fees	$ 4,974,121	$ 4,634,203
Pager and paging equipment sales	932,812	1,058,337
	$ 5,906,933	$ 5,692,540
Expenses:		
Sales and marketing	$ 4,245,273	$ 3,749,794
General and administrative	3,980,880	3,371,291
Depreciation and amortization	3,946,001	3,674,623
	$12,172,154	$10,795,708
Operating income	$ 2,663,313	$ 1,801,151
Other income (expense):		
Interest and other income	$ 42,585	$ 105,590
Gain on sale of assets	—	106,185
Interest expense	(284,623)	(302,455)
	$ (242,038)	$ (90,680)
Income before income taxes	$ 2,421,275	$ 1,710,471
Provision for income taxes	886,530	—
Net income	$1,534,745	$ 1,710,471
Net income per share	.38	.42

CALABRO PAGING SERVICES
Consolidated Statement of Retained Earnings

Balance at December 31, 1998	**$(1,945,891)**
Net income	1,710,471
Balance at December 31, 1999	**$ (235,429)**
Net income	1,535,745
Less dividends	209,140
Balance at December 31, 2000	**$ 1,090,185**

Required:

a. Determine the preliminary judgment about materiality for Calabro Paging Services using the worksheet included in Exhibit 3–1.

b. Allocate the preliminary judgment about materiality to the balance sheet accounts using the relative size of the accounts as the basis for allocation. Assume that Jones has decided that long-term debt, deferred income taxes, common stock and paid-in capital, and treasury stock will be audited 100 percent.

c. Reallocate the amounts allocated in part (b) based on the following information: (1) controls over both the revenue and purchasing cycles are strong; (2) inventory contains some pagers that may be outdated; and (3) there were approximately $1 million of additions to property, plant, and equipment during 2000.

INTERNET ASSIGNMENTS

[7,8]   3-42   EarthWear Clothiers operates in the retail mail order industry. Use the Internet to gather information to supplement the following assessments:

a. Assess EarthWear's client business risk.

b. Assess the risk of material misstatement due to error or fraud.

[7]   3-43   Calabro Paging Services is a publicly held business services company that uses wireless communications technology to develop solutions for businesses. The company owns and operates paging systems; manufactures, leases, and sells pagers; and provides commercial paging services in 12 major metropolitan areas. The company emphasizes its systems' reliability, solution-oriented marketing, and high level of customer service. The company provides high-quality, low-cost service to the marketplace. Calabro's annual growth rate has been greater than 20 percent over the last five years. Assume that you are the auditor for Calabro Paging Services.

a. Use the Internet to gather information on the paging industry, including information on the factors that are used in assessing client business risk. Note that many paging companies are owned by larger telecommunications companies that are better financed than Calabro Paging Services.

b. Draft a memo describing Calabro Paging Services' client business risk.

Chapter 4

Evidential Matter, Types of Evidence, and Working Paper Documentation

LEARNING OBJECTIVES

Upon completion of this chapter you will

[1] Understand the relationship between evidential matter and the auditor's report.

[2] Know management assertions about components in the financial statements.

[3] Know the audit objectives that relate to management assertions.

[4] Define audit procedures and understand their relationship to audit objectives.

[5] Learn the basic concepts of evidential matter.

[6] Identify and define the types of audit evidence.

[7] Understand the reliability of the types of evidence.

[8] Understand the relationship of types of evidence to audit objectives and audit activities.

[9] Develop an understanding of the contents, types, organization, and ownership of working papers.

RELEVANT ACCOUNTING AND AUDITING PRONOUNCEMENTS

FASB Statement of Financial Accounting Concepts No. 2, "Qualitative Characteristics of Accounting Information" (CON2)

SAS No. 22, "Planning and Supervision" (AU 311)

SAS No. 31, "Evidential Matter" (AU 326)

SAS No. 41, "Working Papers" (AU 339)

SAS No. 47, "Audit Risk and Materiality in Conducting an Audit" (AU 312)

SAS No. 55, "Consideration of Internal Control in a Financial Statement Audit" (AU 319)

SAS No. 56, "Analytical Procedures" (AU 329)

SAS No. 67, "The Confirmation Process" (AU 330)

SAS No. 80, "Amendment to Statement on Auditing Standards No. 31, Evidential Matter" (AU 326)

SAS No. 82, "Considerations of Fraud in a Financial Statement Audit" (AU 316)

This chapter covers the third important concept underlying the entire audit process: *evidential matter*. Evidential matter consists of accounting data and all corroborative information that support the amounts included in the financial statements. The third standard of field work states:

> Sufficient, competent evidential matter is to be obtained through inspection, observation, inquiries, and confirmations to afford a reasonable basis for an opinion regarding the financial statements under examination.

This standard indicates that on a typical financial statement audit most of the auditor's work involves obtaining and evaluating evidence using procedures such as inspection and confirmations to test the fair presentation of the financial statements. To perform this task effectively and efficiently, an auditor must thoroughly understand the important aspects of evidential matter. This includes understanding how audit evidence relates to financial statement assertions and the auditor's report, basic concepts of evidential matter, types of audit evidence, and the documentation of evidence in the working papers. Each of these topics is covered in this chapter.

The Relationship of Evidential Matter to the Audit Report

[LO 1] SAS No. 31, "Evidential Matter" (AU 326), provides the basic framework for the auditor's understanding of evidence and its use to support the auditor's opinion on the financial statements. In reaching an opinion on the financial statements, the auditor gathers evidence by conducting audit procedures to test audit objectives and their related management assertions. The evidence gathered from the audit procedures is used to determine the fairness of the financial statements and the type of audit report to be issued. Figure 4–1 presents an overview of the relationships among the financial statements, management assertions about components of the financial statements, audit objectives, audit procedures, and the audit report. More specifically, there is a top-down relationship from the financial statements to the audit procedures. The financial statements reflect management's assertions about the various financial statement components. The auditor develops audit objectives for each relevant management assertion and then conducts audit procedures to gather evidence to test whether the audit objectives are being met. The application of audit procedures provides the evidence that supports the auditor's report.

Auditors typically divide financial statements into components or segments in order to manage the audit. A component can be a financial statement account or a transaction cycle. A number of methods are used to develop components of the financial statements for testing purposes. Some CPA firms use a balance sheet approach and develop components by related

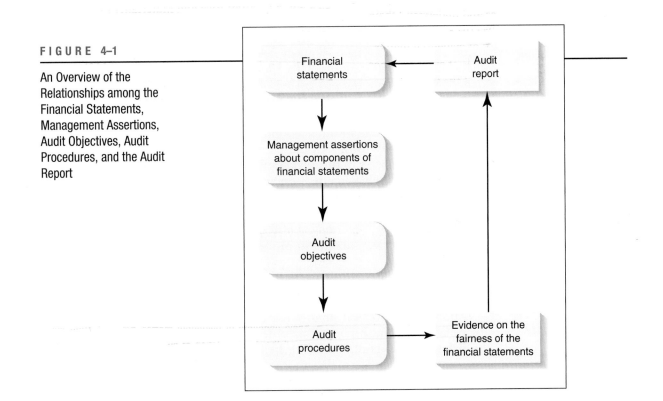

FIGURE 4–1

An Overview of the Relationships among the Financial Statements, Management Assertions, Audit Objectives, Audit Procedures, and the Audit Report

TABLE 4–1	Management Assertions, Audit Objectives, and Illustrative Audit Procedures	

Management Assertions about Components of Financial Statements	Audit Objectives	Sample Audit Procedures for Accounts Receivable
Existence or occurrence	Validity	Confirm accounts receivable.
Completeness	Completeness	Agree total of accounts receivable subsidiary ledger to accounts receivable control account.
	Cutoff	Examine large sales invoices for two days before and after year-end for recording of sales in proper period.
Rights and obligations	Ownership	Inquire of management whether receivables have been sold.
Valuation or allocation	Accuracy	Trace selected accounts from the aged trial balance to the subsidiary accounts receivable records for proper amount and aging.
	Valuation	Test the adequacy of the allowance for doubtful accounts.
Presentation and disclosure	Classification	Examine listing of accounts receivable for amounts due from affiliates, officers, directors, or other related parties.
	Disclosure	Evaluate receivables for footnote disclosure.

financial statement accounts. Other CPA firms use a cycle approach, which focuses on the flow of transactions by functional cycles and the accounts that are affected by those cycles. This text divides the components by transaction cycle, such as the revenue cycle or purchasing cycle, and their related financial statement accounts. This approach allows the auditor to gather evidence by examining the processing of related transactions through the accounting system from their origin to their ultimate disposition in the accounting journals and ledgers. In other words, the auditor can examine the "cradle-to-grave" cycle for an accounting transaction from the time it is initiated by the entity until its final recording in the financial statement accounts. Later chapters in this text cover each of the major transaction cycles that auditors typically encounter on an engagement.

Table 4–1 provides more information on the detailed relationships among management assertions, audit objectives, and audit procedures. The following three sections expand the discussion of management assertions, audit objectives, and audit procedures.

Management Assertions

[LO 2]

Assertions are expressed or implied representations by management that are reflected in the financial statement components. For example, when the balance sheet contains a line item for accounts receivable of $5 million, management asserts that those receivables exist and have a net realizable value of $5 million. Management also asserts that the accounts receiv-

TABLE 4–2	Summary of Management Assertions
• *Existence or occurrence*	The assets and liabilities *exist,* and the recorded transactions have *occurred.*
• *Completeness*	The accounts and transactions that should be included are included; thus, the financial statements are *complete.*
• *Rights and obligations*	The assets are *rights* of the entity, and the liabilities are its *obligations.*
• *Valuation or allocation*	Assets, liabilities, equity, revenues, and expenses are appropriately *valued* and are *allocated* to the proper accounting period.
• *Presentation and disclosure*	Amounts shown in the financial statements are properly *presented* and *disclosed.*

able balance arose from selling goods or services on credit in the normal course of business. In general, the assertions relate to the requirements of generally accepted accounting principles. Auditing standards (AU 326) classify management assertions into five categories:

- Existence or occurrence
- Completeness
- Rights and obligations
- Valuation or allocation
- Presentation and disclosure

Table 4–2 summarizes and explains management assertions.

Existence or Occurrence

Assertions about existence or occurrence address whether assets or liabilities of the entity actually exist at a given date and whether recorded transactions have occurred during a given period. For example, management asserts that inventory shown on the balance sheet physically exists and is available for sale. Similarly, management asserts that revenues reported in the income statement represent valid sales that occurred during the period.

Completeness

Assertions about completeness address whether all transactions and accounts that should be presented in the financial statements are included. For example, management asserts that inventory represents all items on hand at the balance sheet date. Management also implicitly asserts that the amount shown for accounts payable on the balance sheet includes all such liabilities as of the balance sheet date.

Rights and Obligations

Assertions about rights and obligations address whether assets are the rights of the entity and liabilities are the obligations of the entity at a given date. For example, management asserts that the entity has legal title or rights of ownership to the inventory shown on the balance sheet. Similarly, amounts capitalized for leases reflect assertions that the entity has rights to leased property and that the corresponding lease liability represents an obligation of the entity.

Valuation or Allocation

Assertions about valuation or allocation address whether asset, liability, equity, revenue, and expense components have been included in the financial statements at appropriate amounts. For example, management asserts that inventory is carried at the lower of cost or market value on the balance sheet. Similarly, management asserts that the cost of property, plant, and equipment is systematically allocated to appropriate accounting periods by recognizing depreciation expense.

Presentation and Disclosure

Assertions about presentation and disclosure address whether particular components of the financial statements are properly classified, described, and disclosed. For example, management asserts that the portion of long-term debt shown as a current liability will mature in the current year. Similarly, management asserts, through footnote disclosure, that all major restrictions on the entity resulting from debt covenants are disclosed.

Audit Objectives

[LO 3]   In obtaining evidence to support the assertions contained in the financial statements, the auditor develops specific audit objectives that relate to each management assertion. Table 4–1 shows the relationship between management assertions and their related audit objectives. Audit objectives test *components* (such as accounts or transaction cycles) of the financial statements. Table 4–3 lists the audit objectives that apply to the audit of an *account balance.* Once the auditor has sufficient evidence that the set of audit objectives is met, he or she has reasonable assurance that the financial statements are fairly presented.

The application of the audit risk model, as discussed in Chapter 3, should guide the auditor in determining which audit objectives apply to each relevant management assertion for the component (account) being tested. Depending on which account is being tested, some assertions and their related audit objectives may be more important than others. For example, gen-

TABLE 4–3	Audit Objectives for Testing an Account Balance
• *Validity*	Transactions in the accounts are valid.
• *Completeness*	All existing transactions are included in the accounts.
• *Cutoff*	Transactions in the account are recorded in the proper period.
• *Ownership*	Transactions in the account are owned.
• *Accuracy*	Transactions or amounts included in the account are properly accumulated from journals and ledgers.
• *Valuation*	Transactions in the account are properly valued.
• *Classification*	Transactions in the account or financial statements are properly classified.
• *Disclosure*	All proper disclosures are made in the financial statements or footnotes.

erally a test of an asset account will place heavy emphasis on validity, while a test of a liability account will place more emphasis on completeness.

The following sections discuss each audit objective in more detail.

Validity

The validity objective relates to the existence or occurrence assertion and is concerned with whether the transactions included in the accounts are valid or that they exist; that is, should they be included in the financial statements? The auditor's main concern is that the account balances are not overstated due to fictitious amounts. For example, to test the validity of accounts receivable the auditor might confirm the customers' balances. A customer's acknowledgment that the amount is owed provides evidence on the validity of the recorded accounts receivable. Another type of overstatement would be the inclusion of nonexistent inventory in the financial statements. The auditor can observe the client's physical inventory count to ensure that the inventory exists.

Completeness

The completeness objective relates to the management assertion of completeness and addresses whether all transactions are included in the accounts. For example, if the client fails to record sales or purchase transactions, the financial statements will be misstated. Note that the auditor's concern with completeness is opposite the concern for validity. Failure to meet the completeness objective results in an understatement in an account, while invalid recorded amounts result in an account being overstated. For example, to test the completeness objective for accounts receivable, the auditor compares the total of the accounts receivable subsidiary ledger to the accounts receivable control account in the general ledger. If the totals do not agree, some sales transactions, and the related accounts receivable, may not have been included in the client's accounting records.

Cutoff

The cutoff objective is also related to the completeness assertion and is concerned with whether the transactions included in the account are recorded in the proper period. The auditor's procedures must ensure that transactions occurring near year-end are recorded in the financial statements in the proper period. For example, the auditor may want to test proper cutoff of accounts receivable at December 31, 2000. The auditor can examine a sample of shipping documents and sales invoices for a few days before and after year-end to test whether the sales transactions are recorded in the proper period. The objective is to determine that all 2000 sales and no 2001 sales have been recorded in 2000. Thus, the auditor examines the shipping documents to ensure that no 2001 sales have been recorded in 2000 and that no 2000 sales are recorded in 2001. This example also demonstrates that some audit procedures provide evidence on more than one objective. In this example, the primary reason for examining selected sales transactions was to ensure that the sales were recorded in the proper period (cutoff). However, the presence of shipping documents and sales invoices for the sales recorded in 2000 also provides evidence on transaction validity.

Ownership

This objective addresses whether the assets and liabilities belong to the entity and relates directly to management's assertions about rights and obligations. If the entity does not have rights to an asset, or if a liability is not the entity's obligation, it should not be included in the financial statements. For example, the auditor may inquire of management whether any recorded accounts receivable have been sold and therefore no longer belong to the entity. Or a jewelry store may have expensive, precious gems appearing in inventory that are actually held on consignment.

Accuracy

The accuracy objective relates to the valuation or allocation assertion and addresses proper accumulation of transactions and amounts from journals and ledgers. For example, auditors frequently use an aged trial balance to document the detail in a client's accounts receivable subsidiary ledger. To test the aged trial balance's accuracy, the auditor foots the aged trial balance and traces selected customer accounts from the aged trial balance to the accounts receivable subsidiary ledger for proper amount and aging.

Valuation

The valuation objective relates to the valuation or allocation assertion and is concerned with ensuring that the accounts shown in the financial statements are recorded at the proper amount. Generally accepted accounting principles establish the valuation method for a particular transaction or account balance. For example, accounts receivable are accounted for at net realizable value; that is, the allowance for doubtful accounts is used to adjust gross accounts receivable to the amount expected to be collected. The auditor tests the adequacy of the allowance for uncollectible accounts by examining the entity's past bad debt experience relative to the current balance in the allowance account.

Classification

It is important that transactions be included in the correct account and that accounts be properly presented in the financial statements. For example, in auditing accounts receivable, the auditor examines the listing of accounts receivable to ensure that receivables from affiliates, officers, directors, or other related parties are classified separately from trade receivables. The classification objective relates to the presentation and disclosure assertion.

Disclosure

This audit objective relates directly to the presentation and disclosure assertion and is concerned with ensuring that all required financial statement and footnote disclosures are made. For example, if accounts receivable are pledged as security for debt, such information should be disclosed in the financial statements. Similarly, if a long-term debt agreement contains major covenants (such as limits on payment of dividends or issuance of additional debt), that information should be disclosed in the footnotes.

Audit Procedures

[LO 4]   Audit procedures are specific acts performed by the auditor to gather evidence to determine if specific audit objectives are being met. A set of audit procedures prepared to test audit objectives for a component of the financial statements is usually referred to as an *audit program*. Table 4–1 illustrates an audit procedure for each audit objective related to the audit of accounts receivable. The reader should note that there is *not* a one-to-one relationship between audit objectives and audit procedures. In some instances more than one audit procedure is required to meet an audit objective. Conversely, in some cases an audit procedure provides evidence for more than one audit objective. Examples of audit procedures used to test various account balances will be presented in later chapters.

Basic Concepts of Evidential Matter

[LO 5]   From an audit perspective, evidential matter consists of the underlying accounting data and all corroborating information available to the auditor. In presenting evidential matter, auditing standards (AU 326) discuss the following concepts:

- The nature of evidential matter.
- The competence of evidential matter.
- The sufficiency of evidential matter.
- The evaluation of evidential matter.

The Nature of Evidential Matter

Accounting data that can be used as evidence to test audit objectives include the books of original entry (such as general and subsidiary ledgers), related accounting manuals, and records such as worksheets and spreadsheets that support amounts in the financial statements. Many times these data are in electronic form. Corroborating evidential matter includes both written and electronic information such as checks, records of electronic transfers, invoices, contracts, minutes, confirmations, and written representations. Corroborating evidence also includes information obtained by the auditor through inquiry, observation, inspection, and physical examination.

For some entities, accounting data and corroborating evidential matter may be available only in electronic form.[1] Thus, source documents such as purchase orders, bills of lading, invoices, and checks are replaced with electronic messages or electronic images. Two common examples are Electronic Data Interchange (EDI)[2] and image processing systems.[3] A client that uses EDI may process sales or purchase transactions electronically. For example, the client's EDI system can contact a vendor electronically when supplies of a part run low. The vendor will then ship the goods to the client and send an invoice electronically. The client can authorize its bank to make an electronic

---

[1]The AICPA's Audit Practice Release, *The Information Technology Age: Evidential Matter in the Electronic Environment* (AICPA 1997), provides nonauthoritative implementation guidance about electronic evidence and its impact on the audit. See also A. L. Williamson, "The Implications of Electronic Evidence," *Journal of Accountancy* (February 1997), pp. 69-71.

[2]See Chapter 7 for a discussion of EDI.

[3]The AICPA's Audit Practice Release, *Audit Implications of Electronic Document Management* (AICPA 1997), discusses the issues faced by auditors when a client uses electronic document management that includes image processing systems. Discussion of such issues is beyond the scope of this text.

payment directly to the vendor's bank account. In an image processing system, documents are scanned and converted to electronic images to facilitate storage and reference, and the source documents may not be retained after conversion. In such systems, electronic evidence may exist at only a certain point in time and may not be retrievable later. This may require the auditor to select sample items several times during the year rather than at year-end.

The Competence of Evidential Matter

Evidence, regardless of its form, is considered competent when it provides information that is both *relevant* and *reliable*.

Relevance   The competence of evidence depends on its relevance to the audit objective being tested. If the auditor relies on evidence that is unrelated to the audit objective, he or she may reach an incorrect conclusion about a management assertion. For example, suppose the auditor wants to check the completeness objective for recording sales transactions; that is, are all goods shipped to customers recorded in the sales journal? A normal audit procedure for testing this objective is to trace a sample of shipping documents (such as bills of lading) to the related sales invoices and entries in the sales journal. If the auditor samples the population of sales invoices issued during the period, the evidence would not relate to the completeness objective (that is, the auditor would not detect shipments made that are not billed or recorded). The auditor should check the log of prenumbered bills of lading, after ascertaining that such documents were issued for all customer shipments. Any conclusion based on the population of sales invoices would not be based on evidence relevant to testing the completeness objective.

Reliability   *Reliability* refers to whether a particular type of evidence can be relied upon to signal the true state of an assertion or audit objective. Because of varied circumstances on audit engagements, it is difficult to generalize about the reliability of various types of evidence. However, the auditor should consider the following general factors when assessing the reliability or validity of evidence.

- *Independence of the source of the evidence.* Evidence obtained directly by the auditor from an independent source outside the entity is usually viewed as more reliable than evidence obtained solely from within the entity. Thus, a confirmation of the client's bank balance received directly by the auditor would be viewed as more reliable than examination of the cash receipts journal and cash balance as recorded in the general ledger. Additionally, evidence that is obtained from the client, but that has been subjected to verification by an independent source, is viewed as more reliable than evidence obtained solely from within the entity. For example, a canceled check held by the client would be more reliable than a duplicate copy of the check because the canceled check would be endorsed by the payee and cleared through the bank—that is, verified by an independent source.
- *Effectiveness of internal control.* A major objective of a client's internal control is to generate reliable information to assist management decision making. As part of the audit, the effectiveness of

the client's internal control is assessed. When the auditor assesses the client's internal control as effective (that is, low control risk), evidence generated by that accounting system is viewed as reliable. Conversely, if internal control is assessed as ineffective (that is, high control risk), the evidence from the accounting system would not be considered reliable. Thus, the more effective the client's internal control, the more assurance it provides about the reliability of audit evidence.

- *Auditor's direct personal knowledge.* Evidence obtained directly by the auditor is generally considered to be more reliable than evidence obtained indirectly by other means. For example, an auditor's physical examination of a client's inventory is considered to be relatively reliable because the auditor has direct personal knowledge regarding the inventory. There are, of course, exceptions to this general rule. For example, an auditor may competently examine an inventory composed of pagers; however, if the inventory is composed of diamonds or specialty computer chips, the auditor may lack the competence to assess the validity and valuation of such inventory items. In such cases, the auditor may need the skill and knowledge of a specialist to assist with the inventory audit.

The Sufficiency of Evidential Matter

In most instances, the auditor relies on evidence that is *persuasive* rather than *convincing* in forming an opinion on a set of financial statements. This occurs for two reasons. First, because an audit must be completed in a reasonable amount of time and at a reasonable cost, the auditor examines only a sample of the transactions that compose the account balance or class of transactions. Thus, the auditor reaches a conclusion about the account or class based on a subset of the available evidence.

Second, due to the nature of evidence, auditors must often rely on evidence that is not perfectly reliable. As discussed in the next section, the types of audit evidence have different degrees of reliability, and even highly reliable evidence has weaknesses. For example, an auditor can physically examine inventory, but such evidence will not ensure that obsolescence is not a problem. Therefore, the nature of the evidence obtained by the auditor seldom provides absolute assurance about an audit objective.

The *amount* and *type* of evidential matter are determined by the auditor's professional judgment. In judging the sufficiency of evidence, the auditor relies on the materiality and audit risk for the account balance or class of transactions to determine the scope of the audit. For example, when the tolerable misstatement allocated to an account balance is small, the auditor has to collect more evidence than if the amount of tolerable misstatement is large. Determining the sufficiency of evidence is one of the more critical decisions the auditor faces on an engagement.

The Evaluation of Evidential Matter

The ability to evaluate evidence appropriately is another important skill an auditor must develop. Proper evaluation of evidence requires that the auditor understand the types of evidence that are available and their relative reliability or diagnosticity. The auditor must be capable of assessing when a sufficient amount of competent evidence has been obtained in order to determine whether specific audit objectives have been achieved.

In evaluating evidence, an auditor should be *thorough* in searching for evidence and *unbiased* in its evaluation. For example, suppose an auditor decides to mail accounts receivable confirmations to 50 customers. Suppose further that the client has a total of 500 customer accounts receivable. In auditing the 50 customers, the auditor must gather sufficient evidence on *each* of the 50 accounts. In evaluating evidence, the auditor must remain objective and must not allow the evaluation of the evidence to be biased by other considerations. For example, in evaluating a client's response to an audit inquiry, the auditor must not allow any personal factors to influence the evaluation of the client's response.

Types of Audit Evidence

[LO 6]   In conducting audit procedures, the auditor examines various types of audit evidence. For discussion purposes, evidence is categorized into the following types:

- Physical examination.
- Reperformance.
- Documentation.
- Confirmation.
- Analytical procedures.
- Inquiries of client personnel or management.
- Observation.

Physical Examination

Physical examination is a relatively reliable type of evidence that involves the auditor inspecting or counting a *tangible asset*. An audit engagement includes many situations in which the auditor physically examines an entity's assets. Some examples might be counting cash on hand, examining inventory or marketable securities, and examining tangible fixed assets. This type of evidence primarily provides assurance that the asset exists. In some instances, such as examining inventory, physical examination may provide evidence on valuation by identifying obsolete or slow-moving items. However, physical examination provides little or no assurance on the ownership objective.

Reperformance

In reperformance the auditor recalculates information and tests the transfer of information in the accounting system. Examples of this type of evidence include recalculation of depreciation expense on fixed assets and recalculation of accrued interest. Reperformance also includes footing, crossfooting, reconciling subsidiary ledgers to account balances, and testing postings from journals to ledgers. Because the auditor creates this type of evidence, it is normally viewed as highly reliable.

Documentation

Documentary evidence relates to the auditor's examination of the client's accounting data (such as ledgers and journals) and corroborating evidential matter (checks, invoices, and so on). On most audit engagements, documentation makes up the bulk of the evidence gathered by the auditor. Two issues are important in discussion of documentation as a type of evidence: the reliability of documentary evidence and its relationship to specific audit objectives.

Reliability of Documentary Evidence

Reliability of Documentary Evidence   A previous section noted the independence of the source of evidence as a factor that affected the reliability of evidential matter. In particular, evidence obtained from a source outside the entity was generally considered more reliable than evidence obtained solely from within the entity. Typically a distinction is made between internal and external documents. *Internal documents* are generated and maintained within the entity; that is, these documents have not been seen by any party outside the client's organization. Examples include duplicate copies of sales invoices and shipping documents, materials requisition forms, and worksheets for overhead cost allocation. *External documents* are of two forms: documents originating within the entity but circulated to independent sources outside the entity and documents generated outside the entity but included in the client's accounting records. Examples of the first include remittance advices returned with cash receipts from customers and payroll checks, while examples of the second include bank statements and vendors' invoices.

In general, external documentary evidence is viewed as more reliable than internal evidence because a third party either initiated or reviewed it. This difference in reliability between internal and external documents is, however, relative. Internal documents generated by good internal controls are likely to be highly reliable. Conversely, external documents may be manipulated or withheld by client personnel. If this is likely on an engagement, the auditor would discount the reliability of the external documents in the client's possession. In such a situation, the auditor would also discount the reliability of the internal documents. In summary, determining the reliability of documentary evidence involves a good deal of auditor judgment.

Documentary Evidence Related to Audit Objectives

Documentary Evidence Related to Audit Objectives   The second issue concerning documentation relates directly to the validity and completeness objectives and to the *direction of testing* taken when documentary evidence is examined. Figure 4–2 presents an overview of this relationship.

The direction of testing between the accounting records and source documents (such as sales invoices or shipping documents) is important when testing the validity and completeness objectives. *Vouching* refers to first selecting an item for testing from the accounting journals or ledgers and then examining the underlying source document. Thus, the direction of testing is

FIGURE 4–2

Direction of Testing for
Validity and Completeness

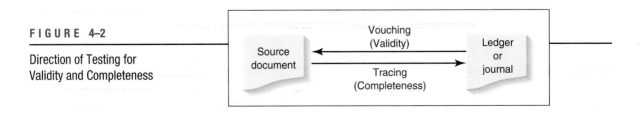

from the ledgers or journals back to the source documents. This approach provides evidence that items included in the accounting records are *valid*. For example, an auditor may want to examine a sample of sales transactions from the sales journal to ensure that sales are not fictitious. If adequate source documents exist for each sales transaction selected from the sales journal, the auditor can conclude that each sale was valid. *Tracing* refers to first selecting an accounting transaction (a source document) and then following it into the journal or ledger. The direction of testing in this case is from the source documents to the ledgers or journals. Testing in this direction ensures that transactions that occurred are recorded (*completeness*) in the accounting records. For example, if the auditor selects a sample of shipping documents and traces them to the related sales invoices and then to the sales journal, he or she would have evidence on the completeness of sales.

Confirmation

SAS No. 67, "The Confirmation Process" (AU 330), defines *confirmation* as the process of obtaining and evaluating a direct communication from a third party in response to a request for information about a particular item affecting financial statement assertions. The requests for such communications are usually written by the client on the auditor's behalf. The reliability of evidence obtained through confirmations is directly affected by factors such as

- The form of the confirmation.
- Prior experience with the entity.
- The nature of the information being confirmed.
- The intended respondent.

Confirmations are used extensively on audits; they generally provide reliable evidence for the validity objective and, in testing certain financial statement components (such as accounts payable), can provide evidence about the completeness objective. Evidence about valuation, cutoff, and ownership can also be obtained through the use of confirmations. For example, an auditor can send a confirmation to a consignee to verify that a client's inventory has been consigned. The returned confirmation provides evidence that the client owns the inventory. Table 4–4 lists selected amounts and information confirmed by auditors. Accounts receivable, accounts payable, and bank confirmations are discussed in more detail in later chapters.

Analytical Procedures

Analytical procedures are an important type of evidence on an audit. They consist of evaluations of financial information made by a study of plausible relationships among both financial and nonfinancial data (AU 329). For example, the current-year accounts receivable balance can be compared to the prior-year balance after adjusting for any increase or decrease in sales and other economic factors. Similarly, the auditor might compare the current-year gross margin percentage to the gross margin percentage for the previous five years. The auditor makes such comparisons either to identify accounts that may contain material misstatements and require more investigation or as a reasonableness test of the account balance. Analytical procedures are an effective and efficient form of evidence.

TABLE 4–4	Amounts and Information Frequently Confirmed by Auditors

Amounts or Information Confirmed	Source of Confirmation
Cash balance	Bank
Accounts receivable	Individual customers
Inventory on consignment	Consignee
Accounts payable	Individual vendors
Bonds payable	Bondholders/trustee
Common stock outstanding	Registrar/transfer agent
Insurance coverage	Insurance company
Collateral for loan	Creditor

The reliability of analytical procedures is a function of (1) the availability and reliability of the data used in the calculations and (2) the plausibility and predictability of the relationship being tested. Because of the growing importance of this type of evidence in auditing, analytical procedures are covered in greater detail in Chapter 5.

Inquiries of Client Personnel or Management

Responses (oral or written) obtained from client personnel or management to questions raised by the auditor are an important source of evidence. In understanding the client's business or internal controls, the auditor makes numerous inquiries of client personnel. For example, the auditor may ask the storeroom manager what control procedures prevent theft of raw materials. The auditor will also require representations by management concerning information such as related-party transactions and contingent liabilities. In assessing the responses to such inquiries, the auditor should use his or her business and client experience to ascertain the reasonableness and reliability of the response. Because this evidence is not from independent sources and is therefore not considered highly reliable, auditors normally gather additional *corroborative* evidence to support the client's responses. In the case of the internal controls over the storeroom, the auditor might follow up the client's responses by testing the control procedures to verify their existence and effectiveness.

Observation

This type of evidence involves the auditor observing the performance of some activity. The actions being observed typically do not leave an audit trail that can be tested by documentation. For example, the auditor can observe the segregation of duties between the person receiving payments from customers and the person recording those payments in the accounts receivable subsidiary ledger. Note that observation provides evidence only on what is currently happening. Client personnel may act differently when the auditor is not observing them. Similar to inquiries made of client personnel, this type of evidence generally requires additional corroboration by the auditor because it is not considered highly reliable.

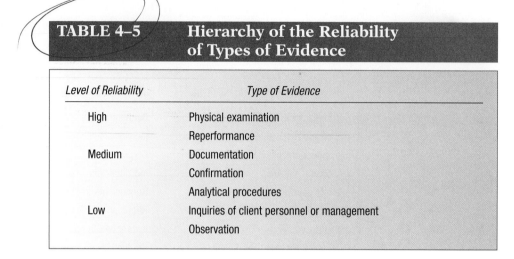

TABLE 4–5	Hierarchy of the Reliability of Types of Evidence	
Level of Reliability	**Type of Evidence**	
High	Physical examination	
	Reperformance	
Medium	Documentation	
	Confirmation	
	Analytical procedures	
Low	Inquiries of client personnel or management	
	Observation	

Reliability of the Types of Evidence

[LO 7]   Table 4–5 presents a hierarchy of the reliability of the types of evidence. Physical examination and reperformance are generally considered of high reliability because the auditor has direct knowledge about them. Documentation, confirmation, and analytical procedures are generally considered to be of medium reliability. The reliability of documentation depends primarily on whether a document is internal or external, and the reliability of confirmation is affected by the four factors listed previously. The reliability of analytical procedures may be affected by the availability and reliability of the data. Finally, inquiries of client personnel or management and observation are generally low-reliability types of evidence because both require further corroboration by the auditor.

The reader should understand, however, that the levels of reliability shown in Table 4–5 are general guidelines. The reliability of the types of evidence may vary considerably across entities, and it may be subject to a number of exceptions. For example, in some circumstances, confirmations may be viewed as a highly reliable source of evidence. This may be true when a confirmation is sent to an independent third party who is highly qualified to respond to the auditor's request for information. Inquiries of client personnel or management provide another example. Audit research has shown that, in certain situations, inquiries of client personnel or management are relatively effective in detecting material misstatement.[4]

Relationship of Evidence to Audit Objectives and Audit Activities

[LO 8]   Each of the seven types of evidence discussed in the previous section is used for different audit objectives. Table 4–6 presents the relationships among the types of audit evidence and the audit objectives. For example,

---

[4]See, for example, A. Wright and R. H. Ashton, "Identifying Audit Adjustments with Attention-Directing Procedures," *The Accounting Review* (October 1989), pp. 710–28.

TABLE 4–6	Relationship of the Types of Evidence to Audit Objectives

Type of Evidence	Audit Objectives							
	Validity	Completeness	Cutoff	Ownership	Accuracy	Valuation	Classification	Disclosure
Physical examination	X	X	X			X		
Reperformance		X			X	X	X	
Documentation	X	X	X	X		X	X	X
Confirmation	X	X	X	X		X		X
Analytical procedures	X	X	X		X	X	X	X
Inquiries of client personnel or management	X	X	X	X		X	X	X
Observation						X		

FIGURE 4–3

Summary of Audit Team, Evidence, and Activities

Audit Team Members	Audit Report	Audit Activities		
		Planning	Execution	Review
Partner				
Manager	Amount of audit evidence examined			
Senior				
Staff				

while physical examination is generally used to provide evidence on validity and completeness, it can also provide evidence on the cutoff and valuation objectives. Similarly, analytical procedures can provide evidence on all audit objectives except ownership. Auditors must understand which audit objectives are tested by the various types of evidence in order to properly plan and evaluate audit tests.

Figure 4–3 presents a summary of the audit team and its evidence-related audit activities. In general, most audit evidence is developed by the audit staff and audit senior, while a smaller amount is created by the manager and partner. Three activities—*planning, execution,* and *reviewing*—encompass the main activities related to audit evidence. Planning for the audit starts at the partner level and proceeds downward through the other team members. All members of the team execute the audit. Finally, the review of working papers that contain the audit evidence proceeds upward through the audit team.

Working Papers

The Nature of Working Papers

[LO 9]

Working papers are the auditor's record of the work performed and the conclusions reached on the audit. The quantity, type, and content of the working papers are a function of the circumstances of the specific engagement. SAS No. 41, "Working Papers" (AU 339), stipulates that working papers have two functions: (1) to aid in the conduct and supervision of the audit and (2) to provide support for the auditor's report.

While working papers are still prepared in hard-copy format, microcomputers and audit software are increasingly being used to prepare them.

Conduct and Supervision of the Audit   The working papers contain the audit evidence that documents the auditor's compliance with GAAS. In particular, working papers document the auditor's compliance with the standards of field work. Figure 4–3 shows the relationships among audit evidence and the audit activities of planning, execution, and review. The planning of the engagement, along with the execution of the plan, is contained in the working papers. The working papers are also the focal point for reviewing the work of subordinates.

Support for the Audit Report   When the engagement is complete, the auditor must decide on the appropriate type of report to issue. The basis for this decision rests in the audit evidence gathered and the conclusions reached and documented in the working papers. The working papers also document that the scope of the audit was adequate for the report issued. Information on the correspondence of the financial statements with GAAP is also included in the working papers.

Contents of Working Papers

Most CPA firms maintain working papers in two types of files: permanent and current. *Permanent files* contain historical data about the client that are of continuing relevance to the audit. *Current files,* on the other hand, include information and data related specifically to the current year's engagement. Table 4–7 contains examples of the types of information included in each type of file.

Types of Working Papers

The auditor's working papers come in a variety of types. The more common of these working papers include the audit plan and programs, working trial balance, account analysis and listings, audit memoranda, and adjusting and reclassification entries.

Audit Plan and Programs   The audit plan contains the strategy to be followed by the auditor in conducting the audit. This document outlines the auditor's understanding of the client and the potential audit risks. It contains the basic framework for how the audit resources (budgeted audit hours) are to be allocated to various parts of the engagement. The audit

TABLE 4–7	Examples of Information Included in Permanent and Current Files

Permanent File:
- Copies of, or excerpts from, the corporate charter.
- Chart of accounts.
- Organizational chart.
- Accounting manual.
- Copies of important contracts (pension contracts, union contracts, leases, etc.).
- Documentation of internal control (e.g., flowcharts).
- Terms of stock and bond issues.
- Prior years' analytical procedure results.

Current File:
- Copy of financial statements and auditor's report.
- Audit plan and audit programs.
- Copies of, or excerpts from, minutes of important committee meetings.
- Working trial balance.
- Adjusting and reclassification journal entries.
- Working papers supporting financial statement accounts.

programs contain the audit procedures that will be conducted by the auditor. Generally, each transaction cycle and account balance has a separate audit program.

Working Trial Balance   The working trial balance links the amounts in the financial statements to the audit working papers. Exhibit 4–1 illustrates a partial working trial balance for EarthWear Clothiers. In addition to a column for account name, the trial balance contains columns for working paper references, the prior year's balances, the unadjusted current-year balances, and columns for adjusting and reclassification entries. The last column would agree to the amounts contained in the financial statements after combining common account balances. A lead schedule is then used to show the detailed general ledger accounts that make up a financial statement category (cash, accounts receivable, and so on). For example, the trial balance would contain only one line for "cash and cash equivalents" and the "C lead" schedule would list all general ledger cash accounts. This approach is described in more detail later in the chapter.

Account Analysis and Listings   Account analysis working papers generally include the *activity* in a particular account for the period. For example, Exhibit 4–2 shows the analysis of legal and audit expense for

EXHIBIT 4-1

An Example of a Partial Working Trial Balance

EARTHWEAR CLOTHIERS
Partial Working Trial Balance
December 31, 2000

Account Description	W/P Ref.	Balance 12/31/99	Balance 12/31/00	Adjustments DR	CR	Adjusted T/B	Reclassification DR	CR	Financial Statements
Cash and cash equivalents	C lead	$ 7,729,150	$ 41,772,345						
Receivables	E lead	3,628,958	3,932,845						
Inventory	F lead	74,167,392	64,100,475						
Prepaid advertising	G lead	7,121,190	4,980,478						
. . . .									

EXHIBIT 4–2

Example of an Account Analysis Working Paper

T20
SAA
2/4/01

EARTHWEAR CLOTHIERS
Analysis of Legal and Audit Expense
12/31/00

Date	Payee	Amount	Explanation
Feb. 1	Katz & Fritz	$ 28,400.00**V**	For services related to a patent infringement suit by Gough Mfg. Co. Lawsuit was dismissed.
April 10	Willis & Adams	516,500.00**V**	Annual audit fee.
Oct. 20	Smoothe, Sylk, Fiels, Goode & Associates	2,100.00**V**	Legal services for a purchase contract with McDonald Merchandise, Inc.
		$547,000.00	

F   T/B

Tick Mark Legend

V = Examined payees' bills for amount and description.
F = Footed.
T/B = Agreed to trial balance.

Conclusion: Based on the audit work performed, EarthWear's legal and audit expense account is not materially misstated.

EarthWear Clothiers for the year ended December 31, 2000. Listings represent a schedule of items remaining in the ending balance of an account and are often called *trial balances.* For example, the auditor may obtain a listing of all amounts owed to vendors that make up the accounts payable balance as of the end of the year. This listing would represent a trial balance of unpaid vendors' invoices.

Audit Memoranda   Much of the auditor's work is documented in written memoranda. These include discussions of items such as internal controls, inventory observation, errors identified, and problems encountered during the audit.

Adjusting and Reclassification Entries   The working papers also include documentation for the adjusting and reclassification entries identified by the auditor or client. Adjusting entries are made to correct errors in the client's records. For example, if the auditor discovered that certain inventory items were improperly valued, an adjusting entry would be proposed to correct the dollar error. Adjusting entries are posted in both the client's records and the working trial balance.

Reclassification entries are made to properly present information on the financial statements. A reclassification entry affects income statement accounts or balance sheet accounts, but not both. For example, a reclassification entry might be necessary to present as a current liability the current portion of long-term debt. Reclassification entries are not posted to the client's records.

Format of Working Papers

Audit working papers should clearly and concisely communicate the auditor's work. While the formatting of working papers may differ from firm to firm, three general characteristics should be recognized.

Heading   All working papers should have a proper heading. The heading should include the name of the client, the title of the working paper, and the client's year-end date. Exhibit 4–2 shows a working paper with a proper heading.

Indexing and Cross-Referencing   Working papers must be organized so that members of the audit team or firm can find relevant audit evidence. Some firms use a lettering system; other firms use some type of numbering system. For example, the general working papers may be labeled "A," internal control systems working papers "B," cash working papers "C," and so on. When the auditor performs audit work on one working paper and supporting information is obtained from another working paper, the auditor cross-references the information on each working paper. This process of indexing and cross-referencing provides a trail from the financial statements to the individual working papers that a reviewer can easily follow. Indexing and cross-referencing are discussed further in the next section.

Tick Marks   Auditors use tick marks to document work performed. Tick marks are simply notations that are made by the auditor near, or next to, an item or amount on a working paper. The tick mark symbol is typically explained or defined at the bottom of the working paper, although many firms use a standard set of tick marks. Exhibit 4–2 shows some examples of tick marks. On this working paper, the tick mark "V" indicates that the auditor examined the bills sent to the client by the payee for proper amount and description.

Many CPA firms document their conclusions about an individual account or component of the financial statements in the working papers. Exhibit 4–2 shows an example of how an auditor might document a conclusion about an individual account.

Organization of Working Papers

The auditor's working papers need to be organized so that any member of the audit team (and others) can find the audit evidence that supports each financial statement account. While no specific guidelines dictate how this should be accomplished, the following discussion presents a general approach that should assist in understanding working paper organization.

The financial statements contain the accounts and amounts covered by the auditor's report. These accounts come from the working trial balance, which summarizes the general ledger accounts contained on each lead schedule. Each lead schedule includes the general ledger accounts that make up the financial statement account. Different types of audit working papers (account analysis, listings, confirmations, and so on) are then used to support each of the general ledger accounts. Each of these working papers is indexed, and all important amounts are cross-referenced between working papers.

Figure 4–4 presents an example of how working papers could be organized to support the cash account. Note that the $15,000 shown on the balance sheet agrees to the working trial balance. The "A lead" schedule in turn contains the three general ledger accounts that are included in the $15,000 balance. Audit working papers then support each of the general ledger accounts. For example, the working papers indexed "A2" provide the audit evidence supporting the general cash balance of $12,000. Also note that each important amount is cross-referenced. For example, the balance per bank of $14,000 on "A2" is referenced to "A2.1" and the cash balance on "A2.1" is referenced back to "A2."

Ownership of Working Papers

The working papers are the property of the auditor. This includes not only working papers prepared by the auditor but also working papers prepared by the client at the request of the auditor. The auditor should retain working papers for a reasonable period of time in order to meet the needs of his or her practice and legal record retention requirements. Some firms microfiche working papers, while other firms destroy them after a predetermined period.

Although the auditor owns the working papers, they cannot be shown, except under certain circumstances, to anyone without the client's consent. Chapter 19 discusses the auditor's ethical considerations concerning the confidentiality of working papers.

FIGURE 4–4

An Example of Working
Paper Organization

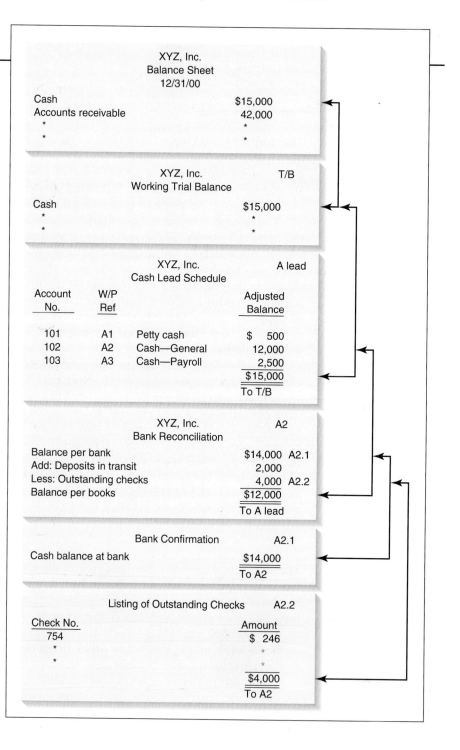

REVIEW QUESTIONS

[handwritten notes in left margin:]
more manageable –
follow through beg to end
evidence used to test the
audit objective – source doc
relevent = relates to audit prob)
reliable = true state
indep. of source, effectiveness
of I/C auditor's direct personal
knowledge
sampling; not perfectly reliable
gather more evidence or issue
qualified opinion because of a scope lim

[LO 1]   4-1 Explain why the auditor divides the financial statements into components or segments in order to test management's assertions.

4-2 Define evidential matter. Give three examples of corroborating evidential matter.

.4-3 Evidence is considered competent when it is both reliable and relevant. What is meant by the terms *relevant* and *reliable*?

4-4 List and discuss the three general factors that the auditor should ✱ consider when assessing the reliability of audit evidence.

[5]   4-5 Explain why in most instances audit evidence is persuasive rather than convincing.

4-6 What actions should the auditor take when doubt exists about major assertions?

[1,5]   4-7 List and define the five categories of management assertions. ✱

[1,3,8]   4-8 How do management assertions relate to the financial statements and audit objectives?

[3]   4-9 List and define the eight audit objectives for testing an account ✱ balance.

[6]   4-10 List and define the seven types of audit evidence. ✱

[6]   4-11 Distinguish between internal and external forms of documentary evidence. Discuss the relative reliability of each.

[6]   4-12 When using documentation as a type of evidence, distinguish between vouching and tracing in terms of the direction of testing and the audit objectives being tested.

[6,7]   4-13 Why is it necessary to obtain corroborating evidence for inquiries of client personnel and management and for observation?

not independent

[7]   4-14 Discuss the relative reliability of the different types of evidence. ✱

[9]   4-15 Define the two major types of working paper files. Give two examples of information contained in each type of file.

[9]   4-16 Why are indexing and cross-referencing important to the documentation of audit working papers?

[9]   4-17 Who owns the audit working papers?
auditor

MULTIPLE-CHOICE QUESTIONS FROM CPA EXAMINATIONS

existence = validity

[2,4]   4-18 Which of the following procedures would an auditor most likely rely on to verify management's assertion of <u>completeness</u>?

everything there that should be

a. Reviewing standard bank confirmations for indications of kiting. *existence*

(b.) Comparing a sample of shipping documents to related sales invoices.

c. Observing the client's distribution of payroll checks. *existence - fraud*

d. Confirming a sample of recorded receivables by direct communication with the debtors. *existence*

[6,7]   4-19 Which of the following procedures would provide <u>the most reliable</u> audit evidence?

a. Inquiries of the client's internal audit staff held in private.

    b. Inspection of prenumbered client purchase orders filed in the vouchers payable department. *internal doc.*

    c. Analytical procedures performed by the auditor on the entity's trial balance.

    d. Inspection of bank statements obtained directly from the client's financial institution. *independent source*

[5,6]   4-20   Which of the following statements concerning audit evidence is correct?

    a. To be competent, audit evidence should be either persuasive or relevant but need *not* be both. ✗

    b. The measure of the validity of audit evidence lies in the auditor's judgment.

    c. The difficulty and expense of obtaining audit evidence concerning an account balance is a valid basis for omitting the test. ✗

    d. A client's accounting data may be sufficient audit evidence to support the financial statements. *not completely*

[5]   4-21   Which of the following statements is generally correct about the competence of evidential matter?

    a. The auditor's direct personal knowledge, obtained through observation and inspection, is more persuasive than information obtained indirectly from independent outside sources. *could be manipulated*

    b. To be competent, evidential matter must be either valid or relevant but need *not* be both. ✗

    c. Accounting data alone may be considered sufficient competent evidential matter to issue an unqualified opinion on financial statements. ✗

    d. Competence of evidential matter refers to the amount of corroborative evidence to be obtained. *relevance & reliability*

[7]   4-22   An auditor would be *least* likely to use confirmations in connection with the examination of

    a. Inventory.

    b. Refundable income taxes. *usually do this*

    c. Long-term debt.

    d. Stockholders' equity.

[6,7]   4-23   Which of the following types of audit evidence is the *least* persuasive?

    a. Prenumbered purchase order forms. *internal*

    b. Bank statements obtained from the client. *outside*

    c. Test counts of inventory performed by the auditor. *direct*

    d. Correspondence from the client's attorney about litigation. *outside*

[6,7]   4-24   Audit evidence can come in different forms with different degrees of persuasiveness. Which of the following is the *most* persuasive type of evidence?

    a. Bank statements obtained from the client. *external*

    b. Computations made by the auditor. *direct*

    c. Prenumbered client sales invoices. *internal*

    d. Vendors' invoices. *external*

[2,6,7]   4-25   In testing the existence assertion for an asset, an auditor ordinarily works from the

    a. Financial statements to the potentially unrecorded items. ✗

    b. Potentially unrecorded items to the financial statements. ✗

what is is   validity
there is   vouching

c. Accounting records to the supporting evidence.

d. Supporting evidence to the accounting records.

[9] 4-26 An auditor's working papers should

a. Not be permitted to serve as a reference source for the client. *ok*

b. Not contain critical comments concerning management. *ok*

c. Show that the accounting records agree or reconcile with the financial statements.

d. Be considered the primary support for the financial statements being audited. *—clients have support*

[9] 4-27 Which of the following statements concerning working papers is incorrect?

a. An auditor may support an opinion by other means in addition to working papers. ✓

b. The form of working papers should be designed to meet the circumstances of a particular engagement. ✓

c. An auditor's working papers may *not* serve as a reference source for the client.

d. Working papers should show that the internal controls have been studied and evaluated to the degree necessary. ✓

[9] 4-28 The current file of the auditor's working papers should generally include

a. A flowchart of the accounting system. *P*

b. Organization charts. *P*

c. A copy of the financial statements.

d. Copies of bond and note indentures. *P*

[9] 4-29 The permanent file section of the working papers that is kept for each audit client most likely contains

a. Review notes pertaining to questions and comments regarding the audit work performed. *C*

b. A schedule of time spent on the engagement by each individual auditor. *C*

c. Correspondence with the client's legal counsel concerning pending litigation. *C*

d. Narrative descriptions of the client's accounting system and control procedures.

[5,9] 4-30 Which of the following factors will most likely affect an auditor's judgment about the quantity, type, and content of working papers?

a. The degree of reliance on internal control.

b. The content of the client's representation letter. *X*

c. The timing of substantive tests completed prior to the balance sheet date. *X*

d. The usefulness of the working papers as a reference source for the client. *X*

[9] 4-31 An audit working paper that reflects the major components of an amount reported in the financial statements is referred to as a(n)

a. Lead schedule.

b. Supporting schedule.

c. Audit control account.

d. Working trial balance.

PROBLEMS

[2]   4-32   Management makes assertions about components of the financial statements. Match the management assertions shown in the following left-hand column with the proper description of the assertion shown in the right-hand column.

Management Assertion	Description
a. Existence or occurrence	1. The accounts and transactions that should be included are included; thus, the financial statements are complete.
b. Completeness	
c. Rights and obligations	2. Assets, liabilities, equity revenues, and expenses are appropriately valued and are allocated to the proper accounting period.
d. Valuation or allocation	
e. Presentation and disclosure	3. Amounts shown in the financial statements are properly presented and disclosed.
	4. The assets are the rights of the entity, and the liabilities are its obligations.
	5. The assets and liabilities exist, and the recorded transactions have occurred.

[6]   4-33   For each of the following audit procedures, indicate which type of evidence is being gathered: (1) physical examination, (2) reperformance, (3) documentation, (4) confirmation, (5) analytical procedures, (6) inquiries of client personnel or management, or (7) observation.

a. Sending a written request to the client's customers requesting that they report the amount owed to the client.

b. Examining large sales invoices for a period of two days before and after year-end to determine if sales are recorded in the proper period.

c. Agreeing the total of the accounts receivable subsidiary ledger to the accounts receivable general ledger account.

d. Discussing the adequacy of the allowance for doubtful accounts with the credit manager.

e. Comparing the current-year gross profit percentage with the gross profit percentage for the last four years.

f. Examining a new plastic extrusion machine to ensure that this major acquisition was received.

g. Watching the client's warehouse personnel count the raw materials inventory.

h. Performing test counts of the warehouse personnel's count of the raw material.

i. Obtaining a letter from the client's attorney indicating that there were no lawsuits in progress against the client.

j. Tracing the prices used by the client's billing program for pricing sales invoices to the client's approved price list.

[3,6]   (4-34) For each of the audit procedures listed in Problem 4-33, identify the primary audit objective being tested.

[1,5]   4-35   a. The first generally accepted auditing standard of field work requires, in part, that "the work is to be adequately planned." An effective tool that aids the auditor in adequately planning the work is an audit program.

Required:

Describe an audit program and the purposes it serves.

b. Auditors frequently refer to "standards" and "procedures." *Standards* are measures of the quality of the auditor's performance. Standards specifically refer to the 10 generally accepted auditing standards. *Procedures* relate to acts that the auditor performs while trying to gather evidence. Procedures specifically refer to the methods or techniques the auditor uses in conducting the examination.

Required:

List at least eight different types of procedures an auditor would use in examining financial statements. For example, a type of procedure an auditor would use frequently is the observation of activities and conditions. Do not discuss specific accounts.

(AICPA, adapted)

[6,7]   (4-36) Evidence comes in various types and has different degrees of reliability. Following are some statements that compare various types of evidence.

a. A bank confirmation versus observation of the segregation of duties between cash receipts and recording payment in the accounts receivable subsidiary ledger.

b. An auditor's recalculation of depreciation versus examination of raw material requisitions. *direct personal knowledge of outcome*

c. A bank statement included in the client's records versus shipping documents. *external*

d. Physical examination of common stock certificates versus physical examination of inventory components for a personal computer.

Required: *prepared by outside entity*

For each situation, indicate whether the first or second type of evidence is more reliable. Provide a rationale for your choice.

[6,7]   (4-37) Documentary evidence relates to the auditor's examination of client accounting data and corroborating evidential matter. One issue that affects the reliability of documentary evidence is whether the documents are *internal* or *external*. Following are examples of documentary evidence:

1. Duplicate copies of sales invoices. I
2. Purchase orders. I
3. Bank statements. E
4. Remittance advices. E
5. Vendors' invoices. E
6. Materials requisition forms. I
7. Overhead cost allocation sheets. I

   8. Shipping documents. I
   9. Payroll checks. E
   10. Long-term debt agreements. E

Required:
a. Classify each document as internal or external evidence.
b. Classify each document as to its reliability (high, moderate, or low).

[6,7]   4-38   The confirmation process is defined as the process of obtaining and evaluating a direct communication from a third party in response to a request for information about a particular item affecting financial statement assertions.

Required:
a. List and describe the factors that affect the reliability of confirmations.

b. Refer back to EarthWear Clothiers' financial statements included in Chapter 1. Identify any information on EarthWear's financial statements that might be verified through the use of confirmations.

[9]   4-39   Working papers are the auditor's record of work performed and conclusions reached on an audit engagement.

Required:
a. What are the purposes of working papers?
b. List and describe the various types of working papers.
c. What factors affect the auditor's judgment about the quantity, type, and content of working papers for a particular engagement? (Hint: Refer to AU 339.)

DISCUSSION CASE

[5,6,7]   4-40   Bentley Bros. Book Company publishes more than 250 fiction and nonfiction titles. Most of the company's books are written by Southern authors and typically focus on subjects popular in the region. The company sells most of its books to major retail stores such as Waldenbooks and B. Dalton.

Your firm was just selected as the new auditors for Bentley Bros., and you have been appointed as the audit manager for the engagement based on your prior industry experience. The prior auditors were removed because the client felt that it was not receiving adequate business advice. The prior auditors have indicated to you that the change in auditors did not result from any disagreements over accounting or auditing issues.

Your preliminary review of the company's financial statements indicates that the allowance for return of unsold books represents an important account (that is, high risk) because it may contain material misstatements. Consistent with industry practice, retailers are allowed to return unsold books for full credit. You know from your prior experience with other book publishers that the return rate for individual book titles can range from 30 to 50 percent. The client develops its allowance for return of unsold books based on internally generated records; that is, it maintains detailed records of all book returns by title.

Required:
a. Discuss how you would assess the reliability of the client's records for developing the allowance for return of unsold books.
b. Discuss how you would determine the return rate for relatively new titles.
c. Consider whether any external evidence can be obtained that would provide additional evidence on the reasonableness of the account.

INTERNET ASSIGNMENT

[5,6,7]   4-41   Use one of the Internet browsers to search for the following terms:
• Audit evidence

• Electronic data interchange (EDI)

• Image processing systems

SCAD⁵ ASSIGNMENT

Assignments 1 and 2 can be completed at this point. Assignment 1 introduces the audit client, Southwest Appliances, and provides detailed guidance on planning and documenting audit work. Assignment 2 provides an introduction to Southwest's sales and collection cycle, including the processing of documents.

---

⁵Refer to W. L. Felix, Jr., M. S. Niles, J. Andrus, and R. G. May, *SCAD IV: A Simulated Case for Audit Decision Making* (New York: McGraw-Hill, 1996).

Part III

PLANNING THE AUDIT AND UNDERSTANDING INTERNAL CONTROL

Chapter 5

Audit Planning and Types of Audit Tests

LEARNING OBJECTIVES

Upon completion of this chapter you will

[1] Know what is required to establish the terms of an engagement.

[2] Identify the steps that are performed in planning an audit engagement.

[3] Know the types of audit tests.

[4] Learn the purposes and types of analytical procedures.

[5] Identify financial ratios that are useful as analytical procedures.

RELEVANT ACCOUNTING AND AUDITING PRONOUNCEMENTS

FASB No. 57, "Related Party Disclosures" (FAS 57)

SAS No. 11, "Using the Work of a Specialist" (AU 336)

SAS No. 22, "Planning and Supervision" (AU 311)

SAS No. 45, "Related Parties" (AU 334)

SAS No. 47, "Audit Risk and Materiality in Conducting an Audit" (AU 312)

SAS No. 54, "Illegal Acts" (AU 317)

SAS No. 55, "Consideration of Internal Control in a Financial Statement Audit" (AU 319)

SAS No. 56, "Analytical Procedures" (AU 329)

SAS No. 61, "Communications with Audit Committees" (AU 380)

SAS No. 65, "The Auditor's Consideration of the Internal Audit Function in an Audit of Financial Statements" (AU 322)

SAS No. 78, "Consideration of Internal Control in a Financial Statement Audit: An Amendment to SAS No. 55" (AU 319)

SAS No. 82, "Consideration of Fraud in a Financial Statement Audit" (AU 316)

SAS No. 83, "Establishing an Understanding with the Client" (AU 310)

SAS No. 84, "Communications between Predecessor and Successor Auditors" (AU 315)

Statement on Quality Control Standards No. 2, "System of Quality Control for a CPA Firm's Accounting and Auditing Practice" (QC 10)

Quality Control Policies and Procedures for CPA Firms, "Establishing Quality Control Policies and Procedures" (QC 90)

Good audit planning can result in an efficient and effective audit. Failure to plan an engagement properly can lead to the issuance of misstated financial statements, an inappropriate audit report, or an audit that is not cost-effective. The first standard of field work states that "the work is to be adequately planned and assistants, if any, are to be properly supervised." SAS No. 22, "Planning and Supervision" (AU 311), provides extensive guidance on the implementation of this field-work standard. Two major categories of planning related to an audit are *preengagement activities* and *engagement-planning activities*. Preengagement activities relate to issues that should be addressed before the engagement formally begins and mainly relates to client acceptance and retention issues (refer to Chapter 2). Engagement-planning activities involve the specific steps that go into developing an overall audit strategy.

This chapter begins by discussing topics that relate to establishing the terms of the engagement and then presents specific issues that are included in engagement planning. The chapter also reviews the major types of audit tests. The last part of the chapter covers analytical procedures, including ratios that are useful for financial statement analysis.

Establishing the Terms of the Engagement

[LO 1]   The auditor and the client must agree on the terms of the engagement, including the type, scope, and timing of the engagement. This understanding reduces the risk that either party may misinterpret what is expected or required of the other party. The terms of the engagement, which are documented in the engagement letter, should include the objectives of the engagement, management's responsibilities, the auditor's responsibilities, and the limitations of the engagement (AU 310.05). In establishing the terms of the engagement,[1] three topics must be discussed: (1) the audit committee, (2) the engagement letter, and (3) the internal auditors.

The Audit Committee[2]

With small privately held companies, the owner-manager and the auditor usually negotiate directly. For large privately held companies and public companies, the auditor is appointed by vote of the stockholders, usually after recommendation by the board of directors or a subcommittee referred to as the *audit committee*. Preferably, the audit committee should be composed of members of the board of directors who do not hold positions with the company. Companies whose stock is traded on the New York Stock Exchange or on the over-the-counter market are required to have audit committees, while the American Stock Exchange recommends that its listed companies have audit committees.

The audit committee has responsibility for the financial reporting and disclosure process. As such, it should encourage fair reporting from the perspective of stockholders, creditors, and employees. In addition, the audit committee should provide for the independence of the external and internal auditors.

The audit committee should meet with the external auditor before the engagement starts to discuss the auditor's responsibilities and significant

---

[1]See K. M. Gibson, K. Pany, and S. H. Smith, "Do We Understand Each Other?" *Journal of Accountancy* (January 1998), pp. 53–59, for more discussion of the importance of establishing terms for the engagement.

[2]See Coopers & Lybrand LLP, *Audit Committee Guide* (New York: Coopers & Lybrand LLP, 1995), and Coopers & Lybrand LLP, *Audit Committee Update 1998* (New York: Coopers & Lybrand LLP, 1998), for detailed discussions of the formation, structure, organization, and activities of audit committees.

accounting policies. It may also provide limited input into the scope of the auditor's work, such as requesting that the external auditor visit certain locations. The audit committee may also engage the external or internal auditors to conduct special investigations. The external auditor is required to make a number of important communications to the audit committee during or at the end of the engagement (AU 380). Most of the required communications are made at the completion of the engagement; Chapter 17 covers them in detail.

The Engagement Letter

An *engagement letter* formalizes the arrangement reached between the auditor and the client. This letter serves as a contract, outlining the responsibilities of both parties and preventing misunderstandings between the two parties. While an engagement letter is not required by auditing standards, good audit practice dictates that firms use such letters with their clients in order to avoid misunderstandings. Exhibit 5–1 shows a sample engagement letter.

In addition to the items mentioned in the sample engagement letter in Exhibit 5–1, the engagement letter may include

- Arrangements involving the use of specialists or internal auditors.
- Any limitation of the liability of the auditor or client, such as indemnification to the auditor for liability arising from knowing misrepresentations to the auditor by management. (Note that regulatory bodies, such as the SEC, may restrict or prohibit such liability-limiting arrangements.)
- Additional services to be provided relating to regulatory requirements.
- Arrangements regarding other services (for example, assurance, tax, or consulting services).

Internal Auditors

When the client has internal auditors, the auditor may request their assistance in conducting the audit. The decision process the auditor follows is based on SAS No. 65, "The Auditor's Consideration of the Internal Audit Function in an Audit of Financial Statements" (AU 322) and is outlined in Figure 5–1. The major issue for the independent auditor is assessing the *competence* and *objectivity* of the internal auditors and the effect of their work on the audit. Table 5–1 presents factors that the auditor should consider when assessing the competence and objectivity of the internal auditors.

The internal auditors' work may affect the nature, timing, and extent of the audit procedures performed by the independent auditor. For example, as part of their regular work, internal auditors may review, assess, and monitor the entity's controls that are included in the various accounting cycles. Similarly, part of their work may include confirming receivables or observing certain physical inventories. If the internal auditors are competent and objective, the independent auditor may use the internal auditors' work in these areas to reduce the scope of audit work. The materiality of the account balance or class of transactions and its related audit risk may also determine how much the independent auditor can rely on the internal auditors' work. When internal auditors provide direct assistance, the auditor should supervise, review, evaluate, and test their work.

EXHIBIT 5–1

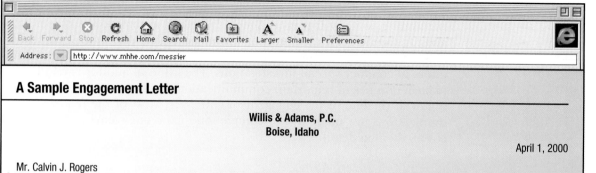

A Sample Engagement Letter

Willis & Adams, P.C.
Boise, Idaho

April 1, 2000

Mr. Calvin J. Rogers
EarthWear Clothiers
P.O. Box 787
Boise, Idaho 83845

Dear Mr. Rogers:

This will confirm our understanding of the arrangements for our audit of the financial statements of EarthWear Clothiers for the year ending December 31, 2000.

We will audit the company's financial statements of the year ending December 31, 2000, for the purpose of expressing an opinion on the fairness with which they present, in all material respects, the financial position, results of operations, and cash flows in conformity with generally accepted accounting principles.

We will conduct our audit in accordance with generally accepted auditing standards. Those standards require that we obtain reasonable, rather than absolute, assurance that the financial statements are free of material misstatement, whether caused by error or fraud. Accordingly, a material misstatement may remain undetected. Also, an audit is not designed to detect error or fraud that is immaterial to the financial statements; therefore, the audit will not necessarily detect misstatements less than this materiality level that might exist due to error, fraudulent financial reporting, or misappropriation of assets. If, for any reason, we are unable to complete the audit or are unable to form or have not formed an opinion, we may decline to express an opinion or decline to issue a report as a result of the engagement.

While an audit includes obtaining an understanding of internal control sufficient to plan the audit and to determine the nature, timing, and extent of audit procedures to be performed, it is not designed to provide assurance on internal control or to identify reportable conditions. However, we are responsible for ensuring that the audit committee (or others with equivalent authority or responsibility) is aware of any reportable conditions that come to our attention.

The financial statements are the responsibility of the company's management. Management is also responsible for (1) establishing and maintaining effective internal control over financial reports, (2) identifying and ensuring that the company complies with the laws and regulations applicable to its activities, (3) making all financial records and related information available to us, and (4) providing to us at the conclusion of the engagement a representation letter that, among other things, will confirm management's responsibility for the preparation of the financial statements in conformity with generally accepted accounting principles, the availability of financial records and related data, the completeness and availability of all minutes of the board and committee meetings, and, to the best of its knowledge and belief, the absence of fraud involving management or those employees who have a significant role in the entity's internal control.

Assistance to be supplied by your personnel, including the preparation of schedules and analyses of accounts, is described on a separate attachment. Timely completion of this work will facilitate the completion of our audit.

As part of our engagement for the year ending December 31, 2000, we will also review the federal and state income tax returns for EarthWear Clothiers.

Our fees will be billed as work progresses and are based on the amount of time required at various levels of responsibility, plus actual out-of-pocket expenses. Invoices are payable upon presentation. We will notify you immediately of any circumstances we encounter that could significantly affect our initial estimate of total fees of $510,000.

If this letter correctly expresses your understanding, please sign the enclosed copy and return it to us.

We appreciate the opportunity to serve you.

Very truly yours,

Willis & Adams

M. J. Willis

M. J. Willis, Partner

APPROVED:

By ___*Calvin J. Rogers*___ Chief Executive Officer

Date ___April 3, 2000___

F I G U R E 5–1
The Auditor's Consideration of the Internal Audit Function in an Audit of Financial Statements

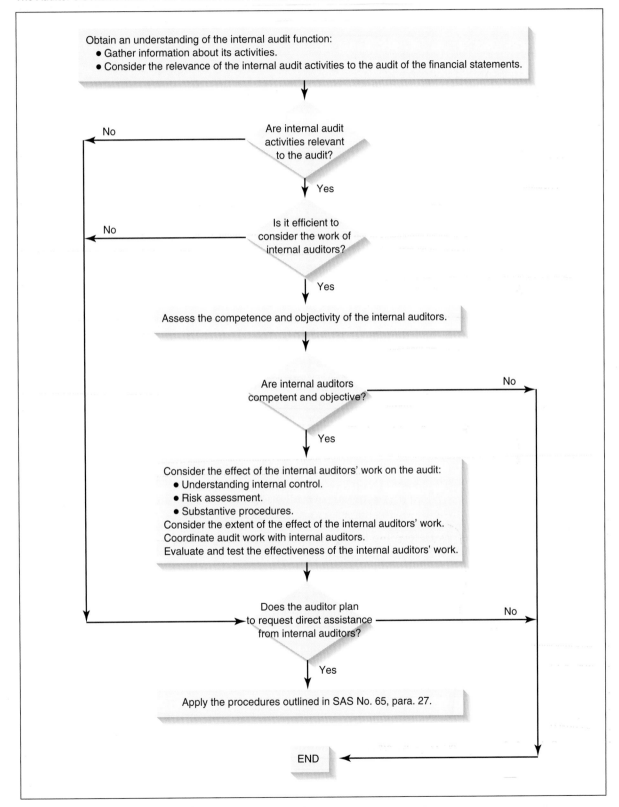

TABLE 5–1	Factors for Assessing the Competence and Objectivity of Internal Auditors

Competence:

- Educational level and professional experience.
- Professional certification and continuing education.
- Audit policies, procedures, and checklists.
- Practices regarding their assignments.
- The supervision and review of their audit activities.
- The quality of their working paper documentation, reports, and recommendations.
- Evaluation of their performance.

Objectivity:

- The organizational status of the internal auditor responsible for the internal audit function (for example, the internal auditor reports to an officer of sufficient status to ensure that the audit coverage is broad and the internal auditor has access to the board of directors or the audit committee).
- Policies to maintain internal auditors' objectivity about the areas audited (for example, internal auditors are prohibited from auditing areas to which they have recently been assigned or are to work upon completion of responsibilities in the internal audit function).

Engagement Planning

Overview

[LO 2]

Engagement planning involves all the issues the auditor should consider in developing an overall strategy for conducting the audit. The objective of the audit plan is to conduct an effective and efficient audit. Basically, this means that the audit is to be conducted in accordance with GAAS and that the risk of material misstatements is reduced to an acceptably low level. The audit plan should also consider how to conduct the engagement in a cost-effective manner.

When preparing an overall audit plan, the auditor should perform each of the following steps:

- Determine the audit staffing requirements.
- Assess independence.
- Obtain knowledge of the client's business and industry.
- Establish materiality and audit risk, and assess inherent risk.
- Assess a preliminary level for control risk.
- Assess the possibility of errors, fraud, and illegal acts.
- Identify related parties.
- Conduct preliminary analytical procedures.
- Develop an overall audit strategy and prepare audit programs.
- Consider additional value-added services.

While these steps are listed in the order in which they are usually completed, the continuous nature of auditing often dictates that a number of them be conducted concurrently.

Determine the Audit Staffing Requirements

Public accounting firms need to ensure that their engagements are completed by auditors having the proper degree of technical training and proficiency given the circumstances of the clients. Factors that should be considered in determining staffing requirements include engagement size and complexity, level of risk, any special expertise, personnel availability, and timing of the work to be performed. For example, if the engagement involves a high level of risk, the firm should staff the engagement with more experienced auditors. Similarly, if the audit involves a specialized industry (banking, insurance, and so on) or if the client uses sophisticated computer processing, the firm must ensure that members of the audit team possess the requisite expertise. Generally, a time budget is prepared in order to assist with the staffing requirements and to schedule the field work.

In some instances, the audit may require consulting with an outside specialist. SAS No. 11, "Using the Work of a Specialist" (AU 336), which provides guidance in this area, defines a *specialist* as a person or firm possessing special skill or knowledge in a field other than accounting or auditing. This would include individuals such as actuaries, appraisers, attorneys, engineers, and geologists. Such specialists may assist the auditor with valuation issues, determination of physical quantities, amounts derived from specialized techniques, or interpretations of regulations or agreements. For example, an auditor might consult an actuary to determine the amount of the client's pension obligations or a geologist to estimate a client's oil and gas reserves.

Assess Independence

The second general standard requires that the auditor be independent of the client in order to issue an opinion. According to the Statements on Quality Control Standards, a public accounting firm should establish policies and procedures to ensure that persons at all organizational levels within the firm maintain independence in accordance with Rule 101 of the Code of Professional Conduct (see Chapter 19). A firm should document compliance with this policy by having all personnel complete an annual independence questionnaire or report. This questionnaire requests information about the auditor's financial or managerial relationships with the firm's clients. Under certain circumstances, family members' financial or managerial relationships are attributable to the auditor. For example, if the spouse of an auditor participating in an engagement was an accounting supervisor for the client, independence would be considered impaired.

At the engagement level, the partner-in-charge should ensure that all individuals assigned to the engagement are independent of the client. This can be accomplished by reviewing the annual independence reports for each member of the audit team.

Another area of concern related to independence is unpaid client fees. If an account receivable from a client takes on the characteristics of a loan, the auditor's independence may be impaired. Many public accounting firms adopt a policy of not completing the current audit until all of the prior year's fees have been paid.

Finally, the CPA firm must be concerned when it also provides consulting services such as systems design for an audit client. While the performance of consulting services does not, in and of itself, impair independence, the audit team must remain objective when evaluating client activities that were developed by their firm's consultants.

In the rare instance where the auditor is not independent of the client, the type of audit opinion should be discussed during the planning stage. As pointed out in Chapter 2, a disclaimer of opinion must be issued when the auditor is not independent.

Obtain Knowledge of the Client's Business and Industry

Chapter 2 discussed the importance of the auditor being a business and industry expert. The auditor needs this expertise in order to plan and conduct the audit properly. This knowledge can be acquired by prior experience with the client or its industry, a tour of the client's facilities, and inquiries of client personnel. The auditor's knowledge of the client should include the nature of the client's business, its organization, and its operating characteristics. This includes matters such as types of products or services, capital structure, number of locations, and production and distribution methods. The auditor must also understand the industry in which the client operates. Issues such as government regulations, economic conditions, competition, and specialized accounting practices must be considered by the auditor. This industry information can be obtained from AICPA accounting and auditing guides, trade publications, textbooks, and periodicals, as well as by attending specialized training programs. For example, an auditor who has a client in the property and casualty insurance industry would need to be more aware of issues affecting this particular industry than would an auditor whose client manufactures some basic product. Additionally, the property and casualty insurance industry is regulated by federal and state agencies and is subject to specialized accounting practices. The information gathered on the client's business and industry is used to assess client business risk as discussed in Chapter 3.

Establish Materiality and Audit Risk, and Assess Inherent Risk

Materiality and audit risk are major concepts that affect the scope of the audit and therefore must be considered when the auditor plans the engagement. Additionally, the auditor must assess the client's inherent risk. Chapter 3 covered the decision processes followed by the auditor in establishing materiality and audit risk, as well as the assessment of inherent risk. The reader should return to Chapter 3 and review the important issues related to these concepts.

Assess a Preliminary Level for Control Risk

Control risk is the risk that material misstatements will not be prevented or detected by internal controls. The auditor evaluates the effectiveness of internal control for preventing material misstatements in the financial statements and prepares a preliminary assessment of control risk. A preliminary assessment of control risk is necessary for the auditor to plan the nature, timing, and extent of testing. A primary concern at this point is the extent to which information technology is used in processing accounting information. In evaluating the effect of information technology on the client's accounting systems, the auditor needs information on the following:

- The extent to which information technology is used in each significant accounting system.
- The complexity of the client's computer operations.
- The organizational structure of the information technology activities.
- The availability of data.
- The need for information technology–assisted techniques to gather data and conduct audit procedures.

The presence of complex information technology may require the use of a computer audit specialist. Chapters 6 and 7 cover these issues in more detail.

Assess the Possibility of Errors, Fraud, and Illegal Acts

Auditing standards (SAS No. 47, 54, and 82) guide the auditor in assessing the possibility of errors, fraud, and illegal acts.

Errors and Fraud   The auditor has a responsibility to plan and perform the audit to obtain reasonable assurance that the financial statements are free from material misstatement, whether caused by error or fraud. As discussed in Chapter 3, *errors* are *unintentional* misstatements or omissions of amounts or disclosures in financial statements.

Fraud refers to *intentional* misstatements that include management fraud and defalcation. Note that the major difference between errors and fraud relates to intent. Although auditors view intentional misstatements as more serious than unintentional errors, it is often difficult for the auditor to determine an individual's intention when a misstatement is detected.

During the planning process, the auditor assesses the risk of material misstatement by considering those risk factors (refer to Chapter 3) that are identified on the engagement. When risk factors are identified during the planning process, the auditor should document those factors and the steps taken to respond to them. However, even a well-planned and -executed audit may not detect material fraud (see Exhibit 5–2). Audit procedures that are effective in detecting errors may not be effective in detecting fraud such as forgery and collusion because GAAS do not require auditors to authenticate documents, nor is the auditor trained to do so. However, if the auditor suspects that documents have been falsified, he or she should expand the audit work or use a specialist to determine the propriety of the documents. Additionally, auditing procedures are not likely to be effective in detecting misstatements when collusion occurs between client personnel and third parties or among management or employees of the client. Thus, the auditor should exercise due care and professional skepticism to achieve reasonable assurance that both material errors and fraud are detected. *Professional skepticism* means that the auditor should remain objective and unbiased by not assuming that management is either honest or dishonest.

During the conduct of the audit, certain conditions or circumstances that may indicate the presence of an error or fraud may come to the auditor's attention. Some examples of such circumstances are shown in Table 5–2. For example, if the auditor selects a sample of vendors' invoices for testing and the client cannot produce authorized requisitions or some

EXHIBIT 5–2

Informix Cites Accounting Irregularities for Restated Earnings

Informix, a once–high-flying database software company, announced that accounting irregularities caused earnings to be restated for the fiscal years ended 1994, 1995, and 1996 and for the first quarter of 1997. After an extended audit, Informix cut reported revenues from January 1994 to June 1997 by $278.2 million and reported net losses totaling $243.3 million. The company disclosed that it improperly booked revenues and profits under its former chief executive officer. The errors and irregularities took numerous forms and primarily resulted from a lack of compliance with the company's procedures and controls and with revenue recognition issues. Informix disclosed that "the earnings process for a significant number of original license agreements with resellers (original equipment manufacturers, distributors, and value-added resellers) was not complete at the time of delivery of the master copy of the software to the reseller. Further, the company has learned that informal or otherwise undisclosed arrangements with a number of resellers have or could result in significant concessions or allowances that were not accounted for when the revenue was originally reported as earned." It would be difficult for an auditor to become aware of such informal arrangements with resellers.

Sources: K. Swisher, "Informix Posts Loss of $110.7 Million, Restates Earnings," *The Wall Street Journal* (November 19, 1997); and *The PointCast Network* (Business Wire), November 18, 1997.

TABLE 5–2   Examples of Circumstances Indicating an Increased Risk of Errors or Fraud

- Analytical procedures disclose differences from expectations.
- Unreconciled differences exist between a control account and subsidiary records.
- Confirmation requests disclose significant differences or a lower-than-expected response rate.
- Transactions lack proper documentation or authorization.
- Errors known to client personnel are not voluntarily disclosed to the auditor.

other form of authorization for the purchases, the auditor should consider the possibility of an error or fraud being present. If the auditor suspects or detects fraud, he or she should consider whether it has a material effect on the financial statements and what its potential implications are for other parts of the audit.

Illegal Acts   The term *illegal acts* refers to violations of laws or governmental regulations. In some instances, fraud as described in the previous section may also consist of illegal acts. SAS No. 54 distinguishes between illegal acts that have *direct and material* effects on the financial statements and those that have *material but indirect* effects. The auditor should consider laws and regulations that are generally recognized as having a direct and material effect on the determination of financial statement amounts. For example, tax laws and laws and regulations that may affect the amount of revenue recognized under a government contract fall into this

TABLE 5–3	Information or Circumstances That May Indicate an Illegal Act

- Unauthorized transactions, improperly recorded transactions, or transactions not recorded in a complete or timely manner.
- An investigation by a government agency, an enforcement proceeding, or payment of unusual fines or penalties.
- Violations of laws or regulations cited in reports of examinations by regulatory agencies.
- Large payments for unspecified services to consultants, affiliates, or employees.
- Sales commissions or agents' fees that appear excessive.
- Large payments in cash or bank cashiers' checks.
- Unexplained payments to government officials.
- Failure to file tax returns or pay government duties.

category. Auditing standards (SAS No. 54) state that the auditor's responsibility for detecting illegal acts having a direct and material effect on the financial statements is the same as that for errors or fraud.

Other illegal acts, such as violations of the securities acts or occupational safety and health, Food and Drug Administration, environmental protection, equal employment, and price-fixing or other antitrust violations, may materially but indirectly affect the financial statements. The auditor should be aware that such illegal acts may have occurred. If specific information comes to the auditor's attention that provides evidence concerning the existence of such material but indirect illegal acts, the auditor should apply audit procedures specifically directed at determining whether illegal acts have occurred. However, an audit conducted in accordance with GAAS provides no assurance that illegal acts will be detected or that any contingent liability that may result will be disclosed.

Table 5–3 presents some examples of specific information or circumstances that indicate the possibility of an illegal act. For example, the business world has seen a number of instances where payments of sales commissions or agent's fees were really bribes to secure contracts. When the auditor becomes aware of such a possible illegal act, he or she should obtain an understanding of the nature of the act, the circumstances in which it occurred, and sufficient other information to evaluate its effects on the financial statements. The auditor should then discuss the matter with the appropriate level of management. If management does not provide satisfactory information, the auditor should consult with the client's legal counsel and apply additional audit procedures, if necessary.

If an illegal act has occurred or is likely to have occurred, the auditor should consider its implications for other aspects of the audit, particularly the reliability of management representations. The auditor should ensure that the audit committee, or other body or person with equivalent authority and responsibility, is adequately informed about significant illegal acts. The auditor should also recognize that, under the circumstances noted previously, he or she may have a duty to notify parties outside the client.

Identify Related Parties

FASB No. 57, "Related Party Disclosures" (FAS 57), defines related parties as

Affiliates of the enterprise; entities for which investments are accounted for by the equity method by the enterprise; trusts for the benefits of the employees, such as pension and profit-sharing trusts that are managed by or under the trusteeship of management; principal owners of the enterprise; its management; members of the immediate families of the principal owners of the enterprise and its management; and other parties with which the enterprise may deal if one party controls or can significantly influence the management or operating policies of the other to the extent that one of the transacting parties might be prevented from fully pursuing its own separate interests. Another party also is a related party if it can significantly influence the management or operating policies of the transacting parties or if it has an ownership interest in one of the transacting parties and can significantly influence the other to an extent that one or more of the transacting parties might be prevented from fully pursuing its own separate interests.

It is important that the auditor attempt to identify all related parties during the planning phase of the audit because transactions between the entity and related parties may not be "at arm's length." For example, the client may lease property from an entity owned by the chief executive officer at lease rates in excess of prevailing market rates. The auditor can identify related parties by evaluating the client's procedures for identifying related parties, requesting a list of related parties from management, and reviewing filings with the Securities and Exchange Commission and other regulatory agencies. Once related parties have been identified, audit personnel should be provided with the names so that transactions with such parties are identified and investigated. Here are some additional audit procedures that may identify transactions with related parties:

- Review the minutes of the board of directors and executive or operating committees for information about material transactions authorized or discussed at their meetings.
- Review conflict-of-interest statements obtained by the company from management.
- Review the extent and nature of business transacted with major customers, suppliers, borrowers, and lenders for indications of previously undisclosed relationships.
- Review accounting records for large, unusual, or nonrecurring transactions or balances, paying particular attention to transactions recognized at or near the end of the reporting period.
- Review confirmations of loans receivable and payable for indications of guarantees. If guarantees are identified, determine their nature and the relationships of the guarantor to the entity.

The reader should refer to SAS No. 45, "Related Parties" (AU 334), for additional guidance on searching for and reporting on related parties.

Conduct Preliminary Analytical Procedures

SAS No. 56, "Analytical Procedures" (AU 329), defines analytical procedures as consisting of evaluations of financial information made by a study of plausible relationships among both financial and nonfinancial data. This standard requires that the auditor apply analytical procedures at the planning phase for all audits. The main objectives of analytical procedures at this point are (1) to understand the client's business and transactions and

(2) to identify financial statement accounts that are likely to contain errors. By identifying where errors are likely, the auditor can allocate more resources to investigate those accounts. Suppose, for example, that an auditor computes a client's inventory turnover ratio for the last five years as follows:

$$\text{Inventory turnover} = \frac{\text{Cost of goods sold}}{\text{Inventory}}$$

The results of this analysis show the following trend, which is compared to industry data:

	1996	*1997*	*1998*	*1999*	*2000*
Client	8.9	8.8	8.5	8.0	7.9
Industry	8.8	8.7	8.8	8.6	8.6

The client's inventory turnover ratio in this case has declined steadily over the five-year period, while the industry turnover ratio shows only a minor decline over the same period. The auditor might suspect that the client's inventory contains slow-moving or obsolete inventory. The auditor would then plan additional testing for selected audit objectives such as valuation, completeness, and validity.

Develop an Overall Audit Strategy and Prepare Audit Programs

Once these planning steps have been completed, the auditor develops an overall audit strategy. This involves decisions about the *nature, extent,* and *timing* of audit tests. The auditor's preliminary decision concerning control risk determines the level of control testing, which in turn affects the auditor's tests of the account balance.

The audit strategy is normally documented in an audit plan. Audit programs containing specific audit procedures are also prepared. Exhibit 5–3 presents a partial audit program for substantive tests of accounts receivable. The types of audit tests are discussed later in this chapter.

Consider Additional Value-Added Services

As part of the planning process, the auditor should look for opportunities to recommend additional value-added services. Traditionally, value-added services have included tax planning, system design and integration, and internal reporting processes. With auditors taking a more global view of the client and its business and industry, there are new opportunities to provide valuable services for the client. For example, the new assurance services (introduced in Chapter 1 and discussed in more detail in Chapter 21) include risk assessment, business performance measurement (benchmarking), and electronic commerce. The auditor also likely can provide recommendations based on the assessment of client business risk. With the knowledge gathered through assessing client business risk, the auditor can provide important feedback to management and the board of directors on the strengths and weaknesses of business processes, strategic planning, and emerging trends. Proper consideration of value-added services during the planning process should alert the audit team to proactively identify opportunities to improve client service.

EXHIBIT 5–3

A Partial Audit Program for Substantive Tests of Accounts Receivable

Audit Procedures	W/P Ref.	Completed by	Date
1. Obtain the December 31, 2000, aged accounts receivable trial balance and			
a. Foot the trial balance and agree total to accounts receivable control account.			
b. Judgmentally select five accounts from the aged trial balance; agree the information per the aged trial balance to the original sales invoice and determine if the invoice was included in the appropriate aging category.			
2. Confirm accounts receivable using a monetary-unit sampling plan. Set the risk for incorrect acceptance = 10%, tolerable misstatement = $50,000, and expected misstatement = $20,000.			
a. For all responses with exceptions, follow up on the cause of the error.			
b. For all nonresponses, examine subsequent cash receipts and/or supporting documents.			
c. Summarize the statistical test results.			
d. Summarize the confirmation results.			
3. Test sales cutoff by identifying the last shipping advice for the year and examining five large sales for three days before and after year-end.			
4. Test the reasonableness of the allowance for doubtful accounts by the following:			
a. Test the reasonableness using past percentages on bad debts.			
b. For any large account in the aged trial balance greater than 90 days old, test for subsequent cash receipts.			
c. For the following financial ratios, compare the current year to prior year and internal budgets:			
• Number of days outstanding in receivable.			
• Aging of receivables.			
• Write-offs as a percentage of sales.			
• Bad debt expense as a percentage of sales.			
5. Prepare a memo summarizing the tests, results, and conclusions.			

Types of Audit Tests

[LO 3] There are two general types of audit tests:

- Tests of controls
- Substantive tests

Tests of Controls

Tests of controls consist of procedures directed toward the evaluation of the effectiveness of the *design* and *operation* of internal controls (AU 319). When tests of controls look at design issues, the auditor evaluates whether the control has been properly designed to prevent or detect material misstatements. Tests of controls directed toward the operational effectiveness of a control are concerned with how the control is applied, the consistency of its application during the period, and by whom it is applied. The following audit procedures are examples of tests of controls:

- Inquiries of appropriate client personnel.
- Inspection of documents, reports, and electronic media indicating performance of the control.
- Observation of the application of specific internal controls.
- Reperformance of the application of the control by the auditor.

Table 5–4 provides examples of internal controls that are normally present in a revenue cycle and tests of controls that the auditor might use to test the operation of the controls.

Substantive Tests

Substantive tests detect material misstatements (that is, dollar errors) in an account balance, transaction class, and disclosure component of the financial statements. There are three categories of substantive tests: *substantive tests of transactions, analytical procedures,* and *tests of account balances.*

Substantive Tests of Transactions Substantive tests of transactions test for errors or fraud in individual transactions. Examining individual transactions provides the auditor with evidence on the validity,

---

TABLE 5–4	Examples of Internal Controls and Tests of Controls
Internal Controls	*Test of Controls*
Create a separation of duties between the shipping function and the order entry and billing functions.	Observe and evaluate whether shipping personnel have access to the order entry or billing activities.
Credit Department personnel initial sales orders, indicating credit approval.	Inspect a sample of sales orders for presence of initials of Credit Department personnel.
Billing Department personnel account for the numerical sequence of sales invoices.	Inquire of Billing Department personnel about missing sales invoices numbers.
Agree sales invoices to shipping document and customer order for product types, price, and quantity.	Recompute the information on a sample of sales invoices.

completeness, valuation, accuracy, and cutoff audit objectives. For example, an auditor may examine a large purchase of inventory by testing that the cost of the goods included on the vendor's invoice is properly recorded in the inventory and accounts payable accounts. This gives the auditor evidence about validity, completeness, valuation, cutoff, and the proper accumulation of the inventory transaction in the client's accounting records. As discussed in the next section, substantive tests of transactions are often conducted along with tests of controls as a dual-purpose test.

Analytical Procedures   Because of their growing importance to auditors, analytical procedures are discussed in more detail later in the chapter.

Tests of Account Balances   Tests of account balances concentrate on the *details* of amounts contained in an account balance. These important tests establish whether any material misstatements are included in the accounts presented in the financial statements. For example, the auditor may want to test accounts payable. To test the details of the accounts payable account, the auditor can examine a sample of the individual vendor invoices that make up the ending balance in accounts payable. In examining this documentation, the auditor is concerned with testing the validity and valuation audit objectives. Additionally, the auditor may send confirmations to vendors with zero balances in their accounts in order to test the completeness objective.

Dual-Purpose Tests

Tests of controls look for errors in the application of controls, while substantive tests of transactions are concerned with monetary errors. However, for some audit tests, it is difficult to determine whether the audit procedure is a test of controls or a substantive test of transactions. For example, in Table 5–4, the last control procedure shown is agreement of sales invoices to shipping documents and customer orders for product type, price, and quantity. The test of controls shown is to recompute the information on a sample of sales invoices. While this test primarily checks the effectiveness of the control, it also provides evidence on whether the sales invoice contains the wrong quantity, product type, or price. Dual-purpose tests can also improve the efficiency of the audit.

This text discusses tests of controls within each cycle when the assessment of control risk is covered. Substantive tests of transactions are discussed along with the other substantive tests when the financial statement accounts affected by the accounting cycle are discussed. The reader should remember, however, that in most audit situations substantive tests of transactions are conducted at the same time as tests of controls.

Analytical Procedures

[LO 4]   SAS No. 56, "Analytical Procedures" (AU 329), defines analytical procedures as consisting of evaluations of financial information made by a study of plausible relationships among both financial and nonfinancial data. Analytical procedures may range from the use of simple comparisons to the use of complex models. The discussion of analytical procedures in this chapter is limited to simple comparisons and basic ratio analyses. The use of regression analysis techniques is covered in advanced auditing texts.[3] Proper application of analytical procedures requires that the auditor have knowledge of the client's business and industry. Without such knowledge, the auditor may be unable to develop appropriate analytical procedures or properly evaluate the results of such tests.

Types of Analytical Procedures

The auditor can use a number of different types of analytical procedures to test a client's financial information. Some common types of analytical procedures include the following.

Comparison of Current-Year Financial Information with Comparable Prior Period(s) After Consideration of Known Changes. This is perhaps the most commonly used analytical procedure. For example, the auditor may compare the amounts shown on this year's trial balance with the prior year's audited balances and investigate those amounts that are out of line by some predetermined cutoff percentage or absolute amount. More specifically, the auditor can compare the current-year accounts receivable balance with the prior year's balance after adjusting for the change in sales during the current period.

Comparison of Current-Year Financial Information with Budgets, Projections, and Forecasts. This type of analytical procedure is similar to the previous type except that the current-year actual results are compared to the client's planned activity. For example, the auditor can test the reasonableness of selected income and expense accounts by comparing their current-year amounts to the client's budget and investigating accounts that are not consistent with the auditor's expectations.

Relationships among Elements of Financial Information within the Current Period. There are many examples of one element in the financial statements relating to another element. This is particularly true for the relationship between certain balance sheet accounts and their related income or expense accounts. For example, there should be a relationship between the balance for long-term debt and interest expense. The auditor can test this relationship by multiplying the average long-term debt for the period by the average interest rate. This estimate of interest expense can be compared to the balance of interest expense shown on the trial balance. See the example for EarthWear Clothiers later in the chapter.

Comparison of the Client's Financial Information with Industry Data. The auditor can, for example, compare the client's financial ratios (receivable turnover, inventory turnover, and so on) to industry averages. The industry

---

[3]See A. D. Bailey, Jr., *Statistical Auditing: Review, Concepts, and Problems* (New York: Harcourt Brace Jovanovich, 1981), chap. 10, for a detailed discussion of regression analysis applied to auditing.

information can serve as a benchmark for assessing how well the client's financial position and performance compare with other companies in the industry. Robert Morris Associates, Dun & Bradstreet, and Standard & Poor's publish this type of industry data. Exhibit 5–4 contains an extract of industry data from *Industry Norms & Key Business Ratios 1997–98*, published by Dun & Bradstreet, Inc.

Relationships of Financial Information to Nonfinancial Information. The auditor may have relevant nonfinancial information available for comparison purposes or for developing estimates of the client's financial information. This might include items such as the number of employees, hours worked, and so on. For example, the auditor can multiply commissioned sales by the average commission rate and compare this estimate to the client's recorded commission expense. Another example would be the number of pagers in service for a company that leases pagers. This number can be multiplied by the average billing rate to test the total pager leasing revenue.

Purposes of Analytical Procedures

Analytical procedures are used for three purposes:

1. To assist the auditor in *planning* the nature, timing, and extent of other audit procedures.
2. As a *substantive test* to obtain evidential matter about particular assertions related to account balances or classes of transactions.
3. As an *overall review* of the financial information in the final review stage of the audit.

Analytical procedures are required for use in the planning and overall review stages of all audits of financial statements made in accordance with GAAS. However, auditors should consider applying analytical procedures for all three purposes because such procedures have been shown to effectively detect errors.[4] Analytical procedures are also relatively inexpensive tests to perform.

Analytical Procedures Used in Planning the Audit

The use of analytical procedures in planning an engagement was discussed earlier in this chapter. To reiterate, the objectives are (1) to enhance the auditor's understanding of the client's business and the transactions and events that have occurred since the last audit and (2) to identify areas that may represent risks relevant to the audit. More specifically, the auditor needs to identify the existence of unusual transactions and events, amounts, and ratios or trends that may indicate matters having financial statement and audit planning implications.

At the planning stage, analytical procedures usually involve data aggregated at a high level. For most entities, analytical procedures consist of reviewing changes in account balances from the prior year using the

---

[4]For example, see A. Wright and R. H. Ashton, "Identifying Audit Adjustments with Attention-Directing Procedures," *The Accounting Review* (October 1989), pp. 710–28. W. R. Kinney, Jr., and R. D. Martin, "Does Auditing Reduce Bias in Financial Reporting? A Review of Audit-Related Adjustment Studies," *Auditing: A Journal of Practice and Theory* (Spring 1994), pp. 149–55, review the audit research on this issue.

EXHIBIT 5–4

An Example of Industry Data Available from Published Sources

SIC 5961
CTLG, ML-ORDER HSES
(No Breakdown)
1997 (451 Establishments)

	$	%
Cash	101,474	16.6
Accounts receivable	94,139	15.4
Notes receivable	3,668	0.6
Inventory	236,570	38.7
Other current	48,292	7.9
Total current	**484,142**	**79.2**
Fixed assets	82,524	13.5
Other noncurrent	44,624	7.3
Total assets	**611,291**	**100.0**
Accounts payable	125,315	20.5
Bank loans	1,834	0.3
Notes payable	14,671	2.4
Other current	97,195	15.9
Total current	**239,015**	**39.1**
Other long-term	59,907	9.8
Deferred credits	—	—
Net worth	312,370	51.1
Total liab and net worth	**611,291**	**100.0**
Net sales	2,386,410	100.0
Gross profit	925,927	38.8
Net profit after tax	78,752	3.3
Working capital	245,127	—

RATIOS	UQ	MED	LQ
Solvency:			
Quick ratio (times)	1.6	0.8	0.3
Current ratio (times)	3.9	2.1	1.4
Curr liab to nw (%)	25.1	68.6	142.6
Curr liab to inv (%)	45.8	92.0	146.8
Total liab to nw (%)	29.7	84.1	178.9
Fixed assets to nw (%)	9.3	22.3	49.4
Efficiency:			
Coll period (days)	4.4	14.1	34.1
Sales to inv (times)	14.6	7.9	5.3
Assets to sales (%)	21.2	31.2	47.3
Sales to nwc (times)	19.6	8.6	4.4
Acct pay to sales (%)	3.8	6.2	9.3
Profitability:			
Return on sales (%)	6.9	2.9	0.6
Return on assets (%)	21.2	7.4	1.2
Return on nw (%)	47.7	17.5	4.9

Source: Dun & Bradstreet, Inc.

unadjusted working trial balance. Material accounts that appear to be out of line, based on the auditor's knowledge of the client's business and industry, are subjected to further inquiry by the auditor. This usually involves discussing these accounts with relevant client personnel and, in some instances, planning additional substantive tests of the accounts.

Analytical Procedures as a Substantive Test

Figure 5–2 presents an overview of the auditor's decision process when conducting analytical procedures as a substantive test. The first step in this process is to develop an *expectation* for the amount or account balance. An expectation can be developed using any of the types of analytical procedures discussed previously. Consider the following example from EarthWear Clothiers:

EarthWear's income statement shows $230,000 of interest expense. To conduct an analytical procedure as a substantive test of this account, the auditor could develop an expectation in the following manner. Obtain the general ledger balance for the short-term line of credit for each month of the year and calculate a monthly average. Determine the average interest rate for the year for the short-term line of credit. Multiply the average monthly balance in the short-term line of credit account by the average interest rate and compare the result to the interest expense.

Suppose that the auditor obtained the following information from EarthWear's general ledger:

Month	Balance
January	$ 500,000
February	1,000,000
March	1,400,000
April	1,500,000
May	2,000,000
June	2,600,000
July	2,700,000
August	5,400,000
September	8,700,000
October	12,000,000
November	4,900,000
December	500,000
Total	$ 43,200,000
Average	$ 3,600,000

Further, assume that interest rates have remained stable over the year, fluctuating between 6 and 7 percent. If the auditor uses 6.5 percent as the average interest rate, the expectation for interest expense is $234,000 ($43,200,000 × .065).

As shown in Figure 5–2, once an expectation is developed, it can be compared to the amount recorded by the client. In the example, the expected interest expense ($234,000) is compared with the recorded interest

FIGURE 5–2

Overview of the Auditor's Decision Process for Analytical Procedures as a Substantive Test

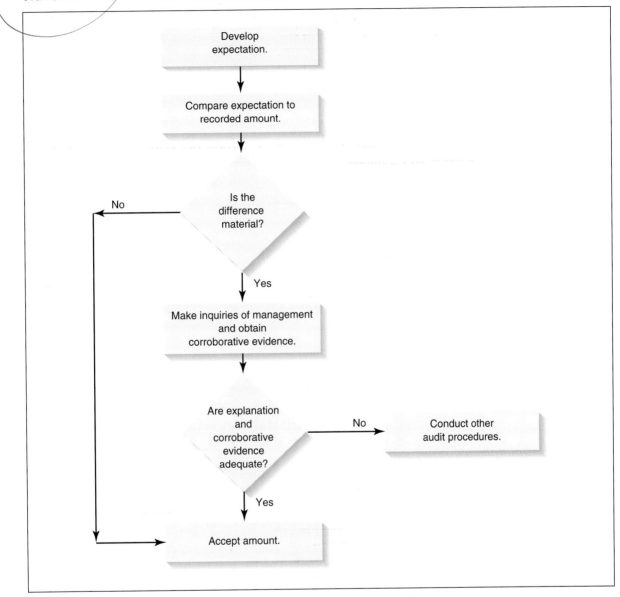

expense ($230,000). The next decision for the auditor is to determine if the difference between the expectation and the recorded amount is material. Because the difference between the auditor's expectation and the recorded amount is only $4,000, the auditor would likely determine that the difference is not material and accept the interest expense account as fairly stated.

However, if the recorded amount is *materially* different from the auditor's expectation, the auditor will normally inquire of management about the cause of the difference. SAS No. 56 points out that the auditor should ordinarily corroborate management's explanation with additional evidence. If the client's explanation and the corroborative evidence are not adequate, or if no corroborative evidence is available, the auditor will need to conduct additional audit procedures. If the explanation and evidence are adequate for resolving the difference, the auditor can accept the amount as being fairly presented.

When analytical procedures are used as direct substantive tests, the auditor is testing one or more particular audit objectives. For example, in the commission expense example, the auditor is testing primarily the valuation objective. The effectiveness and efficiency of analytical procedures in identifying material misstatements depend on

- The nature of the assertion or audit objective.
- The plausibility and predictability of the relationship.
- The availability and reliability of the data used.
- The precision of the expectation.

The Nature of the Assertion or Audit Objective   Analytical procedures can be used to test all audit objectives except ownership (refer to Table 4–6 in Chapter 4). However, they may be more effective at identifying certain types of misstatements than testing individual transactions. For example, they may be more effective at detecting omissions (completeness objective) than examining detailed documentary evidence. The key point is that the auditor needs to be sure that the analytical procedure performed is appropriate for the assertion or audit objective being examined.

The Plausibility and Predictability of the Relationship   The main concern with plausibility is whether the relationship used to test the assertion or audit objective makes sense. In an earlier example, the auditor examined the change in accounts receivable by relating it to the change in sales. It is plausible to expect that an increase in sales should lead to an increase in accounts receivable. Many factors determine the predictability of the relationship. For example, income statement items tend to be more predictable than balance sheet items because income statement accounts involve only transactions from the current period. Similarly, if the client operates in a static environment, the relationships are likely to be more predictable than they are for a client that operates in a dynamic environment.

The Availability and Reliability of Data   The ability to develop expectations for certain audit objectives is a function of the reliability of the available data. The reliability of data for developing expectations depends on the three factors discussed in Chapter 4 under the competence of evidential matter: (1) the independence of the source of the evidence, (2) the effectiveness of internal controls, and (3) the auditor's direct personal knowledge. In addition, data for analytical procedures are more reliable if the data were subjected to audit in the current or prior periods and if the expectation was developed from multiple sources of data. For example, if the auditor is computing ratios based on *audited* data from prior periods, the data used in the computations would be considered reliable.

The Precision of the Expectation

The precision of the expectation is a function of the materiality and detection risk for the objective being tested. If the audit objective being tested requires a low level of detection risk, the precision of the expectation needs to be relatively small. However, as the precision gets smaller, the auditor will probably need to conduct more audit tests. Therefore, the auditor's decisions concerning materiality and detection risk for analytical procedures directly impact the amount of audit work to be performed.

An example will help to explain this further. Suppose the auditor decides to use an analytical procedure to assess the fair presentation of a client's depreciation expense. Suppose further that the auditor expects depreciation expense to be $3,500,000. Based on materiality and detection risk considerations, this expectation does not require tight precision, and a $200,000 difference would be acceptable. If the recorded amount equals $3,350,000, no further investigation would be necessary. Conversely, if the expectation requires a precision of $100,000, the auditor would need to inquire of management and obtain corroborating evidence because the difference between the expectation and the recorded amount is greater than $100,000. If there is no adequate explanation or corroborative evidence, the auditor would have to conduct additional audit procedures because the available evidence does not support management's assertions about depreciation expense.

Analytical Procedures Used in the Overall Review

The objective of analytical procedures at the overall review stage of an audit is to assist the auditor in assessing the conclusions reached and evaluating the overall financial statement presentation. This requires reviewing the trial balance, financial statements, and footnotes in order to (1) judge the adequacy of the evidence gathered to support any unusual or unexpected balances investigated during the audit and (2) determine if any other unusual balances or relationships have not been investigated.

In the first instance, competent evidence in the working papers should support any differences from the auditor's expectations. For example, the auditor can compare the audited balances from the current year with the audited balances from the prior year. If there is a material difference, the auditor's working papers should explain the difference. In the second instance, this comparison of audited values may reveal some unusual items that have not been investigated and explained. Assuming that the difference between the auditor's expectation and the recorded amount is material, the auditor will have to perform additional audit work before an audit report can be issued.

Selected Financial Ratios Useful as Analytical Procedures

[LO 5]   A number of financial ratios are used by auditors as analytical procedures. These ratios are broken down into four categories: short-term liquidity, activity, profitability, and coverage ratios. Although the ratios discussed apply to most entities, auditors may also use other industry-specific ratios. As follows, each ratio is calculated for EarthWear Clothiers for the year ended December 31, 2000.

A few points are worth mentioning before the financial ratios are discussed. First, in many instances, the auditor may compare the client's ratios with industry averages (see Exhibit 5–4). While the industry averages serve as useful benchmarks, certain limitations should be recognized. Because the industry ratios are averages, they may not capture operating or geographical factors that may be specific to the client. The use of different accounting principles for valuing inventory or calculating depreciation may also result in differences from industry averages for certain ratios. Finally, the industry data may not be available in sufficient detail for a particular client. For example, if the auditor was looking for industry information on a company in the paging industry (see Problem 3–43, which includes Calabro Paging Services), such ratio data is combined with the telecommunications industry data.

Second, audit research has shown that material misstatements may not significantly affect certain ratios.[5] This is particularly true for activity ratios. Third, the auditor must be careful not to evaluate a financial ratio in isolation. In certain cases, a ratio may be favorable because its components are unfavorable. If related ratios are not examined, the auditor may draw an incorrect conclusion. For example, suppose that a client's days outstanding in accounts receivable is getting larger and the inventory turnover ratio is getting smaller. The negative trend in these ratios may indicate that accounts receivable are getting older and that some inventory may be obsolete. However, both of these factors positively affect the current ratio. If the auditor calculates only the current ratio, he or she may reach an incorrect conclusion about the entity's ability to meet current obligations.

Short-Term Liquidity Ratios

Short-term liquidity ratios indicate the entity's ability to meet its current obligations. Three ratios commonly used for this purpose are the *current ratio, quick* (or *acid test*) *ratio,* and the *operating cash flow ratio.*

Current Ratio   The current ratio is calculated as follows:

$$\text{Current ratio} = \frac{\text{Current assets}}{\text{Current liabilities}} = \frac{122,418}{65,505} = 1.87$$

It includes all current assets and current liabilities and is usually considered acceptable if it is 2 to 1 or better. Generally, a high current ratio indicates an entity's ability to pay current obligations. However, if current assets include old accounts receivable or obsolete inventory, this ratio can be distorted.

---

[5]See W. R. Kinney, Jr., "Attention-Directing Analytical Review Using Accounting Ratios: A Case Study," *Auditing: A Journal of Practice and Theory* (Spring 1987), pp. 59–73, for a discussion of this limitation of analytical procedures.

Quick Ratio   The quick ratio includes only assets that are most readily convertible to cash and is calculated as follows:

$$\text{Quick ratio} = \frac{\text{Liquid assets}}{\text{Current liabilities}} = \frac{(41{,}722 + 3{,}933)}{65{,}505} = .70$$

Thus, inventories and prepaid items are not included in the numerator of the quick ratio. The quick ratio may provide a better picture of the entity's liquidity position if inventory contains obsolete or slow-moving items. A ratio greater than 1 generally indicates that the entity's liquid assets are sufficient to meet the cash requirements for paying current liabilities.

Operating Cash Flow Ratio   The operating cash flow ratio measures the entity's ability to cover its current liabilities with cash generated from operations and is calculated as follows:

$$\text{Operating cash flow ratio} = \frac{\text{Cash flow from operations}}{\text{Current liabilities}} = \frac{54{,}807}{65{,}505} = .84$$

The operating cash flow ratio uses the cash flows as opposed to assets to measure short-term liquidity. It provides a longer-term measure of the entity's ability to meet its current liabilities. If cash flow from operations is small or negative, the entity will likely need alternative sources of cash, such as additional borrowings or sales of assets, to meet its obligations.

Activity Ratios

Activity ratios indicate how effectively the entity's assets are managed. Only ratios related to accounts receivable and inventory are discussed here because for most wholesale, retail, or manufacturing companies these two accounts represent the assets that have high activity. Activity ratios may also be effective in helping the auditor determine if these accounts contain material misstatements.

Receivables Turnover and Days Outstanding in Accounts Receivable   These two ratios provide information on the activity and age of accounts receivable. The receivables turnover ratio and days outstanding in accounts receivable are calculated as follows:

$$\text{Receivables turnover} = \frac{\text{Credit sales}}{\text{Receivables}} = \frac{503{,}434}{3{,}933} = 128.0$$

$$\text{Days outstanding in accounts receivable} = \frac{365 \text{ days}}{\text{Receivables turnover}} = 2.85 \text{ days}$$

The receivables turnover ratio indicates how many times accounts receivable are turned over during a year. However, the days outstanding in accounts receivable may be easier to interpret because this ratio can be compared to the client's terms of trade. For example, if an entity's terms of trade are 2/10, net/30, the auditor would expect that if management was doing a good job of managing receivables, the value for this ratio would be 30 days or less. If the auditor calculates the days outstanding to be 43 days, he or she might suspect that the account contains a material amount of bad debts. Comparing the days outstanding to industry data may be helpful in detecting a slowdown in payments by customers that is affecting the entire industry. EarthWear's ratio is 2.85 days because most sales are paid in cash or by credit card.

Inventory Turnover and Days of Inventory on Hand   These activity ratios provide information on the inventory and are calculated as follows:

$$\text{Inventory turnover} = \frac{\text{Cost of goods sold}}{\text{Inventory}} = \frac{274,126}{64,100} = 4.28$$

$$\text{Days of inventory on hand} = \frac{365 \text{ days}}{\text{Inventory turnover}} = 85.3 \text{ days}$$

Inventory turnover indicates the frequency with which inventory is consumed in a year. The higher the ratio, the better the entity is at liquidating inventory. This ratio can be easily compared to industry standards. Suppose that the auditor calculates the inventory turnover to be 4.7 times a year. If the industry average is 8.2 times a year, the auditor might suspect that inventory contains obsolete or slow-moving goods. The days of inventory on hand measures how much inventory the entity has available for sale to customers.

Profitability Ratios

Profitability ratios indicate the entity's success or failure for a given period. A number of ratios measure the profitability of an entity, and each ratio should be interpreted by comparison to industry data.

Gross Profit Percentage   The gross margin percentage ratio is generally a good indicator of potential misstatements and is calculated as follows:

$$\text{Gross profit percentage} = \frac{\text{Gross profit}}{\text{Net sales}} = \frac{229,308}{503,434} = 45.5\%$$

If this ratio varies significantly from previous years or differs significantly from industry data, the entity's financial data may contain errors. Numerous errors can affect this ratio. For example, if the client has failed to record sales, the gross profit percentage will be less than in previous years. Similarly, any errors that affect the inventory account can distort this ratio. For example, if the client has omitted goods from the ending inventory, this ratio will be smaller than in previous years.

Profit Margin   The profit margin ratio is calculated as follows:

$$\text{Profit margin} = \frac{\text{Net income}}{\text{Net sales}} = \frac{22,929}{503,434} = 4.5\%$$

While the gross profit percentage ratio measures profitability after cost of goods sold is deducted, the profit margin ratio measures the entity's profitability after all expenses are considered. Significant fluctuations in this ratio may indicate that misstatements exist in the selling, general, or administrative expense accounts.

Return on Assets This ratio is calculated as follows:

$$\text{Return on assets} = \frac{\text{Net income}}{\text{Total assets}} = \frac{22,929}{170,121} = 13.5\%$$

This ratio indicates the return earned on the resources invested by both the stockholders and the creditors.

Return on Equity The return on equity ratio is calculated as follows:

$$\text{Return on equity} = \frac{\text{Net income}}{\text{Stockholders' equity}} = \frac{22,929}{100,405} = 22.8\%$$

This ratio is similar to the return on assets ratio except that it shows only the return on the resources contributed by the stockholders.

Coverage Ratios

Coverage ratios provide information on the long-term solvency of the entity. These ratios give the auditor important information on the ability of the entity to continue as a going concern.

Debt to Equity This ratio is calculated as follows:

$$\text{Debt to equity} = \frac{\text{Short-term debt} + \text{Long-term debt}}{\text{Stockholders' equity}} = \frac{(65,505 + 297)}{100,405} = .655$$

This ratio indicates what portion of the entity's capital comes from debt. The lower the ratio, the less debt pressure on the entity. If the entity's debt to equity ratio is large relative to the industry's, it may indicate that the entity is too highly leveraged and may not be able to meet its debt obligations on a long-term basis.

Times Interest Earned This ratio is calculated as follows:

$$\text{Times interest earned} = \frac{\text{Net income} + \text{Interest expense}}{\text{Interest expense}}$$

$$= \frac{(22,929 + 230)}{230} = 100.7$$

The times interest earned ratio indicates the ability of current operations to pay the interest that is due on the entity's debt obligations. The more times that interest is earned, the better the entity's ability to service the interest on long-term debt.

REVIEW QUESTIONS

[LO 1] 5-1 In establishing the terms of the engagement, what topics should the auditor consider? AC, EL, IA

[1,2] 5-2 What is the purpose of an engagement letter? contract List the important information that the engagement letter should contain.

[1,2] 5-3 What factors should an external auditor use to assess the competence and objectivity of internal auditors?

[1,2] 5-4 What is an audit committee, and what are its responsibilities?

[2] 5-5 What is the objective of the audit plan?

[2] 5-6 List the matters an auditor should consider when developing an overall audit plan.

[2] 5-7 Discuss the knowledge an auditor must obtain about a client's business and industry and how that information can be gathered.

[2] 5-8 Distinguish between errors and fraud. Give two examples of each.

[2] 5-9 What is meant by the term *professional skepticism?*

[2,3] 5-10 During the conduct of an audit, information that indicates that a material misstatement may be present may be uncovered. If an auditor discovers a larger-than-expected number of differences in accounts receivable confirmations, what types of errors or fraud might have led to such differences?

[2,3] 5-11 Distinguish between illegal acts that are "direct and material" and those that are "material but indirect." List five circumstances that may indicate that an illegal act may have occurred.

[2] 5-12 List three audit procedures that may be used to identify transactions with related parties.

[3] 5-13 What are the two general types of audit tests? Define each type of audit test and give two examples.

[3,4] 5-14 Define *analytical procedures.*

[3,4] 5-15 What are the objectives for using analytical procedures at the planning stage of an audit?

[4,5] 5-16 List and discuss the four categories of financial ratios that are presented in the chapter.

MULTIPLE-CHOICE QUESTIONS FROM CPA EXAMINATIONS

[1,2] 5-17 An auditor who accepts an audit engagement and does *not* possess industry expertise pertaining to the business entity should
  a. Engage financial experts familiar with the nature of the business entity.
  b. Obtain knowledge of matters that relate to the nature of the entity's business.
  c. Refer a substantial portion of the audit to another CPA, who will act as the principal auditor.
  d. First inform management that an unqualified opinion cannot be issued.

[2] 5-18 Rogers & Co., CPAs, policies require that all members of the audit staff submit weekly time reports to the audit manager, who then

prepares a weekly summary work report regarding variance from budget for Rogers's review. This provides written evidence of Rogers & Co.'s professional concern regarding compliance with which of the following generally accepted auditing standards?

a. Quality control.

b. Due professional care.

c. Adequate review.

d. Adequate planning. *time budget part of Planning*

[1,2]   5-19   In using the work of a specialist, an understanding should exist among the auditor, the client, and the specialist as to the nature of the work to be performed by the specialist. Preferably, the understanding should be documented and would include all of the following *except*

a. The objectives and scope of the specialist's work.

b. The specialist's representations as to his or her relationship, if any, to the client.

c. The specialist's understanding of the auditor's corroborative use of the specialist's findings in relation to the representations in the financial statements.

d. A statement that the methods or assumptions to be used are *not* inconsistent with those used by the client.

[2]   5-20   Which of the following statements is correct concerning related-party transactions?

a. In the absence of evidence to the contrary, related-party transactions should be assumed to be outside the ordinary course of business.

b. An auditor should determine whether a particular transaction would have occurred if the parties had *not* been related.

c. An auditor should substantiate that related-party transactions were consummated on terms equivalent to those that prevail in arm's-length transactions.

book d. The audit procedures directed toward identifying related-party transactions should include considering whether transactions are occurring but are *not* being given proper accounting recognition.

[2]   5-21   When planning an examination, an auditor should

a. Consider whether the extent of substantive tests may be reduced based on the results of the internal control questionnaire. ✗

b. Make preliminary judgments about materiality levels for audit purposes.

c. Conclude whether changes in compliance with prescribed internal controls justify reliance on them. *can't conclude until tested*

d. Prepare a preliminary draft of the management representation letter. ✗

[2]   5-22   A difference of opinion regarding the results of a sample cannot be resolved between the assistant who performed the auditing procedures and the in-charge auditor. The assistant should

a. Refuse to perform any further work on the engagement.

b. Accept the judgment of the more experienced in-charge auditor.

c. Document the disagreement and ask to be disassociated from the resolution of the matter.

d. Notify the client that a serious audit problem exists.

[2] 5-23 Which of the following statements best describes an auditor's responsibility to detect errors and fraud?

a. The auditor should study and evaluate the client's internal control system and design the audit to provide reasonable assurance of detecting all errors and fraud.

b. The auditor should assess the risk that errors and fraud may cause the financial statements to contain material misstatements and determine whether the necessary internal controls are prescribed and are being followed satisfactorily. *won't detect*

c. The auditor should consider the types of errors and fraud that could occur and determine whether the necessary internal controls are prescribed and are being followed.

d. The auditor should assess the risk that errors and fraud may cause the financial statements to contain material misstatements and design the audit to provide reasonable assurance of detecting <u>material</u> errors and fraud.

[2] 5-24 Morris, CPA, suspects that a pervasive scheme of illegal bribes exists throughout the operations of Worldwide Import-Export, Inc., a new audit client. Morris has notified the audit committee and Worldwide's legal counsel, but neither could assist Morris in determining whether the amounts involved were material to the financial statements or whether senior management is involved in the scheme. Under these circumstances, Morris should

a. Express an unqualified opinion with a separate explanatory paragraph.

b. Disclaim an opinion on the financial statements.

c. Express an adverse opinion on the financial statements.

d. Issue a special report regarding the illegal bribes.

[2] 5-25 Which of these statements concerning illegal acts by clients is correct?

a. An auditor's responsibility to detect illegal acts that have a direct and material effect on the financial statements is the same as that for errors and fraud.

b. An audit in accordance with generally accepted auditing standards normally includes audit procedures specifically designed to detect illegal acts that have an indirect but material effect on the financial statements.

c. An auditor considers illegal acts from the perspective of the reliability of management's representations rather than their relation to audit objectives derived from financial statement assertions.

d. An auditor has *no* responsibility to detect illegal acts by clients that have an indirect effect on the financial statements.

[1,2,3] 5-26 Miller Retailing, Inc., maintains a staff of three full-time internal auditors who report directly to the controller. In planning to use the internal auditors to help in performing the audit, the independent auditor most likely will

a. Place limited reliance on the work performed by the internal auditors.

b. Decrease the extent of the tests of controls needed to support the assessed level of detection risk.

c. Increase the extent of the procedures needed to reduce control risk to an acceptable level.

d. Avoid using the work performed by the internal auditors.

[2,3,4]   5-27   An entity's financial statements were misstated over a period of years due to large amounts of revenue being recorded in journal entries that involved debits and credits to an illogical combination of accounts. The auditor could most likely have been alerted to this fraud by

a. Scanning the general journal for unusual entries.

b. Performing a revenue cutoff test at year-end.

c. Tracing a sample of journal entries to the general ledger.

d. Examining documentary evidence of sales returns and allowances recorded after year-end.

[3,4]   5-28   The primary objective of analytical procedures used in the final review stage of an audit is to

a. Obtain evidence from details tested to corroborate particular assertions.

b. Identify areas that represent specific risks relevant to the audit.

c. Assist the auditor in assessing the validity of the conclusions reached.

d. Satisfy doubts when questions arise about a client's ability to continue in existence.

[3,4,5]   5-29   To help plan the nature, timing, and extent of substantive auditing procedures, preliminary analytical procedures should focus on

a. Enhancing the auditor's understanding of the client's business and of events that have occurred since the last audit date.

b. Developing plausible relationships that corroborate anticipated results with a measurable amount of precision.

c. Applying ratio analysis to externally generated data such as published industry statistics or price indexes.

d. Comparing recorded financial information to the results of other tests of transactions and balances.

[4]   5-30   Which of the following factors would *least* influence an auditor's consideration of the reliability of data for purposes of analytical procedures?

a. Whether the data were processed in a computerized system or in a manual accounting system.

b. Whether sources within the entity were independent of those who are responsible for the amount being audited.

c. Whether the data were subjected to audit testing in the current or prior year.

d. Whether the data were obtained from independent sources outside the entity or from sources within the entity.

[3,4]   5-31   For all audits of financial statements made in accordance with generally accepted auditing standards, the use of analytical procedures is required to some extent

	In the Planning Stage	As a Substantive Test	In the Review Stage
a.	Yes	No	Yes
b.	No	Yes	No
c.	No	Yes	Yes
d.	Yes	No	No

PROBLEMS

[1,2]   5-32   Dodd, CPA, audited Adams Company's financial statements for the year ended December 31, 1999. On November 1, 2000, Adams notified Dodd that it was changing auditors and that Dodd's services were being terminated. On November 5, 2000, Adams invited Hall, CPA, to make a proposal for an engagement to audit its financial statements for the year ended December 31, 2000.

Required:
a. What procedures concerning Dodd should Hall perform before accepting the engagement?
b. What additional procedures should Hall consider performing during the planning phase of this audit (after accepting the engagement) that would *not* be performed during the audit of a continuing client?

(AICPA, adapted)

[1]   5-33   For many years the financial and accounting community has recognized the importance of the use of audit committees and has endorsed their formation. By now the use of audit committees has become widespread. Independent auditors have become increasingly involved with audit committees and consequently have become familiar with their nature and function.

Required:
a. Describe what an audit committee is.
b. Identify the reasons why audit committees have been formed and are currently in operation.
c. Describe the functions of an audit committee.

(AICPA, adapted)

[1,2]   5-34   The audit committee of the board of directors of Unicorn Corporation asked Tish & Field, CPAs, to audit Unicorn's financial statements for the year ended December 31, 2000. Tish & Field explained the need to make an inquiry of the predecessor auditor and requested permission to do so. Unicorn's management agreed and authorized the predecessor auditor to respond fully to Tish & Field's inquiries.

After a satisfactory communication with the predecessor auditor, Tish & Field drafted an engagement letter that was mailed to the audit committee of the board of directors of Unicorn Corporation. The engagement letter clearly set forth the arrangements concerning the involvement of the predecessor auditor and other matters.

Required:
a. What information should Tish & Field have obtained during their inquiry of the predecessor auditor prior to accepting the engagement?
b. What other matters would Tish & Field generally have included in the engagement letter?

(AICPA, adapted)

[1]   5-35 A CPA has been asked to audit the financial statements of a publicly held company for the first time. All preliminary verbal discussions and inquiries among the CPA, the company, the predecessor auditor, and all other necessary parties have been completed. The CPA is now preparing an engagement letter.

Required:
a. List the items that should be included in the typical engagement letter in these circumstances.
b. Describe the benefits derived from preparing an engagement letter.

(AICPA, adapted)

[2,3,4]   5-36 Parker is the in-charge auditor with administrative responsibilities for the upcoming annual audit of FGH Company, a continuing audit client. Parker will supervise two assistants on the engagement and will visit the client before the field work begins.

Parker has started the planning process by listing procedures to be performed prior to the beginning of field work. The list includes
1. Reviewing correspondence and permanent files.
2. Reviewing prior years' audit working papers, financial statements, and auditor's reports.
3. Discussing matters that may affect the examination with the CPA firm personnel responsible for providing audit and nonaudit services to the client.
4. Discussing with management current business developments affecting the client.

Required:
Complete Parker's list of procedures to be performed before the beginning of field work.

(AICPA, adapted)

[1,2,3]   5-37 Kent, CPA, is engaged in the audit of Davidson Corporation's financial statements for the year ended December 31, 2000. Kent is about to commence auditing Davidson's employee pension expense, but Kent's preliminary inquiries concerning Davidson's defined benefit pension plan lead Kent to believe that some of the actuarial computations and assumptions are so complex that they are beyond the competence ordinarily required of an auditor. Kent is considering engaging Park, an actuary, to assist with this portion of the audit.

Required:
a. What are the factors Kent should consider in the process of selecting Park?
b. What are the matters that should be understood among Kent, Park, and Davidson's management as to the nature of the work to be performed by Park?
c. May Kent refer to Park in the auditor's report if Kent decides to issue an unqualified opinion? Why?
d. May Kent refer to Park in the auditor's report if Kent decides to issue other than an unqualified opinion as a result of Park's findings? Why?

(AICPA, adapted)

[3,4,5]   5-38   Analytical procedures consist of evaluations of financial information made by a study of plausible relationships among both financial and nonfinancial data. They range from simple comparisons to the use of complex models involving many relationships and elements of data. They compare recorded amounts, or ratios developed from recorded amounts, to expectations developed by the auditor.

Required:
a. Describe the broad purposes of analytical procedures.
b. Identify the sources of information from which an auditor develops expectations.
c. Describe the factors that influence an auditor's consideration of the reliability of data for the purpose of achieving audit objectives.

(AICPA, adapted)

[3,4]   5-39   At December 31, 2000, EarthWear has $2,333,000 in a liability account labeled "Reserve for returns." The footnotes to the financial statements contain the following policy: "At the time of sale, the company provides a reserve equal to the gross profit on projected merchandise returns, based on prior returns experience." The client has indicated that returns for sales that are six months old are negligible, and gross profit percentage for the year is 45.5 percent. The client has also provided the following information on sales for the last six months of the year:

Month	Monthly Sales (000s)	Historical Return Rate
July	$37,247	.005
August	42,845	.008
September	49,247	.012
October	51,870	.015
November	60,490	.018
December	78,138	.028

Required:
a. Using the information given, develop an expectation for the reserve for returns account.
b. Compare your expectation to the book value and determine if it is greater than tolerable misstatement ($25,000) allocated to the reserve for returns account in Chapter 3.
c. Independent of your answer in part (b), what procedures should the auditor perform if the difference between the expectation and the book value is greater than tolerable misstatement?

[2]   5-40   Post, CPA, accepted an engagement to audit the financial statements of General Company, a new client. General is a publicly held retailing entity that recently replaced its operating management. In the course of applying auditing procedures, Post discovered that General's financial statements may be materially misstated due to the existence of fraud.

Required:
a. Describe Post's responsibilities regarding the circumstance described.

b. Describe Post's responsibilities to report on General's financial statements and other communications if Post is precluded from applying necessary procedures in searching for fraud.

c. Describe Post's responsibilities to report on General's financial statements and other communications if Post concludes that General's financial statements are materially affected by fraud.

d. Describe the circumstances in which Post may have a duty to disclose fraud to third parties outside General's management and its audit committee.

(AICPA, adapted)

[3]   5-41   Exhibit 5–3 contains a partial audit program for substantive tests of accounts receivable.

Required:

For audit procedures 1–4, identify the primary audit objective being tested.

[3,4,5]   5-42   Arthur, CPA, is auditing the RCT Manufacturing Company as of February 28, 2000. As with all engagements, one of Arthur's initial procedures is to make overall checks of the client's financial data by reviewing significant ratios and trends so that he better understands the business and can determine where to concentrate his audit efforts.

The financial statements prepared by the client with audited 1999 figures and preliminary 2000 figures are presented here in condensed form.

RCT MANUFACTURING COMPANY **Condensed Balance Sheets** **February 28, 2000 and 1999**		
Assets	**2000**	**1999**
Cash	$ 12,000	$ 15,000
Accounts receivable, net	93,000	50,000
Inventory	72,000	67,000
Other current assets	5,000	6,000
Plant and equipment, net of depreciation	60,000	80,000
	$242,000	$218,000
Equities		
Accounts payable	$ 38,000	$ 41,000
Federal income taxes payable	30,000	15,000
Long-term liabilities	20,000	40,000
Common stock	70,000	70,000
Retained earnings	84,000	52,000
	$242,000	$218,000

RCT MANUFACTURING COMPANY
Condensed Income Statements
Years Ended February 28, 2000 and 1999

	2000	1999
Net sales	$1,684,000	$1,250,000
Cost of goods sold	927,000	710,000
Gross margin on sales	$ 757,000	$ 540,000
Selling and administrative expenses	682,000	504,000
Income before federal income taxes	$ 75,000	$ 36,000
Income tax expense	30,000	14,400
Net income	$ 45,000	$ 21,600

Additional information:
- The company has only an insignificant amount of cash sales.
- The end-of-year figures are comparable to the average for each respective year.

Required:

For each year, compute the current ratio and a turnover ratio for accounts receivable. Based on these ratios, identify and discuss audit procedures that should be included in Arthur's audit of (1) accounts receivable and (2) accounts payable.

(AICPA, adapted)

DISCUSSION CASES

[2,3]   5-43   Forestcrest Woolen Mills is a closely held North Carolina company that has existed since 1920. The company manufactures high-quality woolen cloth for men's and women's outerwear. Your firm has audited Forestcrest for 15 years.

Five years ago, Forestcrest signed a consent decree with the North Carolina Environmental Protection Agency. The company had been convicted of dumping pollutants (such as bleaching and dyeing chemicals) into the local river. The consent decree provided that Forestcrest construct a water treatment facility within eight years.

You are conducting the current-year audit, and you notice that there has been virtually no activity in the water treatment facility construction account. Your discussion with the controller produces the following comment: "Because of increased competition and lower sales volume, our cash flow has decreased below normal levels. You had better talk to the president about the treatment facility."

The president (and majority shareholder) tells you the following: "Given the current cash flow levels, we had two choices: lay off people or stop work on the facility. This is a poor rural area of North Carolina with few other job opportunities for our people. I decided to stop work on the water treatment facility. I don't think that the state will fine us or close us down." When you ask the president if the company will be able to comply with the consent decree, he informs you that he is uncertain.

Required:
a. Discuss the implications of this situation for the audit and audit report.
b. Would your answer change if these events occurred in the seventh year after the signing of the consent decree?

[4,5]   5-44   Count d'Valeur Entertainment Shops is a chain of science-based toy and novelty stores owned and operated by two brothers from a family of native Iowans with a flamboyant lifestyle. Their business grew from one store in 1996 to 10 stores by the end of 1999. Their strategy is to offer the very latest in science (and science fiction) toys and novelties at low prices with aggressive sales tactics in their well-placed stores (all are in trendy shopping malls).

After a period of substantial growth, competition stiffened during 2000, and the brothers ceased their active expansion in order to tighten their controls over operations. They focused on inventory management and sought assistance from Alex and Louis, CPAs (their independent auditor), in redesigning their system. Management feels that this redesign succeeded because inventory was lower at year-end, resulting in substantially increased inventory turnover (based on ending inventories). Furthermore, management is proud that it has continued to realize its target of 100 percent markup on the cost of its merchandise.

The 1999 and 2000 audited consolidated income statements for Count d'Valeur are shown in Exhibit 1; a statement of store contributions to consolidated earnings is shown in Exhibit 2. The financial statements have been audited by Alex and Louis, CPAs, who gave them a standard three-paragraph audit report for both 1999 and 2000.

EXHIBIT 1

Audited Consolidated Earnings

COUNT D'VALEUR ENTERTAINMENT SHOPS
Summary of Consolidated Earnings
Years Ended April 30, 1999 and 2000 (in thousands)

		1999		2000
Sales		$106,893		$108,299
Cost of sales:				
Beginning inventory	$ 8,972		$ 9,953	
Purchases	54,727		52,986	
	$63,699		$62,939	
Ending inventory	9,953		8,445	
Cost of sales		53,746		54,494
Gross profit		$ 53,147		$ 53,805
Operating expenses (direct)		31,962		29,976
Net contribution of stores		$ 21,185		$ 23,829
Corporate expenses (total)		9,455		9,123
Net income		$ 11,730		$ 14,706

Notes:

1. Count d'Valeur Entertainment Shops is a Subchapter S corporation and is taxed as such under the Internal Revenue Code of 1954.

2. All inventories are valued at the lower of cost or market value. Cost is calculated using the first-in, first-out method.

EXHIBIT 2

Unaudited Contribution to Earnings by Store

COUNT D'VALEUR ENTERTAINMENT SHOPS
Net Contribution by Store
Year Ended April 30, 2000 (in thousands)

	Sales	Beginning Inventory	Purchases	Ending Inventory	Cost of Sales	Gross Profit	Operating Expenses	Net Contribution
Store 1	11,372	1,009	5,456	894	5,571	5,801	3,056	2,745
Store 2	10,990	982	5,370	688	5,664	5,326	2,996	2,330
Store 3	10,615	968	5,133	816	5,285	5,330	2,973	2,357
Store 4	12,052	979	5,938	966	5,951	6,101	3,126	2,975
Store 5	10,488	1,005	5,066	822	5,249	5,239	2,947	2,292
Store 6	11,653	980	5,806	918	5,868	5,785	3,092	2,693
Store 7	11,800	1,035	5,804	838	6,001	5,799	3,111	2,688
Store 8	10,995	1,016	5,468	901	5,583	5,412	3,007	2,405
Store 9	9,509	1,022	4,667	915	4,774	4,735	2,864	1,871
Store 10	8,825	957	4,278	687	4,548	4,277	2,804	1,473
Consolidated	$108,299	$9,953	$52,986	$8,445	$54,494	$53,805	$29,976	$23,829

Your client, We're Easy Money, Inc. (WEMI), is considering acquiring Count d'Valeur Entertainment Shops as of June 30, 2000. WEMI wants you to conduct a preacquisition review and inform it of any accounting or auditing problems. Due to the nature of the business, WEMI is especially concerned about the inventory. To facilitate negotiation of the sale, the brothers have given Alex and Louis permission to waive confidentiality and cooperate fully with you in answering questions about the company and their audit.

Your partner has met with the Alex and Louis partner in charge of the Count d'Valeur audit. Her notes are attached as Exhibit 3. You are to finish her work by evaluating her review as well as conducting analytical procedures that you believe proper.

Required:

a. Prepare a list of misstatements that might have occurred in inventory and cost of sales and, if they had occurred, how they would affect the account values and ratios of account values.

b. Develop expectations about the likely audited value of inventory and cost of sales at each store based on your overall knowledge.

c. Does inventory appear to be "materially" overstated at any store or in the aggregate? What additional investigation, if any, would you recommend?

EXHIBIT 3

Partner's Notes of Meeting with Alex and Louis and Her Review of Their Work Papers

Count d'Valeur's Inventory Procedures:

Purchasing: Accounting for purchasing is conducted at the firm's home office in Sioux City, Iowa, but store managers are allowed great discretion in ordering unique items that they believe will sell in their own stores. Thus, there is no common chainwide product list, and inventory is established on a physical or periodic basis.

Inventory quantities: To strengthen control and to allow its store personnel to concentrate on operations, Count d'Valeur relies on an independent inventory-counting firm to determine inventory quantities at each store. At fiscal year-end, the outside firm sends two count specialists to each store. Each specialist has a handheld computer designed for efficient recording of product codes and counts. Each specialist walks the aisles counting every product code item encountered. The count and item code are then entered into the handheld computer.

At the end of the counting process, the memory contents of each handheld computer are read into a PC program that matches the two sets of counts and identifies discrepancies. The two specialists locate the items in question, recount the stock, and enter a corrected amount. The PC then prepares a written inventory quantity summary for the store manager. It also prepares a diskette with the same information that is forwarded to the home office in Sioux City, Iowa.

Pricing and obsolescence: In Sioux City, the inventory quantities on the diskettes are matched by computer against purchase records to price the inventory at first-in, first-out cost. Items without purchase records are noted for follow-up to complete the purchase/accounts payable records. The extended amounts are then summarized and entered as the general ledger amounts. A lower-of-cost-or-market (LCM) assessment is made by calculating inventory turnover by product groupings summarized across stores. All items with more than four months' supply are then reviewed by one of the brothers to assess whether an accounting adjustment is needed and whether the store manager should be contacted to discuss the overstock problem.

Alex and Louis's Auditing Procedures:

Alex and Louis's auditors reviewed Count d'Valeur's internal controls over inventory and were satisfied that they were well designed. The auditors arranged with Count d'Valeur management to observe the outside count team procedures at stores 2 and 7. Also at both locations, Alex and Louis auditors randomly selected a substantial number of items, independently counted them,

E X H I B I T 3 (concluded)

and noted the counts in their work papers. They observed no exceptions in procedure by the outside count personnel and only inconsequential quantity differences when their own counts were traced and compared with those in the final inventory summary that supported the Count d'Valeur financial statements. During their store visit, Alex and Louis's auditors also looked for out-of-the-way, musty, or dusty inventory and found none. This was followed by a testing of the "months' supply on hand" calculation that Count d'Valeur personnel made at the home office. They were satisfied that the LCM adjustment was adequate.

Alex and Louis conducted overall analytical procedures by comparing the Count d'Valeur balances and ratios with those for toy and novelty stores nationwide. Their comparison revealed that Count d'Valeur has lower merchandise markup percentages than 80 percent of the industry but has been able to maintain its gross profit rate during 2000 while the industry average has fallen by about 1.5 percent. Also, median inventory turnover for the industry has risen from 4.5 to 4.8 over the same period.

(Adapted and used with permission of W. R. Kinney, Jr.)

INTERNET ASSIGNMENTS

[2] 5-45 EarthWear Clothiers makes high-quality clothing for outdoor sports. It sells most of its products through mail order. Use the Internet to obtain information about the retail mail order industry.

[3,4,5] 5-46 Using the information from the text, EarthWear Clothiers' home page (www.mhhe.com/earthwear), and Willis & Adams's home page (www.mhhe.com/willisandadams) prepare an audit planning memo. In preparing the memo, include information on each of the following items:

- Obtain knowledge of the client's business and industry.
- Establish audit risk and materiality (refer to Chapter 3), and assess inherent risk (cite all important factors and their possible effects on the audit).
- Assess a preliminary level of control risk (limit the assessment to the control environment and order entry).
- Assess the possibility of errors, fraud (refer to SAS No. 82), and illegal acts.
- Conduct preliminary analytical procedures, including industry data.

[2] 5-47 Visit the Institute of Internal Auditors (IIA) home page (www.theiia.org) and familiarize yourself with the information contained there. Search the site for information about the IIA's requirements for the objectivity and independence of internal auditors.

SCAD ASSIGNMENT

Assignment 3 can be completed at this point. It requires an assessment of inherent risk and materiality. It also requires the computation and documentation of analytical procedures for Southwest Appliances.

Internal Control in a Financial Statement Audit

LEARNING OBJECTIVES

Upon completion of this chapter you will

[1] Understand the importance of internal control to management and auditors.

[2] Identify the components of internal control.

[3] Learn how to plan an audit strategy.

[4] Learn how to develop an understanding of an entity's internal control.

[5] Identify the tools available for documenting the understanding of internal control.

[6] Learn the types of tests of controls.

[7] Know how to assess and document the level of control risk.

[8] Understand audit strategies for the nature, timing, and extent of substantive tests based on different levels of detection risk.

[9] Understand the considerations for the timing of audit procedures.

[10] Learn about the auditor's communication of internal control–related matters.

[11] Learn how to flowchart an accounting cycle.

RELEVANT ACCOUNTING AND AUDITING PRONOUNCEMENTS

COSO, *Internal Control—Integrated Framework* (New York: AICPA, 1992)

SAS No. 22, "Planning and Supervision" (AU 311)

SAS No. 47, "Audit Risk and Materiality in Conducting an Audit" (AU 312)

SAS No. 55, "Consideration of Internal Control in a Financial Statement Audit" (AU 319)

SAS No. 56, "Analytical Procedures" (AU 329)

SAS No. 60, "Communication of Internal Control–Related Matters Noted in an Audit" (AU 325)

SAS No. 65, "The Auditor's Consideration of the Internal Audit Function in an Audit of Financial Statements" (AU 322)

SAS No. 70, "Reports on the Processing of Transactions by Service Organizations" (AU 324)

SAS No. 78, "Consideration of Internal Control in a Financial Statement Audit: An Amendment to SAS No. 55 (AU 319)

SAS No. 87, "Restricting the Use of an Auditor's Report" (AU 532)

Chapter 3 identified control risk as a component of the audit risk model. Additionally, Chapter 5 cited assessing of control risk as a major step in the auditor's planning activities. This chapter provides detailed coverage of the auditor's assessment of control risk. It addresses the importance of internal control and its components, as well as how evaluating internal control relates to substantive testing. It also discusses the timing of audit procedures and the required communications of internal control–related matters. 🌊

Internal Control

Definition of Internal Control

[LO 1]

Internal control is a process effected by an entity's board of directors, management, and other personnel that is designed to provide reasonable assurance regarding the achievement of objectives in the following categories: (1) effectiveness and efficiency of operations, (2) reliability of financial reporting, and (3) compliance with applicable laws and regulations.

While an entity's internal controls address objectives in each category, not all of these objectives and their related internal controls are relevant to a financial statement audit. Generally, internal controls pertaining to the preparation of financial statements for external use are relevant to an audit. For example, controls that relate to the safeguarding of assets are relevant because omitting assets will result in misstated financial statements. Other controls may be relevant when they relate to data the auditor uses to apply auditing procedures. For example, the internal controls that relate to operating or production statistics may be utilized by the auditor as nonfinancial data for analytical procedures. On the other hand, some controls that relate to management's planning or operating decisions may not be relevant for audit purposes. For example, controls related to issues such as product design or production locations are not likely to be relevant to a financial statement audit.

Management's Perspective

From management's perspective, the internal control system provides a way to meet its stewardship or agency responsibilities. For example, management must maintain controls that provide reasonable assurance that adequate control exists over the entity's assets and records. This can be accomplished by developing internal controls that require employees to follow corporate policies and procedures such as proper authorization for transactions. Such an internal control system not only ensures that assets and records are safeguarded but also creates an environment in which efficiency and effectiveness are encouraged and monitored. This is becoming more important as entities automate their information systems and operate more globally.

Management also needs a control system that generates reliable information for decision making. If the information system does not generate reliable information, management may be unable to make informed decisions about issues such as product pricing, cost of production, and profit information. In summary, management has numerous incentives for establishing and maintaining a strong system of internal controls.

The Auditor's Perspective

The importance of internal control to the auditor is rooted in the second standard of field work, which states

A sufficient understanding of internal control is to be obtained to plan the audit and to determine the nature, timing, and extent of tests to be performed.

The controls that are relevant to the entity's ability to record, process, summarize, and report financial data consistent with management's assertions (existence or occurrence, completeness, rights and obligations, valuation or allocation, and presentation and disclosure) are the auditor's main concern. More specifically, the auditor needs assurance about the reliability of the data generated within the internal control system in terms of how it affects the fairness of the financial statements and how well the assets and records of the entity are safeguarded.

As we shall see in this chapter, the auditor's understanding of internal controls is a major factor in determining the overall audit strategy. The auditor's responsibilities for internal control are discussed under two major topics: (1) the components of internal control and (2) the auditor's consideration of internal control in planning and performing an audit.

The Components of Internal Control

[LO 2]   An entity's internal control consists of five interrelated components:

- Control environment
- Risk assessment
- Control activities
- Information and communication
- Monitoring

Partitioning internal control into these five components provides a useful framework for auditors to consider the impact of an entity's internal control on an audit. In planning the audit, the auditor should obtain an understanding of these five components of internal control sufficient to plan the audit by performing procedures to understand the design of controls relevant to the preparation of financial statements and whether they have been placed in operation.

Control Environment

The control environment sets the tone of an organization, influencing the control consciousness of its people. It is the foundation for all other components of internal control, providing discipline and structure. Factors that affect the control environment are shown in Table 6–1. Note that Table 3–2 listed a number of risk factors that can affect the control environment. This reinforces the discussion in that chapter about the interrelationship between inherent risk and control risk.

TABLE 6–1	Factors Affecting the Control Environment

- Integrity and ethical values.
- A commitment to competence.
- Participation of the board of directors or audit committee.
- Management's philosophy and operating style.
- Organizational structure.
- Assignment of authority and responsibility.
- Human resource policies and practices.

The importance of control to an entity is reflected in the overall attitude to, awareness of, and actions of the board of directors, management, and owners regarding control. The control environment can be thought of as an umbrella that covers the entire entity and establishes the framework for implementing the entity's accounting systems and internal controls.

Integrity and Ethical Values   The effectiveness of an entity's internal controls is a function of the integrity and ethical values of the individuals who create, administer, and monitor the controls. An entity needs to establish ethical and behavioral standards that are communicated to employees and are reinforced by day-to-day practice. For example, management should remove incentives or temptations that might lead personnel to engage in dishonest, illegal, or unethical acts. Some examples of incentives that may lead to unethical behavior are pressures to meet unrealistic performance targets and high performance-dependent rewards. Examples of temptations include an ineffective board of directors, a weak internal audit function, and insignificant penalties for improper behavior. Management can best communicate integrity and ethical behavior within an entity through the use of policy statements and codes of conduct.

A Commitment to Competence   Competence is the knowledge and skills necessary to accomplish the tasks that define an individual's job. Conceptually, management must specify the competence level for a particular job and translate it into the required level of knowledge and skills. For example, an entity should have a formal or informal job description for each job. Management then must hire employees who have the appropriate competence for their jobs. Good human resource policies (discussed later in this section) help to attract and retain competent and trustworthy employees.

Participation of the Board of Directors or Audit Committee[1]
The board of directors and its audit committee significantly influence the control consciousness of the entity. As mentioned in Chapter 5, the audit committee is a subcommittee of the board of directors that is normally composed of directors who are not part of the management team. The board of directors and the audit committee must take their fiduciary responsibilities seriously and actively oversee the entity's accounting and reporting policies and procedures. Factors that affect the effectiveness of the board or audit committee include the following:

- Its independence from management.
- The experience and stature of its members.
- The extent of its involvement with and scrutiny of the entity's activities.
- The appropriateness of its actions.

---

[1]See Deloitte & Touche LLP, *Audit Committees—A Pivotal Role* (Wilton, CT: Deloitte & Touche LLP, 1995), for a detailed discussion of the changing corporate governance of audit committees.

- The degree to which difficult questions are raised and pursued with management.
- Its interaction with the internal and external auditors.

Management's Philosophy and Operating Style   Establishing, maintaining, and monitoring the entity's internal controls are management's responsibility. Management's philosophy and operating style may significantly affect the quality of internal control. Characteristics such as the following may signal important information to the auditor about management's philosophy and operating style:

- Management's approach to taking and monitoring business risks.
- Management's attitudes and actions toward financial reporting (conservative or aggressive selection from available alternative accounting principles and the conscientiousness and conservatism with which accounting estimates are developed).
- Management's attitudes toward information processing and accounting functions and personnel.

Organizational Structure   The organizational structure defines how authority and responsibility are delegated and monitored. It provides a *framework* for planning, executing, controlling, and monitoring operations. Establishing a relevant organizational structure includes considering key areas of authority and responsibility and appropriate lines of reporting.

   An entity develops an organizational structure that depends on its size and the nature of its business. Factors such as the level of technology in the entity's industry and external influences such as regulation play a major role in the type of organizational structure used. For example, an entity in a high-technology industry may need an organizational structure that can respond quickly to technological changes in the marketplace. Similarly, an entity that operates in a highly regulated industry, such as banking, may be required to maintain a very tightly controlled organizational structure in order to comply with federal or state laws.

Assignment of Authority and Responsibility   This control environment factor includes *how* authority and responsibility for operating activities are assigned and *how* reporting relationships and authorization hierarchies are established. It includes the policies regarding acceptable business practices, the knowledge and experience of key personnel, and the resources provided for carrying out duties. It also includes policies and communications directed at ensuring that all personnel understand the entity's objectives, know how their individual actions interrelate and contribute to those objectives, and recognize how and for what they will be held accountable.

   An entity can use a number of controls to meet the requirements of this control environment factor. First, the entity can have a well-specified organizational chart that indicates the lines of authority and responsibility. Second, management and supervisory personnel should have job descriptions that include their control-related responsibilities.

Human Resource Policies and Procedures   The quality of internal control is a direct function of the quality of the personnel operating the system. The entity should have sound personnel policies for hiring, training, evaluating, counseling, promoting, compensating, and taking remedial action. For example, in hiring employees, standards that emphasize seeking the most qualified individuals, with emphasis on educational background, prior work experience, and evidence of integrity and ethical behavior, demonstrate an entity's commitment to employing competent and trustworthy people. Research into the causes of errors in accounting systems has shown personnel-related issues to be a major cause of error.[2]

Risk Assessment

An entity's risk assessment for financial reporting is the identification, analysis, and management of risks relevant to the preparation of financial statements that are fairly presented in conformity with GAAP. This risk assessment process should consider external and internal events and circumstances that may arise and adversely affect the entity's ability to record, process, summarize, and report financial data consistent with the assertions of management in the financial statements. Client business risks can arise or change due to the following circumstances:

- *Changes in the operating environment.* Changes in the regulatory or operating environment can alter competitive pressures and create significantly different risks.
- *New personnel.* New personnel may have a different focus on or understanding of internal control.
- *New or revamped information systems.* Significant and rapid changes in information systems can change the risk relating to internal control.
- *Rapid growth.* Significant and rapid expansion of operations can strain controls and increase the risk of a breakdown of controls.
- *New technology.* Incorporating new technologies into production processes or information systems may change the risk associated with internal control.
- *New lines, products, or activities.* Entering business areas or transactions with which an entity has little experience may introduce new risk associated with internal control.
- *Corporate restructuring.* Restructuring may be accompanied by staff reductions and changes in supervision and segregation of duties that may change the risk associated with internal control.
- *Foreign operations.* The expansion or acquisition of foreign operations carries new and often unique risks that may impact internal control.
- *Accounting pronouncements.* Adopting new accounting principles or changing accounting principles may affect the risk involved in preparing financial statements.

---

[2]For example, see A. Wright and R. H. Ashton, "Identifying Audit Adjustments with Attention-Directing Procedures," *The Accounting Review* (October 1989), pp. 710–28. This study indicates that approximately 55 percent of the errors detected by auditors resulted from personnel problems, insufficient accounting knowledge, and judgment errors.

Control Activities

Control activities are the policies and procedures that help ensure that necessary actions are taken to address the risks involved in achieving the entity's objectives. Control activities that are relevant to the audit include

- Performance reviews
- Information processing
- Physical controls
- Segregation of duties

Performance Reviews   A strong accounting system should have controls that independently check the performance of the individuals or processes in the system. Some examples include comparing actual performance with budgets, forecasts, and prior-period performance; investigating the relationship of operating and financial data followed by analysis, investigation of unexpected differences, and corrective actions; and reviewing functional or activity performance.

Information Processing   There are two broad categories of information systems control activities: general controls and application controls. *General controls* relate to the overall information processing environment and include controls over data center operations, system software acquisition and maintenance, access security, and application system development and maintenance. For example, an entity's controls for developing new programs for existing accounting systems should include adequate documentation and testing before implementation.

Application controls apply to the processing of individual applications and help to ensure the completeness and accuracy of transaction processing, authorization, and validity. Two examples are (1) the entity should have controls that ensure that each transaction that occurs in an entity's accounting system is properly authorized and (2) the entity should design documents and records so that all relevant information is captured in the accounting system.

General and application controls are covered in more detail in Chapter 7.

Physical Controls   These controls include the physical security of assets. Physical controls include adequate safeguards, such as secured facilities, authorization for access to computer programs and data files, and periodic counting of assets such as inventory and comparison to control records.

Segregation of Duties   It is important for an entity to segregate the authorization of transactions, recording of transactions, and custody of the related assets. Independent performance of each of these functions reduces the opportunity for any one person to be in a position to both perpetrate and conceal errors or fraud in the normal course of his or her duties. Two examples will help to demonstrate the importance of good segregation of duties. First, if an employee can authorize the sale of marketable securities and has access to the stock certificates, the assets can be misappropriated. Second, if an employee receives payment from customers on account and has access to the accounts receivable subsidiary ledger, it is possible for that employee to misappropriate the cash and cover the shortage in the accounting records.

Information and Communication

The information system relevant to the financial reporting objectives, which includes the accounting system, consists of methods and records established to record, process, summarize, and report an entity's transactions and to maintain accountability for the related assets and liabilities. An effective accounting system gives appropriate consideration to establishing methods and records that will

- Identify and record all valid transactions.
- Describe on a timely basis the transactions in sufficient detail to permit proper classification of transactions for financial reporting.
- Measure the value of transactions in a manner that permits recording their proper monetary value in the financial statements.
- Determine the time period in which transactions occurred to permit recording of transactions in the proper accounting period.
- Properly present the transactions and related disclosures in the financial statements.

A careful examination of these characteristics of an effective information system reveals a direct relationship with audit objectives. Later in this chapter, the audit objectives for internal control are discussed. The basis for such objectives comes from these characteristics.

Communication involves providing an understanding of individual roles and responsibilities pertaining to internal control over financial reporting. It includes the extent to which personnel understand how their activities in the financial reporting information system relate to the work of others and the means of reporting exceptions to an appropriate higher level within the entity. Policy manuals, accounting and reporting manuals, and memoranda communicate policies and procedures to the entity's personnel. Communications can also be made orally or through the actions of management.

Monitoring

To provide reasonable assurance that an entity's objectives will be achieved, management should monitor internal control to determine whether it is operating as intended and that it is modified as appropriate for changes in conditions. Monitoring is a process that assesses the quality of internal control over time. It involves appropriate personnel assessing the design and operation of controls on a timely basis and taking necessary action.

Monitoring can be done through ongoing activities or separate evaluations. Ongoing monitoring procedures are built into the normal, recurring activities of the entity and include regular management and supervisory activities. For example, production managers at the corporate or divisional levels of an entity can monitor operations at lower levels by reviewing activity reports and questioning reported activity that differs significantly from their knowledge of the operations.

Management uses internal auditors or personnel performing similar functions to monitor the operating effectiveness and efficiency of internal controls. An effective internal audit function has clear lines of authority and reporting, qualified personnel, and adequate resources to enable these personnel to carry out their assigned duties. The presence of a strong internal audit function strengthens the control environment.

The Effect of Entity Size on Internal Control

The size of an entity may affect how the various components of internal control are implemented. While large entities may be able to implement the components in the fashion just described, small to midsize entities may use alternative approaches that may not adversely affect their internal control. One of the control environment factors that might differ between small and large entities is the use of a written code of conduct. While a large entity may have a written code of conduct, a small or midsize entity may not. However, a small entity may develop a culture that emphasizes integrity and ethical behavior through oral communication and the example of the owner-manager.

While the basic concepts of the risk assessment, control activities, and information and communication components should be present in all entities, they are likely to be less formal in a small or midsize entity than in a large entity. For example, in a small entity, the owner-manager's involvement in day-to-day activities can provide a highly effective control that identifies risks that may affect the entity and monitors activities. A small entity can also have effective communication channels due to its size, the fact that there are fewer levels in the organizational hierarchy, and management's greater visibility. The monitoring component can also be effective in a small to midsize entity as a result of management's close involvement in operations. For example, the owner may review all daily cash disbursements to ensure that only authorized payments are made to vendors. By being involved in day-to-day operations, management may be better able to identify variances from expectations and inaccuracies in financial data.

The Limitations of an Entity's Internal Control

An internal control system should be designed and operated to provide reasonable assurance that an entity's objectives are being achieved. The concept of reasonable assurance recognizes that the cost of an entity's internal control system should not exceed the benefits that are expected to be derived. The necessity of balancing the cost of controls with the related benefits requires considerable estimation and judgment on the part of management. The effectiveness of any internal control system is subject to certain inherent limitations, including management override of internal control, personnel errors or mistakes, and collusion. For example, in a recent survey by KPMG (see Figure 6–1), management override and collusion were reasons why fraud occurred in many companies.

Management Override of Internal Control   An entity's controls may be overridden by management. For example, a senior-level manager can require a lower-level employee to record entries in the accounting records that are not consistent with the substance of the transactions and

FIGURE 6–1

Reasons Why Fraud
Occurred

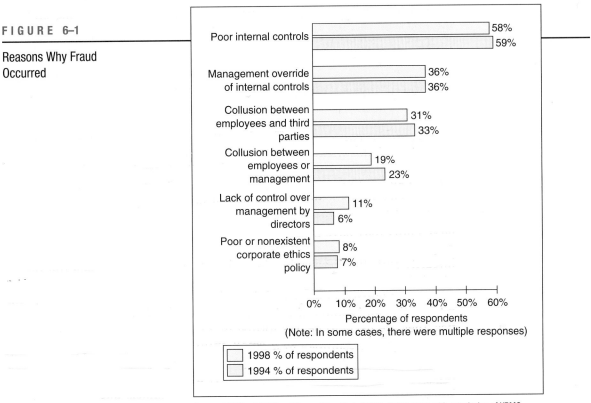

Source: KPMG, *1998 Fraud Survey* (New York: KPMG, 1998). Used with permission of KPMG.

violate the entity's controls. The lower-level employee may record the transaction, even though he or she knows that it violates the entity's controls, out of fear of losing his or her job.

The auditor is particularly concerned when senior management is involved in such activities because it raises serious questions about management's integrity. Violations of control procedures by senior management, however, may be difficult to detect with normal audit procedures.

Personnel Errors or Mistakes   The internal control system is only as effective as the personnel who implement and perform the controls. For example, employees may misunderstand instructions or make errors of judgment. Employees may also make mistakes because of personal carelessness, distraction, or fatigue. The auditor should carefully consider the quality of the entity's personnel when evaluating internal control.

Collusion   The effectiveness of segregation of duties lies in individuals' performing only their assigned tasks or in the performance of one person being checked by another. There is always a risk that collusion between individuals will destroy the effectiveness of segregation of duties. For example, an individual who receives cash receipts from customers can collude with the one who records those receipts in the customers' records in order to steal cash from the entity.

Consideration of Internal Control in Planning and Performing an Audit

The audit risk model states that $AR = IR \times CR \times DR$. In applying the audit risk model, the auditor must assess control risk. How the auditor assesses *CR* is described in the remainder of this chapter. Figure 6–2 presents a flowchart of the auditor's decision process when considering internal control in planning an audit. The following sections discuss the various steps in this decision process.

Planning an Audit Strategy

[LO 3]

Overview   As shown in Figure 6–2, the auditor's initial step is obtaining a preliminary understanding of internal control. With a recurring engagement, the auditor is likely to possess substantial knowledge about the client's internal control system. In that case, the auditor may be able to choose an audit strategy that includes little updating of the understanding of the entity's internal control system. For a new client, the auditor may delay making a judgment about an audit strategy until a more detailed understanding of internal control is obtained.

The auditor can choose from two audit strategies: a *no-reliance*, or *substantive, strategy* and a *reliance strategy*. However, there is no one audit strategy for the entire audit; rather the auditor establishes a strategy for individual accounting cycles (such as revenue or purchasing) or by specific assertion or audit objective (validity, valuation, and so on) within a cycle.

Substantive Strategy   Following the left-hand side of Figure 6–2, the auditor first obtains an understanding of internal control sufficient to plan a substantive audit approach. A substantive audit approach means that the auditor has decided not to rely on the entity's controls and to directly audit the related financial statement accounts. The auditor next documents the understanding of internal control, sets control risk at the maximum, and documents the control risk assessment. Finally, substantive tests are designed and performed based on the assessment of a maximum level of control risk.

Reliance Strategy   Following the right-hand side of Figure 6–2, the auditor first obtains an understanding of internal control as the basis for assessing a level of control risk that is less than the maximum. The reliance strategy requires a more detailed understanding of internal control than the substantive strategy does because the auditor intends to rely on the controls. The auditor next documents his or her understanding of internal control and plans and performs tests of controls. Control risk is then assessed based on the results of the tests. If the assessed level of control risk does not support the planned level of control risk, the planned substantive tests are revised. If the planned level of control risk is supported, no revisions of the planned substantive tests are required. The assessed level of control risk is

FIGURE 6–2

Flowchart of the Auditor's Consideration of Internal Control and Its Relation to Substantive Tests

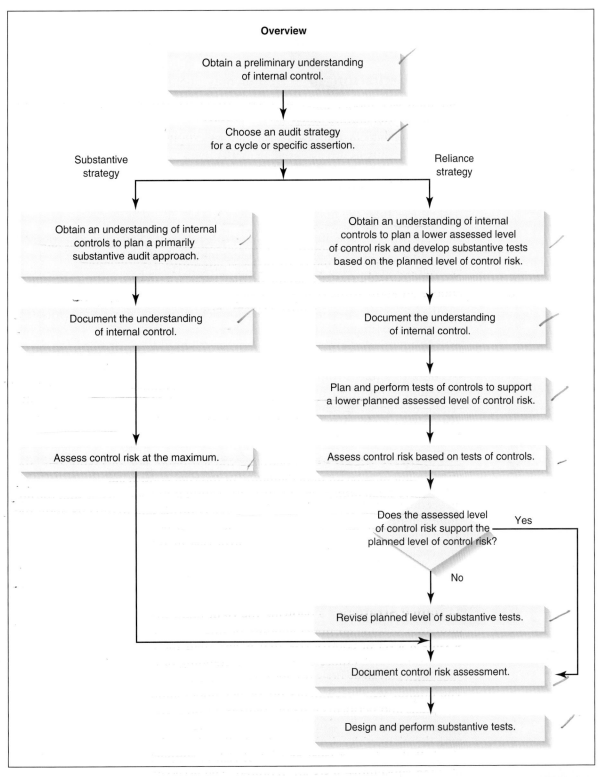

documented, and substantive tests are designed and performed. If the planned level of control risk is not supported, the auditor normally increases the planned substantive tests and documents the revised control risk assessment. The reader should remember that there may be different degrees of reliance for different accounting cycles or audit objectives within a cycle.

Implementation   The auditor may decide to follow a substantive strategy and set control risk at the maximum for some or all assertions because of one or all of the following factors:

- The controls do not pertain to an assertion.
- The controls are assessed as ineffective.
- Evaluating the effectiveness of controls is inefficient.

The auditor's decision to follow a reliance strategy and assess control risk at less than the maximum involves

- Identifying specific internal controls relevant to specific assertions that are likely to prevent or detect material misstatements.
- Testing controls to evaluate their effectiveness.

Assessing control risk at less than the maximum implies that the internal controls are effective in preventing, or detecting and correcting, misstatements in the financial statements.

As mentioned previously, control risk should be assessed for an accounting cycle or for relevant assertions or audit objectives related to an accounting cycle. From a practical standpoint, control risk is normally assessed in terms of the audit objectives that relate to the relevant assertions. Table 6–2 lists the internal control objectives. Each of these objectives is identical, or similar, to the audit objectives used for testing account balances that were discussed in Chapter 4. The only exception is the disclosure objective, which applies only to account balances. Table 6–3 shows the relationship between these two sets of audit objectives.

Table 6–4 shows the internal control objectives and the basic control procedures that are normally in place for each objective to protect against material misstatements. For example, the use of prenumbered documents that are accounted for is a basic control procedure found in each accounting cycle to ensure validity and completeness. In a revenue cycle, prenum-

TABLE 6–2	Internal Control Objectives
Validity	All transactions processed are valid.
Completeness	All transactions are included.
Timeliness	All transactions are recorded on a timely basis.
Authorization	All transactions are properly authorized.
Valuation	All transactions are properly valued.
Classification	All transactions are classified into the proper account.
Posting and summarization	All transactions are properly recorded in journals and properly posted in special and general journals.

bered shipping documents that are normally accounted for provide reasonable assurance that all revenue is recorded. Similarly, reconciliation of the accounts receivable subledger to the general ledger accounts receivable provides a control to ensure proper posting and summarization. Later chapters show these basic control procedures for each accounting cycle.

TABLE 6–3   The Relationship between Internal Control Objectives and Audit Objectives

Internal Control Objective	Audit Objective	Discussion
Validity	Validity	Identical relationship.
Completeness	Completeness	Identical relationship.
Timeliness	Cutoff	Similar relationship. Timeliness ensures that transactions are recorded in the accounting system on a timely basis. Cutoff ensures that the transactions are recorded in the proper period.
Authorization	Ownership	Limited relationship. Authorization relates to approval of transactions, including the acquisition of assets. Ownership relates to an ownership right in the asset.
Valuation	Valuation	Identical relationship.
Classification	Classification	Identical relationship.
Posting and summarization	Accuracy	Identical relationship.
	Disclosure	Internal control provides little or no assurance that proper financial statement disclosures will be made.

TABLE 6–4   Internal Control Objectives and Basic Control Procedures

Internal Control Objective	Basic Control Procedures
Validity	• Segregation of duties. • Prenumbered documents that are accounted for. • Daily or monthly reconciliation of subsidiary records with independent review.
Completeness	• Prenumbered documents that are accounted for. • Segregation of duties. • Daily or monthly reconciliation of subsidiary records with independent review.
Timeliness	• Procedures for prompt recording of transactions. • Internal review and verification.
Authorization	• General and specific authorization at important control points.
Valuation	• Internal verification of amounts and calculations.
Classification	• Chart of accounts. • Internal review and verification.
Posting and summarization	• Segregation of duties. • Monthly reconciliation of subsidiary records by an independent person. • Internal review and verification.

Understanding Internal Control

[LO 4]

The auditor must understand the entity's internal control in order to plan the financial statement audit. This understanding includes knowledge about the design of relevant internal controls and whether they have been placed in operation by the entity. This knowledge is used to

- Identify the types of potential misstatements.
- Determine control risk, which in turn affects detection risk.
- Assist in the design of substantive tests.

In deciding on the *nature* and *extent* of the understanding of internal control needed for the engagement, the auditor should also consider the following items:

- Knowledge from previous audits.
- Understanding of the entity's industry.
- Assessment of inherent risk.
- Judgments about materiality.
- The complexity and sophistication of the entity's operations and systems.

Each of these items needs to be considered explicitly when the auditor is examining a client's internal control. For example, the auditor will devote more attention to understanding internal control as the complexity and sophistication of the entity's operations and systems increase. If an entity utilizes sophisticated data processing techniques, the auditor may find it necessary to follow a reliance strategy.

To properly understand a client's internal control, an auditor must understand the five components of internal control (control environment, risk assessment, control activities, information and communication, and monitoring). The main difference between the reliance and substantive audit strategies, in terms of the understanding of internal control, is the *extent* of required knowledge about each of the components; a greater understanding is normally required if a reliance strategy is followed.

Understanding the Control Environment   The auditor should learn enough about the control environment to understand management's and the board of directors' attitude, awareness, and actions concerning the control environment, considering both the substance of controls and their collective effect. This includes knowledge of the factors contained in Table 6–1. Exhibit 6–1 presents a questionnaire that includes the type of information the auditor would document about EarthWear's control environment (see Problem 6–42 for additional information). The auditor should concentrate on the substance of controls rather than on their form because controls may be established but not acted on. For example, management may establish formal conflict-of-interest policies but seldom follow up on whether employees are really complying with these policies.

Understanding Risk Assessment   The auditor should obtain sufficient information about the entity's risk assessment process to understand how management considers risks relevant to financial reporting objectives and decides what to do to address those risks. For example, suppose a

EXHIBIT 6–1

Address: http://www.mhhe.com/messier

A Partial Questionnaire for Documenting the Auditor's Understanding of the Control Environment

CONTROL ENVIRONMENT QUESTIONNAIRE

Client: EarthWear Clothiers	**Balance Sheet Date:** 12/31/2000
Completed by: *SAA* **Date:** *9/30/00*	**Reviewed by:** *DRM* **Date:** *10/15/00*

INTEGRITY AND ETHICAL VALUES

The effectiveness of controls cannot rise above the integrity and ethical values of the people who create, administer, and monitor them. Integrity and ethical values are essential elements of the control environment, affecting the design, administration, and monitoring of other components. Integrity and ethical behavior are the product of the entity's ethical and behavioral standards, how they are communicated, and how they are reinforced in practice.

	Yes, No, N/A	Comments
Have appropriate entity policies regarding such matters as acceptable business practices, conflicts of interest, and codes of conduct been established, and are they adequately communicated?	Yes	*The permanent work papers contain a copy of EarthWear's conflict-of-interest policy.*
Does management demonstrate the appropriate "tone at the top," including explicit moral guidance about what is right or wrong?	Yes	*EarthWear's management maintains high moral and ethical standards and expects employees to act accordingly.*
Are everyday dealings with customers, suppliers, employees, and other parties based on honesty and fairness?	Yes	*EarthWear's management maintains a high degree of integrity in dealing with customers, suppliers, employees, and other parties; it requires employees and agents to act accordingly.*
Does management document or investigate deviations from established controls?	Yes	*To our knowledge, management has not attempted to override controls. Employees are encouraged to report attempts to bypass controls to appropriate individuals within the organization.*

COMMITMENT TO COMPETENCE

Competence is the knowledge and skills necessary to accomplish tasks that define the individual's job. Commitment to competence includes management's consideration of the competence levels for particular jobs and how those levels translate into requisite skills and knowledge.

Does the company maintain formal or informal job descriptions or other means of defining tasks that comprise particular jobs?	Yes	*EarthWear has formal written job descriptions for all supervisory personnel, and job duties for nonsupervisory personnel are clearly communicated.*
Does management determine to an adequate extent the knowledge and skills needed to perform particular jobs?	Yes	*The job descriptions specify the knowledge and skills needed. The Human Resources Department uses this information in hiring, training, and promotion decisions.*
Does evidence exist that employees have the requisite knowledge and skills to perform their job?	Yes	*Our prior experiences with EarthWear personnel indicate that they have the necessary knowledge and skills.*

client operates in the oil industry, where there is always some risk of environmental damage. The auditor should obtain sufficient knowledge about how the client manages such environmental risk, because environmental accidents can result in costly litigation against the entity. Exhibit 6–2 presents a questionnaire that includes the type of information the auditor would document about EarthWear's risk assessment process.

Understanding Control Activities   As the auditor learns about the other components (control environment, risk assessment, information and communication, and monitoring) he or she is also likely to obtain information about some control activities. For example, in examining the information system that pertains to accounts receivable, the auditor is likely to see how the entity grants credit to customers. The auditor should consider the knowledge gained about the presence or absence of control activities that has been obtained from learning about the other four components in determining whether it is necessary to investigate control activities in order to plan the audit. Auditing standards (AU 319) do not require the auditor to understand control activities related to each class of transaction or account balance in the financial statements or to every assertion or audit objective relevant to them.

The extent of the auditor's understanding of control activities is a function of the audit strategy adopted. When the auditor decides to follow a substantive strategy approach, little or no work is done on understanding control activities. When a reliance strategy is followed, the auditor has to understand the control activities that relate to audit objectives for which a lower level of control risk is expected.

Exhibit 6–3 presents a questionnaire that includes the type of information the auditor would document on EarthWear's control activities.

Understanding the Information System and Communications
The auditor should obtain sufficient knowledge of the information system relevant to financial reporting to understand the following:

- The classes of transactions in the entity's operations that are significant to the financial statements.
- How those transactions are initiated.
- The accounting records, supporting information, computer media, and specific accounts in the financial statements that are involved in the processing and reporting of transactions.
- The accounting processing involved in the initiation of a transaction to its inclusion in the financial statements, including how the computer is used to process data.
- The financial reporting process used to prepare the entity's financial statements, including significant accounting estimates and disclosures.

A well-designed information system that is operating effectively can reduce the risk of material misstatement. The auditor must learn about each accounting cycle that affects significant account balances in the financial statements. This includes understanding how transactions are initiated, how documents and records are generated, and how the documents and

EXHIBIT 6–2

A Partial Questionnaire for Documenting the Auditor's Understanding of Risk Assessment

RISK ASSESSMENT QUESTIONNAIRE

Client: EarthWear Clothiers		Balance Sheet Date: 12/31/2000	
Completed by: *SAA*	Date: *9/30/00*	Reviewed by: *DRM*	Date: 10/15/00

A risk assessment process should consider external and internal events and circumstances that may occur and adversely affect its ability to record, process, summarize, and report financial data consistent with management's assertions. Management should initiate plans, programs, or actions to address significant, identified risks or accept the risk because of cost considerations.

	Yes, No, N/A	Comments
Does the entity set entitywide objectives that state what the entity desires to achieve, and are they supported by strategic plans?	*Yes*	*EarthWear has established broad objectives. Management has prepared a five-year business plan that includes goals for the company's products, responsibilities, and growth plans.*
Does the entity have a risk analysis process that includes estimating the significance of the risks, assessing the likelihood of their occurring, and determining the actions needed to respond to the risks?	*Yes*	*The company's business plan and budgeting process include analyzing risks that might affect the company. Senior management meets monthly to discuss recent events and how they may affect the company.*
Does the entity have mechanisms to identify and react to changes that may dramatically and pervasively affect the entity?	*Yes*	*Management has a number of mechanisms to identify risks that may affect the company. These include review of business and industry publications, participation in industry trade groups, and a strategic analysis group.*

records flow to the general ledger and financial statements. Understanding the information system also requires knowing how the computer is used to process data. Finally, understanding the information system requires knowledge about how the client prepares accounting estimates and gathers information for significant disclosures.

The level of understanding of the information system will, in many cases, be similar for both the substantive and reliance strategies. In some instances, the basic knowledge required for a substantive strategy approach may be sufficient to allow the auditor to plan a lower assessed level of control risk. In other instances, however, the auditor may have to learn more about the information system in order to reach a lower level of control risk. For example, suppose a sales report is generated by sales region and type of

EXHIBIT 6–3

A Partial Questionnaire for Documenting the Auditor's Understanding of Control Activities

CONTROL ACTIVITIES QUESTIONNAIRE

Client: EarthWear Clothiers		**Balance Sheet Date:** 12/31/2000
Completed by: *SAA* **Date:** *9/30/00*		**Reviewed by:** *DRM* **Date:** *10/15/00*

Control activities include the policies and procedures that ensure that management's directives are effective in processing and preparing financial statements. Control activities ensure that the entity's financial reporting objective is carried out.

	Yes, No, N/A	Comments
Does management have clear objectives in terms of budget, profit, and other financial and operating goals?	Yes	*EarthWear has a very sophisticated budgeting process that includes monitoring activities. All significant budget variances are summarized and explained in a monthly controller's report. See A20 for extracts of significant items from the controller's report.*
Are such objectives • Clearly written? • Actively communicated throughout the entity? • Actively monitored?	Yes	
Does the appropriate level of management • Adequately investigate variances? • Take appropriate and timely corrective actions?	Yes	
Has management established procedures to prevent unauthorized access to, or destruction of, documents, records, assets, programs, and data files?	Yes	*See B10 for a description of the IT Department's controls over access to (1) the computer operations area and (2) data programs and files.*

---

product. If the auditor does not intend to rely on that report, an understanding of how that report is generated would not be necessary to plan the audit. However, if the auditor decides that such a report would be useful in valuing inventory, an understanding of how the information included in the report is captured, processed, and reported would be necessary.

In addition, the auditor should obtain sufficient knowledge of how the entity communicates financial reporting roles and responsibilities and significant matters relating to financial reporting.

Exhibit 6–4 presents a questionnaire that includes the type of information the auditor would gather to document EarthWear's information and communications component.

EXHIBIT 6–4

A Partial Questionnaire for Documenting the Auditor's Understanding of Information and Communications

INFORMATION AND COMMUNICATIONS QUESTIONNAIRE

Client: EarthWear Clothiers		Balance Sheet Date: 12/31/2000	
Completed by: *SAA* Date: *9/30/00*		Reviewed by: *DRM* Date: *10/15/00*	

INFORMATION

Information systems record, process, summarize, and report information. Relevant information includes industry, economic, and regulatory information obtained from external sources, as well as internally generated information.

	Yes, No, N/A	Comments
Does the information system give management the necessary reports on the entity's performance relative to established objectives, including relevant external and internal information?	Yes	*The strategic plan and the budgeting process identify information that is needed to analyze and monitor the entity's objectives.*
Is the information provided to the right people in sufficient detail and in time to enable them to carry out their responsibilities effectively?	Yes	*All department groups within EarthWear are required to provide timely and adequate financial reporting. Actual performance is reported on a weekly and monthly basis. Performance is monitored by the controller's office.*
Is the development or revision of information systems over financial reporting based on a strategic plan?	Yes	*There is a strategic plan for updating the information systems over financial reporting that is revised on an annual basis.*

COMMUNICATIONS

Communications include the extent to which personnel understand how their activities in the financial reporting information system relate to the work of others and the means of reporting exceptions to an appropriate level within the entity.

	Yes, No, N/A	Comments
Does management communicate employees' duties and control responsibilities in an effective manner?	Yes	*Employees are given information regarding their duties during their initial training.*
Are communication channels established for people to report suspected improprieties?	Yes	*EarthWear's employee manual states that suspected violations of company policies should be reported to a vice president. Procedures allow such suspected violations to be reported anonymously.*
Does communication flow across the organization adequately to enable people to discharge their responsibilities effectively?	Yes	*There are good communications channels across departments.*

EXHIBIT 6–5

A Partial Questionnaire for Documenting the Auditor's Understanding of Monitoring

MONITORING QUESTIONNAIRE

Client: EarthWear Clothiers		**Balance Sheet Date:** 12/31/2000
Completed by: *SAA* **Date:** *9/30/00*		**Reviewed by:** DRM **Date:** 10/15/00

Management should monitor internal control in the ordinary course of operations. This monitoring includes regular management and supervisory activities and other actions personnel take in performing their duties that assess the quality of internal control.

	Yes, No, N/A	Comments
How many customer complaints are received about billings? Are complaints investigated for underlying causes and any internal control deficiencies corrected?	Yes	*Customer complaints are generally very low (1 out of every 5,000 invoices). Most complaints relate to delays in receiving goods that are on order by the company.*
Does the entity have an internal audit function?	Yes	
Are internal control recommendations made by internal and external auditors implemented?	Yes	*Recommendations that management and the board feel are cost-beneficial are implemented.*
Does the entity conduct separate evaluations of internal control?	Yes	*The board of directors focuses on the control environment and monitoring activities. The audit committee meets regularly with the internal and external auditors about control-related activities.*

Understanding Monitoring   The auditor should know how the entity monitors the performance of internal control over financial reporting, including how corrective action is initiated. For example, if the client has an internal audit function, the external auditor should understand how management uses the internal auditors to monitor internal control.

Exhibit 6–5 presents a questionnaire that includes the type of information the auditor would document about EarthWear's monitoring process.

Audit Procedures   In addition to previous experience with a client, an auditor may use the following audit procedures to learn about internal control:

- Inquiry of appropriate management, supervisory, and staff personnel.
- Inspection of entity documents and reports.
- Observation of entity activities and operations.

An Example   Table 6–5 presents two account balances from EarthWear Clothiers' financial statements that differ in terms of their nature, size, and complexity. The differences in these characteristics result in different levels of understanding of internal control and different control risk assessments. In this example, inventory is a material account balance that is composed of numerous products. This account also contains significant inherent risk, and the data for this account are generated by a sophisticated computer system. For inventory, the auditor must understand the control environment factors, risk management factors, monitoring activities, significant classes of transactions, inventory pricing policies, the flow of transactions, and what control activities will be relied upon. The auditor will likely use all of the audit procedures just discussed to obtain an understanding of internal control for inventory. In contrast, prepaid advertising is a significant account; however, it contains few transactions. There is little or no inherent risk and the accounting records are simple, so the knowledge needed about risk assessment, the information system and communications, and monitoring is minimal. In this instance, the auditor needs only to understand the control environment factors, the nature of the account balance, and the monitoring activities. No knowledge of control activities is necessary for this account. Audit procedures for the prepaid advertising account would likely be limited to recalculation of amortization of advertising.

Documenting the Understanding of Internal Control

[LO 5]

A number of tools are available to the auditor for documenting the understanding of internal control. These include

- Copies of the entity's procedures manuals and organizational charts.
- Narrative description.
- Internal control questionnaires.
- Flowcharts.

Auditing standards (AU 319) require that the auditor document the understanding of the entity's internal control components using these tools. On many engagements, auditors combine these tools to document their understanding of the components of internal control. The combination depends on the complexity of the entity's internal control system and the extensiveness of the audit procedures to be performed. For example, in a complex entity, the auditor may document the control environment, assessment of risk, and monitoring activities using a memorandum and internal control questionnaire. Documentation of the information system and communications, as well as control activities, may be accomplished through the use of an internal control questionnaire and a flowchart. For a small entity, documentation using a memorandum may be sufficient.

An auditor should also document his or her understanding of an entity's internal control to provide protection in the event he or she is sued. Proper documentation can provide evidence that the auditor conducted the audit in conformity with GAAS.

TABLE 6-5 Account Characteristics and Their Effect on the Auditor's Understanding of Internal Control

EarthWear Account Balance	Account Characteristics	Extent of Understanding Needed to Plan the Audit	Control Risk Assessment	Planned Substantive Testing
Inventory ($64,100,000)	• Material balance. • Numerous transactions from a large product base. • Significant inherent risk related to overstock and out-of-style products. • Sophisticated computer processing.	• Entity control environment factors. • Risk assessment factors. • Monitoring activities. • Significant classes of transactions. • Inventory pricing policies. • Initiation, processing, and recording of transactions. • Control activities to be relied upon.	• Tests of controls conducted on relevant controls in the purchasing and inventory cycles were consistent with the planned assessment of control risk. • Control risk is assessed to be *low*.	Substantive tests will include • Physical examination of inventory. • Information technology–assisted audit techniques to audit the inventory compilation.
Prepaid advertising ($4,980,000)	• Significant balance. • Few transactions. • Little or no inherent risk. • Simple accounting procedures.	• Entity control environment factors. • Nature of the account balance. • Monitoring activities.	• Because there are few transactions and the procedures for amortizing advertising expenditures are simple, a substantive strategy is selected. • Control risk is assessed at the *maximum*.	• Substantive testing will recalculate the amortization of the advertising expenditures.

Procedures Manuals and Organizational Charts   Many organizations prepare procedures manuals that document the entity's policies and procedures. Portions of such manuals may include documentation of the accounting systems and related control procedures. The entity's organizational chart presents the designated lines of authority and responsibility. Copies of both of these documents can help the auditor document his or her understanding of the internal control system.

Narrative Description   The understanding of internal control may be documented in a memorandum. This documentation approach is most appropriate when the entity has a simple internal control system because a narrative description will be difficult to follow and analyze for a more complex entity, such as EarthWear Clothiers. Exhibit 6–6 presents an example of a partial memorandum for documenting the auditor's understanding of the control environment of a small client.

Internal Control Questionnaires   Internal control questionnaires are one of many types of questionnaires used by auditors. Questionnaires serve as "memory joggers" in that they provide a systematic means for the auditor to investigate areas such as internal control. An internal control questionnaire is generally used for entities with more complex internal control. It contains questions about the important factors or characteristics of the five components discussed earlier in this chapter. Exhibits 6–1 through 6–5 provide examples of the use of such questionnaires. As shown in those exhibits,

E X H I B I T 6–6	**An Example of a Partial Audit Memorandum for Documenting the Auditor's Understanding of an Entity's Control Environment**

WORCESTER WOOLEN MILLS
Audit Memo—Control Environment
December 31, 2000

The company manufactures high-quality woolen cloth for women's outerwear. There is one location in Starkeville, Mississippi. Jonathan Worcester is chairman of the board and chief executive officer. His son Wally is chief operating officer. The family controls 97 percent of the common stock. The board of directors is composed of family members, but Jonathan and Wally monitor the business and make most of the business decisions.

Jim Johansen, the controller, and Mary Margarita, the bookkeeper, handle most of the significant accounting functions. Wally reviews cash receipts and cash disbursements. Jonathan and Wally have conservative attitudes toward accounting, and they consider lower taxes to be important. Our firm is consulted on the accounting for unusual transactions, and there are rarely any adjustments for errors from routine transaction processing.

The company uses a microcomputer and a standard accounting software package. Access to the computer and files is limited to Wally, Jim, and Mary. Jonathan and Wally review the computerized prepared financial statements and monitor revenues and expenses as compared to budget and prior-year results.

the auditor's responses to the questions included in the internal control questionnaire provide the documentation for his or her understanding.

Flowcharts   Flowcharts provide a diagrammatic representation, or "picture," of the entity's accounting system. The flowchart outlines the configuration of the system in terms of functions, documents, processes, and reports. This documentation facilitates an auditor's analysis of the system's strengths and weaknesses. Figure 6–3 presents a simple example of a flowchart for the order entry portion of a revenue cycle. The appendix to this chapter provides detailed coverage of flowcharting techniques. Flowcharts are used extensively in this book to represent accounting systems.

Tests of Controls

[LO 6]

As discussed in Chapter 5, audit procedures directed toward evaluating the effectiveness of either the *design* or the *operation* of an internal control are referred to as *tests of controls*. When the auditor decides to follow a substantive strategy, control risk is set at the maximum and tests of controls are normally not performed (refer to Figure 6–2). However, if the auditor chooses a reliance strategy, tests of controls are performed in order to provide evidence to support the lower level of control risk. Tests of controls directed toward the effectiveness of the design of a control are concerned with evaluating whether that control is suitably designed to prevent material misstatements. Tests of controls directed toward the operating effectiveness are concerned with assessing how the control was applied, the consistency with which it was applied during the audit period, and by whom it was applied. A number of audit procedures are used as tests of controls, including

- Inquiry of appropriate client personnel.
- Inspection of documents, reports, and electronic media indicating the performance of the policy or procedure.
- Observation of the application of the policies and procedures.
- Reperformance of the application of the policy or procedure by the auditor.

When the auditor decides to test controls, he or she must also determine the nature, extent, and timing of those tests. The nature of the tests of controls relates to the type of tests to be performed. For example, some controls, such as segregation of duties, can be tested only via inquiry or observation. For other controls, documentary evidence may exist, and the auditor can inspect source documents. Finally, in some instances, the auditor may reperform the control either manually or with a computer. For example, the auditor may recompute an employee's gross wages by multiplying the number of hours shown on the employee's time card by the employee's wage rate and compare the amount to the payroll register.

The extent of the auditor's tests of controls is a function of how low control risk is to be assessed. The more extensive the tests of controls, the more evidence there is to support a lower control risk assessment. The timing decision is concerned with whether controls are to be tested at an interim date or at year-end. The general issue of the timing of audit procedures is discussed later in this chapter.

An Example of a Flowchart for the Order Entry Portion of the Revenue Cycle

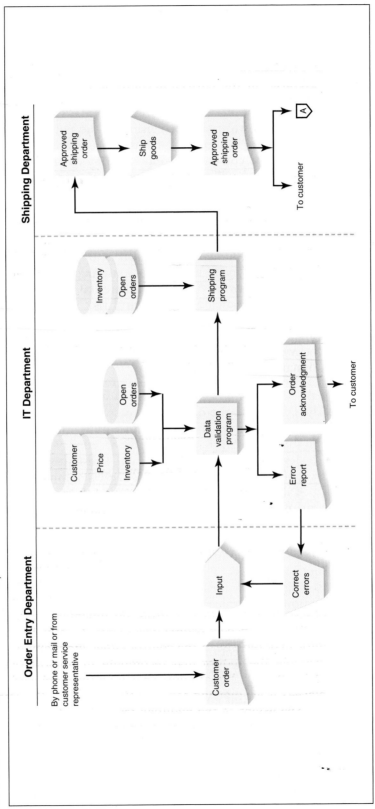

Assessing and Documenting the Level of Control Risk

[LO 7]

Assessing control risk involves evaluating the effectiveness of an entity's internal controls in preventing or detecting material misstatements in the financial statements. If the auditor is following a substantive strategy, control risk is assessed at the maximum. If a reliance strategy is being followed, the results of the tests of controls must be evaluated. The conclusion that results from this step is referred to as the *assessed level of control risk*.

If the tests of controls are consistent with the auditor's planned assessment of control risk, no revision in the nature, extent, or timing of substantive tests is necessary. On the other hand, if the tests of controls indicate that the controls are not operating as preliminarily assessed, the level of control risk will have to be increased, and the nature, extent, and timing of planned substantive testing will have to be modified.

Auditing standards (AU 319) state that the auditor should document the basis for his or her conclusions about the assessed level of control risk. The auditor should also document the assessed level of control risk so that the audit risk model can be used as discussed in Chapter 3. This assessment may be made in either quantitative or qualitative terms. A quantitative scale might be 0.0 to 1.0, where 0.0 indicates that there is no control risk and 1.0 indicates that control risk is at the maximum. A qualitative scale might utilize the terms *maximum*, *high*, *moderate*, and *low*. The auditor's assessment of control risk and the basis for that assessment can be documented using a structured working paper, an internal control questionnaire, or a memorandum.

Substantive Tests

[LO 8]

The last step in the decision process is performing substantive tests. Detection risk is the risk that substantive audit procedures will not detect a material misstatement that exists in an account balance or class of transactions. The level of detection risk used for a substantive test is based on the planned level of audit risk and the assessed levels of inherent and control risk.

Table 6–6 presents two examples of how the nature, timing, and extent of substantive testing may vary as a function of the detection risk level for a purchasing cycle and inventory account. Assume that audit risk is set low for both clients but that client 1 has a high level of inherent risk and control risk while client 2 has a low level of inherent risk and control risk. The use of the audit risk model results in setting detection risk at low for client 1 and high for client 2. For client 1, the low detection risk requires that (1) more reliable types of evidence, such as confirmation and reperformance, be obtained, (2) most of the audit work be conducted at year-end, and (3) the tests be extensive. In contrast, client 2 has a high detection risk, which means that (1) less reliable types of evidence, such as analytical procedures, can be obtained, (2) most of the audit work can be conducted at an interim date, and (3) tests of the inventory account can be limited. Another major difference between the two strategies involves the physical examination of the inventory on hand. For the low-detection-risk strategy, physical inventory would be examined at year-end because the control risk was assessed to be high. For the high-detection-risk strategy, the auditor can examine the physical inventory at an interim date because the control risk assessment indicates little risk of material misstatement.

TABLE 6–6	Audit Strategies for the Nature, Timing, and Extent of Substantive Testing Based on Different Levels of Detection Risk for Inventory

Low-Detection-Risk Strategy—Client 1

Nature	Audit tests for all significant audit objectives using the following types of audit procedures:
	• Physical examination (conducted at year-end).
	• Review of external documents.
	• Confirmation.
	• Reperformance.
Timing	All significant work completed at year-end.
Extent	Extensive testing of significant accounts or transactions.

High-Detection-Risk Strategy—Client 2

Nature	Corroborative audit tests using the following types of audit tests:
	• Physical examination (conducted at an interim date).
	• Analytical procedures.
	• Substantive tests of transactions and balances.
Timing	Interim and year-end.
Extent	Limited testing of accounts or transactions.

FIGURE 6–4

A Timeline for Planning and Performing the Audit of EarthWear Clothiers

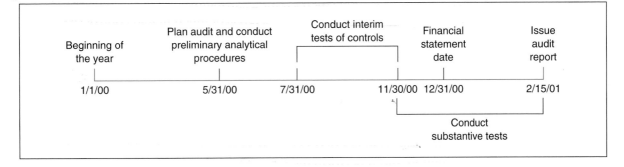

Timing of Audit Procedures

[LO 9]   Audit procedures may be conducted at an interim date or at year-end. Figure 6–4 presents a timeline for planning and performing a midsize to large audit for an entity such as EarthWear Clothiers with a 12/31/00 year-end. In this example, the audit is planned and preliminary analytical procedures are conducted around 5/31/00. The interim tests of controls are conducted sometime during the time frame 7/31/00 to 11/30/00. Substantive tests are planned for the time frame 11/30/00 to

2/15/01, when the audit report is to be issued. The auditor's considerations of conducting tests of controls and substantive tests at an interim date are discussed in turn.

Interim Tests of Controls

An auditor might test controls at an interim date because the internal control objective being tested may not be significant, the control has been effective in prior audits, or it may be more efficient to conduct the tests at that time. A reason why it may be more efficient to conduct interim tests of controls is that staff accountants may be less busy at the time, and it may minimize the amount of overtime needed at year-end. Additionally, if the controls are found not to be operating effectively, testing them at an interim date gives the auditor more time to reassess the control risk and modify the audit plan. It also gives the auditor time to inform management so that likely misstatements can be located and corrected before the rest of the audit is performed.

An important question the auditor must address is the need for additional audit work in the period following the interim testing period. For example, suppose the auditor examines a sample of sales transactions for the period 1/1/00 to 8/31/00. What testing, if any, should the auditor conduct for the period 9/1/00 to 12/31/00? The auditor should consider factors such as the significance of the internal control objective, the evaluation of the design and operation of the control, the results of tests of controls, the length of the remaining period, and the planned substantive tests in determining the nature and extent of audit work for the remaining period. At a minimum, the auditor would inquire about the nature and extent of changes in policies, procedures, or personnel that occurred subsequent to the interim period. If significant changes have occurred, or if the results of tests of controls are unfavorable, the auditor may need to conduct additional audit procedures for the period not included in the interim testing.

Interim Substantive Tests

Conducting substantive tests at an interim date may increase the risk that material misstatements are present in the financial statements. The auditor can control for this potential problem by considering when it is appropriate to examine an account at an interim date and by performing selected audit procedures for the period between the interim date and year-end.

The auditor should consider the following factors when substantive tests are to be completed at an interim date:

- The level of control risk.
- Changing business conditions or circumstances that may cause management to misstate financial amounts in the remaining period.
- Control procedures for ensuring that the account is properly analyzed and adjusted, including proper cutoff procedures.
- The auditor's ability to investigate the remaining period.

For example, the level of control risk is an important factor in deciding whether to conduct substantive tests at an interim date. If the entity's accounting system has control weaknesses that result in a high level of assessed control risk, it is unlikely that the auditor would conduct substantive tests at an interim date. In this instance, the auditor has little assurance that the accounting system will generate accurate information during the remaining period. Similarly, the auditor must consider the controls followed by the entity to ensure that the account is properly analyzed and adjusted, including cutoff procedures. The auditor must have some assurance that these controls are performed both at the interim date and at year-end.

When the auditor conducts substantive tests of an account at an interim date, some additional substantive tests are ordinarily conducted in the remaining period. Generally, this would include comparing the year-end account balance with the interim account balance. It might also involve conducting some analytical procedures or reviewing related journals and ledgers for large or unusual transactions. If misstatements are detected during interim testing, the auditor will have to revise the planned substantive tests for the remaining period or reperform some substantive tests at year-end.

Communication of Internal Control–Related Matters

[LO 10]   During the engagement, the auditor may identify certain matters related to the entity's internal control. SAS No. 60, "Communication of Internal Control–Related Matters Noted in an Audit" (AU 325), requires that the auditor report to the audit committee, or to a similar level of authority when the entity does not have an audit committee, matters that are referred to as *reportable conditions.* Reportable conditions are significant deficiencies in the design or operation of internal control that could adversely affect the organization's ability to record, process, summarize, and report financial data consistent with management's assertions. Table 6–7 presents examples of possible reportable conditions.

Reportable conditions may be identified as part of the auditor's consideration of the five components of internal control or through substantive tests. The auditor may also identify matters that are less significant than reportable conditions. These matters may be communicated to the audit committee if the auditor chooses or if the client requests it.

It is preferable for the auditor to communicate reportable conditions to the audit committee in writing. Exhibit 6–7 illustrates a report on reportable conditions. The following items should be included in the report:

- A statement that the purpose of the audit was to report on the financial statements and not to provide assurance on internal control.
- A definition of reportable conditions.
- A statement of restrictions on the distribution of the report.

This information may be communicated orally; however, the auditor should document the communication in the working papers.

In some cases, the reportable condition may be of such magnitude as to be considered a *material weakness.* A material weakness in internal control is defined as

> a reportable condition in which the design or operation of one or more of the specific internal control components does not reduce to a relatively low level the risk that errors or fraud in amounts that would be material in relation to the financial statements being audited may occur and not be detected within a timely period by employees in the normal course of performing their assigned functions. (AU 325.15)

TABLE 6–7   Examples of Reportable Conditions

Deficiencies in Internal Control Design:
- Inadequate overall internal control design.
- Absence of appropriate segregation of duties consistent with appropriate control objectives.
- Absence of appropriate reviews and approvals of transactions, accounting entries, or systems output.
- Inadequate procedures for appropriately assessing and applying accounting principles.
- Inadequate provisions for safeguarding assets.
- Absence of other control techniques considered appropriate for the type and level of transaction activity.
- Evidence that a system fails to provide complete and accurate output that is consistent with objectives and current needs because of design flaws.

Failures in the Operation of Internal Control:
- Evidence of failure of identified controls in preventing or detecting misstatements of accounting information.
- Evidence that a system fails to provide complete and accurate output consistent with the entity's control objectives because of the misapplication of control procedures.
- Evidence of failure to safeguard assets from loss, damage, or misappropriation.
- Evidence of intentional override of internal control by those in authority to the detriment of the overall objectives of the system.
- Evidence of failure to perform tasks that are part of internal control, such as reconciliations not prepared or not prepared in a timely fashion.
- Evidence of willful wrongdoing by employees or management.
- Evidence of manipulation, falsification, or alteration of accounting records or supporting documents.
- Evidence of intentional misapplication of accounting principles.
- Evidence of misrepresentation by client personnel to the auditor.
- Evidence that employees or management lack the qualifications and training to fulfill their assigned functions.

Other:
- Absence of a sufficient level of control consciousness within the organization.
- Failure to follow up and correct previously identified internal control deficiencies.
- Evidence of significant or extensive undisclosed related-party transactions.
- Evidence of undue bias or lack of objectivity by those responsible for accounting decisions.

EXHIBIT 6–7

Example of a Report on Reportable Conditions

In planning and performing our audit of the financial statements of the Worcester Woolen Mills for the year ended December 31, 2000, we considered its internal control in order to determine our auditing procedures for the purpose of expressing our opinion on the financial statements and not to provide assurance on internal control. However, we noted certain matters involving internal control and its operation that we consider to be reportable conditions under standards established by the American Institute of Certified Public Accountants. Reportable conditions involve matters coming to our attention relating to significant deficiencies in the design or operation of internal control that, in our judgment, could adversely affect the organization's ability to record, process, summarize, and report financial data consistent with the assertions of management in the financial statements.

Our review of internal control indicated that there was not adequate segregation of duties in the billing and cash receipts departments.

This report is intended solely for the information and use of the audit committee, board of directors, management, and others within the organization and is not intended to be and should not be used by anyone other than these specified parties.

The auditor may choose to separately identify reportable conditions that are material weaknesses. In reporting on such matters, the auditor is allowed to report that none of the reportable conditions were material weaknesses. However, the auditor is precluded from reporting that no reportable conditions were noted during the audit. Chapter 21 discusses additional types of reporting on internal control.

The auditor may also want to communicate to the client other issues identified during the audit that go beyond internal control. A *management letter* can be used to communicate to the client suggestions for matters such as operational efficiencies or business strategies. Providing the client with suggestions in these areas is part of the auditor's client service activities. Chapter 17 provides an example of a management letter.

APPENDIX:

[LO 11]

Flowcharting Techniques

From the auditor's perspective, a flowchart is a diagrammatic representation of the entity's accounting system. The information systems literature typically discusses three types of flowcharts: document flowcharts, systems flowcharts, and program flowcharts. A document flowchart represents the flow of documents among departments in the entity. A systems flowchart extends this approach by including the processing steps, including computer processing, in the flowchart. A program flowchart illustrates the operations performed by the computer in executing a program. Flowcharts that are typically used by public accounting firms combine document and systems flowcharting techniques. Such flowcharts show the path from the origination of the transactions to their recording in the accounting journals and ledgers. While there are some general guidelines on preparing flowcharts for documenting accounting systems, the reader should understand that a public accounting firm often modifies these techniques to correspond with their firm's audit technologies.

Following are a number of common guidelines that are used in preparing flowcharts.

Symbols

A standard set of symbols is used to represent documents and processes. Figure 6–5 presents examples of the more commonly used symbols. Note that the symbols are divided into three groups: input/output symbols, processing symbols, and data flow and storage symbols.

Organization and Flow

A well-designed flowchart should start in the upper left part of the page and proceed to the lower right part of the page. When it is necessary to show the movement of a document or report back to a previous function, an on-page connector should be used. When the flowchart continues to a subsequent page, the movement of documents or reports can be handled by using an off-page connector. Flow arrows should show the movement of documents, records, or information. When processes or activities cannot be fully represented by flowchart symbols, the auditor should supplement the flowchart with written comments. This can be accomplished by using the annotation symbol or just writing the comment directly on the flowchart.

FIGURE 6–5

Flowcharting Symbols

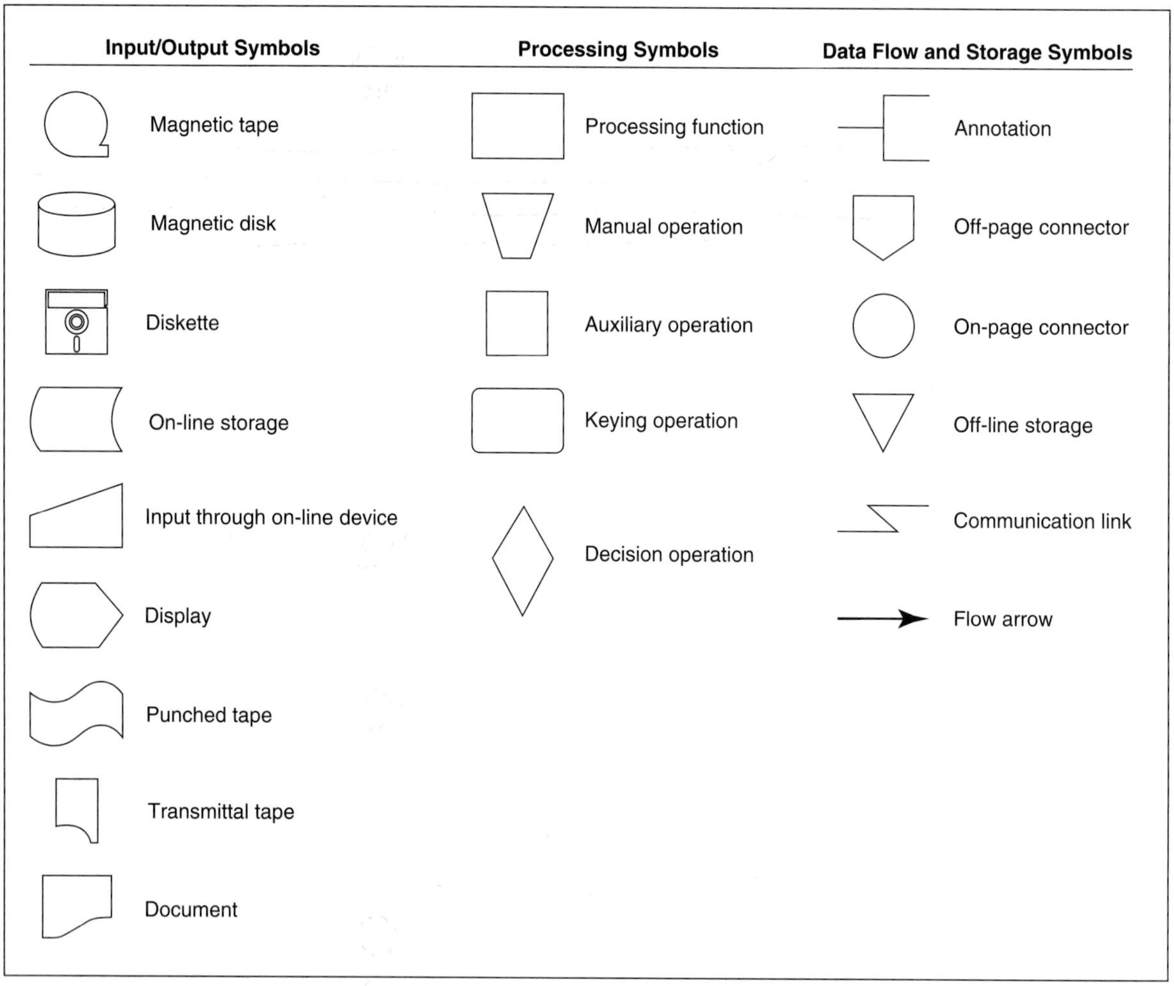

Input/Output Symbols	Processing Symbols	Data Flow and Storage Symbols
Magnetic tape	Processing function	Annotation
Magnetic disk	Manual operation	Off-page connector
Diskette	Auxiliary operation	On-page connector
On-line storage	Keying operation	Off-line storage
Input through on-line device	Decision operation	Communication link
Display		Flow arrow
Punched tape		
Transmittal tape		
Document		

A flowchart is typically designed along the lines of departments or functions. It is thus important to indicate the delineation of activities between the departments or functions. As shown in Figure 6–3, this can be accomplished by using a vertical dashed line.

REVIEW QUESTIONS

[LO 1] 6-1 What are management's incentives for establishing and maintaining strong internal control? What are the auditor's main concerns with internal control?

[2] 6-2 Describe the five components of internal control.

[2] 6-3 What are some of the factors that affect the control environment?

[2] 6-4 Why is it important to maintain proper segregation of duties among the authorization of transactions, the recording of transactions, and the custody of assets?

[2] 6-5 How does the size of an entity affect internal control?

[2] 6-6 What is meant by the concept of reasonable assurance in terms of internal control? What are the inherent limitations of internal control?

[3] 6-7 What are the major differences between a substantive strategy and a reliance strategy when the auditor considers internal control in planning an audit?

[3,4] 6-8 List the audit objectives for assessing control risk. How do the internal control objectives differ from the audit objectives for tests of account balances?

[4] 6-9 Why must the auditor obtain an understanding of internal control?

[4] 6-10 What knowledge is necessary for sufficient understanding of the information system and communications component?

[5] 6-11 List the tools that can document the understanding of internal control.

[6] 6-12 Distinguish between tests of controls for testing the design and those for testing the operation of an internal control.

[7,8] 6-13 What are the requirements under auditing standards for documenting the assessed level of control risk?

[9] 6-14 What factors should the auditor consider when substantive tests are to be completed at an interim date? If the auditor conducts tests at an interim date, what audit procedures would normally be completed for the remaining period?

[10] 6-15 Distinguish between a reportable condition and a material weakness in internal control. List two examples of reportable conditions.

[10] 6-16 What is the auditor's responsibility for communicating reportable conditions?

MULTIPLE-CHOICE QUESTIONS FROM CPA EXAMINATIONS

[2] 6-17 Which of the following is *not* a component of an entity's internal control system?

    a. Control risk.

    b. Risk assessment.

    c. Control activities.

    d. Control environment.

[4,5,6]   6-18   After obtaining an understanding of an entity's internal control system and assessing control risk, an auditor may

a. Perform tests of controls to verify management's assertions that are embodied in the financial statements. *test of account balances*

b. Consider whether evidential matter is available to support a further reduction in the assessed level of control risk.

c. Apply analytical procedures as substantive tests to validate the assessed level of control risk. *sub. strategy – test of a.b.*

d. Evaluate whether the internal controls detected material misstatements in the financial statements. *sub strategy – test of a.b.*

[1,4]   6-19   Which of the following statements about internal control is correct?

a. A properly maintained internal control system reasonably ensures that collusion among employees cannot occur.

b. The establishment and maintenance of internal control is an important responsibility of the internal auditor. *BOD – IA tests*

c. An exceptionally strong internal control system is enough for the auditor to eliminate substantive tests on a significant account balance.

d. The cost–benefit relationship is a primary criterion that should be considered in designing an internal control system.

[4,6,7]   6-20   After obtaining an understanding of an entity's internal control system, an auditor may assess control risk at the maximum level for some assertions because he or she

a. Believes the internal controls are unlikely to be effective.

b. Determines that the pertinent internal control components are *not* well documented.

c. Performs tests of controls to restrict detection risk to an acceptable level.

d. Identifies internal controls that are likely to prevent material misstatements.

[3,4]   6-21   During consideration of internal control in a financial statement audit, an auditor is *not* obligated to

a. Search for significant deficiencies in the operation of internal control. *sub. strategy*

b. Understand the internal control environment and the information system.

c. Determine whether the controls relevant to audit planning have been placed in operation. *preliminary understanding*

d. Perform procedures to understand the design of internal control.

[1,2]   6-22   An auditor's primary consideration regarding an entity's internal controls is whether they

a. Prevent management override.

b. Relate to the control environment.

c. Reflect management's philosophy and operating style.

d. Affect the financial statement assertions.

[6]   6-23   Evidential matter concerning proper segregation of duties ordinarily is best obtained by

a. Inspection of third-party documents containing the initials of those who applied control procedures. *auth.*

b. Direct personal observation of the employee who applies control procedures.

c. Preparation of a flowchart of duties performed and available personnel.

d. Making inquiries of co-workers about the employee who applies control procedures.

[3,7] 6-24 In planning an audit of certain accounts, an auditor may conclude that specific procedures used to obtain an understanding of an entity's internal control system need *not* be included because of the auditor's judgments about materiality and assessments of

a. Control risk.

b. Detection risk.

c. Sampling risk.

d. Inherent risk.

[3,7] 6-25 As the acceptable level of detection risk increases, an auditor may change the

a. Assessed level of control risk from below the maximum to the maximum level.

b. Assurance provided by tests of controls by using a larger sample size than planned.

c. Timing of substantive tests from year-end to an interim date.

d. Nature of substantive tests from a less effective to a more effective procedure.

[6,7] 6-26 Regardless of the assessed level of control risk, an auditor would perform some

a. Tests of controls to determine the effectiveness of internal controls.

b. Analytical procedures to verify the design of internal controls.

c. Substantive tests to restrict detection risk for significant transaction classes.

d. Dual-purpose tests to evaluate both the risk of monetary misstatement and preliminary control risk.

[6] 6-27 Which of the following audit techniques would most likely provide an auditor with the most assurance about the effectiveness of the operation of an internal control?

a. Inquiry of client personnel.

b. Recomputation of account balance amounts.

c. Observation of client personnel.

d. Confirmation with outside parties.

[3,4,7] 6-28 When control risk is assessed at the maximum level for all financial statement assertions, an auditor should document the auditor's

	Understanding of the Entity's Internal Control Components	Conclusion That Control Risk Is at the Maximum Level	Basis for Concluding That Control Risk Is at the Maximum Level
a.	Yes	No	No
b.	Yes	Yes	No
c.	No	Yes	Yes
d.	Yes	Yes	Yes

[10]   6-29   Which of the following statements concerning material weaknesses and reportable conditions is correct?
   a. An auditor should identify and communicate material weaknesses separately from reportable conditions.
   b. All material weaknesses are reportable conditions.
   c. An auditor should immediately report material weaknesses and reportable conditions discovered during an audit.
   d. All reportable conditions are material weaknesses.

[10]   6-30   When communicating internal control–related matters noted in an audit, an auditor's report issued on reportable conditions should indicate that
   a. Errors or fraud may occur and *not* be detected because there are inherent limitations in any internal control system.
   b. The issuance of an unqualified opinion on the financial statements may depend on corrective follow-up action.
   c. The deficiencies noted were *not* detected within a timely period by employees in the normal course of performing their assigned functions.
   d. The purpose of the audit was to report on the financial statements and *not* to provide assurance on internal control.

[11]   6-31   An advantage of using systems flowcharts to document information about internal control instead of using internal control questionnaires is that systems flowcharts
   a. Identify internal control weaknesses more prominently.
   b. Provide a visual depiction of clients' activities.
   c. Indicate whether controls are operating effectively.
   d. Reduce the need to observe clients' employees performing routine tasks.

[11]   6-32   An auditor's flowchart of a client's accounting system is a diagrammatic representation that depicts the auditor's
   a. Program for tests of controls.
   b. Understanding of the system.
   c. Understanding of the types of fraud that are probable, given the present system.
   d. Documentation of the study and evaluation of the system.

PROBLEMS

[1,2,4]   6-33   Johnson, CPA, has been engaged to audit the financial statements of Rose, Inc., a publicly held retailing company. Before assessing control risk, Johnson is required to obtain an understanding of Rose's control environment.

Required:
   a. Identify additional control environment factors (excluding the factor illustrated in the following example) that set the tone of an organization, influencing the control consciousness of its people.
   b. For each control environment factor identified in part (a), describe the components and why each component would be of interest to the auditor.

Use the following format:

Integrity and Ethical Values

The effectiveness of controls cannot rise above the integrity and ethical values of the people who create, administer, and monitor them. Integrity and ethical values are essential elements of the control environment, affecting the design, administration, and monitoring of other components. Integrity and ethical behavior are the product of the entity's ethical and behavioral standards, how they are communicated, and how they are reinforced in practice.

[2,3,4,5,7]   6-34   An auditor is required to obtain sufficient understanding of each component of an entity's internal control system to plan the audit of the entity's financial statements and to assess control risk for the assertions embodied in the account balance, transaction class, and disclosure components of the financial statements.

Required:
a. What are the components of an entity's internal control system?
b. For what purpose should an auditor's understanding of the internal control components be used in planning an audit?
c. Why may an auditor assess control risk at the maximum level for one or more assertions embodied in an account balance?
d. What must an auditor do to support an assessment of control risk at less than the maximum level when he or she has determined that controls have been placed in operation?
e. What should an auditor consider when seeking a further reduction in the planned assessed level of control risk?
f. What are an auditor's documentation requirements concerning an entity's internal control system and the assessed level of control risk?

[2,4]   6-35   TameBird Industries produces meals for airlines and nursing homes. For the prior two audit engagements, your firm has written a management letter recommending that TameBird establish better segregation of duties in the accounts receivable and accounts payable functions. Tom Tuffnut, controller for TameBird, has received authorization to hire an additional clerk to work in the accounting area. Tom now has three accounting clerks available, and he has asked you to provide advice on how to best assign the following functions:
1. Responsibility for petty cash fund.
2. Opening of mail and listing of cash receipts.
3. Depositing cash receipts in bank.
4. Maintaining accounts receivable subsidiary records.
5. Determining which accounts receivable are uncollectible.
6. Maintaining cash disbursements journal.
7. Preparing checks for signature.
8. Reconciling bank statements.

Required:
Prepare a recommendation to Tom Tuffnut on how best to distribute the various functions among the three accounting clerks.

[5,11]   6-36   Auditors use various tools to document their understanding of an entity's internal control system, including narrative descriptions, internal control questionnaires, and flowcharts.

Required:

a. Identify the relative strengths and weaknesses of each tool.

b. Briefly describe how the complexity of an entity's internal control system affects the use of the various tools.

[11]   6-37   Following is a *partial* description of an entity's revenue cycle.

Orders are received by mail or phone from customers. Customer service agents prepare a sales order, which is forwarded to the sales department for credit authorization and terms of trade. Normal terms of trade are 2/10, net 30. After approval, the sales order is sent to the shipping department, where a bill of lading or shipping document (two copies) is prepared. One copy accompanies the goods, while the other copy is sent to the billing department. The billing department prepares a sales invoice (two copies) using the company's authorized price list. The original copy of the sales invoice is sent to the customer, and one copy is forwarded to the accounts receivable department.

Required:

Prepare a flowchart for this portion of the entity's revenue cycle.

[10]   6-38   During an audit made in accordance with generally accepted auditing standards, an auditor may become aware of matters relating to the client's internal control that may interest the client's audit committee or individuals with an equivalent level of authority and responsibility, such as the board of directors, the board of trustees, or the owner in an owner-managed enterprise.

Required:

a. What are meant by the terms *reportable conditions* and *material weakness*?

b. What are an auditor's responsibilities in identifying and reporting these matters?

(AICPA, adapted)

[10]   6-39   Ken Smith, the partner in charge of the audit of Houghton Enterprises, identified the following reportable conditions during the audit of the December 31, 2000, financial statements:

1. Controls for granting credit to new customers were not adequate. In particular, the credit department did not adequately check the creditworthiness of customers with an outside credit agency.

2. There were not adequate physical safeguards over the company's inventory. No safeguards prevented employees from stealing high-value inventory parts.

Required:

a. Draft the required communications to the management of Houghton Enterprises, assuming that both items are reportable conditions.

b. Assume that Smith determined that the second item was a material weakness. How would the required communication change?

[9]   6-40   Cook, CPA, has been engaged to audit the financial statements of General Department Stores, Inc., a continuing audit client, which is a chain of medium-sized retail stores. General's fiscal year will end on June 30, 2000, and General's management has asked Cook

to issue the auditor's report by August 1, 2000. Cook will not have sufficient time to perform all of the necessary field work in July 2000 but will have time to perform most of the field work as of an interim date, April 30, 2000.

After the accounts are tested at the interim date, Cook will also perform substantive tests covering the transactions of the final two months of the year. This will be necessary to extend Cook's conclusions to the balance sheet date.

Required:
a. Describe the factors Cook should consider before applying principal substantive tests to General's balance sheet accounts at April 30, 2000.
b. For accounts tested at April 30, 2000, describe how Cook should design the substantive tests covering the balances as of June 30, 2000, and the transactions of the final two months of the year.

(AICPA, adapted)

DISCUSSION CASE

[2,4,6]   6-41   Preview Company, a diversified manufacturer, has five divisions that operate throughout the United States and Mexico. Preview has historically allowed its divisions to operate autonomously. Corporate intervention occurred only when planned results were not obtained. Corporate management has high integrity, but the board of directors and audit committee are not very active. Preview has a policy of hiring competent people. The company has a code of conduct, but there is little monitoring of compliance by employees. Management is fairly conservative in terms of accounting principles and practices, but employee compensation packages depend highly on performance. Preview Company does not have an internal audit department, and it relies on your firm to review the controls in each division.

Chip Harris is the general manager of the Fabricator Division. The Fabricator Division produces a variety of standardized parts for small appliances. Harris has been the general manager for the last seven years, and each year he has been able to improve the profitability of the division. He is compensated based largely on the division's profitability. Much of the improvement in profitability has come through aggressive cost cutting, including a substantial reduction in control procedures over inventory.

During the last year a new competitor has entered Fabricator's markets and has offered substantial price reductions in order to grab market share. Harris has responded to the competitor's actions by matching the price cuts in the hope of maintaining market share. Harris is very concerned because he cannot see any other areas where costs can be reduced so that the division's growth and profitability can be maintained. If profitability is not maintained, his salary and bonus will be reduced.

Harris has decided that one way to make the division more profitable is to manipulate inventory because it represents a large amount of the division's balance sheet. He also knows that controls over inventory are weak. He views this inventory manipulation as a short-run solution to the profit decline due to the competitor's price cutting. Harris is certain that once the competitor stops cutting prices or goes bankrupt, the misstatements in inventory can be corrected with little impact on the bottom line.

Required:

a. Evaluate the strengths and weaknesses of Preview Company's control environment.

b. What factors in Preview Company's control environment have led to and facilitated Harris's manipulation of inventory?

(Used with permission of the PricewaterhouseCoopers LLP Foundation)

INTERNET ASSIGNMENT

 [2,4,5]   **6-42**   Complete the following control environment questionnaire for each of the control environment factors shown for EarthWear Clothiers. Refer to the information in the text and EarthWear Clothiers home page (www.mhhe.com/earthwear) for the necessary information to answer each question. If the information needed to answer the question is not available, list how the missing information would be obtained by the auditor.

CONTROL ENVIRONMENT QUESTIONNAIRE

Client: EarthWear Clothiers		**Balance Sheet Date:** 12/31/2000
Completed by: _____ **Date:** _____		**Reviewed by:** _____ **Date:** _____

BOARD OF DIRECTORS AND AUDIT COMMITTEE

An entity's control consciousness is influenced significantly by the entity's board of directors or audit committee. Attributes include the board or audit committee's independence from management, the experience and stature of its members, the extent of its involvement and scrutiny of activities, the appropriateness of its actions, the degree to which difficult questions are raised and pursued with management, and its interaction with internal and external auditors.

	Yes, No, N/A	Comments
Are there regular meetings of the board of directors (or comparable bodies) to set policies and objectives, review the entity's performance, and take appropriate action, and are minutes of such meetings prepared and signed on a timely basis?		
Does an audit committee exist?		
Does the audit committee adequately assist the board in maintaining a direct line of communication with the entity's external and internal auditors?		
Does the audit committee have adequate resources and authority to discharge its responsibilities?		
Is this evidenced by • Regular meetings? • The appointment of qualified members? • Minutes of meetings?		

MANAGEMENT PHILOSOPHY AND OPERATING STYLE

Management's philosophy and operating style significantly influence the control environment—particularly when management is dominated by one or a few individuals. Management's philosophy and operating style should create a positive atmosphere that reduces the risk of misstatement and that is conducive to the effective operation of internal control.

Are management and operating decisions dominated by one or a few individuals?		
Are business risks adequately monitored?		
Is management willing to adjust the financial statements for misstatements that approach a material amount?		
Does management adequately consult with its auditors on accounting issues?		
Has management been responsive to prior recommendations from its auditors?		
Is a high priority given to internal control?		

ORGANIZATIONAL STRUCTURE

An entity's organizational structure provides the framework within which its activities for achieving entitywide objectives are planned, executed, controlled, and monitored. Establishing a relevant organizational structure includes considering key areas of authority and responsibility and appropriate lines of reporting.

	Yes, No, N/A	Comments
Is the organization of the entity clearly defined in terms of lines of authority and responsibility?		
Are controls for authorization of transactions established at an adequately high level?		
Are such controls adequately adhered to?		
Is the organizational structure appropriate for the size and complexity of the entity?		
Has management established policies for developing and modifying accounting systems and control activities?		
Are accounting and data processing centralized or decentralized?		

ASSIGNMENT OF AUTHORITY AND RESPONSIBILITY

The methods of assigning authority and responsibility should result in clear understanding of reporting relationships and responsibilities established within the entity.

Is there a clear assignment of responsibility and delegation of authority to deal with such matters as organizational goals and objectives, operating functions, and regulatory requirements?		
Are employee job responsibilities, including specific duties, reporting relationships, and constraints, clearly established and communicated to employees?		
Has management clearly communicated the scope of authority and responsibility to data processing management?		
Does adequate computer systems documentation indicate the controls for authorizing transactions and approving systems changes?		
Is there adequate documentation of data processing controls?		

```
                                                                              ⊟⊟
  ◄      ►►     ⊗     C    ⌂     ◎     📇     ▣     A     A     📇
Back  Forward  Stop  Refresh  Home  Search  Mail  Favorites  Larger  Smaller  Preferences            e

Address: ▼  http://www.mhhe.com/messier
```

HUMAN RESOURCE POLICIES AND PROCEDURES

Human resource policies and practices relate to hiring, orientation, training, evaluating, counseling, promoting, compensating, and remedial actions. The entity's human resource policies and practices should positively influence the entity's ability to employ sufficiently competent personnel to accomplish its goals and objectives.

	Yes, No, N/A	Comments
Do client accounting personnel appear to have the background and experience for their duties?		
Do client accounting personnel understand the duties and procedures applicable to their jobs?		
Is the turnover of accounting personnel relatively low?		
Does the entity adequately train new accounting personnel?		
Does the workload of accounting personnel appear to permit them to control the quality of their work?		
Does previous experience with the client indicate sufficient integrity on the part of personnel?		

SCAD ASSIGNMENT

Assignment 4, "Evaluation of Control Structure" for Southwest Appliances, can be assigned at this time.

The Effects of Information Technology on the Audit Function

LEARNING OBJECTIVES

Upon completion of this chapter you will

[1] Learn about changing information technology (IT) and its implications for auditing.

[2] Understand the level of complexity in IT systems.

[3] Identify and understand general and application controls.

[4] Understand the effect of IT on internal control.

[5] Learn the audit process in an IT environment.

[6] Learn how to plan an audit strategy.

[7] Learn about computer-assisted audit techniques.

[8] Identify and understand the ways in which auditors use microcomputers.

[9] Understand how to assess control risk when an entity's accounting transactions are processed by a service organization.

RELEVANT ACCOUNTING AND AUDITING PRONOUNCEMENTS

SAS No. 22, "Planning and Supervision" (AU 311)

SAS No. 31, "Evidential Matter" (AU 326)

SAS No. 47, "Audit Risk and Materiality in Conducting an Audit" (AU 312)

SAS No. 55, "Consideration of Internal Control in a Financial Statement Audit" (AU 319)

SAS No. 65, "The Auditor's Consideration of the Internal Audit Function in an Audit of Financial Statements" (AU 322)

SAS No. 70, "Reports on the Processing of Transactions by Service Organizations" (AU 324)

SAS No. 78, "Consideration of Internal Control in a Financial Statement Audit: An Amendment to SAS No. 55" (AU 319)

SAS No. 80, "Amendment to Statement on Auditing Standards No. 31, Evidential Matter" (AU 326)

The effect of information technology on the audit function is the focus of this chapter. The last decade has seen an explosive growth in information technology, and auditors must be aware of its implications. The major changes in information technology and their effect on auditing are therefore discussed. This chapter also discusses auditing in a computerized environment. While audit objectives do not change as a result of information technology, the nature, extent, and timing of audit procedures may be affected (AU 326.12). The use of a microcomputer as an audit tool and the assessment of control risk when an entity's transactions are processed by a service organization are also covered in this chapter. 🌐

Changing Information Technology (IT) and Its Effect on Auditing

[LO 1] The power of computers has increased exponentially, while the cost of such technology has decreased. For example, today's microcomputers possess the same amount of power as a mainframe computer did 20 years ago. This period has also seen the development of powerful software packages that are truly user-friendly. Other technological advances include distributed data processing, telecommunications, advanced networking capabilities, and electronic commerce.

Such technology presents both challenges and opportunities for auditors. One of the challenges for auditors is to understand this technology and how it impacts the audit process. This may require additional education and training on the part of auditors. The application of computer technology to accounting systems may also offer significant opportunities for auditors. For example, computerized accounting systems may make the conduct of some parts of the audit less mundane, more interesting to audit staffs, and perhaps more efficient. Many auditing firms now provide their staff auditors with microcomputers and audit software, which facilitate tasks such as trial balance and working paper preparation. Audit software allows auditors to use more sophisticated and powerful analytical procedures, such as regression analysis. Audit software also lets auditors download client data files and perform more extensive tests.[1]

Table 7–1 lists technological changes that may affect the audit function. This section discusses these changes along with their implications for the audit function.

Distributed Data Processing, Networking, and Electronic Data Interchange

Distributed data processing organizes and coordinates data processing by decentralizing computer functions and computing power. Distributed data processing places selected information processing capabilities at the division or user department level. This can enhance user productivity through easier access to data and computer programs. For example, minicomputers that are connected to the entity's mainframe computer may be installed at the division level so that each division can control the processing and maintenance of its own data. Selected information can then be sent to the central computer at predetermined times to update corporate records. Figure 7–1 presents a schematic of a distributed data processing system. A smaller-scale version of distributed data processing might involve a *client/server system* where the *client* is a desktop PC or workstation. When the user requests information or processing, the *server*, which can be another PC or workstation, a minicomputer, or possibly a mainframe computer, does the processing, holds and updates the data, and sends back the results to the user-client.

There are two major levels of networking. At one level, networking occurs within an entity and is called a *local area network* (LAN). This allows various groups *within* the organization to communicate (such as, via e-mail) with one another. It also provides a way for various groups to access the en-

---

[1]Richard B. Lanza, "Take My Manual Audit, Please," *Journal of Accountancy* (June 1998), pp. 33–36.

TABLE 7–1	**Technological Changes That May Affect the Audit Function**

- Distributed data processing, networking, and electronic data interchange.
- Real-time systems.
- Intelligent systems.
- End-user computing.
- Electronic (Internet) commerce.

FIGURE 7–1

An Example of a Distributed
Data Processing System

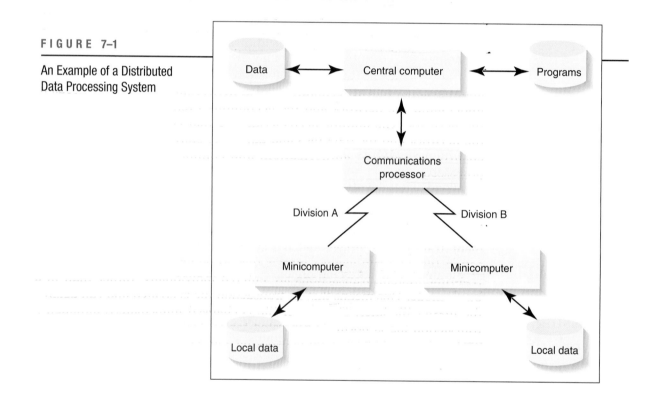

tity's data, whether centralized in one location or distributed among many locations throughout the organization.

The other level of networking provides communication *outside* the organization. An entity can send data to various groups (such as suppliers or customers) outside the organization directly by the computer via connection to *wide area networks* (WANs). This includes the initiation and execution of transactions.

Another innovation in this area is the use of *electronic data interchange* (EDI),[2] which allows organizations to transmit business transactions over

---

[2]For more information on EDI, see American Institute of Certified Public Accountants, *Audit Implications of EDI* (Auditing Practice Release) (New York: AICPA, 1996).

telecommunications networks. The benefits of EDI include a reduction in paperwork and faster turnaround times for transactions. For example, a number of large business organizations such as General Motors use just-in-time inventory systems. These organizations have developed their inventory systems so that raw materials are automatically ordered from suppliers via computer-generated purchase orders that are sent to the vendor electronically. Upon shipment and delivery, the vendor bills the organization through EDI and is paid through an electronic funds transfer system.

Audit Implications   The auditor's major concerns with distributed data processing are the controls that limit access to the system and the telecommunications controls that transmit data to and from the central computer. If unauthorized individuals can access the system at either the division or corporate levels, assets and records may be misappropriated. The auditor must also be concerned about the completeness and accuracy of the data that are sent back and forth between the central (server) and divisional (client) computers. With networking, the auditor needs to understand the network and the accounting cycles that are affected by the network. The auditor needs assurance that controls limit access to the network and the data files and databases stored there. Such controls ensure the validity, authorization, and completeness of transactions processed.

Real-Time Systems

On-line systems, which provide immediate responses to an inquiry without changing data files, have been in use for some time. In a batch environment, transactions are entered as a group, validated, batched onto a transaction file, and run against master files to be updated. With an on-line, real-time system, transactions are entered individually, rather than in a batch mode. This means that no transaction file is created and run against the master file later. The master file is changed immediately, although a transaction log is normally generated for control purposes. On-line, real-time systems rely heavily on networking and database technology. Examples of real-time processing include just-in-time inventory systems, insurance claims settlements, airline reservation systems, and optical scanning of purchases in retail stores.

Audit Implications   On-line, real-time systems significantly affect how audits are performed. Such systems likely have fewer source documents in hard-copy form, and there may also be no batch-type controls to ensure completeness. Thus the concern for controls over access to the system is increased. Another concern relates to the fact that transactions may be authorized by controls included in the programs. In an on-line, real-time system, the auditor must rely more on the entity's controls, and auditing needs to be conducted more continuously.

Intelligent Systems

Innovations in programming languages have provided tools for developing specialized computer systems referred to as *decision support systems* (DSSs) or *expert systems* (ESs). These systems place the knowledge and decision processes of experts into a computer program. In many entities, DSSs and ESs are used as part of the accounting systems. Examples include credit approval, pricing of insurance policies, and valuation of loan-loss reserves. *Neural networks*, which can learn from examples and cases, are also increasingly used in areas such as bankruptcy prediction. Auditors use DSSs and ESs to gather and evaluate evidence.

Audit Implications   A client's use of DSS and ES technology poses potential control problems for the auditor. If important organizational decisions are made by these systems, the auditor must be concerned with the integrity of the knowledge captured in the system and how the system makes decisions. For example, if a client uses an expert system to value loan-loss reserves, the auditor must "audit" the knowledge and logic of the program to ensure that the expert system's decisions are appropriate.

End-User Computing[3]

Developments in microcomputer technology, high-level computer languages, and packaged software have allowed user departments to develop their own applications and data files. Two of the major advantages of end-user computing are a shorter development time for applications and a reduction in the conflicts that sometimes arise between the user department and the IT department. The major problem with end-user computing is that it may not be subjected to the same IT controls that are applied at the main computer center.

Audit Implications   While end-user computing offers advantages to user departments, it may represent some real risks for both the client and the auditor. Control over end-user computing is an important issue for the auditor (and management) because weak controls at the user department may allow users to inappropriately access and modify data at the main computer center. If such controls are not present, the auditor will have concerns about the safeguarding of assets and data integrity.

Electronic (Internet) Commerce

There has been a tremendous growth of electronic commerce involving individuals and organizations engaging in business transactions without paper documents, using computers and telecommunications networks. EDI, which was previously discussed, is one example of this type of commerce. In EDI, business is conducted between entities that have a prearranged contractual relationship. More recently, electronic commerce through the Internet or World Wide Web ("the Web") has included business between individuals and entities that were not previously known to each other. For example, many companies (such as, Amazon.com) now sell products directly to consumers over the Internet. As this form of commerce becomes a source of revenues for audit clients, auditors must be aware of the associated risks.

---

[3]See American Institute of Certified Public Accountants, *Auditing in Common Computer Environments* (Auditing Practice Release) (New York: AICPA, 1995), for a detailed discussion of end-user computing.

Audit Implications   When a client sells products or services over the Internet, the auditor's main concerns are transaction integrity, protection of information, and unauthorized access to the entity's network. If the client does not have adequate controls, electronic transactions can be changed, lost, duplicated, or processed incorrectly. The entity must also have sufficient controls to ensure that consumer information is protected from unauthorized use. Additionally, the entity must have strong access controls that prevent security breaches of the corporate network or Internet servers.

The Complexity of IT Systems

[LO 2]   One way of focusing the discussion of the effects of IT on the audit function is to consider the complexity of the IT systems the auditor may encounter. There are a number of computer types and equipment configurations. For discussion purposes, IT systems are categorized into three types: low-complexity, medium-complexity, and advanced systems. The reader should keep in mind that real-world IT systems cannot be easily classified into one of the three categories.

Low-Complexity Systems

A low-complexity IT system would normally be composed of a stand-alone microcomputer or a small number of microcomputers that are connected to a network. The system would generally be used for maintaining journals, subsidiary ledgers, and the general ledger. The system might also be used for preparing basic accounting documents (such as sales invoices or checks). Most of the software used by the system would be purchased from vendors with little or no modification.

Systems of this type generally have few controls. Typically, there is a lack of segregation of duties because of cost considerations, limited security or access controls, and limited data and operation controls. For most entities with a low-complexity IT system, the auditor will not be able to rely on internal control. However, the auditor may be able to use data retrieval software to perform substantive tests.[4]

Medium-Complexity Systems

A system of medium complexity would, at a minimum, include a minicomputer or server and might include a number of microcomputers or terminals networked to the minicomputer or server. The recent increase in the power of computers sometimes blurs the distinction between the types of computers. For example, some microcomputers are almost as powerful as low-end minicomputers, while some minicomputers have nearly the power of mainframe computers. The types of software used in a medium-complexity system would be more advanced, with utility programs used to enter and change data and purchased software used and modified to meet the entity's needs.

---

[4]AICPA, *Auditing in Common Computer Environments* (Auditing Practice Release) (New York: AICPA, 1995).

A medium-complexity system may also lack a number of important controls. For example, there may be limited segregation of duties within the IT department and between the IT and user departments. There may or may not be a separate, secure location for the computer. Last, the documentation of the system may be limited. In a medium-complexity IT environment, the auditor may be able to reduce control risk if sufficient controls are present.

Advanced Systems

Most large entities today depend heavily on IT for handling their information processing needs. The technological advances just discussed are implemented into advanced systems. An advanced system contains one or more of the following characteristics:

- Telecommunications.
- Extensive database systems.
- On-line, real-time processing.
- Distributed data processing.
- Automatic transaction initiation, EDI, and electronic commerce.
- No visual audit trail.

One or more mainframe computers control the entity's information processing capabilities.

Advanced systems should contain most, if not all, of the general and application controls discussed in the next section. Such systems are very complex with significant interactions between the accounting and operating cycles. In an advanced system, the traditional controls are programmed with the processing trail existing only in machine-readable form. For a client utilizing an advanced IT system, an auditor may need to rely on the system to conduct the audit. In such cases, the audit team will include an auditor who is specially trained in IT auditing. Auditing an advanced system will also require the use of computer-assisted audit techniques to gather evidential matter.

Types of Controls in an IT Environment

[LO 3]   There are two broad categories of information systems control activities: general controls and application controls. *General controls* relate to the overall information processing environment and have a *pervasive* effect on the entity's computer operations. General controls are sometimes referred to as supervisory, management, or information technology controls. *Application controls* apply to the processing of specific computer applications and are part of the computer programs used in the accounting system (for example, revenues or purchasing). Figure 7–2 shows the relationship between general and application controls.

General Controls

General controls can be classified into five categories:

- Organizational controls.
- Systems development and modification controls.

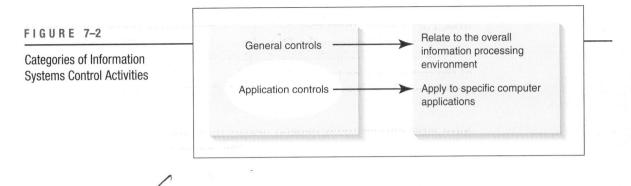

FIGURE 7–2

Categories of Information Systems Control Activities

- Hardware and systems software controls.
- Security and access controls.
- Operations and data controls.

Organizational Controls   The use of IT eliminates many of the traditional segregation of duties functions that are present in a manual system. As with a manual system, the size of the entity affects the extent to which segregation of duties can be achieved. Complete segregation of duties is usually found only in large entities that rely extensively on IT for information processing. In a small to medium-size IT operation, the auditor will continue to have concerns about proper segregation of duties. Figure 7–3 shows an organizational chart for a large IT department. Table 7–2 briefly describes the duties of each function identified in Figure 7–3.

Possible modifications to the organizational chart shown in Figure 7–3 can maintain good segregation of duties. For example, the systems analysis and application programming functions can be combined. Normally this will not lead to a significant control risk as long as the programmers have access only to programs being developed or maintained and not to the production (application) programs used in regular operations. However, if possible, the systems programming function should remain separate from the application programming function. If this segregation is not maintained, it is possible for systems programmers to change production programs in order to record fictitious transactions or to misappropriate assets. Some IT departments have the librarian and data control group report to operations with little loss of control.

The most important separation of duties in the IT department is between operations and the systems analysis and programming functions, because these groups have the most knowledge about how the system works. If the systems analysts or programmers have access to computer operations, they may be able to make unauthorized changes to programs or files. Again, this may result in fictitious transactions and misappropriated assets. For example, if a systems analyst can access the computer, he or she could alter his or her own payroll records.

Cost considerations may not allow for complete segregation of duties in small or medium-size IT departments. Figure 7–4 presents an organizational chart for a small or medium-size IT department. Note that the separation of duties between systems analysis and programming and computer

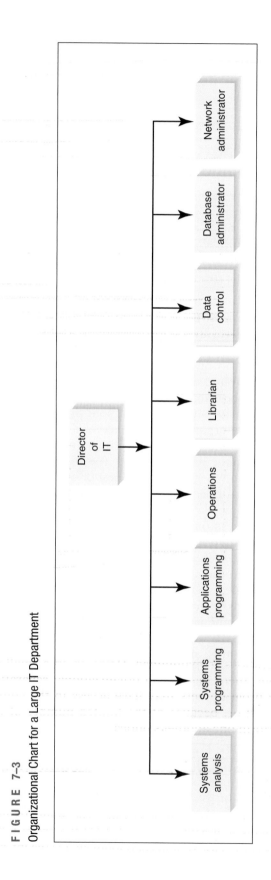

FIGURE 7–3

Organizational Chart for a Large IT Department

TABLE 7–2	Assigned Duties for the Major Functions in a Large IT Department

Function	*Brief Description of Assigned Duties*
Systems analysis	Responsible for determining the requirements for new and existing systems, including specifications for programmers and preparation of systems documentation
Systems programming	Responsible for systems software (such as operating system, library, security packages)
Applications programming	Responsible for writing and testing application programs and preparation of program documentation
Operations	Responsible for proper operation of the computer equipment
Librarian	Responsible for maintaining custody of files, programs, and documentation
Data control	Responsible for control over data received from user departments, including error correction, and for control over distribution of output
Database administrator	Responsible for all activities related to the database
Network administrator	Responsible for data communication activities

FIGURE 7–4

Organizational Chart for a Small or Medium-Size IT Department

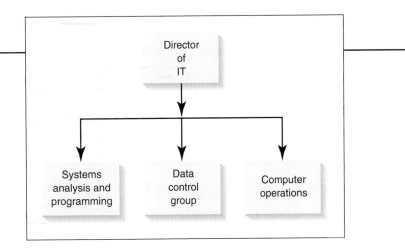

operations is maintained. However, in a small or medium-size IT department, there may be an organizational separation of these functions, but the programmers may have access to the computer console to run programs; or, because of the limited number of personnel, employees may perform one another's duties.

Systems Development and Modification Controls   Another general control is the development of new information systems and the modification of existing systems. These controls are critical for ensuring the reliability of information processing. The ability to audit accounting information systems is greatly improved if (1) the entity follows common policies and procedures for systems development, (2) the internal and/or external auditors are involved in the development process, and (3) proper user, system operator, and program documentation is provided for each application. For example, having internal or external auditors involved early in the design of the system can ensure that proper controls are built into the system.

The entity should establish written policies and procedures for planning, developing, and implementing new systems. Normally, a request for a new system is submitted by the user department to the IT department or an information services committee. A feasibility study may be conducted that includes cost/benefit analysis, hardware and software needs, and the system's impact on current applications and operations. Next, the system is designed, programmed, tested, and implemented. Last, the entity should prepare good documentation, including flowcharts, file layouts, source code listings, and operator instructions. This level of documentation is necessary for the auditors to understand the accounting systems, including application controls, so that tests of controls and substantive testing can be properly planned and conducted.

The entity must also have strong controls to ensure that once programs are placed into operation, all authorized changes are made and unauthorized changes are prevented. Although not as detailed, the controls for program changes are similar to those followed for new systems development. From the auditor's perspective, the important issue here is whether changes to programs are properly authorized, tested, and implemented.

Hardware and Systems Software Controls
Hardware controls are built into the equipment by the manufacturer and are intended to ensure that the reliability of information processing is not affected by equipment failure. Table 7–3 contains some examples of hardware controls. Normally, auditors do not have to verify the hardware controls.

Systems software is computer programs that control the computer functions and allow the application programs to run. These programs include operating systems, library and security packages, and database management systems. For example, the operating system controls the operations of the computer and allocates computer resources among the application programs. The operating system also detects and corrects processing errors.

Security and Access Controls
These general controls are concerned with (1) physical protection of computer equipment, software, and data and (2) loss of assets and information through theft or unauthorized use.

TABLE 7–3	Examples of Hardware Controls
Hardware Control	*Description*
Duplicate circuitry	A computation is performed twice by the central processing unit, and the two results are compared.
Parity check	A parity or check bit verifies the transmission of data.
Echo check	The transmission of data to and from the components of the system is verified.
Dual read	Input to the system is read twice by separate components and compared for accuracy.

Security controls include locating the computer facilities in a separate building or in a secure part of a building. They also include limiting access to the computer facilities through the use of locked doors with authorized personnel being admitted through use of a conventional key, an authorization card, or physical recognition. Control must also be enforced within the computer facility. For example, programmers must not be allowed access to the computer room; this restriction will prevent them from making unauthorized modifications to systems and application programs.

There must also be adequate protection against events such as fire and water damage, electrical problems, and sabotage. Proper construction of computer facilities can minimize the damage from such events. In order to ensure that the entity's operations are not interrupted by such events, the entity should have an operational disaster recovery plan, which may include an off-site backup location for processing critical applications.

Unauthorized access to programs or data can cause loss of assets and information. Physical control over programs and data can be maintained by a separate library function that controls access and use of files. In advanced computer systems with on-line, real-time database systems and telecommunications technologies, programs and data can be accessed from outside the computer facility. Access controls in advanced systems should thus include physical security over remote terminals, authorization controls that limit access only to authorized information, user identification controls such as passwords, and data communication controls such as encryption of data. Without such controls, an unauthorized user could access the system, with a resulting loss of assets or a decrease in the reliability of data.

Operations and Data Controls   These general controls ensure that the computer hardware and the application systems operate as planned on an ongoing basis. Operations and data controls include controls over computer operations, data preparation, work flow control, and library functions. Important controls over computer operations should prevent unauthorized access to programs, files, and systems documentation by computer operators. In advanced IT systems, traditional controls such as rotation of operator duties and mandatory vacations should be implemented. The operating systems log, which documents all program and operator activities, should be regularly reviewed to ensure that operators have not performed any unauthorized activities.

Controls over data preparation include proper entry of data into an application system and proper oversight of error correction. Controls over work flow include scheduling of application programs, proper setup for programs, and use of the correct files. The library function needs controls to ensure that (1) the correct files are provided for specific applications, (2) files are properly maintained, and (3) backup and recovery procedures exist.

Application Controls

Application controls apply to the processing of individual accounting applications, such as sales or payroll, and help ensure the completeness and accuracy of transaction processing, authorization, and validity. Although application controls are typically discussed under the categories of input, processing, and output controls, changes in technology have blurred the distinctions among input, processing, and output. For example, many of the data validation checks that were once performed as part of production programs are now accomplished with sophisticated editing routines and intelligent data entry equipment. As a result, application controls are discussed under the following categories:

- Data capture controls
- Data validation controls
- Processing controls
- Output controls
- Error controls

Data Capture Controls   Data capture controls must ensure that (1) all transactions are recorded in the application system, (2) transactions are recorded only once, and (3) rejected transactions are identified, controlled, corrected, and reentered into the system. Thus, data capture controls are concerned primarily with *validity, completeness,* and *valuation* internal control objectives. For example, checking that all transactions are recorded in the system relates to the completeness objective.

There are three ways of capturing data in an information system: (1) source documentation, (2) direct data entry, or (3) a combination of the two. When source documents are present, batch processing is an effective way of controlling data capture. Batching is simply the process of grouping similar transactions for data entry. It is important that each batch be well controlled. This can be accomplished by assigning each batch a unique number and recording it in a batch register or log. A cover sheet should also be attached to each batch with spaces for recording the batch number, the date, the signatures of various persons who processed the batch, and information on errors detected. To ensure complete processing of all transactions in a batch, some type of batch total should be used. Table 7–4 presents the three most common types of information used for batch totals.

Direct data entry, on the other hand, involves on-line processing of the data with no source documents. The combination method may involve entry of the data from source documents directly through on-line processing. If direct data entry or a combination of source documents and direct

 TABLE 7–4	Types of Information Used for Batch Totals	
Batch Total	*Description of Information*
Financial total	A total of some dollar field in the set of transactions (such as total sales or total amount of vouchers to be recorded)
Hash total	A total of some nonfinancial field in the batch of transactions (such as total number of units sold or total number of employee Social Security numbers)
Record count	A total of the number of transactions included in the batch

data entry is used, the system should create a *transaction log*. The log should contain a detailed record of each transaction, including date and time of entry, terminal and operator identification, and a unique number (such as customer order number).

Data Validation Controls   These controls can be applied at various stages, depending on the entity's IT capabilities, and are mainly concerned with the *valuation* internal control objective. When source documents are batch processed, the data are taken from source documents and transcribed to tape or disk. The data are then validated by an edit program or by routines that are part of the production programs. When the data are entered directly into off-line storage through an intelligent terminal or directly into an edit (validation) program with subsequent (delayed or real-time) processing into the application system, each individual transaction should be subjected to a number of programmed edit checks. Table 7–5 lists common validation tests. For example, a payroll application program may have a limit test that subjects any employee payroll transaction involving more than 80 hours worked to review before processing.

Some entities use *turnaround documents* to improve data accuracy. Turnaround documents are output documents from the application that are used as source documents in later processing. For example, a monthly statement sent to a customer may contain two parts; one part of the monthly statement is kept by the customer, while the other part is returned with the payment. The latter part of the statement contains encoded information that can be processed using various input devices. By using a turnaround document, the entity does not have to reenter the data, thus avoiding data capture and data validation errors.

With direct data (on-line) entry, accuracy can be improved by special validation routines that may be programmed to *prompt* the data entry personnel. Here the system requests the desired input data and then waits for an acceptable response before requesting the next piece of input data. In many cases, the screen displays the document format with blanks that are completed by data entry personnel. The validation routine should include

TABLE 7–5	Common Data Validation Controls

Data Validation Control	Description
Limit test	A test to ensure that a numerical value does not exceed some predetermined value
Range test	A check to ensure that the value in a field falls within an allowable range of values
Sequence check	A check to determine if input data are in proper numerical or alphabetical sequence
Existence (validity) test	A test of an ID number or code by comparison to a file or table containing valid ID numbers or codes
Field test	A check on a field to ensure that it contains either all numeric or alphabetic characters
Sign test	A check to ensure that the data in a field have the proper arithmetic sign
Check-digit verification	A numeric value computed to provide assurance that the original value was not altered

a completeness test to ensure that all data items are completed before processing. Airline reservation systems and catalog retailers (like EarthWear) that take phone orders use this type of entry system.

Processing Controls   These are controls that ensure proper processing of transactions. In some information systems, many of the controls discussed under data validation may be performed as part of data processing. General controls play an important role in providing assurance about the quality of processing controls. If the entity has strong general controls (such as systems development and modification controls, library controls, personnel practices, separation of duties), it is likely that programs will be properly written and tested, correct files will be used for processing, and unauthorized access to the system will be limited. Table 7–6 presents a number of processing controls.

Output Controls   Output includes reports, checks, documents, and other printed or displayed (on terminal screens) information. Controls over output from computer systems are important application controls. The main concern here is that computer output may be distributed or displayed to unauthorized users. A number of controls should be present to minimize the unauthorized use of output. A report distribution log should contain a schedule of when reports are prepared, the names of individuals who are to receive the report, and the date of distribution. Some type of transmittal sheet indicating the intended recipients' names and addresses should be attached to each copy of the output. A release form may be part of the transmittal sheet and should be signed by the individual acknowledging receipt of the report.

The data control group should be responsible for reviewing the output for reasonableness and reconciling the control or batch totals to the output. The user departments should also review the output for completeness and accuracy because they may be the only ones with sufficient knowledge to recognize certain types of errors.

Error Controls   Errors can be identified at any point in the system. While most transaction errors should be identified by data capture and data validation controls, some errors may be identified by processing or output

TABLE 7–6	Types of Processing Controls

Processing Control	Description
File or volume labels	Internal and external file labels should be assigned. The application program should check to ensure that the correct file is used for processing.
Control totals	Control totals ensure the accuracy and completeness of processing. For example, run-to-run totals are control totals that reconcile two processing runs.
Reasonableness tests	These are programmed controls that determine if the processing results are outside some predetermined value.

controls. After identification, errors must be corrected and resubmitted to the application system at the correct point in processing. For example, if a transaction was entered with an incorrect customer number, it should be rejected by a validity test. After the customer number is corrected, it should be resubmitted into the system. Given the separation of the IT department's data control group from the user departments, internal control is improved by dividing the responsibility for handling errors. Errors that result from processing transactions (such as data entry errors) should be corrected and resubmitted by the data control group. Errors that occur outside the IT department (like omitted or invalid data) should be corrected by the appropriate user department and resubmitted. This segregation of duties prevents the data control group from processing invalid transactions.

There are a number of ways of effectively identifying, correcting, and resubmitting errors. Figure 7–5 provides a flowchart of how errors can be

FIGURE 7–5

A Flowchart of Processing
for Error Transactions

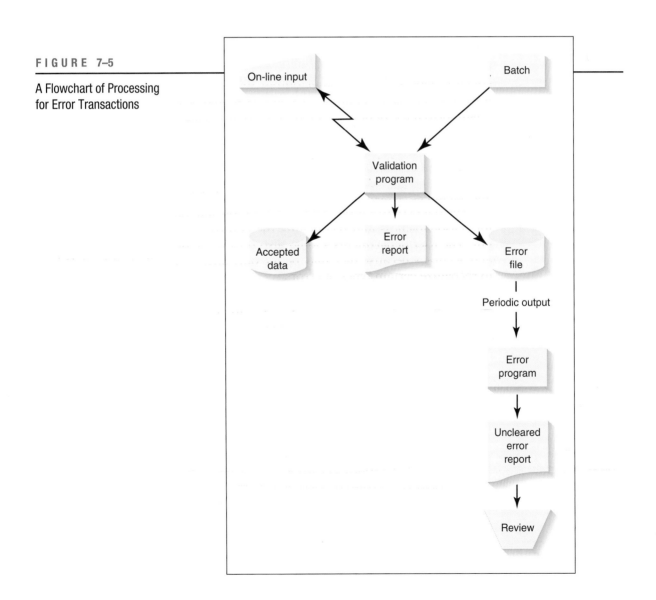

handled in a data validation program within an application system. In this example, errors are maintained in an error file and printed on an error report. The errors noted on the error report should be corrected by either the data control group or the user departments. When these transactions are resubmitted, they are "closed out" on the error file. Periodically, the error file should be printed out; items that have not been cleared within a pre-specified period of time should be investigated.

The Effect of IT on Internal Control

[LO 4] The five components of internal control were presented in Chapter 6. In particular, we discussed (1) the factors that affect the control environment, (2) risks relevant to the achievement of entity objectives, (3) control activities that ensure that actions have been taken to address those risks, (4) information and communication requirements, and (5) monitoring activities. The presence of computer processing for significant accounting applications affects how an entity implements its internal control system. Table 7–7 lists factors within the control environment and selected control activities that are affected by IT. For example, Chapter 6 mentioned a new or revamped information system as a circumstance that affects risk assessment.

Control Environment Factors

Assignment of Authority and Responsibility Clear lines of authority and responsibility are important so that the entity's objectives are met. In a manual system, each user department is normally responsible for its own data. However, a database management system centralizes these responsibilities in a database administrator, so these lines may be blurred because of the interaction between user departments and the IT department. For example, in a database management system, multiple users may have access to a particular database. Authorization to access the database and determination of who is responsible for the integrity of the data become important. If the data in such a system are altered, it may be very difficult for management to determine who was responsible.

TABLE 7–7	Control Environment Factors and Control Activities Affected by IT

Control Environment Factors
- Assignment of authority and responsibility.
- Human resource policies and practices.

Control Activities
- Information processing.
- Proper segregation of duties.
- Physical controls.

Additionally, in a manual system, management can easily supervise employees because they are generally in the same physical location. Data communication capabilities, however, allow employees to perform their duties in remote locations. It is important, then, for management to be sure that sufficient supervisory controls and monitoring processes are built into computer systems to ensure that employees follow corporate policies.

Human Resource Policies and Practices   Competent, trustworthy employees are a key ingredient in any internal control system. In a computerized environment, it is even more important to have personnel who possess the skills and knowledge needed to operate the information systems. Further, in such environments, fewer individuals monitor the integrity of the data.

Control Activities

Information Processing   Two areas in which control activities can be affected by computer processing are (1) authorization of transactions and (2) the keeping of adequate documents and records. Authorization policies are easy to observe in manual systems because the individual who authorizes the transaction usually signs his or her name to document approval. In a computerized environment, however, many of the authorization procedures for transactions are part of the computer program. For example, credit for an existing customer's sales transaction may be approved automatically by comparing the total of the current order plus the customer's prior balance to a predefined credit limit. The sales transaction may also be priced by the computer program. Another concern relates to who is granted authority to access confidential information. Unauthorized individuals may be able to gain access to critical client data, and it may be very difficult for an organization to know that such access has occurred.

In an IT system, there may not be a hard copy of source documents and records. Thus, the normal paper audit trail may not be present for the auditor to examine. For example, some retail catalog organizations have a customer service representative record a customer's telephone orders directly into the computer via a terminal. In such a situation, there is no hard copy of a customer's sales order as there is when the order is mailed to the organization. However, a well-designed computer system should include a record in machine-readable form stored on disk or tape of the processing steps that took place. In such a case, the auditor has to rely on computer-assisted audit procedures to obtain evidence on the processing of transactions.

Segregation of Duties   One of the biggest concerns in a computerized system is ensuring proper segregation of duties within the IT department. In a manual system, the initiation of transactions, authorization of transactions, recording of transactions, and custody of assets can be separated by having different individuals perform those tasks. In a computerized environment, the programs within the system may perform all of these functions. Thus, it is important to have adequate controls within the IT department to compensate for this situation. However, many small to medium-size computer systems may not segregate duties adequately because the cost of doing so may be prohibitive.

Physical Controls   Physical control over assets and records is important in any type of system. In a computerized environment, however, many of the assets and records may be concentrated in the IT department or be accessible through the computer system. It may also be easier to hide the theft of assets. For example, if controls over access to the system are not adequate, an employee may be able to enter fictitious purchases of goods or services into the entity's records. A check may then be mailed to a fictitious vendor with the employee later converting the cash disbursement to his or her personal funds.

It is also important to have proper backup controls for computer programs and data files in case original copies are destroyed or damaged. For example, an entity should have a disaster recovery plan, which may include backup copies of programs and data files stored at a different location.

The Audit Process in an IT Environment[5]

Overview

[LO 5]

In planning the engagement, the auditor must consider how the entity uses IT to process accounting information. The auditor's knowledge of the entity's computer processing must include the following factors:

- The extent to which the computer is used in each significant accounting application.
- The complexity of the entity's computer operations.
- The organizational structure of the computer's processing activities.
- The availability of data for evidential matter.

As the entity's computer applications become more complex because of the use of sophisticated information technology, the auditor may need to devote more effort to understanding internal control in order to conduct tests of controls and substantive tests. This is particularly important where transactions or accounting records may be available for only a short period of time or may exist only in machine-readable form. In such situations, specialized skills may be required to assess the effect of computer processing on the audit. As mentioned earlier, a computer audit specialist may need to be part of the audit team in order to evaluate internal control properly and to plan audit tests.

It is important to remember that audit objectives do not change when accounting information is processed by a computer. What may change,

---

[5]For a detailed example, see American Institute of Certified Public Accountants, *Consideration of the Internal Control in a Financial Statement Audit* (Auditing Practice Release) (New York: AICPA, 1996).

however, are the methods of applying specific audit procedures. While the auditor may continue to use manual audit procedures for some tests, in computerized accounting systems it may be necessary to use computer-assisted audit techniques to obtain audit evidence. Examples of computer-assisted audit techniques are discussed later in this chapter.

Audit Strategy Decisions

✐ [LO 6]

Figure 7–6 relates the auditor's consideration of general and application controls to the assessment of control risk and to the nature, extent, and timing of substantive tests. Figure 7–6 parallels the logic outlined in Figure 6–2, except that general and application controls are substituted for the components of internal control. Following the approach shown in Figure 7–6 leads to a choice of the same audit strategies (substantive or reliance) discussed in Chapter 6. The preliminary review of general controls is necessary under either audit strategy, but the level of required understanding of the general controls is greater when the auditor plans to rely on internal controls. Each of these strategies is discussed briefly.

Substantive Strategy   Following a substantive audit strategy is sometimes referred to as *auditing around the computer*. Two conditions are necessary before this approach can be followed:

1. There must be adequate source documents and accounting reports in non–machine-readable form.
2. The transactions must be traceable from the source documents to the accounting reports and from the reports back to the source documents.

By following a substantive audit strategy approach, the auditor concentrates on agreeing the input with the output, without directly verifying the processing of the data. The auditor is therefore relying on controls in the user departments rather than on the application controls included in the computer programs. The auditor may choose this approach because it is less costly and requires limited IT knowledge. While a substantive audit strategy implies that application controls will not be relied upon, the auditor may still use the computer for audit procedures such as selecting and printing accounts receivable confirmations.

Reliance Strategy   When a reliance strategy is followed, the auditor reviews and tests general and application controls and determines their effectiveness. While the auditor uses inquiry of client personnel, observation, and documentation to gather evidence about the general controls, the reliance strategy results in the auditor using computer-assisted audit techniques to test application controls. Table 7–8 lists the categories of general controls and some typical audit procedures used to test their effectiveness.

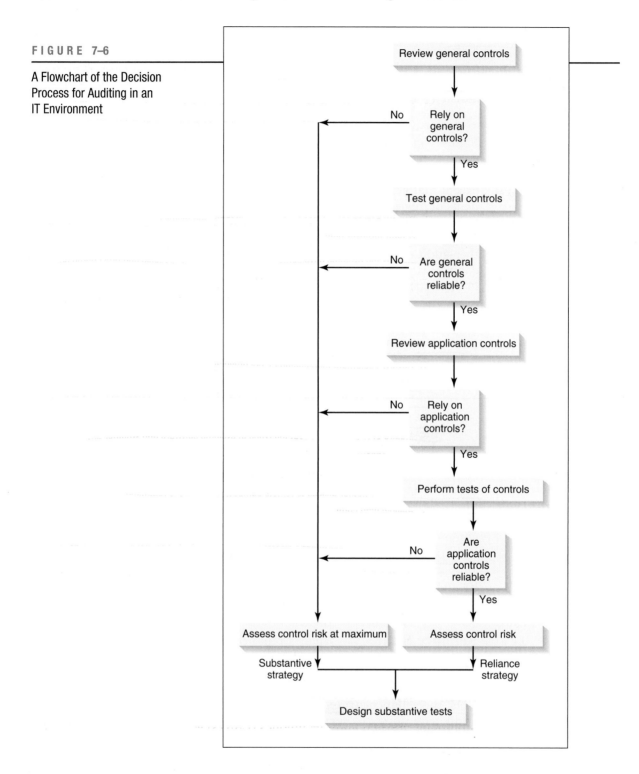

TABLE 7–8	**Selected Audit Procedures for Testing General Controls**
General Controls	*Selected Audit Procedures*
Organizational controls	1. Review the IT department's organizational chart to determine if any incompatible functions exist among systems analysis, systems programming, applications programming, operations, librarian, and data control. 2. Review job descriptions of key IT personnel to ensure that there are no incompatible duties. 3. Observe IT operations to ensure that systems analysts and programmers do not have access to the computer or files. 4. Review personnel policies for hiring, promoting, and dismissing IT employees. Review IT staff turnover data.
Systems development and modification controls	1. Review the systems development standards manual for policies and procedures for development and maintenance of application systems. 2. Review the documentation of a sample of application systems to determine if systems development and modification policies and procedures are being followed. 3. Review documentation for approval of new applications by management, users, and IT groups.
Hardware and systems software controls	1. Review equipment manufacturers' documentation to determine what hardware controls are available. 2. Review equipment failure logs or other operating reports on the equipment's reliability. 3. Review maintenance contracts with computer equipment manufacturers. 4. Inquire of IT personnel about the types of systems software and whether any modifications have been made to the programs.
Security and access controls	1. Inquire of IT management about and observe physical security controls. 2. Observe whether access to remote computer terminals is restricted. 3. Review data communication access controls. 4. Inquire of IT management about fire detection devices. 5. Review the IT department's disaster recovery plan, including insurance coverage.
Operations and data controls	1. Review and test whether authorization to gain access to the system is consistent with the segregation of duties in IT. 2. Review controls over work flow and error correction procedures. 3. Review backup and recovery procedures.

Computer-Assisted Audit Techniques[6]

[LO 7] Computer-assisted audit techniques (CAATs) generally assist the auditor in testing application controls. Many of these controls are embedded into the client's computer programs. Additionally, the auditor may need to use

---

[6]For more information on computer-assisted audit techniques, see American Institute of Certified Public Accountants, *Auditing with Computers* (Auditing Practice Release) (New York: AICPA, 1994).

CAATs to execute substantive tests when the information is maintained in machine-readable form. The following types of CAATs are discussed:

- Generalized audit software
- Custom audit software
- Test data
- Integrated test facility
- Parallel simulation
- Concurrent auditing techniques

Generalized Audit Software

Generalized audit software (GAS) includes programs that allow the auditor to perform tests on computer files and databases. GAS was developed so that auditors would be able to conduct similar computer-assisted audit techniques in different computer environments. For example, GAS permits an auditor to select and prepare accounts receivable confirmations from a variety of computer systems. This type of software provides a high-level computer language that allows the auditor to easily perform various functions on a client's computer files and databases. A sample of functions that can be performed by GAS is shown in Table 7–9.

The following steps are completed by the auditor in a typical GAS application. An accounts receivable application is used as an example.

1. Set the objectives of the application:
   - Test the mathematical accuracy of the accounts receivable subsidiary database.
   - Select for confirmation all accounts receivable customer accounts with balances greater than $10,000 plus a random sample of 50 accounts with balances less than $10,000.
   - Print out the confirmation and monthly statement for all selected customer accounts.
2. Design the application:
   - Identify the data structures used in the database.
   - Specify the format for the confirmation.

TABLE 7–9	Functions Performed by Generalized Audit Software

Function	Description
File or database access	Reads and extracts data from a client's computer files or databases for further audit testing
Selection operators	Select from files or databases transactions that meet certain criteria
Arithmetic functions	Perform a variety of arithmetic calculations (addition, subtraction, and so on) on transactions, files, and databases
Statistical analyses	Provide functions supporting various types of audit sampling
Report generation	Prepares various types of documents and reports

3. Code the instructions for the application:
   - Prepare the GAS specification sheets or enter the code directly into the GAS for the confirmation application.
4. Process the application:
   - Access the client's accounts receivable database with the GAS. Generally, a work file is extracted from the database for processing on the GAS.
5. Evaluate the results of the application:
   - Verify the output that tested the mathematical accuracy of the accounts receivable subsidiary ledger database.
   - Review the confirmations and monthly statements.
   - Mail confirmations and monthly statements to customers.

GAS offers several advantages: (1) it is easy to use, (2) limited IT expertise or programming skills are required, and (3) the time required to develop the application is usually short. Among the disadvantages of GAS are that (1) it involves auditing *after* the client has processed the data rather than while the data is being processed and (2) it provides a limited ability to verify programming logic because its application is usually directed to testing client files or databases.

Custom Audit Software

Custom audit software is generally written by auditors for specific audit tasks. Such programs are necessary when the entity's computer system is not compatible with the auditor's GAS or when the auditor wants to conduct some testing that may not be possible with the GAS. It may also be more efficient to prepare custom programs if they will be used in future audits of the entity or if they may be used on similar engagements. The major disadvantages of custom software are that (1) it is expensive to develop, (2) it may require a long development time, and (3) it may require extensive modification if the client changes its accounting application programs.

Inventory observation and testing provide a good example of where such a program might be useful. Suppose a client maintains computerized perpetual inventory records that are updated by the sales and purchasing systems. Further assume that the client conducts a physical inventory once a year, at which time the perpetual records are corrected by a physical count. At the time of the physical inventory, the client's employees record the physical counts on special computer forms that are optically scanned to create a physical inventory file. The quantities on hand are priced using an approved price file. What results from this analysis is the inventory balance used for updating the perpetual records and the financial statements.

The auditors who observe the client's physical inventory record the counts on special computer forms that are optically scanned and used as input to the custom program. The custom program would perform the following audit procedures: (1) trace the test counts into the client's perpetual inventory file and print out any exceptions; (2) perform a complete mathematical test, including extensions, footings, crossfootings, and use of approved prices; (3) summarize the inventory by type; and (4) print out items in excess of a predetermined amount for review.

Test Data

The auditor uses test data for testing the application controls in the client's computer programs. In using this method, the auditor first creates a set of simulated data (that is, test data) for processing. The data should include both valid and invalid data. After calculating the expected results of processing the test data, the auditor uses the client's computer to process the data. The valid data should be properly processed, while the invalid data should be identified as errors. The results of this processing are compared to the auditor's predetermined results. Figure 7–7 flowcharts this process. This technique can be used to check

- Data validation controls and error detection routines.
- Processing logic controls.
- Arithmetic calculations.
- The inclusion of transactions in records, files, and reports.

The objective of using the test data method is to ensure the accuracy of the computer processing of transactions.

The main advantage of the test data method is that it provides direct evidence on the effectiveness of the controls included in the client's application programs. However, the test data method has a number of potential disadvantages. First, it can be very time-consuming to create the test

FIGURE 7–7

Flowchart of the Test Data Method

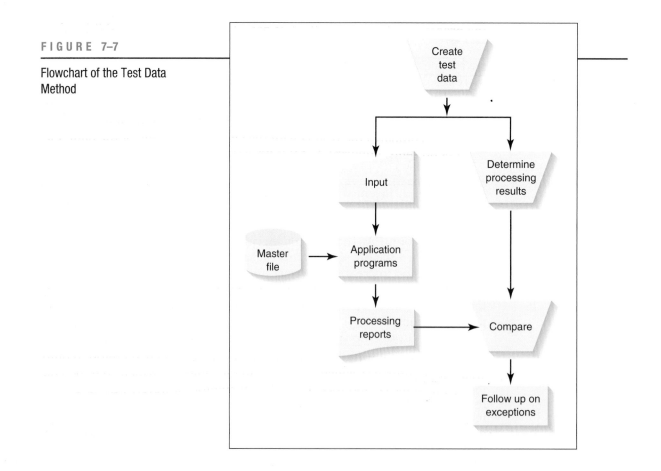

data. Second, the auditor may not be certain that all relevant conditions or controls are tested. The use of special computer programs called *test data generators* may help alleviate these potential disadvantages. Third, the auditor must be certain that the test data are processed using the client's regular production programs. This concern can be alleviated if the client's general controls for program changes, access, and library functions are reliable. Last, the auditor must be sure to remove the valid test data from the client's files.

Integrated Test Facility

Closely related to the test data method is the use of an integrated test facility (ITF). Unlike the test data method, in which the test data are processed separately, the ITF technique enters test data along with actual data in a normal application run. The test data relate to a "minicompany" or "dummy" entity that has been created within the client's records. The auditor then examines the processing of the test data related to the "dummy" entity. The ITF technique has the same objectives as the test data method except that the testing takes place under *actual* operating conditions. This provides added assurance that the auditor is testing the computer programs actually used by the client.

In addition to the cost of using this technique, the major disadvantage of an ITF is removal of the test data from the client's records. Test data are usually removed by reversing or canceling the transactions. The auditor must be very careful to ensure that all the test data are removed and that the process used to remove the test data does not create any additional errors in the client's system.

Parallel Simulation

The use of parallel simulation requires that the auditor construct a computer simulation that mimics the client's production programs. With this method the auditor processes actual client data through the simulated program and compares the results with the client's processing of the data. Figure 7–8 presents a flowchart of this process.

The main advantages of the use of a parallel simulation are that (1) it provides evidence on the controls used in the client's application programs and (2) it allows the auditor to test the accuracy of large volumes of transactions. The major disadvantage is the cost of developing the simulation. However, some generalized audit software may provide a cost-effective tool for developing the simulation.

Concurrent Auditing Techniques

With the exception of the ITF, all of the CAATs just discussed involve gathering audit evidence either outside the actual processing cycle or after processing has been completed. Advanced systems with on-line, real-time processing, extensive database systems, and distributed processing require continuous monitoring. Advanced computer systems may therefore require that the auditor use concurrent auditing techniques, which may be conducted by internal auditors. The external auditor, however, will have to review the internal auditors' work if he or she intends to rely on it in order to reduce control risk. (Detailed discussion of concurrent auditing techniques is beyond the scope of this book; however, such techniques are briefly

FIGURE 7–8

Flowchart of a Parallel
Simulation

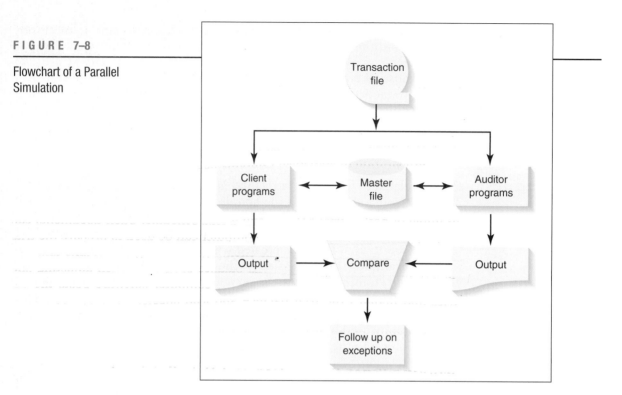

described here. The reader should consult a specialized textbook[7] on IT auditing for more information about concurrent auditing techniques.)

Three concurrent auditing techniques are (1) snapshot, (2) system control audit review file (SCARF), and (3) expert systems. The snapshot technique is sometimes referred to as *tagging and tracing*. The auditor embeds routines at various points in the application computer programs. Selected transactions are tagged, and "snapshots" are taken of the transactions at various processing points. SCARF involves embedding audit modules into the application software. The module can sample or continuously monitor transactions that do not meet certain criteria. The selected transactions are copied to a file that is reviewed by the auditor. Last, expert systems can be used by the auditor in collecting and evaluating evidence on the client's computer system. As computer technology continues to evolve, concurrent audit techniques will play a larger role in the audit process.

The Use of Microcomputers as an Audit Tool

Public accounting firms use microcomputers and audit software extensively in conducting audits. For example, auditors take portable microcomputers to the client's premises for use as an audit tool and often use specialized software programs to perform various audit tasks.

---

[7]For example, see J. D. Warren, Jr., L. W. Edelson, X. L. Parker, and R. M. Thurun, *Handbook of IT Auditing* (Boston, MA: RIA Group/WG&L, 1998).

Audit Tasks

[LO 8]

A number of important audit tasks can be performed using a microcomputer. These include

- Trial balance and lead schedule preparation.
- Working paper preparation and data retrieval and analysis.
- Audit program preparation.
- Analytical procedures.
- Documentation of internal control.
- Preparation of statistical sampling applications.

Trial Balance and Lead Sheet Preparation   Chapter 4 presented an example of both a trial balance and a lead schedule. Such documents can be prepared manually, or a microcomputer can be used to prepare the trial balance and lead schedules. The client's general ledger accounts and balances can be entered into the trial balance program. When adjusting and reclassification entries are entered, the computer software posts the entries and updates the trial balance and lead sheets. The microcomputer software can also be used to consolidate financial statements and prepare the final drafts of the financial statements.

Working Paper Preparation and Data Retrieval and Analysis
The microcomputer can also be helpful in preparing working papers, particularly when standard working paper format is applicable. Examples include accounts receivable confirmation control, details of property, plant, and equipment, and interest computations. Additionally, the auditor may be able to download information from the client's computer files directly into the working papers for further analysis and testing. For example, the auditor can use software such as ACL Software or Interactive Data Extraction and Analysis (IDEA) to scan a client's cash disbursements file and select all items over a specified dollar amount for further analysis.

Audit Program Preparation   Numerous software packages have been developed to assist the auditor in preparing audit programs. These are sometimes referred to as *audit program generators*. Program generators allow the auditor to develop an audit program for testing an accounting cycle and its related account balances by reviewing a menu of suggested audit procedures and selecting the procedures that are most appropriate for auditing that particular cycle and its accounts. The audit program can be stored in the working papers or printed out for use by the auditor.

Analytical Procedures   Most of the microcomputer software used for trial balance preparation also provides the capability of performing analytical procedures on the financial statement data. The software allows the auditor to (1) maintain prior years' financial statement data so that absolute and percentage comparisons can be made and (2) calculate financial statement ratios for current and prior years. Electronic spreadsheets can also be used to perform this type of analysis.

Documentation of Internal Control   Chapter 6 discussed the use of narrative descriptions, internal control questionnaires, and flowcharts for documenting internal control. Microcomputers can assist with each of these. For example, a word processor can be used to prepare a narrative description of the accounting system. Internal control questionnaires can be automated as part of the firm's computer software to provide documentation of the responses; and in some instances the software will help the auditor evaluate the system. Finally, computer software exists for preparing flowcharts of a client's accounting system.

Preparation of Statistical Sampling Applications   Software is also available to help the auditor prepare and document statistical sampling applications. This includes support for designing the sampling application and selecting the sample items. An example of statistical sampling software is shown in Chapters 8 and 9.

Types of Microcomputer Software

Various types of microcomputer software are available for use by the auditor. Spreadsheets, word processors, and data extraction software are three examples of software available from commercial vendors. Spreadsheets allow the auditor to perform mathematical functions such as calculating financial ratios on a set of data. Word processors help the auditor create and save text. They can be used to prepare internal control descriptions and memoranda. Data extraction software allows the auditor to extract client files and then perform various functions on the data, including recalculating various fields on the file and stratifying the transactions or balances.

Another type of software is general-purpose audit software. A number of vendors, including the larger public accounting firms, have developed software to maintain trial balance information and working papers. In some cases, the larger firms are automating their entire audit methodology. Audit-related expert systems may be incorporated in the firm's software.

Auditing Accounting Applications Processed by Outside Service Organizations

[LO 9]   In some instances, a client may have some or all of its accounting transactions processed by an outside service organization. Examples of such service organizations include mortgage bankers that service mortgages for others and trust departments that invest or hold assets for employee benefit plans. More frequently, however, service organizations are IT service centers that process transactions such as payroll and the related accounting reports. SAS No. 70, "Reports on the Processing of Transactions by Service Organizations" (AU 324), provides guidance to the auditor when a client uses a service organization to process certain transactions.

Because the client's transactions are subjected to the controls of the service organization, one of the auditor's concerns is the internal control system in place at the service organization. The auditor should consider the following factors in determining the significance of these controls on planning the audit:

- The inherent risk and significance of the audit assertion affected by the controls.
- The extent of the interaction between the client's controls and the service organization's controls.
- Controls applied by the client to transactions processed by the service organization.
- The auditor's prior experience with the service organization.
- The extent of auditable data within the client's internal control.

Based on these factors, the auditor may sufficiently understand the client's internal control. However, in some cases the auditor may need additional information from the service organization. This information may be obtained by contacting the service organization through the client.

After obtaining an understanding of internal control, the auditor identifies controls that are applied by the client or the service organization that will allow an assessment of reduced control risk. The auditor may obtain evidence to support the lower assessment of control risk by testing the client's controls over the activities performed by the service organization or by tests of controls at the service organization.

Because service organizations process data for many customers, it is not uncommon for them to have an auditor issue a report on their operations. Such reports can be distributed to the auditors of a service organization's customers. SAS No. 70 provides for two types of reports by a service organization's auditor on its internal control. One type of report is a description of the service organization's controls and an assessment of whether they are suitably designed to achieve specified internal control objectives. The other type of report goes further by testing whether the controls provide reasonable assurance that the related control objectives were achieved during the period. An auditor may reduce control risk below the maximum only on the basis of a service auditor's report that includes tests of the controls.

REVIEW QUESTIONS

[LO 1]   7-1   Discuss three technological changes that are occurring in information technology and their implications for the audit function.

[4]   7-2   What control environment factors and control activities are affected by IT?

[4]   7-3   How do authorization procedures differ between a manual and a computerized system?

[3]   7-4   Define the two categories of IT controls.

[3]   7-5   List the five categories of general controls. Why is segregation of duties important in an IT department?

[3]   7-6   Why is it important to maintain separation of duties between IT operations and programmers?

[3]   7-7   Why are controls over program changes so important? List controls that can ensure that all program changes are proper.

[3]   7-8   Give two examples of hardware controls.

[3]   7-9   List two controls over physical access and two controls over access to programs and data.

[3]   7-10   What are the categories of application controls? What are the objectives of data capture controls?

[3]   7-11   Identify and explain four data validation controls. What are turnaround documents, and how do they improve data accuracy?

[2]   7-12   Discuss the complexity of IT systems and the characteristics that distinguish each type of system.

[2,3]   7-13   What knowledge of a client's computer processing must the auditor possess?

[6]   7-14   Briefly describe the substantive and reliance strategies for auditing in an IT environment.

[7]   7-15   Distinguish between generalized and custom audit software. List the functions that can be performed by generalized audit software.

[7]   7-16   What are the advantages and disadvantages of generalized audit software and the test data method?

[7]   7-17   How does the test data method differ from using an ITF?

[8]   7-18   List five audit tasks that can be performed using a microcomputer.

MULTIPLE-CHOICE QUESTIONS FROM CPA EXAMINATIONS

[3,4]   7-19   Which of the following most likely represents a weakness in internal control of an IT system?

a. The systems analyst reviews output and controls the distribution of output from the IT department.

b. The accounts payable clerk prepares data for computer processing and enters the data into the computer.

c. The systems programmer designs the operating and control functions of programs and participates in testing operating systems.

d. The control clerk establishes control over data received by the IT department and reconciles control totals after processing.

[3,7] 7-20 When an accounting application is processed by computer, an auditor *cannot* verify the reliable operation of programmed control procedures by

a. Manually comparing detailed transaction files used by an edit program to the program's generated error listings to determine that errors were properly identified by the edit program.

b. Constructing a processing system for accounting applications and processing actual data from throughout the period using both the client's program and the auditor's program.

c. Manually reperforming, as of a point in time, the processing of input data and comparing the simulated results to the actual results.

d. Periodically submitting auditor-prepared test data to the same computer process and evaluating the results.

[3,4] 7-21 An auditor anticipates assessing control risk at a low level in a computerized environment. Under these circumstances, on which of the following procedures would the auditor initially focus?

a. Programmed control procedures.

b. Application control procedures.

c. Output control procedures.

d. General control procedures.

[3,7] 7-22 Which of the following types of evidence would an auditor most likely examine to determine whether internal controls are operating as designed?

a. Confirmations of receivables verifying account balances.

b. Letters of representation corroborating inventory pricing.

c. An attorney's responses to the auditor's inquiries.

d. Client records documenting the use of IT programs.

[3] 7-23 Which of the following controls would most likely ensure that an entity could reconstruct its financial records?

a. Hardware controls are built into the computer by the computer manufacturer.

b. Backup diskettes or tapes of files are stored away from originals.

c. Personnel who are independent of data input perform parallel simulations.

d. System flowcharts provide accurate descriptions of input and output operations.

[1,3] 7-24 An auditor would most likely be concerned with which of the following controls in a distributed data processing system?

a. Hardware controls.

b. Systems documentation controls.

c. Access controls.

d. Disaster recovery controls.

[1,3,7] 7-25 To obtain evidence that on-line access controls are properly functioning, an auditor most likely would

a. Create checkpoints at periodic intervals after live data processing to test for unauthorized use of the system.

b. Examine the transaction log to discover whether any transactions were lost or entered twice due to a system malfunction.

c. Enter invalid identification numbers or passwords to ascertain whether the system rejects them.

d. Vouch a random sample of processed transactions to ensure proper authorization.

[3]   7-26   Which of the following computer documents would an auditor most likely utilize in obtaining an understanding of internal control?

a. Systems flowcharts.

b. Record counts.

c. Program listings.

d. Record layouts.

[3]   7-27   Which of the following statements most likely represents a disadvantage for an entity that keeps microcomputer-prepared data files rather than manually prepared files?

a. Random error associated with processing similar transactions in different ways is usually greater. ✗

b. It is usually more difficult to compare recorded accountability with a physical count of assets. ✗

c. Attention is focused on the accuracy of the programming process rather than on errors in individual transactions. ✗

d. It is usually easier for unauthorized persons to access and alter the files.

[3,7]   7-28   An auditor would most likely test for the presence of unauthorized IT program changes by running a

a. Program with test data.

b. Check-digit verification program.

c. Source code comparison program.

d. Program that computes control totals.

[3]   7-29   Errors in data processed in a batch computer system may *not* be detected immediately because

a. Transaction trails in a batch system are available for only a limited period of time.

b. There are time delays in processing transactions in a batch system.

c. Errors in some transactions cause rejection of other transactions in the batch.

d. Random errors are more likely in a batch system than in an online system.

[3,7]   7-30   To obtain evidence that user identification and password controls are functioning as designed, an auditor would most likely

a. Attempt to sign on to the system using invalid user identifications and passwords.

b. Write a computer program that simulates the logic of the client's access control software.

c. Extract a random sample of processed transactions and ensure that the transactions were appropriately authorized.

d. Examine statements signed by employees stating that they have *not* divulged their user identifications and passwords to any other person.

[7]   7-31   Which of the following statements is *not* true of the test data approach to testing an accounting system?

a. The test data are processed by the client's computer programs under the auditor's control.

b. The test data need consist of only those valid and invalid conditions that interest the auditor. ✓

c. Only one transaction of each type need be tested. ✓

d. The test data must consist of all possible valid and invalid conditions.

[8]   7-32   Using microcomputers in auditing may affect the methods used to review the work of staff assistants because

a. The audit field work standards for supervision may differ. ✗

b. Documenting the supervisory review may require assistance of consulting services personnel. ✗

c. Supervisory personnel may not understand the capabilities and limitations of microcomputers. ✗

d. Working paper documentation may not contain readily observable details of calculations.

[7]   7-33   Which of the following computer-assisted auditing techniques allows fictitious and real transactions to be processed together without client operating personnel being aware of the testing process?

a. Parallel simulation.

b. Generalized audit software programming.

c. Integrated test facility.

d. The test data approach.

[7]   7-34   A primary advantage of using generalized audit software packages to audit the financial statements of a client that uses an IT system is that the auditor may

a. Consider increasing the use of substantive tests of transactions in place of analytical procedures.

b. Substantiate the accuracy of data through self-checking digits and hash totals.

c. Reduce the level of required tests of controls to a relatively small amount.

d. Access information stored on computer files while having a limited understanding of the client's hardware and software features.

PROBLEMS

[3]   7-35   A number of controls exist in an entity's IT system. Select the type of control from the following list and enter it in the appropriate place on the grid.

Control policy or procedure:

1. Echo check
2. Limit test
3. Existence test
4. Parity check
5. Hash total
6. Control total
7. Check-digit verification
8. Sequence check
9. Financial total

	Description of Control	Control
4	a. A check bit used to verify the transmission of data	
3	b. A test of an ID number or code by comparing it to a file that contains valid ID numbers or codes	
5	c. A total of some nonfinancial field in a batch of transactions	
1	d. Verification of the transmission of data to and from the components of the system	
2	e. A test to ensure that a numeric value does not exceed some predetermined value	
6	f. Totals that ensure the accuracy and completeness of processing	
7	g. A numeric value computed to provide assurance that the original value was not altered	

[7]   7-36   Auditors use various audit techniques to gather evidence when a client's accounting information is processed by a computer. Select the audit procedure from the following list and enter it in the appropriate place on the grid.

Audit procedure:
1. Test data method
2. Custom audit software
3. Auditing around the computer
4. Parallel simulation
5. Integrated test facility
6. Generalized audit software

	Description of Audit Technique	Audit Technique
4	a. Processing client data through a computer program developed by the auditor and comparing it to the client's processing results	
5	b. Processing fictitious and real data along with client data as part of normal processing	
2	c. Program written by the auditor to perform a specific task for a particular client	
3	d. The auditor's auditing of the inputs and outputs of the system without verification of the processing of the data	
1	e. Processing fictitious and real data separately through the client's IT system	

[3]   7-37   Johnson, CPA, was engaged to examine the financial statements of Horizon, Inc., which has its own computer installation. During the preliminary review, Johnson found that Horizon lacked proper segregation of the programming and operating functions. As a result, Johnson intensified the study and evaluation of internal control and concluded that the existing compensating general controls provided reasonable assurance that the objectives of internal control were being met.

Required:
a. In a properly functioning IT environment, how is the separation of the programming and operating functions achieved?
b. What are the compensating general controls that Johnson most likely found? Do *not* discuss hardware and application controls.

(AICPA, adapted)

[3,4,7,8]   7-38   After determining that computer controls are valid, Hastings is reviewing the sales system of Rosco Corporation in order to determine how a computerized audit program may assist in performing tests of Rosco's sales records.

Rosco sells crude oil from one central location. All orders are received by mail and indicate the preassigned customer identification number, desired quantity, proposed delivery date, method of payment, and shipping terms. Because price fluctuates daily, order forms do not indicate a price. Price sheets are printed daily, and details are stored in a permanent diskette file. The details of orders are also maintained in a permanent diskette file.

Each morning the shipping clerk receives a computer printout that indicates details of customers' orders to be shipped that day. After the orders have been shipped, the shipping details are input to the computer, which simultaneously updates the sales journal, perpetual inventory records, accounts receivable, and sales accounts.

The details of all transactions, as well as daily updates, are maintained on diskettes that are available for use by Hastings in the performance of the audit.

Required:
a. How may a computerized audit program be used by Hastings to perform substantive tests of Rosco's sales records in their machine-readable form? Do *not* discuss accounts receivable and inventory.
b. After having performed these tests with the assistance of the computer, what other auditing procedures should Hastings perform in order to complete the examination of Rosco's sales records?

(AICPA, adapted)

[8]   7-39   Microcomputer software has been developed to improve the efficiency and effectiveness of audits. Electronic spreadsheets and other software packages are available to aid in the performance of audit procedures otherwise performed manually.

Required:
Decribe the potential benefits to an auditor of using microcomputer software in an audit as compared to performing an audit without the use of a computer.

(AICPA, adapted)

[7,8]   7-40   Brown, CPA, is auditing the financial statements of Big Z Wholesaling, Inc., a continuing audit client, for the year ended January 31, 2000. On January 5, 2000, Brown observed the tagging and counting of Big Z's physical inventory and made appropriate test counts. These test counts have been recorded on a computer file. As in prior years, Big Z gave Brown two computer files. One file represents the perpetual inventory (first-in, first-out) records for the year ended January 31, 2000. The other file represents the January 5 physical inventory count.

Assume:
1. Brown issued an unqualified opinion on the prior year's financial statements.
2. All inventory is purchased for resale and located in a single warehouse.
3. Brown has appropriate computerized audit software.
4. The perpetual inventory file contains the following information in item number sequence:
   a. Beginning balances at February 1, 1999: item number, item description, total quantity, and price.
   b. For each item purchased during the year: date received, receiving report number, vendor item number, item description, quantity, and total dollar amount.
   c. For each item sold during the year: date shipped, invoice number, item number, item description, quantity, and dollar amount.
   d. For each item adjusted for physical inventory count differences: date, item number, item description, quantity, and dollar amount.
5. The physical inventory file contains the following information in item number sequence: tag number, item number, item description, and count quantity.

Required:
Decribe the substantive auditing procedures Brown may consider performing with computerized audit software using Big Z's two computer files and Brown's computer file of test counts. The substantive auditing procedures described may indicate the reports to be printed out for Brown's follow-up by subsequent application of manual procedures. Do *not* describe subsequent manual auditing procedures.

   Group the procedures by those using (a) the perpetual inventory file and (b) the physical inventory and test count files.

(AICPA, adapted)

[3,7,8]   **7-41** A manufacturer is planning to automate its entire accounting system. All computer hardware will be purchased from a national vendor. All software will be written by members of the organization's IT staff. The automation of the accounting function will take place in phases, with the payroll function being automated first.

The automated payroll system will function as follows: An employee's immediate supervisor will review and approve the employee's time card. All time cards will then be sent to the payroll department, where they will be reviewed for completeness and obvious errors. They will then be batched by department and sent to data processing. Data processing operations will convert the time card data to a transaction file by a key-to-disk operation. The transaction file will then be input to the payroll application. Hard-copy output will include checks, a payroll journal, payroll summary, and error listings.

Required:
a. For the development and operation of this payroll system, list the general and application control areas required.
b. For each type of control listed in part (a), (1) list specific controls, (2) state the purpose each control serves, and (3) identify the audit techniques that would be used to assess each control. Use the following format for your answer:

General Controls			
Major Control Area	*Specific Control*	*Purpose of Control*	*Applicable Audit Technique*
1. Plan of organization and operation of the IT activity.	1. Separation of duties of analysts, programmers, operators, library, and central control group.	1. Avoid incompatible functions, prevent manipulation.	1. Observation of operations or review of organizational charts.

Application Controls			
Major Control Area	*Specific Control*	*Purpose of Control*	*Applicable Audit Technique*

(CIA, adapted)

[3,4]   **7-42** You have been assigned to conduct an audit of your client's database system. Through previous work you know that the system includes a centralized database shared by all users. Access to the database is direct by the users through remote terminals and is controlled by the database software system. The IT department includes a manager of operations and a manager of computer programming, both of whom report to the IT director.

Your preliminary understanding of the database system includes the following points:

1. There are no restrictions regarding the type of transaction or access to the on-line terminals.
2. All users and IT personnel have access to the extensive system documentation.
3. Before being entered into the user authorization table, user passwords and access codes are established by user management and approved by the manager of computer programming.
4. The manager of computer programming established and controls the database directory. Users approve any changes in data definition.
5. User requests for data are validated by the system against a transactions–conflict matrix to ensure that data is transmitted only to authorized users.
6. System access requires the users to input their passwords, and terminal activity logs are maintained.
7. Input data are edited for reasonableness and completeness, transaction control totals are generated, and transaction logs are maintained.
8. Processing control totals are generated and reconciled to changes in the database.
9. Output is reconciled to transaction and input control totals. The resulting reports are printed and placed in a bin outside the IT room for pickup by the users at their convenience.
10. Backup copies of the database are generated daily and stored in the file library area, access to which is restricted to IT personnel.

Required:
a. From the results of your preliminary review, describe five controls in the system.
b. List five specific audit steps you would include in your audit program to determine whether transaction input is properly authorized.
c. Evaluate the relative strengths of the general and application controls for the database system.

(CIA, adapted)

[9] 7-43 Learn Laser Corporation uses Penny's Payroll Service Corporation to process its payroll transactions. All original payroll data are reviewed by Learn's payroll clerks, and batch totals of hours worked by department are prepared before the payroll is sent to Penny's for processing. When the payroll data, checks, and reports are returned from Penny's, the payroll clerks agree the batch totals and randomly test five payroll checks for proper gross pay and deductions.

Penny uses the same basic payroll software for all its customers. It has engaged a public accounting firm to test the operation of its control. The public accounting firm has issued a report that provides reasonable assurance that Penny's control policies and procedures are operating effectively.

Required:
As the auditor of Learn Laser Corporation, what audit procedures would you conduct in order to reduce the control risk over Learn's payroll cycle?

DISCUSSION CASE

[3,4]   7-44   Ajax, Inc., an audit client, recently installed a new computerized system to process more efficiently the shipping, billing, and accounts receivable records. During interim work, an assistant completed the review of the accounting system and the internal controls. The assistant determined the following information concerning the new IT system and the processing and control of shipping notices and customer invoices.

Each major computerized function—shipping, billing, accounts receivable, and so on—is permanently assigned to a specific computer operator, who is responsible for making program changes, running the program, and reconciling the computer log. Responsibility for the custody and control of the magnetic tapes and system documentation is randomly rotated among the computer operators monthly to prevent any one person from having access to the tapes and documentation at all times. Each computer programmer and operator has access to the computer room via a magnetic card and a digital code that is different for each card. The systems analyst and the supervisor of the computer operators do not have access to the computer room.

The system's documentation consists of the following items: program listing, error listing, logs, and record layout. To increase efficiency, batch totals and processing controls are omitted from the system.

Ajax ships products directly from two warehouses, which forward shipping notices to General Accounting. There, the billing clerk enters the price of the item and accounts for the numerical sequence of shipping notices. The billing clerk also prepares daily adding machine tapes of the units shipped and the sales amounts. Shipping notices and adding machine tapes are forwarded to the IT department for processing. The computer output consists of

- A three-copy invoice that is forwarded to the billing clerk.
- A daily sales register showing the aggregate totals of units shipped and sales amounts that the computer operator compares to the adding machine tapes.

The billing clerk mails two copies of each invoice to the customer and retains the third copy in an open invoice file that serves as a detailed accounts receivable record.

Required:
a. Identify each weakness in the internal controls in the new computerized system and each weakness or inefficiency in the procedures for processing and controlling shipping notices and customer invoices.
b. Prepare a management letter to Ajax's chief financial officer that contains one specific recommendation for correcting the weaknesses identified in part (a).

(AICPA, adapted)

Part IV

STATISTICAL TOOLS FOR AUDITING

Chapter 8

Audit Sampling: An Overview and Application to Tests of Controls

LEARNING OBJECTIVES

Upon completion of this chapter you will

[1] Learn the definition of audit sampling.

[2] Learn the types of audit procedures that do not involve sampling.

[3] Understand basic sampling terminology.

[4] Learn the types of audit sampling.

[5] Learn the sampling requirements of SAS No. 39.

[6] Learn how to apply attribute sampling to tests of controls.

[7] Work through an example of attribute sampling.

[8] Learn how to apply nonstatistical sampling to tests of controls.

This chapter has two overall objectives: (1) to provide an overview of audit sampling and (2) to apply statistical and nonstatistical sampling techniques to tests of controls.

RELEVANT ACCOUNTING AND AUDITING PRONOUNCEMENTS

AICPA, *Audit Sampling* (Audit Practice Release) (New York: AICPA, 1999)

SAS No. 22, "Planning and Supervision" (AU 311)

SAS No. 39, "Audit Sampling" (AU 350)

SAS No. 47, "Audit Risk and Materiality in Conducting an Audit" (AU 312)

SAS No. 82, "Consideration of Fraud in a Financial Statement Audit" (AU 316)

Chapter 9 presents statistical and nonstatistical sampling techniques for substantive tests of account balances.

Introduction

In the early days of auditing, it was not unusual for the independent auditor to examine all of the records of the company being audited. However, as companies grew in size and complexity, it became uneconomical to examine all of the accounting records and supporting documents. Auditors found it necessary to draw conclusions about the fairness of a company's financial statements based on an examination of a subset of the records and transactions. As a result, the auditor provides reasonable, not absolute, assurance (refer to the third standard of field work) that the financial statements are fairly presented. The justification for accepting some uncertainty is the trade-off between the cost of examining all of the data and the cost of making an incorrect decision based on a sample of the data. As noted in Chapter 2, this concept of reasonable assurance is addressed in the auditor's report.

However, recent years have seen an apparent decline in the use of statistical sampling by auditors. Two studies have reported that auditors use statistical sampling in only 10 percent of their sampling applications, while nonstatistical sampling is used in the remaining 90 percent.[1] There are a few possible explanations for the decline in use of statistical sampling. First, auditors have found that other types of evidence, such as analytical procedures, are nearly as effective as statistical sampling and not as costly to conduct. Second, companies have developed well-controlled accounting systems that process few routine transactions erroneously.[2] In such cases, auditors can test the systems' controls and focus their substantive testing on nonroutine transactions. Last, the advent of powerful microcomputer audit software allows auditors to perform 100 percent testing rather than sampling.[3] However, the author believes that the study of audit sampling is important for auditing students. While the use of statistical sampling may be declining, concepts (such as sampling risk) that underlie sampling provide a sound basis for making audit judgments and reaching conclusions about the fair presentation of the financial statements.

Sampling Defined

[LO 1]

SAS No. 39, "Audit Sampling," defines *audit sampling* as the application of an audit procedure to less than 100 percent of the items within an account balance or class of transactions for the purpose of evaluating some characteristic of the balance or class (AU 350.01). The fact that an audit involves sampling is expressed to users of the financial statements by the phrase "An audit includes examining, on a test basis" contained in the scope paragraph of the auditor's report.

---

[1]See N. Hitzig, "Audit Sampling: A Survey of Current Practice," *The CPA Journal* (July 1995), pp. 54–57; and W. F. Messier, Jr., S. J. Kachelmeier, and K. Jensen, "An Experimental Assessment of Recent Professional Developments in Nonstatistical Sampling Guidance," Working paper, Georgia State University, November 1998.

[2]See R. K. Elliott, "The Future of Audits," *Journal of Accountancy* (September 1994), pp. 74–82; R. K. Elliott, "Confronting the Future: Choices for the Attest Function," *Accounting Horizons* (September 1994) pp. 106–124; and the Report of the Special Committee on Assurance Services (www.aicpa.org).

[3]R. B. Lanza, "Take My Manual Audit, Please," *Journal of Accountancy* (June 1998), pp. 33–36.

When sampling is used by an auditor, an element of uncertainty enters into the auditor's conclusions. This element of uncertainty, referred to as *sampling risk,* was discussed briefly under detection risk in Chapter 3. Sampling risk refers to the possibility that the sample drawn is not representative of the population and that, as a result, the auditor will reach an incorrect conclusion about the account balance or class of transactions based on the sample.

The use of sampling also introduces another type of risk, *nonsampling risk.* Nonsampling risk arises from the possibility that the auditor may use inappropriate audit procedures, fail to detect a misstatement when applying an audit procedure, or misinterpret an audit result. While statistical sampling allows the auditor to quantify sampling risk, no sampling method allows the auditor to measure nonsampling risk. The uncertainty related to nonsampling risk can be controlled by adequate training, proper planning, and effective supervision.

Audit Evidence Choices That Do Not Involve Sampling

🖋 **[LO 2]**

In assessing inherent risk or control risk, or in auditing an account balance or a class of transactions, the auditor seldom relies on a single test. Generally, the auditor applies a number of audit procedures in order to reach a conclusion. Some audit tests involve sampling as defined in SAS No. 39 (AU 350.01), while others do not involve sampling. Table 8–1 lists evidence choices that generally do not involve sampling.

Inquiry and Observation   Inquiry and observation are used extensively as a source of evidential matter. For example, auditors use inquiry and observation to understand the components of internal control. Inquiry of upper-level management is also used to evaluate many of the inherent risk factors discussed in Chapter 3. Finally, auditors use observation to establish the existence of inventories. Because of the nature of inquiry and observation, they do not involve sampling.

Analytical Procedures   Most simple analytical procedures utilized by auditors do not involve sampling or similar statistical tests. This includes the analytical procedures discussed in Chapter 5, such as simple comparison of last year's balances with the current year's balances and comparison of ratios across accounting periods. However, auditors use statistical techniques such as regression analysis as analytical procedures

TABLE 8–1	Audit Evidence Choices That Do Not Involve Audit Sampling

- Inquiry and observation.
- Analytical procedures.
- Procedures applied to every item in the population.
- Classes of transactions or account balances not tested.

to predict account balances. Such statistical techniques are subject to both sampling and nonsampling risks.

Procedures Applied to Every Item in the Population   Sometimes the auditor examines all the items that constitute a class of transactions or an account balance. Because the entire class or balance is subjected to a 100 percent examination, such an audit procedure does not involve sampling. The population for audit sampling purposes, however, does not need to be the entire class of transactions or account balance. For example, the auditor may decide to audit all accounts receivable customer balances greater than a specified dollar amount, such as $10,000, and then use sampling for customer account balances less than $10,000. Alternatively, the auditor could decide to apply analytical procedures to the receivable accounts under $10,000 or to apply no audit procedures to them because an acceptably low risk of material misstatement exists in this group. In these instances, the auditor is not using sampling for either group of accounts receivable.

Classes of Transactions or Account Balances Not Tested   In some instances, the auditor may decide that a class of transactions or an account balance does not need to be examined, either because it is not material or because an acceptably low risk of material misstatement exists. Such untested transactions or account balances are not subject to audit sampling.

Terminology

[LO 3]   The terminology used in this text is consistent with that of SAS No. 39. However, the labels attached to these terms may differ from those used in a basic statistics class. This section explains SAS No. 39 terminology in basic statistical terminology. Three terms are discussed: *sampling risk, Type I* and *Type II errors,* and *precision.*

Sampling Risk

Auditors use the concept of risk instead of that of reliability or confidence level. A *confidence level* measures the proportion of all such intervals that would contain the unknown population characteristic. Risk is the *complement* of reliability or confidence level. For example, the auditor may set sampling risk for a particular sampling application at 5 percent. The reliability or confidence level is therefore specified as 95 percent. In auditing terms, sampling risk arises from the possibility that, when a test of controls or a substantive test is restricted to a sample, the auditor's conclusions may differ from the conclusions he or she would reach if the test were applied to all items in the population. Sampling risk is a function of sample size: the larger the sample, the lower the sampling risk.

Type I and Type II Errors

Type I and Type II errors are the two types of decision errors an auditor can make when deciding that sample evidence supports or does not support a test of controls or a substantive test based on a sampling application. These errors are sometimes referred to as *alpha* and *beta* risks. In relation to tests of controls, SAS No. 39 refers to Type I and Type II errors as follows:

- ***Risk of assessing control risk too high (Type I).*** The risk that the assessed level of control risk based on the sample is greater than the true operating effectiveness of the control.
- ***Risk of assessing control risk too low (Type II).*** The risk that the assessed level of control risk based on the sample is less than the true operating effectiveness of the control.

In relation to substantive tests, SAS No. 39 refers to these types of errors as

- ***Risk of incorrect rejection (Type I).*** The risk that the sample supports the conclusion that the recorded account balance is materially misstated when it is not materially misstated.
- ***Risk of incorrect acceptance (Type II).*** The risk that the sample supports the conclusion that the recorded account balance is not materially misstated when it is materially misstated.

The risk of assessing control risk too high and the risk of incorrect rejection relate to the *efficiency* of the audit. Both of these decision errors can result in the auditor conducting more audit work than necessary in order to reach the correct conclusion. The risk of assessing control risk too low and the risk of incorrect acceptance relate to the *effectiveness* of the audit. These decision errors can result in the auditor failing to detect a material misstatement in the financial statements. This can lead to litigation against the auditor by parties that rely on the financial statements.

Precision

In normal statistical terms, precision measures the closeness between a sample estimate and the population characteristic being estimated, given a specified sampling risk. SAS No. 39 uses the term *allowance for sampling risk* to reflect the concept of precision in a sampling application. Thus, the allowance for sampling risk at the planning stage of a sampling application is the *difference* between the expected mean of the population and the tolerable deviation or misstatement. For example, if an auditor expected that a control would have a 2 percent deviation (failure) rate and he or she was willing to tolerate a deviation rate of 5 percent, the allowance for sampling risk would be 3 percent. At the evaluation stage, the allowance for sampling risk is the difference between the mean of the sample tested and the computed limit for the sample result. Following the previous example, if the auditor tested 100 items and found one deviation, the sample deviation rate is 1 percent. If the auditor calculated the upper limit for the test to be 3.5 percent, the allowance for sampling risk is 2.5 (3.5 – 1.0) percent.

Types of Audit Sampling

Nonstatistical versus Statistical Sampling

There are two general approaches to audit sampling: *nonstatistical* and *statistical*. In nonstatistical (or judgmental) sampling the auditor considers sampling risk when evaluating the results of an audit sample without using statistical theory to measure sampling risk. Statistical sampling, on the other hand, uses the laws of probability to select and evaluate the results of an audit sample, thereby permitting the auditor to quantify the sampling

[LO 4] risk for the purpose of reaching a conclusion about the population. Both approaches require the use of the auditor's professional judgment to plan, perform, and evaluate the sample evidence. The major advantages of statistical sampling are that it helps the auditor (1) design an efficient sample, (2) measure the sufficiency of evidence obtained, and (3) quantify sampling risk. The disadvantages of statistical sampling include additional costs of (1) training auditors in the proper use of sampling techniques and (2) designing and conducting the sampling application. With a nonstatistical sampling application, the auditor must rely on his or her professional judgment rather than the laws of probability to reach a conclusion about the audit test. Therefore, the disadvantage of nonstatistical sampling is that it may not be as effective as statistical sampling.

This chapter and Chapter 9 provide detailed coverage of both statistical and nonstatistical sampling. However, the reader should realize that many of the tests conducted on an audit use nonstatistical sampling.

Types of Statistical Sampling Techniques

Auditors use three major categories of statistical sampling techniques: *attribute sampling, monetary-unit sampling,* and *classical variables sampling.*

Attribute Sampling   Attribute sampling is used to estimate the proportion of a population that possesses a specified characteristic. The most common use of attribute sampling is for tests of controls. In this case, the auditor wants to determine the deviation rate for a control implemented within the client's accounting system. For example, the auditor may want to estimate how often a credit check is not performed on customer orders before shipment. Measurement of the deviation rate determines whether the control can be relied upon to process accounting transactions properly and therefore support the auditor's assessed level of control risk. Attribute sampling may also be used with a substantive test of transactions when such a test is conducted with a test of controls as a dual-purpose test.

Monetary-Unit Sampling   Monetary-unit sampling uses attribute sampling theory and techniques to estimate the dollar (or other currency) amount of misstatement for a class of transactions or an account balance. Variations of monetary-unit sampling are known as *probability-proportional-to-size sampling, cumulative monetary amount sampling,* and *combined attribute variables sampling.* Auditors use this sampling technique extensively because it has a number of advantages over classical variables sampling.

Classical Variables Sampling   Classical variables sampling includes the sampling techniques typically taught in an undergraduate statistics class. The auditor's purpose in using classical variables sampling is (1) to estimate a dollar amount for a class of transactions or account balance or (2) to determine if a class of transactions or account balance is materially misstated. While auditors sometimes use variables sampling to estimate the dollar value of a class of transactions or account balance, it is more frequently used to determine whether an account is materially misstated.

Chapter 9 demonstrates the application of monetary-unit sampling and classical variables sampling to substantive tests of account balances.

Requirements of SAS No. 39

 [LO 5]   SAS No. 39 (AU 350) contains requirements that auditors must follow when planning, selecting a sample for, and performing and evaluating an audit sampling application.

Planning

The audit sampling application must be well planned and give adequate consideration to (1) the relationship of the sample to the objective(s) of the test; (2) the maximum deviation rate from a control that would support the planned level of control risk for a test of controls, or the amount of monetary misstatement in an account balance that may exist without causing the financial statements to be misstated in a substantive test; and (3) the risk of assessing control risk too low or the risk of incorrect acceptance.

Sample Selection

SAS No. 39 requires that the sample items be selected in such a way that the sample can be expected to represent the population. Thus, all items must have an opportunity to be selected. Following is an overview of sample selection methods.

Random-Number Selection

The auditor may select a random sample using a random-number table or random numbers generated by audit sampling computer software.[4] Using this method of selection, every sampling unit (such as a document or customer account) has the same probability of being selected as every other sampling unit in the population. This selection method can be used for both nonstatistical and statistical sampling. Statistical sampling requires that the auditor be able to measure the probability of selecting the sampling units selected. Thus, random-number selection is used in many statistical sampling applications.

Systematic Selection

When using a systematic selection approach to select a sample, the auditor determines a sampling interval by dividing the physical population by the sample size. A starting number is selected in the first interval, and then every nth item is selected. When a random starting point is used, systematic selection provides a sample where every sampling unit has an equal chance of being selected. For example, suppose the auditor wishes to select 100 items from a population of 15,000 items. The sampling interval in this case is 150 (15,000 ÷ 100). The auditor chooses a random number, say 125, and that item is selected for testing. The second item is 375 (125 + 150), the third item is 525, and so on. To avoid any possible bias in the population, the auditor should use several random starting points. In our example, after selecting 10 items, the auditor could use a new random start to select the 11th item. Systematic selection can be used for both nonstatistical and statistical sampling.

---

[4]See H. Arkin, *Handbook of Sampling for Auditing and Accounting* (New York: McGraw-Hill, 1974), for an example of a random-number table.

Haphazard Selection   When a haphazard selection approach is used, sampling units are selected without any conscious bias—that is, without a special reason for including or omitting items from the sample. This does not imply that the items are selected in a careless manner; rather, the sampling units are selected to represent the population. Haphazard selection may be useful for nonstatistical sampling, but it should not be used for statistical sampling because the auditor cannot measure the probability of an item being selected.

Performance and Evaluation

The performance and evaluation of a sampling application must address four issues. First, the auditor must consider the effect of not being able to apply a planned audit procedure to a sample item. This may occur, for example, because supporting documentation for the sample item is missing. The auditor's treatment of unexamined items depends on their effect on the evaluation of the sample. If the evaluation of the sample results is not altered by the missing items, it is not necessary for the auditor to examine the items. However, if the fact that these items are missing leads to a conclusion that the control is not effective or the account balance is materially misstated, the auditor should consider alternative procedures that would provide sufficient evidence to form a conclusion on the control or account balance.

Second, the auditor should project the sample results to the population being tested and compare those results with the planned amounts. For a test of controls, the computed upper deviation rate is compared to the maximum or tolerable deviation rate. For a substantive test of an account balance, the projected misstatement plus an allowance for sampling risk would be compared to the tolerable misstatement. For example, if the projected misstatement plus the allowance for sampling risk based on the sample was $15,000 and the tolerable misstatement was $45,000, the auditor would be reasonably assured that there is an acceptably low risk that the true monetary misstatement for the population exceeds the tolerable misstatement.

Third, the auditor must give appropriate consideration to sampling risk. With a statistical sampling application, sampling risk can be quantified, while the auditor must use sound judgment to assess sampling risk in a nonstatistical sampling application.

Finally, SAS No. 39 requires that the auditor adequately consider qualitative aspects of misstatements. These include (1) the nature and cause of the misstatements and (2) the possible relationship of the misstatements to other phases of the audit. For example, if the auditor's sample showed that a client's control for product pricing does not always operate effectively, he or she should determine the potential cause of the control failure. The auditor should also consider how the ineffectiveness of this control might affect substantive tests of accounts receivable.

The remainder of this chapter presents an application of attribute sampling to tests of controls, followed by a discussion of nonstatistical sampling applied to tests of controls. Discussing attribute or statistical sampling first makes it easier to identify the differences between statistical and nonstatistical sampling applications.

Attribute Sampling Applied to Tests of Controls

[LO 6]   Attribute sampling is a statistical sampling method used to estimate the proportion of a characteristic in a population. In applying this technique to tests of controls, the auditor normally attempts to determine the operating effectiveness of a control in terms of deviations from a prescribed internal control policy.

In conducting a statistical sample for a test of controls, the auditor must properly plan, perform, and evaluate the sampling application and adequately document each phase of the sampling application in the working papers. The following sections discuss the steps that are included in the three phases of an attribute-sampling application. The discussion utilizes examples from the revenue cycle. Table 8–2 lists each step of the three phases in the sampling application.

Planning

Proper planning of an attribute-sampling application involves completing a number of important steps. Each of these steps, in turn, requires the use of professional judgment on the part of the auditor.

Step 1: Determine the Objective(s) of the Tests of Controls

The objective of attribute sampling when applied to tests of controls is to evaluate the operating effectiveness of the internal control that the auditor

---

TABLE 8–2   Steps in an Attribute-Sampling Application

Planning
1. Determine the objective(s) of the tests of controls.
2. Define the deviation from the control policy or procedure.
3. Define the population.
4. Define the sampling unit.
5. Determine the sample size.
   a. Determine the acceptable risk of assessing control risk too low.
   b. Determine the tolerable deviation rate.
   c. Determine the expected population deviation rate.
   d. Consider the effect of population size.

Performance
6. Randomly select the sample items.
7. Perform the audit procedures.

Evaluation
8. Calculate the sample results.
9. Perform error analysis.
10. Draw final conclusions.

intends to rely upon to reduce control risk below the maximum. Thus, the auditor assesses the deviation or error rate that exists for each control selected for testing. Audit sampling for tests of controls is generally appropriate when the application of the control leaves documentary evidence. For example, in most revenue cycles, goods are billed after they are shipped. Therefore, no sales transaction should be recorded unless a properly authorized shipping document is present prior to recording in the sales journal. The auditor can test a sample of sales invoices for proper recording by examining the corresponding shipping documents.

Step 2: Define the Deviation from the Control Policy or Procedure

For tests of controls, a deviation is a departure from adequate performance of the internal control. It is important for the auditor to define carefully what is considered a deviation. For example, suppose the client has implemented a specified policy for granting credit to customers that is performed in the following manner. For *new* customers, the client has the credit department conduct a background credit check. Based on this credit check, the customer is either granted a line of credit or denied credit. For *existing* customers, when a new order is received, the amount of the current sales transaction is added to the customer's account receivable balance and compared to the customer's approved line of credit. If the total is less than the line of credit, the sale is made. If the total exceeds the credit limit, the sale is subjected to management review before it is completed. For this control policy, the auditor would have to define a deviation in terms of how the policy is applied to a new customer versus an existing customer. For a new customer, a deviation would involve the credit department's failing to complete a credit check properly or granting credit to an unworthy customer. For an existing customer, a deviation would involve a sale that exceeds the customer's credit limit at the time of sale without additional approval by management.

Step 3: Define the Population

The items that constitute the account balance or class of transactions make up the population. The auditor must determine that the population from which the sample is selected is appropriate for the specific audit objective because sample results can be projected only to the population from which the sample was selected. For example, suppose the auditor is interested in testing whether all shipments to customers were billed. If the auditor uses the population of sales invoices, he or she is not likely to detect goods shipped but not billed. The population of sales invoices includes only recorded sales. In this example, the correct population for testing the completeness audit objective would be the population of all shipped goods as documented by bills of lading.

Once the population has been defined, the auditor must determine that the physical representation (referred to as the *frame*) of the population is complete. Because the auditor selects the sample from the frame, any conclusions relate only to that physical representation of the population. If the frame and the population differ, the auditor might draw the wrong conclusion about the population. For example, in a revenue cycle, a typical control employed to fulfill the completeness objective is the use of prenumbered documents that are accounted for by client personnel. If the population for the sampling application is defined as all sales in the period, the auditor could review the numeric file that contains the copies of the sales invoices and reconcile those numbers to the numbers included in the sales journal. Alternatively, the auditor might be able to rely on the client's control for ensuring that the frame that represents the population is intact.

Another decision the auditor must make when defining the population is the period to be covered by the test. An application of attribute sampling for tests of controls can cover either the entire period under audit or some interim period. On some audits, it may not be efficient to define the population as all transactions executed throughout the audit period. In such cases, the auditor can define the population to be the period from the first day of the year to some interim date. The results of the sampling application in this case would apply only to the period tested. However, the auditor must also consider whether to conduct additional tests in the remaining period. Some of the factors the auditor might consider when deciding whether additional evidence needs to be obtained for the remaining period are shown in Table 8–3. For example, the auditor may decide that no additional detailed work is necessary on the basis of favorable results of the tests of controls for the interim period. However, at a minimum, the auditor should inquire whether any changes have been made to the accounting system or controls during the remaining period. In other situations, the auditor may decide to review journals or ledgers affected by the accounting cycle for unusual transactions or adjustments during the remaining period.

Step 4: Define the Sampling Unit   The individual members of the population are called the *sampling units*. A sampling unit may, for example, be a document, an entry, or a line item. Each sampling unit makes up one item in the population. The sampling unit should be defined in relation to the control being tested. In a previous example, the control for granting credit was presented. In this case the sampling unit can be defined as the sales invoice packet that contains the customer order, sales

---

TABLE 8–3	Factors Influencing the Decision to Gather Additional Evidence in the Remaining Period

- The significance of the assertion being tested.
- Any changes in the internal controls that were tested during the interim period.
- Employee turnover.
- The results of the tests of controls performed during the interim period.
- The length of the remaining period.
- The evidential matter about the design or operation that may result from the substantive tests to be performed during the remaining period.

order, bill of lading, and sales invoice. The sales order would typically show some indication that the credit department had followed the client's credit-granting procedures.

Step 5: Determine the Sample Size

While the auditor uses statistical sampling as a way of quantifying the risk associated with the test, considerable judgment is required in choosing the factors for determining the sample size. The auditor should consider the following four factors when determining the sample size:

- The acceptable risk of assessing control risk too low.
- The tolerable deviation rate.
- The expected population deviation rate.
- The population size.

The first three factors affect the sample size significantly. The fourth factor, population size, typically has a limited effect except when the population is relatively small.

a. ***Determine the acceptable risk of assessing control risk too low.***
The risk of assessing control risk too low is the risk that the sample will support the auditor's planned degree of reliance on the control when the true deviation rate for the population does not justify such reliance (a Type II error). This risk influences the effectiveness of the audit. If the auditor assesses control risk too low and overrelies on the controls, the level of substantive tests may be too low to detect material misstatements that may be present in the financial statement account because detection risk was set too high. In setting the acceptable risk of assessing control risk too low, the auditor considers the importance of the audit objective on which the control provides assurance and the degree of reliance to be placed on the control. Generally, when the auditor has decided to rely on controls, the risk of assessing control risk too low is set at 5 or 10 percent. However, the auditor must remember that there is an *inverse* relationship between the risk of assessing control risk too low and sample size: the smaller the risk of assessing control risk too low, the larger the sample size must be. For example, assuming a tolerable deviation rate of 5 percent, an expected population deviation rate of 1 percent, and a large population, the effect on the sample size is substantial (a 21 percent increase) when the risk of assessing control risk too low changes from 10 percent to 5 percent. Thus, the auditor must balance effectiveness concerns with efficiency concerns when setting the acceptable risk of assessing control risk too low. It is not uncommon for auditors to establish one level of acceptable risk for all tests of controls.

Acceptable Risk of Assessing Control Risk Too Low	Sample Size
10%	77
5%	93

TABLE 8–4	Suggested Tolerable Deviation Rates for Assessed Levels of Control Risk

Planned Assessed Level of Control Risk	*Tolerable Deviation Rate*
Low	2–6%
Moderate	7–10%
Slightly below maximum	11–20%
Maximum	Omit test

b. ***Determine the tolerable deviation rate.*** The tolerable deviation rate is the maximum deviation rate that the auditor is willing to accept and still rely on the control procedure. Table 8–4 provides some examples of the relationship between the planned level of control risk and the tolerable deviation rate.

A low tolerable rate (such as 2–6%) would be used when the auditor plans to place substantial reliance on the control and thus plans to assess control risk low. A higher tolerable rate (7–10%) would be used when the auditor plans a moderate level of control risk.

The tolerable deviation rate is *inversely* related to the sample size. The lower the tolerable deviation rate, the larger the sample size. For example, assuming an acceptable risk of assessing control risk too low of 5 percent, an expected population deviation rate of 0 percent, and a large population, the effect of tolerable deviation rate on sample size is

Tolerable Deviation Rate	*Sample Size*
2%	149
6%	49
10%	29

In evaluating the results of testing a control, the auditor is normally concerned only with whether the true deviation rate exceeds the tolerable deviation rate. This is sometimes referred to as the *upper-limit approach.* Thus, the statistical test is a one-tailed test that measures whether the estimated deviation rate is understated.

c. ***Determine the expected population deviation rate.*** The expected population deviation rate is the rate the auditor expects to exist in the population. The auditor can develop this expectation based on prior years' results or on a pilot sample. If the auditor believes that the expected population deviation rate exceeds the tolerable deviation rate, the statistical test should be omitted and substantive tests should be used. The expected population deviation rate has a *direct* relationship to sample size: the larger the expected population deviation rate, the larger the sample size must be. For example, assuming an acceptable risk of assessing control risk too low of 5 percent, a tolerable deviation rate of 5 percent, and a large population, the effect of the expected population deviation rate on sample size is

Expected Population Deviation Rate	Sample Size
1%	93
1.5%	124
2%	181
3%	Sample size is too large to be cost-effective for most audit applications.

d. ***Consider the effect of the population size.*** The population size generally has little or no effect on the sample size. If the population contains more than 5,000 units, the effect on the sample size is negligible. The following examples assume an acceptable risk of assessing control risk too low of 5 percent, a tolerable deviation rate of 5 percent, and an expected population deviation rate of 1 percent.

Population Size	Sample Size
100	64
500	87
1,000	90
5,000	93
100,000	93

The tables used in this chapter assume a large population. When the population size is smaller than 5,000, the sample size taken from the tables can be adjusted by the *finite population correction factor (FPCF)* as follows:

$$FPCF = \sqrt{1 - \frac{n}{N}}$$

where

n = the sample size from the tables
N = the number of units in the population

For example, the sample size shown in the preceding table is 93 when population size is 100,000. If the population size were 1,000, the sample size of 93 could be adjusted as follows:

$$\text{Sample size} = 93 \sqrt{1 - \frac{n}{N}}$$

$$90 = 93 \sqrt{1 - \frac{93}{1,000}}$$

Table 8–5 summarizes the effect of the four factors on the size of the sample to be selected.

Performance

After the sampling application has been planned, the auditor performs each of the following steps.

TABLE 8–5	The Effect of Sample Selection Factors on Sample Size

		Examples	
Factor	*Relationship to Sample Size*	*Change in Factor*	*Effect on Sample*
Acceptable risk of assessing control risk too low	Inverse	Lower	Increase
		Higher	Decrease
Tolerable deviation rate	Inverse	Lower	Increase
		Higher	Decrease
Expected population deviation rate	Direct	Lower	Decrease
		Higher	Increase
Population size	Increases sample size only when population size is small (5,000 or fewer items). Therefore, population size generally has no effect on sample size.		

Step 6: Randomly Select the Sample Items   When a statistical sampling application is used, the sample must be selected randomly. Auditors typically use unrestricted random sampling *without* replacement for sampling applications. This means that once an item is selected, it is removed from the frame and cannot be selected a second time. Given the auditor's objective, it seems sensible for an auditor to include an item only once in the sample. To generate a random sample, the auditor can use a random-number table, a computer program that generates random numbers, or systematic selection with a random start. Generating a random sample using a computer program is relatively easy and will be demonstrated later in the chapter.

Step 7: Perform the Audit Procedures   After the sample items have been selected, the auditor conducts the planned audit procedures. Using the control discussed earlier for testing the completeness of sales transactions, the auditor would examine the sales invoice packet for the presence of a shipping document to support each sales invoice. If the shipping document is present, the auditor considers the control properly applied. If the shipping document is not present, the sample item is considered a deviation from the control procedure.

In conducting the audit procedures for tests of controls, the auditor may encounter the following situations:

- **Voided documents.** The auditor may occasionally select a voided document in a sample. If the transaction has been properly voided, it does not represent a deviation. The item should be replaced with a new sample item.
- **Unused or inapplicable documents.** Sometimes a selected item is not appropriate for the definition of the control. For example, the auditor may define a deviation for a purchase transaction as a

vendor's bill not supported by a receiving report. If the auditor selects a telephone or utility bill, there will not be a receiving report to examine. In such a case, the absence of the receiving report would not be a deviation. The auditor would simply replace the item with another purchase transaction.

- *Missing documents.* For most tests of controls, the auditor examines documents for evidence of the performance of the control. If the auditor is unable to examine a document or to use an alternative procedure to test whether the control was adequately performed, the sample item is a deviation for purposes of evaluating the sample results.

- *Stopping the test before completion.* If a large number of deviations are detected early in the tests of controls, the auditor should consider stopping the test, as the results of the test will not support the planned assessed level of control risk. In such a case, the auditor may rely on other internal controls or set control risk at the maximum for the audit objective affected, and revise the related substantive tests.

After the audit procedures have been completed, the auditor proceeds with his or her evaluation of the sample results.

Evaluation

The evaluation phase includes the following steps.

Step 8: Calculate the Sample Results   After completing the audit procedures, the auditor should summarize the deviations by the controls tested and evaluate the results. Determining the sample results for an attribute-sampling application can be accomplished by the use of a computer program or attribute-sampling tables. The auditor calculates the *sample deviation rate* and the *computed upper deviation rate.* The sample deviation rate is the number of deviations found in the sample divided by the number of items in the sample. The sample deviation rate represents the auditor's best estimate of the population's deviation rate. However, because this result is based on a sample, the auditor must consider an allowance for sampling risk. The computed upper deviation rate is the sum of the sample deviation rate and the allowance for sampling risk. It represents the upper one-sided limit for the population deviation rate based on the sample size, the number of deviations, and the planned level of risk for assessing control risk too low. As mentioned earlier, attribute-sampling tests are typically one-sided because the auditor is generally concerned only with the maximum deviation rate in the population.

Step 9: Performing Error Analysis   The auditor should evaluate the qualitative aspects of the deviations identified. This involves two considerations. First, the nature of each deviation and its cause should be considered. For example, the auditor should determine if a deviation is an unintentional error or a fraud. Relatedly, the auditor should attempt to determine whether a deviation resulted from a cause such as misunderstanding of instructions or carelessness. Understanding the nature and cause of a deviation helps the auditor better assess control risk. Second, the auditor should consider how the deviations may impact the other phases of the audit. For example, suppose that most of the deviations found in a test of the revenue cycle resulted from improper granting of credit. As a result, the auditor would expect that the valuation objective was not met for accounts receivable and would therefore increase the amount of audit work for the substantive tests of the allowance for uncollectible accounts.

Step 10: Draw Final Conclusions

In drawing a conclusion about the statistical sampling application for tests of controls, the auditor compares the tolerable deviation rate to the computed upper deviation rate. If the computed upper deviation rate is less than the tolerable deviation rate, the auditor can conclude that the controls can be relied upon. If the computed upper deviation rate exceeds the tolerable deviation rate, the auditor must conclude that the controls are not operating at an acceptable level.

However, the final conclusion about control risk for the accounting system being tested is based on the auditor's professional judgment of the sample results and other relevant tests of controls such as inquiry and observation. If the auditor concludes that the evidence supports the planned level of control risk, no modifications of the planned substantive tests are necessary. On the other hand, if the planned level of control risk is not supported by the sample results and other tests of controls, the auditor should either (1) test other control procedures that could support the planned level of control risk or (2) increase the assessed level of control risk and modify the nature, extent, or timing of substantive tests.

Table 8–6 shows the auditor's risks when evaluating sample evidence on the planned level of control risk. If the evidence supports the planned level of control risk and the internal control is reliable, the auditor has made a correct decision. Similarly, if the evidence does not support the planned level of control risk and the internal control is not reliable, a correct decision has been made. The other two combinations result in decision errors by the auditor. If the evidence supports the planned level of control risk and the internal control is not reliable, the auditor will have

TABLE 8–6	The Auditor's Risks When Evaluating Sample Evidence on the Planned Level of Control Risk	
Auditor's Decision Based on Sample Evidence	**True State of Internal Control**	
	Reliable	*Not Reliable*
Supports the planned level of control risk	Correct decision	Risk of assessing control risk too low
Does not support the planned level of control risk	Risk of assessing control risk too high	Correct decision

set control risk too low and overrelied on internal control (Type II error). This results in the auditor establishing detection risk too high and leads to a lower level of evidence being gathered through substantive tests. Thus, the auditor's risk of not detecting material misstatement is increased. This can lead to a lawsuit against the auditor. If the evidence does not support the planned level of control risk and the internal control is reliable (Type I error), the auditor will not have placed sufficient reliance on internal control and detection risk will have been set too low. Thus, a higher level of evidence will be gathered by substantive tests, leading to overauditing and an inefficient audit.

An Example of an Attribute-Sampling Plan

[LO 7]   Calabro Paging Services, the company included in Discussion Case 3–41 in Chapter 3, will be used to demonstrate an attribute sampling plan. Don Jones, senior-in-charge of the Calabro Paging Services audit, developed an understanding of Calabro's revenue cycle and has decided to rely on selected controls to reduce control risk below the maximum. Jones intends to test the entire year and has determined that the population is complete. The following subsections document Jones's sampling plan. Typically, a CPA firm uses a formal working paper to document the steps in the sampling plan.

Determine the Objective of the Test (Step 1)

The objective of this test is to determine if Calabro's revenue cycle is functioning as documented. In particular, Jones wants to determine if the controls identified as reliable are operating effectively and thus allow control risk to be set below the maximum.

Define the Deviation from the Control Policy or Procedure (Step 2)

Calabro's revenue transactions arise in the following manner:

Subscribers may lease a pager from the company or purchase a pager and pay only an access fee for the company paging system. Each subscriber enters into a service contract with the company, which provides for the payment of the access fee and the purchase or lease of one or more pagers. The company's contracts with customers with large numbers of pagers are typically for three- to five-year terms, while contracts for smaller quantities are typically for one-year terms with annual renewal.

For this sampling application, Jones has decided to rely on three controls in Calabro's revenue cycle. The three control procedures and their definitions are as follows:

1. **Sales and service contracts are properly authorized for credit approval.** Calabro's credit department personnel check the creditworthiness of new customers and establish a credit limit based on that evaluation. For existing customers, the amount of the new sale or lease is added to the existing accounts receivable balance, and the total is compared to the customer's credit limit. If the amount is less than the credit limit, the transaction is processed. If the total is more than the credit limit, the transaction is subjected to review by the credit manager before the sale is approved. Therefore, a deviation in

this test is defined as the failure of Calabro's credit department personnel to follow proper credit approval procedures for new and existing customers.

2. ***Sales are not recorded without an approved sales and lease contract.*** Calabro's revenue cycle contains a control that no revenue transactions are to be recorded unless an approved sales or lease contract is sent to the billing department. For this control, a deviation is defined as the absence of an approved sales or lease contract.

3. ***Sales and lease contracts are properly priced.*** Calabro's revenue cycle also includes a control that requires billing department personnel to use an authorized price list for the sale of pagers. Access and lease fees are determined based on a fee structure that includes volume discounts for large unit subscribers. A deviation in this case is the use of an unauthorized price for a pager or an incorrect access or lease fee.

Define the Population (Step 3)

For the current test, Jones has decided to test the entire year. The physical representation of the population is the numeric file of sales and lease contracts maintained in the sales department. Based on a review of the client's procedures for completeness, Jones has determined that the frame is complete. The population of sales and lease transactions for the year contains 125,000 items that are numbered from 1 to 125,000.

Define the Sampling Unit (Step 4)

The sampling unit for this test is defined as the sales or lease contract. Jones can perform all tests for the controls selected by examining this set of documents.

Determine the Sample Size (Step 5)

Table 8–7 shows Jones's decision for each of the parameters required to determine sample size. Jones decides to set the risk of assessing control risk too low at 5 percent, the tolerable deviation rate at 6 percent, and the expected population deviation rate at 1 percent for control 1. For control 1,

| TABLE 8–7 | The Auditor's Decisions for Sample Size |

	Control*		
Parameters	1	2	3
Risk of assessing control risk too low	5%	10%	5%
Tolerable deviation rate	6%	8%	5%
Expected population deviation rate	1%	2%	1%
Sample size	78	48	93

*Control 1: Sales or lease contracts are properly authorized for credit approval.
Control 2: Sales are not recorded without an approved sales and lease contract.
Control 3: Sales and lease contracts are properly priced.

TABLE 8–8　　**Statistical Sample Sizes for Attribute Sampling—5 Percent Risk of Assessing Control Risk Too Low**

Expected Population Deviation Rate	Tolerable Deviation Rate										
	2%	3%	4%	5%	6%	7%	8%	9%	10%	15%	20%
0.00%	149(0)	99(0)	74(0)	59(0)	49(0)	42(0)	36(0)	32(0)	29(0)	19(0)	14(0)
.25	236(1)	157(1)	117(1)	93(1)	78(1)	66(1)	58(1)	51(1)	46(1)	30(1)	22(1)
.50	*	157(1)	117(1)	93(1)	78(1)	66(1)	58(1)	51(1)	46(1)	30(1)	22(1)
.75	*	208(2)	117(1)	93(1)	78(1)	66(1)	58(1)	51(1)	46(1)	30(1)	22(1)
1.00	*	*	156(2)	93(1)	78(1)	66(1)	58(1)	51(1)	46(1)	30(1)	22(1)
1.25	*	*	156(2)	124(2)	78(1)	66(1)	58(1)	51(1)	46(1)	30(1)	22(1)
1.50	*	*	192(3)	124(2)	103(2)	66(1)	58(1)	51(1)	46(1)	30(1)	22(1)
1.75	*	*	227(4)	153(3)	103(2)	88(2)	77(2)	51(1)	46(1)	30(1)	22(1)
2.00	*	*	*	181(4)	127(3)	88(2)	77(2)	68(2)	46(1)	30(1)	22(1)
2.25	*	*	*	208(5)	127(3)	88(2)	77(2)	68(2)	61(2)	30(1)	22(1)
2.50	*	*	*	*	150(4)	109(3)	77(2)	68(2)	61(2)	30(1)	22(1)
2.75	*	*	*	*	173(5)	109(3)	95(3)	68(2)	61(2)	30(1)	22(1)
3.00	*	*	*	*	195(6)	129(4)	95(3)	84(3)	61(2)	30(1)	22(1)
3.25	*	*	*	*	*	148(5)	112(4)	84(3)	61(2)	30(1)	22(1)
3.50	*	*	*	*	*	167(6)	112(4)	84(3)	76(3)	40(2)	22(1)
3.75	*	*	*	*	*	185(7)	129(5)	100(4)	76(3)	40(2)	22(1)
4.00	*	*	*	*	*	*	146(6)	100(4)	89(4)	40(2)	22(1)
5.00	*	*	*	*	*	*	*	158(8)	116(6)	40(2)	30(2)
6.00	*	*	*	*	*	*	*	*	179(11)	50(3)	30(2)
7.00	*	*	*	*	*	*	*	*	*	68(5)	37(3)

*Sample size is too large to be cost-effective for most audit applications. The number in parentheses represents the maximum number of deviations in a sample of that size that allows the auditor to conclude that the tolerable deviation rate is not exceeded.

Jones has planned a low assessed level of control risk (see Table 8–4). A similar strategy is followed for control 3. For control 2, Jones has planned a moderate assessed level of control risk. In this sampling plan, the effect of the size of the population can be ignored because the population contains 125,000 transactions.

Tables 8–8 and 8–9 are used to determine the sample size for each of the controls. For control 1, Jones uses Table 8–8 to determine the sample size because the risk of assessing control risk too low is 5 percent. Jones identifies the column for a 6 percent tolerable deviation rate and reads down that column until the row for a 1 percent expected population deviation rate is found. The sample size for control 1 is 78 items. For control 2, Jones uses Table 8–9 because the risk of assessing control risk too low is

TABLE 8–9	Statistical Sample Sizes for Attribute Sampling— 10 Percent Risk of Assessing Control Risk Too Low

Expected Population Deviation Rate	Tolerable Deviation Rate										
	2%	3%	4%	5%	6%	7%	8%	9%	10%	15%	20%
0.00%	114(0)	76(0)	57(0)	45(0)	38(0)	32(0)	28(0)	25(0)	22(0)	15(0)	11(0)
.25	194(1)	129(1)	96(1)	77(1)	64(1)	55(1)	48(1)	42(1)	38(1)	25(1)	18(1)
.50	194(1)	129(1)	96(1)	77(1)	64(1)	55(1)	48(1)	42(1)	38(1)	25(1)	18(1)
.75	265(2)	129(1)	96(1)	77(1)	64(1)	55(1)	48(1)	42(1)	38(1)	25(1)	18(1)
1.00	*	176(2)	96(1)	77(1)	64(1)	55(1)	48(1)	42(1)	38(1)	25(1)	18(1)
1.25	*	221(3)	132(2)	77(1)	64(1)	55(1)	48(1)	42(1)	38(1)	25(1)	18(1)
1.50	*	*	132(2)	105(2)	64(1)	55(1)	48(1)	42(1)	38(1)	25(1)	18(1)
1.75	*	*	166(3)	105(2)	88(2)	55(1)	48(1)	42(1)	38(1)	25(1)	18(1)
2.00	*	*	198(4)	132(3)	88(2)	75(2)	48(1)	42(1)	38(1)	25(1)	18(1)
2.25	*	*	*	132(3)	88(2)	75(2)	65(2)	42(1)	38(1)	25(1)	18(1)
2.50	*	*	*	158(4)	110(3)	75(2)	65(2)	58(2)	38(1)	25(1)	18(1)
2.75	*	*	*	209(6)	132(4)	94(3)	65(2)	58(2)	52(2)	25(1)	18(1)
3.00	*	*	*	*	132(4)	94(3)	65(2)	58(2)	52(2)	25(1)	18(1)
3.25	*	*	*	*	153(5)	113(4)	82(3)	58(2)	52(2)	25(1)	18(1)
3.50	*	*	*	*	194(7)	113(4)	82(3)	73(3)	52(2)	25(1)	18(1)
3.75	*	*	*	*	*	131(5)	98(4)	73(3)	52(2)	25(1)	18(1)
4.00	*	*	*	*	*	149(6)	98(4)	73(3)	65(3)	25(1)	18(1)
5.00	*	*	*	*	*	*	160(8)	115(6)	78(4)	34(2)	18(1)
6.00	*	*	*	*	*	*	*	182(11)	116(7)	43(3)	25(2)
7.00	*	*	*	*	*	*	*	*	199(14)	52(4)	25(2)

*Sample size is too large to be cost-effective for most audit applications. The number in parentheses represents the maximum number of deviations in a sample of that size that allows the auditor to conclude that the tolerable deviation rate is not exceeded.

10 percent. Reading down the 8 percent tolerable deviation rate column until the 2 percent expected population deviation rate is found, Jones determines that the sample size is 48. Finally, the sample size for control 3 is 93. This is found by using Table 8–8 and reading down the 5 percent tolerable deviation rate column until the 1 percent expected deviation rate row is reached.

As mentioned previously, auditors typically establish one set of parameters for all controls tested within an accounting cycle. This is particularly true when all the tests of controls are to be conducted on the same sampling units. The parameters are usually chosen for the control that requires the largest sample size. Therefore, in this example, the sample size that would be used for testing the three controls would be 93. The sample sizes shown in Table 8–7 are used in the following example for illustrative purposes.

EXHIBIT 8–1

Sample Screens from PricewaterhouseCoopers's Statistical Sampling Software

Screen 1

PricewaterhouseCoopers's Statistical Sampling Program   APSS

1. Classical Variable Sampling Data Entry—Ratio & Difference
2. Classical Variable Sampling Data Entry—Direct Projection
3. Classical Variable Sampling Evaluation—Ratio & Difference
4. Classical Variable Sampling Evaluation—Direct Projection
5. Attribute Sampling
6. Sampling Proportionate to Size
7. Random Number Generator
8. Documentation Forms 1—Compliance (Attributes) Test
9. Documentation Forms 2—Substantive (Variables) Set (Including SPS)

Screen 2

PricewaterhouseCoopers   Attributes Sampling   APSS

1. Sample Size Determination
2. Sample Evaluation

Enter menu selection number

Screen 3

ATTRIBUTE SAMPLING—SAMPLE SIZE DETERMINATION—AUDIT APPLICATION

Allowable Risk of Incorrect Acceptance (1, 5, 10, 20, 30, 40, or 50%)	5
Conservative Expected Deviation Rate [CEDR] (%)	1.00*
Maximum Tolerable Deviation Rate [MTDR] (%)	5.00
Population Size (0 assumes infinite)	125000
Required Sample Size	93
Allowable Number of Deviations	1

Therefore, if you find 1 or fewer deviations in the sample of 93, you may conclude at a Risk of Incorrect Acceptance of 5% that the Deviation Rate for the Population does not exceed the Tolerable Rate.

*Because the Number of Deviations must be a whole number, the Conservative Expected Deviation Rate is adjusted from 1.00% to 1.08%.

Exhibit 8–1 shows screen displays from PricewaterhouseCoopers's statistical sampling audit software[5] for determining the sample size for control 3.

---

[5]This material is used with the permission of PricewaterhouseCoopers LLP. The author is grateful to the firm for allowing the use of this material.

Screen 1 shows the introductory menu. Item 5, "Attribute Sampling," is selected. Screen 2 shows the menu for choosing sample size determination or sample evaluation. Item 1 is chosen, and the auditor responses to the queries are shown on screen 3. The responses to the queries about the allowable risk of incorrect acceptance, expected deviation rate, tolerable deviation rate, and population size lead to a sample of 93.

Randomly Select the Sample Items (Step 6)

Jones randomly selects the sample items. Exhibit 8–2 shows an example of the output from the random-number generator in the Pricewaterhouse-Coopers statistical sampling software. The auditor enters the first and last numbers in the sequence of sales and lease contracts (1–125,000), the sample size (93), and the number of extra items to be selected (5). Extras are added in case some selected items do not meet the sample guidelines. The output provides the random numbers by smallest to largest document number and also indicates the order in which the items were selected.

Perform the Audit Procedures (Step 7)

Jones examines each of the sample items for the presence of a deviation. Thus, for control 1, Jones tests the 78 sales and lease contracts for proper credit authorization procedures by credit department personnel. When conducting the specific audit procedures, Jones must be careful not to commit nonsampling errors, for example, failing to detect a misstatement in a sample item. The results of the audit procedures can be recorded on a working paper similar to the one shown in Exhibit 8–3.

Calculate the Sample Results (Step 8)

Exhibit 8–3 shows the results of the tests of the three controls. Jones calculates the sample deviation rate and the computed upper deviation rate for each control tested. To determine the computed upper deviation rate, Jones uses either Table 8–10 or Table 8–11, depending on the risk of assessing control risk too low that has been assigned to the test. Therefore, for control 1, Jones uses Table 8–10 in the following way: The column for the actual number of deviations found (2 deviations) is read down until the appropriate row for sample size is found. If the exact sample size is not found, the closest smaller sample size is used. This approach provides a conservative (larger) computed upper deviation rate. For control 1, the row for a sample size of 75 is used. The computed upper deviation rate for control 1 is 8.2 percent. Thus, for control 1, the sample deviation rate is 2.6 percent and the allowance for sampling risk is 5.6 percent (8.2 – 2.6). For control 2, Table 8–11 is used because the risk of assessing control risk too low is 10 percent. In this case, no deviations were found, so the sample deviation rate is 0 percent and the upper computed deviation rate (and allowance for sampling risk) is 5 percent. No control deviations were found for control 3; therefore, the sample deviation rate is 0 percent. Table 8–10 shows a computed upper deviation rate (and allowance for sampling risk) of 3.3 percent.

EXHIBIT 8–2

An Example of a Random Sample Drawn from a Computer Program

Total Population   125000

Sample Size   93

Number of Extras   5

Random Start   42211461

Random Numbers Generated

Order	Document	Order	Document	Order	Document
28	372	26	54234	79	111678
49	1283	68	56523	44	112305
48	1347	3	57757	29	112770
47	1378	23	58305	20	114244
81	1442	65	58678	59	114618
54	2377	71	59485	50	116688
43	2867	72	59605	64	120058
80	3883	74	59647	45	120353
51	4815	18	61573	14	121809
7	5838	17	62459	6	122607
90	7152	11	62837	93	122891
30	12183	41	65620	82	124737
46	13640	35	66410	73	124850
39	13653	25	67753		Extra Sample Items
61	15008	70	71611	Order	Document
36	15941	89	73326	94	103176
13	16472	24	77595	95	86589
92	17080	34	80164	96	1305
32	24742	52	81092	97	88699
55	25029	57	81347	98	43242
16	25464	2	82765		Random Numbers Printed 98
62	25787	21	83877		
15	27765	66	85023		
9	28064	38	85244		
67	28349	8	85800		
58	28612	78	88878		
5	29480	85	89130		
22	30501	84	89652		
19	32181	27	89741		
83	32434	60	91121		
10	32896	31	92799		
1	35381	76	93062		
69	37002	53	96509		
63	46044	4	97127		
56	46540	87	98255		
40	47842	33	102148		
37	48920	12	103753		
77	52140	42	103775		
75	52222	91	107409		
88	53702	86	107585		

EXHIBIT 8–3

A Sample Working Paper for Recording the Results of Tests of Controls

CPS

B20
DLJ
2/3/01

CALABRO PAGING SERVICES
Controls Tested—Revenue Cycle
12/31/00

		Control Procedure		
Sample Item	Sales Invoice Number	1	2	3
1	35381	✓	✓	✓
2	82765	E	✓	✓
•		•	•	•
•		•	•	•
48	1347	✓	✓	✓
49	1283	E		✓
•		•		•
•		•		•
77	52140	✓		✓
78	88878	✓		✓
•				•
•				•
91	107409			✓
92	17080			✓
93	122891			✓
Number of deviations		2	0	0
Sample size		78	48	93
Sample deviation rate		2.6%	0%	0%
Computed upper deviation rate		8.2%	5.0%	3.3%
Tolerable deviation rate		6%	8%	5%
Auditor's decision		Does not support reliance	Supports reliance	Supports reliance

Tick Mark Legend
✓ = Sales or lease contract examined for proper performance of control procedure. No exception.
E = Control *not* performed properly.

TABLE 8–10 Statistical Sample Results Evaluation Table (Computed Upper Deviation Rates) for Attribute Sampling— 5 Percent Risk of Assessing Control Risk Too Low

Sample Size	Actual Number of Deviations Found										
	0	1	2	3	4	5	6	7	8	9	10
25	11.3	17.6	*	*	*	*	*	*	*	*	*
30	9.5	14.9	19.6	*	*	*	*	*	*	*	*
35	8.3	12.9	17.0	*	*	*	*	*	*	*	*
40	7.3	11.4	15.0	18.3	*	*	*	*	*	*	*
45	6.5	10.2	13.4	16.4	19.2	*	*	*	*	*	*
50	5.9	9.2	12.1	14.8	17.4	19.9	*	*	*	*	*
55	5.4	8.4	11.1	13.5	15.9	18.2	*	*	*	*	*
60	4.9	7.7	10.2	12.5	14.7	16.8	18.8	*	*	*	*
65	4.6	7.1	9.4	11.5	13.6	15.5	17.4	19.3	*	*	*
70	4.2	6.6	8.8	10.8	12.6	14.5	16.3	18.0	19.7	*	*
75	4.0	6.2	8.2	10.1	11.8	13.6	15.2	16.9	18.5	20.0	*
80	3.7	5.8	7.7	9.5	11.1	12.7	14.3	15.9	17.4	18.9	*
90	3.3	5.2	6.9	8.4	9.9	11.4	12.8	14.2	15.5	16.8	18.2
100	3.0	4.7	6.2	7.6	9.0	10.3	11.5	12.8	14.0	15.2	16.4
125	2.4	3.8	5.0	6.1	7.2	8.3	9.3	10.3	11.3	12.3	13.2
150	2.0	3.2	4.2	5.1	6.0	6.9	7.8	8.6	9.5	10.3	11.1
200	1.5	2.4	3.2	3.9	4.6	5.2	5.9	6.5	7.2	7.8	8.4

*Over 20 percent.

TABLE 8–11 Statistical Sample Results Evaluation Table (Computed Upper Deviation Rates) for Attribute Sampling— 10 Percent Risk of Assessing Control Risk Too Low

Sample Size	Actual Number of Deviations Found										
	0	1	2	3	4	5	6	7	8	9	10
20	10.9	18.1	*	*	*	*	*	*	*	*	*
25	8.8	14.7	19.9	*	*	*	*	*	*	*	*
30	7.4	12.4	16.8	*	*	*	*	*	*	*	*
35	6.4	10.7	14.5	18.1	*	*	*	*	*	*	*
40	5.6	9.4	12.8	16.0	19.0	*	*	*	*	*	*
45	5.0	8.4	11.4	14.3	17.0	19.7	*	*	*	*	*
50	4.6	7.6	10.3	12.9	15.4	17.8	*	*	*	*	*
55	4.1	6.9	9.4	11.8	14.1	16.3	18.4	*	*	*	*
60	3.8	6.4	8.7	10.8	12.9	15.0	16.9	18.9	*	*	*
70	3.3	5.5	7.5	9.3	11.1	12.9	14.6	16.3	17.9	19.6	*
80	2.9	4.8	6.6	8.2	9.8	11.3	12.8	14.3	15.8	17.2	18.6
90	2.6	4.3	5.9	7.3	8.7	10.1	11.5	12.8	14.1	15.4	16.6
100	2.3	3.9	5.3	6.6	7.9	9.1	10.3	11.5	12.7	13.9	15.0
120	2.0	3.3	4.4	5.5	6.6	7.6	8.7	9.7	10.7	11.6	12.6
160	1.5	2.5	3.3	4.2	5.0	5.8	6.5	7.3	8.0	8.8	9.5
200	1.2	2.0	2.7	3.4	4.0	4.6	5.3	5.9	6.5	7.1	7.6

*Over 20 percent.

Exhibit 8–4 shows the output from PricewaterhouseCoopers's statistical sampling software for the evaluation of control 3. Screen 1 shows the introductory menu for sample evaluation. Item 1, "Audit Application—Unstratified Sampling," is chosen, and the auditor inputs the parameters shown on screen 2 for the allowable risk of incorrect acceptance (5 percent), the maximum tolerable deviation rate (5 percent), the population size (125,000), the sample size (93), and the number of deviations (0). The estimated maximum deviation rate is determined to be 3.17 percent.

E X H I B I T 8–4

Evaluation Results from PricewaterhouseCoopers's Statistical Sampling Software

Screen 1

PricewaterhouseCoopers	Attributes Sampling	APSS
	Sample Evaluation	

1. Audit Application—Unstratified Sampling
2. Audit Application—Stratified Sampling
3. Audit Application—Two-step Sequential Sampling
4. Accounting Application—Unstratified Sampling
5. Accounting Application—Stratified Sampling

Enter menu selection number

Screen 2

Calabro Paging Services

AUDIT APPLICATION—UNSTRATIFIED SAMPLE EVALUATION

Allowable Risk of Incorrect Acceptance (1, 5, 10, 20, 30, 40, or 50%)	5%
Maximum Tolerable Deviation Rate [MTDR]	5.00%
Population Size	125000
Sample Size	93
Number of Deviations	0
Sample Deviation Rate	0.00%
Estimated Maximum Deviation Rate	3.17%

Therefore, based on the sample evidence, you may conclude at a Risk of Incorrect Acceptance of 5% that the deviation rate for the population does not exceed the Tolerable Rate of 5.00%.

Source: PricewaterhouseCoopers LLP. Used by permission.

Perform Error Analysis (Step 9)

Before drawing final conclusions on the sampling plan, Jones investigates the nature and cause of the errors. Jones also considers whether the deviations may impact the other phases of the audit. In the current example, two deviations were detected for control 1, which relates to proper authorization of credit. Jones's investigation indicates that both deviations had occurred when sales in excess of credit limits were made to existing customers. Further investigation disclosed that the sales manager instead of the credit manager had approved the sale. Jones now knows the nature and cause of the errors. The effect of the control deviations is likely to be an increase in the amount of audit work conducted on the allowance for uncollectible accounts.

Draw Final Conclusions (Step 10)

The statistical conclusion about each control is made by comparing the tolerable deviation rate to the computed upper deviation rate. If the computed upper deviation rate is less than the tolerable deviation rate, the statistical tests indicate that the control is reliable. If the computed upper deviation rate is greater than the tolerable deviation rate, the sample evidence does not support the reliability of the control. Exhibit 8–3 shows that the sample evidence does not support the operating effectiveness of control 1 (credit authorization) because the computed upper deviation rate (8.2 percent) exceeds the tolerable deviation rate (6 percent). In this case, the sample deviation rate was 2.6 percent and the allowance for sampling risk was 5.6 percent. The sample evidence supports the reliability of controls 2 and 3 because the computed upper deviation rate is less than the tolerable deviation rate. In this example, there appear to be no other controls or other evidence to support the operating effectiveness of control 1. Thus, Jones increases both the assessed level of control risk and the substantive tests related to the authorization and valuation audit objectives.

Nonstatistical Sampling for Tests of Controls

When conducting a nonstatistical sampling application for tests of controls, the auditor considers each of the steps shown in Table 8–2. The only differences between nonstatistical and statistical sampling occur in the following steps:

- Determining the sample size.
- Randomly selecting the sample items.
- Calculating the sample results.

Determining the Sample Size

When a nonstatistical sampling application is used, the auditor should consider the acceptable risk of assessing control risk too low, the tolerable deviation rate, and the expected population deviation rate when determining sample size. However, the auditor does not use a statistical formula or table to determine sample size. Instead, professional judgment is used to relate these factors and determine the appropriate sample size for the application; for example, an auditor might consider each of these factors and determine that a sample size of 30 is adequate.

A number of public accounting firms establish guidelines for nonstatistical sample sizes for tests of controls. For example, a firm might establish guidelines as follows:

Planned Assessed Level of Control Risk	Sample Size
Slightly below the maximum	10–15
Moderate	20–35
Low	30–60

In using such guidelines, if one or more deviations are found in the sample, the auditor needs to expand the sample or increase the assessed level of control risk.

Randomly Selecting the Sample Items

While random-sample or systematic-sample selection is required for attribute sampling, nonstatistical sampling allows the use of those selection methods as well as other selection methods such as haphazard sampling, which was described earlier in this chapter. The haphazard sample should be selected in such a way that it is likely to be representative of the population. The auditor should avoid distorting the sample by selecting only items that are unusual or large, or items that are the first or last items in the frame.

Calculating the Sample Results

With a nonstatistical sample, the auditor can calculate the sample deviation rate but cannot quantify the computed upper deviation rate and the sampling risk associated with the test. The AICPA Audit Pactice Release *Audit Sampling* provides the following advice for considering sampling risk in a nonstatistical test of controls:

> [I]t is generally appropriate for the auditor to assume that the sample results do not support the planned assessed level of control risk if the rate of deviation identified in the sample exceeds the expected population deviation rate used in designing the sample. In that case there is likely to be an unacceptably high risk that the true deviation rate in the population exceeds the tolerable rate. If the auditor concludes that there is an unacceptably high risk that the true population deviation rate could exceed the tolerable rate, it might be practical to expand the test to sufficient additional items to reduce the risk to an acceptable level. Rather than testing additional items, however, it is generally more efficient to increase the auditor's assessed level of control risk to the level supported by the results of the original sample.[6]

Suppose an auditor planned a nonstatistical sampling application by setting the acceptable risk of assessing control risk too low at 5 percent, the expected population deviation rate at 2 percent, and the tolerable deviation rate at 6 percent. Assume the auditor judgmentally chooses a sample size of 30 items. If the auditor detects no control deviations, the sample deviation rate is 0 percent. In this instance, the sample deviation rate (0 percent) is less than the expected population deviation rate (2 percent), and

---

[6]American Institute of Certified Public Accountants, *Audit Sampling* (Audit Practice Release), (New York: AICPA, 1999), Chapter 5.

there is an acceptable risk that the true population deviation rate exceeds the tolerable deviation rate. If one control deviation is detected, the sample deviation rate is 3.3 percent. Because the sample deviation rate is greater than the expected population deviation rate (2 percent), there is an unacceptably high risk that the true population deviation rate exceeds the tolerable deviation rate. The use of a statistical evaluation table illustrates why the results of the nonstatistical sample are not likely to support the effectiveness of the control. Table 8–10 shows that if one deviation is found in a sample of 30 items, the computed upper deviation rate is 14.9 percent. This greatly exceeds the tolerable deviation rate of 6 percent.

REVIEW QUESTIONS

[LO 1]	8-1	Define *audit sampling*. Why do auditors sample instead of examining every transaction?
[2]	8-2	List audit evidence choices that do not involve sampling.
[3]	8-3	Distinguish between Type I and Type II errors. What terms are used to describe these errors when the auditor is conducting tests of controls and substantive tests? What costs are potentially incurred by auditors when such decision errors occur?
[5]	8-4	Discuss the requirements of SAS No. 39 for a sampling application.
[4]	8-5	Distinguish between nonstatistical and statistical sampling. What are the advantages and disadvantages of using statistical sampling?
[4]	8-6	Briefly describe the three types of statistical sampling techniques.
[6,7]	8-7	Define *attribute sampling*. Why is this sampling technique appropriate for tests of controls?
[6,7,8]	8-8	After defining the population, the auditor must make what additional decisions concerning the population?
[6,7,8]	8-9	In some instances, a sampling application may apply to only a portion of the year being audited. List three factors that the auditor might consider when deciding whether to gather additional evidence for the remaining period.
[7]	8-10	List the four factors that enter into the sample size decision. What is the relationship between sample size and each of these factors?
[6,7,8]	8-11	In performing certain audit procedures the auditor may encounter voided documents, inapplicable documents, or missing documents. How should each of these situations be handled within the attribute-sampling application?
[6,7,8]	8-12	The auditor should perform error analysis when deviations are found in a sampling application. What are the purposes of performing error analysis?
[6,7,8]	8-13	If the planned level of control risk is not supported by the sampling results, what should the auditor do?
[8]	8-14	List the three steps that differ when a nonstatistical sampling application is performed.
[8]	8-15	How should the results of a nonstatistical sample be evaluated in terms of considering sampling risk?

MULTIPLE-CHOICE QUESTIONS FROM CPA EXAMINATIONS

[6,7]   8-16   An auditor plans to examine a sample of 20 purchase orders for proper approval as prescribed by the client's internal accounting control procedures. One of the purchase orders in the chosen sample of 20 cannot be found, and the auditor is unable to use alternative procedures to test whether that purchase order was properly approved. The auditor should
a. Choose another purchase order to replace the missing purchase order in the sample.
b. Consider this compliance test invalid and proceed with substantive tests because internal control cannot be relied upon.
c. Treat the missing purchase order as a deviation for the purpose of evaluating the sample.
d. Select a completely new set of 20 purchase orders.

[6,7]   8-17   Which of the following combinations results in a decrease in sample size in an attribute sample for a test of controls?

	Risk of Assessing Control Risk Too Low	Tolerable Deviation Rate	Expected Population Deviation Rate
a.	Increase	Decrease	Increase
b.	Decrease	Increase	Decrease
c.	Increase	Increase	Decrease
d.	Increase	Increase	Increase

[3,6]   8-18   The likelihood of assessing control risk too high is the risk that the sample selected to test controls
a. Does *not* support the tolerable deviation rate for some or all of management's assertions.
b. Does *not* support the auditor's planned assessed level of control risk when the true operating effectiveness of the control justifies such an assessment.
c. Contains misstatements that could be material to the financial statements when aggregated with misstatements in other account balances or transaction classes.
d. Contains proportionately fewer monetary errors or deviations from prescribed internal controls than exist in the balance or class as a whole.

[4]   8-19   An advantage of statistical sampling over nonstatistical sampling is that statistical sampling helps an auditor to
a. Eliminate the risk of nonsampling errors.
b. Reduce audit risk and materiality to a relatively low level.
c. Measure the sufficiency of the evidential matter obtained.
d. Minimize the failure to detect errors and fraud.

[6,7]   8-20   To determine the sample size for a test of controls, an auditor should consider the tolerable deviation rate, the allowable risk of assessing control risk too low, and the
a. Expected population deviation rate.
b. Computed upper precision limit.
c. Risk of assessing control risk too high.
d. Risk of incorrect rejection.

Questions 8–21 and 8–22 are based on the following information:

An auditor desired to test credit approval on 10,000 sales invoices processed during the year. The auditor designed a statistical sample that would provide 1 percent risk of assessing control risk too low that not more than 7 percent of the sales invoices lacked approval. The auditor estimated from previous experience that about 2½ percent of the sales invoices lacked approval. A sample of 200 invoices was examined, and 7 of them were lacking approval. The auditor then determined the computed upper deviation rate to be 8 percent.

[6,7]   8-21   In the evaluation of this sample, the auditor decided to increase the level of the preliminary assessment of control risk because the
a. Tolerable deviation rate (7 percent) was less than the computed upper deviation rate (8 percent).
b. Expected population deviation rate (7 percent) was more than the percentage of errors in the sample (3½ percent).
c. Computed upper deviation rate (8 percent) was more than the percentage of errors in the sample (3½ percent).
d. Expected population deviation rate (2½ percent) was less than the tolerable deviation rate (7 percent).

[6,7]   8-22   The allowance for sampling risk was
a. 5½ percent.
b. 4½ percent.
c. 3½ percent.
d. 1 percent.

[4]   8-23   In performing tests of controls over authorization of cash disbursements, which of the following sampling methods would be most appropriate?
a. Monetary unit.
b. Attributes.
c. Variables.
d. Probability-proportional-to-size.

[4,6]   8-24   Samples to test internal controls are intended to provide a basis for an auditor to conclude whether
a. The controls are operating effectively.
b. The financial statements are materially misstated.
c. The risk of incorrect acceptance is too high.
d. Materiality for planning purposes is at a sufficiently low level.

[3,6]   8-25   The following table depicts the auditor's estimated computed upper deviation rate compared with the tolerable deviation rate, and also depicts the true population deviation rate compared with the tolerable deviation rate.

	True State of Population	
Auditor's Estimate Based on Sample Results	*Deviation Rate Is Less Than Tolerable Deviation Rate*	*Deviation Rate Exceeds Tolerable Deviation Rate*
Computed upper deviation rate is less than tolerable deviation rate.	I	III
Computed upper deviation rate exceeds tolerable deviation rate.	II	IV

As a result of tests of controls, the auditor assesses control risk higher than necessary and thereby increases substantive testing. This is illustrated by situation

a. I.
b. II.
c. III.
d. IV.

[6]   8-26   In planning a statistical sample for a test of controls, an auditor increased the expected population deviation rate from the prior year's rate because of the results of the prior year's tests of controls and the overall control environment. The auditor would most likely then increase the planned

a. Tolerable deviation rate.
b. Allowance for sampling risk.
c. Risk of assessing control risk too low.
d. Sample size.

[6]   8-27   Which of the following statements is correct concerning statistical sampling in tests of controls?

a. Deviations from controls at a given rate usually result in misstatements at a higher rate.
b. As the population size doubles, the sample size should also double.
c. The qualitative aspects of deviations are *not* considered by the auditor.
d. There is an inverse relationship between the sample size and the tolerable deviation rate.

[3,6]   8-28   What is an auditor's evaluation of a statistical sample for attributes when a test of 50 documents results in 3 deviations if the tolerable deviation rate is 7 percent, the expected population deviation rate is 5 percent, and the allowance for sampling risk is 2 percent?

a. The planned assessed level of control risk should be modified because the tolerable deviation rate plus the allowance for sampling risk exceeds the expected population deviation rate.
b. The sample results should be accepted as support for the planned assessed level of control risk because the sample deviation rate plus the allowance for sampling risk exceeds the tolerable deviation rate.
c. The sample results should be accepted as support for the planned assessed level of control risk because the tolerable deviation rate less the allowance for sampling risk equals the expected population deviation rate.
d. The planned assessed level of control risk should be modified because the sample deviation rate plus the allowance for sampling risk exceeds the tolerable deviation rate.

[3,6]   8-29   As a result of sampling procedures applied as tests of controls, an auditor incorrectly assesses control risk lower than appropriate. The most likely explanation for this situation is that

a. The deviation rates of both the auditor's sample and the population exceed the tolerable deviation rate.
b. The deviation rates of both the auditor's sample and the population are less than the tolerable deviation rate.

c. The deviation rate in the auditor's sample is less than the tolerable deviation rate, but the deviation rate in the population exceeds the tolerable deviation rate.

d. The deviation rate in the auditor's sample exceeds the tolerable deviation rate, but the deviation rate in the population is less than the tolerable deviation rate.

PROBLEMS

[1]   8-30   One of the generally accepted auditing standards states that sufficient competent evidential matter is to be obtained through inspection, observation, inquiries, and confirmation to afford a reasonable basis for an opinion regarding the financial statements under examination. Some degree of uncertainty is implicit in the concept of "a reasonable basis for an opinion," because the concept of sampling is well established in auditing practice.

Required:
a. Explain the auditor's justification for accepting the uncertainties that are inherent in the sampling process.
b. Discuss the uncertainties that collectively embody the concept of audit risk.
c. Discuss the nature of sampling risk and nonsampling risk. Include the effect of sampling risk on substantive tests of details and on tests of controls.

(AICPA, adapted)

[2]   8-31   Following is a list of audit procedures used as tests of controls in the revenue cycle.
1. Observing and evaluating segregation of duties.
2. Testing of whether sales invoices are supported by authorized customer orders and shipping documents.
3. Reviewing client's procedures for accounting for the numerical sequence of shipping documents.
4. Examining sales orders for proper credit approval.
5. Recomputing the information on copies of sales invoices.
6. Comparing the average days outstanding in accounts receivable with industry averages.

Required:
Indicate those audit procedures that do not involve sampling.

[6,7]   8-32   Jenny Jacobs, CPA, is planning to use attribute sampling in order to determine the degree of reliance to be placed on an audit client's system of internal control over sales. Jacobs has begun to develop an outline of the main steps in the sampling plan as follows:
1. State the objective(s) of the audit test (for example, to test the reliability of internal controls over sales).
2. Define the population (the period covered by the test, the sampling unit, the completeness of the population).
3. Define the sampling unit (for example, client copies of sales invoices).

Required:
a. What are the remaining steps in the outline that Jacobs should include in the statistical test of sales invoices?
b. How does statistical methodology help the auditor develop a satisfactory sampling plan?

(AICPA, adapted)

[6]   8-33   Determine the sample size for each of the control procedures shown in the following table:

Parameters	Control Procedure			
	1	*2*	*3*	*4*
Risk of assessing control risk too low	5%	5%	10%	10%
Tolerable deviation rate	4%	5%	7%	8%
Expected population deviation rate	1%	2%	3%	4%
Sample size				

[6]   8-34   Using the sample sizes determined in Problem 8–33 and the number of deviations shown here, determine the sample deviation rate, the computed upper deviation rate, and the auditor's decision for each control procedure.

Results	Control Procedure			
	1	*2*	*3*	*4*
Number of deviations	0	5	4	3
Sample size				
Sample deviation rate				
Computed upper deviation rate				
Auditor's decision				

[6]   8-35   Determine the sample size for each of the control procedures shown in the following table:

Parameters	Control Procedure			
	1	*2*	*3*	*4*
Risk of assessing control risk too low	5%	5%	10%	10%
Tolerable deviation rate	6%	7%	4%	3%
Expected population deviation rate	2%	2%	1%	0%
Sample size				

[6]   8-36   Using the sample sizes determined in Problem 8–35 and the number of deviations shown here, determine the sample deviation rate, computed upper deviation rate, and the auditor's decision for each control procedure.

	Control Procedure			
Results	*1*	*2*	*3*	*4*
Number of deviations	4	2	2	0
Sample size				
Sample deviation rate				
Computed upper deviation rate				
Auditor's decision				

[8]   8-37   Calgari Clothing Company manufactures high-quality silk ties that are marketed under a number of copyrighted names. Winkle & Huss have been the company's auditors for five years. Lisa Austen, the senior-in-charge of the audit, has reviewed Calgari's control system over purchasing and inventory, and she determined that a number of controls can be relied upon to reduce control risk. Austen has decided to test two control procedures over purchases and inventory: (1) purchase orders are agreed to receiving reports and vendor's invoices for product, quantity, and price; and (2) inventory is transferred to raw material stores using an approved, prenumbered receiving report.

Austen decided to use a nonstatistical sampling approach based on the following judgments for each control procedure and has judgmentally decided to use a sample size of 40 purchase orders for control 1 and 20 receiving reports for control 2.

	Control Procedure	
Parameters	*1*	*2*
Risk of assessing control risk too low	5%	10%
Tolerable deviation rate	7%	9%
Expected population deviation rate	3%	4%

After completing the examination of the sample items, Austen noted one deviation for each control procedure.

Required:
What conclusion should Austen reach about each control procedure? Justify your answer.

[8]   8-38   Doug Iceberge, senior-in-charge of the audit of Fisher Industries, has decided to test the following two controls for Fisher's revenue cycle.
1. All sales invoices are supported by proper documentation, that is, a sales order and a shipping document.
2. All sales invoices are mathematically correct.

Iceberge has decided to use a nonstatistical sampling approach based on the following judgments for each control and has judgmentally decided to use a sample size of 50 sales invoice packets.

	Control Procedure	
Parameters	*1*	*2*
Risk of assessing control risk too low	5%	10%
Tolerable deviation rate	6%	8%
Expected population deviation rate	3%	3%

After completing the examination of the 50 sample items, Iceberge noted one deviation for control 1 and two deviations for control 2.

Required:

What should Iceberge conclude about each control? Justify your answer.

DISCUSSION CASE

[3,5,6]   8-39   Baker, CPA, was engaged to audit Mill Company's financial statements for the year ended September 30. After studying Mill's internal control, Baker decided to obtain evidential matter about the effectiveness of both the design and the operation of the controls that may support a low assessed level of control risk concerning Mill's shipping and billing functions. During the prior years' audits, Baker had used nonstatistical sampling, but for the current year Baker used a statistical sample in the tests of controls to eliminate the need for judgment.

Baker wanted to assess control risk at a low level, so a tolerable deviation rate of 20 percent was established. To estimate the population deviation rate and the computed upper deviation rate, Baker decided to apply a discovery sampling technique of attribute sampling that would use an expected population deviation rate of 3 percent for the 8,000 shipping documents and to defer consideration of the allowable risk of assessing control risk too low until the sample results were evaluated. Baker used the tolerable deviation rate, the population size, and the expected population deviation rate to determine that a sample size of 80 would be sufficient. When it was subsequently determined that the actual population was about 10,000 shipping documents, Baker increased the sample size to 100.

Baker's objective was to ascertain whether Mill's shipments had been properly billed. Baker took a sample of 100 invoices by selecting the first 25 invoices from the first month of each quarter. Baker then compared the invoices to the corresponding prenumbered shipping documents.

When Baker tested the sample, eight deviations were discovered. Additionally, one shipment that should have been billed at $10,443 was actually billed at $10,434. Baker considered this $9 to be immaterial and did not count it as an error.

In evaluating the sample results, Baker made the initial determination that a 5 percent risk of assessing control risk too low was desired and, using the appropriate statistical sampling table, determined that for eight observed deviations from a sample size of 100, the computed upper deviation rate was 14 percent. Baker then calculated the allowance for sampling risk to be 5 percent, the difference between the actual sample deviation rate (8 percent) and the expected error rate (3 percent). Baker reasoned that the actual sample deviation rate (8 percent) plus the allowance for sampling risk (5 percent) was less than the computed upper deviation rate (14 percent); therefore, the sample supported a low level of control risk.

Required:

Describe each incorrect assumption, statement, and inappropriate application of attribute sampling in Baker's procedures.

(AICPA, adapted)

SCAD ASSIGNMENT

Assignment 6, "Tests of Transactions," can be assigned at this time.

Audit Sampling: An Application to Substantive Tests of Account Balances

LEARNING OBJECTIVES

Upon completion of this chapter you will

[1] Develop a sampling plan for substantive tests of account balances.

[2] Learn to apply monetary-unit sampling.

[3] Work through an extended example of monetary-unit sampling.

[4] Learn to apply nonstatistical sampling techniques.

[5] Learn to apply classical variables difference estimation.

[6] Work through an example of classical variables difference estimation.

This chapter demonstrates the application of audit sampling to substantive tests of account balances. In Chapter 8, attribute sampling was used to determine whether controls were operating effectively and could therefore be relied on by the auditor to generate accurate accounting information. Thus, the objective of attribute sampling was to determine the reliability of the client's controls. In this chapter, the purpose of the sampling application is to determine if a financial statement account is not materially misstated. The basic statistical concepts discussed in Chapter 8 are also applicable for sampling applications for substantive tests of account balances.

RELEVANT ACCOUNTING AND AUDITING PRONOUNCEMENTS

AICPA, *Audit Sampling* (Audit Practice Release) (New York: AICPA, 1996)

SAS No. 22, "Planning and Supervision" (AU 311)

SAS No. 39, "Audit Sampling" (AU 350)

SAS No. 47, "Audit Risk and Materiality in Conducting an Audit" (AU 312)

SAS No. 82, "Consideration of Fraud in a Financial Statement Audit" (AU 316)

Two statistical sampling techniques, *monetary-unit sampling* and *classical variables sampling,* and nonstatistical sampling are demonstrated in this chapter. While both statistical sampling methods can provide sufficient, competent evidential matter, monetary-unit sampling may be more practical for most audit applications. The chapter starts by discussing a sampling plan for substantive tests of account balances. This is followed by an introduction of monetary-unit sampling and an extended example. Nonstatistical sampling is then covered. The appendix contains a discussion and example of classical variables sampling. 🌐

A Sampling Plan for Substantive Tests of Account Balances

[LO 1]   In conducting audit sampling for substantive testing of an account balance, the auditor follows the basic steps outlined in Chapter 8 for attribute sampling. Table 9–1 lists each step by the three phases in the sampling application. Again, the auditor should adequately document the sampling application in the working papers.

Planning

In planning a statistical or nonstatistical sampling application for substantive testing, an auditor must apply considerable judgment during each step.

Step 1: Determine the Objective(s) of the Test   Sampling may be used for substantive testing (1) to test the reasonableness of assertions about a financial statement amount or (2) to develop an estimate of some amount. The first use, which is the most frequent application of sampling as a substantive test on a financial statement audit, tests the hypothesis that a financial statement account is not materially misstated. The second use is less frequent but is occasionally used to develop an estimate of an amount as part of a consulting engagement or to review a client's application in an audit. The discussion in this chapter is limited to the use of audit sampling for hypothesis testing. Therefore, the objective or purpose

TABLE 9–1	Steps in a Sampling Application for Substantive Testing

Planning
1. Determine the objective(s) of the test.
2. Define the population.
3. Define the sampling unit.
4. Choose an audit sampling technique.
5. Determine the sample size.
   a. Consider the variation within the population.
   b. Determine the acceptable risk of incorrect acceptance.
   c. Determine the tolerable misstatement.
   d. Determine the expected amount of misstatement.
   e. Consider the population size.

Performance
6. Determine the method of selecting the sample items.
7. Perform the audit procedures.

Evaluation
8. Calculate the sample results.
9. Perform error analysis.
10. Draw final conclusions.

of sampling for substantive testing is to test the hypothesis that no material misstatements exist in an account balance, a class of transactions, or a disclosure component of the financial statements.

Step 2: Define the Population

The auditor must define the population so that the selected sample is appropriate for the audit objective(s) being tested because sample results can be projected only to the population from which the sample was selected. If the auditor is concerned about understatements that result from omitted items (the completeness objective), the sample cannot be drawn from a population of *recorded* transactions. In order to detect such understatements, the auditor should select the items from a population that included the omitted items. For example, if the auditor is concerned about goods shipped but not billed, the population of shipping documents rather than sales invoices is the appropriate population for drawing the sample.

As in the discussion in Chapter 8, once the population has been defined, the auditor must determine that the physical representation, or *frame*, of the population is complete. For example, if the auditor is testing the accounts receivable account, he or she might foot the accounts receivable subsidiary ledger and agree the total to the general ledger account to verify the completeness of the frame. Because the auditor selects the sample from the frame, any conclusions about the population relate only to that physical representation of the population. If the frame and the population differ, the auditor might draw the wrong conclusion about the population.

Step 3: Define the Sampling Unit

Items that make up the population can be used as the sampling unit. Therefore, a sampling unit might be a customer account, an individual transaction, a line item on a transaction, or an individual dollar in an account. For example, in a sampling application on an accounts receivable balance at year-end, the sampling unit might be the balance in a customer's account or an invoice that makes up the customer's balance. Similarly, if sampling is applied to ending inventory, the sampling unit might be a line item on the physical inventory listing or an item from the perpetual inventory records. As we shall see later in the chapter, when monetary-unit sampling is used, the sampling unit is an individual dollar (or other currency) contained in the population.

Step 4: Choose an Audit Sampling Technique

The auditor has to decide on the appropriate sampling method to use for the substantive test. The first decision is whether to use a statistical or a nonstatistical approach. The main difference between statistical and nonstatistical sampling is the auditor's ability to quantify sampling risk using a statistical approach. If a statistical sampling approach is chosen, the auditor must choose between monetary-unit sampling and a classical variables method. Both monetary-unit sampling and classical variables sampling have advantages and disadvantages, and the auditor must use his or her knowledge about the population being tested to select the technique that is most appropriate. The advantages and disadvantages of each method are discussed later in the chapter.

Step 5: Determine the Sample Size   Considerable judgment is required in determining the sample size. The following five factors must be considered:

a. The variation within the population.
b. The acceptable risk of incorrect acceptance.
c. The tolerable misstatement.
d. The expected misstatement.
e. The population size.

a. ***Consider the variation within the population.*** In most accounting populations, the amounts of the individual items vary significantly. For example, a population may contain a small number of large dollar amounts and a large number of small dollar amounts. A measure of this variability is called the *standard deviation*. The auditor can estimate population variation by taking a pilot sample or using the results of prior years' tests. As the population variation increases, the sample size must also be increased. One way of reducing the effect of variability is to stratify the population into groups that are more homogeneous. Each group into which the population is divided is called a *stratum*. Separate samples are taken from each stratum, and the results are combined to form an overall conclusion about the population. Population variation does not affect the sample size when monetary-unit sampling is used because the sample selection method considers it indirectly. However, when classical variables sampling is used, the population variation does affect sample size because the sampling unit is normally a balance such as a customer's account receivable or a transaction such as a sales invoice, and there will be variability among such sampling units. Population variation should also be considered when the auditor uses a nonstatistical sampling approach.

b. ***Determine the acceptable risk of incorrect acceptance.*** The risk of incorrect acceptance is the risk that the sample supports the conclusion that the recorded account balance is not materially misstated when in fact it is (a Type II error). This risk is the same as the risk of assessing control risk too low, as discussed in Chapter 8, except that it relates to a decision about an account balance instead of a control procedure. This risk relates to the effectiveness of the audit. In determining an acceptable risk of incorrect acceptance, the auditor should consider the components of the audit risk model: the acceptable level of audit risk and the assessed levels of inherent and control risk. For practical purposes, the acceptable risk of incorrect acceptance is the same as detection risk (*DR*) after considering the assessed level of detection risk based on other substantive tests such as analytical procedures. If the auditor incorrectly accepts an account balance as being fairly presented when it is materially misstated, he or she will allow the issuance of financial statements that are not fairly presented. The users of those financial statements may then sue the auditor for damages that result from relying on those financial statements.

There is an *inverse* relationship between the risk of incorrect acceptance and sample size: the lower the acceptable risk for incorrect acceptance, the larger the sample size must be.

c. ***Determine the tolerable misstatement.*** The tolerable misstatement is the amount of the preliminary judgment about materiality that is allocated to an account. It represents the maximum amount by which the account can be misstated with the auditor still accepting the account as being fairly presented. Chapter 3 showed how the preliminary judgment about materiality can be allocated to an account. Tolerable misstatement is also *inversely* related to sample size: the lower the amount of tolerable misstatement, the larger the sample size must be.

d. ***Determine the expected misstatement.*** The expected misstatement is the amount of misstatement that the auditor believes exists in the population. The auditor can develop this expectation based on the assessment of inherent risk, prior years' results, a pilot sample, the results of related substantive tests, or the results of tests of controls. As the expected misstatement approaches the tolerable misstatement, the auditor needs more precise information from the sample. Therefore, there is a *direct* relationship to sample size: the larger the expected misstatement, the larger the sample size must be.

e. ***Consider the effect of population size.*** Population size has a *direct* effect on sample size. Other factors being constant, larger populations will require larger sample sizes.

Table 9–2 summarizes the effect of the five factors on sample size.

TABLE 9–2	The Effect of Sample Selection Factors on Sample Size		
		Examples	
Factor	*Relationship to Sample Size*	*Change in Factor*	*Effect on Sample*
Population variability	With monetary-unit sampling, the population variability, or standard deviation, has no effect on the sample size. With nonstatistical sampling and classical variables sampling, variability affects the sample size, but its effects can be controlled through stratification of the population.		
Acceptable risk of incorrect acceptance	Inverse	Lower	Increase
		Higher	Decrease
Tolerable misstatement	Inverse	Lower	Increase
		Higher	Decrease
Expected misstatement	Direct	Lower	Decrease
		Higher	Increase
Population size	Direct	Lower	Decrease
		Higher	Increase

Performance

After planning the sampling application, the auditor performs each of the following steps.

Step 6: Determine the Method of Selecting the Sample Items
In selecting the sample items, the auditor attempts to draw the sample in such a way that it represents the population. Random-sample selection was discussed in Chapter 8 and is used for classical variables sampling. Probability-proportional-to-size sample selection can be used with monetary-unit sampling and is discussed later in this chapter. Random and judgmental selection techniques can be used with nonstatistical sampling.

Step 7: Perform the Audit Procedures
After the sample items have been selected, the auditor conducts the planned audit procedures. In some instances, the auditor may not be able to conduct the planned procedures on a sampling unit. This may occur, for example, because a supporting document is missing. Unless other evidence is available, such items should be considered in error. The auditor must also be careful to conduct the audit procedures so as to avoid nonsampling errors. After all audit procedures have been completed, the auditor evaluates the sample results.

Evaluation

The evaluation phase of the sampling application includes the following steps.

Step 8: Calculate the Sample Results
After completing the audit procedures, the auditor should project the misstatements detected in the sample to the population. The projected misstatement represents the mean misstatement for the sample. To determine the misstatement limits, the auditor calculates an allowance for sampling risk (precision) and adds it to the projected misstatement. The approach to calculating the sample results and evaluating the results differs according to the sampling method used. Each approach is discussed later in this chapter.

Step 9: Perform Error Analysis
The auditor should evaluate the qualitative aspects of the misstatements identified. This involves two considerations. First, the nature of the misstatements and their causes should be considered. For example, the auditor should determine if the misstatements are unintentional errors or fraud. The auditor should also attempt to determine whether the misstatements resulted from causes such as misunderstanding of instructions or carelessness. Understanding the nature and causes of misstatements helps the auditor better assess detection risk. Second, the auditor should consider how these misstatements may impact the other phases of the audit. For example, the nature of the misstatements may provide additional evidence that certain controls are not operating as effectively as previously assessed. This may require the auditor to reassess control risk and expand substantive tests for the audit objectives that are affected by the control that is not operating effectively.

TABLE 9–3	The Auditor's Risks When Evaluating a Financial Statement Account Based on Sample Evidence

| | True State of Financial Statement Account | |
Auditor's Decision Based on Sample Evidence	*Not Materially Misstated*	*Materially Misstated*
Supports the fairness of the account balance	Correct decision	Risk of incorrect acceptance
Does not support the fairness of the account balance	Risk of incorrect rejection	Correct decision

Step 10: Draw Final Conclusions   In drawing a conclusion about a statistical sampling application for substantive testing, tolerable misstatement is compared to the total projected misstatement plus an allowance for sampling risk. If the total projected misstatement plus an allowance for sampling risk is less than the tolerable misstatement, the auditor can generally conclude that the account is not materially misstated for the tested assertion. If the total projected misstatement plus an allowance for sampling risk exceeds the tolerable misstatement, the auditor must conclude that the account is materially misstated. If the account is materially misstated, the auditor can increase the sample, perform other substantive procedures, or adjust the account balance.

Table 9–3 shows the auditor's risks when evaluating an account balance based on sample evidence. If the evidence supports the fairness of the account balance based on the sample evidence and the account is not materially misstated, the auditor has made a correct decision. If the evidence does *not* support the fairness of the account based on the sample evidence and the account is materially misstated, a correct decision has also been made. The other two combinations result in decision errors by the auditor. If the evidence supports the account as fairly stated when it contains a material misstatement, the auditor will have incorrectly accepted the account (Type II error). This can lead to lawsuits against the auditor for issuing a report on misleading financial statements. If the evidence does not support the fairness of the account when it is not materially misstated (Type I error), the auditor will have incorrectly rejected the account. This can lead to overauditing and an inefficient audit.

Monetary-Unit Sampling

[LO 2]   Monetary-unit sampling uses attribute-sampling theory to express a conclusion in dollar amounts rather than as a rate of occurrence. Because monetary-unit sampling has a number of advantages over classical variables sampling, auditors have found important applications for this sampling technique. Some of these applications include auditing accounts receivable, loans receivable, investment securities, and inventory. Monetary-unit sampling is designed primarily to test for *overstatement* errors. However, it can accommodate understatement errors if special considerations are made during the evaluation of the sample results. Monetary-unit sampling is most appropriate for low-error-rate populations because it provides as effective a test as classical variables sampling does but has a more efficient sample size. Following are some advantages and disadvantages of monetary-unit sampling.

Advantages

- When the auditor expects no misstatements, monetary-unit sampling usually results in a smaller sample size than classical variables sampling.
- The calculation of the sample size and the evaluation of the sample results are *not* based on the variation (that is, the standard deviation) between items in the population. The standard deviation is required to compute the sample size for a classical variables sampling application because it relies on the central limit theorem.
- When applied using a probability-proportional-to-size sample selection procedure as outlined in this text, monetary-unit sampling automatically results in a stratified sample because sampled items are selected in proportion to their dollar amounts. Thus, larger dollar items have a higher probability of being selected. With classical variables sampling, the population must be stratified in order to get an efficient sample size.

Disadvantages

- The selection of a zero or negative balances generally requires special design consideration. For example, if examining zero balances (for example, searching for unrecorded liabilities in accounts payable) is important, the auditor must test those items separately because such items will not be selected using a probability-proportional-to-size selection method. Alternatively, if an account such as accounts receivable contains credit balances, the auditor should segregate those items and test them separately.
- The general approach to monetary-unit sampling assumes that the audited amount of the sample item is not in error by more than 100 percent. If the auditor detects items that are in error by more than 100 percent, special adjustments will be necessary when calculating sample results. For example, suppose an accounts receivable account contains a book value of $1,500. If the auditor determines that the correct value for the account should be a credit balance of $3,000, the account will be in error by 300 percent. Such an item would require special consideration when the auditor projects the amount of misstatement.
- When more than one or two misstatements are detected using a monetary-unit sampling approach, the sample results calculations as shown in the textbook may overstate the allowance for sampling risk. This occurs because the methods used to determine the amount of misstatement are very conservative. Thus, an auditor is more likely to reject an acceptable recorded book value and overaudit.[1]

---

[1]There are alternative methods that overcome this disadvantage. However, these methods are more complex. See D. A. Leslie, A. D. Teitlebaum, and R. J. Anderson, *Dollar Unit Sampling: A Practical Guide for Auditors* (Toronto: Copp, Clark and Pitman, 1979), and W. L. Felix, Jr., R. A. Grimlund, F. J. Koster, and R. S. Roussey, "Arthur Andersen's New Monetary-Unit Sampling Approach," *Auditing: A Journal of Practice & Theory* (Fall 1990), pp. 1–16, for a discussion of alternative approaches.

Applying Monetary-Unit Sampling

In Chapter 8 and earlier in this chapter, general considerations as to the use of sampling for substantive tests were discussed along with the steps in a sampling application. In this section, the discussion focuses on those steps that require additional explanation in applying monetary-unit sampling.

Defining the Sampling Unit (Step 3)

With monetary-unit sampling, an individual dollar represents the sampling unit. However, the auditor tests not the individual dollar but rather the account or transaction that contains the selected dollar. The account or transaction that contains the selected dollar is called the *logical unit.*

Determining the Sample Size (Step 5)

A monetary-unit sample size can be determined by using the attribute sample size tables shown in Chapter 8. The auditor first determines the risk for incorrect acceptance and then converts the tolerable misstatement and the expected misstatement to percentages of the book value. For example, suppose the auditor has established a tolerable misstatement of $125,000 and an expected misstatement of $25,000 for an accounts receivable account with a book value of $2,500,000. The tolerable misstatement would be 5 percent ($125,000 ÷ $2,500,000), and the expected misstatement would be 1 percent ($25,000 ÷ $2,500,000). If the risk of incorrect acceptance for this application is 5 percent, the auditor would use Table 8–8 in Chapter 8. In this example, the sample size is 93.

Instead of the attribute-sampling tables, the following formula can be used. However, this formula is not as exact as using the tables.

$$n = \frac{BV}{\left[TM - (EM \times EF)\right] / RF}$$

where

n = Sample size
BV = Book value
TM = Tolerable misstatement
EM = Expected misstatement
EF = Expansion factor
RF = Reliability factor

Using the previous example, the sample size would be 88 using the following formula:

$$n = \frac{\$2,500,000}{\left[\$125,000 - (\$25,000 \times 1.6)\right] / 3.0} = 88$$

The reliability factor of 3.0, which relates to a risk of incorrect acceptance of 5 percent, is taken from Table 9–4. The expansion factor for 5 percent is 1.6, which is taken from Table 9–5. The expansion factor adjusts the expected misstatement for the risk of incorrect acceptance.

| TABLE 9–4 | Reliability Factors for Overstatement and Understatement Errors | | | |

Number of Over- or Understatement Errors	5% Risk of Incorrect Acceptance		10% Risk of Incorrect Acceptance	
	Reliability Factor	Incremental Change*	Reliability Factor	Incremental Change
0	3.00	0.00	2.31	0.00
1	4.75	1.75	3.89	1.58
2	6.30	1.55	5.33	1.44
3	7.76	1.46	6.69	1.36
4	9.16	1.40	8.00	1.31
5	10.52	1.36	9.28	1.28
6	11.85	1.35	10.54	1.26

*The incremental change is calculated by subtracting the reliability factor for the current number of errors from the reliability factor for the previous number of errors. For example, for a 5% risk of incorrect acceptance, the incremental change from 0 errors to 1 error is 1.75 (4.75 – 3.00).

| TABLE 9–5 | Expansion Factors for Expected Errors |

Risk of Incorrect Acceptance	Expansion Factor
1%	1.9
5%	1.6
10%	1.5

Selecting the Sample (Step 6)

The auditor can select a sample for monetary-unit sampling by using a computer program and applying a systematic selection approach. This selection method is referred to as *probability proportional to size*. Probability-proportional-to-size sample selection gives each individual dollar in the population an equal chance of being selected and divides the population into equal groups of dollars. Each group of dollars represents a *sampling interval*. The sampling interval is determined by dividing the book value of the population by the sample size. Figure 9–1 provides an example of how probability-proportional-to-size selection is applied.

In the prior example, the client's accounts receivable had a book value of $2,500,000 and the auditor determined a sample size of 93. To select a probability-proportional-to-size sample, the auditor arranges the client's accounts receivable records (or computer file) in some order. In Figure 9–1, the customer records are arranged in alphabetical order. The auditor selects a random number between 1 and the sampling interval ($2,500,000 ÷ 93 = $26,882), such as 4,000, as a random start, and the customer account that contains the 4,000th dollar is selected for testing. In this case, Admington

FIGURE 9–1

An Example of Probability-Proportional-to-Size Sample Selection

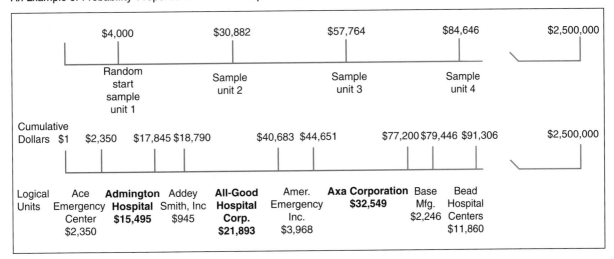

Hospital, with a balance of $15,495, is selected for testing. The auditor then begins to add, either manually or with the aid of a computer program, through the population and selects each logical unit that contains the *n*th dollar. Following this process, the second customer account selected would be All-Good Hospital Corp., which contains the 30,882nd dollar (4,000 + 26,882) and has a balance of $21,893. The third account would be Axa Corporation, which contains the 57,764th dollar (30,882 + 26,882), and so on until the entire population has been subjected to sampling. The advantage of using this approach to selecting the sample is that while each dollar in the population has an equal chance of being selected, logical units containing more dollars have a higher chance of being selected. From an audit perspective, this means that larger accounts are more likely to be examined. Note that all logical units with a book value larger than the sampling interval (such as Axa Corporation) are certain to be selected under this selection method. When the logical unit exceeds the sampling interval, the logical unit may be selected more than once. If this happens, the logical unit is included only once when the sample results are evaluated. Thus, the number of logical units examined may be less than the computed sample size.

Calculating Sample Results (Step 8)   The misstatements detected in the sample must be projected to the population. As mentioned earlier, a monetary-unit sampling application is designed primarily to test for overstatement errors. The projection of the overstatement errors to the population is referred to as the *projected misstatement;* it is equivalent to the sample mean. The auditor calculates an allowance for sampling risk and adds it to the projected misstatement. The total of the projected misstatement and the allowance for sampling risk is referred to as the *upper limit on misstatement* (ULM). If understatement errors are detected, a *net* upper limit on misstatement is calculated by adjusting the ULM for the understatements detected.

The remaining discussion focuses first on samples in which no misstatements are detected and then on samples that contain misstatements.

No Misstatements Detected.   If no misstatements are found in the sample, the projection would be 0 dollars plus an allowance for sampling risk. This amount of misstatement is referred to as the *basic precision* and would be less than or equal to the tolerable misstatement used to design the sample. Basic precision represents the minimum allowance for sampling risk, given no errors. For example, if the auditor finds no errors in auditing the client's accounts receivable, he or she would calculate the upper limit on misstatement by multiplying the reliability factor for the risk of incorrect acceptance by the sampling interval. In the previous example, the sample size was 93 and the sampling interval was $26,882. From Table 9–4, the reliability factor for a 5 percent risk of incorrect acceptance is 3.0. The ULM (and basic precision) is thus $80,646 (3.0 × $26,882).

Misstatements Detected.   If errors are found in the sample, the auditor needs to calculate a projected misstatement and an allowance for sampling risk. Because the selected dollar represents a group of dollars, the percentage of misstatement in the logical unit represents the percentage of misstatement in the sampling interval. Three types of situations can occur with detected errors.

1. ***The logical unit is equal to or greater than the sampling interval.*** In this situation, the projected misstatement is equal to the actual misstatement detected in the logical unit. For example, the Axa Corporation account in Figure 9–1 contained a balance of $32,549, which is larger than the sampling interval of $26,882. Suppose that the auditor detects a $2,500 misstatement. The projected misstatement would be $2,500, and no sampling risk is added because the entire sampling interval was audited.

2. ***The book value of the logical unit is less than the sampling interval, and it is 100 percent misstated.*** Because the logical unit represents the group of dollars in the sampling interval, the sampling interval is assumed to be 100 percent in error. For example, suppose the Bead Hospital Centers account in Figure 9–1 was audited and it had an audited value of 0. In this example, the projected error for this logical unit is $26,882, which is determined by multiplying the percentage misstated (100%) by the sampling interval ($26,882). An allowance for sampling risk would be added to this amount (see the example in the next section).

3. ***The logical unit's book value is less than the sampling interval, and it is misstated by less than 100 percent.*** This is probably the most common situation. The percentage of misstatement in the logical unit is referred to as the *tainting factor*. The tainting factor is calculated using the following formula:

$$\text{Tainting factor} = \frac{\text{Book value} - \text{Audit value}}{\text{Book value}}$$

Suppose that the auditor determined that the All-Good Hospital Corp. account was overstated by $3,284. Thus, the tainting factor for the account would be 15% [(21,893 – 18,609) / 21,893]. The projected misstatement for this logical unit would be $4,032 (15% × $26,882). An allowance for sampling risk would again be added to this amount (see the example in the next section).

An Extended Example

[LO 3]

An extended example is used to demonstrate the final evaluation of a monetary-unit sampling application. The following information relates to the audit of a client's accounts receivable balance:

Example Information

- Book value = $2,500,000
- Tolerable misstatement = $125,000
- Sample size = 93
- Risk of incorrect acceptance = 5%
- Expected amount of misstatement = $25,000
- Sampling interval = $26,882

The calculations of sample size and sampling interval were shown previously. Assume further that, based on the audit work conducted on internal control, the auditor anticipated finding only overstatement errors.

Three separate cases are presented. Cases 1 and 2 contain only overstatement errors. Case 3 considers the detection of both overstatement and understatement errors.

Case 1 Assume that the auditor has completed auditing the 93 sample items selected from the client's accounts receivable account and detected the following overstatement errors:

Overstatement Errors

Error Number	Book Value	Audit Value	Tainting Factor
1-All-Good Hospital	$21,893	$18,609	.15
2-Axa Corp.	32,549	30,049	Not applicable; book value is greater than sampling interval.
3-Learn Heart Centers	15,000	8,250	.45

To calculate the ULM, the auditor ranks the detected errors based on the size of the tainting factor from the largest tainting factor to the smallest. Making the calculation in this manner results in multiplying the largest tainting factor by the largest incremental change in the reliability factor. This approach leads to a ULM that is very conservative; there is a higher risk that an acceptable account balance will be rejected by the auditor (see footnote 1). Calculation of the ULM for the three overstatement errors is as follows:

ULM for Overstatement Errors

Tainting Factor	Sampling Interval	Projected Misstatement	Incremental Change	Projected Misstatement Plus Allowance for Sampling Risk
.45	$26,882	$12,097	1.75 (4.75 – 3.0)	$ 21,170
.15	26,882	4,032	1.55 (6.3 – 4.75)	6,250
Total—errors 1 and 3				$ 27,420
Actual misstatement for error 2				2,500
Basic precision (3.0 × $26,882)				80,646
ULM				$110,566

The ULM in this case is $110,566 and is calculated as follows. First, the projected misstatement for errors 1 and 3 is calculated by multiplying the sampling interval by the tainting factor. This calculation is based on the assumption that the dollar selected for testing represents the sampling interval. In turn, it is assumed that the extent of misstatement in the logical unit that contains the sampled dollar represents the amount of misstatement in the sampling interval. An allowance for sampling risk is added to the projected misstatement by multiplying the projected misstatement by the incremental change in the reliability factor for the risk of incorrect acceptance used to design the sampling application. The incremental change is taken from Table 9–4. Thus, for error 3, the projected misstatement is $12,097, and the allowance for sampling risk is $9,073 (21,171 – 12,097). The allowance for sampling risk for error 1 is $2,218 (6,250 – 4,032). Second, because the book value of error 2 ($32,549) is larger than the sampling interval ($26,882), the amount of misstatement does not require projection or the consideration of sampling risk. The amount of misstatement included in the ULM for error 2 is the known misstatement of $2,500 ($32,549 – $30,049). Last, the basic precision of $80,646 is added to the amounts, resulting in the ULM of $110,566.

For this example, the final decision on whether the accounts receivable balance is materially misstated is made by comparing the tolerable misstatement to the ULM. If the ULM is less than the tolerable misstatement, the evidence supports the conclusion that the account balance is not materially misstated. In this case the ULM of $110,566 is less than the tolerable misstatement of $125,000. Thus, at a 5 percent risk of incorrect acceptance, the ULM in the population does not exceed the tolerable misstatement.

The reader should be aware that alternative methods of calculating the upper limit on misstatement are available and used by public accounting firms.[2] Exhibit 9–1 shows the evaluation of the sample results using

---

[2]See Felix et al., "Arthur Andersen's New Monetary Unit Sampling Approach," for an example of how Arthur Andersen calculates the ULM.

EXHIBIT 9–1

Sample Results Using PricewaterhouseCoopers's LLP Statistical Software

SAMPLING PROPORTIONATE-TO-SIZE—SAMPLE EVALUATION

Allowable Risk of Incorrect Acceptance (1, 5, 10, 20, 30, 40, or 50%)   5%
Maximum Tolerable Error Amount   125000
Sampling Interval   26882

Stratum	Population Recorded Amount	Sample Recorded Amount	Sample Size	Number of Errors Found
Upper	32549	32549	1	1
Lower	2467451	1098330	92	2
Total	2500000	1130879	93	3

Upper Stratum

Error No.	Audited Amount	Recorded Amount	Error %
1	30049.00	32548.00	7.68
Total	30049.00	32548.00	

Lower Stratum

Error No.	Audited Amount	Recorded Amount	Error %
2	18609.00	21893.00	15.00
3	8250.00	15000.00	45.00
Total	26859.00	36893.00	60.00

	Total Error in Sample	Projected Error	Upper Error Limit
Upper Stratum	2500	2500	2500
Lower Stratum	10034	16129	92,559
Total	12533	18622	95,059
Maximum Tolerable Error Amount			125000

At a Risk of Incorrect Acceptance of 5%, the total Upper Error Limit in the population does not exceed the Maximum Tolerable Error Amount.

Source: PricewaterhouseCoopers LLP. Used by permission.

PricewaterhouseCoopers's statistical software. The ULM is calculated to be $95,059. This calculation of the ULM uses a methodology that corrects for the overstatement of sampling risk.

Case 2   Case 1 is extended by assuming the same information, except that the audited value of error 3 is 0 instead of $8,250. The tainting factor for this error is now 100 percent, and the calculation of the ULM is as follows:

ULM for Overstatement Errors

Tainting Factor	Sampling Interval	Projected Misstatement	Incremental Change	Projected Misstatement Plus Allowance for Sampling Risk
1.00	$26,882	$26,882	1.75 (4.75 − 3.0)	$ 47,044
.15	26,882	4,032	1.55 (6.3 − 4.75)	6,250
Total—errors 1 and 3				$ 53,294
Actual misstatement for error 2				2,500
Basic precision (3.0 × $26,882)				80,646
ULM				$136,440

In this case the projected misstatement ($26,882) plus an allowance for sampling risk ($20,162) for error 3 is $47,044, and the ULM is $136,440. Using the prior decision rule, the ULM is compared to the tolerable misstatement. Because the ULM of $136,440 exceeds the tolerable misstatement of $125,000, the auditor has evidence that the accounts receivable account is materially misstated. The auditor now has three options. First, the sample size can be increased. However, this approach is possible in theory but not practical in many audit settings. Second, other substantive tests can be performed. This approach might be followed if the auditor's qualitative analysis of the detected errors indicates that there is a systematic problem with the population. For example, the auditor might determine that the three errors occurred in the pricing of one product line sold by the client. In this instance, he or she might design a substantive test that examines the pricing of all sales in that product line. Finally, the auditor can request that the client adjust the accounts receivable balance. In our example, the minimum adjustment would be $11,440 ($136,440 − $125,000). If the client adjusts the account by $11,440, the ULM will be equal to or less than the tolerable misstatement at a 5 percent risk of incorrect acceptance.

Case 3   The final case considers the possibility that the auditor has detected understatement errors. The methodology used earlier for determining the sample size is based on the auditor's assumption, at the time of planning the sampling application, that all errors in the population are overstatements. When understatement errors are detected, the auditor can calculate a *net* upper limit on misstatement.[3] This approach is followed when the auditor believes that the overall misstatement in the population is in the direction of overstatement. The understatements identified are used to adjust the ULM. To demonstrate this approach, assume that the auditor detected the three overstatement errors shown for case 1, where the ULM was $110,566. Now assume that the following understatement errors were also detected:

Understatement Errors

Error Number	Book Value	Audit Value	Tainting Factor
4	$ 2,000	$ 2,200	.10
5	10,000	10,300	.03

The adjustment for understatement errors is calculated separately from the ULM. The projected misstatement is calculated for each misstatement and netted against the ULM for the overstatements. The adjustment in our example is $3,494, which is determined as follows:

Adjustment for Understatement Errors

Tainting Factor	Sampling Interval	Projected Misstatement
.10	$26,882	$2,688
.03	26,882	806
Adjustment to ULM		$3,494

In this example, the net ULM is $107,072 ($110,566 − $3,494). Using the previous decision rule, the auditor would conclude that the account was not materially misstated because the net ULM of $107,072 is less than the tolerable misstatement of $125,000. When the ULM is adjusted for understatement errors as described here, the risk of incorrect acceptance for the test is no longer 5 percent. However, as mentioned previously, this calculation of the ULM is conservative, and statistical sampling software used by public accounting firms calculates the ULM while holding the risk for incorrect acceptance at 5 percent.

---

[3]This approach to handling understatements is taken from Leslie et al., *Dollar Unit Sampling.* Alternative approaches are also used in practice. For example, if the direction of the errors in the population is unknown, a two-sided confidence interval can be constructed by separating the understatements and calculating a lower limit on misstatements. See A. D. Bailey, Jr., *Statistical Auditing: Review, Concepts, and Problems* (New York: Harcourt Brace Jovanovich, 1981), for a discussion of this approach.

Nonstatistical Sampling for Tests of Account Balances[4]

[LO 4]   When conducting a nonstatistical sampling application for testing an account balance, the auditor considers each of the steps shown in Table 9–1. The sampling unit for nonstatistical sampling is normally a customer account, an individual transaction, or a line item on a transaction. When a nonstatistical sampling application is used, the following items need further explanation:

- Identifying individually significant items.
- Determining the sample size.
- Calculating the sample results.

Identifying Individually Significant Items

In many nonstatistical sampling applications, the auditor determines which items should be tested individually and which items should be subjected to sampling. The items that will be tested individually are items that may contain potential misstatements that individually exceed the tolerable misstatement. These items are tested 100 percent because the auditor is not willing to accept any sampling risk. For example, an auditor may be examining a client's accounts receivable balance in which 20 customer accounts make up 60 percent of the account balance. The auditor may decide to examine the 20 large accounts and sample from the remaining customer accounts. In this case, the remaining 40 percent of the accounts receivable account is subjected to audit sampling.

Determining the Sample Size

When determining the sample size, the auditor should consider the variation in the population, the risk of incorrect acceptance, the tolerable and expected misstatements, and the population size. While an auditor may determine a nonstatistical sample size by using professional judgment, the following formula, based on the AICPA Audit Practice Release *Audit Sampling*, can be used:[5]

$$\text{Sample size} = \left(\frac{\text{Population book value}}{\text{Tolerable misstatement}} \right) \text{Assurance factor}$$

where "Population book value" excludes the amount of items to be individually audited and "Tolerable misstatement" represents the amount of materiality allocated to the account being audited. The assurance factor is determined by assessing inherent and control risk and the risk that other relevant substantive auditing procedures will fail to detect material misstatements. Table 9–6 contains the assurance factors for various combinations of these two assessments.

---

[4]The approach presented here for nonstatistical sampling is based on the American Institute of Certified Public Accountants, *Audit Sampling* (Audit Practice Release) (New York: AICPA, 1999).

[5]This formula is based on the statistical theory underlying monetary-unit sampling.

TABLE 9–6	Assurance Factors for Nonstatistical Sampling

Combined Assessment of Inherent and Control Risk	Risk That Other Substantive Procedures Will Fail to Detect Material Misstatements			
	Maximum	*Slightly below Maximum*	*Moderate*	*Low*
Maximum	3.0	2.7	2.3	2.0
Slightly below maximum	2.7	2.4	2.1	1.6
Moderate	2.3	2.1	1.6	1.2
Low	2.0	1.9	1.2	1.0

Risk that other substantive procedures will fail to detect a material misstatement:
Maximum: No other substantive procedures are performed to test the same assertion(s).
Slightly below maximum: Other substantive procedures that are performed to test the assertion(s) are expected to be slightly effective in detecting material misstatements in those assertion(s).
Moderate: Other substantive procedures that are performed to test the assertion(s) are expected to be moderately effective in detecting material misstatements in those assertion(s).
Low: Other substantive procedures that are performed to test the assertion(s) are expected to be highly effective in detecting material misstatements in those assertion(s).

Calculating the Sample Results

Auditing standards require that the auditor project the amount of misstatement found in the sample to the population. *Audit Sampling* describes two acceptable methods of projecting the amount of misstatement found in a nonstatistical sample.

One method of projecting the amount of misstatement is to divide the amount of misstatement by the fraction of the dollars of the population included in the sample. For example, if the auditor finds misstatements in a sample totaling $1,500 and the sample items constitute 10 percent of the population, the projected misstatement will be $15,000 ($1,500 ÷ 10%).

The second method projects the average misstatement between the audited and recorded amounts of each item in the sample to all items in the population. For example, if the misstatements in a sample of 100 items total $300 and the population contains 10,000 items, the projected misstatement will be $30,000. This amount is determined by calculating the average misstatement in the sample of $3 ($300 ÷ 100 items) and multiplying it by the number of items in the population ($3 × 10,000 items).

These two methods of projecting misstatements give identical results if the sample includes the same proportion of items in the population as the proportion of the population's recorded amount included in the sample. If the proportions are different, the auditor chooses between the two methods on the basis of his or her understanding of the magnitude and distribution of misstatements in the population. If the auditor expects the amount of misstatement to relate closely to the size of the item, the first method should be used. If the auditor expects the misstatements to be relatively constant for all items in the population, the second method should be used.

In evaluating the results of a nonstatistical sample, the auditor uses professional judgment and experience to draw a conclusion. Because a nonstatistical sampling approach is used, the allowance for sampling risk cannot be quantified. The Audit Practice Release provides the following guidance. If the projected misstatement is close to or exceeds the tolerable misstatement, the auditor should conclude that there is an unacceptably high risk that the account is misstated. If the projected misstatement is considerably less than the tolerable misstatement, the auditor should compare the projected misstatement to the expected misstatement. If the projected misstatement is less than the expected misstatement, the auditor can conclude that there is an acceptably low sampling risk that the projected misstatement exceeds the tolerable misstatement. Conversely, if the projected misstatement significantly exceeds the expected misstatement, the auditor would generally conclude that there is an unacceptably high risk that the true misstatement exceeds the tolerable misstatement.

An Example

This example extends the example shown in Chapter 8 for the tests of controls of the revenue cycle for Calabro Paging Services. The senior-in-charge of the audit, Don Jones, has decided to design a *nonstatistical* sampling application to examine the accounts receivable balance of Calabro Paging Services at December 31, 2000. As of December 31, there were 11,800 accounts receivable accounts with a balance of $3,717,900 ($3,582,600 + $135,300 for the allowance for doubtful accounts), and the population is composed of the following strata:

Number and Size of Acounts	Book Value of Stratum
15 accounts > $25,000	$ 550,000
250 accounts > $3,000	850,500
11,535 accounts < $3,000	2,317,400

Jones has made the following decisions:

- Based on the results of the tests of controls, a low assessment is made for inherent and control risk.
- The tolerable misstatement allocated to accounts receivable is $40,000, and the expected misstatement is $15,000.
- There is a moderate risk that other auditing procedures will fail to detect material misstatements.
- All customer account balances greater than $25,000 are to be audited.

Based on these decisions, the sample size is determined as follows: First, individually significant items are deducted from the account balance, leaving a balance of $3,167,900 ($3,717,900 − $550,000) to be sampled. Second, the sample size for the remaining balance is determined using the AICPA's sample size formula:

$$\text{Sample size} = \left(\frac{\$3,167,900}{\$40,000} \right) 1.2 = 95$$

The assurance factor of 1.2 is determined by using Table 9–6 and a low assessment for inherent and control risk and a moderate risk that other auditing procedures will fail to detect material misstatements. The 95 sample items are divided between the two strata based on the recorded amount for each stratum. Accordingly, 26 of the 95 [($850,500 ÷ $3,167,900)95] are allocated to the stratum of accounts greater than $3,000 and 69 to the stratum of accounts less than $3,000. The total sample size for this test is 110, composed of 15 individually significant accounts and a sample of 95 items.

Jones mailed positive confirmations to each of the 110 accounts selected for testing. Either the confirmations were returned to Jones, or he was able to use alternative procedures to determine that the receivables were valid. Four customers indicated that their accounts were overstated, and Jones determined that the misstatements had resulted from unintentional errors by client personnel. The results of the sample are summarized as follows.

Stratum	Book Value of Stratum	Book Value of Sample	Audit Value of Sample	Amount of Overstatement
>$25,000	$ 550,000	$550,000	$549,500	$ 500
>$3,000	850,500	425,000	423,000	2,000
<$3,000	2,317,400	92,000	91,750	250

Based on analysis of the misstatements found, Jones concluded that the amount of misstatement in the population was likely to correlate to the total dollar amount of the items in the population and not to the number of items in the population. Thus, he decided to use the first method (misstatements divided by the fraction of dollars sampled) for projecting the results. His projection of the misstatements follows:

Stratum	Amount of Misstatement	Percentage of Stratum Sampled	Projected Misstatement
>$25,000	$ 500	100%	$ 500
>$3,000	2,000	$425,000 ÷ $850,500 = .50	4,000
<$3,000	250	$92,000 ÷ $2,317,400 = .04	6,250
Total projected misstatement			$10,750

The total projected misstatement is $10,750. Jones should conclude that there is an acceptably low risk that the true misstatement exceeds the tolerable misstatement because the projected misstatement of $10,750 is less than the expected misstatement of $15,000.

Before reaching a final conclusion on the fair presentation of Calabro's accounts receivable balance, Jones would consider the qualitative characteristics of the misstatements detected and the results of other auditing procedures. If these steps are successfully completed, Jones can conclude that the accounts receivable balance is fairly presented in conformity with GAAP.

APPENDIX: **[LO 5]**

Classical Variables Sampling

Classical variables sampling uses normal distribution theory to evaluate the characteristics of a population based on sample data. The mathematical computations used for classical variables sampling are more complex than the monetary-unit sampling approach discussed previously, and auditors typically use computer software to perform the computations. A number of classical variables sampling estimators are available to the auditor for projecting the sample results. These include mean-per-unit, difference, ratio, and regression estimators. These estimators differ basically on the assumed relationship between the book value and the audit value. Only the difference estimator is presented in this text.[6]

Classical variables sampling can easily handle both overstatement and understatement errors. It is most appropriate for populations that contain a moderate to high rate of misstatement. Some applications of this sampling approach include auditing accounts receivable in which unapplied credits exist or a large amount of misstatement is expected, and inventory in which significant audit differences are expected between test counts and pricing tests. Following are some of the advantages and disadvantages of classical variables sampling.

Advantages

- When the auditor expects a large number of differences between book and audited values, classical variables sampling will normally result in a smaller sample size than monetary-unit sampling.
- Classical variables sampling techniques are effective for both overstatements and understatements. No special evaluation considerations are necessary if the sample data include both types of misstatements.
- The selection of zero balances generally does not require special sample design considerations because the sampling unit will be not an individual dollar but rather an account, a transaction, or a line item.

Disadvantages

- In order to determine the sample size, the auditor must estimate the standard deviation of the audited value or differences. However, the auditor may be able to develop a reasonably good estimate of the standard deviation by measuring the standard deviation of the book values, calculating the standard deviation from a pilot sample, or basing the estimate on prior years' audit results.
- If few misstatements are detected in the sample data, the true variance tends to be underestimated, and the resulting projection of the misstatements to the population is likely not to be reliable.

Applying Classical Variables Sampling

The discussion in this section focuses on the special features that apply to classical variables sampling. A detailed example is included to demonstrate the application of classical variables sampling.

[LO 6]

Defining the Sampling Unit (Step 3)
When an auditor uses classical variables sampling techniques, the sampling unit can be a customer account, an individual transaction, or a line item. For example, in auditing accounts receivable, the auditor can define the sampling unit to be a customer's account balance or an individual sales invoice included in the account balance.

---

[6]See D. M. Roberts, *Statistical Auditing* (New York: AICPA, 1978), or Bailey, *Statistical Auditing,* for a discussion of the other classical variables sampling estimators.

TABLE 9–7	Z Values for Levels of Risk of Incorrect Acceptance and Risk of Incorrect Rejection	
Risk of Incorrect Acceptance	Risk of Incorrect Rejection	Z Value
2.5%	5%	1.96
5%	10%	1.64
10%	20%	1.28
15%	30%	1.04
20%	40%	.84

Determining the Sample Size (Step 5)   The following formula can be used to determine the sample size for a classical variables sample:

$$n = \left[\frac{N\left(Z_{IA} + Z_{IR}\right)SD}{TM - EM} \right]^2$$

where

N = Population size

Z_{IA} = One-tailed Z value for the specified level of the risk of incorrect acceptance

Z_{IR} = Two-tailed Z value for the specified level of risk of incorrect rejection

SD = Estimated standard deviation

TM = Tolerable misstatement

EM = Expected misstatement

The risk of incorrect acceptance is a one-tailed test because the account balance can be overstated or understated, but not both. The risk of incorrect rejection[7] is a two-tailed test because the auditor can draw a nonrepresentative sample from either side of the distribution. Table 9–7 shows the Z values for various levels of each risk.

The following example demonstrates how to determine sample size using this formula. Assume that the auditor has decided to apply classical variables sampling to a client's accounts receivable account. Based on the results of testing internal controls over the revenue cycle, the auditor expects to find a moderate level of misstatement in accounts receivable due mainly to improper pricing of products on sales invoices. The year-end balance for accounts receivable contains 4,500 customer accounts and has a book value of $5,500,000. The tolerable misstatement for accounts receivable has been established at $50,000, and the expected misstatement has been judged to be $20,000. The auditor sets the risk of incorrect acceptance

---

[7]Sample size can be determined without controlling for the risk of incorrect rejection (Z_{IR}). If this term is omitted from the formula, a smaller sample size will be selected.

at 5 percent and the risk of incorrect rejection at 20 percent. Based on the results of last year's audit work, the standard deviation is set at $25. Using these parameters, a sample size of 120 is calculated:

$$n = \left[\frac{4,500(1.64+1.28)\$25}{\$50,000-\$20,000}\right]^2 = 120$$

In calculating the sample size, the Z values for the risk of incorrect acceptance and the risk of incorrect rejection are taken from Table 9–7. The Z value for a 5 percent risk of incorrect acceptance is 1.64, and the Z value for a 20 percent risk of incorrect rejection is 1.28.

Selecting the Sample (Step 6)

Sample selection normally relies on random-selection techniques. If the sampling unit is defined to be a customer account, the accounts to be examined can be selected randomly from the aged trial balance of accounts receivable. In this example, a random sample of 120 customer accounts is selected.

Calculating the Sample Results (Step 8)

The difference estimator is used to develop the sample results. Continuing with the prior example, assume that the auditor has examined the 120 accounts receivable customer accounts and that 30 accounts contain misstatements. Table 9–8 presents the details of the 30 misstatements and the data necessary for calculating the sample results. The difference between the book value and the audited value is shown in the fifth column. The sixth column contains the square of each difference (d_i^2). The sum of the squared difference is needed to calculate the standard deviation.

The first calculation is that of the mean misstatement ($\bar{d}$) in an individual account, which is calculated as follows:

$$\bar{d} = \frac{\Sigma d_i}{n} = \frac{\$330.20}{\$120} = \$2.75$$

Thus, the average misstatement in a customer account based on the sample data is an overstatement of $2.75.

The mean misstatement must then be projected to the population. The projected mean misstatement for the population ($\overline{D}$) is an overstatement of $12,375, which is determined as follows:

$$\overline{D} = N\left(\frac{\Sigma d_i}{n}\right) = 4,500(\$2.75) = \$12,375$$

The mean misstatement for the population is the "best estimate" of the misstatement present in the account. This is usually referred to as the *point estimate*. Therefore, the point estimate ($\overline{X}$) for the accounts receivable account is determined by subtracting the projected population misstatement ($\overline{D}$) from the book value (BV) of the account:

$$\overline{X} = BV - \overline{D} = \$5,500,000 - \$12,375 = \$5,487,625$$

However, the auditor has sampled the population, and this uncertainty must be recognized by calculating an allowance for sampling risk. The

TABLE 9–8		Summary of Misstatements Detected			
Sample Item Number	Account Number	Book Value	Audit Value	Audit Difference d_i	d_i^2
1	3892	$ 1,221.92	$ 1,216.40	$ 5.52	$ 30.47
4	1982	2,219.25	2,201.34	17.91	320.77
8	893	1,212.00	1,204.34	7.66	58.68
9	25	5,201.51	5,190.21	17.11	292.75
13	1703	7,205.40	7,188.29	−11.00	121.00
19	4258	3,685.62	3,725.62	−40.00	1,600.00
22	765	58.30	50.64	7.66	58.65
34	1256	17,895.15	17,840.30	54.85	3,008.52
36	3241	542.95	525.98	16.97	287.98
45	895	895.24	823.70	71.54	5,117.97
47	187	10,478.60	10,526.40	−47.80	2,284.84
55	4316	95.00	90.00	5.00	25.00
57	2278	1,903.51	1,875.00	28.51	812.82
59	1843	185.23	200.25	−15.02	225.60
61	64	4,759.65	4,725.32	34.33	1,178.55
69	2371	2,549.61	2,540.26	9.35	87.42
70	1982	12,716.50	12,684.23	32.27	1,041.35
72	2350	361.45	375.50	14.05	197.40
75	349	11,279.40	11,250.40	29.00	841.00
87	2451	74.23	95.40	−21.17	448.17
88	3179	871.58	837.96	33.62	1,130.30
91	1839	571.13	590.00	−18.87	356.08
93	4080	9,467.24	9,504.50	−37.26	1,388.31
97	13	45.20	40.75	4.45	19.80
100	1162	524.90	515.15	9.75	95.06
101	985	7,429.09	7,356.21	72.88	5,311.49
108	304	12,119.60	12,043.60	76.00	5,776.00
110	1977	25.89	26.89	−1.00	1.00
115	1947	1,982.71	2,025.87	−43.16	1,862.79
118	1842	6,429.35	6,384.20	45.15	2,038.52
Total		$123,995.91	$123,665.71	$330.20	$36,018.32

allowance for sampling risk is sometimes referred to as the *achieved precision*. To calculate the achieved precision, the auditor first calculates the standard deviation (*SD*), using the following formula:

$$SD = \sqrt{\frac{\sum\left(d_i^2\right) - n\overline{d}^2}{n-1}} = \sqrt{\frac{\$36,018.32 - 120\left(\$2.75\right)^2}{120-1}} = \$17.34$$

FIGURE 9–2

A Comparison of the Client's Book Value to the Precision Interval

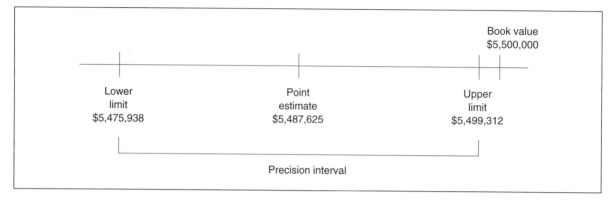

In our example, the standard deviation is $17.34. The achieved precision (AP) is then calculated using the following formula:

$$AP = NZ_{IA} \frac{SD}{\sqrt{n}} = 4,500(1.64)\frac{\$17.34}{\sqrt{120}} = \$11,687$$

In calculating the achieved precision, the auditor uses the Z value for the risk of incorrect acceptance. In our example, the achieved precision is $11,687. The auditor then calculates a precision interval (PI) as follows:

$$PI = \overline{X} \pm AP = \$5,487,625 \pm \$11,687$$

where $5,475,938 is the lower limit and $5,499,312 is the upper limit. Based on the precision interval, the auditor can conclude that there is a 5 percent risk that the true population value falls outside the precision interval. The auditor decides that the evidence supports or does not support the account balance by determining whether the recorded book value is included within the precision interval. If the precision interval includes the book value, the evidence supports the conclusion that the account is not materially misstated. If the book value is not included in the precision interval, the evidence supports the conclusion that the account is materially misstated. In our example, the book value of $5,500,000 lies outside the precision interval. Figure 9–2 graphically displays this result.

When the evidence indicates that the account may be materially misstated, as in our example, the auditor must consider the same three options discussed under monetary-unit sampling: (1) increasing sample size, (2) performing additional substantive tests, or (3) adjusting the account. In our example, if the client adjusts the account by $688, the auditor can accept the account as not being materially misstated.

REVIEW QUESTIONS

[LO 1]   9-1   List the steps in a statistical sampling application for substantive testing.

[1]   9-2   What are the two uses of statistical sampling for substantive testing?

[1]   9-3   How is the sampling unit defined when monetary-unit sampling is used for statistical sampling? How is the sampling unit defined when classical variables sampling is used?

[1]   9-4   How are the risk of incorrect acceptance, the tolerable misstatement, and the expected misstatement related to sample size?

[2]   9-5   Identify the advantages and disadvantages of monetary-unit sampling.

[2,3]   9-6   How does the use of probability-proportional-to-size selection provide an increased chance of sampling larger items?

[2,3]   9-7   What are the three types of error situations that can occur when misstatements are detected using monetary-unit sampling, and how is each projected to the population?

[2,3]   9-8   What is the decision rule for determining the acceptability of sample results when monetary-unit sampling is used?

[3]   9-9   How are understatement errors handled when they are detected in a monetary-unit sampling application?

[4]   9-10   What items considered by an auditor differ when a nonstatistical sampling application is used rather than a statistical sampling application?

[1,4]   9-11   How do changes in the variation of items in the population, the risk of incorrect acceptance, and the tolerable and expected misstatements affect the sample size in a nonstatistical sampling application?

[4]   9-12   Describe the two methods suggested for projecting a nonstatistical sample result. How does an auditor determine which method should be used?

[5]   9-13   What are the advantages and disadvantages of classical variables sampling?

[5,6]   9-14   How should the sampling units be selected in a classical variables sampling application?

[5,6]   9-15   What is the decision rule for determining the acceptability of sample results when classical variables sampling is used?

MULTIPLE-CHOICE QUESTIONS FROM CPA EXAMINATIONS

[2,3]   9-16   In a probability-proportional-to-size sample with a sampling interval of $5,000, an auditor discovers that a selected account receivable with a recorded amount of $10,000 has an audit amount of $8,000. If this were the only error discovered by the auditor, the projected misstatement for this sample would be
a. $1,000.
b. $2,000.
c. $4,000.
d. $5,000.

[1,2,4,5]   **9-17**   An auditor may decide to increase the risk of incorrect rejection when
- a. Increased reliability based on the sample is desired.
- b. Many differences (audit value minus recorded value) are expected.
- c. The initial sample results do *not* support the planned level of control risk.
- d. The cost and effort of selecting additional sample items are low.

[2,3]   **9-18**   Which of the following statements concerning monetary-unit sampling is correct?
- a. The sampling distribution should approximate the normal distribution.
- b. Overstated units have a lower probability of sample selection than units that are understated.
- c. The auditor controls the risk of incorrect acceptance by specifying the risk level for the sampling plan.
- d. The sampling interval is calculated by dividing the number of physical units in the population by the sample size.

[1,5]   **9-19**   Which of the following sampling methods would be used to estimate a numeric measurement of a population, such as a dollar value?
- a. Random sampling.
- b. Numeric sampling.
- c. Attribute sampling.
- d. Variable sampling.

[1]   **9-20**   The risk of incorrect acceptance and the likelihood of assessing the control risk too low relate to the
- a. Effectiveness of the audit.
- b. Efficiency of the audit.
- c. Preliminary estimates of materiality levels.
- d. Allowable risk of tolerable misstatement.

[1]   **9-21**   When planning a sample for a substantive test of details, an auditor should consider the tolerable misstatement for the sample. This consideration should
- a. Be related to the auditor's business risk.
- b. Not be adjusted for qualitative factors.
- c. Be related to preliminary judgments about materiality levels.
- d. Not be changed during the audit process.

[2,5]   **9-22**   An auditor is performing substantive tests of pricing and extensions of perpetual inventory balances consisting of a large number of items. Past experience indicates that there may be numerous pricing and extension errors. Which of the following statistical sampling approaches is most appropriate?
- a. Classical variables sampling.
- b. Monetary-unit sampling.
- c. Stop or go sampling.
- d. Attribute sampling.

[1,2,5]   **9-23**   Which of the following statements concerning the auditor's use of statistical sampling is correct?

a. An auditor needs to estimate the dollar amount of the standard deviation of the population in order to use classical variables sampling.

b. An assumption of monetary-unit sampling is that the underlying accounting population is normally distributed.

c. A classical variables sample needs to be designed with special considerations to include negative balances in the sample.

d. The selection of zero balances usually does *not* require special sample design considerations when using monetary-unit sampling.

[1]   9-24   In assessing the sampling risk, the risk of incorrect rejection and the risk of assessing control risk too high relate to the

a. Efficiency of the audit.

b. Effectiveness of the audit.

c. Selection of the sample.

d. Audit quality controls.

[1,5]   9-25   In estimation sampling for variables, which of the following must be known in order to estimate the appropriate sample size required to meet the auditor's needs in a given situation?

a. The qualitative aspects of misstatements.

b. The total dollar amount of the population.

c. The acceptable level of risk.

d. The estimated rate of misstatement in the population.

[1,2,4,5]   9-26   Which of the following sample planning factors would influence the sample size for a substantive test of details for a specific account?

	Expected Misstatement	Tolerable Misstatement
a.	No	No
b.	Yes	Yes
c.	No	Yes
d.	Yes	No

[1]   9-27   A number of factors influence the sample size for a substantive test of details of an account balance. All other factors being equal, which of the following would lead to a larger sample size?

a. Greater reliance on internal controls.

b. Greater reliance on analytical procedures.

c. Smaller expected frequency of misstatements.

d. Smaller amount of tolerable misstatement.

[2,5]   9-28   Which of the following would most likely be an advantage in using classical variables sampling rather than monetary-unit sampling?

a. An estimate of the standard deviation of the population's recorded amounts is *not* required.

b. The auditor rarely needs the assistance of a computer program to design an efficient sample.

c. Inclusion of zero and negative balances generally does *not* require special design considerations.

d. Any amount that is individually significant is automatically identified and selected.

PROBLEMS

[1,2,5]   9-29   Edwards has decided to use MUS in the audit of a client's accounts receivable balance. Few, if any, misstatements of account balance overstatement are expected.

Required:
a. Identify the advantages of using monetary-unit sampling over classical variables sampling.
b. Calculate the sample size and the sampling interval Edwards should use for the following information:

Tolerable misstatement	$ 15,000
Expected misstatement	$ 6,000
Risk of incorrect acceptance	5%
Recorded amount of accounts receivable	$300,000

c. Calculate the ULM assuming that the following three misstatements were discovered in an MUS sample.

Misstatement Number	Book Value	Audit Value
1	$ 400	$ 320
2	500	0
3	3,000	2,500

(AICPA, adapted)

[2,3]   9-30   The firm of Le and Lysius was conducting the audit of Coomes Molding Corporation for the fiscal year ended October 31. Michelle Le, the partner in charge of the audit, decides that monetary-unit sampling (MUS) is the appropriate sampling technique to use in order to audit Coomes's inventory account. The balance in the inventory at October 31 was $4,250,000. Michelle has established the following: risk of incorrect acceptance = 5%, tolerable misstatement = $212,500, and expected misstatement = $63,750.

Required:
a. Calculate the sample size and sampling interval.
b. Hon Zhu, staff accountant, performed the audit procedures listed in the inventory audit program for each sample item. Calculate the upper limit on misstatement based on the following misstatements. What should Hon conclude about Coomes's inventory account?

Error Number	Book Value	Audit Value
1	$ 6,000	$ 2,000
2	24,000	20,000
3	140,000	65,000

[2,3] 9-31 McMullen and Mulligan, CPAs, were conducting the audit of Cusick Machine Tool Company for the year ended December 31. Jim Sigmund, senior-in-charge of the audit, plans to use MUS to audit Cusick's inventory account. The balance at December 31 was $9,000,000.

Required:

a. Based on the following information, compute the required MUS sample size:
   Tolerable misstatement = $360,000
   Expected misstatement = $90,000
   Risk of incorrect acceptance = 5%

b. Nancy Van Pelt, staff accountant, used the sample items selected in part (a) and performed the audit procedures listed in the inventory audit program. She notes the following misstatements:

Misstatement Number	Book Value	Audit Value
1	$10,000	$7,500
2	9,000	6,000
3	60,000	0
4	800	640

Using this information, calculate the upper limit on misstatement. What conclusion should Van Pelt make concerning the inventory?

c. Assume that, in addition to the four misstatements identified in part (b), Van Pelt had identified the following two understatements:

Misstatement Number	Book Value	Audit Value
5	$6,000	$6,500
6	750	800

Calculate the net upper limit on misstatement.

[4] 9-32 The progressive public accounting firm of Johnson and Johnson has decided to design a nonstatistical sample to examine the accounts receivable balance of Francisco Fragrances, Inc., at October 31. As of October 31, there were 1,500 accounts receivable accounts with a balance of $5.5 million. The accounts receivable population can be segregated into the following strata:

Number and Size of Accounts	Book Value of Stratum
10 accounts > $50,000	$ 750,000
440 accounts > $5,000	3,000,000
1,050 accounts < $5,000	1,750,000

Scott Weller, senior-in-charge of the audit, has made the following decisions:

- Based on the results of the tests of controls, a low assessment is made for inherent and control risk.
- There is a moderate risk that other substantive procedures will fail to detect material misstatements.
- The tolerable misstatement allocated to accounts receivable is $155,000, and the expected misstatement is $60,000.
- All the balances greater than $50,000 will be audited.

Required:

a. Using the formula included in the textbook, compute the suggested sample size for this test.

b. Weller confirmed the accounts receivable accounts selected and noted the following results:

Stratum	Book Value of Stratum	Book Value of Sample	Audit Value of Sample	Amount of Overstatement
>$50,000	$ 750,000	$ 750,000	$ 746,500	$ 3,500
>$5,000	3,000,000	910,000	894,750	15,250
<$5,000	1,750,000	70,000	68,450	1,550

What is the total projected misstatement? In projecting the misstatement, use the amount of misstatement found in the sample divided by the fraction of total dollars from the population included in the sample. What conclusion should Weller make concerning the accounts receivable balance?

[5,6]   **9-33**   World-famous mining mogul Steve Wilsey hired the public accounting firm of Joe Paonessa Associates, P.C., to conduct an audit of his new acquisition, Gator Goldust, Inc. The gold inventory was scheduled to be taken on November 30. The perpetual records show only the *weight* of the gold in various inventory bins. Paonessa has decided to use a variables sampling approach (difference estimation) to determine the correct weight of the gold on hand. (Note that the pricing of the inventory is straightforward because the market value on November 30, determines the price for balance sheet purposes.) There are 4,000 bins in the Gator warehouse. The bins will serve as the sampling units. Paonessa wants to have a 5 percent risk of incorrect acceptance and a 10 percent risk of incorrect rejection. The tolerable misstatement is set at 35,000 ounces, and the expected misstatement is 10,000 ounces. The perpetual record shows 700,000 ounces on hand.

Required:

[Note: Parts (a) and (b) are independent of each other.]

a. Compute the preliminary sample size. The estimated standard deviation is 25 ounces.

b. Assume that Paonessa examined a sample of 100 bins. The following information summarizes the results of the sample data gathered by Paonessa:

Difference Number	Recorded Weight	Audited Weight	d_i	d_i^2
1	445	440	5	25
2	174	170	4	16
•	•	•	•	•
•	•	•	•	•
•	•	•	•	•
29	217	215	2	4
30	96	97	(1)	1
Total	24,000	23,600	400	17,856

Compute the sample results and indicate what conclusion Paonessa should make concerning the inventory balance.

[5,6]   9-34   You are in charge of the audit of Hipp Supply Company for the year ended December 31. In prior years, your firm observed the inventory and tested compilation and pricing. Various misstatements were always found. About 10 percent of the dollar value of the inventory is usually tested.

This year you have established the tolerable misstatement to be $5,000. The client's book value is $97,500. The client has 960 inventory items, the number of which has been determined by examining inventory codes. Each item will be tagged with a prenumbered inventory tag numbered from 1 to 960. You plan to evaluate the results using classical variables sampling (difference estimation).

Assume you have selected a sample of 100 items randomly. For each sample item, audit tests are performed to make sure that the physical count is correct, the pricing is accurate, and the extensions of unit price and quantity are correct. The results are summarized as follows:

Inventory Tag Number	Book Value	Audit Value	d_i	d_i^2
6	$ 100	$ 100	$ 0	$ 0
42	85	85	0	0
46	120	120	0	0
51	420	450	30	900
55	18	18	0	0
56	10	10	0	0
•	•	•	•	•
•	•	•	•	•
•	•	•	•	•
851	25	25	0	0
854	152	150	2	4
857	85	85	0	0
862	76	86	10	100
Total	$10,147	$9,666	$481	$8,895

There were 50 differences, making up the net difference of $481. The recorded total of the client's inventory sheets is $97,500.

Required:
Determine the results of the audit tests using a risk of incorrect acceptance of 10 percent. Indicate whether the evidence supports the fair presentation of the inventory account.

DISCUSSION CASE

[1,2,5]   9-35   Mead, CPA, was engaged to audit Jiffy Company's financial statements for the year ended August 31. Mead is applying sampling procedures.

During the prior years' audits Mead used classical variables sampling in performing tests of controls on Jiffy's accounts receivable. For the current year Mead decided to use monetary-unit sampling (MUS) in confirming accounts receivable because MUS uses each account in the population as a separate sampling unit. Mead expected to discover many overstatements but presumed that the MUS sample would still be smaller than the corresponding size for classical variables sampling.

Mead reasoned that the MUS sample would automatically result in a stratified sample because each account would have an equal chance of being selected for confirmation. Additionally, the selection of negative (credit) balances would be facilitated without special considerations.

Mead computed the sample size using the risk of incorrect acceptance, the total recorded book amount of the receivables, and the number of misstated accounts allowed. Mead divided the total recorded book amount of the receivables by the sample size to determine the sampling interval. Mead then calculated the standard deviation of the dollar amounts of the accounts selected for evaluation of the receivables.

Mead's calculated sample size was 60, and the sampling interval was determined to be $10,000. However, only 58 different accounts were selected because two accounts were so large that the sampling interval caused each of them to be selected twice. Mead proceeded to send confirmation requests to 55 of the 58 customers. Three selected accounts each had insignificant recorded balances under $20. Mead ignored these three small accounts and substituted the three largest accounts that had not been selected in the sample. Each of these accounts had a balance in excess of $7,000, so Mead sent confirmation requests to those customers.

The confirmation process revealed two differences. One account with an audited amount of $3,000 had been recorded at $4,000. Mead projected this to be a $1,000 misstatement. Another account with an audited amount of $2,000 had been recorded at $1,900. Mead did not count the $100 difference because the purpose of the test was to detect overstatements.

In evaluating the sample results, Mead determined that the accounts receivable balance was not overstated because the projected misstatement was less than the allowance for sampling risk.

Required:
Describe each incorrect assumption, statement, and inappropriate application of sampling in Mead's procedures.

(AICPA, adapted)

Part **V**

AUDITING ACCOUNTING APPLICATIONS AND RELATED ACCOUNTS

Chapter 10

Auditing the Revenue Cycle and Related Accounts

LEARNING OBJECTIVES

Upon completion of this chapter you will

[1] Understand why knowledge of an entity's revenue recognition policies is important to the audit.

[2] Understand the revenue cycle.

[3] Identify the types of transactions in the revenue cycle and the financial statement accounts affected.

[4] Identify and describe the types of documents and records used in the revenue cycle.

[5] Understand the functions in the revenue cycle.

[6] Know the appropriate segregation of duties for the revenue cycle.

[7] Identify and evaluate inherent risks relevant to the revenue cycle and related accounts.

[8] Assess control risk for a revenue cycle.

[9] Identify key internal controls and develop relevant tests of controls for revenue, cash receipts, and sales returns transactions.

[10] Relate the assessment of control risk to substantive testing.

[11] Identify substantive tests of transactions used to audit accounts receivable and revenue-related accounts.

[12] Identify analytical procedures used to audit accounts receivable and revenue-related accounts.

[13] Identify tests of account balances used to audit accounts receivable and revenue-related accounts.

[14] Describe the confirmation process and how confirmations are used to obtain evidence about accounts receivable.

[15] Learn how to audit other types of receivables.

[16] Evaluate the audit findings and reach a final conclusion on accounts receivable and revenue-related accounts.

RELEVANT ACCOUNTING AND AUDITING PRONOUNCEMENTS

FASB Statement of Financial Accounting Concepts No. 5, "Recognition and Measurement in Financial Statements of Business Enterprises" (CON5)

FASB Statement of Financial Accounting Concepts No. 6, "Elements of Financial Statements" (CON6)

FASB No. 57, "Related Parties Disclosures" (FAS 57)

SAS No. 22, "Planning and Supervision" (AU 311)

SAS No. 31, "Evidential Matter" (AU 326)

SAS No. 41, "Working Papers" (AU 339)

SAS No. 45, "Omnibus Statement on Auditing Standards—1983" (AU 313 and 334)

SAS No. 47, "Audit Risk and Materiality in Conducting an Audit" (AU 312)

SAS No. 55, "Consideration of Internal Control in a Financial Statement Audit" (AU 319)

SAS No. 56, "Analytical Procedures" (AU 329)

SAS No. 57, "Auditing Accounting Estimates" (AU 342)

SAS No. 65, "The Auditor's Consideration of the Internal Audit Function in an Audit of Financial Statements" (AU 322)

SAS No. 67, "The Confirmation Process" (AU 330)

SAS No. 78, "Consideration of Internal Control in a Financial Statement Audit: An Amendment to SAS No. 55" (AU 319)

SAS No. 80, "Amendment to Statement on Auditing, Standards No. 31, *Evidential Matter*" (AU 326)

SAS No. 82, "Consideration of Fraud in a Financial Statement Audit" (AU 316)

Auditors generally divide an entity's overall information system into transaction cycles. By using a cycles approach, the auditor is able to gather evidence by examining the processing of related transactions from their origin to their ultimate disposition in accounting journals and ledgers. In this chapter, the concepts and techniques learned in the previous chapters are applied to the assessment of inherent risk and control risk for the revenue cycle and related accounts. The revenue cycle focuses on the sale of goods and services to customers. For virtually all entities, the revenue and purchasing cycles represent the two major accounting cycles that affect the financial statements.

The chapter starts by reviewing the basic concepts related to revenue recognition. An overview of the revenue cycle is then presented as an aid in providing the reader with an understanding of the cycle. This is followed by a discussion of the specific factors that affect the assessment of inherent risk for the revenue cycle and the auditor's assessment of control risk. The presentation concentrates on the decision process the auditor follows in making this important assessment. The remainder of the chapter discusses the substantive audit procedures conducted by the auditor to reach the appropriate level of detection risk for the accounts affected by the revenue cycle. While the main emphasis is on the accounts receivable account, the discussion also covers the allowance for uncollectible accounts, bad-debt expense, and sales returns and allowances. Because the cash account is affected by other accounting cycles, it is covered separately in Chapter 16. 🌐

Revenue Recognition

[LO 1]   Revenue recognition is briefly reviewed at the beginning of this chapter because knowledge of this underlying concept is fundamental to auditing the revenue cycle. Additionally, revenue must be recognized in conformity with GAAP in order for an auditor to issue an unqualified opinion. A revenue-producing transaction generally consists of the sale of a product or the rendering of a service. FASB Statement of Financial Accounting Concepts No. 6, "Elements of Financial Statements" (CON6), defines revenues as

> inflows or other enhancements of assets of an entity or settlements of its liabilities (or a combination of both) from delivery or producing goods, rendering services, or other activities that constitute the entity's major or central operations. (para. 78)

Revenues are measured by the exchange value of the goods and services provided. In general, the entity receives cash or claims to cash for the goods or services provided. Claims to cash are usually referred to as trade accounts receivable. FASB Statement of Financial Accounting Concepts No. 5, "Recognition and Measurement in Financial Statements of Business Enterprises" (CON5, para. 83), requires that before revenue is recognized (recorded), it must be *realized* and *earned*. Revenue is realized when a product or service is exchanged for cash, a promise to pay cash, or other assets that can be converted into cash. Revenue is earned when an entity has substantially completed the earning process, which generally means a product has been delivered or a service has been provided (see Exhibit 10–1). For most entities, this revenue recognition process occurs over a short period of time, but in certain industries, such as construction or defense, the revenue recognition process may extend over a period of years.

An entity's revenue recognition policies affect how transactions are processed and how they are accounted for in the financial statements. Thus, an auditor must understand an entity's revenue recognition policies in order to audit the revenue cycle.

EXHIBIT 10–1

Discount-Club Retailers Revise Revenue Recognition of Membership Fees

The accounting fraud at Cendant Corp. seems to have led to increased scrutiny by the SEC of the accounting methods used by discount-club retailers to recognize revenue. Cendant had recognized some membership fees when they were received and some over the membership period. It changed its policy to not record membership fees until the end of the membership term because it offers a full refund at any point during the term. Other discount-club retailers (such as BJ's Wholesale Club Inc. and Costco Cos.) have also made their revenue recognition policies more conservative. For example, BJ's had recognized membership fees when received but now has changed its policy to record revenue incrementally over the life of the membership term, typically 12 months. Auditors must understand how clients recognize revenue to ensure that the financial statements do not contain material misstatements.

Sources: E. MacDonald, L. Johannes, and E. Nelson, "Discount-Club Retailers Shift Accounting," *The Wall Street Journal* (October 20, 1998); E. Nelson and J. S. Lublin, "How Whistle-Blowers Set Off a Fraud Probe That Crushed Cendant," *The Wall Street Journal* (August 8, 1998); and "Cendant Restates Past Results, Includes Membership Acct. Change," *The PointCast Network* (September 29, 1998).

Overview of the Revenue Cycle

[LO 2] In this section an overview of the revenue cycle for EarthWear Clothiers, Inc., is presented, beginning with an order from a customer, proceeding to the exchange of goods or services for a promise to pay, and ending with the receipt of cash. Exhibit 10–2 describes EarthWear's revenue cycle. Figure 10–1 presents the flowchart of Earth-Wear's revenue cycle, which will provide a framework for discussing controls and tests of controls in more detail. The discussion of the revenue cycle in this chapter can be applied equally well to manufacturing, wholesale, and service organizations. It should be kept in mind, however, that an accounting system must be tailored to meet the specific needs of an entity. Therefore, the reader should concentrate on understanding the basic concepts presented so that they can be applied to specific revenue cycles. Problem 10-37 presents an example of a document flowchart for a revenue cycle that is basically a manual system. If the reader has limited knowledge of information technology (IT), this flowchart provides a simpler example of a revenue cycle.

The reader should also notice that the revenue cycle shown in Figure 10–1 interacts with the inventory cycle. Many accounting systems integrate the revenue, purchasing, payroll, and inventory cycles. The flowcharts used in this text to represent those cycles show the points where the cycles interact with one another. As entities use more advanced IT technology, it is becoming easier to integrate the information flow among the various accounting cycles.

We now discuss the following topics related to the revenue cycle:

- Types of transactions and financial statement accounts affected.
- Types of documents and records.
- The major functions.
- The key segregation of duties.

EXHIBIT 10–2

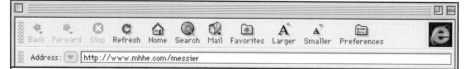

Description of EarthWear's Revenue Cycle

EarthWear provides 24-hour toll-free telephone numbers that may be called seven days a week (except Christmas Day) to place orders. Telephone calls are answered by the company's sales representatives, who use on-line computer terminals to enter customer orders and to retrieve information about product characteristics and availability. The company's sales representatives enter orders into an on-line order entry and inventory control system. Customers using the company's Internet site complete a computer screen that requests information on product code, size, color, and so forth. When the customer finishes shopping for products, he or she enters delivery and credit card information into a computer-based form. EarthWear provides assurance through CPA *WebTrust* that the Web site has been evaluated and tested to meet *WebTrust* Principles and Criteria.

Computer order processing is performed each night on a batch basis, at which time shipping tickets are printed with bar codes for optical scanning. Inventory is picked based on the location of individual products rather than orders, followed by computerized sorting and transporting of goods to multiple packing stations and shipping zones. The computerized inventory control system also handles items that customers return. Orders are generally shipped by United Parcel Service (UPS) at various tiered rates, depending upon the total dollar value of each customer's order. Other expedited delivery services are available for additional charges.

With the exception of sales to groups and companies for corporate incentive programs, customers pay in cash (in stores) or with credit cards. EarthWear's major bank is reimbursed directly by credit card companies, usually within three days. Group and corporate accounts are granted credit by the credit department. When group or corporate orders are received from new customers, the credit department performs a credit check following corporate policies. A credit authorization form is completed with the credit limit entered into the customer database. When a group or corporate order is received from an existing customer, the order is entered, and the data validation program performs a credit check by comparing the sum of the existing order and the customer's balance to the customer's credit limit.

Types of Transactions and Financial Statement Accounts Affected

Three types of transactions are typically processed through the revenue cycle:

*   The sale of goods or rendering of a service for cash or credit.
*   The receipt of cash from the customer in payment for the goods or services.
*   The return of goods by the customer for credit or cash.

[LO 3]

The key controls involved in each of these transactions are discussed later in the chapter. For some entities, other types of transactions that may occur as part of the revenue cycle include scrap sales, intercompany sales, and related-party sales. Although such transactions are not covered specifically in this textbook, the auditor should be aware of how these transactions are processed and their related controls when they represent material amounts in the financial statements.

FIGURE 10–1

Flowchart of the Revenue Cycle–EarthWear Clothiers, Inc.

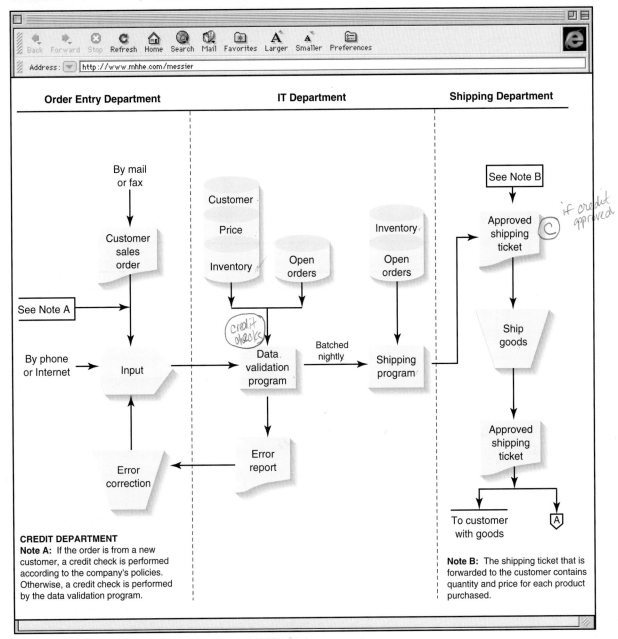

The revenue cycle affects numerous accounts in the financial statements. The most significant accounts affected by each type of transaction are as follows:

1. Sales transactions:
   - Trade accounts receivable.
   - Sales.

F I G U R E   10–1 (*continued*)

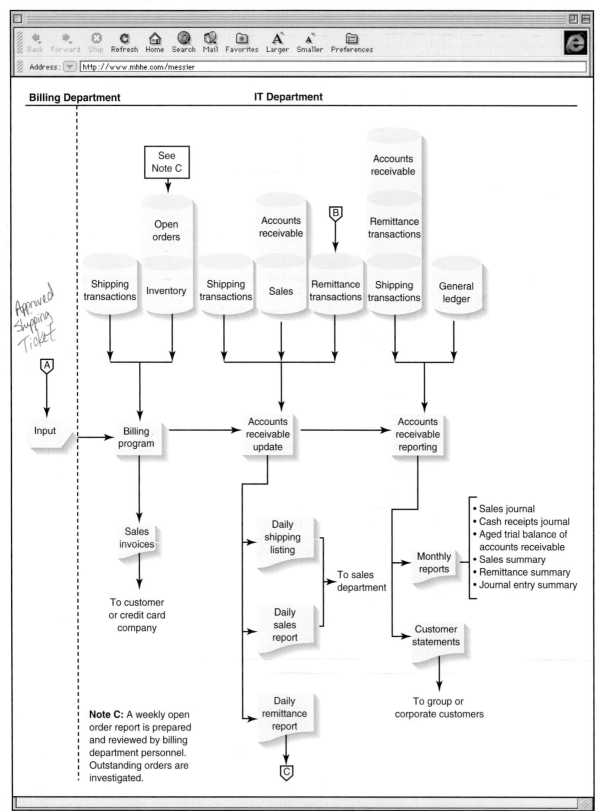

FIGURE 10–1 (*concluded*)

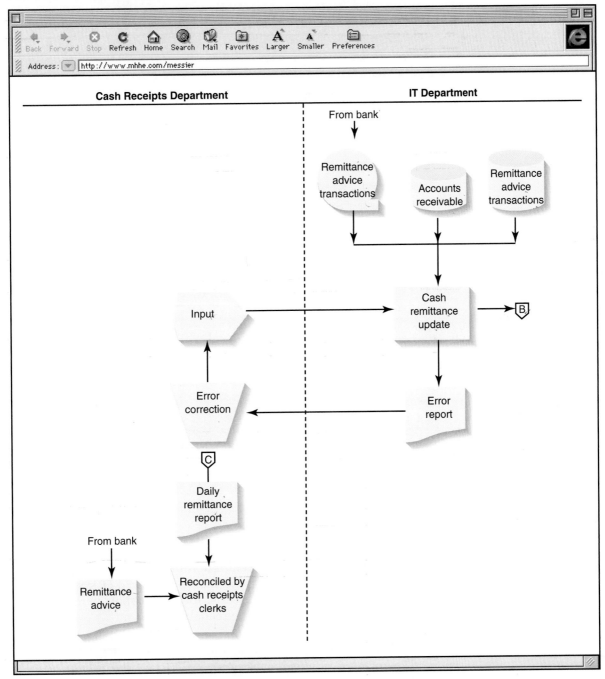

TABLE 10–1	Documents and Records Included in the Revenue Cycle

- Customer sales order.
- Credit approval form.
- Open-order report.
- Shipping document.
- Sales invoice.
- Sales journal.
- Customer statement.
- Accounts receivable subsidiary ledger.
- Aged trial balance of accounts receivable.
- Remittance advice.
- Cash receipts journal.
- Credit memorandum.
- Write-off authorization.

- Allowance for uncollectible accounts.
- Bad-debt expense.
2. Cash receipts transactions:
- Cash.
- Trade accounts receivable.
- Cash discounts.
3. Sales return and allowance transactions:
- Sales returns.
- Sales allowances.
- Trade accounts receivable.

Types of Documents and Records

[LO 4]

Table 10–1 lists the more important documents and records that are normally contained in the revenue cycle. Each of these items is discussed briefly. The reader should keep in mind that in advanced IT systems some of these documents and records may exist for only a short period of time or may be maintained only in machine-readable form.

Customer Sales Order   This document contains the details of the type and quantity of products or services ordered by the customer. Customer sales orders may be prepared and forwarded by a salesperson, mailed or faxed, or received over the Internet. In the EarthWear example (Figure 10–1), order entry personnel enter the mailed or faxed information from customer sales orders into the revenue system. Phone or Internet sales are entered directly into the data validation program.

Credit Approval Form   When a customer purchases products on credit from the client for the first time, the client should have a formal procedure for investigating the creditworthiness of the customer. The result of this procedure should be documented on some type of credit approval form. When the customer plans to purchase additional products in the future, this procedure should be used to establish the customer's credit limit. The amount of the credit limit should be documented on the approval form. When credit limits are included in the client's computer files, the approval forms represent the source documents authorizing the amounts contained in the information system. EarthWear follows such a policy for its group and corporate customers (see Exhibit 10–2).

Open-Order Report   This is a report of all customer orders for which processing has not been completed. In the typical revenue cycle, once a customer's order has been accepted, the order is entered into the system. After the goods have been shipped and billed, the order should be noted as filled. This report should be reviewed daily or weekly, and old orders should be investigated to determine if any goods have been shipped but not billed or to determine why orders have not been filled. Testing for shipments for which the customer has not been billed provides evidence as to the completeness objective. Figure 10–1 shows that EarthWear has an open order file. Note C indicates that an open order report is prepared weekly and reviewed by billing department personnel for long overdue orders.

Shipping Document   A shipping document must be prepared anytime goods are shipped to a customer. This document generally serves as a *bill of lading* and contains information on the type of product shipped, the quantity shipped, and other relevant information. In some revenue systems, the shipping document and bill of lading are separate documents. A copy of the shipping document is sent to the customer, while another copy of the shipping document is used to initiate the billing process. Figure 10–1 shows that EarthWear follows a similar process using a shipping ticket.

Sales Invoice   This document is used to bill the customer. The sales invoice contains information on the type of product or service, the quantity, the price, and the terms of trade. The original sales invoice is usually forwarded to the customer, and copies are distributed to other departments within the organization. The sales invoice is typically the source document that signals the recognition of revenue. The majority of EarthWear's sales are made to customers using credit cards, and they do not receive a bill directly from the company. However, the shipping ticket that accompanies the goods contains the quantity and prices for products purchased. That amount shows up on the customer's credit card statement.

Sales Journal   Once a sales invoice has been issued, the sale needs to be recorded in the accounting records. The sales journal is used to record the necessary information for each sales transaction. Depending on the complexity of the entity's operation, the sales journal may contain information classified by type of sale (for example, product line, intercompany sales, related parties). The sales journal contains columns for debiting accounts receivable and crediting the various sales accounts. EarthWear maintains such a journal.

Customer Statement   This document is usually mailed to a customer monthly. It contains the details of all sales, cash receipts, and credit memorandum transactions processed through the customer's account for the period. EarthWear prepares monthly statements only for group or corporate customers who have accounts receivable with the company.

Accounts Receivable Subsidiary Ledger   The accounts receivable subsidiary ledger contains an account and the details of transactions with each customer. A transaction recorded in the sales journal and cash receipts journal is posted to the appropriate customer's account in the accounts receivable subsidiary ledger. For computerized systems such as EarthWear's, this information is maintained in the accounts receivable file (see Figure 10–1).

Aged Trial Balance of Accounts Receivable   This report, which is normally prepared monthly, summarizes all the customer balances in the accounts receivable subsidiary ledger. Customers' balances are reported in categories (such as, less than 30 days, 30–60 days, 60–90 days, more than 90 days old) based on the time expired since the date of the sales invoice. The aged trial balance of accounts receivable is used to monitor the collection of receivables and to ensure that the details of the accounts receivable subsidiary ledger agree with the general ledger control account. The auditor uses this report for conducting much of the substantive audit work in accounts receivable. EarthWear prepares an aged trial balance of accounts receivable for group and corporate customers.

Remittance Advice   This document is usually mailed with the customer's bill and returned with the customer's payment for goods or services. A remittance advice contains information regarding which invoices are being paid by the customer. Many entities use turnaround documents, where a portion of the sales invoice serves as a remittance advice that is returned with the customer's payment. EarthWear receives remittance advices from group and corporate customers after the payment has been processed by the company's bank. Payments from credit card companies are also made directly to the bank, and a listing similar to a remittance advice is forwarded to EarthWear.

Cash Receipts Journal   This journal is used to record the entity's cash receipts. The cash receipts journal contains columns for debiting cash, crediting accounts receivable, and crediting other accounts such as scrap sales or interest income. EarthWear maintains such a journal.

Credit Memorandum   This document is used to record credits for the return of goods in a customer's account or to record allowances that will be issued to the customer. Its form is generally similar to that of a sales invoice, and it may be processed through the system in the same way as a sales invoice. Exhibit 10–3 describes how EarthWear handles goods returned from customers. The process of customer returns is not shown in the revenue flowchart (Figure 10–1).

EXHIBIT 10–3

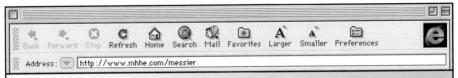

Description of EarthWear Clothiers' Process for Handling Customer Returns

In order to receive credit for returned goods, customers must mail the goods to EarthWear's receiving department. There the goods are inspected, and a receiving document, which also serves as a credit memorandum, is prepared. Credit memoranda are entered into the revenue cycle along with the normal batching of customer orders. The customer receives either a replacement product, a cash refund, or a credit to his or her credit card.

The returned goods are placed back into inventory if they are not defective or damaged. If the goods are defective or damaged they are listed as "seconds" and sold at reduced prices. The inventory records are updated to reflect either the original cost or the reduced price.

TABLE 10–2	Functions in the Revenue Cycle

- *Order entry* — Acceptance of customer orders for goods and services into the system in accordance with management criteria.
- *Credit authorization* — Appropriate approval of customer orders for creditworthiness.
- *Shipping* — Shipping of goods that has been authorized.
- *Billing* — Issuance of sales invoices to customers for goods shipped or services provided; also, processing of billing adjustments for allowances, discounts, and returns.
- *Cash receipts* — Processing of the receipt of cash from customers.
- *Accounts receivable* — Recording of all sales invoices, collections, and credit memoranda in individual customer accounts.
- *General ledger* — Proper accumulation, classification, and summarization of revenues, collections, and receivables in the financial statement accounts.

Write-Off Authorization   This document authorizes the write-off of an uncollectible account. It is normally initiated in the credit department, with final approval for the write-off coming from the treasurer. Depending on the entity's accounting system, this type of transaction may be processed separately or as part of the normal stream of sales transactions. EarthWear has negligible bad debts because most sales are made by credit card. Any bad debts related to group or corporate sales are written off by the credit department after approval by the treasurer.

The Major Functions

[LO 5]

The principal objective of the revenue cycle is selling the entity's goods or services at prices and terms that are consistent with management's policies. Table 10–2 summarizes the functions that normally take place in a typical revenue cycle.

Order Entry   The initial function in the revenue cycle is the entry of new sales orders into the system. It is important that sales or services be consistent with management's authorization criteria before entry into the revenue cycle. In most entities, there is a separate order entry department (see Figure 10–1).

Credit Authorization   The credit authorization function must determine that the customer is able to pay for the goods or services. Failure to perform this function properly may result in bad-debt losses. In many entities, customers have preset credit limits. The credit authorization function must ensure that the credit limit is not exceeded without additional authorization. Where credit limits are programmed into the computer system, a sale that causes a customer's balance to exceed the authorized credit limit should not be processed. The system should also generate an exception report or review by the credit function prior to further processing. Periodically, each customer's credit limits should be reviewed to ensure that the amount is consistent with the customer's ability to pay.

The credit authorization function also has responsibility for monitoring customer payments. An aged trial balance of accounts receivable should be prepared and reviewed by the credit function. Payment should be requested from customers who are delinquent in paying for goods or services. The credit function is usually responsible for preparing a report of customer accounts that may require write-off as bad debts. However, the final approval for writing off an account should come from an officer of the company who is not responsible for credit or collections. If the authorization for bad-debt write-off is part of the credit function, it is possible for credit personnel who have access to cash receipts to conceal misappropriation of cash by writing off customers' balances. In many large organizations, the treasurer approves the write-off of customer accounts because this individual is responsible for cash management activities and the treasurer's department is usually separate from the credit function. In some entities, the accounts written off are turned over to a collection agency for continuing collection efforts. By following this procedure, an entity discourages the use of fictitious bad-debt write-offs to conceal the misappropriation of cash. Most entities have a separate credit department.

Shipping   Goods should not be shipped, nor should services be provided, without proper authorization. The main control that authorizes shipment of goods or performance of services is payment or proper credit approval for the transaction. The shipping function must also ensure that customer orders are filled with the correct product and quantities. To ensure timely billing of customers, completed orders must be promptly forwarded to the billing function. The shipping function is normally completed within a separate shipping department.

Billing   The main responsibility of the billing function is to ensure that all goods shipped and all services provided are billed at authorized prices and terms. The entity's controls should prevent goods from being shipped to customers who are not being billed. In an IT system, an open-order report should be prepared and reviewed for orders that have not been filled on a timely basis. In other systems, all prenumbered shipping documents should be accounted for and matched to their related sales invoices. Any open or unmatched transactions should be investigated by billing department or sales department personnel.

The billing function is also responsible for handling goods returned for credit. The key control here is that a credit memorandum should not be issued unless the goods have been returned. A receiving document should first be issued by the receiving department to acknowledge receipt of the returned goods.

Cash Receipts   The collection function must ensure that all cash collections are properly identified and promptly deposited intact at the bank. Many companies use a lockbox system, in which customers' payments are sent directly to the entity's bank. The bank then forwards a file of cash receipts transactions and remittance advices to the entity. In situations where payments are sent directly to the entity, the checks should be restrictively endorsed and a "prelisting" or control listing prepared. All checks should be deposited daily.

Accounts Receivable   The accounts receivable function is responsible for ensuring that all billings, adjustments, and cash collections are properly recorded in customers' accounts receivable records. Any entries in customers' accounts should be made from authorized source documents such as sales invoices, remittance advices, and credit memoranda. In an IT system, the entries to the customers' accounts receivable records may be made directly as part of the normal processing of these transactions. The use of control totals and daily activity reports provides the control for ensuring that all transactions are properly recorded. The accounts receivable function is normally performed within the billing department or a separate accounts receivable department.

General Ledger   The main objective of the general ledger function in terms of a revenue cycle is to ensure that all revenues, collections, and receivables are properly accumulated, classified, and summarized in the accounts. In an IT system, the use of control or summary totals ensures that this function is performed correctly. One important function is the reconciliation of the accounts receivable subsidiary ledger to the general ledger control account. The general ledger function is also normally responsible for mailing the monthly customer account statements.

Key Segregation of Duties

[LO 6]

One of the most important controls in any accounting system is proper segregation of duties. This is particularly important in the revenue cycle because of the potential for theft and fraud. Therefore, individuals involved in the order entry, credit, shipping, or billing functions should not have access to the accounts receivable records, the general ledger, or any cash receipts activities. If IT is used extensively in the revenue application, there

TABLE 10–3	Key Segregation of Duties in the Revenue Cycle and Possible Errors or Fraud

Segregation of Duties	Possible Errors or Fraud Resulting from Conflicts of Duties
The credit function should be segregated from the billing function.	If one individual has the ability to grant credit to a customer and also has responsibility for billing that customer, it is possible for sales to be made to customers who are not creditworthy. This can result in bad debts.
The shipping function should be segregated from the billing function.	If one individual who is responsible for shipping goods is also involved in the billing function, it is possible for unauthorized shipments to be made and for the usual billing procedures to be circumvented. This can result in unrecorded sales transactions and theft of goods.
The accounts receivable function should be segregated from the general ledger function.	If one individual is responsible for the accounts receivable records and also for the general ledger, it is possible for that individual to conceal unauthorized shipments. This can result in unrecorded sales transactions and theft of goods.
The cash receipts function should be segregated from the accounts receivable function.	If one individual has access to both the cash receipts and the accounts receivable records, it is possible for cash to be diverted and the shortage of cash in the accounting records to be covered. This can result in theft of the entity's cash.

should be proper segregation of duties in the IT department, as discussed in Chapter 7. Table 10–3 contains some of the key segregation of duties for the revenue cycle, as well as examples of possible errors or fraud that can result from conflicts in duties.

Table 10–4 shows the proper segregation of duties for individual revenue functions across the various departments that process revenue transactions.

Inherent Risk Assessment

[LO 7]   In examining the revenue cycle, the auditor should consider the inherent risk factors that may affect both the revenue and cash receipts transactions processed by the cycle and the financial statement accounts affected by those transactions. Chapter 3 categorized risk factors that relate to possible misstatements into three groups: management's characteristics and influence over the control environment, industry conditions, and operating characteristics and financial stability. Management's characteristics and influence over the control environment are pervasive and are likely to affect all of the accounting cycles. Specific inherent risk factors that may affect the revenue cycle include the following:

- Industry-related factors.
- The complexity and contentiousness of revenue recognition issues.
- The difficulty of auditing transactions and account balances.
- Misstatements detected in prior audits.

TABLE 10–4   Segregation of Duties for Revenue and Accounts Receivable Functions by Department

Revenue and Accounts Receivable Functions	Order Entry	Credit	Shipping	Accounts Receivable	Cash Receipts	IT
				Department		
Receiving and preparing customer order	X					
Approving credit		X				
Shipping goods to customer and completing shipping document			X			
Preparing customer invoice *BILLING*						X
Updating accounts receivable records for sales				X		X
Receiving customer's remittance					X	
Updating accounts receivable for remittances				X		X
Preparing accounts receivable aged trial balance				X		X

363

Industry-
Related Factors

Factors such as the profitability and health of the industry in which an entity operates, the level of competition within the industry, and the industry's rate of technological change affect the potential for misstatements in the revenue cycle (see Table 3–3). For example, if the industry is experiencing a lack of demand for its products, the entity may be faced with a declining sales volume, which can lead to operating losses and poor cash flow. Similarly, competition within the industry can affect the entity's pricing policies, credit terms, and product warranties. If such industry-related factors are present, management may engage in activities that can result in misstatements.

The level of governmental regulation within the industry may also affect sales activity. While all industries are regulated by legislation restricting unfair trade practices such as price fixing, a number of industries are more highly regulated. For example, banks and insurance companies are subject to both state and federal laws that may limit an entity's operations. The products developed and sold by pharmaceutical companies are regulated by the Food and Drug Administration. Finally, most states have consumer protection legislation that may affect product warranties, returns, financing, and product liability. Industry-related factors directly impact the auditor's assessment of inherent risk for audit objectives such as authorization and valuation.

The Complexity
and
Contentious-
ness of Revenue
Recognition
Issues

For most entities the recognition of revenue is not a major problem because revenue is recognized when a product is shipped or a service is provided. However, for some entities the recognition of revenue may involve complex calculations (see Table 3–4). Examples include recognition of revenue on long-term construction contracts, long-term service contracts, lease contracts, and installment sales. There may be disputes between the auditor and management over when revenue, expenses, and related profits should be recognized. In such circumstances, the auditor should assess the possibility of material misstatement to be high. Revenue recognition may also have a significant impact on the timeliness and valuation internal control objectives.

The Difficulty
of Auditing
Transactions
and Account
Balances

Accounts that are difficult to audit can pose inherent risk problems for the auditor. In addition to the issues related to revenue recognition discussed previously, the allowance for uncollectible accounts can be difficult to audit because of the subjectivity involved in determining its proper value. Thus, the estimation of this account directly affects the valuation of receivables on the financial statements. The risk of a material misstatement in the estimate of the allowance is also a function of factors such as the complexity of the customer base and the reliability of the data available to test the allowance account. For example, the only evidence available to determine the collectibility of a customer's account may be past payment history or a credit agency report. Such evidence is not as reliable as payments by the customer. The audit considerations for the allowance for uncollectible accounts are discussed later in this chapter.

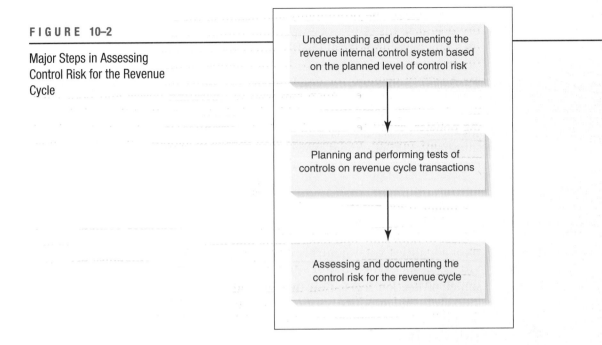

FIGURE 10–2

Major Steps in Assessing Control Risk for the Revenue Cycle

Misstatements Detected in Prior Audits

As previously discussed, the presence of misstatements in previous audits is a good indicator that misstatements are likely to be present during the current audit. With a continuing engagement, the auditor has the results of prior years' audits to help in assessing the potential for misstatements in the revenue cycle.

Control Risk Assessment

[LO 8] The concepts involved in control risk assessment were discussed in Chapters 6 and 7. The following sections apply the approach outlined in those chapters to the revenue cycle. For discussion purposes, it is assumed that the auditor has decided to follow a reliance strategy. Figure 10–2 summarizes the three steps for assessing control risk when a reliance strategy is being followed. Each of these steps is briefly reviewed within the context of the revenue cycle.

Understanding and Documenting Internal Control

In order to assess the control risk for the revenue cycle, the auditor must understand the five components of internal control.

Control Environment Table 6–1 in Chapter 6 listed the factors that are important in understanding the control environment. Because these factors have a pervasive effect on all accounting cycles, understanding the control environment is generally completed on an overall entity basis. The auditor should, however, consider how the various control environment factors may affect the individual accounting cycles. In the remaining discussion of the revenue cycle, it is assumed that the control environment factors, including general IT controls, are reliable.

Risk Assessment   The auditor must understand how management considers risks that are relevant to the revenue cycle, estimates their significance, assesses the likelihood of their occurrence, and decides what actions to take to address those risks. Some of these risks include a new or revamped information system, rapid growth, and new technology. Each of these factors can represent a serious risk to an entity's internal controls over revenues.

Control Activities   When a reliance strategy is adopted for the revenue cycle, the auditor needs to understand the controls that exist to ensure that management's objectives are being met. More specifically, the auditor identifies what controls ensure that the internal control objectives are being met. The auditor's understanding of the revenue cycle can be documented using procedures manuals, narrative descriptions, internal control questionnaires, and flowcharts.

Information and Communication   For each major class of transactions in the revenue cycle, the auditor needs to obtain the following knowledge:

- The process by which sales, cash receipts, and credit memoranda transactions are initiated.
- The accounting records, supporting documents, and accounts that are involved in processing sales, cash receipts, and sales returns and allowances transactions.
- The flow of each type of transaction from initiation to inclusion in the financial statements, including computer processing of the data.
- The process used to prepare estimates for accounts such as the allowance for uncollectible accounts and sales returns.

The auditor typically develops an understanding of an accounting (information) system such as the revenue cycle by conducting a transaction walk-through. This involves the auditor's "walking" a transaction through the accounting system and documenting the various functions that process it. In the case of a continuing audit, the auditor has the prior years' cycle documentation to assist in the walk-through, although the possibility of changes in the system must be considered. If the system has been changed substantially, or the audit is for a new client, the auditor should prepare new documentation of the system.

Monitoring   The auditor needs to understand the client's monitoring processes over the revenue cycle. This includes understanding how management assesses the design and operation of controls in the revenue cycle. It also involves understanding how supervisory personnel within the cycle review the personnel who perform the controls and evaluate the performance of the entity's data processing system.

Planning and Performing Tests of Controls

In performing this step, the auditor systematically examines the client's revenue cycle to identify relevant controls that help to prevent, or detect and correct, material misstatements. Because these controls are relied upon in order to assess a lower level of control risk, the auditor conducts tests of controls to ensure that the controls in the revenue cycle operate effectively. Audit procedures used to test controls in the revenue cycle include inquiry of client personnel, inspection of documents and records, observation of the operation of the control, and reperformance by the auditor of the control procedures.

Subsequent sections examine tests of controls for each major type of transaction in the revenue cycle more specifically. Chapter 8 presented a statistical sampling approach to conducting tests of controls.

Assessing and Documenting the Control Risk

Once the tests of controls in the revenue cycle have been completed, the auditor judges the assessed level of control risk. If the results of the tests of controls support the planned level of control risk, the auditor conducts the planned level of substantive tests for the related account balances. If the results of the tests of controls do not support the planned level of control risk, the auditor should assess control risk at a level higher than planned. Additional substantive tests in the accounts affected by the revenue cycle must then be conducted.

The auditor should document both the *assessed level* of control risk and the *basis* for his or her conclusion. The level of control risk for the revenue cycle can be assessed using either quantitative amounts or qualitative terms such as "low," "medium," and "high." The documentation of the assessed level of control risk for the revenue cycle would include documentation of the accounting system such as the flowchart included in Figure 10–1, the results of the tests of controls, and a memorandum indicating the overall conclusions about control risk.

Internal Control Procedures and Tests of Controls— Revenue Transactions

[LO 9] Table 10–5 summarizes the internal control objectives, possible misstatements, internal control procedures, and selected tests of controls for revenue transactions. Most of these controls exist within EarthWear's revenue cycle (Figure 10–1).

The auditor's decision process on planning and performing tests of controls involves considering the seven internal control objectives and the possible misstatements that can occur if internal control does not operate effectively. The auditor evaluates the client's accounting system to determine the controls that will prevent or detect such misstatements. When controls are present and the auditor decides to rely on them, they must be tested to evaluate their effectiveness. For example, suppose the auditor's evaluation of the entity's revenue cycle indicates that monthly statements are mailed to customers by the accounts receivable department with complaints being handled by the billing department. This control is intended to prevent the recording of fictitious sales transactions. The auditor can review and test

Internal Control Objective	Possible Misstatement	Internal Control Procedure	Test of Controls
Validity	Fictitious sales	Segregation of duties	Observation and evaluation of proper segregation of duties
		Sales recorded only with approved customer order and shipping document	Testing of a sample of sales invoices for the presence of authorized customer order and shipping document; if IT application, examination of programmed controls
		Accounting for numerical sequences of sales invoices	Review and testing of client procedures for accounting for numerical sequence of sales invoices; if IT application, examination of programmed controls
		Monthly customer statements; complaints handled independently	Review and testing of client procedures for mailing and handling complaints about monthly statements
	Sales recorded, goods not shipped, or services not performed	Same control procedures as above	Same test of controls as above
Completeness	Goods shipped or services performed, revenue not recorded	Accounting for numerical sequences of shipping documents and sales invoices	Review and testing of client's procedures for accounting for numerical sequence of shipping documents and sales invoices; if IT application, examination of programmed controls
		Shipping documents matched to sales invoices	Tracing of a sample of shipping documents to their respective sales invoices and to the sales journal
		Sales invoices reconciled to daily sales report	Testing of a sample of daily reconciliations
		An open-order file that is maintained currently and reviewed periodically	Examination of the open-order file for unfilled orders
Timeliness	Revenue transactions recorded in the wrong period	All shipping documents forwarded to the billing function daily	Comparison of the dates on sales invoices with the dates of the relevant shipping documents
		Daily billing of goods shipped	Comparison of the dates on sales invoices with the dates they were recorded in the sales journal

(*continued*)

TABLE 10–5 *(concluded)*

Internal Control Objective	Possible Misstatement	Internal Control Procedure	Test of Controls
Authorization	Goods shipped or services performed for a customer who is a bad credit risk	Proper procedures for authorizing credit and shipment of goods	Review of client's procedures for granting credit
			Examination of sales orders for evidence of proper credit approval; if IT application, examination of programmed controls for credit limits
	Shipments made or services performed at unauthorized prices or on unauthorized terms	Authorized price list and specified terms of trade	Comparison of prices and terms on sales invoices to authorized price list and terms of trade; if IT application, examination of programmed controls for authorized prices and terms
Valuation	Revenue transaction recorded at an incorrect dollar amount	Authorized price list and specified terms of trade	Same as above
		Each sales invoice agreed to shipping document and customer order for product type and quantity; mathematical accuracy of sales invoice verified	Examination of sales invoice for evidence that client personnel verified mathematical accuracy
			Recomputation of the information on a sample of sales invoices; if IT application, examination of programmed controls and consideration of use of computer-assisted audit techniques
Classification	Sales transaction not properly classified	Chart of accounts	Review of sales journal and general ledger for proper classification
		Proper codes for different types of products or services	Examination of sales invoices for proper classification; if IT application, testing of programmed controls for proper codes
Posting and summarization	Sales transactions not posted correctly to the sales journal or customers' accounts in accounts receivable subsidiary ledger	Sales invoices reconciled to daily sales report	Examination of reconciliation of sales invoices to daily sales report
		Daily postings to sales journal reconciled with posting to subsidiary ledger	Examination of reconciliation of entries to sales journal with entries to subsidiary ledger
	Amounts from sales journal not posted correctly to general journal	Subsidiary ledger reconciled to general ledger control account	Review of reconciliation of subsidiary ledger to general ledger control account
		Monthly customer statements with independent review of complaints	Review and testing of client procedures for mailing and handling complaints related to monthly statements

the client's procedures for mailing customer statements and handling complaints. If no exceptions or an immaterial number are noted, the auditor has evidence that the control is operating effectively.

Each of the internal control objectives shown in Table 10–5 for sales transactions is discussed mainly in terms of control procedures and tests of controls. The following sections also include a discussion of internal control procedures and tests of controls that are relevant for EarthWear's revenue cycle.

Validity of Revenue Transactions

Auditors are concerned about the validity objective for revenue transactions because clients are more likely to overstate sales than to understate them. The auditor is concerned about two major types of material misstatements: sales to fictitious customers and recording of revenue when goods have not been shipped or services have not been performed. The controls shown in Table 10–5 are designed to reduce the risk that revenue is recorded before goods are shipped or services are performed. The major control for preventing fictitious sales is proper segregation of duties between the shipping function and the order entry and billing functions. If these functions are not properly segregated, unauthorized shipments can be made to fictitious customers by circumvention of normal billing control procedures. Requiring an approved customer sales order and shipping document before revenue is recognized also minimizes the recording of fictitious sales in a client's records. Accounting for the numerical sequence of sales invoices can be accomplished manually or by computer. The use of monthly customer statements also reduces the risk of revenue being recorded before goods are shipped or services are performed because customers are unlikely to recognize an obligation to pay in such a circumstance. Figure 10–1 shows that EarthWear's revenue cycle includes these internal control procedures where applicable.

For each of the controls shown, a corresponding test of control is indicated. For example, the auditor can observe and evaluate the segregation of duties. The auditor can also examine a sample of sales invoices for the presence of an authorized customer order and shipping document for each one. In an IT environment, such as EarthWear's revenue cycle, the auditor can test the application controls to ensure that sales are recorded only after an approved customer order has been entered and the goods shipped.

Completeness of Revenue Transactions

The major misstatement that concerns both management and the auditor is that goods are shipped or services are performed and no revenue is recognized. Failure to recognize revenue means that the customer may not be billed for goods or services and the client does not receive payment. Internal control procedures that ensure that the completeness internal control objective is being met include accounting for the numerical sequence of shipping documents and sales invoices, matching shipping documents with sales invoices, reconciling the sales invoices to the daily sales report, and maintaining and reviewing the open-order file. For example, Earth-Wear (Figure 10–1) reconciles the batch totals of orders entered and provides a reconciliation of the daily shipping listing and the daily sales report. Additionally, the open-order file is reviewed periodically with follow-up on any order older than some predetermined date.

Tests of controls for these internal control procedures are listed in Table 10–5. For example, in a manual system, the auditor could select a sample of bills of lading and trace each one to its respective sales invoice and to the sales journal. If all bills of lading in the sample were matched to sales invoices and included in the sales journal, the auditor would have evidence that all goods shipped are being billed. The auditor could also use a generalized audit software package to print the items in the open-order file that are older than the client's predetermined time frame for completing a transaction. These transactions would then be investigated to determine why the sales were not completed.

Timeliness of Recording of Revenue Transactions

If the client does not have adequate controls to ensure that revenue transactions are recorded on a timely basis, sales may be recorded in the wrong accounting period. The client should require that all shipping documents be forwarded to the billing function daily for timely processing. The auditor can test this control by comparing the date on a bill of lading with the date on the respective sales invoice and the date the sales invoice was recorded in the sales journal. All billing should occur with only a minimum delay. In EarthWear's revenue cycle, the shipping department forwards the approved shipping order to the billing department for entry into the billing program. In such a system, sales should be billed and recorded within one or two days of shipment.

Authorization of Revenue Transactions

Possible misstatements due to improper authorization include shipping goods to or performing services for customers who are bad credit risks and making sales at unauthorized prices or terms. As discussed earlier in this chapter, management should establish procedures for authorizing credit, prices, and terms. Additionally, no goods should be shipped without a properly authorized sales order. Table 10–5 lists a number of tests of controls for this internal control objective. In a computerized revenue cycle such as EarthWear's, the auditor may need to review the application controls and use computer-assisted audit techniques (CAATs) to test the proper authorization of revenue transactions.

Valuation of Revenue Transactions

Valuation is an important internal control objective because revenue transactions that are not properly valued result in misstatements that directly affect the amounts reported in the financial statements. Again, the presence of an authorized price list and terms of trade reduces the risk of improper valuation. There should also be controls that ensure proper verification of the information contained on the sales invoice, including type of goods and quantities shipped, prices, and terms. The sales invoice should also be verified for mathematical accuracy before being sent to the customer. In a manual system, the sales invoice may contain the initials of the client personnel who verified the mathematical accuracy. In an IT application such as EarthWear's, most of these controls would be programmed. For example, the price list is maintained in a master file. However, the client still needs controls to ensure that the authorized price list is updated promptly and that only authorized changes are made to the master file. The auditor can verify the programmed and processing controls by using CAATs.

Classification of Revenue Transactions

For most entities this is not an important internal control objective in the revenue cycle. The use of a chart of accounts and proper codes for recording transactions should provide adequate assurance about this objective. The auditor can review the sales journal and general ledger for proper classification, and can test sales invoices for proper classification by examining programmed controls to ensure that sales invoices are coded by type of product or service.

Posting and Summarization of Revenue Transactions

In any accounting system there is always a possibility that transactions are not properly summarized from source documents or posted properly from journals to the subsidiary and general ledgers. In the revenue cycle, control totals should be utilized to reconcile sales invoices to the daily sales report, and the daily recordings in the sales journal should be reconciled with the posting to the accounts receivable subsidiary ledger. The accounts receivable subsidiary ledger should periodically be reconciled to the general ledger control account. In a properly designed computerized revenue system, such controls are programmed and reconciled by the control groups in the IT Department and the user departments. The auditor can examine and test the programmed controls and various reconciliations. The use of monthly customer statements may also identify posting errors.

Internal Control Procedures and Tests of Controls— Cash Receipts Transactions

[LO 9]   Table 10–6 summarizes the internal control objectives, possible misstatements, internal control procedures, and selected tests of controls for cash receipts transactions. In assessing the control risk for cash receipts transactions, the auditor follows the same decision process as described for revenue transactions. Each of the internal control objectives shown in Table 10–6 is discussed with an emphasis on the control procedures and tests of controls.

Validity of Cash Receipts Transactions

The possible misstatement that concerns the auditor when considering the validity internal control objective is that cash receipts are recorded but not deposited in the client's bank account. In order to commit such a fraud, an employee needs access to both the cash receipts and the accounts receivable records; segregation of duties normally prevents this type of defalcation. Thus, proper segregation of duties between the cash receipts function and the accounts receivable function is one internal control procedure that can prevent such misstatements. Another very strong control that prevents such misstatements is the use of a lockbox system, such as the system used by EarthWear (Figure 10–1). With a lockbox system, the customers' cash receipts are mailed directly to the client's bank, thereby preventing the

TABLE 10–6   Summary of Internal Control Objectives, Possible Misstatements, Internal Control Procedures, and Tests of Controls for Cash Receipts Transactions

Internal Control Objective	Possible Misstatement	Internal Control Procedure	Test of Controls
Validity	Cash receipts recorded but not received or deposited	Segregation of duties	Observation and evaluation of proper segregation of duties
		Use of lockbox system	Inquiry of management about lockbox policy
		Monthly bank reconciliations prepared and independently reviewed	Review of monthly bank reconciliation for indication of independent review
Completeness	Cash receipts stolen or lost before recording	Same control procedures as above	Same tests of controls as above
		Checks restrictively endorsed when received and daily cash list prepared	Observation of the endorsement of checks
		Daily cash receipts reconciled with posting to accounts receivable subsidiary ledger	Testing of the reconciliation of daily cash receipts with posting to accounts receivable subsidiary ledger
		Customer statements prepared on a regular basis; complaints handled independently	Inquiry of client personnel about handling of monthly statements and examination of resolution of complaints
Timeliness	Cash receipts recorded in wrong period	Use of a lockbox system or a control procedure to deposit cash receipts daily	Examination of cash receipts for daily deposit
Authorization	Cash discounts not properly taken	Procedures specifying policies for cash discounts	Testing of a sample of cash receipts transactions for proper cash discounts
Valuation	Cash receipts recorded at incorrect amount	Daily remittance report reconciled to control listing of remittance advices	Review and testing of reconciliation
		Monthly bank statement reconciled and independently reviewed	Examination of monthly bank reconciliation for independent review
Classification	Cash receipts recorded in wrong financial statement account	Chart of accounts	Tracing of cash receipts from listing to cash receipts journal for proper classification
			Review of cash receipts journal for unusual items

(continued)

TABLE 10–6 *(concluded)*

Internal Control Objective	Possible Misstatement	Internal Control Procedure	Test of Controls
Posting and summarization	Cash receipt posted to wrong customer account	Daily remittance report reconciled daily with postings to cash receipts journal and accounts receivable subsidiary ledger	Review and testing of reconciliation; if IT application, testing of programmed controls for posting
		Monthly customer statements with independent review of complaints	Review and testing of client procedures for mailing statements and handling complaints from customers
	Cash receipts not properly posted to general ledger accounts	Monthly cash receipts journal agreed to general ledger posting	Review of posting from cash receipts journal to the general ledger
		Accounts receivable subsidiary ledger reconciled to general ledger control account	Examination of reconciliation of accounts receivable subsidiary ledger to general ledger control account

client's employees from having access to cash. The cash is deposited in the client's account, and the bank forwards the remittance advices and a file of the cash receipts transactions to the client for processing. Finally, preparation of monthly bank reconciliations that are independently reviewed reduces the possibility that cash receipts will be recorded but not deposited. Table 10–6 lists the tests of controls the auditor could conduct to assess the effectiveness of the client's controls over the validity internal control objective.

Completeness of Cash Receipts Transactions

A major misstatement related to the completeness internal control objective is that cash or checks are stolen or lost before being recorded in the cash receipts records. Proper segregation of duties and a lockbox system are strong controls for ensuring that this objective is met. When a lockbox system is not used, checks should be restrictively endorsed when received, and a daily cash listing should be prepared. An additional control is reconciliation of the daily cash receipts with the amounts posted to customers' accounts in the accounts receivable subsidiary ledger. An example of this control is shown in EarthWear's system, where the total of the remittance advices is reconciled with the daily remittance report by the cash receipts department.

In terms of tests of controls, the controls conducted for the validity internal control objective also provide some evidence about completeness. In addition, the auditor can observe the client's personnel endorsing the checks and preparing the cash listing. The reconciliation of the daily cash receipts with the postings to the accounts receivable subsidiary ledger can be tested by the auditor on a sample basis.

When the client does not have adequate segregation of duties or if collusion is suspected, the possibility of defalcation is increased. An employee who has access to both the cash receipts and the accounts receivable records has the ability to steal cash and manipulate the accounting records to hide the misstatement. This is sometimes referred to as *lapping.* When lapping is used, the perpetrator covers the cash shortage by applying cash from one customer's account against another customer's account. For example, suppose customer 1 has a balance of $5,000 and mails a check for $3,000 as payment on the account. A client's employee who has access to both the cash receipts and the accounts receivable records can convert the $3,000 payment to his or her personal use. The theft of the cash can be covered in the following way: The $3,000 payment is not reflected in the customer's account. When a payment is subsequently received from customer 2, the payment is deposited in the client's cash account but applied to customer 1's accounts receivable account. Now the shortage of cash is reflected in customer 2's accounts receivable account. The client employee who stole the cash keeps hiding the theft by shifting the $3,000 difference from one customer's accounts receivable account to another's. If cash is stolen *before* it is recorded as just described, the fraud is difficult and time-consuming for the auditor to detect. If the auditor suspects that this has occurred, the individual cash receipts have to be traced to the customers' accounts receivable accounts to ensure that each cash receipt has been posted to the correct account. If a cash receipt is posted to a different account, this may indicate that someone is applying cash to different accounts to cover a cash shortage. However, if duties are not properly segregated, that person may also be able to hide the theft through use of a credit memorandum, bad-debt write-off, or no recognition of the revenue transaction. For example, the employee could issue a credit memorandum for $3,000 against the customer's accounts receivable account to cover the $3,000 difference.

Timeliness of Recording of Cash Receipts Transactions

If the client uses a lockbox system or if cash is deposited daily in the client's bank, there is a small possibility of cash being recorded in the wrong period. Generally, the auditor has little concern with this type of misstatement because most entities use such internal control procedures.

Authorization of Cash Discounts

Terms of trade generally include discounts for payment within a specified period as a way of encouraging customers to pay on time. Controls in the accounting system should ensure that management's policies concerning cash discounts are followed. For example, the client may establish terms of trade of 2/10, net/30 days. Customers paying within 10 days are then entitled to a 2 percent discount. When the cash is received, client personnel should check to be sure that the customer is complying with the payment terms. The auditor can test this control by examining a sample of cash receipts transactions to determine if the client's cash discount policies are being followed.

Valuation of Cash Transactions

There are several reasons why cash receipts might be recorded at an incorrect amount. For example, the wrong amount could be recorded from the remittance advice, or the receipt could be incorrectly processed during data entry. The controls listed in Table 10–6 provide reasonable assurance that such errors would be detected and corrected. The corresponding tests of controls involve examining and testing the various reconciliations that take place in this part of the revenue cycle.

Classification of Cash Receipts

The auditor seldom has major concerns about cash receipts being recorded in the wrong financial statement account. The major control for preventing cash from being recorded in the wrong account is a chart of accounts. The auditor's concern is with applying appropriate account codes to the individual cash receipts, especially cash receipts from unusual sources such as scrap sales, notes receivable, and proceeds from sales of equipment. The auditor can trace a sample of remittance advices to the cash receipts journal to ensure proper classification. The cash receipts journal can also be reviewed for unusual items.

Posting and Summarization of Cash Receipts Transactions

The major misstatements that can occur for this internal control objective are cash receipts being posted to the wrong customer account or the wrong general ledger account. This last misstatement should not be confused with the misstatement discussed under the classification objective. For the classification objective, the misstatement results from the wrong financial statement accounts being credited in the cash receipts journal. The misstatement related to the posting and summarization objective involves posting to the accounts receivable subsidiary ledger or from the totals in the cash receipts journal to the general ledger accounts.

The use of monthly customer statements provides a check on posting to the correct customer account because a customer who has made a payment and whose monthly statement does not reflect it will complain to the client. The other controls mainly involve the use of various reconciliations that ensure that cash receipts transactions are properly summarized and posted to the general ledger. Tests of controls that may be used by the auditor are presented for each control procedure shown in Table 10–6.

Internal Control Procedures and Tests of Controls— Sales Returns and Allowances Transactions

[LO 9]   For most entities, sales returns and allowances transactions are few and do not represent a material amount in the financial statements. As a result, this text does not cover them in as much detail as revenue or cash receipts transactions. However, credit memoranda that are used to process sales returns and allowances transactions can also be used to cover an unauthorized shipment of goods or conceal a misappropriation of cash.

Two important controls should be present regarding the processing of credit memoranda. First, each credit memorandum should be approved by someone other than the individual who initiated it. This provides proper segregation of duties between access to the customer's record and authorization for issuing a credit memorandum. Second, a credit for returned goods should be supported by a receiving document indicating that the goods have been returned. The auditor can perform tests of controls on credit memoranda by examining a sample of credit memoranda for proper approval and the presence of the respective receiving documents. For a credit memorandum issued for a reason other than a return of goods, approval by an appropriate individual is the critical control. See Exhibit 10–3 for a discussion of the internal control procedures used by EarthWear to control sales returns.

For entities with few or immaterial sales returns and allowances transactions, the auditor may decide only to gain an understanding of how such transactions are processed and not to conduct tests of controls. Analytical procedures (discussed later in this chapter) can then be used to provide sufficient evidence on the fairness of the sales returns and allowances account.

Relating the Assessed Level of Control Risk to Substantive Testing

[LO 10] The results of the auditor's testing of internal control for the revenue cycle directly impact detection risk and therefore the level of substantive testing that will be required for the accounts affected by the cycle. This includes balance sheet accounts such as accounts receivable, allowance for uncollectible accounts, and cash, as well as income statement accounts such as bad-debt expense and sales returns and allowances.

When the results of testing controls support the planned level of control risk, the auditor can conduct substantive tests of these accounts at the planned level. If the results of testing controls indicate that the control risk can be further reduced, the auditor can increase the detection risk. This might lead to a reduction in the amount or the mix of the substantive tests. For example, if the tests of controls indicate that control risk is lower than planned, the auditor might plan to perform more analytical procedures and fewer tests of account balances. However, if the results of the tests of controls do not support the planned level of control risk, the detection risk will have to be set lower. This normally leads to an increase in the amount of substantive testing. For example, if controls for the validity assertion are weaker than planned for revenue transactions, the auditor might increase the number of accounts receivable confirmations mailed to customers.

Auditing Accounts Receivable and Related Accounts

The auditor uses substantive tests to detect material misstatements in accounts receivable and related accounts. Table 10–7 lists the audit objectives for substantive tests of accounts receivable. These same audit objectives apply to other accounts affected by the revenue cycle.

As discussed in Chapter 5, there are three categories of substantive tests: *substantive tests of transactions, analytical procedures,* and *tests of account*

TABLE 10–7	Audit Objectives for Substantive Tests of Accounts Receivable

• *Validity*	Determine whether recorded accounts receivable are valid receivables.
• *Completeness*	Determine whether all accounts receivable are included.
• *Cutoff*	Determine whether all accounts receivable (that is, sales transactions, credit memos) are recorded in the correct period.
• *Ownership*	Determine whether all accounts receivable are owned by the entity.
• *Accuracy*	Determine whether accounts receivable are properly accumulated from journals and ledgers.
• *Valuation*	Determine whether accounts receivable are properly valued in accordance with GAAP.
• *Classification*	Determine whether accounts receivable are properly classified in the financial statements.
• *Disclosure*	Determine whether all disclosures (such as liens or restrictions) related to accounts receivable are included in the financial statements.

balances. Substantive tests of transactions in the revenue cycle focus mainly on the sales and cash receipts transactions that flow through the accounting system. Analytical procedures are used to examine plausible relationships among accounts receivable and related accounts. Tests of account balances concentrate on the detailed amounts or estimates that make up the ending balances for accounts receivable and related accounts.

Substantive Tests of Transactions

[LO 11]   Substantive tests of transactions are tests conducted to detect monetary misstatements in the individual transactions processed through all accounting cycles. As discussed in Chapter 5, the auditor often conducts substantive tests of transactions at the same time as tests of controls. Additionally, it is often difficult to distinguish a substantive test of transactions from a test of controls because the specific audit procedure may both test the operation of an internal control procedure and a test for monetary misstatement. Table 10–8 presents substantive tests of transactions that can be used to test the audit objectives for accounts receivable. Not all audit objectives are tested using substantive tests of transactions. In the case of accounts receivable, it is usually more efficient and effective to test audit objectives such as ownership, classification, and disclosure using tests of account balances.

One audit test procedure, by itself, may not be sufficient to satisfy an audit objective. For example, while the substantive test of transactions listed in Table 10–8 for the valuation audit objective provides evidence on prices and terms, the auditor's primary concern over the valuation of accounts receivable is with the adequacy of the allowance for uncollectible accounts. This is generally tested using a test of account balance.

TABLE 10–8	Examples of Substantive Tests of Transactions for Accounts Receivable

Audit Objective	Substantive Test of Transactions _vouch_
Validity	For a sample of sales transactions recorded in the sales journal, tracing of sales invoices back to customer orders and shipping documents*
Completeness	Tracing of a sample of shipping documents to the details of the sales invoices and to the sales journal and customers' accounts receivable subsidiary ledger
Cutoff	Comparison of the dates on a sample of sales invoices with the dates of shipment and with the dates they were recorded in the sales journal
Valuation	Comparison of prices and terms on a sample of sales invoices with the authorized price list and terms of trade*
Accuracy	Testing of the postings to the sales journal and accounts receivable subsidiary ledger for the correct amounts for a sample of sales transactions

*These are good examples of substantive tests of transactions that serve as dual-purpose tests. See the similar tests of controls shown in Table 10-5 for the validity and valuation internal control objectives. The substantive tests of transactions shown for the completeness, cutoff, and accuracy objectives would also serve as dual-purpose tests.

Analytical Procedures

[LO 12]　Analytical procedures are useful audit tests for examining the fairness of accounts such as sales, accounts receivable, allowance for uncollectible accounts, bad-debt expense, and sales returns and allowances because such tests provide sufficient evidence at low cost. When performed as part of audit planning, analytical procedures can effectively identify accounts that may contain material misstatements. Analytical procedures are also useful as an overall review for the revenue-related accounts. Table 10–9 lists analytical procedures that are useful in auditing accounts receivable and related accounts either at the planning stage or as an overall review.

For example, a comparison of gross profit percentage to previous years' or industry data may provide valuable evidence on unrecorded revenue (an understatement) or fictitious revenue (an overstatement) and related accounts receivable when this ratio is significantly higher or lower than previous years' or industry data. This ratio may also provide information on changes in pricing policies.

The five ratios shown under the "Accounts Receivable" subheading in Table 10–9 provide evidence on whether accounts receivable properly reflect net realizable value. Each ratio aids the auditor in assessing the fairness of the allowance for uncollectible accounts, which in turn affects the fairness of accounts receivable and bad-debt expense. The days outstanding in accounts receivable ratio for EarthWear provides a good example of an analytical procedure that provides strong evidential support for the valuation of accounts receivable. The days outstanding in accounts receivable ratio is 2.85 days for both 1999 and 2000, suggesting that EarthWear collects its accounts receivable quickly. This result is consistent with the

TABLE 10–9 Analytical Procedures for Accounts Receivable and Related Accounts

Analytical Procedure	Possible Misstatement Detected
Revenue	
Comparison of gross profit percentage by product line with previous years and industry data	Unrecorded (understated) revenue
	Fictitious (overstated) revenue
Comparison of reported revenue to budgeted revenue	Changes in pricing policies
	Product-pricing problems
Accounts Receivable, Allowance for Uncollectible Accounts, and Bad-Debt Expense	
Comparison of receivables turnover and days outstanding in accounts receivable to previous years' and/or industry data	Under- or overstatement of allowance for uncollectible accounts and bad-debt expense
Comparison of aging categories on aged trial balance of accounts receivable to previous years	
Comparison of bad-debt expense as a percentage of revenue to previous years' and/or industry data	
Comparison of the allowance for uncollectible accounts as a percentage of accounts receivable or credit sales to previous years' and/or industry data	
Examination of large customer accounts individually and comparison to previous year	
Sales Returns and Allowances and Sales Commissions	
Comparison of sales returns as a percentage of revenue to previous years' or industry data	Under- or overstatement of sales returns
Comparison of sales discounts as a percentage of revenue to previous years' and/or industry data	Under- or overstatement of sales discounts
Estimation of sales commission expense by multiplying net revenue by average commission rate and comparison of recorded sales commission expense	Under- or overstatement of sales commission expense and related accrual

majority of the company's sales being made with credit cards. EarthWear is reimbursed in approximately three days by its credit card providers. Given this result, EarthWear's auditors may do no further audit work on accounts receivable.

Last, comparing the ratio of sales returns or sales discounts to revenue with previous years' and industry data provides the auditor with evidence on whether all sales returns or sales discounts have been recorded. The auditor can also estimate sales commission expense by multiplying the average commission rate by net sales and comparing that amount with recorded commission expense. In many situations, the auditor may be able to accept the sales returns, sales discounts, and sales commission expense as fairly presented without conducting any additional substantive tests if such analytical procedures produce results that are consistent with the auditor's expectations.

TABLE 10–10	Summary of Audit Objectives and Tests of Account Balances—Accounts Receivable, Allowance for Uncollectible Accounts, and Bad-Debt Expense

Audit Objective	Tests of Account Balances
Validity	Confirmation of selected accounts receivable
	Performance of alternative procedures for accounts receivable confirmation exceptions and nonresponses
Completeness	Obtaining of aged trial balance of accounts receivable and agreeing of total to general ledger
	Review of results of testing the completeness objective for assessing control risk; tracing of shipping documents into sales journal and to accounts receivable subsidiary ledger if such testing was not performed as a test of controls
Cutoff	Examination of a sample of sales invoices and shipping documents for a few days before and after year-end for recording sales in proper period
	Performance of analytical procedures for reasonableness of sales returns cutoff or examination of a sample of receiving documents for a few days before and after year-end for recording sales returns in proper period
Ownership	Review of bank confirmations for any liens on receivables
	Inquiry of management, review of any loan agreements, and review of board of directors' minutes for any indication that accounts receivables have been sold
Accuracy	Obtaining of an aged trial balance of accounts receivable and agreeing of total to general ledger control account
	Tracing of selected items from the aged trial balance to the subsidiary records and sales invoices for proper amount and aging
	Obtaining of an analysis of the allowance for uncollectible accounts and bad-debt expense; tracing of totals to general ledger and individual items to subsidiary records
Valuation	Examination of the results of the confirmations of selected accounts receivable
	Examination of the adequacy of the allowance for uncollectible accounts
Classification	Review of aged trial balance for material credits, long-term receivables, and nontrade receivables
Disclosure	Inquiry about related-party receivables and assurance that they are properly disclosed
	Review of receivables for any accounts that have been pledged, assigned, or discounted

Tests of Account Balances

[LO 13]   Table 10–10 summarizes the audit objectives and tests of account balances for accounts receivable, the allowance for uncollectible accounts, and bad-debt expense. Accuracy is discussed first because the auditor must establish that the detailed records that support the account to be audited agree with the general ledger account.

Accuracy   The amounts contained in the financial statements are derived from the general ledger balances. To test the fairness of a financial statement amount, the auditor tests the general ledger account by examining the amounts or estimates that compose the balance. For many accounts, the general ledger balance is supported by a subsidiary ledger or listing of the

EXHIBIT 10–4

Example of an Aged Trial Balance of Accounts Receivable Working Paper

		CALABRO PAGING SERVICES **Aged Trial Balance—Accounts Receivable** **12/31/00**			**E10** **DLJ** **2/15/2001**
Customer Name	Total	<30 Days	30–60 Days	60–90 Days	>90 Days
Abbott Construction	$ 10,945¥	$ 9,542	$ 1,403		
Acton Labs	9,705		5,205	$ 4,500	
•	•	•	•	•	•
•	•	•	•	•	•
•	•	•	•	•	•
Wright Industries	29,875¥	18,875	11,000		
Zorcon, Inc.	4,340				$ 4,340
Total	$3,717,900	$2,044,895	$1,301,215	$260,253	$111,537
	F T/B	F	F	F	F

F = Footed.
T/B = Agreed to trial balance.
 ¥ = Customer account traced to subsidiary ledger; agreed to total and proper aging tested.

details that make up the balance. Normally, the auditor performs a number of accuracy tests on the subsidiary ledger or listing before conducting other tests of the account balance.

This process is followed when accounts receivable are audited. For example, the auditor agrees the accounts receivable subsidiary ledger of customer accounts to the general ledger accounts receivable (control) account. This is typically accomplished by obtaining a copy of the aged trial balance of accounts receivable and comparing the total balance with the general ledger accounts receivable account balance. Exhibit 10–4 presents an aged trial balance of accounts receivable working paper for Calabro Paging Services (see Problem 3-41). An aged trial balance of the subsidiary ledger is used because the auditor will need this type of data to examine the allowance for uncollectible accounts.

The auditor must also have assurance that the detail making up the aged trial balance is accurate. This can be accomplished in a number of ways. One approach involves mainly manual audit procedures. First, the aged trial balance is footed and crossfooted. *Footing* and *crossfooting* mean that each column of the trial balance is added, and the column totals are then added to ensure that they agree with the total balance for the account. Then a sample of customer accounts included in the aged trial balance is selected for testing. For each selected customer account, the auditor traces the customer's balance back to the subsidiary ledger detail and verifies the total amount and the amounts included in each column for proper aging. A second approach might involve the use of computer-assisted audit techniques. If the general controls over IT are adequate, the auditor can use a generalized audit software package to examine the accuracy of the aged trial balance generated by the client's accounting system.

Validity

The validity of accounts receivable is one of the more important audit objectives because the auditor wants assurance that this account balance is not overstated through the inclusion of fictitious customer accounts or amounts. The major audit procedure for testing the validity objective for accounts receivable is confirmation of customers' account balances. If a customer does not respond to the auditor's confirmation request, additional audit procedures may be necessary. The confirmation process is discussed later in this chapter.

Completeness

The auditor's concern with completeness is whether all accounts receivable have been included in the accounts receivable subsidiary ledger and the general ledger accounts receivable account. The reconciliation of the aged trial balance to the general ledger account should detect an omission of a receivable from *either* the accounts receivable subsidiary ledger or the general ledger account. If the client's accounting system contains proper control totals and reconciliations, such errors should be detected and corrected by the relevant internal control procedures. For example, in Earth-Wear's revenue cycle (Figure 10–1), control totals exist for daily shipping and billing. Personnel in the billing department would be responsible for reconciling the two totals. If such control procedures do not exist in a client's accounting system, or if they are not operating effectively, the auditor will have to trace a sample of shipping documents to sales invoices, the sales journal, and the accounts receivable subsidiary ledger to ensure that the transactions were included in the accounting records. Note that this step is listed in Tables 10–8 and 10–10.

Cutoff

The cutoff objective attempts to determine whether all sales transactions and related accounts receivable are recorded in the proper period. On most audits, sales cutoff is coordinated with inventory cutoff because the shipment of goods normally indicates that the earnings process is complete. The auditor wants assurance that if goods have been shipped in the current period, the resulting sale has been recorded, and also that if the sales have been recorded, the corresponding inventory has been removed from the accounting records. In addition, the auditor needs to determine if there is proper cutoff for sales returns.

Sales Cutoff If there is not a proper cutoff of sales transactions, both revenue and accounts receivable will be misstated for the current and following years. In most instances, errors related to sales cutoff are unintentional and are due to delays in recognizing the shipment of goods or the recognition of the sale. In other instances, the client may intentionally fail to recognize sales transactions in the current period or may recognize sales from the next period in the current period (see Exhibit 10–5). The first situation can occur by the sales transactions not being recorded in

EXHIBIT 10–5

Sunbeam Corporation Restates Financial Results

Sunbeam Corporation restated its financial results for 1996, 1997, and the first quarter of 1998 based on an extensive audit by its audit committee and two public accounting firms. The special audit found that the previously issued financial statements overstated the loss for 1996, overstated profits for 1997, and understated the loss for the first quarter of 1998. Sunbeam reported that, for certain periods, revenue was incorrectly recognized in the wrong period, partly because of the company's "bill and hold" practice of billing customers in the current period for products that were delivered in a later period. The company also booked a significant amount of sales that were made to customers under such liberal terms that they did not constitute valid sales at all, but rather appeared to be consignments or guaranteed sales. In 1997 revenue was restated from $1,186 million to $1,073 million, and earnings were reduced from $123.1 million to $52.3 million. The reporting of these financial irregularities led to the resignation of Sunbeam's CEO, Al Dunlap.

Sources: J. R. Liang, "Dangerous Games: Did "Chainsaw Al" Dunlap Manufacture Sunbeam's Earnings Last Year?" *Barron's* (June 8, 1998), pp. 17–19; M. Brannigan, "Sunbeam Audit to Repudiate '97 Turnaround," *The Wall Street Journal* (October 20, 1998), p. A3; and "Sunbeam to Restate Financial Results; Discloses Adjustments for 1996, 1997, and First Quarter 1998," *The PointCast Network* (October 20, 1998).

the sales journal until the next period. For example, sales that take place on the last two days of the current year are recorded as sales in the next year by delaying entry until the current-year sales journal is closed. The second situation is generally accomplished by leaving the sales journal "open" and recognizing sales from the first few days of the next period as current-period sales.

The client's accounting system should have controls that ensure timely recording of sales transactions. The results of tests of controls, if performed, should provide evidence on the timeliness internal control objective. Additionally, the client should have end-of-period internal control procedures for ensuring a proper sales cutoff between accounting periods.

The test of sales cutoff is straightforward. The auditor first identifies the number of the last shipping document issued in the current period. Then a sample of sales invoices and their related shipping documents is selected for a few days just prior to, and subsequent to, the end of the period. Assuming that sales are recorded at the time of shipment (FOB–shipping point), sales invoices representing goods shipped prior to year-end should be recorded in the current period, and invoices for goods shipped subsequent to year-end should be recorded as sales in the next period. Any transaction recorded in the wrong period should be corrected by the client. For example, suppose the last shipping document issued in the current period was numbered 10,540. None of the recorded sales transactions sampled from a few days prior to year-end should have related shipping document numbers higher than 10,540, and none of the sampled sales transactions recorded in the first few days of the subsequent period should have related shipping document numbers lower than 10,540. In a computerized system such tests are still necessary because a delay in entering data may occur, or management may manipulate the recognition of the transactions.

Sales Returns Cutoff   The processing of sales returns may differ across entities. When sales returns are not material, or if they occur regularly, the entity may recognize a sales return at the time the goods are returned. However, for entities like EarthWear, sales returns may represent a material amount or may occur irregularly. In this instance, the client may estimate an allowance for sales returns. When sales returns represent a material amount, the auditor needs to test for proper cutoff.

Analytical procedures may be used to test cutoff for sales returns. The ratio of sales returns to sales may indicate to the auditor that sales returns are consistent with expectations and therefore that the sales returns cutoff is adequate. If the auditor decides to conduct more detailed tests, the receiving documents used to acknowledge receipt of the returned goods must be examined. Using procedures similar to those for testing sales cutoff, the auditor selects a sample of receiving documents for a few days prior to and subsequent to the end of the period. The receiving documents are traced to the related credit memoranda. Sales returns recorded in the wrong period should be corrected, if material.

Ownership

The auditor must determine whether the accounts receivable are owned by the entity because accounts receivable that have been sold should not be included in the entity's financial statements. For most audit engagements, this does not represent a problem because the client owns all the receivables. However, in some instances a client may sell its accounts receivable. The auditor can detect such an action by reviewing bank confirmations, cash receipts for payments from organizations that factor accounts receivable, or corporate minutes for authorization of the sale or assignment of receivables.

Valuation

Two major valuation issues are related to accounts receivable. The first issue relates to the valuation of the revenue and cash receipts transactions that make up the details of the gross amount of accounts receivable. The concern here is with the quantity and pricing of the items included on the sales invoices and the proper recording of cash received, including any discounts. This affects the gross amount of accounts receivable as well as sales. Tests of controls and substantive tests of transactions normally provide evidence about these types of pricing errors. Pricing errors, especially when the customer has been overcharged or proper payment has not been recorded, may also be detected via confirmations.

The second valuation issue relates to the net realizable value of accounts receivable. The auditor is concerned with determining that the allowance for uncollectible accounts, and thus bad-debt expense, is fairly stated. The allowance for uncollectible accounts is affected by internal factors such as the client's credit-granting and cash collection policies and external factors such as the state of the economy, conditions in the client's industry, and the financial strength of the client's customers.

In verifying the adequacy of the allowance for uncollectible accounts, the auditor starts by assessing the client's policies for granting credit and collecting cash. If the client establishes strict standards for granting credit, the likelihood of a large number of bad debts is reduced. Generally, the auditor assesses the adequacy of the allowance account by first examining the aged trial balance for amounts that have been outstanding for a long time. The probability of collecting these accounts can be assessed by discussing them with the credit manager, examining the customers' financial statements, obtaining credit reports (such as, from Dun & Bradstreet), or reviewing the customers' communications with the client related to payment.

The second step in assessing the adequacy of the allowance account involves examining the client's prior experience with bad debts. The problem with examining only delinquent accounts is that no consideration is given to accounts that are current but that may result in bad debts. By maintaining good statistics on bad debts, the client can determine what percentage of each aging category will become uncollectible. The auditor can test these percentages for reasonableness. Following is an example of how this approach would work.

Suppose Calabro Paging Services developed the following historical data on bad debts:

Aging Category	Percentage as Bad Debts
<30 days	.001
30–60 days	.025
60–90 days	.14
>90 days	.55

The allowance for uncollectible accounts can be determined in the following manner, using the data from Exhibit 10–4:

<30 days	30–60 days	60–90 days	>90 days	Total
$2,044,895	$1,301,215	$260,253	$111,537	$3,717,900
× .001	× .025	× .14	× .55	
$ 2,045	$ 32,530	$ 36,435	$ 61,345	$ 132,355

The balance in the allowance for doubtful accounts on Calabro's general ledger is $135,300 and appears reasonable, given the auditor's calculation of $132,355. While determining the proper amount for the allowance for uncollectible accounts may seem relatively straightforward, considerable judgment on the part of the auditor is involved. As mentioned, the auditor must evaluate the collectibility of individual problem accounts and consider whether the historically derived percentages are reasonable, given the current economic and industry conditions.

Classification

The major issues related to the classification objective are (1) identifying and reclassifying any material credits contained in accounts receivable, (2) segregating short-term and long-term receivables, and (3) ensuring that different types of receivables are properly classified. In many entities, when a customer pays in advance or a credit is issued, the amount is credited to the customer's accounts receivable account. The auditor should determine the amount of such credits and, if material, reclassify them as either a deposit or another type of liability. The second issue requires that the auditor identify and separate short-term receivables from long-term receivables. Long-term receivables should not be included with trade accounts receivable. The auditor must also ensure that nontrade receivables are properly separated from trade accounts receivable. For example, receivables from officers, employees, or related parties should not be included with trade accounts receivable because users might be misled if such receivables are combined. The last two issues are also related to the disclosure audit objective.

Disclosure

Disclosure is an important audit objective for accounts receivable and related accounts. While management is responsible for the financial statements, the auditor must ensure that all necessary disclosures are made. Most public accounting firms use some type of financial statement reporting checklist to ensure that all necessary disclosures are made for each account. Table 10–11 presents some examples of disclosure items for the revenue cycle and related financial statement accounts. Exhibit 10–6 presents two examples of common disclosures for revenue-related accounts. The

---

TABLE 10–11   Example Disclosure Items for the Revenue Cycle and Related Accounts

- Revenue recognition basis.
- Revenues recognized under the percentage-of-completion method.
- Long-term sales contracts.
- Revenues by reportable segment of the business.
- Revenues and receivables from related parties.
- Receivables by type (trade, officer, employee, affiliate, and so on).
- Short- and long-term receivables.
- Pledged or discounted receivables.

EXHIBIT 10–6

Sample Disclosures for Revenue Recognition and Related-Party Transactions

Revenue Recognition
Sales are recognized when the company's products are shipped. Sales to customers with whom the company has reciprocal purchase agreements are accounted for in the same manner as intercompany transactions and are eliminated in the financial statements.

Related-Party Transactions
The company's chairman of the board is also chairman of the board of Dayco Industries. Net sales to Dayco were $990,000 and $1,244,000 for the two years ended 2000 and 1999. Accounts receivable from Dayco were $243,000 and $489,000 at December 31, 2000 and 1999, respectively. The company believes that the terms of sale were substantially the same as those available to unrelated parties for similar products.

first disclosure relates to the basis for recognizing revenue. This disclosure is normally included in a footnote that describes significant accounting policies. The second example presents disclosure of related-party transactions. Disclosures about related-party transactions normally discuss the nature of the transactions, the amounts, and whether the transactions were similar in terms to those for unrelated parties.

The Confirmation Process—Accounts Receivable[1]

[LO 14]   Confirmation is the process of obtaining and evaluating a direct communication provided by a third party in response to an auditor's request for information about a particular item affecting financial statement assertions (AU 330). Confirmation of accounts receivable is considered a generally accepted auditing procedure (AU 330.34), and therefore auditors normally request confirmation of accounts receivable during an audit. However, auditing standards allow the auditor to omit confirming accounts receivable in the following circumstances:

- The accounts receivable are immaterial to the financial statements.
- The use of confirmations would not be effective as an audit procedure. (This might occur if, based on prior experience, the auditor determines that the response rate might be low or the responses might not be reliable.)
- The auditor's assessment of inherent risk and control risk is low, and evidence gathered from other substantive tests is sufficient to reduce audit risk to an acceptably low level.

Because of the importance of accounts receivable confirmations, the auditor should document completely the decision not to gather such evidence.

Confirmations can address more than one audit objective. However, confirmations normally provide different levels of assurance for different audit objectives. Accounts receivable confirmations are generally a good source of evidence for testing the validity objective. If the customer confirms the amount owed to the client, the auditor has competent evidence that the account receivable is valid.[2] Accounts receivable confirmations may also provide evidence on the completeness, cutoff, and valuation objectives. For example, a customer's confirmation of the dollar amount owed provides some evidence on the valuation objective.

A number of factors affect the reliability of accounts receivable confirmations. The auditor should consider each of the following factors when using confirmations to test accounts receivable:

---

[1]See D. K. McConnell, Jr., and G. Y. Banks, "A Common Peer Review Problem," *Journal of Accountancy* (June 1998), pp. 39–44, for a discussion of deficiencies identified by the AICPA's practice-monitoring division in the use of accounts receivable confirmations by auditors.

[2]Research has shown that accounts receivable confirmations are not always a reliable source of evidence. See P. Caster, "An Empirical Study of Accounts Receivable Confirmations as Audit Evidence," *Auditing: A Journal of Practice and Theory* (Fall 1990), pp. 75–91, and P. Caster, "The Role of Confirmations as Audit Evidence," *Journal of Accountancy* (February 1992), pp. 73–76, for a discussion of these findings.

- The type of confirmation request.
- Prior experience with the client or similar engagements.
- The intended respondent.

The types of confirmations are discussed in the next section. The auditor should consider prior experience with the client in terms of confirmation response rates, misstatements identified, and the accuracy of returned confirmations when assessing the reliability of accounts receivable confirmations. For example, if response rates were low in prior audits, the auditor might consider obtaining evidence using alternative procedures. The intended respondents to accounts receivable confirmations may vary from individuals with little accounting knowledge to large corporations with highly qualified accounting personnel. The auditor should consider each respondent's competence, knowledge, ability, and objectivity when assessing the reliability of confirmation requests. For example, if an auditor is confirming accounts receivable for a small retail organization, it is possible that the respondents may not have the knowledge or ability to respond appropriately to the confirmation request. On the other hand, if confirmations are sent to medium-size or large corporations with well-controlled accounts payable systems, the information received in response to such confirmation requests is likely to be reliable. However, some large organizations and government agencies do not respond to confirmations because it may be difficult to accumulate the necessary data since they are on a voucher system. Such nonresponses must be tested using procedures discussed later in the chapter.

Types of Confirmations

There are two types of confirmations: *positive* and *negative.* A positive accounts receivable confirmation requests that customers indicate whether they agree with the amount due to the client stated in the confirmation. Thus, a response is required regardless of whether the customer believes the amount is correct or incorrect. Sometimes an auditor will use a "blank" form of positive confirmation, in which the request requires the customer to provide the amount owed to the client. Positive confirmations are generally used when an account's individual balances are large or if errors are anticipated because the control risk has been judged to be high. Exhibit 10–7 presents an example of a positive confirmation request.

A negative confirmation requests that customers respond only when they disagree with the amount due to the client. An example of a negative confirmation request is shown in Exhibit 10–8. Negative confirmation requests are used when there are many accounts with small balances, control risk is assessed to be low, and the auditor believes that the customers will devote adequate attention to the confirmation. On many audit engagements, a combination of positive and negative confirmations is used to test accounts receivable because of materiality considerations and a mix of customers. For example, positive confirmations may be sent to selected large-dollar customer accounts and negative confirmations sent to a sample of small-dollar customer accounts.

Because positive accounts receivable confirmations require that customers respond to the auditor, any amounts for which responses are not received must be verified by the auditor using alternative procedures. Negative accounts receivable confirmations require a response only when the

EXHIBIT 10–7

Example of a Positive Confirmation Request

CPS   **CALABRO PAGING SERVICES**

Wright Industries
8440 S.W. 97 Boulevard
Starke, FL 32690

Dear Customers:

Please examine the accompanying statement carefully and either confirm its correctness or report any differences to our auditors

> Abbott & Johnson, LLP
> P.O. Box 669
> Tampa, FL 32691

who are auditing our financial statements.
    Your prompt attention to this request will be appreciated. An envelope is enclosed for your reply. Please do not send your payments to the auditors.

Sincerely,
Jan Rodriguez
Controller, Calabro Paging Services

Confirmation:

The balance receivable from us for $29,875 as of December 31, 2000, is correct except as noted below:

_____

_____

_____

Wright Industries

Date _____   By _____

---

information about the customer's balance is incorrect. Therefore, a nonresponse to a negative confirmation request is generally assumed to represent a valid accounts receivable. This can be a major drawback to the use of negative confirmations.

    The accuracy of the accounts receivable confirmation request can generally be improved if a copy of the customer's monthly statement is enclosed with the confirmation request.

Timing

Accounts receivable may be confirmed at an interim date or at year-end. Such considerations were discussed in Chapter 6. The confirmation request should be sent soon after the end of the accounting period in order to maximize the response rate. Sending the confirmations at the end of the accounting period reduces the chance of timing differences arising due to processing of purchases and cash disbursements by the customers.

EXHIBIT 10–8

Example of a Negative Confirmation Request

CPS

CALABRO PAGING SERVICES

Zorcon, Inc.
P.O. Box 1429
Melrose, FL 32692-1429

Dear Customers:

Please examine the accompanying statement carefully. If it does NOT agree with your records, please report any differences directly to our auditors

> Abbott & Johnson, LLP
> P.O. Box 669
> Tampa, FL 32691

who are auditing our financial statements.
 Your prompt attention to this request will be appreciated. An envelope is enclosed for your reply. Please do not send your payments to the auditors.

Sincerely,

Jan Rodriguez
Controller, Calabro Paging Services

Confirmation Procedures

The auditor must maintain control over the accounts receivable confirmations so as to minimize the possibility that direct communication between the customers and the auditor is biased by interception or alteration of the receivable confirmation by the client. For control purposes, the auditor should mail the confirmations outside the client's facilities. Direct mailing from the CPA's office generally provides the best control. To ensure that any confirmations that are undeliverable by the post office are returned to the auditors and not the client, the confirmations should be mailed in envelopes with the CPA firm's address listed as the return address. The envelope used by customers for returning the confirmation response should also be addressed to the CPA firm.[3] The fact that undeliverable confirmations are returned directly to the auditor also provides some assurance that fictitious customers are identified.

 The auditor should maintain a record of the confirmations mailed and those returned. When positive confirmations are used, the auditor generally follows up with second, and possibly third, requests to customers who do not reply, in an attempt to increase the response rate to the confirmation requests. In some cases, a customer may respond using electronic

---

[3]R. H. Ashton and R. E. Hylas, "The Return of 'Problem' Confirmation Requests by the US Postal Service," *The Accounting Review* (October 1980), pp. 275–85, shows that the US Postal Service does an excellent job of returning undeliverable confirmations to the return address.

media (such as e-mail or fax) or orally. In such situations the auditor should verify the source and contents of the communication. For example, a fax response may be verified by a telephone call to the respondent, and an oral response can be verified by requesting a written communication from the respondent.

Each confirmation exception (that is, difference between the recorded balance and the balance confirmed by the customer) should be carefully examined by the auditor to determine the reason for the difference. In many cases, exceptions result from what are referred to as *timing differences.* Such differences occur because of delays in recording transactions in either the client's or the customer's records. For example, the client may ship goods to a customer on the last day of the period and record it as a current-period sale. The customer will probably receive and record the goods as a purchase in the next period. Such situations are not errors and result only because of a delay in recording the transaction. Payment for goods by a customer at the end of the period can result in a timing difference if the customer prepares and records the check in the current period but the client receives and records the check in the following period. Again, the difference in the confirmed amount results from a timing difference. Table 10–12 presents some examples of exceptions and their potential causes.

The need to maintain control over accounts receivable confirmations and responses does not preclude the use of internal auditors in the confirmation process. For example, internal auditors may confirm accounts receivable as part of their normal duties, or they may directly assist the auditor in performing accounts receivable confirmations as part of the annual audit

TABLE 10–12	**Examples of Exceptions to Confirmation Requests**
Type of Difference	*Potential Cause*
Goods not received by customer	Timing difference
	Goods delivered to wrong customer
	Invoice sent to wrong customer
	Fictitious sale
Payment not recorded in client's records	Timing difference
	Payment applied to wrong customer account
	Cash misappropriated
Goods returned for credit by customer	Timing difference
Processing error	Incorrect quantity or price
	Recording error
Amount in dispute	Price of goods in dispute
	Goods do not meet specifications
	Goods damaged in transit

(AU 322). If internal auditors are used in this capacity, their work should be supervised, reviewed, evaluated, and tested by the independent auditor.

Alternative Procedures

When the auditor does not receive responses to positive confirmations, he or she must apply alternative procedures to determine the validity and valuation of the accounts receivable. Auditors normally send second and third requests; they also perform the following alternative audit procedures:

- Examination of subsequent cash receipts.
- Examination of customer orders, shipping documents, and duplicate sales invoices.
- Examination of other client documentation.

Examination of subsequent cash receipts involves checking the accounts receivable subsidiary ledger for payments of the specific sales invoices included in the customers' accounts receivable balances that were outstanding at the date of the confirmation. If the client has strong controls for recording cash receipts, the auditor may stop at this point. If the client's controls are weak, the auditor may extend the testing by tracing the payment in the subsidiary ledger to the cash receipts journal and to the bank statement. If the customer has paid for the goods, the auditor has strong evidence concerning the validity and valuation of the accounts receivable.

If a customer has not paid the account receivable, the auditor can examine the underlying documentation that supports the sales transaction. This documentation includes the original customer order, shipping document, and duplicate sales invoice. If this documentation indicates that the customer ordered the goods and the goods were shipped, then the auditor would have evidence supporting the validity of the accounts receivable. Last, the auditor may need to examine other correspondence between the client and the customer to obtain adequate evidence on the validity and valuation of the accounts receivable.

Auditing Other Receivables

[LO 15] Up to this point the discussion has concentrated on trade accounts receivable. Most entities, however, have other types of receivables that are reported on the balance sheet. Some examples include

- Receivables from officers and employees.
- Receivables from related parties.
- Notes receivable.

The auditor's concern with satisfying the eight audit objectives for these receivables is similar to that for trade accounts receivable. Typically, each of these types of receivables is confirmed and evaluated for collectibility. The transactions that result in receivables from related parties are examined to determine if they were at "arm's length." Notes receivable would also be confirmed and examined for repayment terms and whether interest income has been properly recognized.

Evaluating the Audit Findings—Accounts Receivable and Related Accounts

[LO 16]   When the auditor has completed the planned substantive tests, the likely misstatement (the projected misstatement plus an allowance for sampling risk) for accounts receivable is determined using either statistical or non-statistical sampling techniques. The likely misstatement is then compared to the tolerable misstatement allocated to the account. If the likely misstatement is less than the tolerable misstatement, the auditor may accept the account as fairly presented. Conversely, if the likely misstatement exceeds the tolerable misstatement, the auditor may conclude that the account is not fairly presented. For example, in Chapter 3 (Exhibit 3–4), a tolerable misstatement of $45,000 was allocated to EarthWear's net accounts receivable balance of $3,933,000. Suppose that, after completing the substantive tests, EarthWear's auditor determines that the likely misstatement is $20,000. In this case, the auditor may conclude that EarthWear's accounts receivable are not materially misstated. However, if the likely misstatement is $60,000, the auditor's conclusion will be that the account is materially misstated.

The auditor should also analyze the misstatements discovered through substantive tests of transactions, analytical procedures, and tests of account balances. In some instances, these misstatements may provide additional evidence on control risk. By identifying the causes of the misstatements, the auditor may determine that the original assessment of control risk was too low. For example, the auditor may lower his or her evaluation of the effectiveness of the control for granting credit (that is, may increase control risk) based on a large number of misstatements detected during tests of the allowance for uncollectible accounts. This may impact the auditor's assessment of audit risk.

If the auditor concludes that audit risk is unacceptably high, additional audit procedures should be performed, the client should adjust the related financial statement accounts to an acceptable level, or a qualified report should be issued. In the previous example, in which EarthWear's auditor determined that the likely misstatement was $60,000, additional audit procedures might be required. Such audit procedures would typically be directed at the *systematic* errors detected by the substantive tests. For example, if the substantive tests of transactions indicated that sales invoices were priced incorrectly, the auditor's additional audit procedures would focus on determining the extent of pricing misstatements. Alternatively, the auditor could conclude that accounts receivable are fairly presented if EarthWear's management adjusts the financial statements by $15,000 or more ($60,000 – $45,000). This would result in the likely misstatement being equal to or less than the tolerable misstatement of $45,000.

In summary, the final decision about accounts receivable and the related accounts is based on whether sufficient competent evidence has been obtained from the substantive tests conducted.

REVIEW QUESTIONS

[LO 1]   10-1   Accounting standards require that revenue must be earned and realized before it can be recognized. Discuss what is meant by the terms *earned* and *realized*.

[5,6,9]   10-2   Describe the credit function's duties for monitoring customer payments and handling bad debts.

[5,6,9]   10-3   Describe how the collection function should be controlled when a lockbox system is not utilized.

[8]   10-4   In understanding the accounting system in the revenue cycle, the auditor typically performs a walk-through to gain knowledge of the system. What knowledge should the auditor try to obtain about the accounting system?

[9]   10-5   Identify three tests of controls that could be performed using CAATs for revenue transactions.

[6,9]   10-6   When a client does not adequately segregate duties, the possibility of cash being stolen before it is recorded is increased. If the auditor suspects that this type of defalcation is possible, what type of audit procedures can he or she use to test this possibility?

[7]   10-7   The auditor needs to understand how selected inherent risk factors affect the transactions processed by the revenue cycle. Discuss the potential effect that industry-related factors and misstatements detected in prior periods have on the inherent risk assessment of the revenue cycle.

[9]   10-8   What are the two major controls for sales returns and allowances transactions?

[11,12,13]   10-9   What are the three types of substantive tests? Define each type.

[12]   10-10   List four analytical procedures that can be used to test revenue-related accounts. What potential misstatements are indicated by each of these analytical procedures?

[13]   10-11   Describe how the auditor verifies the accuracy of the aged trial balance.

[13]   10-12   What are the two major issues related to the valuation of accounts receivable?

[13]   10-13   Describe how the auditor tests the adequacy of the allowance for uncollectible accounts. Why is examination of only the delinquent accounts typically not adequate for assessing the adequacy of the allowance for uncollectible accounts?

[13]   10-14   Describe how the auditor tests sales cutoff. Why would a test of sales cutoff typically be coordinated with the test of inventory cutoff?

[14]   10-15   List and discuss the three factors mentioned in the chapter that may affect the reliability of confirmations of accounts receivable.

[14]   10-16   Distinguish between positive and negative confirmations. Under what circumstances would positive confirmations be more appropriate than negative confirmations?

[14]   10-17   What is meant by a *timing difference* when a confirmation exception is noted? Provide two examples.

[15]   10-18   Identify three other types of receivables the auditor should examine. What audit procedures would typically be used to audit other
receivables?

MULTIPLE-CHOICE QUESTIONS FROM CPA EXAMINATIONS

[2,9]   10-19   Mill Company uses a batch-processing method to process its sales
transactions. The data on Mill's sales transaction file are electronically sorted by customer number and are subjected to programmed
edit checks when the company's invoices, sales journals, and updated customer account balances are prepared. One of the direct
outputs of the creation of this file most likely would be a
a. Report showing exceptions and control totals.
b. Printout of the updated inventory records.
c. Report showing overdue accounts receivable.
d. Printout of the sales price master file.

[2,9]   10-20   The completeness of IT-generated sales figures can be tested by
comparing the number of items listed on the daily sales report with
the number of items billed on the actual invoices. This process uses
a. Check digits.
b. Control totals.
c. Validity tests.
d. Process-tracing data.

[6,9]   10-21   For the internal control procedures to be effective, employees
maintaining the accounts receivable subsidiary ledger should *not*
also approve
a. Employee overtime wages.
b. Credit granted to customers.
c. Write-offs of customer accounts.
d. Cash disbursements.

[2,9]   10-22   An auditor selects a sample from the file of shipping documents to
determine whether invoices were prepared. This test is performed
to satisfy the audit objective of
a. Accuracy.
b. Completeness.
c. Control.
d. Existence.

[2,9]   10-23   Which of the following controls is most likely to help ensure that
all credit sales transactions of an entity are recorded?
a. The billing department supervisor sends a copy of each approved
sales order to the credit department for comparison to the customer's authorized credit limit and current account balance.
b. The accounting department supervisor independently reconciles
the accounts receivable subsidiary ledger to the accounts receivable control account each month.
c. The accounting department supervisor controls the mailing of
monthly statements to customers and investigates any differences reported by customers.
d. The billing department supervisor matches prenumbered shipping documents with entries in the sales journal.

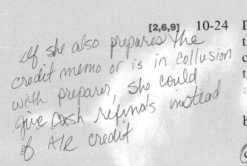

If she also prepares the credit memo or is in collusion with preparer, she could give cash refunds instead of A/R credit

[2,6,9]   **10-24**   During a review of a small business client's internal control system, the auditor discovered that the accounts receivable clerk <u>approves</u> credit memos and has <u>access to cash.</u> Which of the following controls would be most effective in offsetting this weakness?

    a. The owner reviews errors in billings to customers and postings to the subsidiary ledger.

    b. The controller receives the monthly bank statement directly and reconciles the checking accounts. ✗

    ⓒ The owner reviews credit memos after they are recorded.

    d. The controller reconciles the total of the detailed accounts receivable accounts to the amount shown in the ledger. ✗

[2,6,9]   **10-25**   Cash receipts from sales <u>on account</u> have been misappropriated. Which of the following acts would conceal this defalcation and be *least* likely to be detected by an auditor?

    ⓐ Understating the sales journal. *(CR A/R, DR Sales)* *these are reconciled*

    b. Overstating the accounts receivable control account.

    c. Overstating the accounts receivable subsidiary ledger.

Would find in A/R conf.   d. Understating the cash receipts journal. *(not recording at all)*

[2,6,9]   **10-26**   An auditor would consider a cashier's job description to contain compatible duties if the cashier receives remittances from the mailroom and also prepares

    a. The prelisting of individual checks. *(done in mailroom)*

    b. The monthly bank reconciliation. *(independent)*

    ⓒ The daily deposit slip.

    d. Remittance advices. ✗

[2,6,9]   **10-27**   Which of the following internal controls would be most likely to deter the <u>lapping</u> of collections from customers?

    a. Independent internal verification of dates of entry in the cash receipts journal with dates of daily cash summaries. ✗

    b. Authorization of write-offs of uncollectible accounts by a supervisor independent of the credit approval function. ✗

    ⓒ Segregation of duties between receiving cash and posting the accounts receivable ledger.

    d. Supervisory comparison of the daily cash summary with the sum of the cash receipts journal entries. ✗

[9,10]   **10-28**   Smith Corporation has numerous customers. A customer file is kept on disk. Each customer file contains a name, an address, a credit limit, and an account balance. The auditor wishes to test this file to determine whether credit limits are being exceeded. The best procedure for the auditor to follow would be to

    a. Develop test data that would cause some account balances to exceed the credit limit and determine if the system properly detects such situations. *Too hard*

    ⓑ Develop a program to compare credit limits with account balances and print out the details of any account with a balance exceeding its credit limit. *easy*

    c. Request a printout of all account balances so that they can be manually checked against the credit limits.

    d. Request a printout of a sample of account balances so that they can be individually checked against the respective credit limits. *OK – harder*

[13,14]   10-29   When there are many relatively small account balances, negative confirmation of accounts receivable is feasible if the internal control is
a. Strong and the individuals receiving the confirmation requests are unlikely to give them adequate consideration.
b. Weak and the individuals receiving the confirmation requests are unlikely to give them adequate consideration.
c. Weak and the individuals receiving the confirmation requests are likely to give them adequate consideration.
d. Strong and the individuals receiving the confirmation requests are likely to give them adequate consideration.

[13]   10-30   Which of the following is most likely to be detected by an auditor's review of a client's sales cutoff?
a. Unrecorded sales for the year.
b. Lapping of year-end accounts receivable.
c. Excessive sales discounts.
d. Unauthorized goods returned for credit.

[13,14]   10-31   Negative confirmation of accounts receivable is less effective than positive confirmation of accounts receivable because
a. A majority of recipients usually lack the willingness to respond objectively.
b. Some recipients may report incorrect balances that require extensive follow-up.
c. The auditor cannot infer that all nonrespondents have verified their account information.
d. Negative confirmations do not produce evidential matter that is statistically quantifiable.

[13,14]   10-32   An auditor should perform alternative procedures to substantiate the existence of accounts receivable when
a. No reply to a positive confirmation request is received.
b. No reply to a negative confirmation request is received.
c. The collectibility of the receivables is in doubt.
d. Pledging of the receivables is probable.

[13,16]   10-33   An auditor's purpose in reviewing credit ratings of customers with delinquent accounts receivable is most likely to obtain evidence concerning management's assertions about   *Bad debts*
a. Presentation and disclosure.
b. Existence or occurrence.
c. Rights and obligations.
d. Valuation or allocation.

[13,14]   10-34   The negative request form of accounts receivable confirmation is useful particularly when

	The Assessed Level of Control Risk Relating to Receivables Is	The Number of Small Balances Is	Consideration by the Recipient Is
a.	Low	High	Likely
b.	Low	Low	Unlikely
c.	High	Low	Likely
d.	High	High	Likely

[13,16]   10-35   In evaluating the <u>adequacy of the allowance for doubtful accounts,</u> an auditor most likely reviews the entity's aging of receivables to support management's financial statement assertion of
a. Existence or occurrence.
b. Valuation or allocation.
c. Completeness.
d. Rights and obligations.

PROBLEMS

[2,4,5,6,9]   10-36   Taylor, CPA, has been engaged to audit the financial statements of Johnson's Coat Outlet, Inc., a medium-size mail-order retail store that sells a wide variety of coats to the public.

Required:
Prepare the "Shipments" segment of Taylor's internal control questionnaire. Each question should elicit either a yes or no response. Do *not* prepare questions relating to cash receipts, sales returns and allowances, billing, inventory control, or other segments. Use the following format:

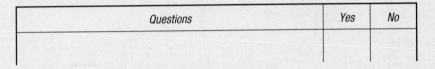

Questions	Yes	No

(AICPA, adapted)

[2,6,9]   10-37   The flowchart on the following page depicts activities relating to the sales, shipping, billing, and collection processes used by Newton Hardware, Inc.

Required:
Identify the weaknesses in internal control relating to the activities of (a) the warehouse clerk, (b) bookkeeper A, and (c) the collections clerk. Do not identify weaknesses relating to the sales clerk or bookkeepers B and C. Do not discuss recommendations concerning the correction of these weaknesses.

(AICPA, adapted)

[2,5,6,9]   10-38   A CPA's audit working papers include the following narrative description of the cash receipts and billing portions of internal control of Parktown Medical Center, Inc. Parktown is a small health care provider that is owned by a publicly held corporation. It employs seven salaried physicians, 10 nurses, three support staff in a common laboratory, and three clerical workers. The clerical workers perform such tasks as reception, correspondence, cash receipts, billing, and appointment scheduling and are adequately bonded. They are referred to in the narrative as "office manager," "clerk 1," and "clerk 2."

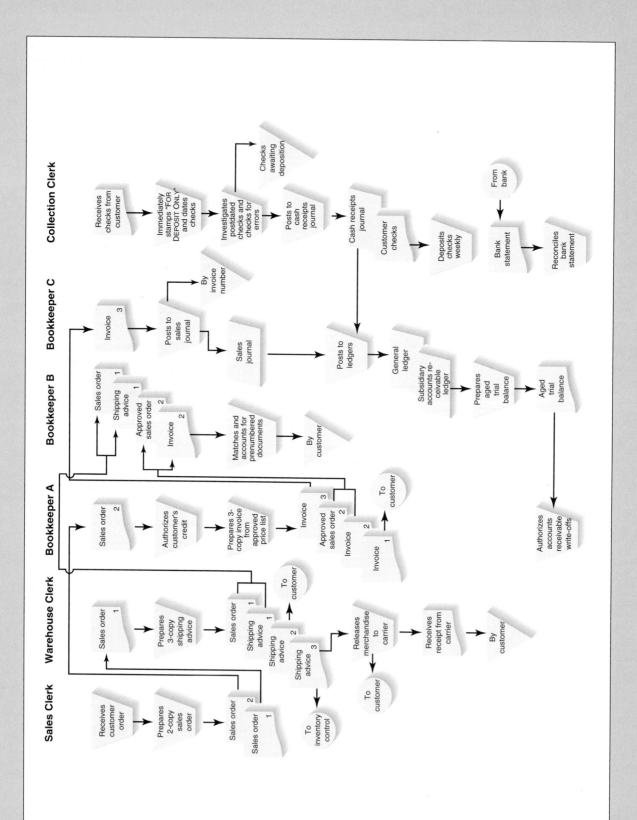

Cash Receipts and Billing

Most patients pay for services by cash or check at the time services are rendered. Credit is not approved by the clerical staff. The physician who is to perform the respective services approves credit based on an interview. When credit is approved, the physician files a memo with the billing clerk (clerk 2) to set up the receivable from data generated by the physician.

The servicing physician prepares a charge slip that is given to clerk 1 for pricing and preparation of the patient's bill. Clerk 1 transmits a copy of the bill to clerk 2 for preparation of the revenue summary and for posting in the accounts receivable subsidiary ledger.

The cash receipts functions are performed by clerk 1, who receives cash and checks directly from patients and gives each patient a prenumbered cash receipt. Clerk 1 opens the mail, immediately stamps all checks "FOR DEPOSIT ONLY," and lists cash and checks for deposit. The cash and checks are deposited daily by the office manager. The list of cash and checks, together with the related remittance advices, is forwarded by clerk 1 to clerk 2. Clerk 1 also serves as receptionist and performs general correspondence duties.

Clerk 2 prepares and sends monthly statements to patients with unpaid balances. Clerk 2 also prepares the cash receipts journal and is responsible for the accounts receivable subsidiary ledger. No other clerical employee is permitted access to the accounts receivable subsidiary ledger. Uncollectible accounts are written off by clerk 2 only after the physician who performed the respective services believes the account to be uncollectible and communicates the write-off approval to the office manager. The office manager then issues a write-off memo that clerk 2 processes.

The office manager supervises the clerks, issues write-off memos, schedules appointments for the doctors, makes bank deposits, reconciles bank statements, and performs general correspondence duties.

Additional services are performed monthly by a local accountant, who posts summaries prepared by the clerks to the general ledger, prepares income statements, and files the appropriate payroll forms and tax returns directly with the parent corporation.

Required:

a. Prepare a flowchart of Parktown Medical Center's cash receipts and billing internal control system.

b. Based only on the information in the narrative, describe the reportable conditions and one resulting misstatement that could occur and not be prevented or detected by Parktown's internal control system concerning the cash receipts and billing function. Do *not* describe how to correct the reportable conditions and potential misstatements. Use the format illustrated on the next page.

(AICPA, adapted)

Reportable Condition	Potential Misstatement
1. There is no control to verify that fees are recorded and billed at authorized rates and terms.	1. Accounts receivable could be overstated and uncollectible accounts understated because of the lack of controls.

[2,6,9]   10-39   The Art Appreciation Society operates a museum for the benefit and enjoyment of the community. During the hours the museum is open to the public, two clerks who are positioned at the entrance collect a five-dollar admission fee from each nonmember patron. Members of the Art Appreciation Society are permitted to enter free of charge upon presentation of their membership cards.

At the end of each day one of the clerks delivers the proceeds to the treasurer. The treasurer counts the cash in the presence of the clerk and places it in a safe. Each Friday afternoon the treasurer and one of the clerks deliver all cash held in the safe to the bank and receive an authenticated deposit slip, which provides the basis for the weekly entry in the cash receipts journal.

The board of directors of the Art Appreciation Society has identified a need to improve the internal control system over cash admission fees. The board has determined that the cost of installing turnstiles or sales booths or otherwise altering the physical layout of the museum would greatly exceed any benefits that might be derived. However, the board has agreed that the sale of admission tickets must be an integral part of its improvement efforts.

Smith has been asked by the board of directors of the Art Appreciation Society to review the internal control over cash admission fees and suggest improvements.

Required:

Indicate weaknesses in the existing internal control system over cash admission fees, which Smith should identify, and recommend one improvement for each of the weaknesses identified. Organize your answer as indicated in the following example:

Weakness	Recommendation
1. There is no basis for establishing the documentation of the number of paying patrons.	1. Prenumbered admission tickets should be issued upon payment of the admission fee.

(AICPA, adapted)

[2,4,5,6,8,9] 10-40 Harris, CPA, has been engaged to audit the financial statements of Spartan Drug Store, Inc. Spartan is a medium-size retail outlet that sells a wide variety of consumer goods. All sales are for cash or check. Cashiers utilize cash registers to process these transactions. There are no receipts by mail, and there are no credit card or charge sales.

Required:

Construct the "Processing Cash Collections" segment of the internal control questionnaire on "Cash Receipts" to be used in evaluating internal control for Spartan Drug Store, Inc. Each question should elicit either a yes or no response. Do *not* discuss the internal controls over cash sales. Use the following format:

Questions	Yes	No

(AICPA, adapted)

[13,14] 10-41 Adam Signoff-On, CPA, was auditing Defense Industries, Inc. Signoff-On sent positive accounts receivable confirmations to a number of Defense's government customers. He received a number of returned confirmations marked "We do not confirm balances because we are on a voucher system."

Required:

List three audit procedures that Signoff-On might use to ensure the validity of these accounts.

[13,14,16] 10-42 The "Accounts Receivable—Confirmation Statistics" working paper on the next page was prepared by an audit assistant during the calendar year 2000 audit of Lewis County Water Company, Inc., a continuing audit client. The engagement supervisor is reviewing the working papers.

Required:

Describe the deficiencies in the working paper that the engagement supervisor should discover. Assume that the accounts were selected for confirmation on the basis of a sample that was properly planned and documented on the working paper.

(AICPA, adapted)

LEWIS COUNTY WATER CO., INC.
Accounts Receivable—Confirmation Statistics
12/31/00

					Index	B-3

	Accounts		Dollars	
	Number	Percent	Amount	Percent
Confirmation requests sent:				
Positives	54	2.7%	$ 260,000	13.0%
Negatives	140	7.0	20,000	10.0
Total sent	194	9.7	$ 280,000	23.0
Accounts selected/client asked us not to confirm	6	0.3		
Total selected for testing	200	10.0		
Total accounts receivable at 12/31/00, confirm date	2,000	100.0	$2,000,000✓★	100.0
Results:				
Replies received through 2/25/01:				
Positives—no exception	44**C**	2.2	$ 180,000	9.0
Negatives—did not reply or replied "no exception"	120**C**	6.0	16,000	0.8
Total confirmed without exception	164	8.2	$ 196,000	9.8
Differences reported and resolved, no adjustment:				
Positives	6φ	0.3	$ 30,000	1.5
Negatives	12	0.6	2,000	0.1
Total	18‡	0.9	$ 32,000	1.6
Differences found to be potential adjustments:				
Positives	2**CX**	0.1	$ 10,000	0.5
Negatives	8**CX**	0.4	2,000	0.1
Total .6% adjustment, immaterial	10	0.5	$ 12,000	0.6
Accounts selected/client asked us not to confirm	6	0.3		

Tick Mark Legend
✓ = Agreed to accounts receivable subsidiary ledger.
★ = Agreed to general ledger and lead schedule.
φ = Includes one related-party transaction.
C = Confirmed without exception, W/P B-4.
CX = Confirmed with exception, W/P *B-5*.

Conclusion: The potential adjustment of $12,000, or .6%, is below materially threshold; therefore, the accounts receivable balance is fairly stated.

[13,14] 10-43 Dodge, CPA, is examining the financial statements of a manufacturing company with a significant amount of trade accounts receivable. Dodge is satisfied that the accounts are properly summarized and classified and that allocations, reclassification, and valuations are made in accordance with generally accepted accounting principles. Dodge is planning to use accounts receivable confirmation requests to satisfy the third standard of field work as to trade accounts receivable.

Required:

a. Identify and describe the two forms of accounts receivable confirmation requests, and indicate what factors Dodge will consider in determining when to use each.

b. Assume Dodge has received a satisfactory response to the confirmation requests. Describe how Dodge could evaluate the collectibility of the trade accounts receivable.

(AICPA, adapted)

[13,16]   10-44   During the year Strang Corporation began to encounter cash-flow difficulties, and a cursory review by management revealed receivable collection problems. Strang's management engaged Stanley, CPA, to perform a special investigation. Stanley studied the billing and collection cycle and noted the following:

- The accounting department employs one bookkeeper, who receives and opens all incoming mail. This bookkeeper is also responsible for depositing receipts, filing remittance advices on a daily basis, recording receipts in the cash receipts journal, and posting receipts in the individual customer accounts and the general ledger accounts. There are no cash sales. The bookkeeper prepares and controls the mailing of monthly statements to customers.

- The concentration of functions and the receivable collection problems caused Stanley to suspect that a systematic defalcation of customers' payments through a delayed posting of remittances (lapping of accounts receivable) is present. Stanley was surprised to find that no customers complained about receiving erroneous monthly statements.

Required:

Identify the procedures Stanley should perform to determine whether lapping exists. *Do not discuss deficiencies in the internal control system.*

(AICPA, adapted)

[11,12,13,16]   10-45   In obtaining evidential matter in support of financial statement assertions, the auditor develops specific audit objectives in light of those assertions. Audit procedures are then selected to accomplish audit objectives.

Required:

Your client is All's Fair Appliance Company, an appliance wholesaler. Select the most appropriate audit procedure from the following list and enter the number in the appropriate place on the grid. (An audit procedure may be selected once, more than once, or not at all.)

Audit Procedure:

1. Review of bank confirmations and loan agreements.
2. Review of drafts of the financial statements.
3. Selection of a sample of revenue transactions and determination that they have been included in the sales journal and accounts receivable subsidiary ledger.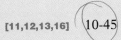
4. Selection of a sample of shipping documents for a few days before and after year-end.

5. Confirmation of accounts receivable.
6. Review of aging of accounts receivable with the credit manager.

Specific Audit Objective	Audit Procedure
a. Ensure that the entity has legal title to accounts receivable. ownership	1
b. Confirm that recorded accounts receivable include all amounts owed to the client. completeness — tracing	3
c. Verify that all accounts receivable are recorded in the correct period. timeliness/cutoff	4
d. Confirm that the allowance for uncollectible accounts is properly stated. Valuation	6
e. Confirm that recorded accounts receivable are valid. validity	5

[13,16]   10-46   You are engaged to audit the Ferrick Corporation for the year ended January 31, 2000. Only merchandise shipped by the Ferrick Corporation to customers up to and including January 30, 2000, has been eliminated from inventory. The inventory as determined by physical inventory count has been recorded on the books by the company's controller. No perpetual inventory records are maintained. All sales are made on an FOB–shipping point basis. You are to assume that all purchase invoices have been correctly recorded.

The following lists of sales invoices are entered in the sales journal for the months of January 2000 and February 2000, respectively.

	Sales Invoice Amount	Sales Invoice Date	Cost of Merchandise Sold	Date Shipped
		January 2000		
a.	$ 3,000	Jan. 21	$2,000	Jan. 31
b.	2,000	Jan. 31	800	Dec. 13
c.	1,000	Jan. 29	600	Jan. 30
d.	4,000	Jan. 31	2,400	Feb. 3
e.	10,000	Jan. 30	5,600	Jan. 29*
		February 2000		
f.	$6,000	Jan. 31	$4,000	Jan. 30
g.	4,000	Feb. 2	2,300	Feb. 2
h.	8,000	Feb. 3	5,500	Jan. 31

*Shipped to consignee.

Required:
You are to ensure that there is proper cutoff of sales and inventory. If an item is not properly recorded, prepare the necessary adjusting entries.

DISCUSSION CASES

[11,12,13,14]   10-47   In the past, the records to be evaluated in an audit have been printed reports, listings, documents, and written papers, all of which are visible output. However, in fully computerized systems that update transaction files daily, output and files are frequently in machine-readable form such as cards, tapes, or disks. Thus, the auditor often has an opportunity to use the computer in performing an audit.

Required:
Discuss how the computer can aid the auditor in examining accounts receivable in such a fully computerized system.

(AICPA, adapted)

[15,16]   10-48   Friendly Furniture, Inc., a manufacturer of fine hardwood furniture, is a publicly held SEC-registered company with a December 31 year-end. During May, Friendly had a flood due to heavy rains at its major manufacturing facility that damaged about $525,000 of furniture. Friendly is insured for the property loss at replacement value and carries business interruption insurance for lost production. The company anticipates that the total insurance proceeds will exceed the carrying value of the destroyed furniture and the cost of repairing the facility will be in the range of $700,000 to $1.75 million. The company believes that the insurance carrier will advance approximately 50 percent of the expected proceeds sometime during July. The company has resumed its operations to about one-half of normal capacity and expects to operate at full capacity by September. The company does not expect to file a formal insurance claim until then, because it expects that the entire cost of the business interruption will not be known until September. Friendly expects to receive the proceeds of the settlement from the insurance carrier during its fourth quarter.

The company is in the process of making a stock offering and will file a registration statement with the SEC at the end of July, in which it will present stub period financial statements covering the six-month period through June 30. Based on the minimum amount of the expected proceeds, Friendly would like to recognize a receivable for the insurance proceeds and to report a gain in its financial statements for the period ended June 30. The company would also like to allocate a portion of the expected proceeds to cost of products sold.

Required:
a. How much of the expected proceeds from insurance coverage, if any, should Friendly include in its June 30 financial statements? Justify your answer with relevant accounting pronouncements.
b. Assuming that Friendly records a receivable from the insurance company at June 30 for the proceeds, what type of audit evidence would the auditor gather to support the amount recorded?

SCAD ASSIGNMENTS

Assignments 5, 7, and 8 can be completed at this time.

Chapter 11

Auditing the Purchasing Cycle and Related Accounts

LEARNING OBJECTIVES

Upon completion of this chapter you will

[1] Understand why knowledge of an entity's expense and liability recognition policies is important to the audit.

[2] Develop an understanding of the purchasing cycle.

[3] Identify the types of transactions in the purchasing cycle and the financial statement accounts affected.

[4] Identify and describe the types of documents and records used in the purchasing cycle.

[5] Understand the functions in the purchasing cycle.

[6] Know the appropriate segregation of duties for the purchasing cycle.

[7] Identify and evaluate inherent risks relevant to the purchasing cycle and related accounts.

[8] Assess control risk for a purchasing cycle.

[9] Identify key internal controls and develop relevant tests of controls for purchasing, cash disbursements, and purchase return transactions.

[10] Relate the assessment of control risk to substantive testing.

[11] Identify substantive tests of transactions used to audit accounts payable and accrued expenses.

[12] Identify analytical procedures used to audit accounts payable and accrued expenses.

[13] Identify tests of account balances used to audit accounts payable and accrued expenses.

[14] Describe how confirmations are used to obtain evidence about accounts payable.

[15] Evaluate the audit findings and reach a final conclusion on accounts payable and accrued expenses.

RELEVANT ACCOUNTING AND AUDITING PRONOUNCEMENTS

FASB Statement of Financial Accounting Concepts No. 5, "Recognition and Measurement in Financial Statements of Business Enterprises" (CON5)

FASB Statement of Financial Accounting Concepts No. 6, "Elements of Financial Statements" (CON6)

SAS No. 31, "Evidential Matter" (AU 326)

SAS No. 45, "Omnibus Statement on Auditing Standards—1983—Substantive Tests Prior to the Balance Sheet Date" (AU 313)

SAS No. 47, "Audit Risk and Materiality in Conducting an Audit" (AU 312)

SAS No. 55, "Consideration of Internal Control in a Financial Statement Audit" (AU 319)

SAS No. 56, "Analytical Procedures" (AU 329)

SAS No. 57, "Auditing Accounting Estimates" (AU 342)

SAS No. 65, "The Auditor's Consideration of the Internal Audit Function in an Audit of Financial Statements" (AU 319)

SAS No. 67, "The Confirmation Process" (AU 330)

SAS No. 78, "Consideration of Internal Control in a Financial Statement Audit: An Amendment to SAS No. 55" (AU 319)

SAS No. 80, "Amendment to Statement on Auditing Standards No. 31, *Evidential Matter*" (AU 326)

SAS No. 82, "Consideration of Fraud in a Financial Statement Audit" (AU 316)

The second major accounting cycle focuses on the purchase of and payment for goods and services from outside vendors. The acquisition of goods and services includes the purchase of raw materials, supplies, manufacturing equipment, furniture, and fixtures, and payment for repairs and maintenance, utilities, and professional services. This cycle does not include hiring and paying employees or the internal allocation of costs within an entity. Chapter 12 covers the payroll cycle and employee-related issues.

This chapter begins by reviewing expense and liability recognition concepts with particular emphasis on the categories of expenses. The framework developed in Chapter 10 on the revenue cycle is used to present the auditor's consideration of internal control. This framework starts with an overview of the purchasing cycle, including the types of transactions, the documents and records involved, and the functions included in the cycle. Inherent risk factors that relate directly to the purchasing cycle are covered next. Assessment of control risk is then presented, followed by a discussion of control procedures and tests of controls. The last sections of the chapter cover the audit of accounts payable and accrued expenses, the major liability accounts affected by the cycle. Auditing the expense accounts affected by the purchasing cycle is covered in Chapter 15. 🌍

Expense and Liability Recognition

🖋 **[LO 1]**   Many transactions processed through a typical purchasing cycle involve the recognition of an expense and its corresponding liability. As a result, the auditor should understand the basic underlying concepts of expense and liability recognition in order to audit the purchasing cycle. FASB Concept Statement No. 6, "Elements of Financial Statements" (CON6), defines expenses and liabilities as follows:

> Expenses are outflows or other using up of assets or incurrences of liabilities (or a combination of both) from delivering or producing goods, rendering services, or carrying out other activities that constitute the entity's ongoing major or central operations. (para. 85)
>
> Liabilities are probable future sacrifices of economic benefits arising from present obligations of a particular entity to transfer assets or provide services to other entities in the future as a result of past transactions or events. (para. 35)

An entity's expense recognition policies and the type of expenses involved affect how the transactions are recorded and accounted for in the financial statements. FASB Statement of Financial Accounting Concepts No. 5, "Recognition and Measurement in Financial Statements of Business Enterprises" (CON5), indicates that expenses can be classified into three categories.

1. Certain expenses can be matched directly with specific transactions or events and are recognized upon recognition of revenue. These types of expenses are referred to as *product costs* and include expenses such as cost of goods sold.

2. Many expenses are recognized during the period in which cash is spent or liabilities incurred for goods and services that are used up at that time or shortly thereafter. Such expenses cannot be directly related to specific transactions and are assumed to provide no future benefit. These expenses are referred to as *period costs*. Examples of such expenses include administrative salaries and rent expense.

3. Some expenses are allocated by systematic and rational procedures to the periods during which the related assets are expected to provide benefits. Depreciation of plant and equipment is an example of such an expense.

EXHIBIT 11–1

Description of EarthWear's Purchasing System

The major purchasing activity for EarthWear involves the purchase of clothing and other products that are styled and quality crafted by the company's design department. All goods are produced by independent manufacturers, except for most of EarthWear's soft luggage. The company purchases merchandise from more than 200 domestic and foreign manufacturers. For many major suppliers, goods are ordered and paid for through the company's electronic data interchange (EDI) system. The computerized inventory control system handles the receipt of shipments from manufacturers, permitting faster access to newly arrived merchandise.

Purchases of other goods and services are made in accordance with EarthWear's purchasing authorization policies. Company personnel complete a purchase requisition, which is forwarded to the purchasing department for processing. Purchasing agents obtain competitive bids and enter the information into the purchase order program. A copy of the purchase order is sent to the vendor. Goods are received at the receiving department, where the information is agreed to the purchase order (receiving report). The receiving report is forwarded to the accounts payable department, which matches the receiving report to the purchase order and vendor invoice. The accounts payable department prepares a voucher packet and enters the information into the accounts payable program.

When payment is due on a vendor invoice, the accounts payable program generates a cash disbursement report that is reviewed by the accounts payable department. Items approved for payment are entered into the cash disbursement program, and a check is printed. The checks are sent to the cashier's department for mailing. Final approval for electronic funds transfer for EDI transactions is made by the accounts payable department.

In general, the liabilities normally incurred as part of the purchasing cycle are trade accounts payable. Other incurred expenses are accrued as liabilities at the end of each accounting period. Most expenses recognized are product or period costs.

Overview of the Purchasing Cycle

[LO 3]   A purchase transaction usually begins with a purchase requisition being generated by a department or support function. The purchasing department prepares a purchase order for the purchase of goods or services from a vendor. When the goods are received or the services have been rendered, the entity records a liability to the vendor. Finally, the entity pays the vendor. Exhibit 11–1 describes EarthWear's purchasing system.

Figure 11–1 presents the flowchart for EarthWear's purchasing system, which serves as a framework for discussing control procedures and tests of controls. As mentioned previously, accounting cycles are tailored to meet the specific needs of the client. The reader should focus on

FIGURE 11-1

Flowchart of the Purchasing Cycle—EarthWear Clothiers, Inc.

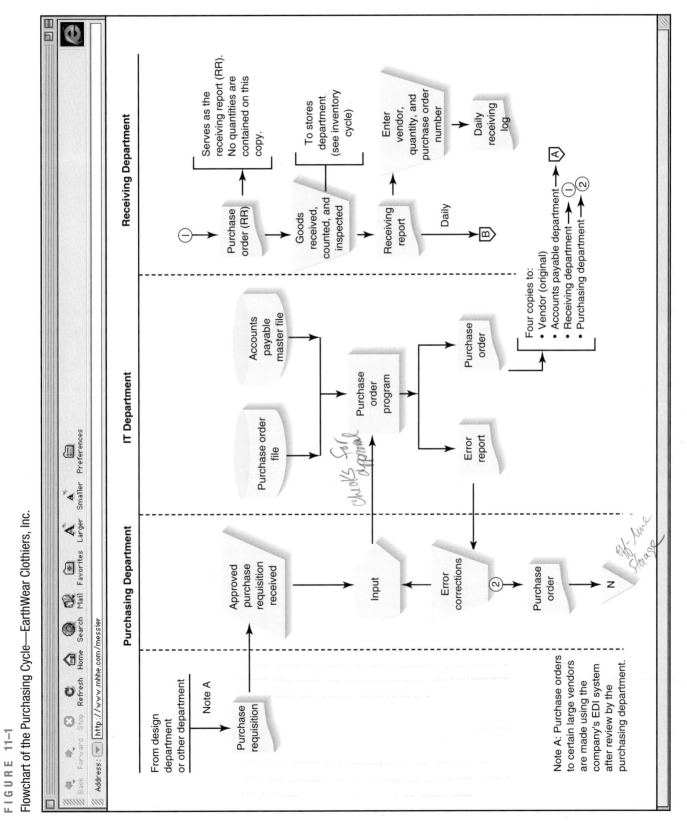

FIGURE 11–1 (concluded)

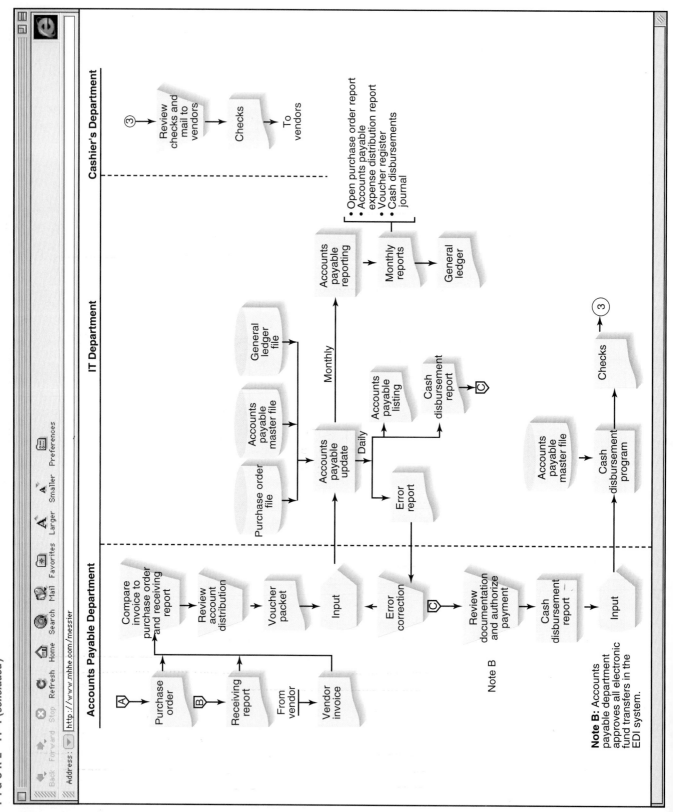

the basic concepts so that they can be applied to the specific purchasing cycles encountered. The following topics related to the purchasing cycle are covered:

- Types of transactions and financial statement accounts affected.
- Types of documents and records.
- The major functions.
- The key segregation of duties.

Types of Transactions and Financial Statement Accounts Affected

[LO 3]

Three types of transactions are processed through the purchasing cycle:

- Purchase of goods and services for cash or credit.
- Payment of the liabilities arising from such purchases.
- Return of goods to suppliers for cash or credit.

The first type is a purchase transaction that includes acquiring goods and services. The second type is a cash disbursement transaction that involves paying the liabilities that result from purchasing goods and services. The final type is a purchase return transaction, in which goods previously purchased are returned to a supplier for cash or credit.

The purchasing cycle affects many accounts in the financial statements. The more common accounts affected by each type of transaction are

1. Purchase transaction:
   - Accounts payable.
   - Inventory.
   - Purchases or cost of goods sold.
   - Various asset and expense accounts.
2. Cash disbursement transaction:
   - Cash.
   - Accounts payable.
   - Cash discounts.
3. Purchase return transaction:
   - Purchase returns.
   - Purchase allowances.
   - Accounts payable.

Types of Documents and Records

Table 11–1 lists the important documents and records that are normally involved in the purchasing cycle. Each of these items is briefly discussed here. The use of an advanced IT system may affect the form of the documents and the auditor's approach to testing the purchasing cycle.

Purchase Requisition This document requests goods or services for an authorized individual or department within the entity. Examples of such requests include an order for supplies from an office supervisor and an order for newspaper advertising space from a marketing manager. In EarthWear's purchasing system, the design department would generate purchase requisitions to acquire goods for sale.

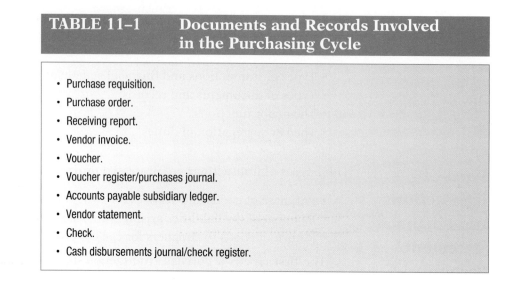

TABLE 11–1	Documents and Records Involved in the Purchasing Cycle

- Purchase requisition.
- Purchase order.
- Receiving report.
- Vendor invoice.
- Voucher.
- Voucher register/purchases journal.
- Accounts payable subsidiary ledger.
- Vendor statement.
- Check.
- Cash disbursements journal/check register.

Purchase Order   This document includes the description, quality, and quantity of, and other information on, the goods or services being purchased. The purchase order also indicates who approved the acquisition and represents the authorization to purchase the goods or services. The purchase order may be mailed, faxed, or placed by telephone with the supplier or vendor. At EarthWear some purchase orders may be generated by the design department, reviewed by a purchasing agent, and then sent to a vendor using the company's EDI system.

Receiving Report   This document records the receipt of goods. Normally, the receiving report is a copy of the purchase order with the quantities omitted. This procedure encourages receiving department personnel to make an adequate, independent count of the goods received. Receiving department personnel record the date, description, quantity, and other information on this document. In some instances, the quality of the goods is determined by receiving department personnel. In other cases, an inspection department determines whether the goods meet the required specifications. The receiving report is important because receiving goods is generally the event that leads to recognition of the liability by the entity.

Vendor Invoice   This document is the bill from the vendor. The vendor invoice includes the description and quantity of the goods shipped or services provided, the price including freight, the terms of trade including cash discounts, and the date billed.

Voucher   This document is frequently used by entities to control payment for acquired goods and services. This document serves as the basis for recording a vendor's invoice in the voucher register or purchases journal. In many purchasing systems, such as EarthWear's, the voucher is attached to the purchase requisition, purchase order, receiving report, and vendor invoice to create a *voucher packet*. The voucher packet thus contains all the relevant documentation supporting a purchase transaction.

Voucher Register/Purchases Journal A voucher register is used to record the vouchers for goods and services. The voucher register contains numerous columns for recording the account classifications for the goods or services, including a column for recording credits to accounts payable, and columns for recording debits to asset accounts such as inventory and expense accounts such as repairs and maintenance. The voucher register also contains columns for miscellaneous debits and credits. Some entities use a purchases journal instead of a voucher register. With a purchases journal, either vouchers or vendors' invoices may be used to record the liability. The major difference between a voucher register and a purchases journal is in the way individual vouchers or vendor invoices are summarized. When a voucher register is used, the details of accounts payable are normally represented by a list of unpaid vouchers. With a purchases journal, subsidiary records are normally maintained by vendor in much the same manner as an accounts receivable subsidiary ledger. However, with computerization of accounts payable records, such distinctions are disappearing. By assigning a vendor number to each voucher, the voucher register can be sorted by vendor to produce a subsidiary ledger for accounts payable.

Accounts Payable Subsidiary Ledger When a purchases journal is utilized, this subsidiary ledger records the transactions with, and the balance owed to, a vendor. When a voucher register system is used, the subsidiary ledger is a listing of the unpaid vouchers. The total in the subsidiary ledger should equal the balance in the general ledger accounts payable account.

Vendor Statement This statement is sent monthly by the vendor to indicate the beginning balance, current-period purchases and payments, and the ending balance. The vendor's statement represents the activity recorded on the vendor's records. It may differ from the client's records because of errors or, more often, timing differences due to delays in shipping goods or recording cash receipts. The client verifies the accuracy of its records by comparing vendor statements with the accounts payable records.

Check This document, signed by an authorized individual, pays for goods or services. Again, in some highly computerized systems, goods and services may be paid for through electronic transfer of funds.

Cash Disbursements Journal/Check Register This journal records disbursements made by check. It is sometimes referred to as a *check register*. The cash disbursements journal contains columns for recording credits to cash and debits to accounts payable and cash discounts. Columns may also record miscellaneous debits and credits. Payments recorded in the cash disbursements journal are also recorded in the voucher register or in the accounts payable subsidiary ledger, depending on which system is used by the entity.

TABLE 11–2	**Functions of the Purchasing Cycle**
• *Requisitioning*	Initiation and approval of requests for goods and services by authorized individuals consistent with management criteria.
• *Purchasing*	Approval of purchase orders and proper execution as to price, quantity, quality, and vendor.
• *Receiving*	Receipt of properly authorized goods or services.
• *Invoice processing*	Processing of vendor invoices for goods and services received; also, processing of adjustments for allowances, discounts, and returns.
• *Disbursements*	Processing of payment to vendors.
• *Accounts payable*	Recording of all vendor invoices, cash disbursements, and adjustments in individual vendor accounts.
• *General ledger*	Proper accumulation, classification, and summarization of purchases, cash disbursements, and payables in the general ledger.

The Major Functions

✐ **[LO 5]**

The principal business objectives of the purchasing cycle are acquiring goods and services at the lowest cost consistent with quality and service requirements and effectively using cash resources to pay for those goods and services. Table 11–2 lists the functions that are normally part of the purchasing cycle.

Requisitioning   The initial function in the purchasing cycle is a request for goods or services by an authorized individual from any department or functional area within the entity (see Figure 11–1). The important issue is that the request meets the authorization procedures implemented by the entity. One frequent organizational control is the establishment of authorization dollar limits for different levels of employees and executives. For example, department supervisors may be authorized to acquire goods or services up to $1,000, department managers up to $5,000, and divisional heads up to $25,000, while any expenditure greater than $100,000 requires approval by the board of directors.

Purchasing   The purchasing function executes properly authorized purchase orders. This function is normally performed by a purchasing department (see Figure 11–1), which is headed by a purchasing manager (or agent) and has one or more buyers responsible for specific goods or services. The purchasing function ensures that goods and services are acquired in appropriate quantities and at the lowest price consistent with quality standards and delivery schedules. Using multiple vendors and requiring competitive bidding are two ways the purchasing function can achieve its objectives.

Receiving   The receiving function is responsible for receiving, counting, and inspecting goods received from vendors. The personnel in the receiving department complete a receiving report that is forwarded to the accounts payable function.

Invoice Processing   The accounts payable department (see Figure 11–1) processes invoices to ensure that all goods and services received are recorded as assets or expenses and that the corresponding liability is recognized. This function involves matching purchase orders to receiving reports and vendor invoices as to terms, quantities, prices, and extensions. The invoice-processing function also compares the account distributions with established account classifications.

The invoice-processing function is also responsible for purchased goods returned to vendors. Appropriate records and control procedures must document the return of the goods and initiate any charges back to the vendor.

Disbursements   The disbursement function is responsible for preparing and signing checks for paying vendors. Adequate supporting documentation must verify that the disbursement is for a legitimate business purpose, that the transaction was properly authorized, and that the account distribution is appropriate. To reduce the possibility that the invoice will be paid twice, all documentation (such as, purchase order, receiving report, and vendor invoice) should be marked "CANCELED" or "PAID" by the cashier's department. Finally, the checks should be mailed to the vendor by the cashier's department or treasurer.

If IT is used to prepare checks, adequate user controls must ensure that only authorized transactions are submitted for payment. Adequate control totals should also be used to agree the amount of payables submitted with the amount of cash disbursed. Checks over a specified limit should be reviewed. For example, in EarthWear's system (see Figure 11–1), the accounts payable department matches the purchase order to the receiving report and the vendor's invoice. The voucher is then input into the accounts payable program. When the vouchers are due for payment, they are printed out on a cash disbursement report. Accounts payable personnel review the items to be paid and input them into the cash disbursement program. The checks are forwarded to the cashier's department for review and mailing to vendors. If a signature plate is used for signing checks, it must be properly controlled within the cashier's department or by the treasurer.

Accounts Payable   The accounts payable department (see Figure 11–1) is also responsible for ensuring that all vendor invoices, cash disbursements, and adjustments are recorded in the accounts payable records. In IT systems, these entries may be made directly as part of the normal processing of purchase, cash disbursement, or returns and allowances transactions. Proper use of control totals and daily activity reports provides controls for proper recording.

General Ledger   The main objective of the general ledger function for the purchasing cycle is to ensure that all purchases, cash disbursements, and payables are properly accumulated, classified, and summarized in the accounts. In an IT system, such as at EarthWear, the use of control or summary totals ensures that this function is performed correctly. The accounting department is normally responsible for this function.

TABLE 11–3	**Key Segregation of Duties in the Purchasing Cycle and Possible Errors or Fraud**

Segregation of Duties	Possible Errors or Fraud Resulting from Conflicts of Duties
The purchasing function should be segregated from the requisitioning and receiving functions.	If one individual is responsible for the requisition, purchasing, and receiving functions, fictitious or unauthorized purchases can be made. This can result in the theft of goods and possibly payment for unauthorized purchases.
The invoice-processing function should be segregated from the accounts payable function.	If one individual is responsible for the invoice-processing and the accounts payable functions, purchase transactions can be processed at the wrong price or terms, or a cash disbursement can be processed for goods or services not received. This can result in overpayment for goods and services or the theft of cash.
The disbursement function should be segregated from the accounts payable function.	If one individual is responsible for the disbursement function and also has access to the accounts payable records, unauthorized checks supported by fictitious documents can be issued, and unauthorized transactions can be recorded. This can result in theft of the entity's cash.
The accounts payable function should be segregated from the general ledger function.	If one individual is responsible for the accounts payable records and also for the general ledger, that individual can conceal any defalcation that would normally be detected by reconciling subsidiary records with the general ledger control account.

The Key Segregation of Duties

[LO 6]

As discussed in previous chapters, proper segregation of duties is one of the most important control procedures in any accounting system. Duties should be assigned so that no one individual can control all phases of processing a transaction in a way that permits errors or fraud to go undetected. Because of the potential for theft and fraud in the purchasing cycle, individuals responsible for requisitioning, purchasing, and receiving should be segregated from the invoice-processing, accounts payable, and general ledger functions. If IT is used extensively in the purchasing application, there should be proper segregation of duties in the IT department, as discussed in Chapter 7. Table 11–3 shows the key segregation of duties for the purchasing cycle and examples of possible errors or fraud that can result from conflicts in duties.

Table 11–4 shows the proper segregation of duties for purchasing and accounts payable functions across the various departments that process purchase transactions.

Inherent Risk Assessment

[LO 7]

At the beginning of the audit of the purchasing cycle and its related accounts, the auditor should consider the relevant inherent risk factors that may impact the transactions processed and the financial statement accounts.

TABLE 11–4	Segregation of Duties for Purchasing and Accounts Payable Functions by Department				

| | **Department** | | | | |
Purchasing and Accounts Payable Function	*Purchasing*	*Receiving*	*Accounts Payable*	*Cashier's*	*IT*
Preparation and approval of purchase order	X				
Receipt, counting, and inspection of purchased materials		X			
Receipt of vendor invoices and matching them with supporting documents			X		
Coding (or checking) of account distributions			X		
Updating of accounts payable records			X		X
Preparation of vendor checks					X
Signing and mailing of vendor checks				X	
Preparation of voucher register					X
Reconciliation of voucher register to general ledger			X		

The following factors taken from Chapter 3 should be considered by the auditor in assessing the inherent risk for the purchasing cycle.

Industry-Related Factors

When auditing the purchasing cycle, the auditor must consider two important industry-related factors in assessing inherent risk: whether the supply of raw materials is adequate and how volatile raw material prices are. If the entity deals with many vendors and prices tend to be relatively stable, there is less risk that the entity's operations will be affected by raw material shortages or that production costs will be difficult to control.

Some industries, however, are subject to such industry-related factors. For example, in the high-technology sector, there have been situations in which an entity has depended on a single vendor to supply a critical component, such as a specialized computer chip or disk drive. When the vendor has been unable to provide the component, the entity has suffered production shortages and shipping delays that have significantly affected financial performance. Other industries that produce basic commodities such as oil, coal, and precious metals can find their financial results significantly affected by swings in the prices of their products. Additionally, industries that use commodities such as oil as raw materials may be subject to both shortages and price instability. The auditor needs to assess the effects of such industry-related inherent risk factors in terms of audit objectives such as valuation.

FIGURE 11–2

Major Steps in Assessing
Control Risk for the
Purchasing Cycle

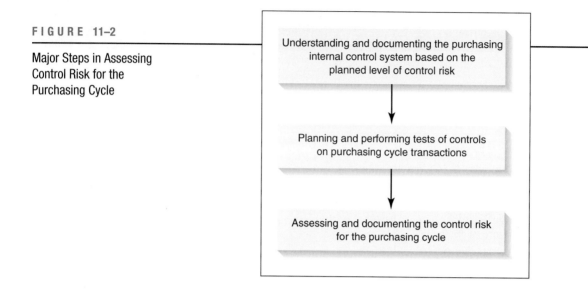

Understanding and documenting the purchasing
internal control system based on the
planned level of control risk

Planning and performing tests of controls
on purchasing cycle transactions

Assessing and documenting the control risk
for the purchasing cycle

Misstatements Detected in Prior Audits

Generally, the purchasing cycle and its related accounts are not difficult to audit and do not result in contentious accounting issues. However, auditing research has shown that the purchasing cycle and its related accounts are more likely than other accounts to contain material misstatements.[1] The auditor's previous experience with the entity's purchasing cycle should be reviewed as a starting point for determining the inherent risk.

Control Risk Assessment

[LO 8]   The discussion of control risk assessment follows the framework outlined in Chapter 6 on internal control and Chapter 10 on the revenue cycle. Again it is assumed that the auditor has decided to follow a reliance strategy. Figure 11–2 summarizes the major steps involved in assessing the control risk for the purchasing cycle.

Understanding and Documenting Internal Control

In order to assess the control risk for the purchasing cycle, the auditor must understand the five components of internal control.

Control Environment   Table 6-1 in Chapter 6 lists factors that affect the control environment. Two factors are particularly important when the auditor considers the control environment and the purchasing cycle: the entity's organizational structure and its methods of assigning authority

---

[1]For example, see A. Wright and R. H. Ashton, "Identifying Audit Adjustments with Attention-Directing Procedures," *The Accounting Review* (October 1989), pp. 710–28. W. R. Kinney, Jr., and R. D. Martin, "Does Auditing Reduce Bias in Financial Reporting? A Review of Audit-Related Adjustment Studies," *Auditing: A Journal of Practice and Theory* (Spring 1994), pp. 149–55, review the audit research studies that have examined sources of accounting errors.

and responsibility. The entity's organizational structure for purchasing may impact the auditor's assessment of control risk because control procedures are implemented within an organizational structure. Authority and responsibility for purchasing are usually granted via procedures that limit the amount of purchases that can be made by various levels of authority within the entity. The remaining discussions of the purchasing cycle assume that the control environment factors are reliable.

Risk Assessment   The auditor must understand how management weighs the risks that are relevant to the purchasing cycle, estimates their significance, assesses the likelihood of their occurrence, and decides what actions to take to address those risks. Some of these risks include a new or revamped information system, rapid growth, and new technology. Each of these factors can represent a serious risk to an entity's internal control system over purchases.

Control Activities   When a reliance strategy is adopted for the purchasing cycle, the auditor needs to understand the controls that exist to ensure that management's objectives are being met. More specifically, the auditor identifies the controls that assure the auditor that the internal control audit objectives are being met.

Information and Communication   For each major class of transactions in the purchasing cycle, the auditor again needs to obtain the following information:

- How purchase, cash disbursements, and purchase return transactions are initiated.
- The accounting records, supporting documents, and accounts that are involved in processing purchases, cash disbursements, and purchase return transactions.
- The flow of each type of transaction from initiation to inclusion in the financial statements, including computer processing of the data.
- The process used to estimate accrued liabilities.

The auditor develops an understanding of the purchasing cycle by conducting a transaction walk-through. In the case of a continuing audit, the auditor has the prior years' documentation of the cycle to assist in the walk-through, although the possibility of changes in the system must be considered. If the system has been changed substantially or the audit is for a new client, the auditor should prepare new documentation of the system.

Monitoring   The auditor needs to understand the client's monitoring processes over the purchasing cycle, including how management assesses the design and operation of controls. It also involves understanding how supervisory personnel within the cycle review the personnel who perform the controls and evaluating the performance of the entity's IT system.

The auditor can document the purchasing cycle using procedures manuals, narrative descriptions, internal control questionnaires, and flowcharts.

Planning and Performing Tests of Controls

The auditor systematically analyzes the purchasing cycle in order to identify controls that ensure that material misstatements are either prevented or detected and corrected. The controls can be relied upon by the auditor to reduce the control risk. For example, the client may have formal procedures for authorizing the acquisition of goods and services. The auditor may decide to rely on these controls to reduce the control risk for the authorization objective. Tests of controls would then be necessary to verify that this control is operating effectively. The auditor would examine a sample of purchase transactions to determine if the acquisition of the goods or services is consistent with the entity's authorization policy.

Assessing and Documenting the Control Risk

After the controls are tested, the auditor assesses the level of control risk. When tests of controls results support the planned level of control risk, no modifications are normally necessary to the planned level of detection risk, and the auditor may proceed with the planned substantive tests. When the tests of controls do not support the planned level of control risk, the auditor must assess a higher level of control risk. This results in a lower level of detection risk and leads to more substantive tests than originally planned.

As discussed earlier, the auditor should establish and document the assessed level of control risk using either quantitative amounts or qualitative terms. Documentation of the control risk for the purchasing cycle might include a flowchart, the results of tests of controls, and a memorandum indicating the auditor's overall conclusion about the control risk.

Internal Control Procedures and Tests of Controls— Purchase Transactions

[LO 9] Table 11–5 summarizes the internal control objectives and possible misstatements for purchase transactions. Most of these controls exist within EarthWear's purchasing cycle (see Figure 11–1). The table also includes key internal control procedures designed to prevent the possible misstatements and examples of tests of controls that can test the effectiveness of the control procedures. The following sections also discuss internal control procedures and tests of controls that are relevant for EarthWear's purchasing cycle.

Validity of Purchase Transactions

The auditor's concern in testing the validity of purchase transactions is that fictitious or nonexistent purchases may have been recorded in the client's records. If fraudulent transactions are recorded, assets or expenses will be overstated. A liability will also be recorded and a resulting payment made, usually to the individual who initiated the fictitious purchase transactions. Proper segregation of duties is the major control for preventing fictitious purchases. The critical segregation of duties is the separation of the requisitioning and purchasing functions from the accounts payable and disbursement functions. If one individual can both process a purchase order and gain access to the accounting records, there is an increased risk that fictitious purchase transactions will be recorded.

The other control procedures shown in Table 11–5 also reduce the risk of purchase transactions being recorded without the goods or services being

TABLE 11–5	Summary of Internal Control Objectives, Possible Misstatements, Internal Control Procedures, and Tests of Controls for Purchase Transactions		
Internal Control Objective	*Possible Misstatement*	*Internal Control Procedure*	*Test of Controls*
Validity	Purchase recorded, goods or services not ordered or received	Segregation of duties	Observe and evaluate proper segregation of duties.
		Purchase not recorded without approved purchase order and receiving report	Test a sample of vouchers for the presence of an authorized purchase order and receiving report; if IT application, examine programmed controls.
		Accounting for numerical sequence of receiving reports and vouches	Review and test client procedures for accounting for numerical sequence of receiving reports and vouchers; if IT application, examine programmed controls.
		Cancellation of documents	Examine paid vouchers and supporting documents for indication of cancellation.
Completeness	Purchases made but not recorded	Accounting for numerical sequence of purchase orders, receiving reports, and vouchers	Review client's procedures for accounting for numerical sequence of purchase orders, receiving reports, and vouchers; if IT application, examine programmed controls.
		Receiving reports matched to vendor invoices and entered in the purchases journal	Trace a sample of receiving reports to their respective vendor invoices and vouchers.
			Trace a sample of vouchers to the purchases journal.
		Vouchers reconciled to daily accounts payable listing	Test a sample of daily reconciliations.
Timeliness	Purchase transactions recorded in the wrong period	All receiving reports forwarded to the accounts payable department daily	Compare the dates on receiving reports with the dates on the relevant vouchers.
		Existence of procedures that require recording the purchases as soon as possible after goods or services are received	Compare the dates on vouchers with the dates they were recorded in the purchases journal.

Note: Receiving reports are used to acknowledge the receipt of tangible goods such as raw materials, office supplies, and equipment. For services such as utilities and advertising, receiving reports are not used.

(*continued*)

TABLE 11–5 (*concluded*)

Internal Control Objective	Possible Misstatement	Internal Control Procedure	Test of Controls
Authorization	Purchase of goods or services not authorized	Approval of acquisitions consistent with the client's authorization dollar limits	Review client's dollar limits authorization for acquisitions.
		Approved purchase requisition and purchase order	Examine purchase requisitions or purchase orders for proper approval; if IT is used for automatic ordering, examine programmed controls.
	Purchase of goods or services at unauthorized prices or on unauthorized terms	Competitive bidding procedures followed	Review client's competitive bidding procedures.
Valuation	Vendor invoice improperly priced or incorrectly calculated	Mathematical accuracy of vendor invoice verified	Recompute the mathematical accuracy of vendor invoice.
		Purchase order agreed to receiving report and vendor's invoice for product, quantity, and price	Agree the information on a sample of voucher packets for product, quantity, and price.
Classification	Purchase transaction not properly classified	Chart of accounts	Review purchases journal and general ledger for reasonableness.
		Independent approval and review of accounts charged for acquisitions	Examine a sample of vouchers for proper classification.
Posting and summarization	Purchase transactions not posted to the purchases journal or the accounts payable subsidiary records	Vouchers reconciled to daily accounts payable listing	Examine reconciliation of vouchers to daily accounts payable report; if IT application, examine programmed controls.
	Amounts from purchases journal not posted correctly to the general ledger	Daily postings to purchases journal reconciled with postings to accounts payable subsidiary records	Examine reconciliation of entries in purchases journal with entries to accounts payable subsidiary records; if IT application, examine programmed controls.
		Voucher register or accounts payable subsidiary records reconciled to general ledger control account	Review reconciliation of subsidiary records to general ledger control account; if IT application, examine programmed controls.

received. Even with proper segregation of duties, no purchase transaction should be recorded without an approved purchase order and a receiving report. The presence of an approved purchase order ensures that the purchase was authorized, and the presence of a receiving report indicates that the goods were received. In an IT environment, such as EarthWear's, the auditor can test the application controls to ensure that purchases are recorded only after an approved purchase order has been entered and the goods received. Accounting for the numerical sequence of receiving reports and vouchers can be accomplished either manually or by the computer. This control prevents the recording of fictitious purchase transactions through the use of receiving documents or vouchers that are numbered outside the sequence of properly authorized documents. Cancellation of all supporting documents ensures that a purchase transaction is not recorded and paid for a second time.

Completeness of Purchase Transactions

If the client fails to record a purchase that has been made, assets or expenses will be understated, and the corresponding accounts payable will also be understated. Controls that ensure that the completeness objective is being met include accounting for the numerical sequences of purchase orders, receiving reports, and vouchers; matching receiving reports with vendor invoices; and reconciling vouchers to the daily accounts payable report. For example, EarthWear uses control totals to reconcile the daily number of vouchers processed with the daily accounts payable listing.

Tests of controls for these control procedures are listed in Table 11–5. For example, the auditor can trace a sample of receiving reports to their corresponding vendor invoices and vouchers. The vouchers can then be traced to the voucher register to ensure that each voucher was recorded. Again, these tests can be performed either manually or with the computer. If each receiving report is matched to a vendor invoice and voucher and the voucher was included in the voucher register, the auditor has a high level of assurance as to the completeness objective.

The auditor's concern with the completeness objective also arises when the accounts payable and accrued expenses accounts are audited at year-end. If the client has strong controls for the completeness objective, the auditor can reduce the scope of the search for unrecorded liabilities at year-end. This issue is discussed in more detail later in this chapter.

Timeliness of Recording of Purchase Transactions

The client should have controls to ensure that purchase transactions are recorded promptly. For example, the client's procedures should require that all receiving reports be forwarded to the accounts payable department daily. There should also be a requirement in the accounts payable department that receiving reports be matched on a timely basis with the original purchase order and the related vendor invoice. In EarthWear's system, the receiving department forwards the receiving report to the accounts payable department daily. Within the accounts payable department, the vendor invoices are matched immediately with the original purchase orders and the receiving reports. The auditor can test these control procedures by comparing the date on the receiving report with the date on the voucher. There should seldom be a long period between the two dates. The auditor also wants to ensure that the vouchers are recorded in the accounting records promptly. This can be tested by comparing the dates on vouchers with the dates the vouchers were recorded in the voucher register.

Authorization of Purchase Transactions

Possible misstatements due to improper authorization include the purchase of unauthorized goods and services and the purchase of goods or services at unauthorized prices or terms. The primary control to prevent these misstatements is the use of an authorization schedule or table that stipulates the amount that different levels of employees are authorized to purchase. Tests of controls include examination of purchase requisitions and purchase orders for proper approval consistent with the authorization table. If the client uses a sophisticated production system that reorders goods automatically, the auditor should examine and test the programmed controls. Competitive bidding procedures should be followed to ensure that goods and services are acquired at competitive prices and on competitive terms.

Valuation of Purchase Transactions

A possible misstatement for the valuation internal control objective is that purchase transactions may be recorded at incorrect amounts due to improper pricing or erroneous calculations. The purchase order should contain the expected price for the goods or services being purchased, based on price quotes obtained by the purchasing agents or prices contained in catalogs or published price lists. If the goods or services are purchased under a contract, the price should be stipulated in the contract. For example, an accounts payable clerk should compare the purchase order with the receiving report and vendor invoice (see Figure 11–1) and investigate significant differences in quantities, prices, and freight charges. The accounts payable clerk also checks the mathematical accuracy of the vendor invoice. The auditor's test of controls for this objective involves reperforming the accounts payable clerk's duties on a sample of voucher packets.

Classification of Purchase Transactions

Proper classification of purchase transactions is an important internal control objective for the purchasing cycle. If purchase transactions are not properly classified, asset and expense accounts will be misstated. Two main controls are used for ensuring that purchase transactions are properly classified. First, the client should use a chart of accounts. Second, there should be independent approval and review of the general ledger accounts charged for the acquisition. A typical procedure is for the department or function that orders the goods or services to indicate which general ledger account to charge. Accounts payable department personnel then review the account distribution for reasonableness (see Figure 11–1). A test of controls for this objective involves examining a sample of voucher packets for proper classification.

Posting and Summarization of Purchase Transactions

In the purchasing cycle, control totals should be used to reconcile vouchers to the daily accounts payable listing, or else the daily postings to the purchases journal should be reconciled to the accounts payable subsidiary records. In addition, the voucher register or accounts payable subsidiary ledger should be reconciled to the general ledger control account. If these control procedures are performed manually, the auditor can review and examine the reconciliations prepared by the client's personnel. In a computerized purchasing cycle, such controls would be programmed and reconciled by the control groups in the IT and accounts payable departments. The auditor can examine the programmed controls and review the reconciliations.

Internal Control Procedures and Tests of Controls— Cash Disbursement Transactions

[LO 9]   Table 11–6 summarizes the internal control objectives and possible misstatements for cash disbursement transactions. The table also includes key internal controls related to each internal control objective and examples of tests of controls that can assess control risk.

Validity of Recorded Cash Disbursement Transactions

For the validity objective, the auditor is concerned with a misstatement caused by a cash disbursement being recorded in the client's records when no payment has actually been made. A number of possibilities exist for the cause of this misstatement. For example, a check may be lost or stolen before it is mailed. The primary control procedures used to prevent such misstatements include proper segregation of duties, independent reconciliation and review of vendor statements, and monthly bank reconciliations. In the purchasing system shown in Figure 11–1, checks are distributed by the cashier's department, which is independent of the accounts payable department (the department authorizing the payment).

Table 11–6 lists tests of controls that the auditor can use to verify the effectiveness of the client's controls. For example, the auditor can observe and evaluate the client's segregation of duties and review the client's procedures for reconciling vendor statements and monthly bank statements.

Completeness of Cash Disbursement Transactions

The major misstatement related to the completeness objective is that a cash disbursement is made but not recorded in the client's records. In addition to the control procedures used for the validity objective, accounting for the numerical sequence of checks and reconciliation of the daily cash disbursements with postings to the accounts payable subsidiary records (see Figure 11–1) helps to ensure that all issued checks are recorded. The auditor's tests of controls may include reviewing and testing the client's procedures for accounting for the sequence of checks and reviewing the client's reconciliation procedures.

Timeliness of Recording of Cash Disbursement Transactions

The client should establish procedures to ensure that when a check is prepared, it is recorded on a timely basis in the cash disbursements journal and the accounts payable subsidiary records. As shown in Figure 11–1, when a check is prepared, it is simultaneously recorded in the accounting records by the computer programs that control transaction processing. The auditor's tests of controls include reviewing the reconciliation of checks with postings to the cash disbursements journal and accounts payable subsidiary records.

TABLE 11–6	**Summary of Internal Control Objectives, Possible Misstatements, Internal Control Procedures, and Tests of Controls for Cash Disbursement Transactions**		
Internal Control Objective	*Possible Misstatement*	*Internal Control Procedure*	*Test of Controls*
Validity	Cash disbursement recorded but not made	Segregation of duties	Observe and evaluate proper segregation of duties.
		Vendor statements independently reviewed and reconciled to accounts payable records	Review client's procedures for reconciling vendor statements.
		Monthly bank reconciliations prepared and reviewed	Review monthly bank reconciliations for indication of independent review.
Completeness	Cash disbursement made but not recorded	Same as above	Same as above.
		Accounting for the numerical sequence of checks	Review and test client's procedures for numerical sequence of checks; if IT application, test programmed controls.
		Daily cash disbursements reconciled to postings to accounts payable subsidiary records	Review procedures for reconciling daily cash disbursements with postings to accounts payable subsidiary records; if IT application, test programmed controls.
Timeliness	Cash disbursement recorded in wrong period	Daily reconciliation of checks issued with postings to the cash disbursements journal and accounts payable subsidiary records	Review daily reconciliations.
Authorization	Cash disbursement not authorized	Segregation of duties	Evaluate segregation of duties.
		Checks prepared only after all source documents have been independently approved	Examine indication of approval on voucher packet.
Valuation	Cash disbursement recorded at incorrect amount	Daily cash disbursements report reconciled to checks issued	Review reconciliation.
		Vendor statements reconciled to accounts payable records and independently reviewed	Review reconciliation.
		Monthly bank statements reconciled and independently reviewed	Review monthly bank reconciliations.

(continued)

TABLE 11–6 (*concluded*)

Internal Control Objective	Possible Misstatement	Internal Control Procedure	Test of Controls
Classification	Cash disbursement charged to wrong account	Chart of accounts	Review cash disbursements journal for reasonableness of account distribution.
		Independent approval and review of general ledger account on voucher packet	Review general ledger account code on voucher packet for reasonableness.
Posting and summarization	Cash disbursement posted to the wrong vendor account	Vendor statements reconciled and independently reviewed	Review reconciliation.
	Cash disbursements journal not summarized properly or not properly posted to general ledger accounts	Monthly cash disbursements journal agreed to general ledger postings	Review postings from cash disbursements journal to the general ledger.
		Accounts payable subsidiary records reconciled to general ledger control account	Review reconciliation.

Authorization of Cash Disbursement Transactions

Proper segregation of duties reduces the likelihood that unauthorized cash disbursements are made. It is important that an individual who approves a purchase not have direct access to the cash disbursement for it. Additionally, the individuals in the accounts payable department who initiate payment should not have access to the checks after they are prepared. In EarthWear's purchasing cycle, the purchasing department functions are segregated from those of the accounts payable and cashier's departments. Checks are forwarded directly from the IT department to the cashier's department for mailing to the vendors. The other major control over unauthorized cash disbursements is that checks are not prepared unless all source documents (purchase requisition, purchase order, receiving report, and vendor's invoice) are included in the voucher packet and approved. For EarthWear's purchasing cycle, a complete voucher packet must be present in order to record the liability and authorize payment.

Valuation of Cash Disbursement Transactions

The potential misstatement related to the valuation objective is that the payment amount is recorded incorrectly. To detect such errors, the client's personnel should reconcile the total of the checks issued on a particular day with the daily cash disbursements report. The client's control procedures should require monthly reconciliation of vendor statements to the accounts payable records. Monthly bank reconciliations also provide controls for detecting misstatements caused by cash disbursements being made in incorrect amounts. Each of these reconciliations should be independently reviewed by the client's personnel. The auditor's test of controls involves reviewing the various reconciliations.

Classification of Cash Disbursement Transactions

The auditor's concern with proper classification is that a cash disbursement may be charged to the wrong general ledger account. In most purchasing systems, purchases are usually recorded through the voucher register or purchases journal. Thus, the only entries into the cash disbursements journal are debits to accounts payable and credits to cash. If these procedures are followed, proper classification of cash disbursements is not a major concern.

Sometimes a client pays for goods and services directly from the cash disbursements journal without recording the purchase transaction in the purchases journal. If a client does pay for goods and services directly from the cash disbursements journal, controls must be present to ensure proper classification. The use of a chart of accounts, as well as independent approval and review of the account code on the voucher packet, should provide an adequate control. The auditor can review the cash disbursements journal for reasonableness of account distribution as well as the account codes on a sample of voucher packets.

Posting and Summarization of Cash Disbursement Transactions

Two possible misstatements are of concern with this internal control objective: (1) cash disbursements are posted to the wrong vendor accounts and (2) the cash disbursements journal is not summarized properly or the wrong general ledger account is posted. The reconciliation of vendors' monthly statements is an effective control procedure for detecting payments posted to the wrong vendor accounts. Agreement of the monthly cash disbursements journal to general ledger postings and reconciliation of the accounts payable subsidiary records to the general ledger control account are effective control procedures for preventing summarization and posting errors (see Figure 11–1). The auditor's tests of controls would include checking postings to the general ledger and reviewing the various reconciliations.

Internal Control Procedures and Tests of Controls—Purchase Return Transactions

[LO 9] The number and magnitude of purchase return transactions are not material for most entities. However, because of the possibility of manipulation the auditor should, at a minimum, inquire about how the client controls purchase return transactions. When goods are returned to a vendor, the client usually prepares a document (sometimes called a debit memo) that reduces the amount of the vendor's accounts payable. This document is processed through the purchasing cycle in a manner similar to the processing of a vendor invoice.

Because purchase returns are often few in number and not material, the auditor normally does not test controls of these transactions. Analytical procedures are usually performed to test the reasonableness of purchase returns. For example, comparison of purchase returns as a percentage of revenue to prior years' and industry data may disclose any material misstatement in this account.

Relating the Assessed Level of Control Risk to Substantive Testing

[LO 10]   The decision process followed by the auditor is similar to that discussed in Chapter 10 for the revenue cycle. If the results of the tests of controls support the assessed level of control risk, the auditor conducts substantive tests at the assessed level. If the results indicate that the control risk can be reduced further, the auditor can increase the detection risk, which will reduce the nature, extent, and timing of substantive tests needed. However, if the results of the tests of controls do not support the assessed level of control risk, the detection risk has to be set lower and the substantive testing increased.

The main accounts affected by the auditor's assessment of control risk for the purchasing cycle include accounts payable, accrued expenses, and most of the expense accounts in the income statement. Additionally, the tests of controls over purchase transactions affect the assessment of detection risk for other cycles. For example, purchase transactions for the acquisition of inventory and property, plant, and equipment are subject to the controls included in the purchasing cycle. If those controls are reliable, the auditor may be able to increase the detection risk for the affected financial statement accounts and therefore reduce the number of substantive tests needed.

Auditing Accounts Payable and Accrued Expenses

The assessments of inherent risk and control risk for the purchasing cycle are used to determine the level of detection risk for conducting substantive tests of accounts payable and accrued expenses. Accounts payable generally represent normal recurring trade obligations. Accrued expenses represent expenses that have been incurred during the period but that have not been billed or paid for as of the end of the period; these include accruals for taxes, interest, royalties, and professional fees. A number of accrued expenses are also related to payroll. Because there is little difference between accounts payable and accrued expenses, they are covered together in this section.

Substantive tests of transactions, analytical procedures, and tests of account balances are used as substantive tests for accounts payable and accrued expenses. The objective of such tests is to detect monetary misstatements.

Table 11–7 shows the audit objectives for testing accounts payable and accrued expenses.

Substantive Tests of Transactions

[LO 11]   Substantive tests of transactions are tests conducted on the individual transactions processed through the purchasing cycle. As previously mentioned, substantive tests of transactions are often conducted with the tests of controls. Table 11–8 presents examples of substantive tests of transactions that can test the audit objectives for accounts payable. Substantive tests of transactions for cash disbursement transactions are covered in Chapter 16.

TABLE 11–7	Audit Objectives for Substantive Tests of Accounts Payable and Accrued Expenses

• Validity	Determine whether recorded accounts payable and accruals are valid liabilities.
• Completeness	Determine whether all accounts payable and accruals are included as liabilities.
• Cutoff	Determine whether accounts payable and accruals are recorded in the correct period.
• Ownership	Determine whether recorded accounts payable and accruals are valid obligations of the entity.
• Accuracy	Determine whether accounts payable and accruals have been properly accumulated from journals and ledgers.
• Valuation	Determine whether accounts payable and accruals are properly valued in accordance with GAAP.
• Classification	Determine whether accounts payable and accruals are properly classified in the financial statements.
• Disclosure	Determine whether all disclosures related to accounts payable and accruals are included in the financial statements.

TABLE 11–8	Examples of Substantive Tests of Transactions for Accounts Payable

Audit Objective	Substantive Test of Transactions
Validity	Test a sample of vouchers for the presence of an authorized purchase order and receiving report.*
Completeness	Trace a sample of vouchers to the purchases journal.
Cutoff	Compare dates on vouchers with the dates transactions were recorded in the purchases journal.
Ownership	Vouch selected purchase transactions recorded in the purchases journal to the voucher packets, thus ensuring that they are obligations of the entity.
Accuracy	Test recordings in the purchases journal for a sample of purchase transactions.
Valuation	Recompute the mathematical accuracy of a sample of vendors' invoices.*
Classification	Verify classification of charges for a sample of purchase transactions.
Disclosure	Test a sample of vouchers to ensure that the nature of the transaction is consistent with the normal course of business.

*These are good examples of substantive tests of transactions that serve as dual-purpose tests. See the similar tests of controls shown in Table 11–5 for the validity and valuation internal control objectives. The substantive tests of transactions shown for the completeness and cutoff objectives would also serve as dual-purpose tests.

Analytical Procedures

[LO 12] Analytical procedures can be useful substantive tests for examining the reasonableness of accounts payable and accrued expenses. When utilized as part of the planning process, analytical procedures can effectively identify accounts payable and accrual accounts that are misstated. Table 11–9 contains some examples of analytical procedures that can be used in the auditing of accounts payable and accrued expenses.

TABLE 11–9	Analytical Procedures for Auditing Accounts Payable and Accrued Expenses

Analytical Procedure	*Possible Misstatement Detected*
Compare payables turnover and days outstanding in accounts payable to previous years' and industry data.	Under- or overstatement of liabilities and expenses
Compare current-year balances in accounts payable and accruals with prior years' balances.	Under- or overstatement of liabilities and expenses
Compare amounts owed to individual vendors in the current year's accounts payable listing to amounts owed in prior years.	Under- or overstatement of liabilities and expenses
Compare purchase returns and allowances as a percentage of revenue or cost of sales to prior years' and industry data.	Under- or overstatement of purchase returns

Tests of Account Balances

[LO 13]   Table 11–10 summarizes the tests of account balances for each audit objective. The discussion of each of these audit objectives is related to accounts payable and accrued expenses. As mentioned in Chapter 10, the auditor first tests accuracy in order to ensure that the detailed records support the general ledger accounts.

Accuracy   The accuracy of accounts payable is determined by obtaining a listing of accounts payable, footing the listing, and agreeing it to the general ledger control account. The items included on this listing are the unpaid individual vouchers (when a voucher system is used) or the balance in the individual vendor accounts in the subsidiary records (when a purchases journal is used). Exhibit 11–2 presents an example of the accounts payable listing for EarthWear in which the information is summarized by vendor from the accounts payable subsidiary ledger. Selected vouchers or vendor accounts are traced to the supporting documents or subsidiary accounts payable records to verify the accuracy of the details making up the listing. For example, the tick mark next to the balance for Aarhus Industries indicates that the auditor has verified the account by tracing the balance to the accounts payable subsidiary records.

For accrued expense accounts, the auditor obtains a detailed account analysis schedule. For example, Exhibit 11–3 shows an account analysis schedule for accrued real estate taxes. The credits to the accrual account represent the recognition of real estate taxes owed at the end of each month. This amount should agree to the amount of real estate taxes expense shown in the income statement. The debits to the account are payments. This schedule is footed and agreed to the accrued real estate taxes account in the general ledger.

TABLE 11-10	Summary of Audit Objectives and Tests of Account Balances—Accounts Payable and Accrued Expenses

Audit Objective	Tests of Account Balances
Validity	Vouch selected amounts from the accounts payable listing and schedules for accruals to voucher packets or other supporting documentation.
	Obtain selected vendors' statements and reconcile to vendor accounts.
	Confirm selected accounts payable.*
Completeness	Obtain listing of accounts payable and agree total to general ledger.*
	Search for unrecorded liabilities by inquiring of management and examining post–balance sheet transactions.
	Obtain selected vendors' statements and reconcile to vendor accounts.
	Confirm selected accounts payable.*
Cutoff	Examine a sample of receiving documents for a few days before and after year-end for recording purchases in proper period.
	Perform analytical procedures for reasonableness of purchase returns.
Ownership	Review voucher packets for presence of purchase requisition, purchase order, receiving report, and vendor invoice.
Accuracy	Obtain a listing of accounts payable and account analysis schedules for accruals; foot listing and schedules and agree totals to general ledger.*
	Trace selected items from the accounts payable listing to the subsidiary records* and voucher packets.
Valuation	Examine the results of the confirmations of selected accounts payable.
	Obtain selected vendors' statements and reconcile to vendor accounts.
	Review accounts payable for items affected by cash discounts.
Classification	Review listing of accounts payable for material debits, long-term payables, and nontrade payables.*
Disclosure	Inquire about related-party payables or accruals, and ensure that they are properly disclosed.
	Review contracts or vendor statements for purchase commitments.

*These tests can be conducted manually or using CAATs.

Validity

The auditor's major concern with this audit objective is whether the recorded liabilities are valid obligations of the entity. To verify the validity of liabilities, the auditor can vouch a sample of the items included on the listing of accounts payable, or the accrued account analysis, to voucher packets or other supporting documents. If adequate source documents are present, the auditor has evidence that the amounts represent valid liabilities (see Exhibit 11–2). In some circumstances, the auditor may obtain copies of the monthly vendor statements or send confirmation requests to vendors to test the validity of the liabilities. Confirmation of accounts payable is discussed later in this chapter.

EXHIBIT 11–2

```
[====================================== ▣▤]
[ ← ←  ⊗   C   ⌂   ◎   ▥   ▣   A   A   ▤          e ]
[ Back Forward Stop Refresh Home Search Mail Favorites Larger Smaller Preferences ]
[ Address: [▼] http://www.mhhe.com/messier                          ]
```

Example of an Accounts Payable Listing Working Paper

EarthWear

N10
DLJ
2/14/2001

EARTHWEAR CLOTHIERS
Accounts Payable Listing
12/31/00

Vendor Name	Amount Due
Aarhus Industries	$ 52,758†**V**
Anderson Clothes, Inc.	237,344 **V**
.	
.	
.	
.	
Washington Mfg., Inc.	122,465†**V**
Zantec Bros.	7,750
Total	$34,463,240
	F T/B

F = Footed.
† = Traced to accounts payable subsidiary records.
V = Voucher packets examined for transaction validity. No exceptions.
T/B = Agreed to trial balance.

Completeness

Completeness is an important audit objective for accounts payable and accruals because auditors are concerned about unrecorded liabilities. Therefore, auditors frequently conduct extensive tests to ensure that all liabilities are recorded. Such tests are commonly referred to as a *search for unrecorded liabilities*. The following audit procedures may be used as part of the search for unrecorded liabilities:

1. Ask management about control procedures used to identify unrecorded liabilities and accruals at the end of an accounting period.
2. Obtain copies of vendors' monthly statements and reconcile the amounts to the client's accounts payable records.

EXHIBIT 11–3

Account Analysis for the Accrued Real Estate Taxes Account Working Paper

EarthWear

N21
DLJ
2/5/2001

EARTHWEAR CLOTHIERS
Analysis of Accrued Real Estate Taxes
12/31/00

Cash disbursements for real estate tax payments	233,911Γ	Beginning balance	$ 22,333‡
		12 monthly accruals for real estate taxes	235,245
		Ending balance	$ 23,667L✓
			F

F = Footed.
‡ = Agreed to prior year's working papers.
✓ = Amount of real estate taxes accrued appears reasonable.
Γ = Payments traced to real estate tax bills and cash disbursements journal.
L = Agreed to general ledger.

3. Confirm vendor accounts, including accounts with small or zero balances.
4. Vouch large-dollar items from the purchases journal and cash disbursements journal for a limited time after year-end; examine the date on each receiving report or vendor invoice to determine if the liability relates to the current audit period.
5. Examine the files of unmatched purchase orders, receiving reports, and vendor invoices for any unrecorded liabilities.

Cutoff

The cutoff objective attempts to determine whether all purchase transactions and related accounts payable are recorded in the proper period. On most audits, purchase cutoff is coordinated with the client's physical inventory count. Proper cutoff should also be determined for purchase return transactions.

Purchase Cutoff   The client should have control procedures to ensure that a proper cutoff takes place. The auditor can test cutoff by first obtaining the number of the last receiving report issued in the current period. A sample of voucher packets is selected for a few days before and after year-end. The receiving reports contained in the voucher packets are examined to determine if the receipt of the goods is consistent with the recording of the liability. For example, suppose that the last receiving report issued by EarthWear in 2000 was number 15,755. A voucher packet recorded in the voucher register or accounts payable in 2000 should have a receiving report numbered 15,755 or less. If the auditor finds a voucher packet recorded in 2000 with a receiving report number higher than 15,755, the liability has been recorded in the wrong period. Accounts payable for 2000 should be adjusted and the amount included as a liability in the next period. For voucher packets recorded in 2001, the receiving reports should be numbered 15,756 or higher. If the auditor finds a voucher packet with a receiving report with a number less than 15,756, the liability belongs in the 2000 accounts payable.

Purchase Returns Cutoff   Purchase returns seldom represent a material amount in the financial statements. If the client has adequate control procedures for processing purchase return transactions, the auditor can use analytical procedures to satisfy the cutoff objective for purchase returns. For example, the prior-year and current-year amounts for purchase returns as a percentage of revenue or cost of sales can be compared. If the results of the analytical procedures are consistent with the auditor's expectation, no further audit work may be necessary.

Ownership

Generally, there is little risk related to this objective because clients seldom have an incentive to record liabilities that are not obligations of the entity. Review of the voucher packets for adequate supporting documents relating liabilities to the client provides sufficient evidence to support this audit objective.

Valuation

The valuation of accounts payable and accruals is generally not a difficult audit objective to test. Accounts payable are recorded at either the gross amount of the invoice or the net of the cash discount if the entity normally takes a cash discount. The substantive tests of account balances noted in Table 11–10 normally provide sufficient evidence as to the proper valuation of accounts payable.

The valuation of accruals depends on the type and nature of the accrued expenses. Most accruals are relatively easy to value, and proper valuation can be tested by examining the underlying source documents. Real estate taxes and interest are examples of accruals that are generally easy to value. In the first case, real estate appraisals or bills usually serve as the basis for the accrual amount (see Exhibit 11–3). In the second case, the amount of interest accrued relates directly to the amount of debt and the interest rate stipulated in the loan agreement. Other accruals, however, may require the auditor to verify the client's estimates. SAS No. 57, "Auditing Accounting Estimates" (AU 342), provides the auditor with guidance in auditing client's estimates. Examples of such estimates include accruals for vacation pay, pension expense, and income taxes.

Classification

The major issues related to the classification objective are (1) identifying and reclassifying any material debits contained in accounts payable, (2) segregating short-term and long-term payables, and (3) ensuring that different types of payables are properly classified. Proper classification can usually be verified by reviewing the accounts payable listing and the general ledger accounts payable account. If material debits are present, they should be reclassified as receivables or as deposits if the amount will be used for future purchases. Any long-term payables should be identified and reclassified to the long-term liability section of the balance sheet. Also, if payables to officers, employees, or related parties are material, they should not be included with the trade accounts payable. The auditor should also ensure that accrued expenses are properly classified.

Disclosure

Even though management is responsible for the financial statements, the auditor must ensure that all necessary financial statement disclosures are made for accounts payable and accrued expenses. Again, a reporting checklist is a useful tool. Table 11–11 presents examples of items that should be disclosed for accounts payable and accrued expenses.

Two disclosures are particularly important. The auditor must ensure that all related-party purchase transactions have been identified. If material, such purchase transactions should be disclosed. The other major disclosure issue is purchase commitments. When the client has entered into a formal long-term purchase contract, adequate disclosure of the terms of the contract should be provided in a footnote. Exhibit 11–4 provides a sample disclosure for a purchase commitment.

TABLE 11–11   Examples of Disclosure Items for Purchasing Cycle and Related Accounts

- Payables by type (trade, officers, employees, affiliates, and so on).
- Short- and long-term payables.
- Long-term purchase contracts, including any unusual or adverse purchase commitments.
- Purchases from and payables to related parties.
- Dependence on a single vendor or a small number of vendors.
- Costs by reportable segment of the business.

EXHIBIT 11–4   **A Sample Disclosure for Purchase Commitments**

The company has various agreements that provide for the purchase at market prices of wood chips, bark, and other residual fiber from trees.

The company also has an agreement to purchase at market prices through 2004 the entire production of an unbleached kraft paper–making machine at Johnson Forest Products Company. The capacity of this machine is estimated to be 30,000 tons a year.

Accounts Payable Confirmations

[LO 14]   Chapter 10 discussed the confirmation process in general and accounts receivable confirmations specifically. This section expands that discussion to include confirmation of accounts payable. Accounts payable confirmations are generally used less frequently by auditors than accounts receivable confirmations because the auditor can test accounts payable by examining vendor invoices and monthly vendor statements. These documents originate from sources external to the client, so this evidence is viewed as reliable. However, if the client has weak internal control, vendor statements may not be available to examine. In such a case, confirmations may be used as a main source of evidence.

While accounts payable confirmations provide evidence on a number of audit objectives, they primarily test the completeness objective. If the client has strong control procedures for ensuring that liabilities are recorded, the auditor focuses on confirmation of large-dollar accounts. However, if the auditor has concerns about liabilities not being recorded, regular vendors with small or zero balances and a sample of other accounts may be confirmed in addition to large-dollar accounts. Small- and zero-balance accounts are confirmed because the client may owe such vendors for purchases but the amounts may not be recorded in the client's accounting records.

When confirming accounts payable, auditors generally use a form of positive confirmation referred to as a *blank or zero-balance* confirmation. This type of positive confirmation does not state the balance owed. Instead, the confirmation requests that the recipient fill in the amount or furnish other information. Exhibit 11–5 presents an example of an accounts payable confirmation request. Note that the confirmation requests the balance owed and a detailed statement of the account. The confirmation also requests additional information on notes payable and consigned inventory.

Generally, accounts payable confirmations are mailed at year-end rather than at an interim date because of the auditor's concerns about unrecorded liabilities. The selection and mailing of accounts payable confirmations should be controlled using the procedures outlined in Chapter 10. When accounts payable confirmations are received, the amounts provided by the vendors must be reconciled with the client's records. Differences are often due to the same types of timing differences noted in Chapter 10 for accounts receivable confirmations. The two major timing differences are due to inventory in transit to the client and cash paid by the client but not yet received by the vendor. Any inconsistencies not due to timing differences normally result in adjustments to the client's records.

Evaluating the Audit Findings—Accounts Payable and Related Accounts

[LO 15]   As discussed in previous chapters, when the auditor has completed the planned substantive tests, all identified misstatements should be aggregated, including known misstatements detected by the auditor and projected misstatements plus an allowance for sampling risk. The likely misstatement is then compared to the tolerable misstatement allocated to the

EXHIBIT 11–5

Example of an Accounts Payable Confirmation Request

EARTHWEAR CLOTHIERS

January 7, 2001

Zantec Bros.
P.O. Box 1469
Macon, GA 35792

Gentlemen:

Our auditors, Willis & Adams, are conducting an audit of our financial statements as of December 31, 2000. Please confirm to them the amount of our accounts payable. Additionally, please provide the following information as of that date:

1. An itemized statement of our account.
2. A list of any notes payable to you including any discounted notes. Please include the original dates and amounts, due dates, and amounts still outstanding.
3. A list of any consigned inventory held by us.

Sincerely,

Sally Jones
Controller, EarthWear Clothiers

Willis & Adams
P. O. Box 4080
Boise, Idaho 79443-4080

   We confirm that EarthWear Clothiers' accounts payable balance at

December 31, 2000, is _____ .

Signature _____   Position _____

---

account. If the likely misstatement is less than the tolerable misstatement, the auditor has evidence that the account is fairly presented. Conversely, if the likely misstatement exceeds the tolerable misstatement, the auditor should conclude that the account is not fairly presented.

For example, in Chapter 3 (Exhibit 3–4), a tolerable misstatement of $200,000 was allocated to EarthWear's accounts payable balance. Exhibit 3–5 showed that Willis & Adams detected a misstatement in recording inventory that amounted to a $27,450 understatement of accounts payable. Because this misstatement ($27,450) is less than the tolerable misstatement of $200,000, Willis & Adams can conclude that the audit evidence supports fair presentation. However, if the misstatement was greater than the tolerable misstatement, the evidence would not support fair presentation. In this case, the auditor would have two choices: adjust the accounts to reduce the misstatement to an amount less than the tolerable misstatement or qualify the audit report.

The auditor should again analyze the misstatements discovered through the application of substantive tests of transactions, analytical procedures, and tests of account balances because these misstatements may provide additional evidence as to the control risk. For example, if most misstatements identified indicate that accounts payable are not properly valued, the auditor may reassess the control procedures used by the client for ensuring proper valuation. If the auditor concludes that the audit risk is unacceptably high, additional audit procedures should be performed, or the auditor must be satisfied that the client has adjusted the related financial statement accounts to an acceptable level. If the client does not adjust the accounts, the auditor should qualify the audit report.

REVIEW QUESTIONS

[LO 1]   **11-1**   Distinguish among the three categories of expenses. Provide an example of each type of expense.

[2,3]   **11-2**   What major types of transactions occur in the purchasing cycle? What financial statement accounts are affected by each type of transaction?

[4]   **11-3**   Briefly describe each of the following documents or records: purchase requisition, purchase order, receiving report, vendor invoice, and voucher. Why would an entity combine all documents related to a purchase transaction into a "voucher packet"?

[4]   **11-4**   Distinguish between a voucher register and a purchases journal. Why is this distinction becoming less important?

[5]   **11-5**   What duties are performed within the purchasing, invoice-processing, and accounts payable functions?

[6]   **11-6**   List the key segregation of duties in the purchasing cycle. What errors or fraud can occur if such duties are not segregated?

[7]   **11-7**   List two inherent risk factors that directly affect the purchasing cycle. Why should auditors be concerned about issues such as the supply of raw materials and the volatility of prices?

[9]   **11-8**   What control procedures typically ensure that the validity, authorization, valuation, and classification internal control objectives are met for a purchase transaction? What tests of controls are performed for each of these internal control objectives?

[9]   **11-9**   Identify two tests of controls that could be performed using computer-assisted audit techniques (CAATs) for purchase transactions.

[9]   **11-10**   What control procedures typically ensure that the validity and authorization internal control objectives are met for a cash disbursement transaction? List one test of controls for each control procedure.

[8,10]   11-11   Describe how detection risk is determined for testing accounts payable and accrued expenses.

[12]   11-12   List two analytical procedures that can test accounts payable. What potential errors or fraud can be identified by each analytical procedure?

[13]   11-13   List the procedures an auditor might use to search for unrecorded liabilities.

[13]   11-14   Describe the tests for purchase cutoff.

[13]   11-15   Identify four possible disclosure issues related to the purchasing cycle and related accounts.

[14]   11-16   What are the differences between accounts receivable and accounts payable confirmations?

MULTIPLE-CHOICE QUESTIONS FROM CPA EXAMINATIONS

[9]   11-17   When goods are received, the receiving clerk should match the goods with
   a. The purchase order and the requisition form *(stored, prepared by clerk)*
   b. The vendor invoice and the receiving report.
   c. The vendor shipping document and the purchase order.
   d. The receiving report and the vendor shipping document.

[9]   11-18   In a properly designed accounts payable system, a voucher is prepared after the invoice, purchase order, requisition, and receiving report are verified. The next step in the system is
   a. Cancellation of the supporting documents.
   b. Entry of the check amount in the check register.
   c. Entering of the voucher into the voucher register.
   d. Approval of the voucher for payment.

[9]   11-19   An internal control questionnaire indicates that an approved receiving report is required to accompany every check request for payment of merchandise. Which of the following procedures provides the greatest assurance that this control is operating effectively?   *validity (vouching)*
   a. Selection and examination of canceled checks and ascertainment that the related receiving reports are dated *no later* than the checks.
   b. Selection and examination of canceled checks and ascertainment that the related receiving reports are dated *no earlier* than the checks.   *backwards*
   c. Selection and examination of receiving reports and ascertainment that the related canceled checks are dated *no earlier* than the receiving reports.   *tracing*
   d. Selection and examination of receiving reports and ascertainment that the related canceled checks are dated *no later* than the receiving reports.   *backwards*

receiving → voucher → payment

payments may include more than one voucher

[9]   11-20   Internal control is strengthened when the quantity of merchandise ordered is omitted from the copy of the purchase order sent to the
   a. Department that initiated the requisition.
   b. Receiving department.

so they verify

    c. Purchasing agent.

    d. Accounts payable department.

[6,9] **11-21** Which of the following internal control procedures is *not* usually performed in the accounts payable department?

    a. Matching the vendor's invoice with the related receiving report. ✓

    b. Approving vouchers for payment by having an authorized employee sign the vouchers. ✓

    c. Indicating the asset and expense accounts to be debited. ✓

    d. Accounting for unused prenumbered purchase orders and receiving reports. *(segr. of duties)*

[9] **11-22** Which of the following is the most effective control procedure to detect vouchers prepared for the payment of goods that were *not* received?

    a. Counting of goods upon receipt in storeroom.

    b. Matching of purchase order, receiving report, and vendor invoice for each voucher in the accounts payable department. ✓

    c. Comparison of goods received with goods requisitioned in receiving department.

    d. Verification of vouchers for accuracy and approval in internal audit department.

[6,9] **11-23** In a properly designed internal control structure, the same employee most likely would match vendors' invoices with receiving reports and also

    a. Post the detailed accounts payable records. ✗

    b. Recompute the calculations on vendors' invoices.

    c. Reconcile the accounts payroll ledger. ? ✗

    d. Cancel vendors' invoices after payment. ✗

[6,9] **11-24** For effective internal control purposes, which of the following individuals should be responsible for mailing signed checks?

    a. Receptionist.

    b. Treasurer.

    c. Accounts payable clerk.

    d. Payroll clerk.

[6,9] **11-25** Budd, the purchasing agent of Lake Hardware Wholesalers, has a relative who owns a retail hardware store. Budd arranged for hardware to be delivered by manufacturers to the retail store on a C.O.D. basis, thereby enabling his relative to buy at Lake's wholesale prices. Budd was probably able to accomplish this because of Lake's poor internal control over

    a. Purchase requisitions.

    b. Cash receipts.

    c. Perpetual inventory records.

    d. Purchase orders. *checks approval, terms (COD)*

[4,9,13] **11-26** To determine whether accounts payable are complete, an auditor performs a test to verify that all merchandise received is recorded. The population of documents for this test consists of all

    a. Vendor invoices

    b. Purchase orders.

    c. Receiving reports.

    d. Canceled checks.

[9] **11-27** Which of the following controls would most effectively ensure that recorded purchases are free of material errors?

a. The receiving department compares the quantity ordered on purchase orders with the quantity received on receiving reports.

b. Vendor invoices are compared with purchase orders by an employee who is independent of the receiving department.

c. Receiving reports require the signature of the individual who authorized the purchase.

d. Purchase orders, receiving reports, and vendor invoices are independently matched in preparing vouchers.

[13] **11-28** Which of the following procedures is *least* likely to be performed before the balance sheet date?

a. Test of internal control over cash.

b. Confirmation of receivables.

c. Search for unrecorded liabilities.

d. Observation of inventory.

[14] **11-29** When using confirmations to provide evidence about the completeness assertion for accounts payable, the appropriate population most likely would be

a. Vendors with whom the entity has previously done business.

b. Amounts recorded in the accounts payable subsidiary ledger.

c. Payees of checks drawn in the month after year-end.

d. Invoices filed in the entity's open invoice file.

[9,13] **11-30** Purchase cutoff procedures should be designed to test whether all inventory

a. Purchased and received before the end of the year was paid for.

b. Ordered before the end of the year was received.

c. Purchased and received before the end of the year was recorded.

d. Owned by the company is in the possession of the company at the end of the year.

[9,13] **11-31** Which of the following audit procedures is best for identifying unrecorded trade accounts payable?

a. Examination of unusual relationships between monthly accounts payable balances and recorded cash payments.

b. Reconciliation of vendors' statements to the file of receiving reports to identify items received just prior to the balance sheet date.

c. Investigation of payables recorded just prior to and just subsequent to the balance sheet date to determine whether they are supported by receiving reports.

d. Review of cash disbursements recorded subsequent to the balance sheet date to determine whether the related payables apply to the prior period.

PROBLEMS

[5,6,9] **11-32** In 2000 Kida Company purchased more than $10 million worth of office equipment under its "special" ordering system, with individual orders ranging from $5,000 to $30,000. "Special" orders entail

low-volume items that have been included in an authorized user's budget. Department heads include in their annual budget requests the types of equipment and their estimated cost. The budget, which limits the types and dollar amounts of office equipment a department head can requisition, is approved at the beginning of the year by the board of directors. Department heads prepare purchase requisition forms for equipment and forward them to the purchasing department. Kida's "special" ordering system functions as follows:

- *Purchasing:* Upon receiving a purchase requisition, one of five buyers verifies that the person requesting the equipment is a department head. The buyer selects the appropriate vendor by searching the various vendor catalogs on file. The buyer then phones the vendor, requests a price quotation, and gives the vendor a verbal order. A prenumbered purchase order is processed with the original sent to the vendor, a copy to the department head, a copy to receiving, a copy to accounts payable, and a copy filed in the open requisition file. When the buyer is orally informed by the receiving department that the item has been received, the buyer transfers the purchase order from the unfilled file to the filled file. Once a month the buyer reviews the unfilled file to follow up on and expedite open orders.

- *Receiving:* The receiving department receives a copy of the purchase order. When equipment is received, the receiving clerk stamps the purchase order with the date received and, if applicable, in red pen prints any differences between the quantity shown on the purchase order and the quantity received. The receiving clerk forwards the stamped purchase order and equipment to the requisitioning department head and orally notifies the purchasing department.

- *Accounts payable:* Upon receiving a purchase order, the accounts payable clerk files it in the open purchase order file. When a vendor invoice is received, the invoice is matched with the applicable purchase order, and a payable is set up by debiting the equipment account of the department requesting the items. Unpaid invoices are filed by due date, and at the due date a check is prepared. The invoice and purchase order are filed by purchase order number in a paid invoice file, and the check is then forwarded to the treasurer for signature.

- *Treasurer:* Checks received daily from the accounts payable department are sorted into two groups: those over $10,000 and those $10,000 and less. Checks for $10,000 and less are machine-signed. The cashier keeps the key and signature plate to the check-signing machine and records all use of the check-signing machine. All checks over $10,000 are signed by the treasurer or the controller.

Required:
a. Prepare a flowchart of Kida Company's purchasing and cash disbursements internal control system.

b. Describe the internal control weaknesses relating to purchases of and payments for "special" orders of Kida Company for the purchasing, receiving, accounts payable, and treasurer functions.

(AICPA, adapted)

[5,6,9]   **11-33**   Katz, CPA, has been engaged to audit the financial statements of Sommer Manufacturing, Inc. Sommer is a medium-size entity that produces a wide variety of household goods. All acquisitions of materials are processed through the purchasing, receiving, accounts payable, and treasurer functions.

Required:
Prepare the "Purchases" segment of the internal control questionnaire to be used in evaluating Sommer's internal control system. Each question should elicit either a yes or no response. Do *not* prepare the receiving, accounts payable, or treasurer segments of the internal control questionnaire. Do *not* discuss the internal controls over purchases. Use the following format:

Questions	Yes	No

(AICPA, adapted)

[4,5,6,9]   **11-34**   The flowchart on the following page depicts the activities relating to the purchasing, receiving, and accounts payable departments of Model Company, Inc.

Required:
Based only on the flowchart, describe the internal control procedures (strengths) that most likely would provide reasonable assurance that specific internal control objectives for the financial statement assertions regarding purchases and accounts payable will be achieved. Do *not* describe weaknesses in internal control.

(AICPA, adapted)

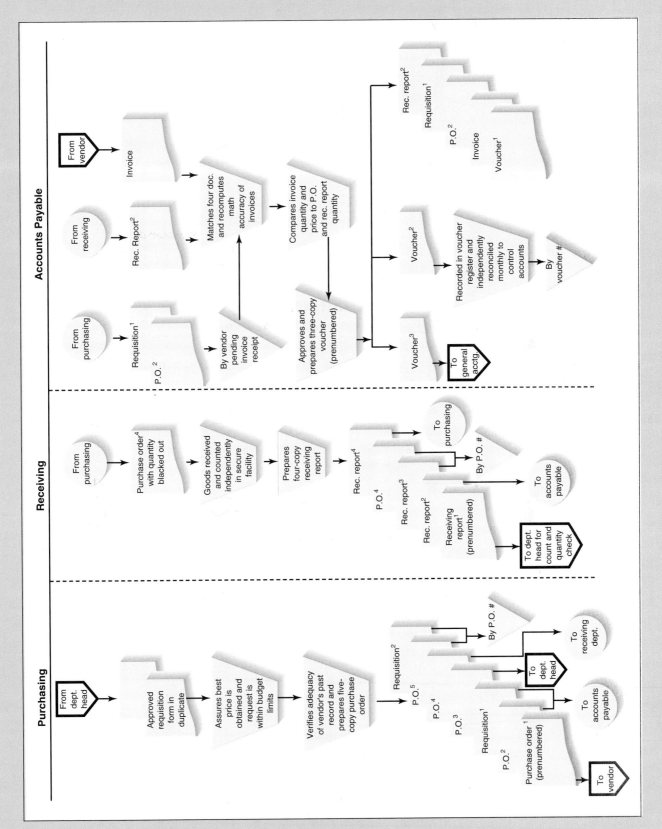

[13,14]   11-35   In obtaining evidential matter in support of financial statement assertions, the auditor develops specific audit objectives in light of those assertions. Audit procedures are then selected to accomplish the audit objectives.

Required:
Your client is All's Fair Appliance Company, an appliance wholesaler. Select the most appropriate audit procedure from the list below and enter the number in the appropriate place on the grid. (An audit procedure may be selected once, more than once, or not at all.)

Audit Procedure:

1. Compare selected amounts from the accounts payable listing with the voucher and supporting documents. *Vouching*
2. Review drafts of the financial statements.
3. Search for unrecorded liabilities.
4. Select a sample of receiving documents for a few days before and after year-end. *cut-off*
5. Confirm accounts payable.
6. Obtain a listing of the accounts payable and agree total to general ledger control account.

	Specific Audit Objective	Audit Procedure
a.	Determine whether all accounts payable are properly valued.	5
b.	Verify that recorded accounts payable include all amounts owed to vendors.	3
c.	Verify that all accounts payable are recorded in the correct period.	4
d.	Determine whether accounts payable have been properly accumulated from the journal to the general ledger.	6
e.	Determine whether recorded accounts payable are valid.	1

[11,12,13,14]   11-36 Coltrane, CPA, is auditing Jang Wholesaling Company's financial statements and is about to perform substantive audit procedures on Jang's trade accounts payable balances. After obtaining an understanding of Jang's internal control for accounts payable, Coltrane assessed the control risk at near the maximum. Coltrane requested and received from Jang a schedule of the trade accounts payable prepared using the trade accounts payable subsidiary ledger (voucher register).

Required:
Describe the substantive audit procedures Coltrane should apply to Jang's trade accounts payable balances. Do *not* include procedures that would be applied only in the audit of related-party payables, amounts withheld from employees, and accrued expenses such as pensions and interest.

(AICPA, adapted)

[4,5,9] 11-37 Dunbar Camera Manufacturing, Inc., manufacturers high-priced precision motion picture cameras in which the specifications of component parts are vital to the manufacturing process. Dunbar buys valuable camera lenses and large quantities of sheet metal and screws. Screws and lenses are ordered by Dunbar and are billed by the vendors on a unit basis. Sheet metal is ordered by Dunbar and is billed by the vendors on the basis of weight. The receiving clerk is responsible for documenting the quality and quantity of merchandise received.

A preliminary review of internal control indicates that these procedures are being followed:

Receiving Report
Properly approved purchase orders, which are prenumbered, are filed numerically. The copy sent to the receiving clerk is an exact duplicate of the copy sent to the vendor. Receipts of merchandise are recorded on the duplicate copy by the receiving clerk.

Sheet Metal
The company receives sheet metal by railroad. The railroad independently weighs the sheet metal and reports the weight and date of receipt on a bill of lading (waybill), which accompanies all deliveries. The receiving clerk checks only the weight on the waybill against the purchase order.

Screws
The receiving clerk opens cartons containing screws, then inspects and weighs the contents. The weight is converted to the number of units by means of conversion charts. The receiving clerk then checks the computed quantity against the amount shown on the purchase order.

Camera Lenses
Each camera lens is delivered in a separate corrugated carton. The receiving clerk counts the cartons and checks the number of cartons against the amounts shown on the purchase orders.

Required:
   a. Explain why the internal control procedures as they apply individually to receiving reports and the receipt of sheet metal, screws, and camera lenses are adequate or inadequate. Do *not* discuss recommendations for improvements.
   b. What financial statement distortions may arise because of the inadequacies in Dunbar's system of internal control, and how may they occur?

(AICPA, adapted)

[11,12,13,14] 11-38 Taylor, CPA, is auditing Rex Wholesaling for the year ended December 31, 2000. Taylor has reviewed internal control relating to the purchasing, receiving, trade accounts payable, and cash disbursement cycles and has decided not to test controls. Based on analytical review procedures, Taylor believes that the trade accounts payable balance on the balance sheet as of December 31, 2000, may be understated.

Taylor has requested and obtained a client-prepared trade accounts payable schedule listing the total amount owed to each vendor.

Required:
What additional substantive audit procedures should Taylor apply in examining the trade accounts payable?

(AICPA, adapted)

DISCUSSION CASE

[13,14]   11-39   Mincin, CPA, is the auditor of the Raleigh Corporation. Mincin is considering the audit work to be performed in the accounts payable area for the current year's engagement. The prior year's working papers show that confirmation requests were mailed to 100 of Raleigh's 1,000 suppliers. The selected suppliers were based on Mincin's sample, which was designed to select accounts with large-dollar balances. A substantial number of hours was spent by Raleigh and Mincin in resolving relatively minor differences between the confirmation replies and Raleigh's accounting records. Alternative audit procedures were used for suppliers who did not respond to the confirmation requests.

Required:
a. Discuss the accounts payable audit objectives that Mincin must consider in determining the audit procedures to be followed.
b. Discuss situations in which Mincin should use accounts payable confirmations, and discuss whether Mincin is required to use them.
c. Discuss why the use of large-dollar balances as the basis for selecting accounts payable for confirmation might not be the most efficient approach, and indicate what more efficient procedures could select accounts payable for confirmation.

(AICPA, adapted)

Chapter **12**

Auditing the Payroll Cycle and Related Accounts

LEARNING OBJECTIVES

Upon completion of this chapter you will

[1] Develop an understanding of the payroll cycle.

[2] Identify the types of transactions in the payroll cycle and the financial statement accounts affected.

[3] Identify and describe the types of documents and records used in the payroll cycle.

[4] Understand the functions in the payroll cycle.

[5] Know the appropriate segregation of duties for the payroll cycle.

[6] Identify and evaluate inherent risks relevant to the payroll cycle and related accounts.

[7] Assess control risk for a payroll cycle.

[8] Identify key internal controls and develop relevant tests of controls for payroll transactions.

[9] Relate the assessment of control risk to substantive testing.

[10] Identify substantive tests of transactions used to audit payroll expense and payroll-related accrued expenses.

[11] Identify analytical procedures used to audit payroll expense and payroll-related accrued expenses.

[12] Identify tests of account balances used to audit payroll expense and payroll-related accrued expenses.

[13] Evaluate the audit findings and reach a final conclusion on payroll expense and payroll-related accrued expenses.

RELEVANT ACCOUNTING AND AUDITING PRONOUNCEMENTS

FASB Statement of Financial Accounting Standards No. 87, "Employer's Accounting for Pensions" (FAS 87)

FASB Statement of Financial Accounting Standards No. 106, "Employer's Accounting for Postretirement Benefits Other Than Pensions" (FAS 106)

SAS No. 31, "Evidential Matter" (AU 326)

SAS No. 47, "Audit Risk and Materiality in Conducting an Audit" (AU 312)

SAS No. 55, "Consideration of Internal Control in a Financial Statement Audit" (AU 319)

SAS No. 56, "Analytical Procedures" (AU 329)

SAS No. 78, "Consideration of Internal Control in a Financial Statement Audit: An Amendment to SAS No. 55" (AU 319)

SAS No. 80, "An Amendment to Statement Auditing Standards No. 31, *Evidential Matter*" (AU 326)

SAS No, 82, "Consideration of Fraud as a Financial Statement Audit" (AU 316)

Compensation and related employee benefit costs represent major expenses for most entities. As a result, organizations tend to have strong control procedures for processing payroll transactions. Additionally, because of the routine nature of these transactions, an entity's payroll cycle may be computerized, or an outside service bureau may be contracted to process the payroll.

This chapter starts with an overview of the payroll cycle and then discusses the three components of the audit risk model. Then the inherent risks that affect the payroll cycle are addressed. This is followed by a discussion of the auditor's control risk assessment. Last, the chapter covers substantive tests for detection risk for payroll and related accounts. 🌏

Overview of the Payroll Cycle

[LO 1] A payroll transaction usually begins with an employee performing some job and recording the time spent on a time card. The time card is approved by a supervisor before being forwarded to the payroll department. The data are then reviewed and sent to the IT department for processing. Finally, payment is made directly to the employee or deposited in the employee's bank account.

Figure 12–1 presents a flowchart of EarthWear's payroll system that serves as a framework for discussing control procedures and tests of controls. Although the description of EarthWear's payroll system is fairly typical, the reader should focus on the basic concepts so that they can be applied to the specific payroll cycles encountered. The following topics related to the payroll cycle are covered:

- Types of transactions and financial statement accounts affected.
- Types of documents and records.
- The major functions.
- The key segregation of duties.

Types of Transactions and Financial Statement Accounts Affected

Two main types of transactions are processed through the payroll cycle:

- Payments to employees for services rendered.
- Accrual and payment of payroll-related liabilities arising from employees' services, including liabilities for Social Security and unemployment taxes.

[LO 2] The discussion of internal control focuses on payments to employees, including a description of how such transactions are processed and the key control procedures that should be present to ensure that no material misstatements occur. The audit of payroll-related accruals is discussed later in the chapter.

The financial statement accounts that are generally affected by the two types of payroll-related transactions are

1. Payroll transactions:
   - Cash.
   - Inventory.
   - Direct and indirect labor expense.
   - Various payroll-related liability and expense accounts.
2. Accrued payroll liability transactions:
   - Cash.
   - Various accruals (such as payroll taxes and pension costs).

FIGURE 12-1

Flowchart of the Payroll Cycle—EarthWear Clothiers

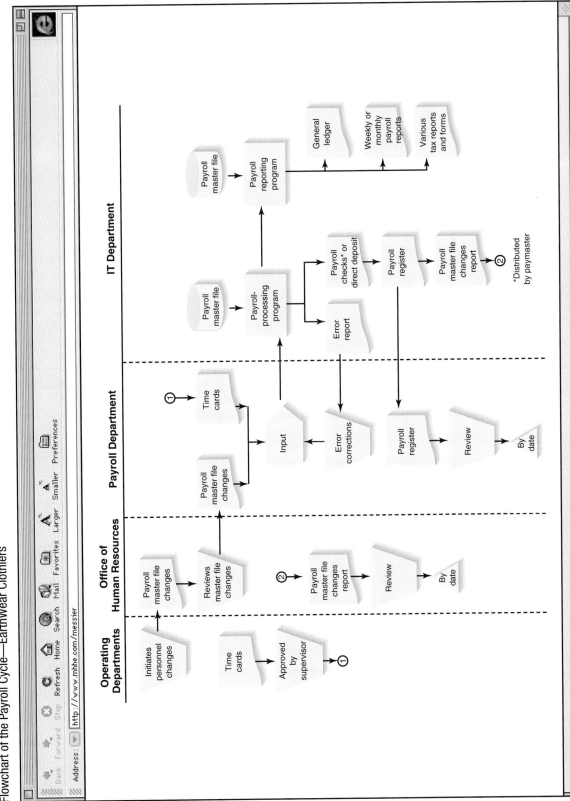

TABLE 12–1	Documents and Records Involved in the Payroll Cycle

- Personnel records, including wage-rate or salary authorizations.
- W-4 and other deduction authorization forms.
- Time card.
- Payroll check.
- Payroll register.
- Payroll master file.
- Payroll master file changes report.
- Periodic payroll reports.
- Various tax reports and forms.

Types of Documents and Records

[LO 3]

Table 12–1 lists the important documents and records that are normally involved in the payroll cycle. Each of these items is briefly discussed here. The use of an advanced IT system may affect the form of the documents and the auditor's approach to testing the payroll cycle.

Personnel Records, Including Wage-Rate or Salary Authorizations

Personnel records contain information on each employee's work history, including hiring date, wage rate or salary, payroll deduction authorization forms, wage-rate and salary adjustment authorizations, performance evaluations, and termination notice, if applicable. Personnel records are normally maintained in the human resources department.

W-4 and Other Deduction Authorization Forms

The employee must authorize deductions from his or her pay. The organization should therefore use authorization forms to document such deductions. For example, the employee must complete a W-4 form to authorize the withholding of federal and state income tax. Similar forms should be used for deductions for medical insurance, retirement contributions, and other benefits.

Time Card

This document records the hours worked by the employee, including the time the employee has started and stopped work. In some cases the employee fills in the time worked; in other cases a time clock records the time.

Payroll Check

This check indicates the amount paid to the employee for services rendered. The amount paid is the gross pay less any deductions.

Payroll Register

This document, which is also referred to as the *payroll journal*, summarizes all payroll checks issued to employees. A payroll register normally indicates employees' gross pay, deductions, and net pay.

TABLE 12–2	Functions in the Payroll Cycle
• *Personnel*	Authorization of hiring, firing, wage-rate and salary adjustments, salaries, and payroll deductions.
• *Supervision*	Review and approval of employees' attendance and time information; monitoring of employee scheduling, productivity, and payroll cost variances.
• *Timekeeping*	Processing of employees' attendance and time information and coding of account distribution.
• *Payroll processing*	Computation of gross pay, deductions, and net pay; recording and summarization of payments and verification of account distribution.
• *Disbursement*	Payment of employees' compensation and benefits.
• *General ledger*	Proper accumulation, classification, and summarization of payroll in the general ledger.

In a computerized environment, the details for this document are maintained in the payroll master file.

Payroll Master File   This computer file maintains all the entity's records related to payroll, including information on each employee such as name, Social Security number, pay rate, and authorized deductions.

Payroll Master File Changes Report   This report contains a record of the changes made to the payroll master file. The office of human resources reviews this report to ensure that all authorized changes have been properly made.

Periodic Payroll Reports   At the end of each week or month, a number of summary payroll reports may be prepared. The type of reports prepared depend on the type of organization. A manufacturing entity might have a payroll expense report that showed the allocation of direct labor to various products. EarthWear Clothiers reports a summary of payroll by various job classifications and departments. Department heads use this report to monitor payroll expense variances.

Various Tax Reports and Forms   Most companies are required to prepare various payroll tax reports for both the federal and state governments. Unemployment compensation forms must also be completed periodically. Additionally, an entity must provide each employee with a W-2 form at the end of the year. Compensation paid to a consultant or independent contractor must be reported on a 1099 form.

The Major Functions

[LO 4]

The principal objectives of the payroll cycle are to (1) record production and other types of payroll costs in the accounts, (2) ensure that payroll costs are for legitimate entity activities, and (3) accrue liabilities for salaries and wages, payroll taxes, and various employee benefit programs. Table 12–2 lists the functions that are normally part of the payroll cycle.

Personnel   The personnel function is responsible for managing the human resource needs of the organization. This includes hiring and terminating employees, setting wage rates and salaries, and establishing and monitoring employee benefit programs. Most large organizations centralize these activities in an office of human resources or personnel department. However, in a small organization, these activities may be combined with the duties of selected operating and administrative personnel. In such organizations, control over human resource activities may not be as strong as when such activities are centralized. The office of human resources maintains employees' personnel records. The office of human resources may also be responsible for defining job requirements and descriptions, administering union contracts, and developing performance criteria and employee evaluation procedures.

Supervision   Supervisors within operating and supporting departments are responsible for reviewing and approving employees' attendance and time information. When time cards or other documents are used to record an employee's time worked and job classification, the supervisor approves this information before processing by the payroll function. Additionally, supervisors should monitor labor productivity and labor cost variances. Standardized labor performance measures, such as standard productivity and wage rates, improve the monitoring of payroll costs. Labor cost variances should be investigated by supervisory personnel and communicated to upper-level management. When employees are not required to complete time cards or job classification documents, the entity needs to have control procedures to notify the timekeeping or payroll-processing function about employees' absences and changes in employees' job classifications. This might be accomplished by having the supervisor submit a periodic attendance and job classification report.

Timekeeping   The timekeeping function prepares employees' time information for payroll processing. When payroll cost distribution is determined at the operating department level, the timekeeping function reviews this information before processing. Otherwise, the timekeeping function should be responsible for coding the payroll costs to appropriate accounts. In some organizations, a separate timekeeping department handles these functions. At EarthWear (see Figure 12–1), the operating and supporting departments are responsible for the timekeeping function.

Payroll Processing   The payroll-processing function is responsible for computing gross pay, deductions, and net pay. This function is also responsible for recording and summarizing payments and verifying account distribution. When IT is used to process payroll, as at EarthWear, the entity must have strong application controls to ensure proper payroll processing.

Disbursement   The disbursement function is responsible for paying employees for services and benefits. In particular, this function oversees the preparation and distribution of payroll checks. Again, check preparation normally occurs in the IT department. Therefore, it is necessary to have control procedures over access to blank checks and check signature plates. Checks are normally distributed by a paymaster, who is typically a member of the treasurer's department. When payments are directly deposited in employees' bank accounts, strong IT application controls are necessary.

General Ledger The general ledger function for the payroll cycle is responsible for properly accumulating, classifying, and summarizing payroll and benefit transactions in the general ledger. When IT is used to process payroll transactions, control totals can help ensure that this function is performed properly. This function is normally performed by the general accounting department.

The Key Segregation of Duties

/ [LO 5]

As discussed in prior chapters, proper segregation of duties is one of the most important control procedures in any accounting system. Duties should be assigned to individuals in such a way that no one individual can control all phases of processing a transaction, thus permitting misstatements to go undetected. Individuals responsible for supervision and timekeeping should be segregated from the personnel, payroll-processing, and general ledger functions. If IT is used extensively in the payroll application, duties should be properly segregated in the IT department. Table 12–3 contains some of the key segregation of duties for the payroll cycle and examples of possible errors or fraud that can result from conflicts in duties.

Table 12–4 shows more detailed segregation of duties for individual payroll functions across the various departments that are involved in processing payroll transactions.

TABLE 12–3	Key Segregation of Duties and Possible Errors or Fraud
Segregation of Duties	*Possible Errors or Fraud Resulting from Conflicts of Duties*
The supervision function should be segregated from the personnel records and payroll-processing functions.	If one individual is responsible for the supervision, personnel records, and payroll-processing functions, fictitious employees can appear on the payroll records or unauthorized payments can be made. This can result in unauthorized payments to existing employees or payments to fictitious employees.
The disbursement function should be segregated from the personnel records, supervision, and payroll-processing functions.	If one individual is responsible for the disbursement function and also has the authority to hire and fire employees, approve time reports, or prepare payroll checks, unauthorized payroll checks can be issued.
The payroll-processing function should be segregated from the general ledger function.	If one individual is responsible for processing payroll transactions and also for the general ledger, that individual can conceal any defalcation that would normally be detected by independent review of accounting entries made to the general ledger.

TABLE 12–4   Segregation of Duties for Payroll Functions by Department

Payroll Function	Operating or Supporting	Personnel	Timekeeping	Payroll	IT	Treasurer
Initiation of wage or salary changes	X					
Initiation of employee hiring and firing	X					
Approval of wage or salary changes		X				
Updating of personnel records		X				
Updating of payroll records		X				
Approval of time cards and job classification	X					
Review of time data and payroll distribution			X			
Preparation of payroll				X	X	
Preparation and signing of payroll checks					X	
Distribution of payroll checks						X
Updating of general ledger for payroll activity					X	
Comparison of monthly departmental payroll expense to budget	X					
Calculation and recording of payroll taxes				X		

Inherent Risk Assessment

[LO 6]   Generally, few inherent risk factors directly affect the payroll cycle and its related accounts. Some factors the auditor might consider are the effect of economic conditions on payroll costs, the supply of skilled workers, and the frequency of employee turnover. Additionally, the presence of labor contracts and legislation such as the Occupational Safety and Health Act may also affect the auditor's assessment of inherent risk. However, because the payroll cycle and its related accounts generally contain few inherent risks, the auditor is normally able to assess the inherent risk as low.

Control Risk Assessment

[LO 7]   The discussion of control risk assessment follows the framework outlined in previous chapters. However, the discussion is not as thorough as the discussion of the revenue or purchasing cycles because it is assumed that the reader has now developed a reasonable understanding of the decision process followed by the auditor when assessing control risk. Figure 12–2 summarizes the three major steps involved in assessing control risk for the payroll cycle.

FIGURE 12–2

Major Steps in Assessing
Control Risk for the Payroll
Cycle

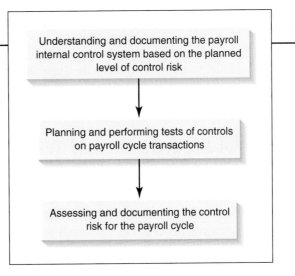

Understanding and Documenting Internal Control

The level of understanding of the five internal control components should be similar to that obtained for the other cycles. The auditor's understanding of the payroll cycle is normally gained by conducting a walk-through of the system to gather evidence about the various functions that are involved in processing the transactions in the cycle. For an ongoing audit, this process merely involves updating prior years' documentation of the payroll system by noting any changes that have occurred. For a new engagement, or if the system has undergone major changes, more time and effort are needed to document the understanding of internal control for the payroll cycle. The auditor's understanding of internal control for the payroll cycle should be documented in the working papers using flowcharts, internal control questionnaires, and memoranda.

Because the control environment pervasively affects all accounting cycles, including the payroll cycle, two factors shown in Table 6–1 in Chapter 6 should be considered. First, the entity's organizational structure, its personnel practices, and its methods of assigning authority and responsibility must be examined. The proper organizational structure for processing payroll transactions was discussed in the previous section. Second, the entity should have sound policies for hiring, training, promoting, and compensating employees. These policies should include specific authority and responsibility for hiring and firing employees, for setting wage rates and making salary changes, and for establishing benefits.

Planning and Performing Tests of Controls

When a reliance strategy is followed, the auditor must identify the control procedures that ensure that material misstatements are either prevented or detected and corrected. For example, the client may have formal procedures for classifying payroll costs in appropriate accounts. The auditor may decide to rely on this control procedure to reduce the control risk for the classification objective. In this case, the client's procedures for classifying payroll transactions by types of payroll costs should be examined by the auditor.

Assessing and Documenting the Control Risk

After the tests of controls are completed, the auditor assesses the level of control risk and documents that assessment using either quantitative amounts or qualitative terms. The documentation supporting the assessed level of control risk for the payroll cycle might include a flowchart, the results of tests of controls, and a memorandum indicating the overall conclusion about control risk.

Internal Control Procedures and Tests of Controls— Payroll Transactions

[LO 8] Table 12–5 summarizes the internal control objectives and possible misstatements for payroll transactions. The table also includes key internal control procedures for each internal control objective and examples of tests of controls that can test the effectiveness of the control procedures. The discussion that follows focuses only on the most important internal control objectives for the payroll cycle. EarthWear's payroll system contains all of the relevant internal control procedures.

Validity of Payroll Transactions

The auditor wants assurance that payments for payroll-related services are being made to valid employees for time actually worked. Thus, the client needs control procedures that prevent payments to fictitious employees and to valid employees who have not worked. Controls must also ensure that payroll payments stop once an employee is terminated. Proper segregation of duties provides the main control against payments to fictitious employees. As noted in Table 12–4, proper segregation of duties among operating and supporting departments, the office of human resources, and the payroll department minimizes the possibility of fictitious employees existing within the system. The maintenance of adequate personnel files should also prevent such misstatements.

The office of human resources approves the termination of an employee and ensures that he or she is removed from the master payroll file. Required completion and approval of a time card also prevent payments to terminated employees. Proper review and approval of time cards by supervisors should prevent valid employees from being paid for work not performed.

Finally, when payroll transactions are processed by an IT system, a payroll check should not be prepared unless the employee transaction has a valid employee number. Review and observation are the main tests of controls the auditor uses to examine the control procedures shown in Table 12–5.

Authorization of Payroll Transactions

As in the discussion of the authorization objective for other accounting cycles, there are key authorization points within the payroll cycle. The client should have authorization procedures for hiring and terminating employees, setting pay rates, making withholdings, awarding benefits, and issuing payroll checks. For example, the department supervisor should approve the amount of time reported by an employee on his or her time card. Similarly, hiring and termination of employees and changes in pay rates should

TABLE 12–5	Summary of Internal Control Objectives, Possible Misstatements, Internal Control Procedures, and Tests of Controls for Payroll Transactions

Internal Control Objective	Possible Misstatement	Internal Control Procedure	Test of Controls
Validity	Payments made to fictitious employees	Segregation of duties	Observe and evaluate proper segregation of duties.
	Payments made to terminated employees	Adequate personnel files	Review and test personnel files.
	Payments made to valid employees who have not worked	Initiation of changes in employment status, wages or salaries, and benefits made by operating departments reported to the office of human resources	Review and test client's procedures for changing employees' records; if IT application, examine programmed controls.
		Time clocks used to record time	Observe employees' use of time clock.
		Time cards approved by supervisors	Inspect time cards presented for approval by supervisor.
		Only employees with valid employee numbers paid	Review and test client's procedures for entering and removing employee numbers from the payroll master file; if IT application, examine programmed controls.
		Use of payroll budgets with review by department supervisors	Review client's budgeting procedures.
Completeness	Employee services provided but not recorded	Prenumbered time cards accounted for by client personnel	Check numerical sequence of time cards; if IT application, examine programmed controls.
Timeliness	Payroll transactions recorded in the wrong period	Notices of additions, terminations, and changes to salaries, wages, and deductions reported promptly to the payroll processing function, after which the changes are updated promptly on the master payroll file	Review and test client's procedures for changes to master payroll file; if IT application, examine programmed controls.
		All time cards forwarded to the payroll department weekly	Review and test procedures for processing time cards.

(continued)

TABLE 12–5 (*concluded*)

Internal Control Objective	Possible Misstatement	Internal Control Procedure	Test of Controls
		Procedures that require recording payroll liabilities as soon as possible after they are incurred	Review and test procedures for recording payroll liabilities.
Authorization	Unauthorized payments made to employees Payments made to employees at a rate in excess of authorized amount or for unauthorized employee benefits	Authorization procedures for • Hiring and terminating employees • Time worked • Wage, salary, and commission rates • Withholdings • Benefits • Issuing payroll check	Review and test authorization procedures for each point of authorization in the payroll cycle; if IT application, examine programmed controls.
Valuation	Employee compensation and payroll deductions computed incorrectly	Verification of payroll amounts and benefit calculations	Review and test client's verification procedures; if IT application, examine programmed controls.
		Review of payroll register for unusual amounts	If IT-prepared, use computer-assisted audit techniques to test computer program logic for calculating amounts.
		Use of payroll budgets with review by department supervisors	Review client's budgeting procedures.
Classification	Payroll transactions not properly classified	Chart of accounts	Review chart of accounts.
		Independent approval and review of accounts charged for payroll	Review and test procedures for classifying payroll costs.
		Use of payroll budgets with review by department supervisors	Review client's budgeting procedures.
Posting and summarization	Payroll transactions not posted correctly to the payroll journal	Changes to master payroll file verified through "before and after" reports	Examine reconciliation of "before and after" reports to payroll master file; if IT application, examine programmed controls.
	Amounts from payroll journal not posted correctly to general ledger	Payroll master file (payroll register) reconciled to general ledger payroll accounts	Review reconciliation of payroll master file to general ledger payroll accounts; if IT application, examine programmed controls.

be authorized by the office of human resources consistent with union contracts or corporate policies. Last, a payroll check should not be issued unless an employee's time card has been approved and that employee has a valid employee number on the payroll master file.

Valuation of Payroll Transactions

The main concern related to the valuation objective is that an employee's gross pay and payroll deductions may be incorrectly computed. For example, an employee may be paid at a higher rate than authorized or payroll deductions may be incorrectly computed. The client should maintain verification procedures to ensure correct payroll and benefit calculations. The auditor can review the client's verification procedures as a test of control. When IT is used to prepare the payroll, the auditor can use computer-assisted audit techniques (CAATs) to test the program logic for proper calculations. In a manual system, or if a service bureau is used, the auditor can recompute the payroll calculations for a sample of payroll transactions.

Classification of Payroll Transactions

Because classification is an important objective for payroll transactions, control procedures must ensure that the appropriate payroll accounts are charged. If payroll expense is charged to the wrong accounts, the financial statements may be misstated. For example, if payroll expense is not properly classified between direct and indirect labor, inventory and cost of goods sold may not be valued properly. The use of an adequate chart of accounts is one control procedure that helps to prevent misclassification. Additionally, the timekeeping function should review the payroll categories assigned by the operating departments. Budgets that compare actual payroll costs to budgeted payroll costs by each category of labor also provide a control over proper classification of payroll. The auditor can review and test the client's control procedures for classifying payroll costs.

Relating the Assessed Level of Control Risk to Substantive Testing

[LO 9] If the results of the tests of controls for the payroll cycle support the assessed level of control risk, the auditor conducts substantive tests of payroll-related accounts at the assessed level. EarthWear, for example, has a strong set of internal control procedures for processing payroll transactions. If the auditor's tests of EarthWear's controls indicate that the controls are operating effectively, then no adjustment of detection risk is necessary. However, if the results of the control tests do not support the assessed level of control risk for EarthWear's payroll cycle, the detection risk will have to be set lower. This would require that the nature and extent of substantive testing of payroll-related accounts be increased.

Auditing Payroll-Related Accounts

Three categories of substantive tests for auditing payroll expense and payroll-related liabilities are discussed here: substantive tests of transactions, analytical procedures, and tests of account balances. Table 12–6

TABLE 12–6	Audit Objectives for Testing Payroll Expense and Payroll-Related Accruals
• *Validity*	Determine whether payroll expense is a valid expense and whether payroll-related accruals are valid liabilities.
• *Completeness*	Determine whether all payroll expense and payroll-related accruals have been recorded.
• *Cutoff*	Determine whether payroll expense and payroll-related accruals are recorded in the correct period.
• *Ownership*	Determine whether recorded payroll expense and accruals are expenses and obligations of the entity.
• *Accuracy*	Determine whether payroll expense has been properly accumulated from journals and ledgers.
• *Valuation*	Determine whether payroll expense and payroll-related accruals are properly valued in accordance with GAAP.
• *Classification*	Determine whether payroll expense and payroll-related accruals are properly classified in the financial statements.
• *Disclosure*	Determine whether all disclosures related to payroll expense and payroll-related accruals are included in the financial statements.

TABLE 12–7	Examples of Substantive Tests of Transactions for Payroll
*Audit Objective**	*Substantive Test of Transactions*
Validity	Test a sample of payroll checks for the presence of an authorized time card.[†]
Completeness	Trace a sample of time cards to the payroll register.
Accuracy	Test postings to the payroll register for a sample of payroll checks.
Valuation	Recompute the mathematical accuracy of a sample of payroll checks; CAATs may be used to test the logic of the computer programs for proper calculation of gross pay, deductions, and net pay.
Classification	Verify classification of charges for a sample of payroll checks.

*The ownership, cutoff, and disclosure objectives are normally tested using tests of account balances. The audit work for these objectives relates mainly to the accruals made for payroll-related expenses.
[†]This is a good example of a substantive test of transactions that serves as a dual-purpose test. The substantive tests of transactions shown for the completeness, valuation, and classification objectives may also serve as dual-purpose tests.

shows the audit objectives for testing payroll expense and payroll-related liabilities, which are often called *accrued payroll expenses*.

Substantive Tests of Transactions

[LO 10]   The intended objective of substantive tests of transactions is to detect monetary misstatements in the individual transactions processed through the payroll cycle. As previously mentioned, substantive tests of transactions are often conducted in conjunction with tests of controls. Table 12–7 presents examples of substantive tests of transactions for selected audit objectives for payroll.

TABLE 12–8	Analytical Procedures for Auditing Payroll Accounts and Payroll-Related Accruals

Analytical Procedure	*Possible Misstatement Detected*
Payroll Expense Accounts	
Compare current-year balances in the various payroll expense accounts with prior years' balances after adjustment for pay changes and number of employees.	Over- or understatement of payroll expense
Compare payroll costs as a percentage of sales with prior years' and industry data.	Over- or understatement of payroll expense
Compare labor utilization rates and statistics with industry data.	Over- or understatement of payroll expense
Compare budgeted payroll expenses with actual payroll expenses.	Over- or understatement of payroll expense
Estimate sales commissions by applying commission formulas to recorded sales totals.	Over- or understatement of sales commissions
Payroll-Related Accrual Accounts	
Compare current-year balances in payroll-related accrual accounts with prior years' balances after adjusting for changes in conditions.	Over- or understatement of accrued liabilities
Test reasonableness of accrual balances.	Over- or understatement of accrued liabilities

Analytical Procedures

[LO 11]   Analytical procedures can be useful substantive tests for examining the reasonableness of payroll expenses and payroll-related accrual accounts. When utilized as part of planning, analytical procedures can effectively identify payroll expense accounts and accrual accounts that may be misstated. Table 12–8 shows examples of analytical procedures that can be used for auditing payroll. Two examples will help to demonstrate their application in practice. First, the auditor can compare budgeted payroll costs with actual payroll costs. Variances due to quantity and wage differences should show up in the client's cost-accounting system (on weekly or monthly reports). If the variances are immaterial, the auditor has some evidence that payroll costs are reasonable. If the variances are material, the auditor should investigate the potential causes of the differences. This analytical procedure also helps the auditor to determine the proper valuation of inventory when standard costs are used to value inventory. Second, the auditor can test the reasonableness of certain accrual balances. For example, if accrued wages represent payroll for two days, the auditor can multiply the total weekly payroll by 40 percent (2 days ÷ 5 days). If the auditor's calculation is close to the accrued amount, no further audit work may be required on the accrued wages account.

Tests Of Account Balances

[LO 12]   Table 12–9 summarizes the tests of account balances for each audit objective. The discussion that follows focuses on tests of payroll expense accounts and accrued payroll liabilities.

TABLE 12–9	Summary of Audit Objectives and Tests of Account Balances—Payroll Expense Accounts and Accruals

Audit Objective	*Tests of Account Balances*
Validity	Vouch selected amounts from the account analysis schedules for the accruals to supporting documentation (payroll tax returns, corporate benefit policies, etc.).
Completeness	Search for unrecorded liabilities (see Chapter 11).
Cutoff	Examine supporting documents for accruals in order to determine proper period for recording expense.
Ownership	Review supporting documentation to determine that the entity is liable for the liability.
Accuracy	Obtain an account analysis schedule for accrued payroll liabilities; foot schedules and agree total to general ledger.
Valuation	Test reasonableness of accrued payroll expenses. Compare amounts accrued to supporting documentation, such as payroll tax returns.
Classification	Review accrued payroll liabilities for proper classification between short-term and long-term liabilities.
Disclosure	Inquire about accruals to ensure that they are properly disclosed. Review benefit contracts for proper disclosure of pension and postretirement benefits.

Payroll Expense Accounts

The payroll cycle affects many expense accounts, including direct and indirect manufacturing expense, general and administrative salaries, sales salaries, commissions, and payroll tax expenses. Some companies account for such expenses by product line or division. In addition, fringe benefits such as medical and life insurance are usually paid for at least partly by the organization. If the entity's internal control is reliable, the auditor generally does not need to conduct detailed tests of these payroll expense accounts. On such audits, sufficient evidence can be gathered through an understanding of internal control, tests of controls, substantive tests of transactions, and analytical procedures. Additional testing is necessary only when control weaknesses exist or when the other types of audit tests indicate that material misstatements may be present.

Several payroll expense accounts may still be examined even when control risk is low. For example, it is common to verify the compensation paid to officers of the company because information on executive salaries and bonuses is needed for the 10K form, proxy statements, and the federal tax return. Limits may also be placed on officers' salaries and bonuses as part of lending agreements. If such limits are exceeded, the entity may be in default on the debt. Officers' compensation is also examined because officers are in a position to override the control procedures and pay themselves more than they are authorized to receive (see Exhibit 12–1). Officers' compensation expense can be verified by comparing the amounts shown in the payroll records with the amounts authorized in either board of directors' minutes or employment contracts.

Accrued Payroll Liabilities

An entity incurs a number of payroll-related liabilities. In addition to these accrued expenses, the entity also withholds various amounts from an employee's pay. These withholdings include payroll taxes (federal and state

EXHIBIT 12–1

Questionable Salary Payments at Lincoln Savings and Loan

One of the most notorious cases noted during the savings-and-loan debacle was Lincoln Savings and Loan. In 1978 Charles Keating, Jr., founded American Continental Corporation (ACC), which acquired Lincoln six years later. In 1989 the Federal Home Loan Bank Board seized control of Lincoln Savings and Loan. The closing of Lincoln cost US taxpayers approximately $2 billion. Exercising his ownership powers over Lincoln, Keating installed his son, Charles Keating III, as chairman of the board at an annual salary of $1 million. An examination report on ACC indicated that "funds sent by Lincoln to ACC were being used by ACC to fund treasury stock transactions [and] pay debt service, consulting fees, and exorbitant management salaries." The report estimated that $34 million had been expended on "Keating family benefits."

Source: The People, Plaintiff and Respondent, v. Charles H. Keating, Jr., Defendant and Appellant (31 Cal., App. 4th 1688, 1993).

income taxes and FICA), medical and life insurance premiums, pension, and other miscellaneous deductions. Some examples of accrued payroll liabilities include

- Accrued wages and salaries.
- Accrued payroll taxes.
- Accrued commissions.
- Accrued bonuses.
- Accrued benefits such as vacation and sick pay.

In auditing accrued payroll liabilities, the auditor is concerned mainly with five audit objectives: *validity, completeness, valuation, cutoff,* and *disclosure.* When control risk is low or the amounts in the accounts are relatively small, the auditor can verify accrued payroll liabilities using analytical procedures. For example, the auditor can compare the prior year's balance in each accrual with the current year's balance after considering changing conditions.

For accrued payroll liability accounts for which the control risk is high or whose amounts are material, the auditor can obtain a detailed account analysis schedule. For example, Exhibit 12–2 shows an account analysis schedule for EarthWear's accrued payroll taxes. The credits to the account represent the recognition of payroll tax expense at the end of each pay period. These amounts can be traced to the various payroll tax returns or other documentation filed by the entity and should agree with the amount of payroll tax expense included in the income statement. The debits to the account represent payments made to relevant government agencies. These payments can be verified by tracing the amounts to the cash disbursements journal.

An interesting aspect of this type of accrual account is that it periodically "clears out" the accrued amount. For example, if the client has to make payments for payroll taxes to the government on the 15th of each month, the accrued payroll taxes account will have a zero balance after the payment. Thus, at the end of any month, the accrued payroll taxes account should contain only an accrual for payroll taxes since the last payment

EXHIBIT 12–2

Account Analysis for Accrued Payroll Taxes Account

EarthWear

N25
DLJ
2/15/01

EARTHWEAR CLOTHIERS
Analysis of Accrued Payroll Taxes
12/31/00

		Beginning balance	$216,950Φ
Disbursements for payment of payroll taxes	$253,275£	Weekly accruals for payroll tax expense	253,540✓
		Ending balance	$217,215λL
			F

F = Footed.
Φ = Traced to prior year's working papers.
L = Agreed to general ledger.
✓ = Traced three weeks' (2/15, 4/20, and 9/30) payroll expense accruals to weekly payroll records.
£ = Traced three payments of payroll taxes to the cash disbursements journal.
λ = Recomputed amount of unpaid payroll taxes for two weeks at the end of December 2000.

(approximately two weeks). In many organizations, these costs are broken down into the various types of payroll taxes (employer's FICA and federal and state unemployment taxes).

Validity and Valuation   The validity and valuation objectives can generally be tested at the same time. The auditor's concerns are whether the recorded liabilities are valid obligations of the entity and whether they are included in the financial statements at the appropriate amount. To verify the validity and valuation of an accrued payroll liability, the auditor can generally trace the amounts included on the account analysis working paper to supporting documentation such as payroll tax reports. If adequate documentation is present, the auditor has evidence that the amount represents a valid liability. The auditor can usually verify the accuracy of the amounts by recalculating the figures.

Completeness   The auditor wants to make sure that all payroll-related liabilities are recorded. The auditor should be aware of the normal payroll-related taxes that are paid by the entity and therefore should be able to determine if accruals have been made for payroll taxes such as Social Secu-

TABLE 12–10	Sample Disclosure Items for the Payroll Cycle and Related Accounts

- Pension disclosures required by FASB No. 87.
- Postretirement benefit disclosures required by FASB No. 106.
- Profit-sharing plans.
- Deferred compensation arrangements.

rity taxes and unemployment insurance. In some instances, the auditor's search for unrecorded liabilities, which was discussed in Chapter 11, may provide evidence that all payroll-related liabilities are recorded.

Cutoff   The auditor also wants to determine whether all payroll-related liabilities are recorded in the proper period. An examination of supporting documentation for the accruals provides evidence on the proper period for recording the expense or liability. For example, an examination of the client's unemployment tax invoices should allow the auditor to determine if a proper accrual for unemployment tax has been made in the current period.

Disclosure   The auditor must ensure that all necessary financial statement disclosures for the payroll cycle and related accounts are made. Table 12–10 presents examples of items that should be disclosed for payroll-related accounts.

Two accounting standards require substantial disclosure. FASB's Nos. 87 and 106 require detailed disclosures of pension costs and postretirement benefits. Although discussion of the audit of these items is beyond the scope of this text, the reader should be aware that such disclosures are important to the fairness of the financial statements. Profit-sharing plans and deferred compensation arrangements also require disclosure in the footnotes.

Evaluating the Audit Findings—Payroll-Related Accounts

[LO 13]   When the auditor has completed the planned substantive tests of the payroll-related accounts, all of the identified misstatements should be aggregated. The likely misstatement is compared to the tolerable misstatement allocated to the payroll-related accounts. If the likely misstatement is less than the tolerable misstatement, the auditor may accept the accounts as fairly presented. Conversely, if the likely misstatement exceeds the tolerable misstatement, the auditor should conclude that the accounts are not fairly presented.

For example, in Chapter 3 (Exhibit 3–4), a tolerable misstatement of $60,000 was allocated to EarthWear's accrued liabilities. Exhibit 3–5 showed that Willis & Adams detected a misstatement in recording payroll expense and bonuses that amounted to a $36,200 understatement of accrued liabilities. Because this misstatement ($36,200) is less than the tolerable misstatement of $60,000, Willis & Adams can conclude that the audit evidence supports fair presentation. However, if the misstatement was greater than the tolerable misstatement, the evidence would not support fair presentation. In this case the auditor would have two choices: adjust the accounts to reduce the misstatement to an amount less than the tolerable misstatement or qualify the audit report.

The auditor should again analyze the misstatements discovered through the application of substantive tests of transactions, analytical procedures, and tests of account balances because these misstatements may provide additional evidence on the control risk for the payroll cycle. If the auditor concludes that the audit risk is unacceptably high, additional audit procedures should be performed, or the auditor must be satisfied that the client has adjusted the payroll-related financial statement accounts to an acceptable level. For example, suppose the auditor's analytical procedures indicate that commissions expense is overstated. The auditor might perform detailed computations of commissions expense or request that the client adjust the account by the amount of the estimated misstatement.

REVIEW QUESTIONS

[LO 1]	12-1	Why is the payroll cycle of most entities computerized?
[2]	12-2	What are the major types of transactions that occur in the payroll cycle? What financial statement accounts are affected by each of these types of transactions?
[3]	12-3	Briefly describe each of the following documents or records: payroll register, payroll master file, and payroll master file changes report.
[4]	12-4	What duties are performed within the personnel, timekeeping, and payroll-processing functions?
[5]	12-5	List the key segregation of duties in the payroll cycle. What errors or fraud can occur if such duties are not segregated?
[7,8]	12-6	Discuss the two control environment factors that an auditor should consider when examining the payroll cycle.
[8]	12-7	What are the key authorization points in a payroll system?
[8]	12-8	Why is it important for the client to establish control procedures over the classification of payroll transactions?
[6]	12-9	List the inherent risk factors that affect the payroll cycle.
[8,10]	12-10	Identify two tests of controls or substantive tests of transactions that can be performed using CAATs for payroll transactions.
[11]	12-11	List two analytical procedures that can be used to test payroll expense accounts and payroll-related liabilities.
[12]	12-12	Discuss how an auditor would audit the accrued payroll taxes account.
[12]	12-13	Identify three possible disclosure issues for payroll expense and payroll-related liabilities.

[7,8] 12-29 Brownstein, CPA, has been engaged to audit the financial statements of Young Computer Outlets, Inc., a new client. Young is a privately owned chain of retail stores that sells a variety of computer software and video products. Young uses an in-house payroll department at its corporate headquarters to compute payroll data and to prepare and distribute payroll checks to its 300 salaried employees.

Brownstein is preparing an internal control questionnaire to assist in obtaining an understanding of Young's internal control and in assessing control risk.

Required:

Prepare a "Payroll" segment of Brownstein's internal control questionnaire that would assist in obtaining an understanding of Young's internal control and in assessing control risk. Do *not* prepare questions relating to cash payroll, IT applications, or payments based on hourly rates, piecework, commissions, employee benefits (pensions, health care, vacations, and so on), or payroll tax accruals other than withholdings. Use the following format:

Internal Control Question	Yes	No
Are paychecks prenumbered and accounted for?		

(AICPA, adapted)

[10,11,12] 12-30 McCarthy, CPA, was engaged to audit the financial statements of Kent Company, a continuing audit client. McCarthy is about to audit Kent's payroll transactions. Kent uses an in-house payroll department to process payroll data and to prepare and distribute payroll checks.

During the planning process, McCarthy determined that the inherent risk of overstatement of payroll expense is high. In addition, McCarthy obtained an understanding of internal control and assessed the control risk for payroll-related assertions at the maximum level.

Required:

Describe the audit procedures McCarthy should consider performing in the audit of Kent's payroll transactions to address the risk of overstatement. Do *not* discuss Kent's internal control.

(AICPA, adapted)

[10,11,12] 12-31 James, who was engaged to examine the financial statements of Talbert Corporation, is about to audit payroll. Talbert uses a computer service center to process weekly payroll as follows.

Each Monday Talbert's payroll clerk inserts data in appropriate spaces on the preprinted service center–prepared input form and sends it to the service center via messenger. The service center extracts new permanent data from the input form and updates its master files. The weekly payroll data are then processed. The weekly payroll register and payroll checks are printed and delivered by messenger to Talbert on Thursday.

Part of the sample selected for audit by James includes the following input form and payroll register:

TALBERT CORPORATION
Payroll Input
Week Ending Friday, November 24, 2000

Employee Data—Permanent File				Current Week's Payroll Data				
				Hours		Special Deductions		
Name	Social Security Number	W-4 Information	Hourly Rate	Regular	Overtime	Bonds	Union	Other
A. Bell	999-99-9991	M-1	$10.00	35	5	$18.75		
B. Carioso	999-99-9992	M-2	10.00	35	4			
C. Deng	999-99-9993	S-1	10.00	35	6	18.75	$4.00	
D. Ellis	999-99-9994	S-1	10.00	35	2		4.00	$50.00
E. Flaherty	999-99-9995	M-4	10.00	35	1		4.00	
F. Gillis	999-99-9996	M-4	10.00	35			4.00	
G. Hua	999-99-9997	M-1	7.00	35	2	18.75	4.00	
H. Jones	999-99-9998	M-2	7.00	35			4.00	25.00
I. King	999-99-9999	S-1	7.00	35	4		4.00	
New Employee:								
J. Smith	999-99-9990	M-3	7.00	35				

TALBERT CORPORATION
Payroll Register
November 24, 2000

Employee	Social Security Number	Hours Regular	Hours Overtime	Payroll Regular	Payroll Overtime	Gross Payroll	FICA	Federal	State	Other Withheld	Net Pay	Check Number
								Taxes Withheld				
A. Bell	999-99-9991	35	5	$ 350.00	$ 75.00	$ 425.00	$ 26.05	$ 76.00	$27.40	$ 18.75	$ 276.80	1499
B. Carioso	999-99-9992	35	4	350.00	60.00	410.00	25.13	65.00	23.60		296.27	1500
C. Deng	999-99-9993	35	6	350.00	90.00	440.00	26.97	100.90	28.60	22.75	260.78	1501
D. Ellis	999-99-9994	35	2	350.00	30.00	380.00	23.29	80.50	21.70	54.00	200.51	1502
E. Flaherty	999-99-9995	35	1	350.00	15.00	365.00	22.37	43.50	15.90	4.00	279.23	1503
F. Gillis	999-99-9996	35		350.00		350.00	21.46	41.40	15.00	4.00	268.14	1504
G. Hua	999-99-9997	35	2	245.00	21.00	266.00	16.31	34.80	10.90	22.75	181.24	1505
H. Jones	999-99-9998	35		245.00		245.00	15.02	26.40	8.70	29.00	165.88	1506
I. King	999-99-9999	35	4	245.00	42.00	287.00	17.59	49.40	12.20	4.00	203.81	1507
J. Smith	999-99-9990	35		245.00		245.00	15.02	23.00	7.80		199.18	1508
Total		350	24	$3,080.00	$333.00	$3,413.00	$209.21	$540.90	$171.80	$159.25	$2,331.84	

Required:

a. Describe how James should verify the information in the payroll input form shown.

b. Describe (but do not perform) the procedures that James should follow in examining of the November 24, 2000, payroll register shown.

(AICPA, adapted)

DISCUSSION CASE

[7,8,9]   12-32   Service Corporation hired an independent computer programmer to develop a simplified payroll application for its newly purchased computer. The programmer developed an on-line database microcomputer system that minimized the level of knowledge required of the operator. It was based on typing answers to input cues that appeared on the terminal's viewing screen, examples of which follow:

A. Access routine:
   1. Operator access number to payroll file?
   2. Are there new employees?

B. New employee routine:
   1. Employee name?
   2. Employee number?
   3. Social Security number?
   4. Rate per hour?
   5. Single or married?
   6. Number of dependents?
   7. Account distribution?

C. Current payroll routine:
   1. Employee number?
   2. Regular hours worked?
   3. Overtime hours worked?
   4. Total employees this payroll period?

The independent auditor is attempting to verify that certain input validation (edit) checks exist to ensure that errors resulting from omissions, invalid entries, or other inaccuracies are detected during the typing of answers to the input cues.

Required:

a. Discuss the various types of input validation (edit) controls that the independent auditor would expect to find in the IT system.

b. Describe the assurances provided by each identified validation check.

(AICPA, adapted)

INTERNET ASSIGNMENT

[11,12]   12-33   Using an Internet browser, search for information on labor costs in the retail catalog industry (for example, labor costs as a percentage of sales).

Chapter **13**

Auditing the Inventory Cycle and Related Accounts

LEARNING OBJECTIVES

Upon completion of this chapter you will

[1] Develop an understanding of the inventory cycle.

[2] Identify and describe the types of documents and records used in the inventory cycle.

[3] Understand the functions in the inventory cycle.

[4] Know the appropriate segregation of duties for the inventory cycle.

[5] Identify and evaluate inherent risks relevant to the inventory cycle and related accounts.

[6] Assess control risk for the inventory cycle.

[7] Identify key internal controls and develop relevant tests of controls for inventory transactions.

[8] Relate the assessment of control risk to substantive testing.

[9] Identify substantive tests of transactions used to audit inventory and related accounts.

[10] Identify analytical procedures used to audit inventory and related accounts.

[11] Know how to audit standard costs.

[12] Know how to observe physical inventory.

[13] Identify tests of account balances used to audit inventory and related accounts.

[14] Evaluate the audit findings and reach a final conclusion on inventory and related accounts.

RELEVANT ACCOUNTING AND AUDITING PRONOUNCEMENTS

FASB Statement of Financial Accounting Concepts No. 5, "Recognition and Measurement in Financial Statements of Business Enterprises" (CON5)

FASB Statement of Financial Accounting Concepts No. 6, "Elements of Financial Statements" (CON6)

SAS No. 1, "Receivables and Inventory" (AU 331)

SAS No. 11, "Using the Work of a Specialist" (AU 336)

SAS No. 31, "Evidential Matter" (AU 326)

SAS No. 45, "Omnibus Statement on Auditing Standards—1983—Substantive Tests Prior to the Balance Sheet Date" (AU 313)

SAS No. 47, "Audit Risk and Materiality in Conducting an Audit" (AU 312)

SAS No. 55, "Consideration of Internal Control in a Financial Statement Audit" (AU 319)

SAS No. 56, "Analytical Procedures" (AU 329)

SAS No. 57, "Auditing Accounting Estimates" (AU 342)

SAS No. 69, "The Confirmation Process" (AU 330)

SAS No. 78, "Consideration of Internal Control in a Financial Statement Audit: An Amendment to SAS No. 55" (AU 319)

SAS No. 80, "Amendment to Statement on Auditing Standards No. 31, *Evidential Matter*" (AU 326)

SAS No. 82, Consideration of Fraud in a Financial Statement Audit (AU 316)

For most manufacturing, wholesale, and merchandising (retail) entities, inventory is a major component of the balance sheet. Inventory also represents one of the most complex parts of the audit. For example, while determining the quantity of inventory on hand is usually an easy audit step to complete, assigning costs to value those quantities is more difficult. Additionally, there

may be other troublesome valuation issues related to inventory such as obsolescence and lower-of-cost-or-market value.

The complexity of auditing inventory may also be affected by the degree of processing required to manufacture products. In a merchandising business, products are purchased directly from vendors with little or no additional processing by the entity before sale. In such cases, verifying inventory is relatively straightforward. On the other hand, determining a proper inventory value may be more difficult when the production process involves numerous steps. The presentation in this chapter mainly discusses inventory in terms of a merchandising company. However, the audit approach followed for merchandising entities is easily adapted to other types of inventory processes.

The coverage of the inventory cycle follows the three components of the audit risk model. An overview of the inventory cycle is presented first, followed by discussion of inherent risk factors and control risk assessment. The last part of the chapter discusses the substantive tests for inventory with particular emphasis on auditing standard costs and observing physical inventory. 🍂

Overview of the Inventory Cycle

[LO 1] The inventory cycle is affected by the internal control procedures previously discussed for the revenue, purchasing, and payroll cycles. Figure 13–1 shows how each of these cycles interacts with the inventory cycle. The acquisition of and payment for inventory are controlled via the purchasing cycle. The cost of both direct and indirect labor assigned to inventory is controlled through the payroll cycle. Last, finished goods are sold and accounted for as part of the revenue cycle. Thus, the "cradle-to-grave" cycle for inventory begins when goods are purchased and stored and ends when the finished goods are shipped to customers.

Exhibit 13–1 describes EarthWear's inventory system, while Figure 13–2 flowcharts the system. This description and flowchart provide a framework for discussing the internal control procedures and tests of controls for the inventory cycle in more detail. However, because of differences in products and their subsequent processing, the inventory cycle usually differs from one entity to the next. The reader should concentrate on understanding the basic concepts of internal control. The following topics related to the inventory cycle are discussed:

FIGURE 13–1

The Relationship of the Inventory Cycle to Other Accounting Cycles

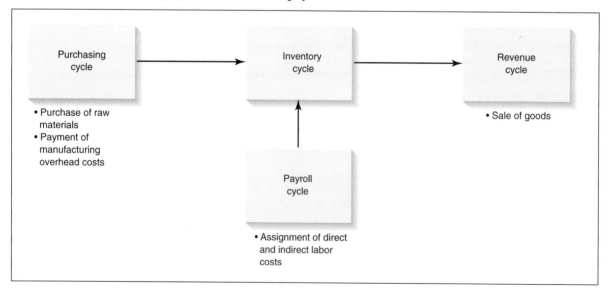

- Types of documents and records.
- The major functions.
- The key segregation of duties.

Types of Documents and Records

 [LO 2]

Table 13–1 lists the more important documents and records that are normally involved in the inventory cycle. Not all of these documents are presented in Figure 13–2. They are discussed here to give the reader information on documents and records that might exist in an inventory cycle of a manufacturing company. The reader should keep in mind that in an advanced IT system some of these documents and records may exist for only a short time or only in machine-readable form.

Production Schedule   A production schedule is normally prepared periodically based on the expected demand for the entity's products. The expected demand may be based on the current backlog of orders or on sales forecasts from the sales or marketing department. In EarthWear's system, this schedule is prepared by the design department. Production schedules determine the quantity of goods needed and the time at which they must be ready in order to meet the production scheduling. Many organizations use material requirements planning or just-in-time inventory programs to assist with production planning. Production schedules give the auditor information on the planned level of operating activity.

EXHIBIT 13–1

Description of EarthWear's Inventory System

Clothing and other products sold by EarthWear are developed by the company's design department. All goods are produced by independent manufacturers, except for most of EarthWear's soft luggage. The company purchases merchandise from more than 200 domestic and foreign manufacturers. For many major suppliers, goods are ordered and paid for through the company's electronic data interchange (EDI) system. The computerized inventory control system handles the receipt of shipments from manufacturers. Goods are received at the receiving department, where the information is agreed to the purchase order (receiving report) and entered into the inventory control system.

The company's sales representatives enter orders into an on-line order entry and inventory control system; customers using the company's Internet site complete a computer screen that enters the orders. Computer processing of orders is performed each night on a batch basis, at which time shipping tickets are printed with bar codes for optical scanning. Inventory is picked based on the location of individual products rather than orders, followed by computerized sorting and transporting of goods to multiple packing stations and shipping zones.

FIGURE 13–2
Flowchart of the Inventory Cycle—EarthWear Clothiers

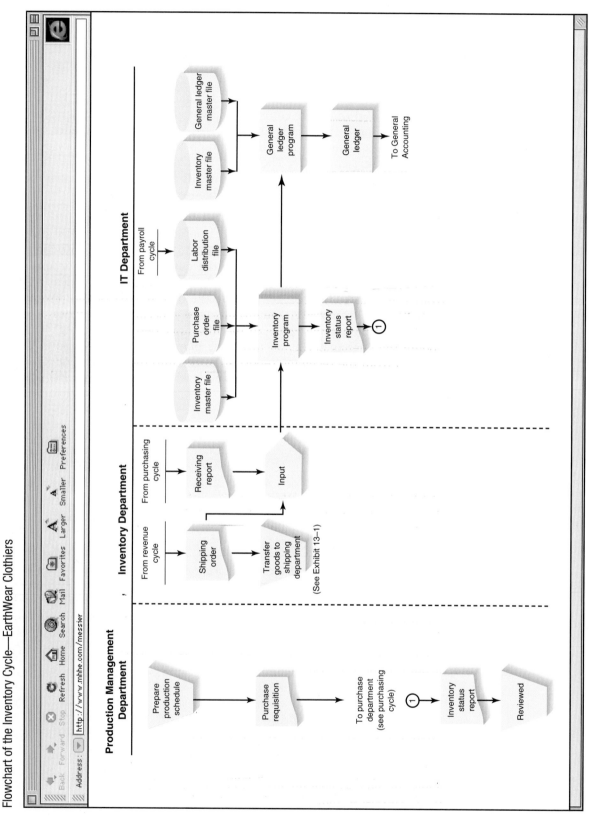

TABLE 13–1	Documents and Records Included in the Inventory Cycle

- Production schedule.
- Receiving report.
- Materials requisition.
- Inventory master file.
- Production data information.
- Cost accumulation and variance report.
- Inventory status report.
- Shipping order.

Receiving Report   The receiving report records the receipt of goods from vendors. This document was discussed as part of the purchasing cycle. It is reconsidered in the inventory cycle because a copy of this document accompanies the goods to the inventory department and is used to update the client's perpetual inventory records. Note in Figure 13–2 that the data from the receiving report are input into the inventory program to update the inventory master file, which contains the information on the client's perpetual records.

Materials Requisition   Materials requisitions are normally used by manufacturing companies to track materials during the production process. Materials requisitions are normally prepared by department personnel as needed for production purposes. For example, the materials requisition is the document that authorizes the release of raw materials from the raw materials department. A copy of the materials requisition may be maintained in the raw materials department, and another copy may accompany the goods to the production departments.

Inventory Master File   The inventory master file contains all the important information related to the entity's inventory, including the perpetual inventory records. In sophisticated inventory systems such as Earth-Wear's, the inventory master file also contains information on the costs used to value inventory. In a manufacturing company, it would not be unusual for the inventory master file to contain the standard costs used to value the inventory at various stages of production.

Production Data Information   In a manufacturing company, production information about the transfer of goods and related cost accumulation at each stage of production should be reported. This information updates the entity's perpetual inventory system. It is also used as input to generate the cost accumulation and variance reports that are produced by the inventory system.

Cost Accumulation and Variance Report   Most inventory control systems in a manufacturing setting produce reports similar to a cost accumulation and variance report. Material, labor, and overhead costs are charged to inventory as part of the manufacturing process. The cost accumulation report summarizes the various costs charged to departments and products. The variance reports present the results of inventory processing in terms of actual costs versus standard or budgeted costs. The cost accounting and manufacturing departments review these reports for appropriate charges.

Inventory Status Report   The inventory status report shows the type and amount of products on hand. Such a report is basically a summary of the perpetual inventory records. This report can also be used to determine the status of goods in process. In sophisticated inventory systems, this type of information can be accessed directly through computer terminals or microcomputers.

Shipping Order   This document was discussed as part of the revenue cycle. It is reconsidered here because a copy of this document is used to remove goods from the client's perpetual inventory records. Note in Figure 13–2 that the inventory master file is updated when open orders are processed and a shipping order is generated.

The Major Functions

Table 13–2 summarizes the functions that normally take place in a typical inventory cycle.

[LO 3]

Inventory Management   At EarthWear, the inventory management function is performed by the design department. This department is responsible for maintaining inventory at appropriate levels. It issues purchase requisitions to the purchasing department and thus represents the point at which the inventory cycle integrates with the purchasing cycle. In a manufacturing company, a production management department would be responsible for managing inventory through planning and scheduling manufacturing activities.

TABLE 13–2	Functions in the Inventory Cycle
• *Inventory management*	Authorization of production activity and maintenance of inventory at appropriate levels; issuance of purchase requisitions to the purchasing department (see Chapter 11 on the purchasing cycle).
• *Raw materials stores*	Custody of raw materials and issuance of raw materials to manufacturing departments.
• *Manufacturing*	Production of goods.
• *Finished goods stores*	Custody of finished goods and issuance of goods to the shipping department (see Chapter 10 on the revenue cycle).
• *Cost accounting*	Maintenance of the costs of manufacturing and inventory in cost records.
• *General ledger*	Proper accumulation, classification, and summarization of inventory and related costs in the general ledger.

Raw Materials Stores   In a manufacturing company, this function is responsible for the receipt, custody, and issuance of raw materials. When goods are received from vendors, they are transferred from the receiving department to the raw materials stores department. Once goods arrive in the raw materials storage area, they must be safeguarded against pilferage or unauthorized use. Finally, when goods are requested for production through the issuance of a materials requisition, this function issues the goods to the appropriate manufacturing department.

Manufacturing   The manufacturing function is responsible for producing the product. From an auditing perspective, there must be adequate control over the physical flow of the goods and proper accumulation of the costs attached to inventory. The manner in which costs are accumulated varies substantially from one entity to another. Entities may produce goods using a job order cost system, a process cost system, or some combination of both.

Finished Goods Stores   This function is responsible for the storage of and control over finished goods. When goods are completed by the manufacturing function, they are transferred to finished goods stores. Again, there must be adequate safeguards against pilferage or unauthorized use. When goods are ordered by a customer, a shipping order is produced by the revenue cycle and forwarded to the finished goods stores department. The goods are then transferred to the shipping department for shipment to the customer. Because EarthWear is a merchandising company, it maintains only finished goods (see Figure 13–2).

Cost Accounting   This function is responsible for ensuring that costs are properly attached to inventory as goods are processed through the manufacturing function. Cost accounting reviews the cost accumulation and variance reports after such data are processed into the accounting records.

General Ledger   The main objective of the general ledger function is to ensure that all inventory and costs of production are properly accumulated, classified, and summarized in the general ledger accounts. In an IT system, control or summary totals ensure that this function is performed correctly. One important control performed by the general ledger function is the reconciliation of the perpetual inventory records to the general ledger inventory accounts.

The Key Segregation of Duties

[LO 4]

Segregation of duties is a particularly important control in the inventory cycle because of the potential for theft and fraud. Therefore, individuals involved in the inventory management and inventory stores functions should not have access to the inventory records, the cost-accounting records, or the general ledger. When the inventory system is highly computerized, there should be proper segregation of duties within the IT department. Table 13–3 shows the key segregation of duties for the inventory cycle and examples of possible errors or fraud that can result from conflicts in duties.

TABLE 13–3	Key Segregation of Duties and Possible Errors or Fraud

Segregation of Duties	*Possible Errors or Fraud Resulting from Conflicts of Duties*
The inventory management function should be segregated from the cost-accounting function.	If the individual responsible for inventory management also has access to the cost-accounting records, production and inventory costs can be manipulated. This may lead to an over- or understatement of inventory and net income.
The inventory stores function should be segregated from the cost-accounting function.	If one individual is responsible for both controlling and accounting for inventory, unauthorized shipments can be made or theft of goods can be covered up.
The cost-accounting function should be segregated from the general ledger function.	If one individual is responsible for the inventory records and also for the general ledger, it is possible for that individual to conceal unauthorized shipments. This can result in the theft of goods, leading to an overstatement of inventory.
The responsibility for supervising physical inventory should be separated from the inventory management and inventory stores functions.	If the individual responsible for production management or inventory stores functions is also responsible for the physical inventory, it is possible that inventory shortages can be covered up through the adjustment of the inventory records to the physical inventory, resulting in an overstatement of inventory.

Table 13–4 shows the proper segregation of duties for individual inventory functions across the various departments that control inventory processing.

Inherent Risk Assessment

[LO 5] In examining the inventory cycle, the auditor needs to consider the inherent risk factors that may affect the transactions processed by the cycle and the financial statement accounts affected by those transactions. The auditor should consider industry-related factors and operating and engagement characteristics (see Chapter 3) when assessing the possibility of a material misstatement.

Industry-Related Factors

A number of industry factors may indicate the presence of material misstatements in inventory. For example, if industry competition is intense, there may be problems with the proper valuation of inventory in terms of lower-of-cost-or-market values. Rapid technology changes in certain industries may also promote material misstatement due to obsolescence (see Exhibit 13–2).

Engagement and Operating Characteristics

A number of engagement and operating characteristics are important to the assessment of inherent risk for inventory. First, the type of product sold by the client can increase the potential for defalcation. For example, products that are small and of high value, such as jewelry, are more susceptible to theft than large products are. Second, inventory is often difficult to audit, and its valuation may result in disagreements with the client. Finally, the auditor must be alert to possible related-party transactions for acquiring raw materials and selling finished product. For example, the client may purchase

TABLE 13–4	Segregation of Duties for Inventory Functions by Department

	Department				
Inventory Function	*Inventory Management*	*Raw Materials Stores*	*Finished Goods Stores*	*Cost Accounting*	*IT*
Preparation of production schedules	X				
Issuance of materials requisitions that accompany goods to the manufacturing department		X			
Updating of cost records with materials, labor, and overhead usage				X	X
Updating of inventory records				X	X
Release of goods to the shipping department			X		
Approval and issuance of purchase requisitions	X				

EXHIBIT 13–2

How Changes in Technology Led to Inventory Obsolescence Problems at MiniScribe

In the computer industry, technological change can significantly affect on inventory obsolescence and poses a major valuation problem for auditors. MiniScribe Corporation was a Colorado-based manufacturer of computer disk drives that went bankrupt, resulting in large payments by a Big 6 firm to stockholders and bondholders. In MiniScribe's case, its 1985 financial statements showed a reserve of $4.85 million for revaluing of computer parts for its inventory that were obsolete. In 1986 revenues increased from $114 million to $185 million, but a reserve of only $2.78 million was established for inventory obsolescence. An accounting expert testified that MiniScribe should have reserved $5.27 million for obsolete inventory in 1986.

Source: L. Berton, "How MiniScribe Got Its Auditor's Blessing on Questionable Sales," *The Wall Street Journal* (May 14, 1992). (See Chapter 20, appendix, for more information on this case.)

raw materials from a company controlled by the chief executive officer at prices in excess of market value. In such a case, the value of inventory will be overstated, and cash will have been misappropriated from the entity.

Audit research has also shown that inventory is likely to contain material misstatements.[1] Therefore, the auditor should consider whether material

---

[1]W. R. Kinney, Jr., and R. D. Martin, "Does Auditing Reduce Bias in Financial Reporting? A Review of Audit-Related Adjustment Studies," *Auditing: A Journal of Practice and Theory* (Spring 1994), pp. 149–55, reviews audit research studies indicating that inventory is likely to contain misstatements. For an example of a specific study, see A. Wright and R. H. Ashton, "Identifying Audit Adjustments with Attention-Directing Procedures," *The Accounting Review* (October 1989), pp. 710–28.

misstatements were found in prior years' audits. If so, the auditor should consider whether such misstatements may be present in the current inventory and plan the audit accordingly.

Control Risk Assessment

[LO 6]   The auditor may follow a substantive strategy when auditing inventory and cost of goods sold. When this is done, the auditor places no reliance on the control procedures in the inventory cycle and sets the level of control risk at the maximum. The auditor then relies on substantive tests to determine the fairness of inventory. Such a strategy may be appropriate when internal control is not adequate.

In many cases, however, the auditor can rely on internal control for inventory. This normally occurs when the client has an integrated cost-accounting/inventory management system. For discussion purposes, it is assumed that the auditor has decided to follow a reliance strategy. Figure 13–3 summarizes the three steps for assessing the control risk following this strategy. Each of these steps is only briefly reviewed within the context of the inventory cycle because the reader should thoroughly understand the control risk assessment process followed by auditors.

Understanding and Documenting Internal Control

In order to assess the control risk for the inventory cycle, the auditor must understand the five internal control components. Two points should be mentioned. First, if the client uses sophisticated IT techniques for monitoring the flow of goods and accumulating costs, the auditor will need to evaluate both the general IT controls and the inventory application controls. Second, the auditor will need a thorough understanding of the process used by the client to value inventory.

FIGURE 13–3

Major Steps in Assessing the
Control Risk in the Inventory
Cycle

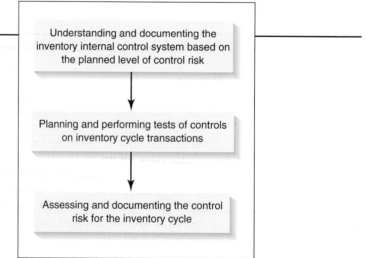

Planning and Performing Tests of Controls

In performing this step, the auditor again must identify the relevant control procedures within the client's inventory cycle that ensure that material misstatements are either prevented or detected and corrected. Audit procedures used to test the client's control procedures in the inventory cycle are discussed in subsequent sections.

Assessing and Documenting the Control Risk

Once the controls in the inventory cycle have been tested, the auditor assesses the level of control risk. The auditor should document the assessed level of control risk using either quantitative amounts or qualitative terms. The documentation supporting the assessed level of control risk for the inventory cycle might include a flowchart such as the one shown in Figure 13–2, the results of the tests of controls, and a memorandum indicating the overall conclusions about control risk.

Internal Control Procedures and Tests of Controls— Inventory Transactions

[LO 7] Table 13–5 provides a summary of the internal control objectives, possible misstatements, internal control procedures, and selected tests of controls for inventory transactions. The discussion includes internal control procedures that are present in a manufacturing setting. Because EarthWear is a retailer, the controls over the production process are not relevant. A number of control procedures in the revenue and purchasing cycles provide assurance for selected internal control objectives for inventory. The discussion that follows is limited to the more important internal control audit objectives.

Validity of Inventory Transactions

The auditor's main concern is that all recorded inventory exists and actually belongs to the client. The major internal control procedure for preventing fictitious inventory transactions from being recorded is proper segregation of duties, in which the inventory management and inventory stores functions are separated from the departments responsible for inventory and cost-accounting records. This control prevents operating personnel from having access to both inventory and the perpetual inventory records. Additionally, prenumbered documents to handle the receipt, transfer, and withdrawal of inventory may prevent the recording of fictitious inventory in the accounting records.

The auditor should also be concerned that goods may be stolen. The auditor's concern about theft of goods varies depending upon the type of product sold or manufactured by the client. Products that are large or cumbersome may be difficult to steal. However, some products that are small and of high value, such as jewelry or computer memory chips, may be susceptible to theft. The client should maintain physical safeguards over inventory that are consistent with the susceptibility and value of the goods.

Review and observation are the main tests of controls used by the auditor to test the control procedures shown in Table 13–5. For example, the auditor can observe and evaluate the employees' segregation of duties. The

TABLE 13–5	Summary of Internal Control Objectives, Possible Misstatements, Internal Control Procedures, and Tests of Controls for Inventory Transactions

Internal Control Objective	Possible Misstatement	Internal Control Procedure	Test of Controls
Validity	Fictitious inventory	Segregation of duties	Observe and evaluate proper segregation of duties.
		Inventory transferred to inventory department using an approved, prenumbered receiving report	Review and test procedures for the transfer of inventory.
		Inventory transferred to manufacturing using prenumbered materials requisitions	Review and test procedures for issuing materials to manufacturing departments.
		Accounting for numerical sequence of materials requisitions	Review and test client procedures for accounting for numerical sequence of materials requisitions.
	Inventory recorded but not on hand due to theft	Physical safeguards over inventory	Observe the physical safeguards over inventory.
Completeness	Inventory received but not recorded	The same as the control procedures for completeness in the purchasing cycle (see Table 11–5)	The same as the tests of controls performed on the control procedures in the purchasing cycle (see Table 11–5)
	Consigned goods not properly accounted for	Procedures to include goods out on consignment and exclude goods held on consignment	Review and test client's procedures for consignment goods.
Timeliness	Inventory transactions recorded in the wrong period	All receiving reports processed daily by the IT department to record the receipt of inventory	Review and test procedures for processing inventory included on receiving reports into the perpetual records.
		All shipping documents processed daily to record the shipment of finished goods	Review and test procedures for removing inventory from perpetual records based on shipment of goods.

(continued)

TABLE 13–5 (*concluded*)

Internal Control Objective	Possible Misstatement	Internal Control Procedure	Test of Controls
Authorization	Unauthorized production activity, resulting in excess levels of inventory	Preparation and review of authorized purchase or production schedules	Review authorized production schedules.
	Inventory obsolescence	Use of material requirements planning and/or just-in-time inventory systems	Review and test procedures for developing inventory levels and procedures used to control them.
		Review of inventory levels by design department	
Valuation	Inventory quantities recorded incorrectly	Periodic or annual comparison of goods on hand with amounts shown in perpetual inventory records	Review and test procedures for taking physical inventory.
	Inventory and cost of goods sold not properly costed	Standard costs that are reviewed by management	Review and test procedures used to develop standard costs.
		Review of cost accumulation and variance reports	Review and test cost accumulation and variance reports.
	Inventory obsolescence	Inventory management personnel review inventory for obsolete, slow-moving, or excess quantities	Review and test procedures for identifying obsolete, slow-moving, or excess quantities.
Classification	Inventory transactions not properly classified among raw materials, work in process, and finished goods	Materials requisitions and production data forms used to process goods through manufacturing	Review the procedures and forms used to classify inventory.
Posting and summarization	Inventory transactions not posted to the perpetual inventory records	Perpetual inventory records reconciled to general ledger control account monthly	Review the reconciliation of perpetual inventory to general ledger control account.
	Amounts for inventory from purchases journal not posted correctly to the general ledger inventory account		

auditor can also review and test the client's procedures for the transfer of raw materials from the receiving department and their issuance to the manufacturing departments.

Completeness of Inventory Transactions

The internal control procedures for the completeness objective relate to recording inventory that has been received. Typically, the control procedures for this objective are contained within the purchasing cycle. These control procedures and the related tests of controls were presented in Table 11–5 in Chapter 11. For example, in some instances, additional control procedures may be used in the raw materials stores department to ensure that the goods are recorded in the perpetual inventory records. This might include comparing a summary of the receiving reports to the inventory status report.

If goods are consigned, the client must have control procedures to ensure that goods held on consignment by other parties are included in inventory and goods held on consignment for others are excluded from inventory. The auditor can review the client's procedures for including or excluding consigned goods.

Authorization of Inventory Transactions

The control procedures for the purchase of materials were discussed in Chapter 11 on the purchasing cycle. The auditor's concern with authorization in the inventory cycle is with unauthorized purchase or production activity that may lead to excess levels of certain types of finished goods. If such goods can quickly become obsolete, ending inventory may be overstated. The preparation and review of authorized purchase schedules by EarthWear's design department should prevent such misstatements. The use of some type of inventory-planning system, such as a material requirements planning system or a just-in-time inventory system, may also limit unauthorized production.

Valuation of Inventory Transactions

Valuation is an important internal control objective because inventory transactions that are not properly valued result in misstatements that directly affect the amounts reported in the financial statements for cost of goods sold and inventory. Proper valuation of inventory involves accurately determining the quantity of goods on hand and assigning the appropriate costs to these goods. The use of a perpetual inventory system in conjunction with a periodic or annual physical inventory count should result in the proper quantities of inventory being shown in the client's perpetual inventory records. EarthWear maintains the purchase cost of its products in its master inventory file. Many manufacturing companies use standard costing systems to value their inventory. Standard costs should approximate actual costs, and the presence of large variances is one signal that the inventory may not be costed at an appropriate value. Auditing the client's physical inventory and standard costs is discussed in more detail later in the chapter.

Proper valuation also involves inventory obsolescence. Inventory management personnel should periodically review inventory on hand for obsolete, slow-moving, or excess inventory. Such inventory should be written down to its fair market value. The auditor can review the client's procedures for identifying obsolete, slow-moving, or excess inventory. EarthWear's design department closely monitors its products to identify any end-of-season merchandise or overstocks, which are then sold at liquidation prices through special catalog inserts.

Classification of Inventory Transactions

Classification is not an important internal control objective for EarthWear because all goods are finished and ready for sale. However, in a manufacturing company, the client must have control procedures to ensure that inventory is properly classified as raw materials, work in process, or finished goods. This can usually be accomplished by determining which departments in the manufacturing process are included in raw materials, work in process, and finished goods inventory. Thus, by knowing which manufacturing department holds the inventory, the client is able to classify it by type.

Relating the Assessed Level of Control Risk to Substantive Testing

[LO 8]   The same judgment process is followed in assessing control risk in the inventory cycle that was used with other cycles. For example, EarthWear has strong controls over the processing of inventory transactions. The auditor can rely on those controls if tests of controls indicate that the controls are operating effectively. If the results of the tests of controls for the inventory cycle do not support the planned level of control risk, the auditor would judge control risk to be higher and set detection risk lower. This would lead to increased substantive tests.

Auditing Inventory

The discussion of the audit of inventory follows the process outlined in prior chapters. Three categories of substantive tests are discussed: substantive tests of transactions, analytical procedures, and tests of inventory account balances. Table 13–6 lists the audit objectives for testing an account balance.

Substantive Tests of Transactions

[LO 9]   The auditor may conduct substantive tests of transactions specifically for inventory. However, because the inventory cycle interacts with the revenue, purchasing, and payroll cycles, transactions involving the receipt of goods, shipment of goods, and assignment of labor costs are normally

TABLE 13–6	Audit Objectives for Testing Inventory
• *Validity*	Determine whether recorded inventory actually exists.
• *Completeness*	Determine whether all inventory is recorded.
• *Cutoff*	Determine whether all transactions that affect inventory are recorded in the correct period.
• *Ownership*	Determine whether all recorded inventory is owned by the entity and whether it is subject to any liens or restrictions.
• *Accuracy*	Determine whether inventory is properly accumulated from journals and ledgers.
• *Valuation*	Determine whether inventory is properly valued in accordance with GAAP.
• *Classification*	Determine whether inventory is properly classified in the general ledger and the financial statements.
• *Disclosure*	Determine whether all disclosures related to inventory are included in the financial statements.

tested as part of those cycles. For example, receiving department personnel prepare a receiving report that includes the quantity and type of goods received. The receiving report and vendor invoice are then used to record the accounts payable. If the auditor intends to obtain substantive evidence on the perpetual inventory records, the tests of receipt and shipment of goods can be extended by tracing the transactions into the perpetual inventory records. For example, the receiving report is generally used by the client to record the goods in the perpetual inventory records or inventory master file (see Figure 13–2). The auditor can perform a substantive test of transactions by tracing a sample of receiving reports into the perpetual inventory records. Labor costs can also be traced to individual inventory transactions and into the cost-accounting records.

Analytical Procedures

[LO 10]   Analytical procedures are useful audit tests for examining the reasonableness of inventory and cost of goods sold. When performed as part of audit planning, analytical procedures can effectively identify whether the inventory and cost of goods sold accounts contain material misstatements. Analytical procedures are also useful as an overall review for inventory and related accounts. In particular, by identifying obsolete, slow-moving, and excess inventory, analytical procedures are useful for testing the valuation objective for inventory. Such tests can also identify problems with improper inclusion or exclusion of costs in overhead. Table 13–7 lists analytical procedures that are useful in auditing inventory and related accounts at either the planning stage or as an overall review.

For example, the inventory turnover ratio (cost of goods sold ÷ inventory) can be compared over time or to an industry average. A high inventory turnover ratio normally indicates efficient inventory policies, while a

TABLE 13–7	**Analytical Procedures for Inventory and Related Accounts**
Analytical Procedure	*Possible Misstatement Indentified*
Compare raw material, finished goods, and total inventory turnover to previous years' and industry averages.	Obsolete, slow-moving, or excess inventory
Compare days outstanding in inventory to previous years' and industry average.	Obsolete, slow-moving, or excess inventory
Compare gross profit percentage by product line with previous years' and industry data.	Unrecorded or fictitious inventory
Compare actual cost of goods sold to budgeted amounts.	Over- or understated inventory
Compare current-year standard costs with prior years' after considering current conditions.	Over- or understated inventory
Compare actual manufacturing overhead costs with budgeted or standard manufacuring overhead costs.	Inclusion or exclusion of overhead costs

low ratio may indicate the presence of slow-moving or obsolete inventory. The gross profit percentage can also be compared to previous years' or industry data and may provide valuable evidence on unrecorded inventory (an understatement) or fictitious inventory (an overstatement). This ratio may also provide information on the proper valuation of inventory. For example, a small or negative gross profit margin may indicate issues related to the lower-of-cost-or-market valuation of inventory.

Prior to presenting the tests of account balances for inventory, this chapter discusses two main audit procedures: auditing standard costs and observing physical inventory.

Auditing Standard Costs

[LO 11] Many manufacturing entities use a standard cost system to measure performance and to value inventory. If a standard cost system is integrated with the general accounting records, cost accumulation and variance reports are direct outputs of the client's inventory-accounting system.

For proper valuation, standard costs should approximate actual costs. To test the standard costs, the auditor should first review the client's policies and procedures for constructing standard costs. Once the policies and procedures are understood, the auditor normally tests the component cost buildup for a representative sample of standard product costs.

Three components make up the cost of producing a product: materials, labor, and overhead. For discussion purposes, suppose that Calabro Paging Services (see problem 3-41) assembles five types of pagers. Assume further that all parts used in the pagers are purchased from outside vendors. The process followed in auditing the three components that make up the standard costs for a type of pager follows.

Materials

Determining the materials costs requires testing the quantity and type of materials included in the product and the price of the materials. The quantity and type of materials are tested by reviewing the engineering specifications for the product. For example, in the case of pagers, the auditor can obtain a set of engineering specifications that includes a blueprint and a list of materials needed to manufacture a particular pager. The auditor can compare the list of materials with the standard cost card or other documentation used to support the cost accumulation. The prices used on the standard cost card can be traced to vendors' invoices as a test of actual costs.

Labor

The determination of labor costs requires evidence about the type and amount of labor needed for production and the labor rate. Following our example, the amount of labor necessary to assemble a pager can be tested by reviewing engineering estimates, which may be based on time-and-motion studies or on historical information. The labor rates for each type of labor necessary to assemble a pager can be tested by examining a schedule of authorized wages.

Overhead

The auditor tests overhead costs by reviewing the client's method of overhead allocation for reasonableness, compliance with GAAP, and consistency. The auditor can examine the costs included in overhead to be sure that such costs can appropriately be assigned to the product. The inclusion or exclusion of such costs should be consistent from one period to the next. Using the pager example, the auditor would obtain a listing of expense accounts used to make up the overhead pool of costs. The auditor can compare the actual costs for the period to the budgeted costs. The auditor can also compare the costs included in the current year's listing with those in the prior year's listing.

Observing Physical Inventory

[LO 12] The auditor's observation of inventory is a generally accepted auditing procedure (AU 331). However, the auditor is not required to observe all inventory, but only inventory that is material. Internal auditors may also observe physical inventory. The primary reason for observing the client's physical inventory is to establish the *validity* or *existence* of the inventory. The observation of the physical inventory also provides evidence on the *ownership* and *valuation* audit objectives. Based on the physical inventory count, the client compiles the physical inventory. While the form of compilation may differ among entities, it normally contains a list of the items by type and quantity, the assigned cost for each item, the inventory value for each item, and a total for the inventory.

Prior to the physical count of inventory, the auditor should be familiar with the inventory locations, the major items in inventory, and the client's instructions for counting inventory. During the observation of the physical inventory count, the auditor should do the following:

- Ensure that no production is scheduled. Or, if production is scheduled, ensure that proper controls are established for movement between departments in order to prevent double counting.
- Ensure that there is no movement of goods during the inventory count. If movement is necessary, the auditor and client personnel must ensure that the goods are not double counted and that all goods are counted.
- Make sure that the client's count teams are following the inventory count instructions. If the count teams are not following the instructions, the auditor should notify the client representative in charge of the area.
- Ensure that inventory tags are issued sequentially to individual departments. For many inventory counts, the goods are marked with multicopy inventory tags. The count teams record the type and quantity of inventory on each tag, and one copy of each tag is then used to compile the inventory. If the client uses another method of counting inventory, such as detailed inventory listings, the auditor should obtain copies of the listings prior to the start of the inventory count.

- Perform test counts and record a sample of counts in the working papers. This information will be used to test the accuracy and completeness of the client's inventory compilation.
- Obtain tag control information for testing the client's inventory compilation. Tag control information includes documentation of the numerical sequence of all inventory tags and accounting for all used and unused inventory tags. If inventory listings are used by the client, copies of the listings will accomplish the objective of documenting the entire inventory count.
- Obtain cutoff information, including the number of the last shipping and receiving documents issued on the date of the physical inventory count.
- Observe the condition of the inventory for items that may be obsolete, slow-moving, or carried in excess quantities.
- Inquire about goods held on consignment for others or held on a "bill-and-hold" basis. Such items should not be included in the client's inventory. The auditor must also inquire about goods held on consignment for the client. These goods should be included in the inventory count.

If these audit procedures are followed, the auditor has reasonable assurance that a proper inventory count has been taken.

Tests of Account Balances

[LO 13]   Table 13–8 summarizes the tests of the inventory account balance for each audit objective. Accuracy is discussed first because the auditor must establish that the detailed records that support the inventory account agree with the general ledger account.

Accuracy

Testing the accuracy of inventory requires obtaining a copy of the compilation of the physical inventory that shows inventory quantities and prices. The inventory compilation is footed, and the mathematical extensions of quantity multiplied by price are tested. Additionally, test counts made by the auditor during the physical inventory and tag control information are traced into the compilation.

Many times the client has adjusted the general ledger inventory balance to agree to the physical inventory amounts (referred to as *book-to-physical adjustment*) before the auditor begins the substantive tests of account balances. If the client has made the book-to-physical adjustment, the totals from the compilation for inventory should agree with the general ledger.

When the client maintains a perpetual inventory system, the totals from the inventory compilation should also be agreed to these records. The auditor can use computer-assisted audit techniques to accomplish these audit steps. For example, the auditor can use a generalized or custom audit software package to trace test counts and tag control information into the client's computer file of the inventory compilation. The extensions and footing can also be tested at the same time.

TABLE 13–8	Summary of Audit Objectives and Tests of Account Balances—Inventory

Audit Objective	Tests of Account Balances
Validity	Observe count of physical inventory (see discussion in chapter for proper inventory observation procedures).
Completeness	Trace test counts and tag control information to the inventory compilation.*
	Confirm or observe any inventory held on consignment by others or in public warehouses.
Cutoff	Examine a sample of receiving documents for a few days before and after year-end for recording of inventory purchases in the proper period (see Chapter 11 for purchase cutoff procedures).
	Examine a sample of shipping documents for a few days before and after year-end for recording of inventory shipments in the proper period (see Chapter 10 for sales cutoff procedures).
Ownership	Verify that inventory held on consignment for others is not included in inventory.
	Verify that "bill-and-hold" goods are not included in inventory.
Accuracy	Obtain a copy of the inventory compilation and agree totals to general ledger.
	Trace test counts and tag control information to the inventory compilation.*
	Test mathematical accuracy of extensions and foot the inventory compilation.*
Valuation	Audit standard costs or other methods used to price inventory (see discussion in the chapter for the audit procedures used to audit standard costs).
	Trace costs used to price goods in the inventory compilation to standard costs or vendors' invoices.
	Perform a lower-of-cost-or-market test on large inventory items or product lines.
	Inquire of management concerning obsolete, slow-moving, or excess inventory.
	Review book-to-physical adjustment for possible misstatements (see Table 13–9).
Classification	Review inventory compilation for proper classification among raw materials, work in process, and finished goods.
Disclosure	Inquire of management and review any loan agreements and board of directors' minutes for any indication that inventory has been pledged or assigned.
	Inquire of management about issues related to LIFO liquidations and warranty obligations.

*CAATs may be used to perform these audit procedures.

Validity

Validity or existence is one of the more important audit objectives for the inventory account. The observation of the physical inventory is the primary audit step used to verify this objective. If the auditor is satisfied with the client's physical inventory count, the auditor has sufficient, competent evidence on the validity or existence of recorded inventory.

Completeness

The auditor must determine whether all inventory has been included in the inventory compilation and the general ledger inventory account. The tests related to the observation of the physical inventory count provide assurance that all goods on hand are included in inventory. Tracing test counts and tag control information into the inventory compilation provides assurance that the inventory counted during the physical inventory observation is included in the compilation. In some cases, inventory is held on consignment by others or is stored in public warehouses (AU 331.14). The auditor normally confirms or physically observes such inventory.

Cutoff

In testing the cutoff objective for inventory, the auditor attempts to determine whether all sales of finished goods and purchases of raw materials are recorded in the proper period. For sales cutoff, the auditor can examine a sample of shipping documents for a few days before and after year-end for recording of inventory shipments in the proper period. For purchases cutoff, the auditor can examine a sample of receiving documents for a few days before and after year-end for recording of inventory purchases in the proper period. Chapters 10 and 11 discuss sales and purchases cutoff.

Ownership

The auditor must determine whether the recorded inventory is actually owned by the entity. Two issues related to ownership can arise. First, the auditor must be sure that the inventory on hand belongs to the client. If the client holds inventory on consignment, such inventory should not be included in the physical inventory. Second, in some industries, goods are sold on a "bill-and-hold" basis. In such cases, the goods are treated as a sale but the client holds the goods until the customer needs them. Again, the auditor must be certain that such goods are segregated and not counted at the time of the physical inventory.

Valuation

A number of important valuation issues are related to inventory. The first issue relates to the costs used to value the inventory items included in the compilation. When the client, such as EarthWear, purchases inventory, valuation of the inventory can normally be accomplished by vouching the costs to vendors' invoices. When the client uses standard costs, the auditor audits the standard costs as discussed previously. The second valuation issue relates to the lower-of-cost-or-market tests for inventory. The auditor normally performs such tests on large-dollar items or on the client's various product lines. At EarthWear, the auditors would likely perform the lower-of-cost-or-market test on merchandise noted by management for liquidation. A third valuation issue relates to obsolete, slow-moving, or excess inventory. The auditor should ask management about such issues. When these issues exist, the inventory should be written down to its current market value. Finally, the auditor should investigate any large adjustments between the amount of inventory shown in the general ledger account and the amount determined from the physical inventory count (book-to-physical adjustments) for possible misstatements. Table 13–9 presents a list of items that may lead to book-to-physical differences.

Classification

Classification of inventory for EarthWear is not an issue because the company sells only finished products. However, in a manufacturing company, the auditor must determine that inventory is properly classified as raw materials, work in process, or finished goods. In most manufacturing

TABLE 13–9	Possible Causes of Book-to-Physical Differences

- Inventory cutoff errors.
- Unreported scrap or spoilage.
- Pilferage or theft.

TABLE 13–10	Sample Disclosure Items for Inventory and Related Accounts

- Cost method (FIFO, LIFO, retail method).
- Components of inventory.
- Long-term purchase contracts.
- Consigned inventory.
- Purchases from related parties.
- LIFO liquidations.
- Pledged or assigned inventory.
- Disclosure of unusual losses from write-downs of inventory or losses on long-term purchase commitments.
- Warranty obligations.

companies, proper classification can be achieved by determining which manufacturing processing department has control of the inventory on the date of the physical count. For example, if inventory tags are used to count inventory and they are assigned numerically to departments, classification can be verified at the physical inventory. The auditor can ensure that each department is using the assigned tags. The tag control information by department can be compared to the information on the inventory compilation to ensure that it is properly classified among raw materials, work in process, and finished goods.

Disclosure

Several important disclosure issues are related to inventory. Table 13–10 presents some examples of disclosure items for inventory and related accounts. For example, management must disclose the cost method, such as LIFO or FIFO, used to value inventory. Management must also disclose the components (raw materials, work in process, and finished goods) of inventory either on the face of the balance sheet or in the footnotes. Finally, if the entity uses LIFO to value inventory and there is a material LIFO liquidation, footnote disclosure is normally required. Exhibit 13–3 presents EarthWear's financial statement disclosure

EXHIBIT 13–3

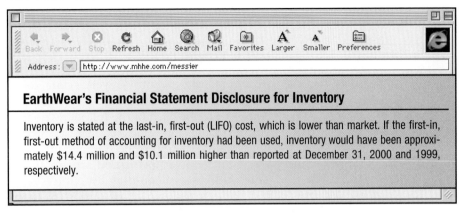

EarthWear's Financial Statement Disclosure for Inventory

Inventory is stated at the last-in, first-out (LIFO) cost, which is lower than market. If the first-in, first-out method of accounting for inventory had been used, inventory would have been approximately $14.4 million and $10.1 million higher than reported at December 31, 2000 and 1999, respectively.

for inventory. Note that the company uses LIFO to value inventory, and it discloses the approximate inventory value if FIFO had been used.

Evaluating the Audit Findings—Inventory

[LO 14] When the auditor has completed the planned substantive tests of the inventory account, all of the identified misstatements should be aggregated. The likely misstatement is compared to the tolerable misstatement allocated to the inventory account. If the likely misstatement is less than the tolerable misstatement, the auditor may accept the inventory account as fairly presented. Conversely, if the likely misstatement exceeds the tolerable misstatement, the auditor should conclude that the inventory account is not fairly presented.

For example, in Chapter 3 (Exhibit 3–4), tolerable misstatement of $250,000 was allocated to EarthWear's inventory. Exhibit 3-5 showed that Willis & Adams detected two misstatements in inventory: one that resulted in an overstatement of inventory by $112,500 based on a projection of a sample and one misstatement that understated inventory by $27,450 due to inventory in transit. Because neither of these misstatements is greater than the tolerable misstatement of $250,000, Willis & Adams can conclude that the audit evidence supports fair presentation. However, if these misstatements, either individually or net, had been greater than the tolerable misstatement, the evidence would not support fair presentation. In this case the auditor would have two choices: adjust the accounts to reduce the misstatement to an amount less than the tolerable misstatement or qualify the audit report.

The auditor should again analyze the misstatements discovered through the application of substantive tests of transactions, analytical procedures, and tests of account balances, because these misstatements may provide additional evidence on the control risk for the inventory cycle. If the auditor concludes that the audit risk is unacceptably high, additional audit procedures should be performed, or the auditor must be satisfied that the client has adjusted the related financial statement accounts to an acceptable level.

REVIEW QUESTIONS

[LO 1] 13-1 Why does inventory represent one of the more complex parts of the audit?

[1] 13-2 How does the inventory cycle relate to the revenue, purchasing, and payroll cycles?

[2] 13-3 Briefly describe each of the following documents or records: production schedule, materials requisition, inventory master file, production data information, and cost accumulation and variance reports.

[3] 13-4 What duties are performed within the inventory management, stores, and cost-accounting functions?

[4] 13-5 List the key segregation of duties in the inventory cycle. What errors or fraud can occur if such segregation of duties is not present?

[5] 13-6 List the inherent risk factors that affect the inventory cycle.

[6] 13-7 List the major steps in assessing control risk in the inventory cycle.

[7] 13-8 What control procedures can a client use to prevent unauthorized inventory production?

[10] 13-9 List three analytical procedures that can test the fairness of inventory and related accounts.

[11] 13-10 Describe how an auditor audits standard costs.

[12] 13-11 List the procedures the auditor should perform during the count of the client's physical inventory.

[13] 13-12 What are some possible causes of book-to-physical inventory differences?

[13] 13-13 List five items for inventory and related accounts that may require disclosure.

MULTIPLE-CHOICE QUESTIONS FROM CPA EXAMINATIONS

[3,7] 13-14 The objectives of internal control for an inventory cycle are to provide assurance that transactions are properly executed and recorded and that
   a. Independent internal verification of activity reports is established.
   b. Transfers to the finished goods department are documented by a completed production report and a quality control report.
   c. Production orders are prenumbered and signed by a supervisor.
   d. Custody of work in process and finished goods is properly maintained.

[4,7] 13-15 Which of the following would most likely be an internal control procedure designed to detect errors and fraud concerning the custody of inventory?
   a. Periodic reconciliation of work in process with job cost sheets.
   b. Segregation of functions between general accounting and cost accounting. *could have collusion*
   c. Independent comparisons of finished goods records with counts of goods on hand.
   d. Approval of inventory journal entries by the storekeeper.

[7] 13-16 Which of the following control procedures would be most likely to assist in reducing the control risk related to the existence or occurrence of manufacturing transactions?
  a. Perpetual inventory records are independently compared with goods on hand.
  b. Forms used for direct materials requisitions are prenumbered and accounted for.
  c. Finished goods are stored in locked limited-access warehouses.
  d. Subsidiary ledgers are periodically reconciled with inventory control accounts.

[4,7] 13-17 Independent internal verification of inventory occurs when employees who
  a. Issue raw materials obtain materials requisitions for each issue and prepare daily totals of materials issued.
  b. Compare records of goods on hand with physical quantities do *not* maintain the records or have custody of the inventory.
  c. Obtain receipts for the transfer of completed work to finished goods prepare a completed production report.
  d. Are independent of issuing production orders update records from completed job cost sheets and production cost reports on a timely basis.

[7] 13-18 An auditor's tests of controls over the issuance of raw materials to production would most likely include
  a. Reconciliation of raw materials and work-in-process perpetual inventory records to general ledger balances.
  b. Inquiry of the custodian about the procedures followed when defective materials are received from vendors.
  c. Observation that raw materials are stored in secure areas and that storeroom security is supervised by a responsible individual.
  d. Examination of materials requisitions and reperformance of client controls designed to process and record issuances.

[7] 13-19 Which of the following internal control procedures is most likely to address the completeness assertion for inventory?
  a. The work-in-process account is periodically reconciled with subsidiary records.
  b. Employees responsible for custody of finished goods do *not* perform the receiving function.
  c. Receiving reports are prenumbered and periodically reconciled.
  d. There is a separation of duties between payroll department and inventory accounting personnel.

[8,12,13] 13-20 A client maintains perpetual inventory records in both quantities and dollars. If the assessed level of control risk were high, an auditor would probably
  a. Insist that the client perform physical counts of inventory items several times during the year.
  b. Apply gross profit tests to ascertain the reasonableness of the physical counts.
  c. Increase the extent of tests of controls of the inventory cycle.
  d. Request that the client schedule the physical inventory count at the end of the year.

[13]   13-21   When auditing merchandise inventory at year-end, the auditor performs a purchase cutoff test to obtain evidence that
   a. All goods purchased before year-end are received before the physical inventory count.   *not necessarily = shipping terms*
   b. No goods held on consignment for customers are included in the inventory balance.
   c. No goods observed during the physical count are pledged or sold.
   d. All goods owned at year-end are included in the inventory balance.

[13]   13-22   An auditor using audit software would probably be _least_ interested in which of the following fields in a computerized perpetual inventory file?
   a. Economic order quantity.
   b. Warehouse location.
   c. Date of last purchase.
   d. Quantity sold.

[12,13] 13-23   Inquiries of warehouse personnel concerning possibly obsolete or slow-moving inventory items provide assurance about management's assertion of
   a. Completeness.
   b. Existence.
   c. Presentation.
   d. Valuation.

[13]   13-24   Which of the following audit procedures would probably provide the most reliable evidence concerning the entity's assertion of rights and obligations related to inventory?
   a. Tracing of test counts noted during the entity's physical count to the entity's summarization of quantities.
   b. Inspection of agreements to determine whether any inventory is pledged as collateral or subject to any liens.
   c. Selection of the last few shipping advices used before the physical count and determination of whether the shipments were recorded as sales.   *cut off*
   d. Inspection of the open-purchase-order file for significant commitments that should be considered for disclosure.

[12,13] 13-25   Periodic or cycle counts of selected inventory items are made at various times during the year rather than via a single inventory count at year-end. Which of the following is necessary if the auditor plans to observe inventory at interim dates?
   a. Complete recounts are performed by independent teams.
   b. Perpetual inventory records are maintained.
   c. Unit cost records are integrated with production-accounting records.
   d. Inventory balances are rarely at low levels.

[12]   13-26   After accounting for a sequence of inventory tags, an auditor traces a sample of tags to the physical inventory listing to obtain evidence that all items   *tracing (completeness)*
   a. Included in the listing have been counted.
   b. Represented by inventory tags are included in the listing.
   c. Included in the listing are represented by inventory tags.
   d. Represented by inventory tags are bona fide.

PROBLEMS

[3,7] 13-27 Yardley, CPA, prepared the flowchart on the following page, which portrays the raw materials purchasing function of one of Yardley's clients, a medium-size manufacturing company, from the preparation of initial documents through the vouching of invoices for payment. The flowchart represents a portion of the work performed on the audit engagement to evaluate internal control.

Required:
Identify and explain the systems and control weaknesses evident from the flowchart. Include the internal control weaknesses resulting from activities performed or not performed. All documents are prenumbered.

(AICPA, adapted)

[1,6,12,13] 13-28 Rasch is the partner-in-charge of the audit of Bonner Distributing Corporation, a wholesaler that owns one warehouse containing 80 percent of its inventory. Rasch is reviewing the working papers that were prepared to support the firm's opinion on Bonner's financial statements, and Rasch wants to be certain that essential audit tests are well documented.

Required:
a. What evidence should Rasch find in the working papers to support the fact that the audit was adequately planned and the assistants were properly supervised?
b. What substantive tests should Rasch expect to find in the working papers to document management's assertion about completeness as it relates to the inventory quantities at the end of the year?

(AICPA, adapted)

[12,13] 13-29 Kachelmeier, CPA, is auditing the financial statements of Big Z Wholesaling, Inc., a continuing audit client, for the year ended January 31, 2000. On January 5, 2000, Kachelmeier observed the tagging and counting of Big Z's physical inventory and made appropriate test counts. These test counts have been recorded on a computer file. As in prior years, Big Z gave Kachelmeier two computer files. One file represents the perpetual inventory (FIFO) records for the year ended January 31, 2000. The other file represents the January 5 physical inventory count.

Assume that:
1. Kachelmeier issued an unqualified opinion on the prior year's financial statements.
2. All inventory is purchased for resale and located in a single warehouse.
3. Kachelmeier has appropriate computerized audit software.
4. The perpetual inventory file contains the following information in item number sequence:
   • Beginning balances at February 1, 1999: item number, item description, total quantity, and price.

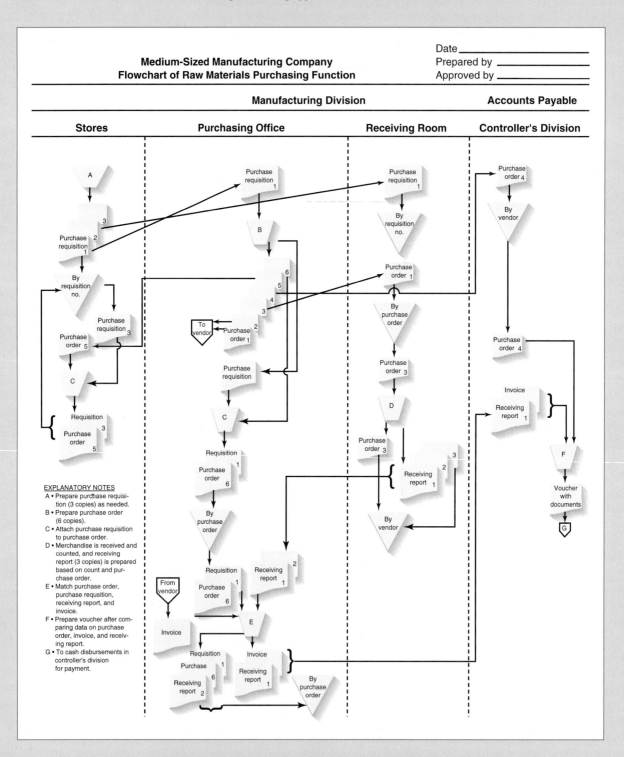

Medium-Sized Manufacturing Company
Flowchart of Raw Materials Purchasing Function

Date _____
Prepared by _____
Approved by _____

Manufacturing Division — Accounts Payable

Stores | Purchasing Office | Receiving Room | Controller's Division

EXPLANATORY NOTES

A • Prepare purchase requisition (3 copies) as needed.
B • Prepare purchase order (6 copies).
C • Attach purchase requisition to purchase order.
D • Merchandise is received and counted, and receiving report (3 copies) is prepared based on count and purchase order.
E • Match purchase order, purchase requisition, receiving report, and invoice.
F • Prepare voucher after comparing data on purchase order, invoice, and receiving report.
G • To cash disbursements in controller's division for payment.

- For each item purchased during the year: date received, receiving report number, vendor item number, item description, quantity, and total dollar amount.
- For each item sold during the year: date shipped, invoice number, item number, item description, quantity, and dollar amount.
- For each item adjusted for physical inventory count differences: date, item number, item description, quantity, and dollar amount.

5. The physical inventory file contains the following information in item number sequence: tag number, item number, item description, and quantity.

Required:

Describe the substantive auditing procedures Kachelmeier may consider performing with computerized audit software using Big Z's two computer files and Kachelmeier's computer file of test counts. The substantive auditing procedures described may indicate the reports to be printed out for Kachelmeier's follow-up by subsequent application of manual procedures. Group the procedures by those using (a) the perpetual inventory file and (b) the physical inventory and test count files. Do *not* describe subsequent manual auditing procedures.

(AICPA, adapted)

[12] 13-30 Abbott Corporation does not conduct a complete annual physical count of purchased parts and supplies in its principal warehouse but instead uses statistical sampling to estimate the year-end inventory. Abbott maintains a perpetual inventory record of parts and supplies and believes that statistical sampling is highly effective in determining inventory values and is sufficiently reliable to make a physical count of each item of inventory unnecessary.

Required:

a. Identify the audit procedures that should be used by the independent auditor that change, or are in addition to, normal required audit procedures when a client utilizes statistical sampling to determine inventory value and does not conduct a 100 percent annual physical count of inventory items.

b. List at least 10 normal audit procedures that should be performed to verify physical quantities whenever a client conducts a periodic physical count of all, or part, of its inventory.

(AICPA, adapted)

[12,13] 13-31 An auditor is examining the financial statements of a wholesale cosmetics distributor with an inventory consisting of thousands of individual items. The distributor keeps its inventory in its own distribution center and in two public warehouses. An inventory computer file is maintained on a computer disk, and at the end of

each business day the file is updated. Each record of the inventory file contains the following data:

- Item number.
- Location of item.
- Description of item.
- Quantity on hand.
- Cost per item.
- Date of last purchase.
- Date of last sale.
- Quantity sold during year.

The auditor plans to observe the distributor's physical count of inventory as of a given date. The auditor will have available a computer tape of the data on the inventory file on the date of the physical count and a general-purpose computer software package.

Required:
The auditor is planning to perform basic inventory-auditing procedures. Identify the basic inventory-auditing procedures and describe how the use of the general-purpose software package and the tape of the inventory file data might help the auditor perform such auditing procedures. Organize your answer as follows:

Basic Inventory-Auditing Procedure	How a General-Purpose Computer Software Package and Tape of the Inventory File Data Might Be Helpful
1. Observation of the physical count, making and recording test counts where applicable	1. By determining which items are to be test counted by selecting a random sample of a representative number of items from the inventory file as of the date of the physical count

(AICPA, adapted)

[9,10,12,13] 13-32 Joan Dunne, CPA, is examining the financial statements of Doo-Right Wholesale Sales, Inc., for the year ended December 31, 2000. Doo-Right has been in business for many years and has never had its financial statements audited. Dunne has gained satisfaction with respect to the ending inventory and is considering alternative audit procedures to verify management's representations concerning the beginning inventory, which was not observed.

Doo-Right sells only one product (bottled Brand X beer) and maintains perpetual inventory records. In addition, Doo-Right takes physical inventory counts monthly. Dunne has already confirmed purchases with the manufacturer and has decided to concentrate on evaluating the reliability of perpetual inventory records and performing analytical procedures to the extent that prior years' unaudited records will allow.

Required:

What audit tests, including analytical procedures, should Dunne apply in evaluating the reliability of perpetual inventory records and verifying the January 1, 2000, inventory?

(AICPA, adapted)

[13]   13-33   In obtaining evidential matter in support of financial statement assertions, the auditor develops specific audit objectives in light of those assertions. Audit procedures are then selected to accomplish audit objectives.

Required:

Your client is Hillmart, a retail department store that purchases all goods directly from wholesalers or manufacturers. Select the most appropriate audit procedure from the list below and enter the number in the appropriate place on the grid. (An audit procedure may be selected once, more than once, or not at all.)

Audit Procedure:

1. Examine current vendor price lists. *LCM - valuation*
2. Review drafts of the financial statements. *classif.*
3. Select a sample of items during the physical inventory count and determine that they have been included on count sheets. *tracing - completeness*
4. Select a sample of recorded items and examine supporting vendor invoices and contracts. *vouching - validity*
5. Select a sample of recorded items on count sheets during the physical inventory count and determine that items are on hand. *validity*
6. Review loan agreements and minutes of board of directors' meetings. *ownership*

Specific Audit Objective	Audit Procedure
a. Ensure that the entity has legal title to inventory.	6
b. Ensure that recorded inventory quantities include all products on hand.	3
c. Verify that inventory has been reduced, when appropriate, to replacement cost or net realizable value.	1
d. Verify that the cost of inventory has been properly determined.	4
e. Verify that the major categories of inventory and their bases of valuation are adequately reported in the financial statements.	2

DISCUSSION CASE

[10,12,13,14]   13-34   The following discussion case extends Discussion Case 6-41 in Chapter 6.

Harris decided that the easiest way to make the Fabricator Division appear more profitable was through manipulating the inventory, which was the largest asset on the books. Harris found that by increasing inventory by 2 percent, income could be increased by 5 percent. With the weakness in inventory control, he felt it would be easy to overstate inventory. Employees count the goods using count sheets, and Harris was able to add two fictitious sheets during the physical inventory, even though the auditors were present and were observing the inventory. A significant amount of inventory was stored in racks that filled the warehouse. Because of their height and the difficulty of test counting them, Harris was able to cover an overstatement of inventory in the upper racks.

After the count was completed, Harris added four additional count sheets that added $350,000, or 8.6 percent, to the stated inventory. Harris notified the auditors of the "omission" of the sheets and convinced them that they represented overlooked legitimate inventory.

The auditors traced the items on these additional sheets to purchase invoices to verify their existence and approved the addition of the $350,000 to the inventory. They did not notify management about the added sheets. In addition, Harris altered other count sheets before sending them to the auditors by changing unit designations (for example, six engine blocks became six "motors"), raising counts, and adding fictitious line items to completed count sheets. These other fictitious changes added an additional $175,000 to the inflated inventory. None of them was detected by the auditors.

Required:
a. What audit procedures did the auditors apparently not follow that should have detected Harris's fraudulent increase of inventory?
b. What implications would there be to an auditor of failure to detect material fraud as described here?
c. What responsibility did the auditors have to discuss their concerns with the client's audit committee?

(Used with the permission of PricewaterhouseCoopers LLP Foundation.)

INTERNET ASSIGNMENT

[10,13]   13-35   Using an Internet browser, search for information on inventory turnover and merchandise liquidations in the retail catalog industry.

Chapter 14

Auditing Selected Asset Accounts: Prepaid Expenses and Property, Plant, and Equipment

LEARNING OBJECTIVES

Upon completion of this chapter you will

[1] Identify the various types of prepaid expenses, deferred charges, and intangible assets.

[2] Understand the auditor's approach to auditing prepaid insurance.

[3] Develop an understanding of the capital asset cycle.

[4] Identify the types of transactions in the capital asset cycle.

[5] Identify and evaluate inherent risks for property, plant, and equipment.

[6] Assess control risk for property, plant, and equipment.

[7] Know the appropriate segregation of duties for property, plant, and equipment.

[8] Identify analytical procedures used to audit property, plant, and equipment.

[9] Identify tests of account balances used to audit property, plant, and equipment.

[10] Evaluate the audit findings and reach a final conclusion on property, plant, and equipment.

RELEVANT ACCOUNTING AND AUDITING PRONOUNCEMENTS

FASB Statement of Financial Accounting Concepts No. 6, "Elements of Financial Statements" (CON6)

FASB Statement of Financial Accounting Standards No. 13, "Accounting for Leases" (FAS 13)

FASB Statement of Financial Accounting Standards No. 34, "Capitalization of Interest Cost" (FAS 34)

SAS No. 31, "Evidential Matter" (AU 326)

SAS No. 47, "Audit Risk and Materiality in Conducting an Audit" (AU 312)

SAS No. 55, "Consideration of Internal Control in a Financial Statement Audit" (AU 319)

SAS No. 56, "Analytical Procedures" (AU 329)

SAS No. 57, "Auditing Accounting Estimates" (AU 342)

SAS No. 78, "Consideration of Internal Control in a Financial Statement Audit: An Amendment to SAS No. 55" (AU 319)

SAS No. 80, "Amendment to Statement on Auditing Standards No. 31, *Evidential Matter*" (AU 326)

SAS No. 82, "Consideration of Fraud in a Financial Statement Audit" (AU 316)

This chapter examines the audit of selected asset accounts. Two categories of asset accounts, prepaid expenses and property, plant, and equipment, are used as examples. While the audit approach taken for each category is similar, differences exist between these two categories of asset accounts. For example, while transactions for both categories are subject to the control procedures in the purchasing cycle, property, plant, and equipment transactions are likely to be subject to additional control procedures because of their complexity or materiality. Additionally, prepaid expenses are normally classified as current assets, while property, plant, and equipment are classified as noncurrent assets.

Auditing Prepaid Expenses

[LO 1] For most entities, accounts receivable and inventory represent the major current assets included in the financial statements. Also included in most financial statements are accounts that are referred to as *other assets*. When such assets provide economic benefit for less than a year, they are classified as current assets and are called *prepaid expenses*. Examples of prepaid expenses include

- Prepaid insurance.
- Prepaid rent.
- Prepaid interest.

Assets providing economic benefit for longer than a year are classified as *deferred charges* or *intangible assets*. Following are examples of deferred charges and intangible assets:

- Organization costs.
- Debt issuance costs.
- Copyrights.
- Trademarks.
- Trade names.
- Licenses.
- Patents.
- Franchises.
- Goodwill.
- Computer software development costs.

One major difference between asset accounts such as accounts receivable or inventory and prepaid expenses is the materiality of the account balances. On many engagements, prepaid expenses, deferred charges, and intangible assets are not highly material. As a result, analytical procedures may be used extensively to verify these account balances.

Inherent Risk Assessment—Prepaid Expenses

The inherent risk for prepaid expenses such as prepaid insurance would generally be assessed as low because these accounts do not involve any complex or contentious accounting issues. Moreover, misstatements that may have been detected in prior audits would generally be immaterial in amount.

Deferred charges and intangible assets, on the other hand, may present serious inherent risk considerations. For example, the valuation and estimation of lives of patents, franchises, and goodwill involve considerable judgment and may lead to disagreements between the auditor and client. In such a situation, the auditor may assess the inherent risk as high.

Control Risk Assessment—Prepaid Expenses

Prepaid expenses, deferred charges, and intangible asset transactions are typically processed through the purchasing cycle. The remaining discussion focuses on the prepaid insurance account because it is encountered on virtually all engagements. Part of the auditor's assessment of control risk for prepaid insurance transactions is based on the effectiveness of the control procedures in the purchasing cycle. For example, the control procedures in the purchasing cycle should ensure that new insurance policies are properly authorized and recorded.

Additional control procedures may be used to control insurance transactions and information. For example, an *insurance register* may maintain a separate record of all insurance policies in force. The insurance register contains important information such as the coverage and expiration date of each policy. This register should be reviewed periodically by an independent person to verify that the entity has insurance coverage consistent with its needs.

The entity also needs to maintain controls over the systematic allocation of prepaid insurance to insurance expense. At the end of each month, client personnel should prepare a journal entry to recognize the expired portion of prepaid insurance. In some cases entities use estimated amounts when recording these journal entries during the year. At the end of the year, the prepaid insurance account is adjusted to reflect the actual amount of unexpired insurance.

Substantive Testing—Prepaid Insurance

[LO 2] On many audits the auditor can gather sufficient, competent evidence on prepaid insurance by performing analytical procedures. Substantive tests of transactions, if performed at all, are conducted as part of testing the purchasing cycle. Substantive tests of the prepaid insurance balance are necessary only when misstatements are expected.

Analytical Procedures

Because there are generally few transactions in the prepaid insurance account and because the amount reported in the financial statements for prepaid insurance is usually immaterial, analytical procedures are effective for verifying the account balance. The following analytical procedures are commonly used to test prepaid insurance:

- Comparing the current-year balance in prepaid insurance and insurance expense with the prior year's balances after considering any changes in operations.
- Computing the ratio of insurance expense to assets or sales and comparing it with the prior year's ratio.

Substantive Tests of the Prepaid Insurance Account

Substantive tests of balances for prepaid insurance and insurance expense may be necessary when the auditor suspects misstatements based on prior years' audits or when analytical procedures indicate that the account balance may be misstated. The auditor begins testing the prepaid insurance account balance by obtaining a schedule from the client that contains a detailed analysis of the policies included in the prepaid insurance account.

 Exhibit 14–1 presents a prepaid insurance schedule for EarthWear Clothiers. The accuracy of this schedule is tested by footing it and tracing the ending balance to the prepaid insurance account in the general ledger. The auditor's work then focuses on testing the validity, completeness, ownership, valuation, and classification audit objectives. The cutoff objective for prepaid insurance is normally tested as part of the search for unrecorded

EXHIBIT 14–1

Example of an Account Analysis Working Paper for Prepaid Insurance

G10
DLJ
2/15/01

EARTHWEAR CLOTHIERS
Analysis of Prepaid Insurance
12/31/00

Insurance Company	Policy Number	Coverage	Term	Premium	Beginning Balance 1/1/00	Additions	Expense	Ending Balance 12/31/00
Babcock, Inc.**C**	46-2074	Liability Umbrella Policy	1/15/99					
			1/15/00	$55,000	$ 2,100	$ 55,000**V**	$ 54,800	$2,300**Ψ**
Evans & Smith**C**	47801-X7	Fire & Casualty	3/30/99					
			3/30/00	33,600	7,500	33,600**V**	32,700	8,400**Ψ**
Nat'l Insurance**C**	8945-X7	Key Executive Term	8/31/99					
		Life Insurance	8/31/00	15,000	5,000	15,000**V**	15,000	5,000**Ψ**
Total					$14,600**¶**	$103,600	$102,500**L**	$15,700**LF**
					F	**F**	**F**	**F**

Reconciliation of insurance expense accounts:

Merchandise overhead insurance expense	$ 69,700**L**
General and administrative overhead insurance expense	32,800**L**
Total	$102,500

F = Footed and crossfooted.
C = Information agreed to insurance company confirmation.
L = Agreed to general ledger.
¶ = Agreed to prior year's working papers.
V = Agreed to insurance company invoice.
Ψ = Amount recomputed by auditor.

liabilities, and no disclosures are generally necessary for prepaid insurance. These steps, along with other audit work, are shown in Exhibit 14–1.

Validity and Completeness   The auditor can test the validity and completeness of insurance policies included in the account analysis by sending a confirmation to the entity's insurance brokers, requesting information on each policy's number, coverage, expiration date, and premiums. This is an effective and efficient way of obtaining evidence on these two audit objectives. An alternative approach is examination of the underlying supporting documents such as the insurance bills and policies. This may be done on a test basis for the policies listed on the schedule. The auditor can also test completeness by comparing the detailed policies in the current year's insurance register with the policies included in the prior year's insurance register.

Ownership   The beneficiary of the policy can be tested by requesting such information on the confirmations sent to the insurance brokers or by examining the insurance policies. If the beneficiary is someone other than the client, the auditor may have evidence of an unrecorded liability or evidence that another party has a claim against the insured assets.

Valuation   The auditor is concerned with whether the unexpired portion of prepaid insurance, and thus insurance expense, is properly valued. This is easily tested by recomputing the unexpired portion of insurance after considering the premium paid and the term of the policy. By verifying the unexpired portion of prepaid insurance, the auditor also verifies the total amount of insurance expense. This is shown in Exhibit 14–1.

Classification   The auditor's concern with classification is that the different types of insurance are properly allocated to the various insurance expense accounts. Normally, an examination of the insurance policy's coverage indicates the nature of the insurance. For example, a fire insurance policy on the main manufacturing and administrative facilities should be charged both to the manufacturing overhead insurance expense account and to the general and administrative insurance expense account. Note in Exhibit 14–1 that the various insurance accounts included in the general ledger are reconciled to total insurance expense. One final procedure that the auditor should perform is asking the client or its insurance broker about the adequacy of the entity's insurance coverage.

Auditing Property, Plant, and Equipment

[LO 3]   For most entities, property, plant, and equipment represent a material amount in the financial statements. When the audit is an ongoing engagement, the auditor is able to focus his or her efforts on the current year's activity because the assets acquired in earlier years were subjected to audit tests at the time of acquisition. On the other hand, for a new engagement, the auditor has to verify the assets that make up the beginning balances in the client's property, plant, and equipment accounts.

The size of the entity may also affect the auditor's approach. If the client is relatively small with few asset acquisitions during the period, it is generally more cost-effective for the auditor to follow a substantive strategy. Following this strategy, the auditor conducts analytical procedures and direct tests of the account balances. Large entities, on the other hand, are likely to have formal procedures for budgeting for and purchasing capital assets. While routine purchases might be processed through the purchasing cycle, as described in Chapter 11, acquisition or construction of specialized assets may be subject to different requisition and authorization procedures. When the entity has a formal control system over capital assets, the auditor may follow a reliance strategy and test the internal control.

Types of Transactions

🖉 **[LO 4]**

Four types of property, plant, and equipment transactions may occur:

- Acquisition of capital assets for cash or other nonmonetary considerations.
- Disposition of capital assets through sale, exchange, retirement, or abandonment.
- Depreciation of capital assets over their useful economic life.
- Leasing of capital assets.

Overview of the Cycle

Larger entities generally use some type of computer-based system to process property, plant, and equipment transactions, maintain subsidiary records, and produce required reports. Figure 14–1 presents a flowchart of EarthWear's accounting system for property, plant, and equipment. Transactions are periodically entered both from the purchasing cycle and through direct input into the system. The property, plant, and equipment master file is then updated, and a number of reports are produced. The periodic report for property, plant, and equipment transactions is reviewed for proper recording by the physical plant department. The property, plant, and equipment subsidiary ledger is a record of all capital assets owned by the entity. It contains information on the cost of the asset, the date acquired, the method of depreciation, and accumulated depreciation. The subsidiary ledger also includes the calculation of depreciation expense for both financial statement and income tax purposes. The general ledger is posted to reflect the new property, plant, and equipment transactions and depreciation expense. The subsidiary ledger should be reconciled to the general ledger control account monthly.

Inherent Risk Assessment—Property, Plant, and Equipment

🖉 **[LO 5]** The assessment of inherent risk for the purchasing cycle provides a starting point for assessing inherent risk for property, plant, and equipment. The following three inherent risk factors classified as operating characteristics require consideration by the auditor:

- Complex accounting issues.
- Difficult-to-audit transactions.
- Misstatements detected in prior audits.

FIGURE 14–1

Flowchart of the Property, Plant, and Equipment (PP&E) Cycle—EarthWear Clothiers

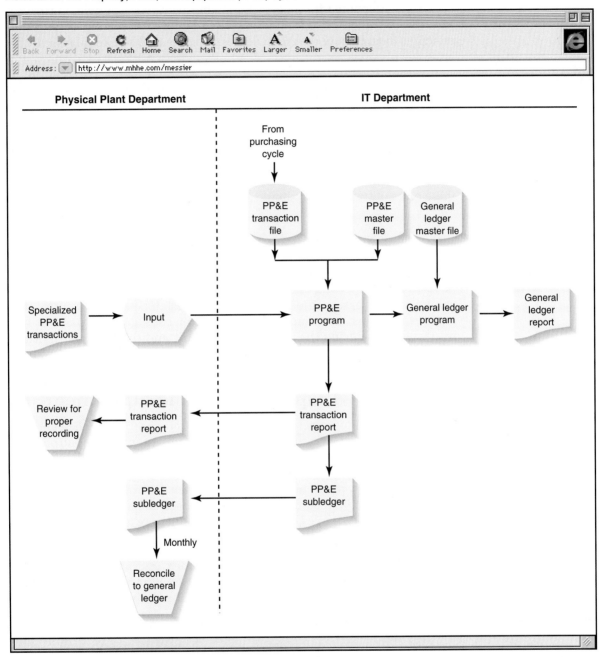

Complex Accounting Issues

A number of different types of property, plant, and equipment transactions involve complex accounting issues. Lease accounting, self-constructed assets, and capitalized interest are examples of such issues. For example, in the case of a lease transaction the auditor must evaluate the client's decision either to capitalize the lease or to treat it as an operating lease. Because of the complexity of the capitalization decision and the subjectivity involved in assessing the capitalization criteria, it is not uncommon for such transactions to be accounted for incorrectly by the client. For example, EarthWear leases store and office space that is accounted for as operating leases. Willis & Adams must be sure that these leases do not qualify as capital leases.

Difficult-to-Audit Transactions

The vast majority of property, plant, and equipment transactions are relatively easy to audit. When assets are purchased directly from vendors, most audit objectives can be tested by examining the source documents. However, transactions involving donated assets, nonmonetary exchanges, and self-constructed assets are more difficult to audit. For example, it may be difficult to verify the trade-in value of an asset exchanged or to properly audit the cost accumulation of self-constructed assets. The presence of these types of transactions should lead to a higher inherent risk assessment.

Misstatements Detected in Prior Audits

If the auditor has detected misstatements in prior audits, the assessment of inherent risk should be set higher than if few or no misstatements have been found in the past.[1] For example, in prior years the auditor may have found numerous client misstatements in accumulating costs for valuing capital assets. Unless the client has established new control procedures over cost accumulation, the auditor should also expect to find misstatements during the current year's audit and therefore set inherent risk as high.

Control Risk Assessment—Property, Plant, and Equipment

[LO 6]   Although the auditor generally follows a substantive strategy when auditing property, plant, and equipment, an understanding of internal control is still required. The presentation that follows focuses on the major internal control objectives, key control procedures, and tests of controls that relate directly to property, plant, and equipment. Other control procedures related to property, plant, and equipment were discussed as part of the purchasing cycle. Important examples of segregation of duties are also presented.

Validity and Authorization

The internal control procedures for the validity and authorization objectives are normally part of the purchasing cycle. Purchase requisitions are initiated in relevant departments and authorized at the appropriate level within the entity. However, large capital asset transactions may be subject to control procedures outside the purchasing cycle. For example, highly specialized technical equipment is likely to be purchased only after passing

---

[1]Research has shown that property, plant, and equipment accounts frequently contain misstatements. See W. R. Kinney, Jr., and R. D. Martin, "Does Auditing Reduce Bias in Financial Reporting? A Review of Audit-Related Adjustment Studies," *Auditing: A Journal of Practice and Theory* (Spring 1994), pp. 149–55, for a review of the audit research studies that have indicated that property, plant, and equipment accounts are likely to contain misstatements.

through a specific capital-budgeting process, which might require that purchase of equipment meet predefined internal rate-of-return criteria. The purchase of equipment may also require that highly skilled engineers approve the technical specifications for the equipment. For such transactions, the auditor may need to examine more than the vendor's invoice to test validity. A review of additional documentation, such as capital-budgeting documents and engineering specifications, may be needed.

Most entities have some type of authorization table for approving capital asset transactions. The client should have internal control procedures to ensure that the authorization to purchase capital assets is consistent with the authorization table. For example, the control procedures should specify dollar limits at each managerial level to ensure that larger projects are brought to the attention of higher levels of management for approval before commitments are made. Lease transactions should be subject to similar control procedures. The entity also needs to have control procedures for authorizing the sale or other disposition of capital assets. This should include a level of authorization above the department initiating the disposition. Control procedures should also identify assets that are no longer used in operations because they may require different accounting treatment. Finally, all major maintenance or improvement transactions should be properly authorized by an appropriate level of management.

Completeness

Most entities use some type of software package to maintain detailed property records (see Figure 14–1). The detailed property, plant, and equipment subsidiary ledger usually includes the following information for each capital asset:

- Description, location, and ID number.
- Date of acquisition and installed cost.
- Depreciation methods for book and tax purposes, salvage value, and estimated useful life.

The control procedures used in the purchasing cycle for ensuring completeness provide some assurance that all capital asset transactions are recorded in the property, plant, and equipment subsidiary ledger and general ledger. One procedure that helps to ensure that this objective is met is monthly reconciliation of the property, plant, and equipment subsidiary ledger to the general ledger control accounts. Figure 14–1 shows this control procedure as it is performed by EarthWear's physical plant department.

Another control procedure that an entity may use to ensure that all capital assets are recorded is periodic comparison of the detailed records in the subsidiary ledger with the existing capital assets. This may be done in a number of ways. The client may take a complete physical examination of property, plant, and equipment on a periodic or rotating basis and compare the physical assets to the property, plant, and equipment subsidiary ledger. Alternatively, the physical examination may be limited to major capital assets or assets that are subject to loss. In both instances the entity's internal auditors may test the reliability of the subsidiary ledger. Larger entities sometimes employ outside specialists to physically examine property, plant, and equipment.

TABLE 14–1	Key Segregation of Duties and Possible Errors or Fraud—Property, Plant, and Equipment

Segregation of Duties	Possible Errors or Fraud Resulting from Conflicts of Duties
The initiation function should be segregated from the final approval function.	If one individual is responsible for initiating a capital asset transaction and also has final approval, fictitious or unauthorized purchases of assets can occur. This can result in purchases of unnecessary assets, assets that do not meet the company's quality control standards, or illegal payments to suppliers or contractors.
The property, plant, and equipment records function should be segregated from the general ledger function.	If one individual is responsible for the property, plant, and equipment records and also for the general ledger functions, that individual can conceal any defalcation that would normally be detected by reconciling subsidiary records with the general ledger control account.
The property, plant, and equipment records function should be segregated from the custodial function.	If one individual is responsible for the property, plant, and equipment records and also has custodial responsibility for the related assets, tools and equipment can be stolen, and the theft can be concealed by adjustment of the accounting records.
If a periodic physical inventory of property, plant, and equipment is taken, the individual responsible for the inventory should be independent of the custodial and record-keeping functions.	If the individual who is responsible for the periodic physical inventory of property, plant, and equipment is also responsible for the custodial and record-keeping functions, theft of the entity's capital assets can be concealed.

Segregation of Duties

[LO 7]

The existence of adequate segregation of duties for property, plant, and equipment within an entity depends on the volume and significance of the transactions processed. For example, if an entity purchases large quantities of machinery and equipment, or if it has large capital projects under construction, it will likely have a formal internal control system. On the other hand, if an entity has few capital asset purchases, it will generally not have a formal control system over such transactions. Table 14–1 shows the key segregation of duties for property, plant, and equipment transactions and examples of possible errors or fraud that can result from conflicts in duties.

Substantive Testing—Property, Plant, and Equipment

As mentioned earlier, when the number of transactions is limited or efficiency is a consideration, auditors often follow a substantive strategy when auditing property, plant, and equipment. Therefore, a detailed discussion of the substantive tests for property, plant, and equipment is provided next. The discussion focuses on analytical procedures and substantive tests of account balances.

Analytical Procedures—Property, Plant, and Equipment

[LO 8]   The following analytical procedures can be used in the audit of property, plant, and equipment:

- Compare prior-year balances in property, plant, and equipment and depreciation expense with current-year balances after consideration of any changes in conditions or asset composition.
- Compute the ratio of depreciation expense to the related property, plant, and equipment accounts and comparison to prior years' ratios.
- Compute the ratio of repairs and maintenance expense to the related property, plant, and equipment accounts and comparison to prior years' ratios.
- Compute the ratio of insurance expense to the related property, plant, and equipment accounts and comparison to prior years' ratios.
- Review capital budgets and comparison of the amounts spent with amounts budgeted.

For example, the auditor can calculate the ratio of depreciation expense to the related property, plant, and equipment accounts and compare it to prior years' ratios. If the ratio is less than prior years' and few assets have been disposed of, the auditor might conclude that depreciation has not been taken on some assets included in the account.

Tests of Account Balances—Property, Plant, and Equipment

[LO 9]   Table 14–2 summarizes the substantive tests of balances for the property, plant, and equipment accounts for each audit objective. The discussion that follows focuses on the major audit procedures conducted by the auditor. Accuracy is discussed first because the auditor must establish that the detailed property, plant, and equipment records agree with the general ledger account.

Accuracy

The auditor verifies the accuracy of property, plant, and equipment by obtaining a lead schedule and detailed schedules for additions and dispositions of assets. This lead schedule is footed, and the individual accounts are agreed to the general ledger. The detailed schedules are also tested for accuracy. Exhibit 14–2 presents a lead schedule for EarthWear's property, plant, and equipment.

Validity

To test validity, the auditor obtains a listing of all major additions and vouches them to supporting documents such as vendors' invoices. If the purchase was properly authorized and the asset has been received and placed in service, the transaction is valid. In addition, the auditor may want to verify that assets recorded as capital assets actually exist. For major acquisitions, the auditor may physically examine the capital asset.

Similarly, disposition of assets must be properly authorized, and the supporting documentation such as sales receipts should indicate how the disposal took place. Generally, the auditor obtains a schedule of all major dispositions and verifies that the asset was removed from the property,

TABLE 14–2	Summary of Audit Objectives and Tests of Account Balances—Property, Plant, and Equipment

Audit Objective	Tests of Account Balances
Validity	Vouch additions and dispositions to vendor invoices or other supporting documentation.
	Verify the existence of major additions by physically examining the capital asset.
	Review lease agreements to ensure that lease transactions are accounted for properly.
Completeness	Physically examine a sample of capital assets and trace of them into the property, plant, and equipment subsidiary ledger.
Cutoff	Examine the purchases and sales of capital assets for a few days before and after year-end.
Ownership	Examine or confirm deeds or title documents for proof of ownership.
Accuracy	Obtain a lead schedule of property, plant, and equipment; foot schedule and agree totals to the general ledger.
	Obtain detailed schedules for additions and dispositions of property, plant, and equipment; agree amounts to totals shown on lead schedule.
Valuation	Vouch additions and dispositions to vendor invoices or other supporting documentation.
	Test depreciation calculations for a sample of capital assets; CAATs can be used to perform this test.
Classification	Vouch transactions included in repairs and maintenance for items that should be capitalized.
	Review lease transactions for proper classification between operating and capital leases.
Disclosure	Examine note or bond agreements to ascertain whether any capital assets are pledged as collateral and require disclosure in the footnotes.
	Review lease transactions and verify that necessary disclosures are made in the footnotes.

plant, and equipment records. If the disposition is the result of a sale or exchange, the auditor would verify the cash receipt for the sale of the asset or documentation that another asset was received in exchange.

The auditor must also ascertain the validity of lease transactions by examining the lease agreements entered into by the entity. If the lease agreement is properly authorized and the asset is placed in service, the evidence supports the validity of the recorded asset.

Completeness

The auditor has some assurance about the completeness objective from the control procedures in the purchasing cycle and, if present, the additional control procedures discussed previously in this chapter. If the auditor still has concerns about the completeness objective, he or she can physically examine a sample of assets and trace them into the property, plant, and equipment subsidiary ledger. If the assets are included in the subsidiary ledger, the auditor has sufficient evidence supporting the completeness objective.

Cutoff

On most engagements, cutoff is tested as part of the audit work in accounts payable and accrued expenses. By examining a sample of vendor invoices from a few days before and after year-end, the auditor can determine if

EXHIBIT 14–2

An Example of a Lead Schedule for Property, Plant, and Equipment

Address: http://www.mhhe.com/messier

K Lead
DLJ
2/15/01

EARTHWEAR CLOTHIERS
Lead Sheet—Property, Plant, and Equipment
12/31/00

Account	W/P Ref.	Cost Beginning Balance	Additions	Deletions	Ending Balance	Accumulated Depreciation Beginning Balance	Additions	Deletions	Ending Balance
Land	K10	$ 5,550,000φ	$ 50,000		$ 5,600,000L				$ 8,066,600L
Buildings	K20	26,962,250φ			26,962,250L	$ 6,988,100φ	$1,078,500		22,653,150L
Fixtures and equipment	K30	37,745,800φ	7,398,650	$755,000	44,389,450L	19,323,950φ	3,799,550	$470,350	858,100L
Leasehold improvements	K40	1,310,300φ	625,550	5,000	1,930,850L	713,250φ	149,850	5,000	0L
Construction in progress	K50	0φ	602,000		602,000L	0φ			
Totals		$71,568,350	$8,676,200	$760,000	$79,484,550F	$27,025,300	$5,027,900L	$475,350	$31,577,850F
		F	F	F	F	F	F	F	F

F = Footed and crossfooted.
L = Agreed to the general ledger.
φ = Agreed to prior year's working papers.

capital asset transactions are recorded in the proper period. Inquiry of client personnel and a review of lease transactions for the same period can provide evidence on proper cutoff for leases.

Ownership

The auditor can test for ownership by examining the vendor's invoices or other supporting documents. In some instances, the auditor may examine or confirm property deeds or title documents for proof of ownership.

Valuation

Capital assets are valued at acquisition cost plus any costs necessary to make the asset operational. The auditor tests the recorded cost of new assets by examining the vendor invoices and other supporting documents used by the client to establish the recorded value of the assets. If the client has material self-constructed assets, the auditor conducts detailed audit work on the construction-in-process account. This includes ensuring that interest is properly capitalized as a cost of the asset (see FASB No. 34, "Capitalization of Interest Cost").

The other valuation issue the auditor must address is the recognition of depreciation expense. If the client uses a computer to process and account for capital assets, the auditor may be able to use computer-assisted audit techniques to verify the calculation of depreciation for various assets. Alternatively, the auditor may recompute the depreciation expense for a sample of capital assets. In making this calculation, the auditor considers the reasonableness of the estimated life of the asset, the depreciation methods used for book and tax purposes, and any expected salvage value.

Classification

First, the classification of a transaction into the correct property, plant, and equipment account is normally examined as part of the testing of the purchasing cycle. The auditor's tests of controls and substantive tests of transactions provide evidence as to the effectiveness of the control procedures for this objective.

Second, the auditor should examine selected expense accounts such as repairs and maintenance to determine if any capital assets have been incorrectly recorded in these accounts. An account analysis of transactions included in the repairs and maintenance account is obtained, and selected transactions are vouched to supporting documents. In examining the supporting documents, the auditor must determine if the transactions are truly expense items or whether it would be more appropriate to capitalize the costs. For example, the auditor may examine an invoice from a plumbing contractor that shows that the water pipe system for a building has been replaced during the current period. If the amount of this transaction was material and improved the building, it should not be expensed as a repair but rather should be capitalized as a building improvement.

Last, the auditor should examine each material lease agreement to verify that the lease is properly classified as an operating or capital lease.

TABLE 14–3	**Examples of Disclosure Items— Property, Plant, and Equipment**

- Classes of capital assets and valuation bases.
- Depreciation methods and useful lives for financial reporting and tax purposes.
- Nonoperating assets.
- Construction or purchase commitments.
- Liens and mortgages.
- Acquisition or disposal of major operating facilities.
- Capitalized and other lease arrangements.

EXHIBIT 14–3	**Sample Disclosure of Nonoperating Property**

In March 1999 the company decided to temporarily idle the Southern Alabama Mill. The decision was made in response to adverse industry conditions, mainly reduced selling prices and increased raw material costs. In September 1999 it was further determined that because of continued deterioration of selling prices and the level of expenditures required to meet environmental restrictions, the Southern Alabama Mill would not resume operations. The assets of the mill cannot be sold for their historical cost, and in the third quarter the company recorded a $15.6 million loss on the mill.

Disclosure

Table 14–3 shows a number of important items that may require disclosure as part of the audit of property, plant, and equipment. Some of these disclosures are made in the "summary of significant accounting policies" footnote, while other items may be disclosed in separate footnotes. Exhibit 14–3 is a sample disclosure for an entity's decision to discontinue operations at one of its operating facilities.

Evaluating the Audit Findings—Property, Plant, and Equipment

[LO 10] The process for evaluating the audit findings for property, plant, and equipment is the same as was discussed in previous chapters. The auditor aggregates the likely misstatements and compares this amount to the tolerable misstatement. If the likely misstatement is less than the tolerable misstatement, the evidence indicates that the property, plant, and equipment accounts are not materially misstated. This is the case with EarthWear. No misstatements were detected for property, plant, and equipment (see Exhibit 3–5). However, if the likely misstatement was greater than the tolerable misstatement, the auditor would either require adjustment of the accounts or issue a qualified audit report.

REVIEW QUESTIONS

[LO 1] 14-1 Distinguish between prepaid expenses and deferred charges, and intangible assets. Give three examples of each of these "other assets."

[1,2] 14-2 Prepaid expenses are generally assessed to have a low inherent risk. Why would deferred charges and intangible assets present serious inherent risk consideration?

[2] 14-3 Describe the type of information that is contained in the insurance register.

[2] 14-4 How does the purchasing cycle affect prepaid insurance and property, plant, and equipment transactions?

[2] 14-5 Why does the auditor normally follow a substantive strategy when auditing prepaid insurance?

[2] 14-6 Identify two analytical procedures that can be used to audit prepaid insurance.

[2] 14-7 Confirmation is a useful audit procedure for verifying information related to prepaid insurance. What type of information would be requested from an entity's insurance broker?

[4] 14-8 List four types of property, plant, and equipment transactions.

[5] 14-9 Describe three factors that the auditor should consider in assessing the inherent risk for property, plant, and equipment.

[6] 14-10 What is a typical control over authorization of capital asset transactions?

[6] 14-11 What type of information is maintained in the property, plant, and equipment subsidiary ledger?

[7] 14-12 What is the key segregation of duties for property, plant, and equipment transactions? What errors or fraud can occur if such segregation of duties is not present?

[8] 14-13 Identify three analytical procedures that can be used to audit property, plant, and equipment.

[9] 14-14 What procedures would an auditor use to verify the completeness, ownership, and valuation audit objectives for property, plant, and equipment?

MULTIPLE-CHOICE QUESTIONS FROM CPA EXAMINATIONS

[2] 14-15 When auditing prepaid insurance, an auditor discovers that the original insurance policy on plant equipment is not available for inspection. The policy's absence most likely indicates the possibility of a(n)
a. Insurance premium due but not recorded.
b. Deficiency in the coinsurance provision.
c. Lien on the plant equipment.
d. Understatement of insurance expense.

[6] 14-16 To strengthen internal control over the custody of heavy mobile equipment, the client would most likely institute a policy requiring a periodic

a. Increase in insurance coverage.

b. Inspection of equipment and reconciliation with accounting records.

c. Verification of liens, pledges, and collateralizations.

d. Accounting for work orders.

[6]   14-17   A weakness in internal control over recording retirement of equipment may cause an auditor to

a. Trace additions to the "other assets" account to search for equipment that is still on hand but no longer being used.

b. Select certain items of equipment from the accounting records and locate them in the plant.

c. Inspect certain items of equipment in the plant and trace those items to the accounting records.

d. Review the subsidiary ledger to ascertain whether depreciation was taken on each item of equipment during the year.

[6]   14-18   When there are few property and equipment transactions during the year, the continuing auditor usually

a. Completely reviews the related control procedures and tests the control procedures being relied upon.

b. Completely reviews the related control procedures and performs analytical procedures to verify current-year additions to property and equipment.

c. Develops a preliminary understanding of internal control and performs a thorough examination of the balances at the beginning of the year.

d. Develops a preliminary understanding of internal control and performs extensive tests of current-year property and equipment transactions.

[6,9]   14-19   Which of the following control procedures would most likely allow for a reduction in the scope of the auditor's tests of depreciation expense?

a. Review and approval of the periodic equipment depreciation entry by a supervisor who does not actively participate in its preparation.

b. Comparison of equipment account balances for the current year with the current-year budget and prior-year actual balances.

c. Review of the miscellaneous income account for salvage credits and scrap sales of partially depreciated equipment.

d. Authorization of payment of vendor's invoices by a designated employee who is independent of the equipment-receiving function.

[6]   14-20   Property acquisitions that are misclassified as maintenance expense would most likely be detected by an internal control system that provides for

a. Investigation of variances within a formal budgeting system.

b. Review and approval of the monthly depreciation entry by the plant supervisor.

c. Segregation of duties of employees in the accounts payable department.

d. Examination by the internal auditor of vendor invoices and canceled checks for property acquisitions.

[6,7] 14-21 Which of the following procedures is most likely to prevent the improper disposition of equipment?

a. Separation of duties between those authorized to dispose of equipment and those authorized to approve removal work orders.

b. The use of serial numbers to identify equipment that could be sold.

c. Periodic comparison of removal work orders to authorizing documentation.

d. Periodic analysis of the scrap sales and the repairs and maintenance accounts.

[9] 14-22 An auditor analyzes repairs and maintenance accounts primarily to obtain evidence in support of the audit assertion that all

a. Noncapitalizable expenditures for repairs and maintenance have been properly charged to expense.

b. Expenditures for property and equipment have *not* been charged to expense.

c. Noncapitalizable expenditures for repairs and maintenance have been recorded in the proper period.

d. Expenditures for property and equipment have been recorded in the proper period.

[8,9] 14-23 When there are numerous property and equipment transactions during the year, an auditor who plans to assess the control risk at a low level usually performs

a. Analytical procedures for property and equipment balances at the end of the year.

b. Tests of controls and extensive tests of property and equipment balances at the end of the year.

c. Analytical procedures for current-year property and equipment transactions.

d. Tests of controls and limited tests of current-year property and equipment transactions.

[9] 14-24 Which of the following combinations of procedures would an auditor be most likely to perform to obtain evidence about fixed-asset additions?

a. Inspecting documents and physically examining assets.

b. Recomputing calculations and obtaining written management representations.

c. Observing operating activities and comparing balances to prior-period balances.

d. Confirming ownership and corroborating transactions through inquiries of client personnel.

[6] 14-25 Which of the following internal controls is most likely to justify a reduced assessed level of control risk concerning plant and equipment acquisitions?

a. Periodic physical inspection of plant and equipment by the internal audit staff.

b. Comparison of current-year plant and equipment account balances with prior-year actual balances.

c. Review of prenumbered purchase orders to detect unrecorded trade-ins.

d. Approval of periodic depreciation entries by a supervisor independent of the accounting department.

PROBLEMS

[1,2] 14-26 Natherson, CPA, is engaged to audit the financial statements of Lewis Lumber for the year ended December 31, 2000. Natherson obtained and documented an understanding of internal control relating to the purchasing cycle and assessed control risk relating to the purchasing cycle at the maximum level. Natherson requested and obtained from Lewis a schedule analyzing prepaid insurance as of December 31, 2000, and sent confirmation requests to Lewis's insurance broker.

Required:
a. Identify two analytical procedures that Natherson could use to verify prepaid insurance.
b. What substantive audit procedures should Natherson conduct on the schedule of prepaid insurance?

[1,2] 14-27 Taylor, CPA, has been engaged to audit the financial statements of Palmer Company, a continuing audit client. Taylor is about to perform substantive audit procedures on Palmer's goodwill (excess of cost over fair value of net assets purchased) that was acquired in prior years' business combinations. An industry slowdown has occurred recently, and the operations purchased have not met profit expectations.

During the planning process, Taylor determined that there was a high risk that material misstatements in the assertions related to goodwill could occur. Taylor obtained an understanding of internal control and assessed the control risk at the maximum level for the assertions related to goodwill.

Required:
a. Describe the substantive audit procedures Taylor should consider performing in auditing Palmer's goodwill. Do *not* discuss Palmer's internal control system.
b. Describe the two significant assertions that Taylor would be most concerned with relative to Palmer's goodwill. Do *not* describe more than two.

(AICPA, adapted)

[6,7] 14-28 Nakamura, CPA, has accepted an engagement to audit the financial statements of Grant Manufacturing Company, a new client. Grant has an adequate control environment and a reasonable segregation of duties. Nakamura is about to assess the control risk for the assertions related to Grant's property and equipment.

Required:
Describe the key internal controls related to Grant's property, equipment, and related transactions (additions, transfers, major maintenance and repairs, retirements, and dispositions) that Nakamura may consider in assessing the control risk.

(AICPA, adapted)

[4,6,9,10] 14-29 Gonzales, CPA, is the auditor for a manufacturing company with a balance sheet that includes the entry "Property, plant, and equipment." Gonzales has been asked by the company's management if audit adjustments or reclassifications are required for the following material items that have been included in or excluded from "Property, plant, and equipment":

1. A tract of land was acquired during the year. The land is to be the future site of the client's new headquarters, which will be constructed next year. Commissions were paid to the real estate agent used to acquire the land, and expenditures were made to relocate the previous owner's equipment. These commissions and expenditures were expensed and are excluded from "Property, plant, and equipment."

2. Clearing costs were incurred to ready the land for construction. These costs were included in "Property, plant, and equipment."

3. During the land-clearing process, timber and gravel were recovered and sold. The proceeds from the sale were recorded as other income and are excluded from "Property, plant, and equipment."

4. A group of machines was purchased under a royalty agreement that provides royalty payments based on units of production from the machines. The costs of the machines, freight costs, unloading charges, and royalty payments were capitalized and are included in "Property, plant, and equipment."

Required:

a. Describe the general characteristics of assets, such as land, buildings, improvements, machinery, equipment, fixtures, and so on, that should normally be classified as "Property, plant, and equipment," and identify audit objectives in connection with the examination of "Property, plant, and equipment." Do not discuss specific audit procedures.

b. Indicate whether each of the items numbered 1 to 4 requires one or more audit adjustments or reclassifications, and explain why such adjustments or reclassifications are required or not required. Organize your answer as follows:

Item Number	Is Auditing Adjustment or Reclassification Required? (Yes or No)	Reasons Why Audit Adjustments or Reclassifications Are Required or Not Required

(AICPA, adapted)

[8,9]   14-30   To support financial statement assertions, an auditor develops specific audit objectives. The auditor then designs substantive tests to satisfy or accomplish each objective.

Required:

Items (a) through (c) represent audit objectives for the property and equipment accounts. Select the most appropriate audit procedure from the following list and enter the number in the appropriate place on the grid. (An audit procedure may be selected once or not at all.)

Audit Procedure

1. Trace opening balances in the summary schedules to the prior year's audit working papers.
2. Review the provision for depreciation expense and determine that depreciable lives and methods used in the current year are consistent with those used in the prior year.
3. Determine that the responsibility for maintaining the property and equipment records is segregated from the responsibility for custody of property and equipment.
4. Examine deeds and title insurance certificates.
5. Perform cutoff tests to verify that property and equipment additions are recorded in the proper period.
6. Determine that property and equipment are adequately insured.
7. Physically examine all major property and equipment additions.

Specific Audit Objective	Audit Procedure
a. Verify that the entity has the legal right to property and equipment acquired during the year.	
b. Verify that recorded property and equipment represent assets that actually exist at the balance sheet date.	
c. Verify that net property and equipment are properly valued at the balance sheet date.	

(AICPA, adapted)

[8,9]   14-31   Pierce, an independent auditor, was engaged to examine the financial statements of Wong Construction, Inc., for the year ended December 31, 2000. Wong's financial statements reflect a substantial amount of mobile construction equipment, used in the firm's operations. The equipment is accounted for in a subsidiary ledger. Pierce developed an understanding of internal control and assessed the control risk as moderate.

Required:
Identify the substantive audit procedures Pierce should utilize in examining mobile construction equipment and related depreciation in Wong's financial statements.

(AICPA, adapted)

[8,9]   14-32   In connection with the annual examination of Sandhu Corporation, a manufacturer of janitorial supplies, you have been assigned to audit property, plant, and equipment. The company maintains a detailed property ledger for all property, plant, and equipment. You prepared an audit program for the balances of property, plant, and equipment but have yet to prepare one for accumulated depreciation and depreciation expense.

Required:
Prepare a separate comprehensive audit program for the accumulated depreciation and depreciation expense accounts.

(AICPA, adapted)

DISCUSSION CASES

[9,10]   14-33   On January 15, 2000, Leno, Inc., which has a March 31 year-end, entered into a transaction to sell the land and building that contained its manufacturing operations for a total selling price of $19,750,000. The book value of the land and the building was $3,420,000. The final closing was not expected to occur until sometime between July 2001 and March 2002.

On March 15, 2000, Leno, Inc., received an irrevocable letter of credit, issued by a major bank, for $5,000,000, which represented more than 25 percent of the sales price. Leno, Inc., would collect the $5,000,000 and would keep the money even if the buyer decided not to complete the transaction. The letter of credit had an option for an extension for up to one year for a total period of two years. At closing, the entire selling price was to be paid in cash.

Leno, Inc., was going to continue its manufacturing operations in the building and would continue to be responsible for all normal occupancy costs until final closing, when it would move to another location. After the sale, the building would be torn down and replaced by a large office building complex.

Required:
a. Based on relevant accounting pronouncements, how should Leno, Inc., account for the transaction at March 31, 2000?
b. What additional types of evidence should the auditor examine prior to recognizing any gain on the transaction?

[9,10]   14-34   Towers Associates was formed as a joint venture on August 16, 2000, between Lynx, Inc., and Francisco, Inc. Lynx contributed a parcel of land with an existing building, tower 1, and an attached annex located on the site. Francisco contributed $125 million in cash. Some floors in tower 1 have been vacated so that it can be renovated floor by floor. The remainder of the building will continue in use, and the remaining tenants will move to vacant floors during the renovation. Tower 2 and a plaza, which will serve both buildings, are under construction on the site on which the annex had been located. Because the parties are joint-venture partners, the assets contributed by Lynx were also valued at $125 million. That amount was allocated between the land and the building.

The value of the total parcel of land was appraised at $98 million, based on its highest and best use if vacant. To determine the fair value of the land in its current state, the value of the land at its highest and best use was reduced by the costs of removing the annex so that the land will be available for another use. The following two types of costs are related to removing the annex:
1. Approximately $4.5 million to demolish the annex.
2. Approximately $60 million for the relocation of tenants whose leases extended beyond 2000.

Relocation costs include the net rent costs of relocating tenants from the annex to buildings not owned by the venture, the costs of moving those tenants, and the costs of improving their new space.

The total cost of $64.5 million to get the land ready for another use has been discounted to $52.5 million at the joint venture's cost of funds and has been subtracted from the value of the land at its highest and best use. The resulting amount, $45.5 million, is the amount recorded as the contributed value of the land, which has been allocated between tower 1 and tower 2 (including the adjacent plaza) based on the relative square footage of the associated land. The contributed value of tower 1 was recorded as $79.5 million. The costs of developing the plaza will be allocated between tower 1 and tower 2 based on square footage.

Your client, Towers Associates, has been accumulating tenant relocation costs as part of construction in progress and would like to charge them to tower 2 and depreciate them over the life of the building. Your client would also like to defer depreciating the costs of renovating tower 1 and the costs of constructing the plaza until the first phase of the project (the renovation of tower 1 and the construction of the plaza) has been completed.

Additional Information

- The value of land was estimated by using the *development method,* where the ultimate sales value of the land as fully developed was estimated at its highest and best use and reduced by the costs of getting the land ready for its future use.

- The term *highest and best use* is defined by the American Institute of Real Estate Appraisers as "that reasonable and probable use that supports the highest present value, as defined as of the effective date of the appraisal."

- The AICPA's Audit and Accounting Guide *Guide for the Use of Real Estate Appraisal Information* explains that "the concept of highest and best use also considers (1) the use of the land that may reasonably be expected to produce the greatest net return over a given period of time and (2) the legal use that will yield the highest present value, sometimes called *optimum* use." The guide states further:

  > The highest and best use of the land or site, if vacant and available for use, may be different from the highest and best use of the improved property. It would be different if the improvement is not appropriate and yet contributes to the total property value in excess of the value of the site.

Required:

a. How should Towers Associates account for the cost of relocating tenants from the annex? Do the costs of relocating tenants have a future benefit to the entity?

b. Indicate how you would audit (1) the $4.5 million in demolition costs and (2) the $60 million in tenant relocation costs.

Auditing Long-Term Liabilities, Stockholders' Equity, and Income Statement Accounts

LEARNING OBJECTIVES

Upon completion of this chapter you will

[1] Understand the types and features of long-term debt.

[2] Assess control risk for long-term debt.

[3] Identify key internal control procedures for long-term debt.

[4] Know how to conduct substantive audit procedures for long-term debt.

[5] Understand the types of stockholders' equity transactions.

[6] Assess control risk for stockholders' equity.

[7] Identify key internal control procedures for stockholders' equity.

[8] Know the appropriate segregation of duties for stockholders' equity.

[9] Know how to conduct substantive audit procedures for capital stock.

[10] Know how to conduct substantive audit procedures for dividends.

[11] Know how to conduct substantive audit procedures for retained earnings.

[12] Know how to conduct substantive audit procedures for income statement accounts.

RELEVANT ACCOUNTING AND AUDITING PRONOUNCEMENTS

FASB Statement of Financial Accounting Concepts No. 5, "Recognition and Measurement in Financial Statements of Business Enterprises" (CON5)

FASB Statement of Financial Accounting Concepts No. 6, "Elements of Financial Statements" (CON6)

SAS No. 1, "Consistency of Application of Generally Accepted Accounting Procedures" (AU 420)

SAS No. 31, "Evidential Matter" (AU 326)

SAS No. 47, "Audit Risk and Materiality in Conducting an Audit" (AU 312)

SAS No. 55, "Consideration of Internal Control in a Financial Statement Audit" (AU 319)

SAS No. 56, "Analytical Procedures" (AU 329)

SAS No. 67, "The Confirmation Process" (AU 330)

SAS No. 78, "Consideration of Internal Control in a Financial Statement Audit: An Amendment to SAS No. 55" (AU 319)

SAS No. 80, "Amendment to Statement on Auditing Standards No. 31, *Evidential Matter*" (AU326)

SAS No. 82, "Consideration of Fraud in a Financial Statement Audit" (AU316)

This chapter presents the audit of long-term liabilities, stockholders' equity, and income statement accounts. Long-term debt and equity are the major sources of financing for most entities. A substantive audit strategy is normally followed when these financial statement accounts are audited, because although the number of transactions is few, each transaction is usually material.

The discussion of auditing the income statement focuses on how the auditor's work on internal control provides evidence on income statement accounts and how most income statement accounts are audited when their related balance sheet accounts are audited. Last, the audit of selected income statement accounts is presented. 🔌

Auditing Long-Term Debt

[LO 1] Common types of long-term debt financing include notes, bonds, and mortgages. More sophisticated types of debt financing include collateralized mortgage obligations, repurchase and reverse repurchase agreements, interest-rate swaps, financial futures, derivatives (see Exhibit 15–1), and myriad other financial instruments. Accounting for such sophisticated debt instruments can be complex and is beyond the scope of this text. Capitalized lease obligations also represent a form of long-term debt. To simplify the presentation of the audit of long-term debt, the discussion focuses on notes and bonds, including the audit of interest payable and interest expense.

Long-term debt may have a number of features that can affect the audit procedures used. For example, debt may be convertible into stock, or it may be combined with warrants, options, or rights that can be exchanged for equity. Debt may be callable under certain conditions, or it may require the establishment of a sinking fund to ensure that the debt can be repaid. Last, debt may be either unsecured or secured by assets of the entity.

The auditor's consideration of long-term debt, however, is no different than for any other financial statement account. The auditor must be assured that the amounts shown on the balance sheet for the various types of long-term debt are not materially misstated. This assurance extends to the proper recognition of interest expense in the financial statements.

The approach to the audit of long-term debt varies depending on the frequency of the entity's financing activities. For entities that engage in frequent financing activities, the auditor may follow a reliance strategy under which internal control is formally evaluated and tests of controls are performed in order to assess the control risk. However, for the vast

---

EXHIBIT 15–1

Derivatives Lead to Losses at Orange County and Major Corporations

Derivatives are contracts that are written between two parties and have a value that is derived from the value of an underlying asset, such as currencies, equities, commodities, or interest rates, or from stock market or other indicators. While derivatives can be used wisely by management to manage risk, in some instances derivatives have actually increased risk.

In 1994 highly leveraged interest-rate derivatives caused a $1.7 billion loss in the Orange County Investment Pool—money managed for the county and its cities, school districts, and other agencies. The loss occurred because the county's treasurer, Robert L. Citron, leveraged the pool's $7.6 billion to almost $20 billion and "bet" that interest rates would decline or remain steady. When the Federal Reserve Bank raised interest rates, Orange County's derivatives unraveled.

Losses on derivatives have also occurred for Procter & Gamble and Gibson Greeting Cards. Both companies entered into derivatives with Bankers Trust. Procter & Gamble announced losses in excess of $150 million and sued Bankers Trust over the transactions. Gibson had an estimated loss of $20 million but settled with Bankers Trust for $6.2 million.

Sources: Carol J. Loomis, "Untangling the Derivatives Mess," *Fortune* (March 20, 1995), pp. 50–68; and R. H. D. Molvar and J. F. Green, "The Question of Derivatives," *Journal of Accountancy* (March 1995), pp. 55–61.

majority of entities, it is more efficient for the auditor to follow a substantive strategy and perform a detailed audit of long-term debt and the related interest accounts.

Control Risk Assessment—Long-Term Debt

[LO 2]   When a substantive strategy is followed, the auditor needs a sufficient understanding of the entity's internal control system over debt to be able to anticipate the types of misstatements that may occur and thus plan the substantive tests. The following discussion of control risk assessment for long-term debt focuses on the general types of control procedures that should be present to minimize the likelihood of material misstatement. The internal control objectives that are of primary concern to the auditor are validity, authorization, completeness, valuation, and classification. Proper segregation of duties is important for ensuring the propriety of long-term debt.

Control Objectives and Related Procedures

[LO 3]   Following are some of the more common internal control procedures that should be present for each of the important control objectives for long-term debt.

Validity and Authorization   The entity should have internal control procedures to ensure that any long-term borrowing is properly initiated by authorized individuals. First, adequate documentation must verify that a note or bond was properly authorized. The presence of adequate documentation, such as a properly signed lending agreement, allows the auditor to determine if the transaction was properly executed. Second, any significant debt commitments should be approved by the board of directors or by executives who have been delegated this authority. Entities that engage in recurring borrowing activities should have both general and specific controls. The board of directors should establish general controls to guide the entity's financing activities. The specific controls for borrowing and repayment may be delegated to an executive, such as the chief financial officer. When the chief financial officer or similar executive is responsible for both executing and accounting for long-term debt transactions, another executive body, such as the finance committee of the board of directors, should provide overall review and approval in the minutes. If the client has proper control procedures for issuing debt transactions, it is generally easy for the auditor to test those transactions for validity and authorization at the end of the period.

Completeness   The client should maintain adequate detailed records of long-term debt transactions to ensure that all borrowings and repayments of principal and interest are recorded. One approach to handling detailed debt transactions is to maintain a subsidiary ledger that contains information about all the long-term debt owed by the client. The debt amount recorded in the subsidiary ledger should be reconciled to the general ledger control account regularly.

Valuation   Note and bond transactions are recorded in the accounting records at their face value plus or minus any premium or discount. Premium or discount should be amortized using the effective interest method to calculate interest expense. Sometimes an entity incurs issuing costs such as underwriter's fees, legal fees, and accounting fees. Such costs should be recorded as deferred charges and amortized over the life of the debt. Valuation issues for sophisticated financing investments are far more complex. Although the client should have control procedures to ensure that long-term debt is properly valued, the client may ask the auditor to assist with recording the debt properly.

Classification   Control procedures should ensure that notes and bonds are properly classified. The major issue is to properly classify as a short-term liability the portion of long-term debt that is due in the next year.

One final issue related to the control risk for long-term debt is that the client should have adequate custodial procedures for any unissued notes or bonds to safeguard against loss from theft. Procedures should provide for periodic inspections by an individual independent of both the custodial and accounting responsibilities for long-term debt.

Substantive Tests of Long-Term Debt

[LO 4]   A substantive strategy for auditing long-term debt involves examining any new debt agreements, determining the status of prior debt agreements, and confirming balances and other relevant information with outside parties.

Analytical procedures are useful in auditing interest expense because of the direct relationship between the stated interest rate and the amount of long-term debt. For example, the auditor could estimate interest expense by multiplying the 12 monthly balances for long-term debt by the average interest rate. The reasonableness of interest expense could then be assessed by comparing this estimate to the interest expense amount recorded in the general ledger. If the two amounts are not materially different, the auditor can conclude that interest expense is fairly stated. If the estimated amount of interest expense is materially higher than the recorded amount, the auditor might conclude that the client has failed to record a portion of interest expense. On the other hand, if the recorded amount of interest expense is materially higher than the estimated amount, the client may have failed to record debt. Refer to the example in Chapter 5 for an example of the use of an analytical procedure to test the relationship between EarthWear's short-term line of credit and related interest expense.

Table 15–1 summarizes the main tests of account balances for long-term debt. The following discussion delineates the general approach to auditing long-term debt.

The auditor generally begins the audit of long-term debt by obtaining an analysis schedule for notes payable, bonds payable, and accrued interest payable. Exhibit 15–2 presents an example of such a schedule. Because Earth-Wear does not have long-term debt, the example in Exhibit 15–2 is based on Calabro Paging Services (see Problem 3-41). If there are numerous transactions during the year, this schedule may include only the debt outstanding at

TABLE 15–1	Summary of Audit Objectives and Tests of Account Balances—Long-Term Debt

Audit Objective	Tests of Account Balances
Validity	Examine copies of new note or bond agreements.
	Examine board of directors' minutes for approval of new lending agreements.
	Confirm notes or bonds directly with creditors (in many instances, creditors are banks, insurance companies, or trustees representing the creditors).
Completeness	Obtain a standard bank confirmation that requests specific information on notes from banks (see Chapter 16 for further discussion of bank confirmations).
	Confirm notes or bonds with creditors.
	Review interest expense for payments to debtholders not listed on the debt analysis schedule.
	Review notes paid or renewed after the balance sheet date to determine if there are unrecorded liabilities at year-end.
Cutoff	Review debt activity for a few days before and after year-end to determine if the transactions are included in the proper period.
Accuracy	Obtain an analysis of notes payable, bonds payable, and accrued interest payable; foot schedule and agree totals to the general ledger.
Valuation	Examine new debt agreements to ensure that they were recorded at the proper value.
	Confirm the outstanding balance for notes or bonds and the last date on which interest has been paid.
	Recompute accrued interest payable.
	Verify computation of the amortization of premium or discount.
Classification	Examine the due dates on notes or bonds for proper classification between current and long-term debt.
	Review debt for related-party transactions or borrowings from major shareholders.
Disclosure	Examine note or bond agreements for any restrictions that should be disclosed in the footnotes.

the end of the period. Note that this schedule includes a considerable amount of information on each debt transaction, including the payee, date due, interest rate, original amount, collateral, and paid and accrued interest.

Exhibit 15–2 also indicates the audit procedures performed on the details of the debt schedule. The most important audit objectives are tested as follows: Each debt instrument is confirmed with the debtholders and includes a request to verify the amount owed and last date on which interest has been paid. Confirmation of the debt and accrued interest provides evidence on the validity, completeness, and valuation objectives. If the client's debt is guaranteed by another party, a confirmation should be sent to the guarantor to confirm the guarantee.

The auditor also examines the due dates for the debt to ensure proper classification between current and long-term liabilities. Last, the auditor examines the debt agreements for any restrictive covenants that require disclosure in the footnotes. Examples of such covenants include restrictions on the payment of dividends or the issuance of additional debt or equity, and the maintenance of certain financial ratios. Exhibit 15–3 is an example of the disclosure of restrictive covenants.

Analysis Schedule for Auditing Long-Term Debt and Accrued Interest Payable

CPS

P10
DLJ
2/27/01

CALABRO PAGING SERVICES
Schedule of Long-Term Debt and Accrued Interest Payable
12/31/00

				Long-Term Debt				Accrued Interest Payable			
Payee	Due Date	Face Amount	Security	Beginning Balance	Additions	Payments	Ending Balance	Beginning Balance	Expenses	Paid	Ending Balance
First National Bank—Line of credit	11/1/03	$ 7,000,000	All assets**C**	$ 200,000	$900,000	$300,000γ	$ 800,000	$ 1,875	$ 22,500λ	$ 22,815	$ 1,560
8.75% lease obligation—Patriot Insurance Co.	12/15/02	$ 2,000,000	Communications equipment**C**	238,637		48,230γ	190,407	5,470	37,541λ	38,461	4,550
7% bonds payable—All American Insurance	6/30/05	$10,000,000	Land and buildings**C**	3,100,000		200,000γ	2,900,000	36,850	224,602λ	219,820	41,632
Total				$3,538,637	$900,000	$548,230	$3,890,407**L**	$44,195	$284,643**L**	$281,096	$47,742**L**
				F	**F**	**F**	**F**	**F**	**F**	**F**	**F**

Less current portion of long-term debt 424,061✓

$3,466,346

L = Agreed to general ledger.
γ = Traced payments to cash disbursements journal.
λ = Recomputed interest expense.
C = Agreed all information to confirmation.
F = Footed.
✓ = Tested amount of current portion of long-term debt.

EXHIBIT 15–3	**Sample Disclosure of Restrictive Loan Covenants**
	The 7 percent bond agreement contains provisions (1) limiting funded debt, security interests, and other indebtedness, (2) requiring the maintenance of defined working capital and tangible net worth, and (3) imposing restrictions on the payment of cash dividends. The company was in compliance with, or received a waiver regarding, each of the agreements during the year ended 2000. Under the terms of these agreements, $825,000 of retained earnings was available for payment of cash dividends at December 31, 2000.

Auditing Stockholders' Equity

[LO 5]   For most entities, stockholders' equity includes common stock, preferred stock, paid-in capital, and retained earnings. In recent years, numerous financial instruments have been developed that contain both debt and equity characteristics and affect the audit of stockholders' equity. Myriad stock options and compensation plans also impact the audit of stockholders' equity. A discussion of these complex equity instruments and stock option plans is beyond the scope of this text.

Following are the three major types of transactions that occur in stockholders' equity:

- *Issuance of stock.* This includes transactions such as sale of stock for cash; the exchange of stock for assets, services, or convertible debt; and issuance of stock for stock splits.
- *Repurchase of stock.* This includes the reacquisition of stock (referred to as *treasury stock*) and the retirement of stock.
- *Payment of dividends.* This includes the payment of cash dividends or issuance of stock dividends.

Control Risk Assessment—Stockholders' Equity

[LO 6]   A substantive strategy is most often used to audit stockholders' equity because the number of transactions is usually small. Although control risk can then be assessed at the maximum, the auditor must still understand the types of control procedures that are in place to prevent the misstatement of equity transactions.

Many large entities, such as publicly traded companies, use an independent *registrar, transfer agent,* and *dividend-disbursing agent* to process and record equity transactions. The registrar is responsible for ensuring that all stock issued complies with the corporate charter and for maintaining the control totals for total shares outstanding. The transfer agent is responsible for preparing stock certificates and maintaining adequate stockholders' records. The dividend-disbursing agent prepares and mails dividend checks to the stockholders of record. When an entity uses an independent registrar, transfer agent, and dividend-disbursing agent, the auditor may be able to obtain sufficient evidence by confirming the relevant information with those parties.

If an entity uses its own employees to perform the stock transfer and dividend disbursement functions, the auditor needs to perform more detailed testing of the stock-related records and transactions that occurred during the period. The following internal control objectives, internal control procedures, and segregation of duties are relevant when client personnel transfer stock and disburse dividends.

Control Objectives and Related Procedures

[LO 7]

Following are the major internal control objectives for stockholders' equity:

- Verify that stock and dividend transactions comply with the corporate charter (validity).
- Verify that stock and dividend transactions have been properly approved (authorization).
- Verify that stock and dividend transactions have been properly valued (valuation).
- Verify that all stock and dividend transactions have been properly posted and summarized in the accounting records (posting and summarization).

Validity   One of the entity's officers, such as the corporate secretary or legal counsel, should ensure that every stock or dividend transaction complies with the corporate charter or any regulatory requirement that affects the entity. This individual should also maintain the stockholders' ledger, which contains the name of each stockholder and the number of shares held by that shareholder.

Authorization   For most entities, the board of directors or stockholders approve stock and dividend transactions. The authorization is normally documented in the minutes of the board of directors' meetings. The auditor can examine the board of directors' minutes for proper authorization.

Valuation   Stock issuances, stock repurchases, and dividends should be recorded by the treasurer's department at an amount that conforms to GAAP. The auditor can recompute the recording of the stock and dividend transactions.

Posting and Summarization   The control procedures for this objective include reconciliation of the stockholders' records with the number of shares outstanding and reconciliation of dividends paid with the total shares outstanding on the dividend record date.

Segregation of Duties

[LO 8]

If the entity has enough personnel, the following segregation of duties should be maintained:

- The individuals responsible for issuing, transferring, and canceling stock certificates should not have any accounting responsibilities.
- The individual responsible for maintaining the detailed stockholders' records should be independent of the maintenance of the general ledger control accounts.
- The individual responsible for maintaining the detailed stockholders' records should not also process cash receipts or disbursements.

- Appropriate segregation of duties should be established among the preparation, recording, signing, and mailing of dividend checks.

Auditing Capital-Stock Accounts

[LO 9]   The capital-stock accounts include common stock, preferred stock, and paid-in capital. When auditing the capital-stock accounts, the auditor is normally concerned with the validity, completeness, valuation, and disclosure objectives. The auditor begins the audit of capital stock by obtaining a schedule of all activity in the accounts for the current period. The beginning balance is agreed to the prior year's working papers, and the ending balance is agreed to the general ledger. The majority of the auditor's work then focuses on the current-period activity in each account.

Validity and Completeness

All valid capital-stock transactions are approved by the board of directors. Therefore, the auditor can test the validity of capital-stock transactions by tracing the transactions recorded in the current year to the board of directors' minutes. When an independent registrar and transfer agent are used by the entity, the auditor confirms the total number of shares outstanding at the end of the period. If the amount of shares listed as outstanding on the confirmation reconciles to the general ledger capital-stock accounts, the auditor has evidence that the total number of shares outstanding at the end of the year is correct.

If the entity does not use outside agents, it will maintain a stock register and/or a stock certificate book. The auditor may perform the following tests:

- Trace the transfers of shares between stockholders to the stock register and/or stock certificate book (valuation and completeness).
- Foot the shares outstanding in the stock register and/or stock certificate book and agree them to total shares outstanding in the general ledger capital-stock accounts (completeness).
- Examine any canceled stock certificates (validity).
- Account for and inspect any unissued stock certificates in the stock certificate book (completeness).

Valuation

When capital stock is issued for cash, the assessment of proper valuation is straightforward. The par, or stated, value for the shares issued is assigned to the respective capital-stock account, while the difference between the price and par, or stated, value is allocated to paid-in capital. The auditor can recompute the values assigned to each transaction. The proceeds from the sale of stock are normally traced to the cash receipts records.

The valuation issue is more complex when capital stock is issued in exchange for assets or services, for a merger or acquisition, for convertible securities, or for a stock dividend. For example, when a stock dividend is declared and the number of shares issued is less than 20 percent of the shares outstanding, the dividend is recorded at fair market value. The fair market value of the stock dividend is charged to retained earnings and credited to common stock and paid-in capital. To test valuation, the auditor can recompute the stock dividend and trace the entries into the general ledger.

TABLE 15–2	**Sample Disclosure Items for Stockholders' Equity**

- Number of shares authorized, issued, and outstanding for each class of stock.
- Call privileges, prices, and dates for preferred stock.
- Preferred-stock sinking funds.
- Stock option or purchase plans.
- Restrictions on retained earnings and dividends.
- Any completed or pending transactions (such as stock dividends or splits) that may affect stockholders' equity.

Disclosure

A number of important disclosures are frequently necessary for stockholders' equity. Table 15–2 contains examples of stockholders' equity disclosures. The normal sources of this information include the corporate charter, minutes of the board of directors' meetings, and contractual agreements.

Auditing Dividends

[LO 10] Generally, all dividends that are declared and paid will be audited because of concerns with violations of corporate bylaws or debt covenants. When the entity uses an independent dividend-disbursing agent, the auditor can confirm the amount disbursed to the agent by the entity. This amount is agreed with the amount authorized by the board of directors. The auditor can recompute the dividend amount by multiplying the number of shares outstanding on the record date by the amount of the per share dividend approved by the board of directors. This amount should agree to the amount disbursed to shareholders and accrued at year-end. If the auditor is concerned about the client's controls over dividend disbursements, he or she may test the payee names and amounts on the individual canceled checks with the stock register or stock certificate book. The auditor also reviews the entity's compliance with any agreements that restrict the payments of dividends.

Auditing Retained Earnings

[LO 11] Under normal circumstances, retained earnings are affected by the current year's income or loss, as well as dividends paid. However, certain accounting standards require that some transactions be included in retained earnings. Prior-period adjustments, correction of errors, valuation accounts for marketable securities and foreign currency translation, and changes in appropriations of retained earnings are examples of such transactions.

The auditor begins the audit of retained earnings by obtaining a schedule of the account activity for the period. The beginning balance is agreed to the prior year's working papers and financial statements. Net income or loss can be traced to the income statement. The amounts for any cash or stock dividends can be verified as described earlier. If there are any prior-period adjustments, the auditor must be certain that the transactions satisfy the requirements of the relevant accounting standards. Any new appropriations or changes in existing appropriations should be traced to the contractual agreements that required the appropriations. Last, the auditor must make sure that all necessary disclosures related to retained earnings are made in the footnotes. For example, many debt agreements restrict the amount of retained earnings that is available for payment as dividends (see Exhibit 15–3).

Auditing Income Statement Accounts

[LO 12]   In auditing income statement accounts, the auditor must be satisfied that the revenue and expense accounts are not materially misstated and that they are accounted for in accordance with GAAP. The income statement is viewed as an important source of information by various users of the financial statements. For example, creditors or potential creditors look to an entity's profitability as one indicator of the entity's ability to repay debt. Potential investors look to the income statement when deciding whether to purchase the entity's stock. Finally, vendors may examine the entity's earnings potential in order to assess whether the entity will be able to pay for goods or services purchased on credit.

The audit of the revenue and expense accounts depends on the extent of work conducted by the auditor on the entity's internal control system and balance sheet accounts. For example, the likelihood of material misstatement in the various revenue and expense accounts is a function of the entity's internal control system. The level of control risk used to assess the different accounting cycles directly affects the extent of testing that the auditor requires to audit the income statement accounts.

Auditing the income statement includes consideration of the results of audit work conducted in other parts of the audit and completion of additional substantive testing on selected income statement accounts, including the following:

- Assessment of the results of testing controls for the various accounting cycles.
- Assessment of the results of the direct tests of balance sheet accounts and the related income statement accounts.
- Performance of analytical procedures on income statement accounts.
- Tests of selected income statement accounts.

Assessing Control Risk for Accounting Cycles

In previous chapters, the auditor's approach to assessing the control risk for various accounting cycles was discussed. If the control risk is set at the maximum, the auditor does not rely on controls but conducts extensive substantive tests of account balances. When a reliance strategy is followed, the auditor conducts tests of controls and substantive tests of transactions to determine if the client's control procedures are operating effectively. If the control procedures operate effectively, the auditor may reduce the control risk below the maximum.

To better understand the effect of a reduced control risk assessment on the audit of the revenue and expense accounts, consider the income statement accounts affected by the revenue and purchasing cycles. For example, a reduced control risk assessment for the revenue cycle provides evidence that the sales, accounts receivable, allowance for uncollectible accounts, and sales returns and allowances accounts are not materially misstated. Similarly, a reduced control risk assessment for the purchasing cycle provides evidence that financial statement accounts such as inventory; property, plant, and equipment; accounts payable; and most expense accounts are not materially misstated. The important point here is that the auditor already has reliable evidence on the accounts included in the income statement. The findings for the purchasing cycle are particularly relevant, since proper control procedures provide evidence on most of the expense accounts. This allows the auditor to do considerably less substantive testing for these income statement accounts.

Direct Tests of Balance Sheet Accounts

Income statement accounts are normally audited in the course of auditing the related balance sheet accounts. Table 15–3 lists balance sheet accounts and the related income statement accounts that are verified in this manner. For example, when the allowance for uncollectible accounts is audited, bad-debt expense is also tested. Similarly, when auditing notes receivable, the auditor can test interest income.

Analytical Procedures

Analytical procedures can be used extensively to test the revenue and expense accounts. One type of analytical procedure involves comparing the current year's dollar amount for each revenue and expense account with the prior year's balances. Any account that deviates from the prior year's by more than a predetermined amount should be investigated. An alternative to this type of analytical procedure involves calculating the ratio of individual expense accounts to net sales and comparing these percentages across years. The auditor can also compare these percentages to industry averages. Individual expense accounts that are judged by the auditor to be out of line are investigated further.

Analytical procedures can also be used to conduct direct substantive tests of *specific* revenue or expense accounts. For example, the auditor can test sales commissions by using the client's commission schedule and multiplying commission rates by eligible sales. This estimate can be compared to the recorded commission expense. Other examples might include overall reasonableness tests for interest and depreciation expense.

TABLE 15–3	Examples of Income Statement Accounts Audited in Conjunction with the Balance Sheet Account	

Balance Sheet Account Audited	*Related Income Statement Account Audited*
Accounts receivable/allowance for uncollectible accounts	Bad-debt expense
Notes receivable/investments/accrued interest receivable	Interest income
Property, plant, and equipment/accumulated depreciation	Depreciation expense, gain/losses on sales or retirements of assets
Prepaid insurance	Insurance expense
Long-term debt/accrued interest payable	Interest expense

Tests of Selected Account Balances

Even though the auditor has gathered considerable evidence about revenue and expense accounts based on the audit procedures just discussed, the auditor may want to examine some accounts further. For these accounts, the auditor typically analyzes in detail the transactions included in each account. The auditor verifies the transactions by examining (vouching) the supporting documentation. Accounts examined in this manner are generally accounts that are not directly affected by an accounting cycle, accounts that may contain sensitive information or unusual transactions, or accounts for which detailed information is needed for the tax return or other schedules included with the financial statements. Some examples of such accounts include legal expense, travel and entertainment, charity expense, other income and expenses, and any account containing related-party transactions. Exhibit 15–4 presents an account analysis for EarthWear's legal expense. In auditing the legal-expense account, the auditor vouches the transactions to the attorneys' invoices. The auditor should examine the invoice not only for the amount but also for information on potential uncertainties, such as lawsuits against the client.

EXHIBIT 15–4

Example of a Detailed Test of an Expense Account

http://www.mhhe.com/messier

T16
DLJ
2/28/01

EARTHWEAR CLOTHIERS
Analysis of Legal Expense
December 31, 2000

Date	Payee	Description	Amount
March 17	Proctor & Finch, PA	Legal fees for patent infringement suit against Marchant, Inc.	$28,500V
June 15	Field, Murray & Forthsye	Fees for copyright of new manual	14,000V
October 1	Proctor & Finch, PA	Legal fees for patent infringement suit against Marchant, Inc.	26,200V
November 30	Hackenbrack, Yost, Amer & Ahmed	Legal fees for land purchase agreement	11,700V
			$80,400L
			F

V = Agreed description and amount to legal invoice.
L = Agreed to general ledger.
F = Footed.

REVIEW QUESTIONS

[LO 1,4,5,9]   15-1   Why does the auditor generally follow a substantive strategy when auditing long-term debt and capital accounts?

[2,3]   15-2   What are the most important internal control objectives for long-term debt? What documents would normally contain the authorization to issue long-term debt?

[3]   15-3   What are the key control procedures when the chief financial officer initiates, approves, and executes debt transactions?

[4]   15-4   Describe how analytical procedures may be used to test interest expense.

[4]   15-5   Confirmations of long-term debt provide evidence about which audit objectives?

[4]   15-6   List three disclosures that may be required for long-term debt.

[5]   15-7   Describe the three major types of transactions that occur in stockholders' equity.

[5]   15-8   What are the functions of the registrar, the transfer agent, and the dividend-disbursing agent?

[8]   15-9   What is the major segregation of duties that should be maintained when the client does not use a registrar or transfer agent and sufficient personnel are available to perform the stock transactions?

[9]   15-10   List two common disclosures for stockholders' equity and why such disclosures are necessary.

[10,11]   15-11   What approach would the auditor follow to audit dividends and retained earnings?

[12]   15-12   Describe the steps followed by the auditor when auditing the income statement.

[12]   15-13   List three analytical procedures that the auditor might use in auditing the income statement.

[12]   15-14   Why would the auditor do an account analysis and vouch selected transactions in income statement accounts such as legal expense, travel and entertainment, and other income/expenses?

MULTIPLE-CHOICE QUESTIONS FROM CPA EXAMINATIONS

[4]   15-15   The auditor can best verify a client's bond sinking fund transactions and year-end balance sheet by
  a. Confirmation of retired bonds with individual holders.
  b. Confirmation with the bond trustee.
  c. Recomputation of interest expense, interest payable, and amortization of bond discount or premium.
  d. Examination and count of the bonds retired during the year.

[3,4]   15-16   Two months before year-end, the bookkeeper erroneously recorded the receipt of a long-term bank loan by a debit to cash and a credit to sales. Which of the following is the most effective procedure for detecting this type of error?
  a. Analysis of the notes payable journal.
  b. Analysis of bank confirmation information.

c. Preparation of a year-end bank reconciliation.

d. Preparation of a year-end bank transfer schedule.

[3] 15-17 Which of the following questions would an auditor most likely include on an internal control questionnaire for notes payable?

a. Are assets that collateralize notes payable critically needed for the entity's continued existence?

b. Are two or more authorized signatures required on checks that repay notes payable?

c. Are the proceeds from notes payable used to purchase noncurrent assets?

d. Are direct borrowings on notes payable authorized by the board of directors?

[4] 15-18 An auditor's program to examine long-term debt would most likely include steps that require

a. Comparing the carrying amount of the debt to its year-end market value.

b. Correlating the interest expense recorded for the period with the outstanding debt.

c. Verifying the existence of the holders of the debt by direct confirmation.

d. Inspecting the accounts payable subsidiary ledger for unrecorded long-term debt.

[4] 15-19 An auditor's purpose in reviewing the renewal of a note payable shortly after the balance sheet date is most likely to obtain evidence concerning management's assertions about

a. Existence or occurrence.

b. Presentation and disclosure.

c. Completeness.

d. Valuation or allocation.

[7,8,9] 15-20 When a client company does *not* maintain its own stock records, the auditor should obtain written confirmation from the transfer agent and registrar concerning

a. Restrictions on the payment of dividends.

b. The number of shares issued and outstanding.

c. Guarantees of preferred stock liquidation value.

d. The number of shares subject to agreements to repurchase.

[9] 15-21 An auditor should trace corporate stock issuances and treasury stock transactions to the

a. Numbered stock certificates.

b. Articles of incorporation.

c. Transfer agent's records.

d. Minutes of the board of directors.

[7,8] 15-22 The primary responsibility of a bank acting as a registrar of capital stock is to

a. Ascertain that dividends declared do *not* exceed the statutory amount allowable in the state of incorporation.

b. Account for stock certificates by comparing the total shares outstanding to the total in the shareholders' subsidiary ledger.

c. Act as an independent third party between the board of directors and outside investors concerning mergers, acquisitions, and the sale of treasury stock.

    d. Verify that stock has been issued in accordance with the authorization of the board of directors and the articles of incorporation.

[12]   **15-23** An auditor compares 2000 revenues and expenses with those of the prior year and investigates all changes exceeding 10 percent. By this procedure the auditor would be most likely to learn that

    a. Fourth-quarter payroll taxes were *not* paid.

    b. The client changed its capitalization policy for small tools in 2000.

    c. An increase in property tax rates has *not* been recognized in the client's accrual.

    d. The 2000 provision for uncollectible accounts is inadequate because of worsening economic conditions.

[12]   **15-24** Which of the following comparisons would be most useful to an auditor in evaluating the results of an entity's operations?

    a. Prior-year accounts payable to current-year accounts payable.

    b. Prior-year payroll expense to budgeted current-year payroll expense.

    c. Current-year revenue to budgeted current-year revenue.

    d. Current-year warranty expense to current-year contingent liabilities.

[9]   **15-25** Although the quantity and content of audit working papers vary with each particular engagement, an auditor's permanent files most likely include

    a. Schedules that support the current year's adjusting entries.

    b. Prior years' accounts receivable confirmations that were classified as exceptions.

    c. Documentation indicating that the audit work was adequately planned and supervised.

    d. Analyses of capital stock and other owners' equity accounts.

PROBLEMS

[4]   **15-26** Maslovskaya, CPA, has been engaged to examine the financial statements of Broadwall Corporation for the year ended December 31, 2000. During the year, Broadwall obtained a long-term loan from a local bank pursuant to a financing agreement that provided that

    1. The loan was to be secured by the company's inventory and accounts receivable.

    2. The company was not to pay dividends without permission from the bank.

    3. Monthly installment payments were to commence July 1, 2000.

    In addition, during the year the company borrowed various short-term amounts from the president of the company, including substantial amounts just prior to year-end.

Required:

    a. For purposes of the audit of the financial statements of Broadwall Corporation, what procedures should Maslovskaya employ in examining the described loans?

    b. What financial statement disclosures should Maslovskaya expect to find with respect to the loans from the president?

(AICPA, adapted)

[8,9]   15-27   Lee, CPA, the continuing auditor of Wu, Inc., is beginning to audit the common stock and treasury stock accounts. Lee has decided to design substantive tests without relying on the company's internal control system.

Wu has no par and no stated-value common stock, and it acts as its own registrar and transfer agent. During the past year Wu both issued and reacquired shares of its own common stock, some of which the company still owned at year-end. Additional common stock transactions occurred among the shareholders during the year.

Common stock transactions can be traced to individual shareholders' accounts in a subsidiary ledger and to a stock certificate book. The company has not paid any cash or stock dividends. There are no other classes of stock, stock rights, warrants, or option plans.

Required:
What substantive audit procedures should Lee apply in examining the common stock and treasury stock accounts?

(AICPA, adapted)

[4]   15-28   Erik Rekdahl, senior-in-charge, is auditing Koonce Katfood, Inc.'s, long-term debt for the year ended July 31, 2000. Long-term debt is composed of two bond issues, which are due in 10 and 15 years, respectively. The debt is held by two insurance companies. Rekdahl has examined the bond indentures for each issue. The indentures provide that if Koonce fails to comply with the covenants of the indentures, the debt becomes payable immediately. Rekdahl identified the following covenants when reviewing the bond indentures:

1. "The debtor company shall endeavor to maintain a working capital ratio of 2 to 1 at all times, and in any fiscal year following a failure to maintain said ratio, the company shall restrict compensation of officers to a total of $650,000. Officers include the chairperson of the board and the president."
2. "The debtor company shall keep all property that is security for these debt agreements insured against loss by fire to the extent of 100 percent of its actual value. Policies of insurance comprising this protection shall be filed with the trustee."
3. "The company is required to restrict 40 percent of retained earnings from availability for paying dividends."
4. "A sinking fund shall be established with the First Morgan Bank of Austin, and semiannual payments of $500,000 shall be deposited in the fund. The bank may, at its discretion, purchase bonds from either issue."

Required:
a. Provide any audit steps that Rekdahl should conduct to determine if the company is in compliance with the bond indentures.
b. List any reporting requirements that the financial statements or footnotes should recognize.

(AICPA, adapted)

[4] 15-29 The long-term debt working paper on the next page (indexed K-1) was prepared by client personnel and audited by Andy Fogelman, an audit assistant, during the calendar year 2000 audit of American Widgets, Inc., a continuing audit client. The engagement supervisor is reviewing the working paper thoroughly.

Required:
Identify the deficiencies in the working paper that the engagement supervisor should discover.

(AICPA, adapted)

DISCUSSION CASES

[4] 15-30 On September 10, Melinda Johnson was auditing the financial statements of a new audit client, Mother Earth Foods, a health-food chain that has a June 30 year-end. The company is privately held and has just gone through a leveraged buyout with long-term financing that includes various restrictive covenants.

In order to obtain debt financing, companies often have to agree to certain conditions, some of which may restrict the way in which they conduct their business. If the borrower fails to comply with the stated conditions, it may be considered in default, which would give the lender the right to accelerate the due date of the debt, add other restrictions, waive the default for a stated period, or revise the covenants. Usually there is a grace period during which the borrower can cure the default.

Johnson believes that it is possible that at August 31 Mother Earth was in violation of the debt covenant restrictions, which became effective on that date. The debt covenants require the company to maintain a certain receivable turnover rate. Johnson is not certain, however, because the accounting records, including period-end cutoffs for sales and purchases, have not been well maintained. Nevertheless, Mother Earth's executives assure Johnson that if they were in violation, the company will be able to obtain a waiver or modification of the covenant.

Required:
a. Discuss the audit procedures that Johnson would conduct to determine if Mother Earth violated the debt covenants. How would Johnson determine whether Mother Earth would be able to obtain a waiver, assuming that the company was in violation of the debt covenants?
b. Based on the case scenario, should Mother Earth continue to classify this debt as noncurrent? Justify your answer.

[5,9] 15-31 Your client, Rosenberg, Inc. (the "Company"), bought certain assets of Howarth, Inc., and accounted for them as a purchase in accordance with APB Opinion No. 16, "Business Combinations." The letter of intent was executed on July 31, 2000, and the transaction closed on October 31, 2000. The purchase price was $8,600,000, payable as $5,100,000 in cash ($2,700,000 of which was borrowed

AMERICAN WIDGETS, INC.
Working Paper
December 31, 2000

	Initials	Date
Prepared By	AF	3/22/01
Approved By		

Lender	Interest Rate	Payment Terms	Collateral	Balance 12/31/99	2000 Borrowings	2000 Reductions	Balance 12/31/00	Interest Paid to	Accrued Interest Payable 12/31/00	Comments
First Commercial Bank φ	12%	Interest only on 25th of month, principal due in full 1/1/04; no prepayment penalty	Inventories	$ 50,000✓	$300,000A 1/31/00	$100,000✺ 6/30/00	$250,000CX	12/25/00	$2,500NR	Dividend of $80,000 paid 9/2/00 (W/P N-3) violates a provision of the debt agreement, which thereby permits lender to demand immediate payment; lender has refused to waive this violation.
Lender's Capital Corporation φ	Prime plus 1%	Interest only on last day of month, principal due in full 3/5/02	2nd mortgage on Park Street Building	100,000✓	50,000A 2/29/00	—	200,000C	12/31/00	—	Prime rate was 8% to 9% during the year.
Gigantic Building & Loan Association φ	12%	$5,000 principal plus interest due on 5th of month, due in full 12/31/09	1st mortgage on Park Street Building	720,000✓	—	60,000θ	660,000C	12/5/00	5,642R	Reclassification entry for current portion proposed (see RJE-3).
J. Lott, majority stockholder φ	0%	Due in full 12/31/03	Unsecured	300,000✓	—	100,000N 12/31/00	200,000C	—	—	Borrowed additional $100,000 from J. Lott on 1/7/01.
				$1,170,000✓ F	$350,000 F	$260,000 F	$1,310,000T/B F		$8,142T/B F	

Interest costs from long-term debt

Interest expense for year	$ 281,333T/B
Average loan balance outstanding	$1,406,667R

Five-year maturities *(for disclosure purposes)*

Year-end	
12/31/01	$ 60,000
12/31/02	260,000
12/31/03	260,000
12/31/04	310,000
12/31/05	60,000
Thereafter	360,000
	$1,310,000
	F

Tick Mark Legend
C = Confirmed without exception, W/P K-2.
F = Readded, foots correctly.
CX = Confirmed with exception, W/P K-3.
NR = Does not recompute correctly.
A = Agreed to loan agreement, validated bank deposit ticket, and board of directors' authorization, W/P W-7.
θ = Agreed to canceled checks and lender's monthly statements.
N = Agreed to cash disbursements journal and canceled check dated 12/31/00, clearing 1/8/01.
T/B = Traced to working trial balance.
✓ = Agreed to 12/31/99 working papers.
φ = Agreed interest rate, term, and collateral to copy of note and loan agreement.
✺ = Agreed to canceled check and board of directors' authorization, W/P W-7.

Conclusions: Long-term debt, accrued interest payable, and interest expense are correct and complete at 12/31/00.

pursuant to a term loan) and 175,000 shares of the company's common stock, which account for approximately 10 percent of the shares issued. It was agreed by the parties that the common stock would be assigned a value of $20 per share.

Rosenberg is a privately held company that plans to go public within two years. Its common stock is thinly traded on the unlisted securities market in Canada. There have been no independent valuations of the company's stock.

In addition to the payment in cash and securities, Rosenberg executed a repurchase agreement with Howarth. The agreement requires Rosenberg to repurchase the stock issued to Howarth on the first anniversary date (October 31, 2001) for $20 per share. In substance, the agreement represents a mandatory "put" on the Rosenberg stock, which was issued to Howarth. The repurchase can be delayed for up to two succeeding anniversary dates if the company pays Howarth an amount equal to $1.80 per share ($315,000) on each anniversary date.

The put can be accelerated if any one of the following occurs: (1) substantially all of the company's assets are sold, (2) Rosenberg merges with another entity and does not survive as the controlling entity, or (3) substantially all of the company's common stock is sold to others.

The put is voided if any one of the following occurs: (1) the stock is sold in connection with a public offering of the company, (2) Howarth declines its right to put the stock, or (3) Howarth sells the stock to a third party. In addition, the company can void the option by redeeming the stock at the guaranteed price of $20 per share.

The repurchase agreement also contains an exchange clause whereby the common stock may be exchanged for a demand promissory note. The exchange right becomes operable if any one of the following occurs: (1) Rosenberg borrows in excess of $15 million, (2) Rosenberg issues equity securities with rights and preferences and limitations senior to the shares given to Howarth, or (3) Rosenberg fails to perform under the repurchase agreement.

The company's controller tells you that she plans to show the common stock issued to Howarth in the shareholders' equity section of the balance sheet. She also tells you that the company's president believes that the fair value of the stock is $20 per share and insists that it be recorded at that amount at inception.

Required:
a. What business reasons may have motivated Rosenberg to structure the transaction in this manner? Should the mandatorily redeemable common stock issued to Howarth be classified in the shareholders' equity section of the balance sheet?
b. At what amount should the common stock be valued? What audit procedures would you use to verify the common stock valuation?

Chapter 16

Auditing Cash and Investments

LEARNING OBJECTIVES

Upon completion of this chapter you will

[1] Understand the relationship of the various accounting cycles to cash.

[2] Know the different types of bank accounts.

[3] Identify substantive tests of transactions used to audit cash.

[4] Identify tests of account balances used to audit cash.

[5] Know how to audit a bank reconciliation.

[6] Understand fraud-related audit procedures for cash.

[7] Understand why clients invest in securities of other entities.

[8] Identify key internal controls for investments.

[9] Know the appropriate segregation of duties for investments.

[10] Identify tests of account balances used to audit investments.

RELEVANT ACCOUNTING AND AUDITING PRONOUNCEMENTS

FASB Statement of Financial Accounting Standards No. 95, "Statement of Cash Flows" (FAS 95)

FASB Statement of Financial Accounting Standards No. 115, "Accounting for Certain Investments in Debt and Equity Securities" (FAS 115)

SAS No. 31, "Evidential Matter" (AU 326)

SAS No. 47, "Audit Risk and Materiality in Conducting an Audit" (AU 312)

SAS No. 55, "Consideration of Internal Control in a Financial Statement Audit" (AU 319)

SAS No. 56, "Analytical Procedures" (AU 329)

SAS No. 67, "The Confirmation Process" (AU 330)

SAS No. 78, "Consideration of Internal Control in a Financial Statement Audit: An Amendment to SAS No. 55" (AU 319)

SAS No. 80, "Amendment to Statement on Auditing Standards No. 31, *Evidential Matter*" (AU 326)

SAS No. 81, "Auditing Investments" (AU 332)

SAS No. 82, "Consideration of Fraud in a Financial Statement Audit" (AU 316)

This chapter covers the audit of cash and investments. These are the last audit areas studied in this text because each of the other accounting cycles interacts with cash. Additionally, the evidence gathered during the audit of other accounting cycles affects the type and amount of evidence required to audit cash.

Proper management of cash and investments is essential to every entity. The principal goal of cash management is to ensure that sufficient cash is available to meet the entity's needs. Achieving this goal requires good forecasting of cash receipts and disbursements. By using sound cash-forecasting techniques, management can plan for (1) investing excess cash and (2) borrowing at favorable interest rates when cash is required. Because cash and investments are so liquid, they normally represent critical audit areas. 🦫

Cash and the Effect of Other Accounting Cycles

 **[LO 1]** The line item "cash" reported in the financial statements represents currency on hand and cash on deposit in bank accounts, including certificates of deposit, time deposits, and savings accounts. Frequently, certain "cash equivalents" are combined with cash for presentation in the financial statements. FASB Statement of Financial Accounting Standards No. 95, "Statement of Cash Flows" (FAS 95), defines *cash equivalents* as short-term, highly liquid investments that are readily convertible to cash or so near their maturity that there is little risk of change in their value (para. 8). Examples of such financial instruments include Treasury bills, commercial paper, and money market funds.

Because virtually all accounting transactions pass through the cash account as part of their "cradle-to-grave" cycle, cash is affected in one way or another by all of the entity's transaction cycles. Figure 16–1 shows the effect each major transaction cycle has on the cash account. Although the main source of cash receipts is the revenue cycle, other sources of cash include (1) the sale of property, plant, and equipment and (2) the proceeds from issuing long-term debt or capital stock. The main sources of disbursements from cash are the purchasing and payroll cycles. Generally, large payments from the purchasing cycle are for acquisitions of inventory and property, plant, and equipment. Payments on long-term debt and repurchase of stock are other types of cash disbursements.

Because of the close relationship of cash to the revenue and purchasing cycles, internal control system issues were discussed in Chapters 10 and 11, respectively. Table 10–5 summarized the internal control objectives, possible misstatements, control procedures, and tests of controls for cash receipt

FIGURE 16–1

The Effects of Major Accounting Transactions/Cycles on Cash

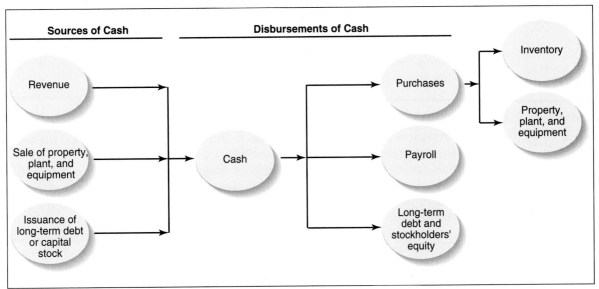

transactions. A similar summary was provided for cash disbursement transactions in Table 11–5. A discussion of the control risk for cash receipt and disbursement transactions will not be repeated in this chapter. However, the auditor's assessment of the control risk for transactions processed through the revenue and purchasing cycles strongly affects the nature and extent of testing for the ending cash balance. For example, if the control risk is below the maximum for both of these cycles, the auditor can reduce the substantive testing of the cash balances. The reader should review the assessment of control risk for cash receipt and cash disbursement transactions.

Types of Bank Accounts

[LO 2]   As mentioned, cash management is an important function in all organizations. In order to maximize its cash position, an entity implements procedures for accelerating the collection of cash receipts and properly delaying the payment of cash disbursements. Such procedures allow the entity to earn interest on excess cash or to reduce the cost of cash borrowings.

In spite of the sophisticated nature of cash management, the entity's management must still be concerned with the control and safekeeping of cash. Using different types of bank accounts aids in controlling the entity's cash. The following types of bank accounts are typically used:

- General cash account
- Imprest cash accounts
- Branch accounts

It is important to understand each of the different types of bank accounts used. While the audit approach to each type of account is similar, the extent of testing varies from one account to the next. Each type of bank account is briefly discussed.

General Cash Account

The general cash account is the principal cash account for most entities. The major source of cash receipts for this account is the revenue cycle, and the major sources of cash disbursements are the purchasing and payroll cycles. This cash account may also be used for receipts and disbursements from other bank accounts maintained by the entity. For many small entities, this is the only cash account maintained.

Imprest Cash Accounts

An imprest bank account contains a stipulated amount of money, and the account is used for limited purposes. Imprest accounts are frequently used for disbursing payroll and dividend checks. In the case of payroll, a separate bank account containing a minimum balance is established for disbursing payroll checks. Prior to the disbursement of payroll checks, a check is drawn or a cash transfer is made from the general cash account to the payroll account for the amount of the net payroll. The payroll checks are then drawn on this imprest account. Thus, the payroll account serves as a clearing account for the payroll checks and facilitates the disbursement of cash while also maintaining adequate control over cash. Use of imprest accounts also minimizes the time required to reconcile the general cash account.

Branch Accounts

Companies that operate branches in multiple locations may maintain separate accounts at local banks. This allows each branch to pay local expenses and to maintain a banking relationship in the local community. Branch cash accounts can be operated in a number of ways. In some cases, the branch accounts are nothing more than imprest accounts for branch payments in which a minimum balance is maintained. The branch submits periodic cash reports to headquarters, and the branch account receives a check or transfer from the general cash account. In other cases, the branch account functions as a general cash account by recording both cash receipts and cash disbursements.

For proper control, the branch should be required to submit periodic cash reports to headquarters, and the entity's management should carefully monitor the cash balances in the branch accounts.

Substantive Tests of Transactions—Cash

[LO 3]   Table 16–1 contains examples of substantive tests of transactions for both cash receipts and cash disbursements. The audit objectives for ownership and disclosure are not included. Questions about the ownership of cash are seldom raised, while the disclosure objective is tested as part of the

TABLE 16–1   Examples of Substantive Tests of Transactions for Cash

| | Substantive Tests of Transactions | |
Audit Objectives	*Cash Receipts*	*Cash Disbursements*
Validity	Trace a sample of entries in the cash receipts journal to remittance advices, daily deposit slips, and bank statement.	Trace a sample of entries from the cash disbursements journal to canceled checks, voucher packet, and bank statement. Examine a sample of canceled checks for authorized signature and proper endorsement.
Completeness	Trace a sample of remittance advices to cash receipts journal and, if necessary, to deposit slips.	Trace a sample of canceled checks to the cash disbursements journal.
Cutoff	Compare the dates for recording a sample of cash receipt transactions in the cash receipt journal with the dates the cash was deposited in the bank (note any significant delays).	Compare the dates for a sample of checks with the dates the checks cleared the bank account (note any significant delays).
Accuracy	Foot cash receipts journal and agree posting to the general ledger.	Foot cash disbursements journal and agree posting to the general ledger.
Valuation	Compare a sample of remittance advices with amount in cash receipts journal.	Compare a sample of canceled checks with amounts in cash disbursements journal.
Classification	Examine a sample of remittance advices for proper account classification.	Examine a sample of canceled checks for proper account classification.

Note: Many of the substantive tests of transactions mentioned also serve as dual-purpose tests (see Tables 10–6 and 11–6).

substantive tests of the cash balances. By testing both cash receipt and cash disbursement transactions, the auditor obtains important evidence about the relevant audit objectives for the cash account. On most audits, the substantive tests of transactions for cash receipts and cash disbursements are conducted together with the tests of controls for the revenue and purchasing cycles, respectively.

Analytical Procedures—Cash

Because of its residual nature, cash does not have a predictable relationship with other financial statement accounts. As a result, the auditor's use of analytical procedures for auditing cash is limited to comparisons with prior years' cash balances and to budgeted amounts. This limited use of analytical procedures is normally offset by (1) extensive tests of controls and/or substantive tests of transactions for cash receipts and cash disbursements or (2) extensive tests of the entity's bank reconciliations.

Tests of Account Balances—Cash

The Effects of Control Procedures

[LO 4]

The reliability of the client's control procedures over cash receipts and cash disbursements affects the nature and extent of the auditor's substantive tests of cash balances. The preceding chapters discussed a number of important control procedures for both cash receipt and cash disbursement transactions. For example, incoming checks are to be restrictively endorsed (stamped "For deposit only to the company's bank account"), and daily cash receipts are to be reconciled with postings to the accounts receivable subsidiary ledger. The effective operation of these control procedures provides strong evidence that the completeness objective is being met. Similarly, outgoing checks are to be signed only when all documents included in the voucher packet have been independently approved. The effective operation of this control procedure provides the auditor with evidence on the authorization objective.

A major internal control procedure that directly affects the audit of cash is the completion of a monthly bank reconciliation by client personnel who are independent of the handling and recording of cash receipts and cash disbursements. Such bank reconciliations ensure that the client's books reflect the same balance as the bank's after reconciling items have been considered. Control can be improved further if an independent party such as the internal auditor reviews the bank reconciliation.

If the client has good bank reconciliation procedures that are promptly performed, the auditor may be able to reduce the audit work on the ending cash balance.

Audit Objectives

Table 16–2 summarizes the audit objectives and substantive tests of account balances for cash accounts. The ownership objective is not included in Table 16–2 because it is seldom important to the audit of the cash balance. The major audit procedures for each cash account involve tests of

TABLE 16–2	Summary of Audit Objectives and Tests of Account Balances—Cash

Audit Objective	Tests of Account Balances
Validity Completeness Valuation	Test bank reconciliation: • Obtain standard bank confirmation and trace balance per bank to the bank reconciliation. • Obtain cutoff bank statement. • Trace deposits in transit, outstanding checks, and other reconciling items to cutoff bank statement. If control risk is high or if fraud is suspected: • Perform extended bank reconciliation procedures. • Perform a proof of cash. • Test for kiting.
Accuracy	Obtain a copy of the bank reconciliation. Foot the reconciliation and the outstanding check listing. Trace balance per book to the general ledger.
Cutoff	Cash receipts: • Observe cash on hand for the last day of the year and trace deposits to cash receipts journal and cutoff bank statement. Cash disbursements: • Record the last check issued on the last day of the year and trace to cash disbursements journal. • Trace outstanding checks on bank reconciliation and investigate any check clearing after a long delay.
Classification Disclosure	Review board of directors' minutes, line-of-credit arrangements, loan agreements, or other documents for any restrictions on cash such as compensating balances or sinking fund requirements.

the bank reconciliation. The approach to auditing a bank reconciliation is basically the same regardless of the type of bank account being examined. However, the type and extent of the audit work are more detailed for the general cash account because it normally represents a material amount and because of the large amount of activity in the account. The audit procedures listed for cash cutoff should be familiar to the reader and are not discussed here.

Auditing the General Cash Account

[LO 5]

Table 16–2 shows that the main source of evidence for the validity, completeness, accuracy, and valuation objectives is the audit work completed on the bank reconciliation. To audit a cash account, the auditor should obtain the following documents:

• A copy of the bank reconciliation.
• A standard form to confirm account balance information with financial institutions (referred to as a *standard bank confirmation*).
• A cutoff bank statement.

Bank Reconciliation Working Paper

Exhibit 16–1 provides an example of a bank reconciliation working paper for EarthWear's general cash account. Note that the difference between the cash balance showed in Exhibit 16–1 and the balance in cash on the financial statements is represented by cash equivalents (Treasury bills and commercial paper). On most audits, the auditor obtains a copy of the bank reconciliation prepared by the client's personnel. The working paper reconciles the balance per the bank with the balance per the books. The major reconciling items are deposits in transit, outstanding checks, and other adjustments, such as bank service charges and any check returned because the customer did not have sufficient cash (NSF check) in its account to cover payment of the check.

Standard Bank Confirmation Form

The auditor generally confirms the account balance information with every bank or financial institution that maintains an account for the client. The American Institute of Certified Public Accountants, American Bankers Association, and Bank Administration Institute have agreed on a standard format for confirming such information.[1] Exhibit 16–2 contains a completed copy of the confirmation form, which is titled "Standard Form to Confirm Account Balance Information with Financial Institutions." This form is also used to obtain information about any loans the client may have with the bank.

Note that the confirmation form does not require bank personnel to conduct a comprehensive, detailed search of the bank's records beyond the account information requested on the confirmation. However, it does request that bank personnel indicate any other deposits or loans that come to their attention while completing the confirmation. As a result, this confirmation request cannot be relied upon to identify *all* information about a client's bank deposits or loans. If the auditor believes that additional information is needed about a client's arrangements with a financial institution, a separate confirmation letter signed by the client should be sent to the official at the financial institution who is responsible for the client's accounts. Details regarding lines of credit and compensating balances are examples of information that might be confirmed in this manner. This issue is discussed later in this chapter.

Cutoff Bank Statement

A major step in auditing a bank reconciliation is verifying the propriety of the reconciling items such as deposits in transit and outstanding checks. The auditor obtains a cutoff bank statement to test the reconciling items included in the bank reconciliation. A cutoff bank statement normally covers the 7- to 10-day period after the date on which the bank account is reconciled. Any reconciling item should have cleared the client's bank account during the 7- to 10-day period. The auditor obtains this cutoff bank statement by having the client request that the bank send the statement, including canceled checks, directly to the auditor.

---

[1]See D. P. Sauter, "Bank Confirmation Form Receives Facelift," *Journal of Accountancy* (March 1991), pp. 82–89, for additional discussion of the new standard form for confirming bank accounts.

EXHIBIT 16–1

Example of a Bank Reconciliation Working Paper

	C10
	DLJ
	2/14/01

EARTHWEAR CLOTHIERS
Bank Reconciliation
12/31/00

General Cash Account

Balance per bank: **C11**		$1,854,890**C**
Add:		
Deposits in transit:		
12/30/00	$156,940✓	
12/31/00	340,875✓	497,815
Deduct:		
Outstanding checks:		
#1243	$121,843φ	
#1244	232,784φ	
#1247	30,431φ	
#1250	64,407φ	
#1251	123,250φ	(572,715)
Balance per books, unadjusted		1,779,990
Adjustments to books:		
Bank service charges	$ 250✓	
NSF check	7,400✓	(7,650)
Balance per books, adjusted		$1,772,340**L**
		F

F = Footed.
C = Traced balance to bank confirmation.
L = Agreed to cash lead schedule and general ledger.
✓ = Traced amount to cutoff bank statement.
φ = Examined canceled check for proper payee, amount, and endorsement.

Note: The controller has signed for the return of the cutoff bank statement.

EXHIBIT 16-2

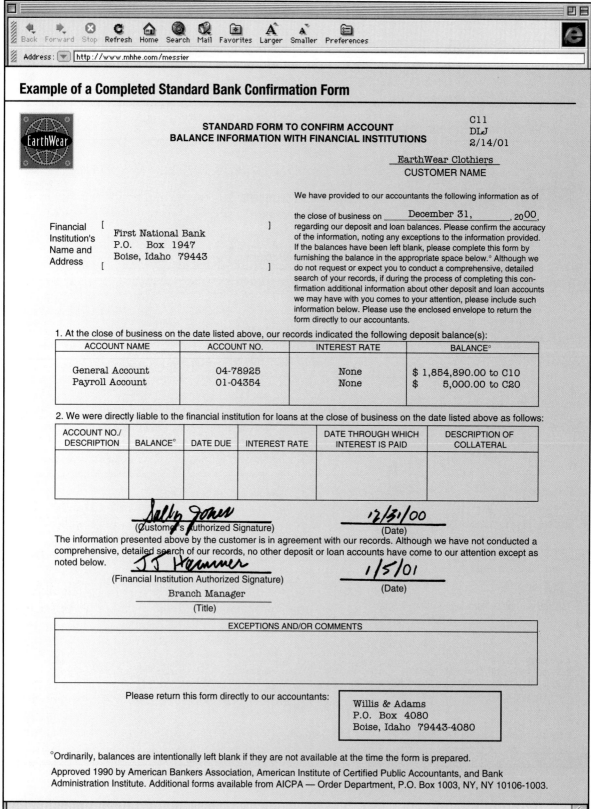

Example of a Completed Standard Bank Confirmation Form

Address: http://www.mhhe.com/messier

EarthWear

STANDARD FORM TO CONFIRM ACCOUNT
BALANCE INFORMATION WITH FINANCIAL INSTITUTIONS

C11
DLJ
2/14/01

EarthWear Clothiers
CUSTOMER NAME

We have provided to our accountants the following information as of the close of business on ____December 31,____, 20 00, regarding our deposit and loan balances. Please confirm the accuracy of the information, noting any exceptions to the information provided. If the balances have been left blank, please complete this form by furnishing the balance in the appropriate space below.° Although we do not request or expect you to conduct a comprehensive, detailed search of your records, if during the process of completing this confirmation additional information about other deposit and loan accounts we may have with you comes to your attention, please include such information below. Please use the enclosed envelope to return the form directly to our accountants.

Financial Institution's Name and Address

[First National Bank
P.O. Box 1947
Boise, Idaho 79443]

1. At the close of business on the date listed above, our records indicated the following deposit balance(s):

ACCOUNT NAME	ACCOUNT NO.	INTEREST RATE	BALANCE°
General Account	04-78925	None	$ 1,854,890.00 to C10
Payroll Account	01-04354	None	$ 5,000.00 to C20

2. We were directly liable to the financial institution for loans at the close of business on the date listed above as follows:

ACCOUNT NO./ DESCRIPTION	BALANCE°	DATE DUE	INTEREST RATE	DATE THROUGH WHICH INTEREST IS PAID	DESCRIPTION OF COLLATERAL

Sally Jones
(Customer's Authorized Signature)   12/31/00
                                            (Date)

The information presented above by the customer is in agreement with our records. Although we have not conducted a comprehensive, detailed search of our records, no other deposit or loan accounts have come to our attention except as noted below.

JJ Hammer
(Financial Institution Authorized Signature)   1/5/01
                                                 (Date)
Branch Manager
(Title)

EXCEPTIONS AND/OR COMMENTS

Please return this form directly to our accountants:

Willis & Adams
P.O. Box 4080
Boise, Idaho 79443-4080

°Ordinarily, balances are intentionally left blank if they are not available at the time the form is prepared.

Approved 1990 by American Bankers Association, American Institute of Certified Public Accountants, and Bank Administration Institute. Additional forms available from AICPA — Order Department, P.O. Box 1003, NY, NY 10106-1003.

Tests of the Bank Reconciliation   The auditor uses the following audit procedures to test the bank reconciliation:

1. *Test the mathematical accuracy of the bank reconciliation working paper and agree the balance per the books to the general ledger.* In Exhibit 16–1, the working paper has been footed and the balance per the books as shown on the reconciliation has been agreed to the general ledger.

2. *Agree the bank balance on the bank reconciliation with the balance shown on the standard bank confirmation.* The bank confirmation shown in Exhibit 16–2 has been prepared so that it corresponds to the bank reconciliation in Exhibit 16–1. The $1,854,890 shown on the bank reconciliation has been agreed to the $1,854,890 balance shown on the bank confirmation in Exhibit 16–2.

3. *Trace the deposits in transit on the bank reconciliation to the cutoff bank statement.* Any deposit in transit shown on the bank reconciliation should be listed as a deposit shortly after the end of the period. The tick mark next to the deposits in transit shown in Exhibit 16–1 indicates that the deposits were traced by the auditor to the cutoff bank statement.

4. *Compare the outstanding checks on the bank reconciliation working paper with the canceled checks contained in the cutoff bank statement for proper payee, amount, and endorsement.* The auditor should also ensure that no checks dated prior to December 31 are included with the cutoff bank statement that are not included as outstanding checks on the bank reconciliation. The tick mark next to the outstanding checks shown in Exhibit 16–1 indicates that the checks were traced by the auditor to the cutoff bank statement and that the canceled checks were examined for propriety.

5. *Agree any charges included on the bank statement to the bank reconciliation.* In some cases, these charges may result in an adjustment to the client's books. For example, the bank service charges of $250 and the NSF check for $7,400 shown in Exhibit 16–1 require adjustment of the client's records.

6. *Agree the adjusted book balance to the cash account lead schedule.* The adjusted book balance would be part of the amount included in the financial statements for cash.

Fraud-Related Audit Procedures

💊 **[LO 6]**

If the client does not have adequate control procedures over cash or the auditor suspects that some type of fraud or defalcation involving cash has occurred, it may be necessary to extend the normal cash audit procedures. Although many types of fraud, such as forgery or collusion, are difficult to detect, SAS No. 82, "Consideration of Fraud in a Financial Statement Audit" (AU 316), indicates that the auditor has a responsibility to plan and perform the audit to obtain reasonable assurance about whether the financial statements are free of material misstatement, whether caused by error or fraud.

Three audit procedures that auditors typically use to detect fraudulent activities in the cash accounts are

- Extended bank reconciliation procedures.
- Proof of cash.
- Tests for kiting.

Extended Bank Reconciliation Procedures   In some instances, the year-end bank reconciliation can be used to cover cash defalcations. This is usually accomplished by manipulating the reconciling items in the bank reconciliation. For example, suppose a client employee was able to steal $5,000 from the client. The client's cash balance at the bank would then be $5,000 less than reported on the client's books. The employee could "hide" the $5,000 shortage in the bank reconciliation by including a fictitious deposit in transit. Thus, the typical approach to searching for possible fraud is to extend the bank reconciliation procedures to examine the disposition of the reconciling items included on the prior months' reconciliations and the reconciling items included in the current bank reconciliation.

For example, assume that the auditor suspected that some type of fraud had been committed. The auditor would examine the November and December bank reconciliations by ensuring that all reconciling items had been properly handled. For deposits in transit on the November bank reconciliation, the auditor would trace the deposits to the November cash receipts journal to verify that they were recorded. The deposits would also be traced to the December bank statement to verify that they were deposited in the bank. Checks listed as outstanding on the November bank reconciliation would be traced to the November cash disbursements journal, and the canceled checks returned with the December bank statement would be examined for propriety. Other reconciling items such as bank charges, NSF checks, and collections of notes by the bank would be similarly traced to the accounting records for proper treatment. The auditor would examine the reconciling items included on the December bank reconciliation in a similar fashion to ensure that such items were not being used to cover a cash defalcation. Further investigation would be required for any reconciling items not properly accounted for. The client's management should be informed if the auditor detects any fraudulent transactions.

Proof of Cash   A proof of cash is used to reconcile the cash receipts and disbursements recorded on the client's books with the cash deposited into and disbursed from the client's bank account for a specific time period. Exhibit 16–3 presents an example of a proof of cash for Calabro Paging Services (Problem 3-41) for one month, although on some audits a proof of cash is performed for the entire period under audit. Because the proof contains four columns, a proof of cash is commonly referred to as a *four-column proof of cash*. The four columns include

- A bank reconciliation for the beginning of the period.
- A reconciliation of the cash deposited in the bank with the cash receipts recorded in the cash receipts journal.

EXHIBIT 16–3

Example of a Proof of Cash

CP5

CALABRO PAGING SERVICES
Proof of Cash—General Cash Account
12/31/00

	11/30/00	December Receipts	December Disbursements	12/31/00
Balance per bank	$513,324	$457,822ϕ	$453,387ϕ	$517,759**F**
Deposits in transit:				
11/30/00	114,240	(114,240)		
12/31/00		116,437		116,437
Outstanding checks:				
11/30/00	(117,385)		(117,385)	
12/31/00			115,312	(115,312)
Collection of note receivableν	(7,500)	7,500		
Balance per books, unadjusted	502,679	467,519γ	451,314μ	518,884**F**
Adjustments to books:				
Bank charges			125	(125)∈
NSF checks		(5,250)		(5,250)∈
Balance per books, adjusted	$502,679	$462,269	$451,439	$513,509**FL**
	F	**F**	**F**	**F**

F = Footed and crossfooted.
L = Agreed to general ledger.
ϕ = Traced to December bank statement.
γ = Agreed to December cash receipts journal.
μ = Agreed to December cash disbursements journal.
ν = Traced to November bank statement and December cash receipts journal.
∈ = Traced to cutoff bank statement.

- A reconciliation of the cash disbursed through the bank account with the cash disbursements recorded in the cash disbursements journal.
- A bank reconciliation for the end of the period.

The primary purposes of the proof of cash are (1) to ensure that all cash receipts recorded in the client's cash receipts journal were deposited in the client's bank account, (2) to ensure that all cash disbursements recorded in the client's cash disbursements journal have cleared the client's bank account, and (3) to ensure that no bank transactions have been omitted from the client's accounting records. The reader should note that a proof of cash will *not* detect a theft of cash when the cash was stolen *before* being recorded in the client's books. If the auditor suspects that cash was stolen before being recorded in the client's books, the audit procedures discussed under the completeness objective for cash receipt transactions in Chapter 10 should be performed.

Tests for Kiting   When cash has been stolen by an employee, it is possible to cover the cash shortage by following a practice known as *kiting*. This involves an employee covering the cash shortage by transferring money from one bank account to another and recording the transactions improperly on the client's books. Concealing the cash shortage can be accomplished by preparing a check on one account before year-end but not recording it as a cash disbursement in the account until the next period. The check is deposited in a second account before year-end and recorded as a cash receipt in the current period. The deposit must occur close enough to year-end that it will not clear the first bank account before the end of the year.

One approach that auditors commonly use to test for kiting is the preparation of an *interbank transfer schedule* such as the one shown in Exhibit 16–4. This exhibit provides six examples of the types of cash transfers

EXHIBIT 16–4

Example of an Interbank Transfer Schedule

Transfer Number*	Amount	Account 1 Disbursement Dates		Account 2 Receipt and Deposit Dates	
		Per Client Books	Per Bank Statement	Per Client Books	Per Bank Statement
1	$15,000	12/28	12/30	12/28	12/29
2	7,500	12/30	1/2	12/30	12/31
3	8,400	12/31	1/2	12/31	1/2
4	10,000	1/2	1/2	12/30	12/31
5	3,000	1/3	1/3	1/3	12/30
6	17,300	1/2	1/4	1/2	1/2

*Explanation for each transfer in determining proper cash cutoff at 12/31/00:
1. The transfer was made on December 28 and recorded on the books as both a receipt and a disbursement on the same date. The check written was deposited on December 28 in the receiving bank account and credited on the bank statement the next day. The check cleared account 1 on December 30. All dates are in the same accounting period, so there are no questions as to the propriety of the cutoff.
2. This transfer is proper. However, the transfer check should appear as an *outstanding check* on the reconciliation of account 1.
3. Transfer 3 is also proper. In this example, the transfer should appear as a *deposit in transit* on the reconciliation of account 2 and as an outstanding check on the reconciliation of account 1.
4. This transfer represents kiting because the receipt was recorded on the books in the period prior to that in which the corresponding disbursement was recorded. Cash is overstated by $10,000.
5. Transfer 5 is also improper. In this case a deposit was made in the receiving bank in one period without the receipt being made in the books until the subsequent period. Unless this matter is explained on the reconciliation for the receiving bank, the transfer was apparently made to temporarily cover a shortage in that account. While the shortage will become apparent in the accounts as soon as the transfer is recorded in the following period, it will be covered by an unrecorded deposit on the balance sheet date.
6. This transfer is proper.

an auditor might encounter. For example, transfer 2 is an example of a proper cash transfer. A check was drawn on account 1 and recorded as a cash disbursement on December 30. It was recorded as a cash receipt in account 2 on December 30 and deposited in that account on December 31. The check cleared account 1 on January 2. The auditor would examine this transfer by tracing the check to the cash disbursements journal, the cash receipts journal, and the December 31 bank reconciliation. Because the check cleared the bank on January 2, it should be listed as an outstanding check on the December 31 bank reconciliation for account 1. The reader will also notice that transfers 1, 3, and 6 are proper transfers.

Transfer 4 represents an example of kiting. A check was written on account 1 before year-end, but the disbursement was not recorded in the disbursements journal until after year-end (January 2). The check was deposited in account 2 and recorded as a cash receipt before year-end. Thus, the cash shortage in account 2 is covered by a cash deposit from account 1, and cash is overstated by $10,000. Transfer 5 represents a different type of impropriety that would also require additional work on the part of the auditor.

In some instances an interbank transfer schedule is used even though control procedures are adequate and no fraud is suspected. When a client maintains many cash accounts, cash transfers may be inadvertently mishandled. The use of an interbank transfer schedule provides the auditor with evidence on the proper cutoff for cash transactions.

Auditing a Payroll or Branch Imprest Account

The audit of any imprest cash account such as payroll or a branch account follows the same basic audit steps discussed under the audit of the general cash account. The auditor obtains a bank reconciliation, along with a standard bank confirmation and a cutoff bank statement. However, the audit testing is less extensive for two reasons. First, the imprest balance in the account is generally not material. An imprest payroll or branch account may contain a balance of only $1,000. Second, the types of disbursements from the account are homogeneous. The checks are for similar types of transactions and for relatively small amounts. For example, there may be a limit on the size of an individual payroll check.

Auditing a Petty Cash Fund

Most entities maintain a petty cash fund for paying certain types of expenses or transactions. Although the balance in the fund is not material, there is a potential for defalcation because a client's employee may be able to process numerous fraudulent transactions through the fund over the course of a year. Auditors seldom perform detailed substantive testing of the petty cash fund, except when fraud is suspected. However, the auditor may document the controls over the petty cash fund, especially for smaller clients.

Control Procedures   A petty cash fund should be maintained on an imprest basis by an *independent* custodian. While it is preferable for the custodian not to be involved in any cash functions, this is not possible for many clients. When the petty cash custodian does have other cash-related functions to perform, another supervisory person such as the controller should review the petty cash activity.

Prenumbered petty cash vouchers should be used for withdrawing cash from the fund, and a limit should be placed on the size of reimbursements made from petty cash. Periodically, the petty cash fund is reimbursed from the general cash account for the amount of the vouchers in the fund. Accounts payable clerks should review the vouchers for propriety before replenishing the petty cash fund. Finally, someone independent of the cash functions should conduct surprise counts of the petty cash fund.

Audit Tests   The first step is for the auditor to gain an understanding of the client's control procedures over petty cash. The adequacy of the client's control procedures determines the nature and extent of the auditor's work. The audit of petty cash focuses on both the transactions processed through the fund during the period and the balance in the fund. The auditor may select a sample of petty cash reimbursements and examine the propriety of the items paid for by the fund. This may be done as part of the auditor's tests of controls or substantive tests of transactions for the cash disbursement functions. The auditor tests the balance in the petty cash fund by counting it. When the count is conducted, the total of cash in the fund plus the vouchers should equal the imprest balance. This count may be done at an interim date or at year-end.

Disclosure Issues for Cash

The auditor must consider a number of important financial statement disclosures when auditing cash. Some of the more common disclosure issues are shown in Table 16–3. The auditor's review of the minutes of board of directors' meetings, line-of-credit arrangements, loan agreements, and similar documents is the primary source of the information for the financial statement disclosures. In addition, the auditor typically confirms items such as compensating balances required under a bank line of credit.

Exhibit 16–5 illustrates a letter for confirmation of compensating balances, while Exhibit 16–6 presents an example of footnote disclosures for compensating balances.

TABLE 16–3   Sample Disclosure Items for Cash
• Accounting policy for defining cash and cash equivalents.
• Any restrictions on cash such as a sinking fund requirement for funds allocated by the entity's board of directors for special purposes.
• Contractual obligations to maintain compensating balances.
• Cash balances restricted by foreign exchange controls.
• Letters of credit.

EXHIBIT 16–5

Illustrative Letter for Confirmation of Compensating Balances

 CALABRO PAGING SERVICES

December 31, 2000

Mr. Frank Lorchian
First National Bank
Tampa, FL 34201

Dear Mr. Lorchian:

In connection with an audit of the financial statements of Calabro Paging Services as of December 31, 2000, and for the year then ended, we have advised our independent auditors that as of the close of business on December 31, 2000, there were compensating balance arrangements as described in our agreement dated June 30, 1996. Withdrawal by Calabro Paging Services of the compensating balance was not legally restricted as of December 31, 2000. The terms of the compensating balance arrangements at December 31, 2000, were:

The company has been expected to maintain a compensating balance, as determined from your bank's ledger records without adjustment for estimated average uncollected funds, of 15% of its outstanding loans plus 10% of its unused line of credit.

The company was in compliance with, and there have been no changes in, the compensating balance arrangements during the year ended December 31, 2000, and subsequently through the date of this letter.

During the year ended December 31, 2000, and subsequently through the date of this letter, no compensating balances were maintained by the company at your bank on behalf of an affiliate, director, officer, or any other third party, and no third party maintained compensating balances at the bank on behalf of the company.

Please confirm whether the information about compensating balances presented above is correct by signing below and returning this letter directly to our independent auditors, Abbott & Johnson, LLP. P.O. Box 669, Tampa, FL 32691.

Sincerely,

Calabro Paging Services

BY: _____
     Jan Rodriguez, Controller

Dear Abbott & Johnson, LLP:

The above information regarding the compensating balance arrangement with this bank agrees with the records of this bank.

BY: _____ Vice President   Date: _____

EXHIBIT 16–6

Sample Disclosure of Compensating Balances

Lines of Credit:
On December 31, 1996, the company established a line of credit with a bank that provides for unsecured borrowings of $7,000,000 at the bank's prime rate (7% at December 31, 2000). At December 31, 1999 and 2000, $200,000 and $800,000, respectively, had been borrowed under this arrangement. Under the credit arrangement, the company is expected to maintain compensating balances equal to 5 percent of the borrowings in excess of $500,000. This requirement is generally met through normal operating cash balances, which are not restricted as to withdrawal.

Investments[2]

[LO 7]   Entities frequently invest in securities of other entities. Such investments might include equity securities such as common and preferred stock, debt securities such as notes and bonds, and hybrid securities such as convertible bonds and stocks. The accounting for such instruments is affected by factors such as the percentage of the other entity owned, the degree of influence exercised over the entity, the classification of the investment as a current or noncurrent asset, and myriad other factors. For example, FASB Statement of Financial Accounting Standards No. 115, "Accounting for Certain Investments in Debt and Equity Securities" (FAS 115), provides detailed guidance on how to account for investments in certain debt and equity securities.

The auditor's consideration of investments is no different than for any other financial statement account. That is, the auditor must be assured that the amounts shown on the balance sheet for the various types of investments are not materially misstated. This includes the proper recognition of interest income, dividends, and changes in value that must be included in the financial statements.

The auditor's approach to the audit of investments varies depending on the size of the investment and the amount of investment activity. For an entity that has a large investment portfolio, the auditor is likely to follow a reliance strategy in which internal control is formally evaluated and tests of controls are performed in order to assess the control risk below the maximum. However, for the vast majority of entities, it is more efficient for the auditor to follow a substantive strategy and perform a detailed audit of the investment securities at year-end.

Control Risk Assessment—Investments

[LO 8]   The discussion of investments that follows focuses on the general types of control procedures that should be present to minimize the likelihood of a material misstatement. Even when a substantive strategy is followed, the auditor must reasonably understand internal control over investments in order to anticipate the types of misstatements that may occur and plan the substantive tests. The main internal control objectives that concern the auditor are validity, authorization, completeness, valuation, and classification. Proper segregation of duties is important in ensuring the propriety of investments and will be discussed briefly.

Control Objectives and Related Procedures

Following are some of the more common control procedures that should be present for each of the important control objectives for investments.

Validity and Authorization   Control procedures must ensure that the purchase or sale of any investment is properly initiated by authorized individuals. First, the client should have adequate documents to verify that

---

[2]See G. F. Patterson, Jr., "New Guidance on Auditing Investments," *Journal of Accountancy* (February 1997), pp. 65–67, for a discussion of SAS No. 81, "Auditing Investments."

a particular purchase or sale of a security was properly initiated and approved. The presence of adequate documentation allows the auditor to determine the validity of the transaction. Second, the commitment of resources to investment activities should be approved by the board of directors or by an executive who has been delegated this authority. An entity engaging in recurring investment activities should have both general and specific control procedures. The board of directors should establish general policies to guide the entity's investment activities, while the specific procedures for the purchase and sale of securities may be delegated to an individual executive, investment committee, or outside investment advisers. If the client has proper control procedures for initiating and authorizing securities transactions, it is generally easy for the auditor to verify security transactions at the end of the period.

Completeness

The client should maintain adequate control procedures to ensure that all securities transactions are recorded. One control procedure for handling the detailed securities transactions is maintenance of a securities ledger that records all securities owned by the client. This subsidiary ledger should be reconciled to the general ledger control account regularly. Personnel responsible for investment activities should periodically review the securities owned to ensure that all dividends and interest have been received and recorded in the entity's records.

Valuation and Classification

Some important valuation and classification issues are related to investment securities. As mentioned previously, FASB Statement of Financial Accounting Standards No. 115, "Accounting for Certain Investments in Debt and Equity Securities" (FAS 115), addresses accounting and reporting for investments in equity securities that have readily determinable fair values and for all investments in debt securities. The standard requires that those investments be classified in three categories and accounted for as follows:

- Debt securities that the entity has the positive intent and ability to hold to maturity are classified as *held-to-maturity securities* and reported at amortized cost.
- Debt and equity securities that are bought and held principally for the purpose of selling them in the near term are classified as *trading securities* and reported at fair value, with unrealized gains and losses included in earnings.
- Debt or equity securities not classified as either held-to-maturity or trading securities are classified as *available-for-sale securities* and are reported at fair value, with unrealized gains and losses excluded from earnings and reported in a separate component of shareholders' equity.

The client's control procedures should ensure that securities are properly classified and that appropriate prices are used to value investments for financial statement.

One final issue related to the control risk for investments is that the client should have adequate custodial procedures to safeguard against

TABLE 16–4	Key Segregation of Duties and Possible Errors or Fraud—Investments
Segregation of Duties	*Possible Errors or Fraud Resulting from Conflicts of Duties*
The initiation function should be segregated from the final approval function.	If one individual is responsible for both the initiating and approving of securities transactions, fictitious transactions can be made or securities can be stolen.
The valuation-monitoring function should be segregated from the acquisition function.	If one individual is responsible for both acquiring and monitoring the valuation of securities, securities values can be improperly recorded or not reported to management.
Responsibility for maintaining the securities ledger should be separate from that of making entries in the general ledger.	If one individual is responsible for both the securities ledger and the general ledger entries, that individual can conceal any defalcation that would normally be detected by reconciliation of subsidiary records with general ledger control accounts.
Responsibility for custody of the securities should be separate from that of accounting for the securities.	If one individual has access both to securities and to the supporting accounting records, a theft of the securities can be concealed.

theft. When securities are held by the client, they should be stored in a safe or safe-deposit box. Procedures should provide for periodic inspections by an individual independent of both the custodial and accounting responsibilities for securities. If an independent custodian such as a broker maintains securities, the client needs to establish procedures for authorizing the transfer of securities. One approach would require dual authorization by appropriate management personnel.

Segregation of Duties

[LO 9]

Only entities that engage in a significant number of investment activities are likely to have adequate segregation of duties. Table 16–4 contains some key segregation of duties for investments and examples of possible errors or fraud that can result from conflicts in duties.

Substantive Tests of Investments

[LO 10]

As discussed earlier, it is generally more efficient to follow a substantive strategy for auditing investments. When the control risk is set at the maximum, the auditor conducts extensive substantive tests to reach the planned level of detection risk. Additionally, because of the nature of the audit work, substantive tests of transactions are seldom used as a source of evidence.

Analytical procedures such as the following can test the overall reasonableness of investments:

TABLE 16–5	Summary of Audit Objectives and Tests of Account Balances—Investments

Audit Objective	Tests of Account Balances
Validity	Inspect securities if maintained by client or obtain confirmation from independent custodian.
Completeness	Search for purchases of securities by examining transactions for a few days after year-end.
	Confirm securities held by independent custodian.
	Review and test securities information to determine if all interest and dividend income has been recorded.
Cutoff	Review purchases and sales of securities for a few days before and after year-end to determine if the transactions are included in the proper period.
Ownership	Examine brokers' advices for a sample of securities purchased during the year.
Accuracy	Obtain a listing of investments by category (held-to-maturity, trading, and available-for-sale); foot listing and agree totals to securities register and general ledger.
Valuation	Review brokers' advices for cost basis of securities purchased.
	Determine basis for valuing investments by tracing values to published quotations for marketable securities.
	Determine whether there has been any permanent impairment in the value of the cost basis of an individual security.
	Examine sales of securities to ensure proper recognition of realized gains or losses.
Classification	Review and inquire of management about proper classification of investments.
Disclosure	Determine that all disclosures required by SFAS No. 115 have been made for debt and equity securities.
	Determine whether any securities have been pledged as collateral by (1) asking management and (2) reviewing board of directors' minutes, loan agreements, and other documents.

- Comparison of the balances in the current year's investment accounts with prior years' balances after consideration of the effects of current-year operating and financing activities on cash and investments.
- Comparison of current-year interest and dividend income with the reported income for prior years and with the expected return on investments.

SAS No. 81, "Auditing Investments" (AU 332), provides guidance concerning substantive auditing procedures the auditor can perform when gathering evidential matter related to audit objectives for investments. Table 16–5 summarizes the tests of investment account balances for each audit objective. The discussion of the investment account tests focuses on the more important audit objectives. The procedures shown for the other audit objectives should be familiar to the reader.

Validity

SAS No. 81 states that the auditor should perform one or more of the following audit procedures when gathering evidence for validity:

- Physical examination.
- Confirmation with the issuer.
- Confirmation with the custodian.

- Confirmation of unsettled transactions with the broker-dealer.
- Confirmation with the counterparty.
- Reading executed partnership or similar agreements.

If the client maintains custody of the securities, the auditor normally examines the securities. During the physical count, the auditor should note the name, class and description, serial number, maturity date, registration in the name of the client, interest rates or dividend payment dates, and other relevant information about the various securities. When the securities are held by an issuer or a custodian such as a broker or investment adviser, the auditor gathers sufficient, competent evidence for the validity objective by confirming the existence of the securities. The information contained in the confirmation needs to be reconciled with the client's investment records.

Valuation

When securities are initially purchased, they are recorded at their acquisition cost. The auditor can verify the purchase price of a security by examining a broker's advice or similar document. Debt securities that are to be held to maturity should be valued at their amortized cost. The auditor should have verified the purchase price of the debt at the time of purchase, and the effective interest rate should be used to recognize the interest income, which the auditor can recompute. The fair value of most equity securities is available from securities exchanges registered with the Securities and Exchange Commission or on the over-the-counter market. The auditor can verify these values by tracing them to sources such as brokers, *The Wall Street Journal*, or other reliable financial literature.

The auditor must also determine if there has been any permanent decline in the value of an investment security. SAS No. 81 provides guidance for determining whether a decline in value below amortized cost is other than temporary. The following factors are cited as indicating other-than-temporary impairment of the investment:

- Fair value is significantly below cost.
- The decline in fair value is attributable to specific adverse conditions affecting a particular investment.
- The decline in fair value is attributable to specific conditions, such as conditions in an industry or in a geographic area.
- Management does not possess both the intent and the ability to hold the investment long enough to allow for any anticipated recovery in fair value.
- The decline in fair value has existed for an extended period.
- A debt security has been downgraded by a rating agency.
- The financial condition of the issuer has deteriorated.
- Dividends have been reduced or eliminated, or scheduled interest payments on debt securities have not been made.

If the investment value is determined to be permanently impaired, the security should be written down and a new carrying amount established. Last, the auditor should examine the sale of any security to ensure that proper values were used to record the sale and any realized gain or loss.

Classification Two issues are important when the auditor examines the proper classification of investments. First, marketable securities need to be properly classified as held-to-maturity, trading, and available-for-sale because both the balance sheet and income statement are affected by misclassification. Second, the financial statement classification requires that all trading securities be reported as current assets. Held-to-maturity securities and individual available-for-sale securities should be classified as current or noncurrent assets based on whether management expects to convert them to cash within the next 12 months. If the security is expected to be converted to cash within 12 months, it should be classified as a current asset. The auditor should ask management about its plans for dispositing of securities.

SAS No. 81 also guides auditors in evaluating both management's intent with regard to an investment and the entity's ability to hold a debt security to maturity. In evaluating management's intent, the auditor should condsider whether investment activities corraborate or conflict with management's stated intent. The auditor should examine evidence such as written and approved records of investment strategies, records of investment activities, instructions to portfolio managers, and minutes of meetings of the board of directors or the investment committee. In evaluating an entity's ability to hold a debt security to maturity, the auditor should consider factors such as the entity's financial position, working capital needs, operating results, debt agreements, guarantees, and other relevant contractual obligations, as well as laws and regulations. The auditor should also consider operating and cash flow projections or forecasts when considering the entity's ability to hold the debt security to maturity.

Disclosure FASB Statement of Financial Accounting Standards No. 115, "Accounting for Certain Investments in Debt and Equity Securities" (FAS 115), requires specific disclosures for securities. For example, the aggregate fair value and gross unrealized holding gains or losses on securities should be presented for securities classified as available-for-sale.

Most of the information necessary for such disclosures is developed as the other audit objectives are being tested. In addition, the amount of any securities pledged as collateral should be disclosed. Asking management and reviewing board of directors' minutes, loan agreements, and other documents would be the auditor's sources of such information.

REVIEW QUESTIONS

[LO 1]   16-1   What types of items are included under the caption "cash and cash equivalents" in the financial statements?

[2]   16-2   Briefly describe each type of bank account. How does an imprest account help to improve control over cash?

[3]   16-3   Why are analytical procedures of limited use in the audit of the cash balance?

[1]   16-4   How do the client's control procedures over cash receipts and disbursements affect the nature and extent of the auditor's substantive tests of cash balances?

[4,5]   16-5   A bank reconciliation provides the auditor with evidence on which audit objectives?

[4,5]   16-6   Explain why the standard bank confirmation form does *not* identify all information about a client's bank accounts or loans.

[4,5]   16-7   Why does an auditor obtain a cutoff bank statement when auditing a bank account? What information is examined on the canceled checks returned with the cutoff bank statement?

[5]   16-8   Briefly describe how a bank reconciliation is audited.

[6]   16-9   List three fraud-related audit procedures for cash.

[6]   16-10   What are the primary purposes of a proof of cash?

[6]   16-11   What approach is used by the auditor to test for kiting?

[4]   16-12   Identify the control procedures that should be present for petty cash. What audit procedures are normally conducted on petty cash?

[8,9]   16-13   What are the main internal control objectives for investments? Identify the key segregation of investment-related duties and possible errors or fraud that can occur if this segregation is not present.

[10]   16-14   Briefly describe the valuation issues related to investments in debt and equity securities.

[10]   16-15   What two classification issues are important for the audit of investments?

MULTIPLE-CHOICE QUESTIONS FROM CPA EXAMINATIONS

[5]   16-16   An auditor ordinarily sends a standard confirmation request to all banks with which the client has done business during the year under audit, regardless of the year-end balance. A purpose of this procedure is to
    a. Provide the data necessary to prepare a proof of cash.
    b. Request that a cutoff bank statement and related checks be sent to the auditor.
    c. Detect kiting activities that may otherwise *not* be discovered.
    d. Seek information about loans from the banks.

[5]   16-17   To gather evidence regarding the balance per bank in a bank reconciliation, an auditor would examine all of the following *except* the
    a. Cutoff bank statement.
    b. Year-end bank statement.
    c. Bank confirmation.
    d. General ledger.

[4]   16-18   When counting cash on hand, the auditor must exercise control over all cash and other negotiable assets to prevent
    a. Theft.
    b. Irregular endorsement.
    c. Substitution.
    d. Deposits in transit.

[5]   16-19   On receiving the cutoff bank statement, the auditor should trace
    a. Deposits in transit on the year-end bank reconciliation to deposits in the cash receipts journal.
    b. Checks dated before year-end to outstanding checks listed on the year-end bank reconciliation.

      c. Deposits listed on the cutoff statement to deposits in the cash receipts journal.

      d. Checks dated after year-end to outstanding checks listed on the year-end bank reconciliation.

[4,6]   16-20   Which of the following cash transfers results in a misstatement of cash at December 31, 2000?

Bank Transfer Schedule

	Disbursement		Receipt	
Transfer	Recorded in Books	Paid by Bank	Recorded in Books	Received by Bank
a.	12/31/00	1/4/01	12/31/00	12/31/00
b.	1/4/01	1/5/01	12/31/00	1/4/01
c.	12/31/00	1/5/01	12/31/00	1/4/01
d.	1/4/01	1/11/01	1/4/01	1/4/01

[5]   16-21   The primary evidence regarding year-end bank balances is documented in the

      a. Standard bank confirmations.

      b. Outstanding check listing.

      c. Interbank transfer schedule.

      d. Bank deposit lead schedule.

Questions 16–22 and 16–23 relate to the following bank transfer schedule.

MILES COMPANY
Bank Transfer Schedule
December 31, 2000

Check Number	Bank Account From	To	Amount	Date Disbursed per Books	Bank	Date Deposited per Books	Bank
2020	First National	Suburban	$32,000	12/31	1/5◆	12/31	1/3▲
2021	First National	Capital	21,000	12/31	1/4◆	12/31	1/3▲
3217	Second State	Suburban	6,700	1/3	1/5	1/3	1/6
0659	Midtown	Suburban	5,500	12/30	1/5◆	12/30	1/3▲

[4,6]   16-22   The tick mark ◆ most likely indicates that the amount was traced to the

      a. December cash disbursements journal.

      b. Outstanding check list of the applicable bank reconciliation.

      c. January cash disbursements journal.

      d. Year-end bank confirmations.

[4,6]   16-23   The tick mark ▲ most likely indicates that the amount was traced
to the
a. Deposits in transit of the applicable bank reconciliation.
b. December cash receipts journal.
c. January cash receipts journal.
d. Year-end bank confirmations.

[8,9]   16-24   Which of the following controls would most effectively ensure that
the proper custody of assets in the investing cycle is maintained?
a. Direct access to securities in the safe-deposit box is limited to
one corporate officer.
b. Personnel who post investment transactions to the general
ledger are *not* permitted to update the investment subsidiary
ledger.
c. Purchase and sale of investments are executed on the specific
authorization of the board of directors.
d. The recorded balances in the investment subsidiary ledger are
periodically compared with the contents of the safe-deposit box
by independent personnel.

[10]   16-25   To establish the existence and ownership of a long-term investment in the common stock of a publicly traded company, an auditor ordinarily performs a security count or
a. Relies on the client's internal controls if the auditor has reasonable assurance that the control procedures are being applied as
prescribed.
b. Confirms the number of shares owned that are held by an independent custodian.
c. Determines the market price per share at the balance sheet date
from published quotations.
d. Confirms the number of shares owned with the issuing company.

[10]   16-26   An auditor testing long-term investments would ordinarily use analytical procedures to ascertain the reasonableness of the
a. Existence of unrealized gains or losses in the portfolio.
b. Completeness of recorded investment income.
c. Classification between current and noncurrent portfolios.
d. Valuation of marketable equity securities.

[10]   16-27   When an auditor is unable to inspect and count a client's investment securities until after the balance sheet date, the bank where
the securities are held in a safe-deposit box should be asked to
a. Verify any differences between the contents of the box and the
balances in the client's subsidiary ledger.
b. Provide a list of securities added and removed from the box between the balance sheet date and the security-count date.
c. Confirm that there has been *no* access to the box between the
balance sheet date and the security-count date.
d. Count the securities in the box so that the auditor will have an
independent direct verification.

[10]   16-28   Which of the following would provide the best form of evidential
matter pertaining to the annual valuation of a long-term investment in which the independent auditor's client owns a 30 percent
voting interest?

a. Market quotations of the investee company's stock.

b. The current fair value of the investee company's assets.

c. Historical costs of the investee company's assets.

d. Audited financial statements of the investee company.

[10] 16-29 Which of the following is the most effective audit procedure for verifying dividends earned on investments in equity securities?

a. Trace deposits of dividend checks to the cash receipts book.

b. Reconcile amounts received with published dividend records.

c. Compare the amounts received with prior-year dividends received.

d. Recompute selected extensions and footings of dividend schedules and compare totals to the general ledger.

[10] 16-30 An auditor would most likely verify the interest earned on bond investments by

a. Vouching the receipt and deposit of interest checks.

b. Confirming the bond interest rate with the issuer of the bonds.

c. Recomputing the interest earned on the basis of face amount, interest rate, and period held.

d. Testing the internal controls over cash receipts.

PROBLEMS

[4,6] 16-31 Sevcik Company's auditor received, directly from the banks, confirmations and cutoff statements with related checks and deposit tickets for Sevcik's three general-purpose bank accounts. The auditor determined that the internal controls over cash are satisfactory and can be relied upon. The proper cutoff of external cash receipts and disbursements was established. No bank accounts were opened or closed during the year.

Required:

Prepare the audit program of substantive procedures to verify Sevcik's bank balances. Ignore any other cash accounts.

(AICPA, adapted)

[7,8,9] 16-32 Cassandra Corporation, a manufacturing company, periodically invests large sums in investment (debt and equity) securities. The investment policy is established by the investment committee of the board of directors, and the treasurer is responsible for carrying out the investment committee's directives. All securities are stored in a bank safe-deposit vault.

The independent auditor's internal control questionnaire with respect to Cassandra's investments in debt and equity securities contains the following three questions:

- Is investment policy established by the investment committee of the board of directors?

- Is the treasurer solely responsible for carrying out the investment committee's directives?

- Are all securities stored in a bank safe-deposit vault?

Required:

In addition to these three questions, what questions should the auditor's internal control questionnaire include with respect to the company's investments in debt and equity securities?

(AICPA, adapted)

[10]   16-33   Phung, CPA, has been engaged to audit the financial statements of Vernon Distributors, Inc., a continuing audit client, for the year ended September 30. After obtaining an understanding of Vernon's internal control system, Phung assessed control risk at the maximum level for all financial statement assertions concerning investments. Phung determined that Vernon is unable to exercise significant influence over any investee and none are related parties. Phung obtained from Vernon detailed analyses of its investments in domestic securities showing

- The classification among held-to-maturity, trading, and available-for-sale securities.
- A description of each security, including the interest rate and maturity date of bonds and the par value and dividend rate of stocks.
- A notation of the location of each security, either in the treasurer's safe or held by an independent custodian.
- The number of shares of stock or face value of bonds held at the beginning and end of the year.
- The beginning and ending balances at cost and at market, and the unamortized premium or discount on bonds.
- Additions to and sales from the portfolios for the year, including date, number of shares, face value of bonds, cost, proceeds, and realized gain or loss.
- Valuation allowances at the beginning and end of the year and changes therein.
- Accrued investment income for each investment at the beginning and end of the year, and income earned and collected during the year.

Phung then prepared the following partial audit program of substantive audit procedures:

1. Foot and crossfoot the analyses.
2. Trace the September 30 balances to the general ledger and financial statements.
3. Trace the beginning balances to the prior year's working papers.
4. Obtain positive confirmation of the investments held by any independent custodian as of the balance sheet date.
5. Determine that income from investments has been properly recorded as accrued or collected by reference to published sources, by computation, and by tracing to recorded amounts.
6. For investments in nonpublic entities, compare carrying value to information in the most recently available audited financial statements.
7. Determine that all transfers among held-to-maturity, trading, and available-for-sale securities have been properly authorized and recorded.

8. Determine that any other-than-temporary decline in the price of an investment has been properly recorded.

Required:

a. For procedures 4 to 8, identify the primary financial statement assertion relative to investments that would be addressed by each procedure and describe the primary audit objective of performing that procedure. Use the following format:

Primary Assertion	Objective

b. Describe three additional substantive auditing procedures Phung should consider in auditing Vernon's investments.

(AICPA, adapted)

[5]   16-34   The following client-prepared bank reconciliation is being examined by Zachary Kallick, CPA, during the examination of the financial statements of Simmons Company.

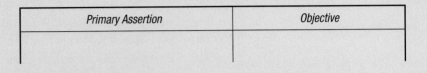

SIMMONS COMPANY
Bank Reconciliation
1st National Bank of U.S. Bank Account
September 30, 2000

Procedure(s)

a. Select 2 procedures	Balance per bank				$28,375
b. Select 5 procedures	Deposits in transit:				
		9/29/00		$4,500	
		9/30/00		1,525	6,025
					$34,400
c. Select 5 procedures	Outstanding checks:				
		988	8/31/00	2,200	
		1281	9/26/00	675	
		1285	9/27/00	850	
		1289	9/29/00	2,500	
		1292	9/30/00	7,225	(13,450)
					$20,950
d. Select 1 procedure	Customer note collected by bank				(3,000)
e. Select 2 procedures	Error:				
	Check 1282, written on 9/26/00 for $270, was erroneously charged by bank as $720; bank was notified on 10/2/00.				450
f. Select 1 procedure	Balance per books				$18,400

Required:

Items (a) through (f) represent items an auditor would ordinarily find on a client-prepared bank reconciliation. The following list of audit procedures shows substantive auditing procedures. For each item, select one or more procedures, as indicated, that the auditor most likely would perform to gather evidence in support of that item. (The procedures on the list may be selected once, more than once, or not at all.)

Assume that

- The client prepared the bank reconciliation on 10/2/00.
- The bank reconciliation is mathematically accurate.
- The auditor received a cutoff bank statement dated 10/7/00 directly from the bank on 10/11/00.
- The 9/30/00 deposit in transit, outstanding checks 1281, 1285, 1289, and 1292, and the correction of the error regarding check 1282 appear on the cutoff bank statement.
- The auditor assessed control risk concerning the financial statement assertions related to cash at the maximum.

Audit Procedure

1. Trace to cash receipts journal.
2. Trace to cash disbursements journal.
3. Compare to 9/30/00 general ledger.
4. Directly confirm with bank.
5. Inspect bank credit memo.
6. Inspect bank debit memo.
7. Ascertain reason for unusual delay.
8. Inspect supporting documents for reconciling item not appearing on cutoff statement.
9. Trace items on bank reconciliation to cutoff statement.
10. Trace items on the cutoff statement to bank reconciliation.

(AICPA, adapted)

[10]   16-35   To support financial statement assertions, an auditor develops specific audit objectives. The auditor then designs substantive tests to satisfy or accomplish each objective.

Required:

Items (a) through (c) represent audit objectives for investments. Select the most appropriate audit procedure from the following list and enter the number in the appropriate place on the grid. (An audit procedure may be selected once or not at all.)

Audit Procedure

1. Trace opening balances in the subsidiary ledgers to the prior year's audit working papers.
2. Determine that employees who are authorized to sell investments do not have access to cash.
3. Examine supporting documents for a sample of investment transactions to verify that prenumbered documents are used.
4. Determine that any impairments in the price of investments have been properly recorded.

5. Verify that transfers from the current to the noncurrent investment portfolio have been properly recorded.
6. Obtain positive confirmations as of the balance sheet date of investments held by independent custodians.
7. Trace investment transactions to minutes of board of directors' meetings to determine that transactions were properly authorized.

Specific Audit Objective	Audit Procedure
a. Verify that investments are properly described and classified in the financial statements.	
b. Verify that recorded investments represent investments actually owned at the balance sheet date.	
c. Verify that investments are properly valued at the lower of cost or market at the balance sheet date.	

(AICPA, adapted)

[10] 16-36 Geller, CPA, who is auditing the financial statements of Bass Corporation for the year ended December 31 is about to commence an audit of the company's noncurrent investment securities. Bass's records indicate that the company owns various bearer bonds that will be held to maturity, as well as 25 percent of the outstanding common stock of Commercial Industrial, Inc. Geller is satisfied with evidence that supports the presumption of significant influence over Commercial Industrial, Inc. The various securities are at two locations, as follows:

- Recently acquired securities are in the company's safe in the custody of the treasurer.
- All other securities are in a safe-deposit box in the company's bank.

All of the securities in Bass's portfolio are actively traded in a broad market.

Required:
a. Assuming that the internal control system over securities is satisfactory and may be relied upon, what are the objectives of examining these noncurrent investment securities?
b. What audit procedures should Geller undertake with respect to examining Bass's noncurrent investment securities?

(AICPA, adapted)

[7,8,10] 16-37 The schedule on the following page was prepared by the controller of World Manufacturing, Inc., for use by the independent auditors during their examination of World's year-end financial statements. All procedures performed by the audit assistant were noted in the "Legend" section; the schedule was properly initialed, dated, and indexed and then submitted to a senior member of the audit staff for review. Internal control was reviewed and is considered to be satisfactory.

WORLD MANUFACTURING, INC.
Marketable Securities
Year Ended December 31, 2000

Description of Security	%	Yr. Due	Serial No.	Face Value of Bonds	General Ledger 1/1	Purchased in 2000	Sold in 2000	Cost	General Ledger 12/31	12/31 Market	Pay Date(s)	Amt. Rec.	Accruals 12/31
Corp. Bonds													
A	6	91	21-7	10,000	9,400a				9,400	9,100	1/15	300b,d	275
D	4	83	73-0	30,000	27,500a				27,500	26,220	7/15	300b,d	100
G	9	98	16-4	5,000	4,000a				4,000	5,080	12/1	1,200b,d	188
Rc	5	85	08-2	70,000	66,000a		57,000b	66,000			8/1	450b,d	
Sc	10	99	07-4	100,000		100,000e			100,000	101,250	7/1	5,000b,d	5,000
				100,000	106,900a	100,000	57,000	66,000	140,900	141,650		7,250	5,563
					a,f	**f**	**f**	**f**	**f,g**	**f**		**f**	**f**
Stocks													
P 1,000 shs. Common			1,044		7,500a				7,500	7,600	3/1	750b,d	
											6/1	750b,d	
											9/1	750b,d	
											12/1	750b,d	250
U 50 shs. Common			8,530		9,700a				9,700	9,800	2/1	800b,d	
											8/1	800b,d	667
					17,200				17,200	17,400		4,600	917
					a,f				**f,g**	**f**		**f**	**f**

Legends and comments relative to above schedule:

a = Beginning balances agreed to 1999 working papers.
b = Traced to cash receipts.
c = Board of directors' minutes examined—purchase and sales approved.
d = Agreed to 1099.
e = Confirmed by tracing to broker's advice.
f = Totals footed.
g = Agreed to general ledger.

Required:

a. What information that is essential to the audit of debt and equity securities is missing from this schedule?

b. What essential audit procedures were not noted as having been performed by the audit assistant?

(AICPA, adapted)

INTERNET ASSIGNMENT

[7,10]   16-38   Both Intel (www.intel.com) and Microsoft (www.microsoft.com) have large amounts of investment securities. Visit their home pages and review their financial statements for information on how they account for investment securities and the amounts of those securities.

Part VI

COMPLETING THE AUDIT AND REPORTING RESPONSIBILITIES

Completing the Engagement

LEARNING OBJECTIVES

Upon completion of this chapter you will

[1] Understand the audit issues related to contingent liabilities.

[2] Know the audit procedures used to identify contingent liabilities.

[3] Understand the audit issues related to a legal letter.

[4] Understand why the auditor must be concerned with commitments.

[5] Know the types of subsequent events.

[6] Understand the effect of subsequent events on the dating of the audit report.

[7] Know the audit procedures used to identify subsequent events.

[8] Know the audit steps included in the auditor's final evidential evaluation process.

[9] Understand the auditor's communication with the audit committee and management and the matters that should be addressed.

[10] Know the auditor's responsibility for subsequent discovery of facts existing at the date of the auditor's report.

RELEVANT ACCOUNTING AND AUDITING PRONOUNCEMENTS

FASB Statement of Financial Accounting Standards No. 5, "Accounting for Contingencies" (FAS 5)

SAS No. 1, "Dating of the Independent Auditor's Report" (AU 530)

SAS No. 1, "Subsequent Events" (AU 560)

SAS No. 1, "Subsequent Discovery of Facts Existing at the Date of the Auditor's Report" (AU 561)

SAS No. 12, "Inquiry of a Client's Lawyer Concerning Litigation, Claims, and Assessments" (AU 337)

SAS No. 31, "Evidential Matter" (AU 326)

SAS No. 56, "Analytical Procedures" (AU 329)

SAS No. 57, "Auditing Accounting Estimates" (AU 342)

SAS No. 59, "The Auditor's Consideration of an Entity's Ability to Continue as a Going Concern" (AU 341)

SAS No. 61, "Communications with Audit Committees" (AU 380)

SAS No. 69, "The Confirmation Process" (AU 330)

SAS No. 80, "Amendment to Statement on Auditing Standards No. 31, *Evidential Matter*" (AU 326)

SAS No. 82, "Consideration of Fraud in a Financial Statement Audit" (AU 316)

SAS No. 85, "Client Representations" (AU 333)

Once the auditor has completed auditing the various accounting cycles and their related financial statement accounts, the evidence is summarized and evaluated. In addition, before choosing the appropriate audit report the auditor considers a number of additional issues that may impact the financial statements. This chapter discusses the following topics:

- Review for contingent liabilities.

- Commitments.
- Review for subsequent events.
- Final evidential evaluation processes.
- Communications with the audit committee and management.
- Subsequent discovery of facts existing at the date of the auditor's report.

Review for Contingent Liabilities

[LO 1]   A *contingent liability* is defined as an existing condition, situation, or set of circumstances involving uncertainty as to possible *loss* to an entity that will ultimately be resolved when some future event occurs or fails to occur. FASB No. 5, "Accounting for Contingencies" (FAS 5), states that when a contingent liability exists, the likelihood that the future event will result in a loss or impairment of an asset or the incurrence of a liability can be classified into three categories:

1. *Probable.* The future event is likely to occur.
2. *Reasonably possible.* The chance of the future event occurring is more than remote but less than likely.
3. *Remote.* The chance of the future event occurring is slight.

If the event is probable and the amount of the loss can be reasonably estimated, the loss is accrued by a charge to income. When the outcome of the event is judged to be reasonably possible or the amount cannot be estimated, a disclosure of the contingency is made in the footnotes to the financial statements. Exhibit 17–1 presents an example of such disclosure taken from a recent annual report. In general, loss contingencies that are judged to be remote are not disclosed in the footnotes.

Examples of contingent liabilities include

- Pending or threatened litigation.
- Actual or possible claims and assessments.
- Income tax disputes.
- Product warranties or defects.
- Guarantees of obligations to others.
- Agreements to repurchase receivables that have been sold.

EXHIBIT 17–1	**Example of Footnote Disclosure for a Contingency**

On October 31, 1998, a class action complaint was filed by a stockholder against the company and certain of its officers and directors in the United States District Court ("the court"). Shortly thereafter, other stockholders filed similar class action complaints. On February 1, 1999, a consolidated amended class action complaint against the company and certain of its officers and directors was filed in the court. In their consolidated complaint, the plaintiffs seek to represent a class consisting generally of persons who purchased or otherwise acquired the company's common stock in the period from March 5, 1998, through August 14, 1998. These actions claim damages related to alleged material misstatements and omissions of fact and manipulative and deceptive acts in violation of federal securities laws and common-law fraud. In December 2000 a motion filed by the plaintiffs to certify a class of purchasers of the company's common stock was approved with limited exceptions, and a class period for certain claims was established from March 5, 1998, to August 14, 1998. Also in December 2000, in response to a motion by the company and individual defendants, claims of common-law fraud, deceit, and negligence, misrepresentation, and certain of the violations of the federal securities laws against certain of the individual defendants were dismissed. At this time, it is not possible to predict the outcome of the pending lawsuit or the potential financial impact on the company of an adverse decision.

Audit Procedures for Identifying Contingent Liabilities

[LO 2]

The auditor may identify contingent liabilities while conducting audit procedures directed at audit objectives related to specific accounting cycles or financial statement accounts. Examples of such audit procedures include

1. Reading the minutes of meetings of the board of directors, committees of the board, and stockholders.
2. Reviewing contracts, loan agreements, leases, and correspondence from government agencies.
3. Reviewing income tax liability, tax returns, and IRS agents' reports.
4. Confirming or otherwise documenting guarantees and letters of credit obtained from financial institutions or other lending agencies.
5. Inspecting other documents for possible guarantees.

For example, the auditor normally reads the minutes of the board of directors' meetings for identification and approval of major transactions. Normally, the board of directors would discuss any material uncertainty that might exist for the entity. Similarly, the auditor examines the entity's income tax expense and accrued liability. The audit procedures for this account include determining if the IRS has audited the entity's prior year's tax returns. If so, the auditor should examine the IRS agents' report for any additional taxes assessed and determine whether the entity will contest the additional assessment.

In addition, near the completion of the engagement the auditor conducts specific audit procedures to identify contingent liabilities. Such procedures include

1. Inquiry of and discussion with management about its policies and procedures for identifying, evaluating, and accounting for contingent liabilities. Management has the responsibility for establishing policies and procedures to identify, evaluate, and account for contingencies. Large entities may implement such policies and procedures within their internal control systems. The management of smaller entities, however, may rely on legal counsel and auditors to identify and account for contingencies.
2. Examining documents in the entity's records such as correspondence and invoices from attorneys for pending or threatened lawsuits. Chapter 15 presented an account analysis of legal expense. Even though the amount of the legal expense account may be immaterial, the auditor normally examines the transactions in the account. The purpose of this examination is to identify actual or potential litigation against the client. The account analysis can also be used to develop a list of attorneys who have been consulted by the entity.
3. Obtaining a legal letter that describes and evaluates any litigation, claims, or assessments. Legal letters are discussed in the next section.
4. Obtaining written representation from management that all litigation, asserted and unasserted claims, and assessments have been disclosed in accordance with FASB No. 5. This information is obtained in a representation letter (see SAS No. 85, "Client Representations") furnished by the client.

TABLE 17–1	Examples of Types of Litigation

- Breach of contract.
- Patent infringement.
- Product liability.
- Violations of government legislation, including
  - Securities laws.
  - Antidiscrimination statutes based on race, sex, age, and other characteristics.
  - Antitrust laws.
  - Income tax regulations.
  - Environmental protection laws.
  - Foreign Corrupt Practices Act.
  - Racketeer Influenced and Corrupt Organizations Act (RICO).

Legal Letters

[LO 3]

A letter of audit inquiry (referred to as a *legal letter*) sent to the client's attorneys is the primary means of obtaining or corroborating information about litigation, claims, and assessments.[1] Auditors typically analyze legal expense for the entire period and send a legal letter to each attorney who has been consulted by management. Auditors should be particularly careful with letters sent to the entity's general counsel and attorneys specializing in patent law or securities laws because the general counsel should be aware of major litigation, and patent infringement and securities laws are major sources of litigation. Additionally, a legal letter should be obtained from the entity's in-house counsel if such a position exists. Table 17–1 provides examples of types of litigation that the auditor may encounter.

The auditor should ask management to send a legal letter to the attorneys, requesting that they provide the following information:

- A list and evaluation of any pending or threatened litigation to which the attorney has devoted substantial attention. The list may be provided by the client.
- A list of unasserted claims and assessments considered by management to be probable of assertion and reasonably possible of unfavorable outcome.
- A request that the attorney describe and evaluate the outcome of each pending or threatened litigation. This should include the progress of the case, the action the entity plans to take, the likelihood of unfavorable outcome, and the amount or range of potential loss.
- A request for additions to the list provided by management or a statement that the list is complete.

---

[1]B. K. Behn and K. Pany, "Limitations of Lawyers' Letters," *The Journal of Accountancy* (February 1995), pp. 61–67.

- A request that the attorney comment on unasserted claims where his or her views differ from management's evaluation.
- A statement by management acknowledging an understanding of the attorney's professional responsibility involving unasserted claims and assessments.
- A request that the attorney indicate if his or her response is limited and the reasons for such limitations.
- A description of any materiality levels agreed upon for the purposes of the inquiry and response.

 Exhibit 17–2 presents an example of a legal letter. Attorneys are generally willing to provide evidence on actual or pending litigation. However, they are sometimes reluctant to provide information on unasserted claims or assessments. An unasserted claim or assessment is one in which the injured party or potential claimant has not yet notified the entity of a possible claim or assessment. The following situation is an example of a possible unasserted claim. Suppose that one of the entity's manufacturing facilities is destroyed by fire and a number of people are killed. Suppose further that a subsequent investigation shows that the client had failed to install proper fire safety equipment. The entity's fiscal year may end and the financial statements for the period that includes the fire may be released. Although the families of the employees have not yet initiated or threatened litigation, an unasserted claim may exist at the financial statement date. In this case, the entity's attorneys may be reluctant to provide the auditor with information about the unasserted claims because of client–attorney privilege. The attorneys may also be concerned that disclosing the unasserted claim in the financial statements may itself result in a lawsuit. This dilemma is generally solved by having the attorneys corroborate management's understanding of their professional responsibility involving unasserted claims and assessments. Refer to the third paragraph in the legal letter shown in Exhibit 17–2 for the manner in which the client requests the attorneys to communicate to the auditor. In general, disclosing an unasserted claim is not required unless it is probable that the claim will be asserted and there is a reasonable possibility that the outcome will prove to be unfavorable.

Attorneys may limit their responses to items to which they have given substantial attention. Attorneys may also be unable to respond to the outcome of a matter because the factors in the case do not allow them to reasonably estimate the likelihood of the outcome or to estimate the possible loss. Finally, refusal to furnish information in a legal letter is a limitation on the scope of the audit sufficient to preclude an unqualified opinion.

Commitments

[LO 4]   Companies often enter long-term commitments to purchase raw materials or to sell their products at a fixed price. The main purpose of entering into such a purchase or sales contract is to obtain a favorable pricing arrangement or to secure the availability of raw materials. Long-term commitments are usually identified through inquiry of client personnel during the audit of

EXHIBIT 17–2

Address: ▼ http://www.mhhe.com/messier

Example of a Legal Letter

EARTHWEAR CLOTHIERS

January 15, 2001

Leon, Leon & Dalton
958 S.W. 77th Avenue
Boise, Idaho 79443

Gentlemen:

In connection with an audit of our financial statements for the year ended December 31, 2000, please furnish our auditors, Willis & Adams, P.O. Box 4080, Boise, Idaho 79443-4080, with the information requested below concerning contingencies involving matters with respect to which you have devoted substantial attention on behalf of the company in the form of legal consultation or representation. For the purposes of your response to this letter, we believe that as to each contingency an amount in excess of $25,000 would be material, and in the aggregate $150,000. However, determination of materiality with respect to the overall financial statements cannot be made until our auditors complete their examination. Your response should include matters that existed at December 31, 2000, and during the period from that date to the date of completion of their examination, which is anticipated to be on or about February 15, 2001.

Regarding pending or threatened litigations, claims, and assessments, please include in your response (1) the nature of each matter; (2) the progress of each matter to date; (3) how the company is responding or intends to respond (for example, to contest the case vigorously or seek an out-of-court settlement); and (4) an evaluation of the likelihood of an unfavorable outcome and an estimate, if one can be made, of the amount or range of potential loss. Please furnish to our auditors such explanation, if any, that you consider necessary to supplement the foregoing information, including an explanation of the matters as to which your views may differ from those stated.

We understand that whenever, in the course of performing legal services for us with respect to a matter recognized to involve an unasserted possible claim or assessment that may call for financial statement disclosure, if you have formed a professional conclusion that we should disclose or consider disclosure concerning such possible claim or assessment, as a matter of professional responsibility to us, you will so advise us and will consult with us concerning the question of such disclosure and the applicable requirements of Statement of Financial Accounting Standards No. 5. Please specifically confirm to our auditors that our understanding is correct.

Please specifically identify the nature of and reasons for any limitation on your response.

Very truly yours,

Calvin J. Rogers
Chief Executive Officer
EarthWear Clothiers

chapter—in particular, analytical procedures and review for subsequent events—are used by the auditor to help in assessing whether the entity will be able to continue as a going concern. If the auditor determines that there is substantial doubt about this, he or she should modify the audit report. Chapter 18 provides detailed coverage of the auditor's approach to the going-concern problem, including reporting requirements.

Representation Letter

During the course of the audit, management makes a number of representations to the auditor as part of the inquiries made to obtain sufficient competent evidence. SAS No. 85, "Client Representations" (AU 333), requires that the auditor obtain a representation letter from management. The purpose of this letter is to corroborate oral representations made to the auditor and to document the continued appropriateness of such representations. The representation letter also reduces the possibility of misunderstanding concerning the responses provided by management to the auditor's inquiries.

For example, during the audit, the auditor may inquire about related parties and conduct specific audit procedures to identify related-party transactions. Even if the results of these audit procedures indicate that such transactions have been properly disclosed, the auditor should obtain written representations that management is not aware of any such transactions that have not been disclosed. In other instances, evidence may not be available to corroborate management's representations. For example, suppose that management indicates an intent to refinance a short-term obligation in the next period and reclassifies it as a long-term liability in the current financial statements. The auditor would obtain written representation from management to confirm that the obligations will be refinanced in the next period.

Exhibit 17–3 presents an example of a representation letter. Note the important types of information that management is asked to represent. The representation letter should be addressed to the auditor and generally given the same date as the auditor's report. Normally, the chief executive officer and chief financial officer sign the representation letter. Management's refusal to provide a representation letter results in a scope limitation that is sufficient to preclude an unqualified opinion and is ordinarily sufficient to cause an auditor to disclaim an opinion or withdraw from the engagement. In such cases, the auditor should also consider management's refusal when assessing whether he or she can rely on other management representations.

Working Paper Review[2]

All audit work should be reviewed by an audit team member senior to the person preparing the working papers. Thus, the senior-in-charge should conduct a detailed review of the working papers prepared by the staff and follow up on any unresolved problems or issues. In turn, the manager

---

[2]See J. S. Rich, I. Solomon, and K. T. Trotman, "Multi-Auditor Judgment/Decision Making Research; A Decade Later," *Journal of Accounting Literature* Vol. 14 (1997), pp. 86–126, for a discussion of practice and research on the audit review process.

EXHIBIT 17–3

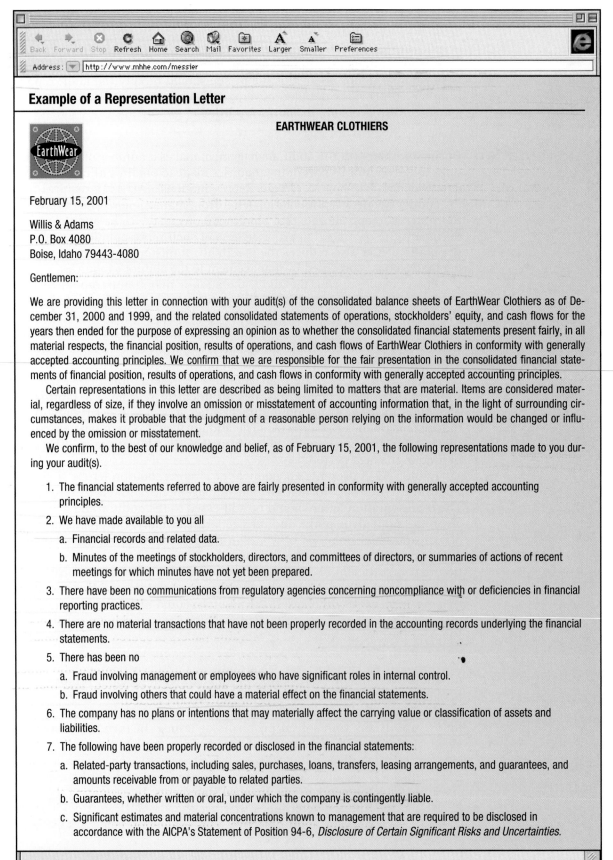

Example of a Representation Letter

EARTHWEAR CLOTHIERS

February 15, 2001

Willis & Adams
P.O. Box 4080
Boise, Idaho 79443-4080

Gentlemen:

We are providing this letter in connection with your audit(s) of the consolidated balance sheets of EarthWear Clothiers as of December 31, 2000 and 1999, and the related consolidated statements of operations, stockholders' equity, and cash flows for the years then ended for the purpose of expressing an opinion as to whether the consolidated financial statements present fairly, in all material respects, the financial position, results of operations, and cash flows of EarthWear Clothiers in conformity with generally accepted accounting principles. We confirm that we are responsible for the fair presentation in the consolidated financial statements of financial position, results of operations, and cash flows in conformity with generally accepted accounting principles.

Certain representations in this letter are described as being limited to matters that are material. Items are considered material, regardless of size, if they involve an omission or misstatement of accounting information that, in the light of surrounding circumstances, makes it probable that the judgment of a reasonable person relying on the information would be changed or influenced by the omission or misstatement.

We confirm, to the best of our knowledge and belief, as of February 15, 2001, the following representations made to you during your audit(s).

1. The financial statements referred to above are fairly presented in conformity with generally accepted accounting principles.

2. We have made available to you all

   a. Financial records and related data.

   b. Minutes of the meetings of stockholders, directors, and committees of directors, or summaries of actions of recent meetings for which minutes have not yet been prepared.

3. There have been no communications from regulatory agencies concerning noncompliance with or deficiencies in financial reporting practices.

4. There are no material transactions that have not been properly recorded in the accounting records underlying the financial statements.

5. There has been no

   a. Fraud involving management or employees who have significant roles in internal control.

   b. Fraud involving others that could have a material effect on the financial statements.

6. The company has no plans or intentions that may materially affect the carrying value or classification of assets and liabilities.

7. The following have been properly recorded or disclosed in the financial statements:

   a. Related-party transactions, including sales, purchases, loans, transfers, leasing arrangements, and guarantees, and amounts receivable from or payable to related parties.

   b. Guarantees, whether written or oral, under which the company is contingently liable.

   c. Significant estimates and material concentrations known to management that are required to be disclosed in accordance with the AICPA's Statement of Position 94-6, *Disclosure of Certain Significant Risks and Uncertainties*.

E X H I B I T 17–3 (*concluded*)

Address: http://www.mhhe.com/messier

8. There are no

  a. Violations or possible violations of laws or regulations whose effects should be considered for disclosure in the financial statements or as a basis for recording a loss contingency.

  b. Unasserted claims or assessments that our lawyer has advised us are probable of assertion and must be disclosed in accordance with Financial Accounting Standards Board (FASB) Statement No. 5, *Accounting for Contingencies.*

  c. Other liabilities or gain or loss contingencies that are required to be accrued or disclosed by FASB Statement No. 5.

9. The company has satisfactory title to all owned assets, and there are no liens or encumbrances on such assets, nor has any asset been pledged as collateral.

10. The company has complied with all aspects of contractual agreements that would have a material effect on the financial statements in the event of noncompliance.

11. Receivables recorded in the financial statements represent valid claims against debtors for sales or other charges arising on or before the balance sheet date and have been appropriately reduced to their estimated net realizable value.

12. Provision has been made to reduce excess or obsolete inventories to their estimated net realizable value.

13. Arrangements with financial institutions involving compensating balances or other arrangements involving restrictions on cash balances, line of credit, or similar arrangements have been properly disclosed.

14. We have fully disclosed to you all sales terms, including all rights of return or price adjustments and all warranty provisions.

To the best of our knowledge and belief, no events have occurred subsequent to the balance sheet date and through the date of this letter that would require adjustment to or disclosure in the aforementioned financial statements.

Calvin J. Rogers
Chief Executive Officer

James C. Watts
Chief Financial Officer

---

should review all working papers, although the extent of the manager's review may vary with how much the manager relies on the senior-in-charge. The engagement partner normally reviews working papers related to critical audit areas as well as working papers prepared by the manager. In reviewing the working papers, the reviewers must ensure that the working papers document that the audit was properly planned and supervised, that the evidence supports the audit objectives tested, and that the evidence is sufficient for the type of audit report issued.

Evaluating Audit Results

In conjunction with the review of the working papers, the auditor must evaluate the results of the audit tests. This evaluation is concerned with two issues: (1) the sufficiency of the audit evidence and (2) the effects of detected misstatements in the financial statements. In evaluating the audit evidence, the auditor determines whether there is sufficient evidence to support each relevant audit objective. This evaluation considers evidence obtained to support the assessment of inherent and control risk, as well as the evidence gathered to reach the planned level of detection risk (substantive tests of transactions, analytical procedures, and tests of account balances). If this evaluation indicates that the evidence is not sufficient to meet the planned level of audit risk, the auditor may need to gather additional evidence. For example, if the final analytical procedures indicate that inventory may still contain material misstatements, the auditor should further test the inventory account balance.

Any misstatements detected during the audit process must be considered in terms of their effects on the financial statements. This involves performing the third step in applying materiality (refer to Chapter 3). In particular, the auditor must estimate the likely misstatements and compare the amount arrived at to the amount of materiality allocated to the relevant component of the financial statement. (*Likely misstatements* include both known and projected misstatements.) The auditor should also consider the effects of unadjusted misstatements on aggregated components of the financial statements such as assets, liabilities, equity, revenues, and expenses.

Exhibit 17–4 is the working paper introduced in Exhibit 3–5. As noted in Chapter 3, none of the errors detected is material in terms of the tolerable misstatement allocated to the individual component of the financial statements affected. Additionally, the overall effect of the misstatements is not material in terms of aggregated components of the financial statements. Even though the misstatements shown in Exhibit 17–4 are not material, it is common practice for the auditor to give those adjustments to the client in order to correct the books. However, the auditor would not require those adjustments to be booked. If the likely error for a particular account is greater than the tolerable misstatement, the account will require adjustment. Similarly, if the unadjusted misstatements affect the aggregated components of the financial statements, the auditor may find it necessary to adjust for these misstatements.

Evaluating Financial Statement Presentation and Disclosure

Either the client or the auditor normally prepares a draft of the financial statements, including footnotes. The auditor reviews the financial statements to ensure compliance with GAAP, proper presentation of accounts, and inclusion of all necessary disclosures. Most public accounting firms use some type of financial statement checklist to assist the auditor in this process.

Independent Partner Review

Most firms have a policy requiring a review by a second partner of the financial statements and audit report for publicly traded companies and those financial statements expected to be widely distributed. The second partner is generally not associated with the details of the engagement and is expected to provide an independent review. The second partner should understand the audit approach, findings, and conclusions for critical audit areas and should review the audit report, financial statements, and footnotes for consistency.

EXHIBIT 17–4

Back Forward Stop Refresh Home Search Mail Favorites Larger Smaller Preferences

Address: http://www.mhhe.com/messier

Example Working Paper for Estimating Likely Misstatements

EarthWear

EARTHWEAR CLOTHIERS
Schedule of Proposed Adjusting Entries
12/31/00

Workpaper Ref.	Proposed Adjusting Entry	Tolerable Misstatement	Assets	Liabilities	Equity	Revenues	Expenses
N10	Payroll expense						12,200
	Bonuses						24,000
	Accrued liabilities	60,000		36,200			
	To accrue payroll through 12/31 and recognize 2000 bonuses.						
F20	Cost of sales	250,000					112,500
	Inventory		(112,500)				
	To adjust ending inventory based on sample results.						
F22	Inventory	250,000	27,450				
	Accounts payable	200,000		27,450			
	To record inventory in transit at 12/31.						
R15	Accounts receivable	45,000	9,850				
	Sales					9,850	
	To record sales cutoff errors at 12/31.						
	Total		(75,200)	63,650		9,850	148,700

Conclusion: Based on the above analysis, the account balances for EarthWear Clothiers are fairly stated in accordance with GAAP.

Communications with the Audit Committee and Management

[LO 9]   SAS No. 61, "Communications with Audit Committees" (AU 380), requires that the auditor communicate certain matters related to the conduct of the audit to those individuals responsible for oversight of the financial reporting process. This communication applies to (1) entities that have an audit committee or similar group, such as a finance committee or budget committee, and (2) all SEC engagements. The intent of this communication is to ensure that the audit committee or similar group receives additional information on the scope and results of the audit. The communication should address the following matters:

- The auditor's responsibility under GAAS.
- Significant accounting policies.
- Management judgments and accounting estimates.
- Significant audit adjustments.
- Disagreements with management.
- Consultation with other accountants.
- Major issues discussed with management before the auditor was retained.
- Difficulties encountered during the audit.
- Fraud involving senior management and fraud that causes material misstatement of the financial statements.

This communication may be oral or written. If communicated orally, a memorandum of the communication should be included in the working papers. When the communication is in writing, the report should indicate that it is intended solely for the use of the audit committee, the board of directors, and, if applicable, management.

Additionally, the auditor normally prepares a *management letter*. The general intent of a management letter is to make recommendations to the client based on observations during the audit; the letter may include areas such as organizational structure and efficiency issues. During the audit, the audit team members should be alert for opportunities to assist the client. Any areas recommended for improvement should be documented in the working papers. Generally, the management letter is addressed to the board of directors, chief executive officer, or chief financial officer. Exhibit 17–5 provides an example of a management letter.

Subsequent Discovery of Facts Existing at the Date of the Auditor's Report

[LO 10]   An auditor has no obligation to make any inquiries or conduct any audit procedures after the financial statements and audit report have been issued. However, facts may come to the auditor's attention after the issuance of the financial statements that might have affected the report had he or she known about them. In Figure 17–1, this would be events occurring

EXHIBIT 17–5

Sample Management Letter

ABBOTT & JOHNSON, LLP
Tampa, Florida

April 5, 2001

Mr. Matthew J. Calabro
Calabro Paging Services
P.O. Box 787
M. K. Vona Industrial Park
Tampa, Florida 32702

Dear Mr. Calabro:

We have audited the financial statements of Calabro Paging Services for the year ended December 31, 2000, and have issued our report thereon dated February 15, 2001. As part of our audit, we studied internal control only to the extent that we considered necessary to determine the nature, timing, and extent of auditing procedures.

Summarized below are suggestions of importance that we believe warrant your attention. Our recommendations were discussed with personnel responsible for the various areas, and many of these recommendations are currently being implemented.

Inventory
The company does not maintain shipping and receiving logs for all pagers sent to and received from vendors for repair. The shipping/receiving log, listing the serial numbers of units sent and the dates the units were sent and received back, should be used to track and monitor the status of repairs and to ensure that the units are returned from vendors promptly.

Receivables
The company does not have procedures to perform timely write-off of receivables balances that are greater than 90 days old unless collectibility can be documented. During our midyear testing we noted multiple receivable balances greater than 90 days outstanding that had not been written off, and there was not adequate support/documentation for maintaining such amounts on the books. These balances were cleared up in December; however, a policy should be implemented to perform this procedure monthly to prevent unusual adjustments to quarterly reports. In conjunction with this monthly review, the allowance for doubtful accounts should be evaluated and revised monthly as appropriate.

We appreciate the opportunity to present these comments for your consideration, and we are prepared to discuss them at your convenience.

Sincerely,

Abbott & Johnson, CPAs

---

after March 5, 2001. SAS No. 1, "Subsequent Discovery of Facts Existing at the Date of the Auditor's Report" (AU 561), provides guidance for the auditor in those circumstances. While a number of situations may apply, the most common situation is where the previously issued financial statements contain material misstatements due to either unintentional or intentional actions by management. For example, the auditor may find out that a material amount of inventory was not included in the financial statements because of a computer error. Alternatively, the auditor may learn

> ### Informix Completes an Extended Audit and Restates Prior Results
>
> In November 1997 Informix Corporation announced that it had completed an extended audit and that it had restated its results for 1994, 1995, 1996, and the first quarter of 1997. The once high-flying database software maker reported that it had improperly booked revenues and profits. Informix's restatements cut reported revenue from January 1994 to June 1997 by $278.2 million. It is not clear how Informix's accounting systems failed to detect the problems. The company frequently recognized revenue from software that was shipped to distributors even though the products were never sold to final customers. Additionally, many recorded sales lacked proper documentation.
>
> *Sources:* K. Swisher, "Informix Posts Loss of $110.7 Million, Restates Results," *The Wall Street Journal* (November 19, 1997); "Informix Completes Extended Audit; Restates Prior Periods and Announces Third Quarter '97 Results," *The PointCast Network* (November 18, 1997).

that management inflated inventory quantities and prices in an effort to increase reported profits. A number of such situations have arisen in recent years (see Exhibit 17–6). Events that occur after the issuance of the auditor's report, such as final settlements of litigation or additional information on accounting estimates becoming available, do not apply to this auditing standard.

When facts are encountered that may affect the auditor's previously issued report, the auditor should consult with his or her attorney because legal implications may be involved and actions taken by the auditor may involve confidential client–auditor communications. The auditor should determine whether the facts are reliable and whether they existed at the date of the audit report. The auditor should discuss the matter with an appropriate level of management and request cooperation in investigating the potential misstatement.

If the auditor determines that the previously issued financial statements are in error and the audit report is affected, he or she should request that the client issue an immediate revision to the financial statements and auditor's report. The reasons for the revisions should be described in the footnotes to the revised financial statements. If the effect on the financial statements cannot immediately be determined, the client should notify persons known to be relying on the financial statements and auditor's report. If the stock is publicly traded or subject to regulatory jurisdiction, the client should contact the SEC, stock exchanges, and other regulatory agencies.

If the client refuses to cooperate and make the necessary disclosures, the auditor should notify the board of directors and take the following steps, if possible:

1. Notify the client that the auditor's report must no longer be associated with the financial statements.
2. Notify any regulatory agencies having jurisdiction over the client that the auditor's report can no longer be relied upon.

EXHIBIT 17–7

Golden Bear Golf Restates 1997 Results; Auditor's Report Not Reliable
Golden Bear Golf, Inc., the golf company controlled by Jack Nicklaus, restated its 1997 results because of an understatement of expenses by a former executive at its Paragon Construction International subsidiary. The company reviewed all Paragon contracts with help from its outside law firm, Arthur Andersen, LLP, and PricewaterhouseCoopers, LLP. As a result of the review, the company found that former Paragon management "falsified records, misrepresented the status of construction projects, and made false statements about Paragon's revenue, costs, and profits to the company's executive management and board of directors on repeated occasions." Based on this information, Golden Bear said that its previously issued financial statements for the periods ended December 31, 1997, and March 31, 1998, as well as Arthur Andersen, LLP's, report, were not reliable. *Sources:* A. Carrns, "Golden Bear Golf to Restate '97 Loss at $24.7 Million," *The Wall Street Journal* (July 28, 1998); and A. Carrns, "Nicklaus's Golf Firm Says Chief Quit; Winslett Named, Some Losses Restated," *The Wall Street Journal* (October 20, 1998).

3. Notify each person known to the auditor to be relying on the financial statements. Usually, notifying a regulatory agency such as the SEC is the only practical way of providing appropriate disclosure.

The practical outcome of these procedures is that the auditor has withdrawn his or her report on the previously issued financial statements (see Exhibit 17–7). In notifying the client, regulatory agencies, and other persons relying on the auditor's report, the auditor should disclose the effect the information would have had on the auditor's report had it been known to the auditor.

REVIEW QUESTIONS

[LO 1] 17-1 Define what is meant by *contingent liability*. What three categories are used to classify a contingent liability in FASB No. 5? Give four examples of a contingent liability.

[3] 17-2 What information does the auditor ask the attorney to provide on pending or threatened litigation? What is meant by an unasserted claim, and why are attorneys reluctant to provide information on unasserted claims in the legal letter?

[4] 17-3 Provide two examples of commitments. Under what conditions do such commitments result in the recognition of a loss in the financial statements?

[5] 17-4 What are the two types of subsequent events, and how is each type accounted for in the financial statements? Give two examples of each type.

[5,6] 17-5 Under what circumstances would the auditor dual date an audit report?

[8]   17-6   Are any analytical procedures required as part of the final overall review of the financial statements? What is the purpose of such analytical procedures?

[8]   17-7   Why does the auditor obtain a representation letter from management?

[8]   17-8   Describe the purposes of an independent partner review.

[9]   17-9   What items should be included in the auditor's communication with an audit committee or similar group?

[10]   17-10   What types of events would generally require revision of the issued financial statements? What procedures should the auditor follow when the client refuses to cooperate and make the necessary disclosures?

MULTIPLE–CHOICE QUESTIONS FROM CPA EXAMINATIONS

[3]   17-11   An auditor should request that an audit client send a letter of inquiry to those attorneys who have been consulted concerning litigation, claims, or assessments. The primary reason for this request is to provide
   a. The opinion of a specialist as to whether loss contingencies are possible, probable, or remote.
   b. A description of litigation, claims, and assessments that have a reasonable possibility of unfavorable outcome.
   c. An objective appraisal of management's policies and procedures adopted for identifying and evaluating legal matters.
   d. Corroboration of the information furnished by management concerning litigation, claims, and assessments.

[3]   17-12   The scope of an audit is *not* restricted when an attorney's response to an auditor as a result of a client's letter of audit inquiry limits the response to
   a. Matters to which the attorney has given substantive attention in the form of legal representation.
   b. An evaluation of the likelihood of an unfavorable outcome of the matters disclosed by the entity.
   c. The attorney's opinion of the entity's experience in recent similar litigation.
   d. The probable outcome of asserted claims and pending or threatened litigation.

[1,2]   17-13   An auditor would be most likely to identify a contingent liability by obtaining a(n)
   a. Accounts payable confirmation.
   b. Transfer agent confirmation.
   c. Standard bank confirmation.
   d. Related-party transaction confirmation.

[7]   17-14   Which of the following procedures would an auditor most likely perform to obtain evidence about the occurrence of subsequent events?
   a. Recompute a sample of large-dollar transactions occurring after year-end for arithmetic accuracy.
   b. Investigate changes in stockholders' equity occurring after year-end.

   c. Inquire of the entity's legal counsel concerning litigation, claims, and assessments arising after year-end.

   d. Confirm bank accounts established after year-end.

[6] **17-15** An auditor issued an audit report that was dual dated for a subsequent event occurring after the completion of field work but before issuance of the auditor's report. The auditor's responsibility for events occurring subsequent to the completion of field work was

   a. Extended to subsequent events occurring through the date of issuance of the report.

   b. Extended to include all events occurring since the completion of field work.

   c. Limited to the specific event referenced.

   d. Limited to events occurring up to the date of the last subsequent event referenced.

[8] **17-16** Analytical procedures used in the overall review stage of an audit generally include

   a. Considering unusual or unexpected amount balances that were *not* previously identified.

   b. Testing transactions to corroborate management's financial statement assertions.

   c. Gathering evidence concerning account balances that have *not* changed from the prior year.

   d. Retesting control procedures that appeared to be ineffective during the assessment of control risk.

[10] **17-17** After issuing a report, an auditor has *no* obligation to make continuing inquiries or perform other procedures concerning the audited financial statements, unless

   a. Information that existed at the report date and may affect the report comes to the auditor's attention.

   b. The management of the entity requests the auditor to reissue the auditor's report.

   c. Information about an event that occurred after the end of field work comes to the auditor's attention.

   d. Final determinations or resolutions are made of contingencies that were disclosed in the financial statements.

[8] **17-18** To which of the following matters would an auditor *not* apply materiality limits when obtaining specific written client representations?

   a. Disclosure of compensating balance arrangements involving restrictions on cash balances.

   b. Information concerning related-party transactions and related amounts receivable or payable.

   c. The absence of errors and unrecorded transactions in the financial statements.

   d. Fraud involving employees with significant roles in the internal control system.

[8] **17-19** Which of the following forms of documentation is required for an audit in accordance with generally accepted auditing standards?

   a. Internal control questionnaire.

   b. Client engagement letter.

   c. Planning memorandum or checklist.

   d. Client representation letter.

[9]   17-20   Which of the following matters is an auditor required to communicate to an entity's audit committee?

	Significant Audit Adjustments	Changes in Significant Accounting Policies
a.	Yes	Yes
b.	Yes	No
c.	No	Yes
d.	No	No

[10]   17-21   After an audit report containing an unqualified opinion on a nonpublic client's financial statements is issued, the auditor hears that the client has decided to sell the shares of a subsidiary that accounts for 30 percent of its revenue and 25 percent of its net income. The auditor should

a. Determine whether the information is reliable and, if it is determined to be reliable, request that revised financial statements be issued.

b. Notify the entity that the auditor's report may no longer be associated with the financial statements.

c. Describe the effects of this subsequently discovered information in communications with persons known to be relying on the financial statements.

d. Take no action because the auditor has no obligation to make any further inquiries.

[8]   17-22   A written representation from a client's management that, among other matters, acknowledges responsibility for the fair presentation of financial statements should normally be signed by the

a. Chief executive officer and the chief financial officer.

b. Chief financial officer and the chairman of the board of directors.

c. Chairman of the audit committee of the board of directors.

d. Chief executive officer, the chairman of the board of directors, and the client's lawyer.

[10]   17-23   Which of the following events occurring after the issuance of an auditor's report would be most likely to cause the auditor to make further inquiries about the previously issued financial statements?

a. A technological development that could affect the entity's future ability to continue as a going concern.

b. The discovery of information regarding a contingency that existed before the financial statements were issued.

c. The entity's sale of a subsidiary that accounts for 30 percent of the entity's consolidated sales.

d. The final resolution of a lawsuit explained in a separate paragraph of the auditor's report.

[9]   17-24   An auditor is obligated to communicate a "proposed" audit adjustment to an entity's audit committee only if the adjustment

a. Has *not* been recorded before the end of the auditor's field work.

b. Has a significant effect on the entity's financial reporting process.

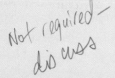

   c. Is a recurring matter that was proposed to management the prior year.

   d. Results from the correction of a prior period's departure from GAAP.

[7] 17-25 Which of the following procedures should an auditor generally perform regarding subsequent events?

   a. Compare the latest available interim financial statements with the financial statements being audited.

   b. Send second requests to the client's customers who failed to respond to initial accounts receivable confirmation requests.

   c. Communicate material weaknesses in internal control to the client's audit committee.

   d. Review the cutoff bank statements for several months after year-end.

PROBLEMS

[1,2,3] 17-26 During an audit engagement, Harper, CPA, has satisfactorily completed an examination of accounts payable and other liabilities and now plans to determine whether there are any loss contingencies arising from litigation, claims, or assessments.

Required:
What audit procedures should Harper follow with respect to the existence of loss contingencies arising from litigation, claims, and assessments? Do *not* discuss reporting requirements.

(AICPA, adapted)

[8] 17-27 Arenas, an assistant accountant with the firm of Better & Best, CPAs, is auditing the financial statements of Tech Consolidated Industries, Inc. The firm's audit program calls for the preparation of a written management representation letter.

Required:
a. In an audit of financial statements, in what circumstances is the auditor required to obtain a management representation letter? What are the purposes of obtaining the letter?

b. To whom should the representation letter be addressed, and when should it be dated? Who should sign the letter, and what would be the effect of his or her refusal to sign the letter?

c. In what respects may an auditor's other responsibilities be relieved by obtaining a management representation letter?

(AICPA, adapted)

[8] 17-28 During the examination of the annual financial statements of Amis Manufacturing, Inc., the company's president, R. Heinrich, and Luddy, the auditor, reviewed the matters that were to be included in a written representation letter. Upon receipt of the following client representation letter, Luddy contacted Heinrich to state that it was incomplete.

To: E. K. Luddy, CPA

In connection with your examination of the balance sheet of Amis Manufacturing, Inc., as of December 31, 2000, and the related statements of income, retained earnings, and cash flows for the year then ended, for the purpose of expressing an opinion as to whether the financial statements present fairly the financial position, results of operations, and cash flows of Amis Manufacturing, Inc., in conformity with generally accepted accounting principles, we confirm, to the best of our knowledge and belief, the following representations made to you during your examination. There were no

- Plans or intentions that may materially affect the carrying value or classification of assets and liabilities.
- Communications from regulatory agencies concerning noncompliance with, or deficiencies in, financial reporting practices.
- Agreements to repurchase assets previously sold.
- Violations or possible violations of laws or regulations whose effects should be considered for disclosure in the financial statements or as a basis for recording a loss contingency.
- Unasserted claims or assessments that our lawyer has advised are probable of assertion and must be disclosed in accordance with Statement of Financial Accounting Standards No. 5.
- Capital-stock repurchase options or agreements or capital stock reserved for options, warrants, conversions, or other requirements.
- Compensating balance or other arrangements involving restrictions on cash balances.

R. Heinrich, President
Amis Manufacturing, Inc.
March 14, 2001

Required:
Identify the other matters that Heinrich's representation letter should specifically confirm.

(AICPA, adapted)

[5,7]   17-29   Namiki, CPA, is auditing the financial statements of Taylor Corporation for the year ended December 31, 2000. Namiki plans to complete the field work and sign the auditor's report about March 10, 2001. Namiki is concerned about events and transactions occurring after December 31, 2000, that may affect the 2000 financial statements.

Required:
a. What general types of subsequent events require Namiki's consideration and evaluation?
b. What auditing procedures should Namiki consider performing to gather evidence concerning subsequent events?

(AICPA, adapted)

[5,6,7]   17-30   For each of the following items, assume that Josh Feldstein, CPA, is expressing an opinion on Scornick Company's financial statements for the year ended December 31, 2000; that he completed field work on January 21, 2001; and that he now is preparing his opinion to accompany the financial statements. In each item a sub-

sequent event is described. This event was disclosed to the CPA either in connection with his review of subsequent events or after the completion of field work. You are to indicate for each item the required accounting of the event. Each of the five items is independent of the other four and is to be considered separately.

1. A large account receivable from Agronowitz Company (material to financial statement presentation) was considered fully collectible at December 31, 2000. Agronowitz suffered a plant explosion on January 25, 2001. Because Agronowitz was uninsured, it is unlikely that the account will be paid.
2. The tax court ruled in favor of the company on January 25, 2001. Litigation involved deductions claimed on the 1997 and 1998 tax returns. In accrued taxes payable Scornick had provided for the full amount of the potential disallowances. The Internal Revenue Service will not appeal the tax court's ruling.
3. Scornick's Manufacturing Division, whose assets constituted 45 percent of Scornick's total assets at December 31, 2000, was sold on February 1, 2001. The new owner assumed the bonded indebtedness associated with this property.
4. On January 15, 2001, R. E. Fogler, a major investment adviser, issued a negative report on Scornick's long-term prospects. The market price of Scornick's common stock subsequently declined by 40 percent.
5. At its January 5, 2001, meeting, Scornick's board of directors voted to increase substantially the advertising budget for the coming year and authorized a change in advertising agencies.

[3] 17-31 Cole & Cole, CPAs, are auditing the financial statements of Consolidated Industries Company for the year ended December 31, 2000. On April 2, 2001, an inquiry letter to J. J. Young, Consolidated's outside attorney, was drafted to corroborate the information furnished to Cole by management concerning pending and threatened litigation, claims, and assessments, as well as unasserted claims and assessments. On May 6, 2001, C. R. Cao, Consolidated's chief financial officer, gave Cole a draft of the inquiry letter below for Cole's review before mailing it to Young.

> May 6, 2001
>
> J. J. Young, Attorney at Law
> 123 Main Street
> Anytown, USA
>
> Dear J. J. Young:
>
> In connection with an audit of our financial statements at December 31, 2000, and for the year then ended, management of the company has prepared, and furnished to our auditors, Cole & Cole, CPAs, 456 Broadway, Anytown, USA, a description and evaluation of certain contingencies, including those set forth below involving matters with respect to which you have been engaged and to which you have devoted substantive attention on behalf of the company in the form of legal consultation or representation. Your response should include matters that existed at December 31, 2000. Because of the confidentiality of all these matters, your response may be limited.

In November 2000 an action was brought against the company by an outside salesman alleging breach of contract for sales commissions and pleading a second cause of action for an accounting with respect to claims for fees and commissions. The salesman's action claims damages of $300,000, but the company believes it has meritorious defenses to the claims. The possible exposure of the company to a successful judgment on behalf of the plaintiff is slight.

In July 2000 an action was brought against the company by Industrial Manufacturing Company ("Industrial") alleging patent infringement and seeking damages of $20 million. The action in U.S. District Court resulted in a decision on October 16, 2000, holding that the company had infringed seven Industrial patents and awarding damages of $14 million. The company vigorously denies these allegations and has filed an appeal with the U.S. Court of Appeals for the Federal Circuit. The appeal process is expected to take approximately two years, but there is some chance that Industrial may ultimately prevail.

Please furnish to our auditors such explanation, if any, that you consider necessary to supplement the foregoing information, including an explanation of those matters as to which your views may differ from those stated and an identification of the omission of any pending or threatened litigation, claims, and assessments or a statement that the list of such matters is complete. Your response may be quoted or referred to in the financial statements without further correspondence with you.

You also consulted on various other matters considered pending or threatened litigation. However, you may not comment on these matters because publicizing them may alert potential plaintiffs to the strengths of their cases. In addition, various other matters probable of assertion that have some chance of an unfavorable outcome, as of December 31, 2000, are unasserted claims and assessments.

C. R. Cao
Chief Financial Officer

Required
Describe the omissions, ambiguities, and inappropriate statements and terminology in Cao's letter.

(AICPA, adapted)

DISCUSSION CASES

[8]   17-32   Medical Products, Inc. (MPI), was created in 1998 and entered the optical equipment industry. Their made-to-order optical equipment requires large investments in research and development. To fund these needs, MPI made a public stock offering, which was completed in 1999. Although the offering was moderately successful, MPI's ambitious management is convinced that they must report a good profit this year (2000) to maintain the current market price of the stock. MPI's president recently stressed this point when he told his controller, Pam Adams, "If we don't make $1.25 million pretax this year, our stock will fall significantly."

Adams was pleased that even after adjustments for accrued vacation pay, 2000 pretax profit was $1.35 million. However, MPI's auditors, Hammer & Bammer (HB), proposed an additional adjustment for inventory valuation that would reduce this profit to $900,000. HB's proposed adjustment had been discussed during the 1999 audit.

An additional issue discussed in 1999 was MPI's failure to accrue executive vacation pay. At that time HB did not insist on the adjustment because the amount ($20,000) was not material to the 1999 results and because MPI agreed to begin accruing vacation pay in future years. The cumulative accrued executive vacation pay amounts to $300,000 and has been accrued at the end of 2000.

The inventory issue arose in 1998 when MPI purchased $450,000 of specialized computer components to be used with their optical scanners for a special order. The order was subsequently canceled, and HB proposed to write down this inventory in 1999. MPI explained, however, that the components could easily be sold without a loss during 2000, and no adjustment was made. However, the equipment was not sold by the end of 2000, and prospects for future sales were considered nonexistent. HB proposed a write-off of the entire $450,000 in 2000.

The audit partner, Johanna Schmidt, insisted that Adams make the inventory adjustment. Adams tried to convince her that there were other alternatives, but Schmidt was adamant. Adams knew the inventory was worthless, but she reminded Schmidt of the importance of this year's reported income. Adams continued her argument, "You can't take both the write-down and the vacation accrual in one year; it doesn't fairly present our performance this year. If you insist on taking that write-down, I'm taking back the accrual. Actually, that's a good idea because the executives are such workaholics, they don't take their vacations anyway."

As Adams calmed down, she said, "Johanna, let's be reasonable; we like you—and we want to continue our good working relationship with your firm into the future. But we won't have a future unless we put off this accrual for another year."

Required:
a. Should the inventory adjustment be taken in 2000?
b. Irrespective of your decision regarding the inventory adjustment, should the auditor insist on accrual of the executives' vacation pay?
c. Consider the conflict between Adams and Schmidt. Assuming that Schmidt believes the inventory adjustment and vacation pay accrual must be made and that she does not want to lose MPI as a client, what should she do?

[1,2,3]   17-33   In February 2000, Ceramic Crucibles of America was notified by the state of Colorado that the state was investigating the company's Durango facility to determine if there were any violations of federal or state environmental laws. In formulating your opinion on the 1999 financial statements, you determined that, based primarily on management's representations, the investigation did not pose a serious threat to the company's financial well-being.

The company subsequently retained a local law firm to represent it in dealing with the state commission. At the end of 2000, you concluded that the action did not represent a severe threat.

However, you have just received the attorney's letter, which is a little unsettling. It states:

> On January 31, 2001, the U.S. Environmental Protection Agency (EPA) listed the Durango site in Durango, Colorado, on the National Priorities List under the Comprehensive Environmental Response, Compensation, and Liability Act (Superfund). The site includes property adjoining the western boundary of Ceramic Crucibles' plant in Durango and includes parts of Ceramic Crucibles' property. The EPA has listed Ceramic Crucibles as one of the three "potentially responsible parties" ("PRPs") that may be liable for the costs of investigating and cleaning up the site. The EPA has authorized $400,000 for a "Remedial Investigation and Feasibility Study" of the site, but that study will not begin until sometime later in 2001. Thus, we do not deem it possible or appropriate at this time to evaluate this matter with regard to potential liability or cost to the company.

You immediately set up a meeting with Dave Buff, Ceramic Crucibles' vice president, Ron Bonner, the company's attorney, and Margaret Osmond, an attorney who specializes in EPA-related issues. At the meeting you ascertain that

- Ceramic Crucibles bought the Durango facility from TW Industries in 1990.
- TW Industries had operated the facility as a manufacturer of ceramic tiles, and they had used lead extensively in incorporating color into the tile.
- The site has been placed on the National Priorities List ("the List") apparently because each state must have at least one site on the List. All sites on the List are rated on a composite score that reflects the relative extent of pollution. The Durango site has a rating of 8.3 compared to a rating of no less than 25 for the other sites on the List.
- The most severe lead pollution (based on toxicity) is in an area located on the other side of a levee behind Ceramic Crucibles' facilities. Although the area close to the building contains traces of lead pollution, the toxicity in this area is about 50 parts per million (ppm), compared to 19,000 ppm beyond the levee.
- Although Ceramic Crucibles used lead in coloring its crucibles until about 1992, the lead was locked into a ceramic glaze that met FDA requirements for appliances used in the preparation of food. Apparently, the acids used in determining the leaching properties of lead for EPA tests are stronger than that used by the FDA. Since 1992, Ceramic Crucibles has used leadfree mud in its crucibles.
- Affidavits taken from present and former employees of Ceramic Crucibles indicate that no wastewater has been discharged though the levee since Ceramic Crucibles acquired the property in 1990.
- The other PRPs and TW Industries are viable companies that should be in a position to meet their responsibilities resulting from any possible EPA action.

Materiality for purposes of evaluating a potential loss is $10 million to $13 million. This is based on the assumption that the loss would be deductible for income tax purposes. In that case, the loss would represent a reduction in stockholders' equity of 4.5 percent to 7.0 percent. Your best guess is that the company's exposure does not exceed that amount. Further, based on the financial strength of the company and its available lines of credit, you believe such an assessment would not result in financial distress to the company.

The creation of the Environmental Protection Agency (EPA) and that of the Comprehensive Environmental Response, Compensation, and Liability Act are a result of the increasing concern of Americans about pollution. An amendment to the act permits the EPA to perform the cleanup. As of the end of 2000, the EPA had a national priorities list of 27,000 sites thought to be severely damaged. The average cost of conducting remedial investigation and feasibility studies ranges from $750,000 to $1 million, and such studies may take as long as three years. Cleanup costs are usually another $10 million to $12 million. It is said that the current estimates that $100 billion will be spent to clean up nonfederal hazardous waste sites may be conservative. The law requires the EPA to identify toxic waste sites and request records from PRPs. The PRPs are responsible for the cost of cleanup, but if they lack the funds, the EPA uses its funds for the cleanup. The EPA has spent $3.3 billion from its trust fund and collected only $65 million from polluters since the passage of the legislation.

Required:
a. How would this type of contingency be classified in the accounting literature, and how should it be accounted for?
b. Would the amount be material to the financial statements?
c. What additional evidence would you gather, and what kinds of representations should you require from the client?
d. Should the investigation affect your opinion on those financial statements?

INTERNET ASSIGNMENTS

[4]   17-34   A number of companies have reported accounting irregularities or fraud in recent years. Some of the companies reporting such fraud include Cendant, Fine Host, Livent, Oxford Health Plans, Sunbeam, Vesta Insurance Group, and Waste Management.

Required:
a. Use an Internet search engine to find information on two of the companies listed. Prepare a memorandum describing the accounting irregularity or fraud.
b. Extend your search to identify two additional companies who have recently reported an accounting irregularity or fraud. Prepare a memorandum describing the accounting irregularity or fraud.

[5]   17-35   It is unusual for an accounting firm to withdraw its opinion on a set of previously issued financial statements. Use an Internet search engine to find a recent example of a company whose public accounting firm has withdrawn its opinion.

Reports on Audited Financial Statements and Special Reporting Issues

LEARNING OBJECTIVES

Upon completion of this chapter you will

[1] Understand the auditor's standard unqualified audit report.

[2] Know the situations that result in modification to the standard unqualified audit report.

[3] Know the conditions that lead to a departure from the standard unqualified audit report.

[4] Know the other types of audit reports.

[5] Understand the effect of materiality on the auditor's choice of audit reports.

[6] Understand the situations that may cause different types of reports on comparative financial statements.

[7] Know the auditor's responsibility for other information in documents containing audited financial statements.

[8] Understand how to identify, assess, and report on entities with going-concern problems.

[9] Understand the auditor's reporting responsibility for financial statements prepared on a comprehensive basis other than GAAP.

[10] Understand the auditor's responsibility for reporting on specified elements, accounts, or items of a financial statement.

[11] Understand the auditor's reporting responsibility for compliance with contractual agreements or regulatory requirements related to financial statements.

[12] Understand the auditor's reporting responsibility for special-purpose financial presentations.

[13] Understand the auditor's reporting responsibility for financial information presented in prescribed forms or schedules that require a prescribed form of auditor's report.

RELEVANT ACCOUNTING AND AUDITING PRONOUNCEMENTS

APB Opinion No. 20, "Accounting Changes" (APB 20)

FASB Statement of Financial Accounting Standards No. 5, "Accounting for Contingencies" (FAS 5)

SAS No. 1, "Consistency of Application of Generally Accepted Accounting Principles" (AU 420)

SAS No. 1, "Part of Audit Performed by Other Independent Auditors" (AU 543)

SAS No. 8, "Other Information in Documents Containing Audited Financial Statements" (AU 550)

SAS No. 26, "Association with Financial Statements" (AU 504)

SAS No. 58, "Reports on Audited Financial Statements" (AU 508)

SAS No. 59, "The Auditor's Consideration of an Entity's Ability to Continue as a Going Concern" (AU 341)

SAS No. 62, "Special Reports" (AU 623)

SAS No. 69, "The Meaning of Present Fairly in Conformity with Generally Accepted Accounting Principles in the Independent Auditor's Report" (AU 411)

SAS No. 75, "Engagements to Apply Agreed-Upon Procedures to Specified Elements, Accounts, or Items of Financial Statements" (AU 622)

SAS No. 79, "Amendment to Statement on Auditing Standards No. 58, Reports on Audited Financial Statements" (AU 508)

SAS No. 87, "Restricting the Use of an Auditor's Report" (AU 532)

The fourth standard of reporting states that whenever the auditor is associated with financial statements, the report shall contain an opinion or, if an opinion cannot be issued, the reasons shall be disclosed in the report. An auditor is *associated* (see SAS No. 26, "Association with Financial Statements" [AU 504]) with financial statements when he or she has consented to the use of his or her name in a document such as an annual report. While other forms of services are covered by the term *association,* for the purposes of this chapter only audit-related engagements are considered.

The purpose of the fourth standard of reporting is to enable shareholders, bondholders, bankers, and other third parties who rely on the financial statements to determine the degree of responsibility taken by the auditor. To assist in accomplishing this goal, the auditing profession has adopted conventional wording for audit reports. This approach helps to prevent misunderstandings in the message being communicated by the auditor to the users of the financial statements. The reader is reminded that the financial statements are the representations of management and that the conformance of their presentation with GAAP is management's responsibility.

SAS No. 58, "Reports on Audited Financial Statements" (AU 508), provides authoritative guidance on audit reporting. 🐾

The Auditor's Standard Unqualified Audit Report

[LO 1]   Chapter 2 presented the auditor's standard unqualified audit report. This report is issued when the auditor has gathered sufficient evidence, the audit was performed in accordance with GAAS, and the financial statements conform to GAAP. Exhibit 18–1 contains the auditor's standard unqualified audit report, which was presented in Exhibit 2–3. This report contains seven elements: (1) the report title, (2) the addressee, (3) the introductory paragraph, (4) the scope paragraph, (5) the opinion paragraph, (6) the name of the auditor, and (7) the audit report date. The reader may wish to return to Chapter 2 to review the detailed discussion of the auditor's standard unqualified audit report.

Explanatory Language Added to the Standard Unqualified Audit Report

[LO 2]   Chapter 2 presented five situations that may require the auditor to modify the wording or add an explanatory paragraph to the standard unqualified audit report:

1. Opinion based in part on the report of another auditor.
2. Going concern.
3. Agreement with a departure from GAAP.
4. Lack of consistency.
5. Emphasis of a matter.

The first situation results in a modification of the wording for the three paragraphs included in the standard unqualified audit report. The other four situations lead to the addition of an explanatory paragraph that *follows* the opinion paragraph without any modifications to the wording of the introductory, scope, or opinion paragraphs. The audit reports that are issued for these situations are still unqualified opinions and are discussed in this section.

EXHIBIT 18-1

The Auditor's Standard Unqualified Audit Report— Comparative Financial Statements

Title:	Report of Ernst & Young LLP, Independent Auditors
Addressee:	The Board of Directors and Stockholders, Intel Corporation
Introductory paragraph:	We have audited the accompanying consolidated balance sheets of Intel Corporation as of December 27, 1997, and December 28, 1996, and the related consolidated statements of income, stockholders' equity, and cash flows for each of the three years in the period ended December 27, 1997. These financial statements are the responsibility of the Company's management. Our responsibility is to express an opinion on these financial statements based on our audits.
Scope paragraph:	We conducted our audits in accordance with generally accepted auditing standards. Those standards require that we plan and perform the audit to obtain reasonable assurance about whether the financial statements are free of material misstatement. An audit includes examining, on a test basis, evidence supporting the amounts and disclosures in the financial statements. An audit also includes assessing the accounting principles used and significant estimates made by management, as well as evaluating the overall financial statement presentation. We believe that our audits provide a reasonable basis for our opinion.
Opinion paragraph:	In our opinion, the consolidated financial statements referred to above present fairly, in all material respects, the consolidated financial position of Intel Corporation at December 27, 1997, and December 28, 1996, and the consolidated results of its operations and its cash flows for each of the three years in the period ended December 27, 1997, in conformity with generally accepted accounting principles.
Name of the auditor:	*Ernst & Young LLP*
	San Jose, California
Date of report:	January 12, 1998

Opinion Based in Part on the Report of Another Auditor

On some audit engagements, parts of the audit may be completed by another CPA firm. For example, in reporting on consolidated financial statements, one of the subsidiaries may be audited by other auditors. In such cases, the auditor for the parent company must be satisfied that he or she is the principal auditor. This is normally determined by the materiality of the portion of the financial statements audited in relation to the portion of the consolidated financial statements audited by the other independent auditors.

The principal auditor at this point must decide whether to refer to the other auditors in the report. The principal auditor must first assess the *professional reputation* and *independence* of the other auditors. If the principal auditor is satisfied as to the professional reputation and independence of the other auditors and their audit work, an opinion may be expressed without referring in the audit report to the work of the other auditors.

However, in most situations, when the subsidiary represents a material amount in the consolidated financial statements, the principal auditor

TABLE 18–1	The Effect on the Audit Report When Part of the Audit Is Completed by Another Auditor

Level of Responsibility of Principal Auditor	*Effect on Audit Report*
Full responsibility	No reference to other auditors
Shared responsibility	Reference made to other auditors

EXHIBIT 18–2

Opinion Based in Part on the Report of Another Auditor

Independent Auditors' Report

To the Stockholders
Collins Company

We have audited the consolidated balance sheets of Collins Company as of December 31, 2000 and 1999, and the related consolidated statements of income, retained earnings, and cash flows for the years then ended. These financial statements are the responsibility of the Company's management. Our responsibility is to express an opinion on these financial statements based on our audits. *We did not audit the financial statements of Furillo Company, a wholly owned subsidiary, whose statements reflect total assets of $25,450,000 and $23,750,000 as of December 31, 2000 and 1999, respectively, and total revenues of $42,781,000 and $40,553,000 for the years then ended. Those statements were audited by other auditors whose report has been furnished to us, and our opinion, insofar as it relates to the amounts included for Furillo Company, is based solely on the report of the other auditors.*

We conducted our audits in accordance with generally accepted auditing standards. Those standards require that we plan and perform the audit to obtain reasonable assurance about whether the financial statements are free of material misstatement. An audit includes examining, on a test basis, evidence supporting the amounts and disclosures in the financial statements. An audit also includes assessing the accounting principles used and significant estimates made by management, as well as evaluating the overall financial statement presentation. We believe that our audits *and the report of the other auditors* provide a reasonable basis for our opinion.

In our opinion, *based on our audits and the report of the other auditors,* the consolidated financial statements referred to above present fairly, in all material respects, the financial position of Collins Company as of December 31, 2000 and 1999, and the results of its operations and its cash flows for the years then ended in conformity with generally accepted accounting principles.

Agassi, Connors, Evert & Co.
February 12, 2001

refers to the other auditors. In referencing the other auditors, the principal auditor is sharing responsibility for the audit report. Table 18–1 summarizes the effect on the audit report of the level of responsibility assumed by the principal auditor.

The portion of the consolidated financial statements, (assets and revenues) audited by the other auditors is disclosed in the report. Exhibit 18–2 is an example of a report in which the principal auditor has referred to the other auditors. Generally, the other auditors are not referenced by name in the report. (For illustrative purposes only, the new wording is shown in italics.)

If the other auditors' report is other than a standard unqualified audit report, the principal auditor needs to determine the nature of the departure and its significance in relation to the *overall* financial statements. If the departure is not material, the principal auditor need not refer to the departure in his or her report. If the principal auditor assesses that the departure is material, it may be necessary to refer to the other auditors' qualification.

Going Concern

A basic assumption that underlies financial reporting is that an entity will continue as a going concern. SAS No. 59, "The Auditor's Consideration of an Entity's Ability to Continue as a Going Concern" (AU 341), states that the auditor has a responsibility to evaluate whether there is substantial doubt about the entity's ability to continue as a going concern for a reasonable period of time, not to exceed one year beyond the date of the financial statements being audited.

When there is substantial doubt about an entity's ability to continue as a going concern, the auditor should modify the standard unqualified report by adding an explanatory paragraph after the opening paragraph. A detailed discussion of the audit and reporting issues related to a going-concern situation is presented later in the chapter.

Auditor Agrees with a Departure from Generally Accepted Accounting Principles

The auditor's standard unqualified audit report states that the financial statements conform to GAAP. However, in unusual circumstances financial statements may be misleading if a promulgated accounting principle was followed. Rule 203 of the Code of Professional Conduct allows the auditor, in such circumstances, to issue an unqualified opinion. However, an explanatory paragraph should be added to the report. The explanatory paragraph should describe the departure, the approximate effects of the departure, if practicable, and the reasons that compliance with the accounting principle results in misleading financial statements. From a practical viewpoint, this situation seldom occurs.

Lack of Consistency

The auditor's standard unqualified audit report implies that the comparability of the financial statements is not affected by changes in accounting principles or that any change is immaterial. Accounting Principles Board Opinion No. 20, "Accounting Changes," governs the accounting for such changes in accounting principles. From the auditor's perspective, accounting changes can be categorized into changes that affect consistency and those that do not affect consistency.

Changes Affecting Consistency   If the change in accounting principle or in the method of its application materially affects the comparability of the financial statements, and the auditor concurs with the change, the auditor should discuss the change in an explanatory paragraph. Auditing standards (AU 420) refer to the following accounting changes as affecting comparability and requiring an explanatory paragraph:

EXHIBIT 18–3

Unqualified Report with an Explanatory Paragraph for a Lack of Consistency
Independent Auditor's Report
[*Standard wording for the introductory, scope, and opinion paragraphs*]
As discussed in Note 7 to the financial statements, the Company changed its method of computing depreciation in 2000.

1. ***Change in accounting principle.*** An example would be a change from straight-line depreciation to an accelerated method for depreciating equipment.
2. ***Change in reporting entity.*** An example would be the consolidation of a major subsidiary's financial statements with the parent company's financial statements in the previous year and accounting for the subsidiary on a cost or equity basis in the current year.
3. ***Correction of an error in principle.*** This refers to a situation in which a client has used an accounting principle that is not acceptable (for example, replacement cost for inventory) in prior years but changes to an acceptable accounting principle (such as, FIFO) in the current year.

Exhibit 18–3 is an example of an unqualified opinion with an explanatory paragraph for an accounting change that results in a lack of consistency.

Changes Not Affecting Consistency   Other changes may affect comparability but do not affect consistency. These include

1. ***Change in accounting estimate.*** A change in the service lives for depreciable assets is an example of a change in estimate.
2. ***Correction of an error that does not involve an accounting principle.*** An example would be a mathematical mistake in a previously issued financial statement.
3. ***Change in classification and reclassification.*** If an item was included in operating expenses last year and included in administrative expenses in the current year, this would be a change in classification.
4. ***Change expected to have a material future effect.*** This would be a change in accounting principle that has an immaterial effect in the current year but is expected to have a material effect in future years.

Changes that do not affect consistency are normally disclosed in the footnotes to the financial statements but do not require recognition in the auditor's report.

Emphasis of a Matter

Under certain circumstances an auditor may want to emphasize a specific matter regarding the financial statements even though he or she intends to express an unqualified opinion. This information should be presented in an explanatory paragraph. Some examples of situations that might cause the auditor to add an explanatory paragraph are significant related-party transactions and important events occurring after the balance sheet date.

Departures from an Unqualified Audit Report

The fourth standard of reporting allows the auditor to assume differing degrees of responsibility on financial statements. The auditor can issue three types of audit reports that depart from the unqualified audit report. The conditions for issuing such reports are discussed next. Figure 18–1 reproduces the overview of audit reporting that was presented in Figure 2–3.

FIGURE 18–1

An Overview of Audit Reporting

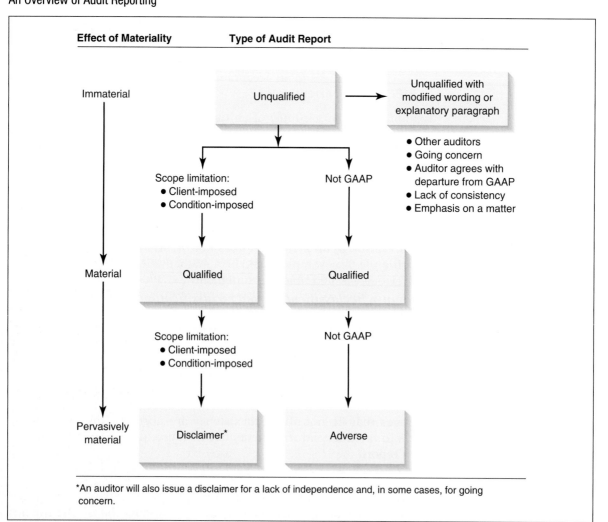

*An auditor will also issue a disclaimer for a lack of independence and, in some cases, for going concern.

Conditions for Departure

[LO 3]

There are three basic reasons that an auditor may be unable to express an unqualified opinion:

1. ***Scope limitation.*** A scope limitation results from a lack of evidence, such as an inability to conduct an audit procedure considered necessary.
2. ***Departure from GAAP.*** The financial statements are affected by a departure from GAAP.
3. ***Lack of independence of the auditor.*** The auditor must comply with the second general standard and the Code of Professional Conduct in order to issue an unqualified opinion.

Other Types of Audit Reports

[LO 4]

There are three types of reports other than unqualified:

1. ***Qualified.*** The auditor's opinion is qualified because of either a scope limitation or a departure from GAAP, but the overall financial statements present fairly.
2. ***Disclaimer.*** The auditor disclaims an opinion on the financial statements either because there is insufficient competent evidence to form an opinion on the overall financial statements or because there is a lack of independence.
3. ***Adverse.*** The auditor's opinion states that the financial statements do not present fairly in conformity with GAAP because the departure materially affects the overall financial statements.

The choice of which audit report to issue depends on the condition and the materiality of the departure.

The Effect of Materiality

[LO 5]

The concept of materiality plays a major role in the auditor's choice of audit reports. If the condition that might lead to the departure is judged by the auditor to be immaterial, a standard unqualified audit report can be issued. As the materiality of the condition increases, the auditor must judge the effect of the item on the *overall* financial statements.

When the auditor is faced with a scope limitation, the assessment of the omitted procedure(s) should consider the nature and magnitude of the potential effects of the item and its significance to the overall financial statements. If the potential effects relate to many items in the financial statements or if the effect of the item is so significant that the overall financial statements are affected, the auditor is more likely to issue a disclaimer than a qualified report. In other words, the *pervasiveness* of the item on the financial statements determines whether the auditor should issue a qualified opinion or disclaim an opinion. For example, suppose an auditor is unable to perform certain audit procedures considered necessary to determining the fairness of a client's inventory balance. Assume further that inventory represents approximately 10 percent of total assets. In such a situation, the auditor would probably consider the item material, but not to the extent that the overall financial statements are not presented fairly, and would most likely issue a qualified opinion. However, if inventory represents a much larger percentage of total assets (such as 30 to 50 percent), the effect is highly material and would lead to the issuance of a disclaimer.

Judgments concerning the effects of a departure from GAAP are not much different. If the departure from GAAP is immaterial, the auditor should issue an unqualified opinion. If the departure from GAAP is material and the overall financial statements still present fairly, the auditor should issue a qualified opinion. If the departure is so pervasive that its effects are highly material, the auditor should issue an adverse opinion. For example, suppose that a client accounted for leased assets as operating leases when proper accounting required that the leases be capitalized. If a client had only one small piece of equipment that was treated in such a manner, the auditor would probably issue an unqualified opinion because the item would be immaterial. However, if the client had many leased assets that were accounted for as operating leases instead of capitalized leases, the auditor would normally issue a qualified or adverse opinion, depending on the pervasiveness of the problem.

Materiality is not a factor that determines an auditor's independence. When an auditor is not independent, a disclaimer should be issued.

Discussion of Conditions Requiring Other Types of Reports

Scope Limitation

A scope limitation results from an inability to obtain sufficient competent evidence about some component of the financial statements. This occurs because the auditor is unable to apply all the audit procedures considered necessary. Such restrictions on the scope of the audit may be imposed by the client or by the circumstances of the engagement. Auditors should be particularly cautious when a client limits the scope of the engagement. In such a situation, the client may be trying to prevent the auditor from discovering material misstatements. Auditing standards suggest that when restrictions imposed by the client significantly limit the scope of the engagement, the auditor should consider disclaiming an opinion on the financial statements. However, if the auditor can overcome a scope limitation by performing alternative procedures, a standard unqualified audit report can be issued.

A number of these types of situations can occur on audit engagements. For example, auditing standards require that the auditor observe inventory (AU 331). However, circumstances may prevent the auditor from doing so. Suppose, for example, that the auditor is not engaged to conduct the audit until *after* year-end. In such a circumstance, the auditor may not be able to perform a number of audit procedures (like observing inventory). If such deficiencies in evidence cannot be overcome by other auditing procedures, the auditor will have to issue a qualified opinion or a disclaimer. Exhibit 18–4 is an example of a disclaimer of opinion because of this type of scope limitation.

Another example occurs when a client requests that the auditor not confirm accounts receivable because of concerns about creating conflicts with customers over amounts owed. If the auditor is satisfied that the client's reasons for not confirming are legitimate and is unable to apply al-

EXHIBIT 18–4

Disclaimer of Opinion—Scope Limitation

Independent Auditor's Report

We were engaged to audit the accompanying balance sheet of Kosar Company as of December 31, 2000 and 1999, and the related statements of income, retained earnings, and cash flows for the years then ended. These financial statements are the responsibility of the Company's management.

[Scope paragraph of standard report should be omitted.]

We were unable to observe the taking of physical inventories stated in the accompanying financial statements at $4,550,000 as of December 31, 2000, and at $4,275,000 as of December 31, 1999, since those dates were prior to the time we were engaged as auditors for the company. The Company's records do not permit the application of other auditing procedures regarding the existence of inventories.

Since we did not observe physical inventories and we were not able to apply other auditing procedures to satisfy ourselves as to inventory quantities, the scope of our work was not sufficient to enable us to express, and we do not express, an opinion on these financial statements.

EXHIBIT 18–5

Qualified Report—Scope Limitation

Independent Auditor's Report

[Standard wording for the introductory paragraph]

Except as discussed in the following paragraph, we conducted our audits in accordance with generally accepted standards. Those standards require that . . . *[same wording as for the remainder of the standard scope paragraph]*.

We were unable to obtain audited financial statements supporting the Company's investment in a foreign affiliate stated at $12,500,000 and $11,700,000 at December 31, 2000 and 1999, respectively, or its equity in earnings of that affiliate of $1,200,000 and $1,050,000, which is included in net income for the years then ended as described in Note 10 to the financial statements; nor were we able to satisfy ourselves as to the carrying value of the investment in the foreign affiliate or the equity in its earnings by other auditing procedures.

In our opinion, except for the effects of such adjustments, if any, as might have been determined to be necessary had we been able to examine evidence regarding the foreign affiliate and earnings, the financial statements referred to . . . *[same wording as for the remainder of the standard opinion paragraph]*.

ternative audit procedures to determine fairness of the receivables, he or she would qualify the opinion or disclaim an opinion.

Finally, the auditor may be unable to obtain audited financial statements for a long-term investment that is accounted for using the equity method. Exhibit 18–5 is an example of a qualified report for such a scope limitation.

Note that in both examples the paragraph that explains the scope limitation is presented *before* the opinion or disclaimer paragraph.

EXHIBIT 18–6

Qualified Report—Not in Conformity with Generally Accepted Accounting Principles

Independent Auditor's Report

[Standard wording for the introductory and scope paragraphs]

The Company has excluded, from property and debt in the accompanying balance sheets, certain lease obligations that, in our opinion, should be capitalized in order to conform with generally accepted accounting principles. If these lease obligations were capitalized, property would be increased by $7,500,000 and $7,200,000, long-term debt by $6,900,000 and $6,600,000, and retained earnings by $1,420,000 and $1,290,000 as of December 31, 2000 and 1999, respectively. Additionally, net income would be increased by $250,000 and $220,000 and earnings per share would be increased by $.25 and $.22, respectively, for the years then ended.

In our opinion, except for the effects of not capitalizing certain lease obligations as discussed in the preceding paragraph, the financial statements referred to . . . *[same wording as for the remainder of the standard opinion paragraph]*.

Statements Not in Conformity with GAAP

If the financial statements are materially affected by an unacceptable departure from GAAP, the auditor should express a qualified or adverse opinion. Examples of these types of departures are an accounting principle that is not acceptable, inadequate disclosure, or a lack of justification for a change in accounting principle.

When the financial statements contain an accounting principle that is not acceptable, the auditor should issue a qualified or adverse opinion depending on materiality. When the auditor expresses a qualified opinion, a separate explanatory paragraph should be added to the report *before* the opinion paragraph. The explanatory paragraph should disclose the effects of the departure on the financial statements. Exhibit 18–6 is an example of a report that has been qualified because of the use of an unacceptable accounting principle.

If the departure's effect is so pervasive that the financial statements taken as a whole are not presented fairly, the auditor should issue an adverse opinion. When an adverse opinion is issued, the auditor should add an explanatory paragraph that *precedes* the opinion paragraph. The explanatory paragraph should discuss the reasons for the adverse opinion and the effects of the departure on the financial statements. The opinion paragraph is modified to state that the financial statements *do not present fairly* in conformity with GAAP. Exhibit 18–7 is an example of an adverse report.

If a client fails to disclose information in the financial statements or footnotes that is required by GAAP, the auditor should issue a qualified or adverse report. The auditor should provide the information in the report, if practicable, unless omission is allowed by auditing standards. One situation in which the auditor would *not* have to provide the information is where the client has declined to include a statement of cash flows. Auditing standards do not require that the auditor prepare a statement when one has been omitted by the client. Exhibit 18–8 is a qualified report for inadequate disclosure.

EXHIBIT 18–7

Adverse Opinion—Not in Conformity with Generally Accepted Accounting Principles

Independent Auditor's Report

[Standard wording for the introductory and scope paragraphs]

As discussed in Note 6 to the financial statements, the Company carries its property, plant, and equipment accounts at appraisal values and determines depreciation on the basis of such values. Generally accepted accounting principles require that property, plant, and equipment be stated at an amount not in excess of cost, reduced by depreciation based on such amount. Because of the departures from generally accepted accounting principles identified above, as of December 31, 2000 and 1999, respectively, inventories have been increased $1,500,000 and $1,340,000 by inclusion in manufacturing overhead of depreciation in excess of that based on cost; property, plant, and equipment, less accumulated depreciation, is carried at $13,475,000 and $12,950,000 in excess of an amount based on the cost to the Company. For the years ended December 31, 2000 and 1999, cost of goods sold has been increased $4,200,000 and $3,600,000, respectively, because of the effects of the depreciation accounting referred to above, resulting in a decrease in net income of $2,520,000 and $2,160,000, respectively.

In our opinion, because of the effects of the matters discussed in the preceding paragraph, the financial statements referred to above do not present fairly, in conformity with generally accepted accounting principles, the financial position of Morton Company as of December 31, 2000 and 1999, or the results of its operation or its cash flows for the years then ended.

EXHIBIT 18–8

Qualified Report—Inadequate Disclosure

Independent Auditor's Report

We have audited the accompanying balance sheets of O'Dea Company as of December 31, 2000 and 1999, and the related statements of income and retained earnings for the years ended. These financial statements are the responsibility of the Company's management. Our responsibility is to express an opinion on these financial statements based on our audit.

[Standard wording for the scope paragraph]

The Company declined to present a statement of cash flows for the years ended December 31, 2000 and 1999. Presentation of such statement summarizing the Company's operating, investing, and financing activities is required by generally accepted accounting principles.

In our opinion, except that the omission of a statement of cash flows results in an incomplete presentation as explained in the preceding paragraph, the financial statements referred to . . . *[same wording as for the remainder of the standard opinion paragraph].*

Auditor Not Independent

Much of the value that users of an auditor's report place on the report is based on the assumption of an unbiased relationship between the auditor and the client. There are few situations in which an auditor would be engaged to audit a client and independence between the two parties would not exist. It is possible that an auditor could be engaged by a client, believing that all members of the audit team were independent of the client. At

EXHIBIT 18–9

Disclaimer of Opinion When the Auditor Is Not Independent
Accountant's Report
We are not independent with respect to Jordan Company, Inc., and the accompanying balance sheet as of December 31, 2000, and the related statements of earnings, retained earnings, and cash flows for the year then ended were not audited by us; accordingly, we do not express an opinion on them.

the end of the engagement, it might come to the audit partner's attention that a member of the audit team had a financial interest in the client. This situation might jeopardize the audit firm's independence and result in the issuance of a report similar to the one shown in Exhibit 18–9.

If an auditor is not independent, a disclaimer of opinion should be issued. In the disclaimer, the auditor should *not* state the reasons for the lack of independence nor describe any audit procedures performed. Note in Exhibit 18–9 that the title of the report does not contain the word *independent.* A title is not required for the disclaimer.

Special Reporting Issues

In addition to the types of audit reports just discussed, auditors often encounter a number of special reporting issues that affect the audit report. Four topics are covered in the remainder of this chapter:

- Reports on comparative financial statements.
- Other information in documents containing audited financial statements.
- Going-concern evaluation.
- Special reports.

Reports on Comparative Financial Statements

[LO 6]   The fourth standard of reporting requires that the auditor either express an opinion on the financial statements taken as a whole or assert that an opinion cannot be expressed. When a client presents financial statements for the current period and one or more prior periods, the auditor must update the audit report on the financial statements presented on a comparative basis. Exhibit 18–1 shows an unqualified standard audit report on Intel's comparative financial statements that covers the balance sheets for two years and statements of income, stockholders' equity, and cash flows for three years. Normally, the date of the auditor's report on the comparative statements is the date of the most recently completed audit.

During the current-year audit, the auditor should be alert for events that may affect prior-period financial statements. Three common situations are discussed.

EXHIBIT 18–10

Comparative Report—Unqualified in Prior Years but Qualified in Current Year for Not Being in Conformity with Generally Accepted Accounting Principles

Independent Auditor's Report

[Standard wording for the introductory and scope paragraphs]

The Company has excluded, from property and debt in the accompanying 2000 balance sheet, certain lease obligations that were entered into in 2000 which, in our opinion, should be capitalized in order to conform with generally accepted accounting principles. If these lease obligations were capitalized, property would be increased by $7,500,000, long-term debt by $6,900,000, and retained earnings by $1,420,000 as of December 31, 2000; net income would be increased by $250,000 and earnings per share would be increased by $.25, respectively, for the year then ended.

In our opinion, except for the effects on the 2000 financial statements of not capitalizing certain lease obligations as discussed in the preceding paragraph, the financial statements referred to . . . *[same wording as for the remainder of the standard opinion paragraph]*.

Different Reports on Comparative Financial Statements

A number of situations may cause the auditor to express different reports on the comparative financial statements. One example is when the auditor expressed a standard unqualified opinion on prior years' financial statements but qualifies the current-year opinion. Exhibit 18–10 is an example of a report issued when a company decided not to capitalize certain lease obligations in the current year. In prior years, the company did not have capitalized lease obligations, so the financial statements for those years conformed to GAAP.

Another common situation occurs when the report on the current year is unqualified but prior-period financial statements were qualified or were disclaimed. Exhibit 18–11 is an example of a report issued when an auditor was hired subsequent to the observation of the physical inventory in the prior year and a disclaimer of opinion was issued for that period. In the current year, the auditor was able to conduct the audit without any scope limitation and issues an unqualified opinion.

A Change in Report on the Prior-Period Financial Statements

During the course of the current year's audit, the auditor may encounter circumstances or events that require updating the report issued on the prior-period financial statements. For example, the auditor may have issued a qualified or adverse opinion in the prior year because the client had not followed GAAP. If the client conforms to GAAP in the current year and restates the prior-period results, the auditor should express an unqualified opinion on the comparative financial statements. Exhibit 18–12 is an example of such a report. Note that the paragraph that precedes the opinion paragraph contains the date of the previous report, the type of opinion previously issued, the reasons for the previous report being issued, and mention of the fact that the current report differs from the previously issued report. In this example, after the client conformed to GAAP in accounting for property, plant, and equipment and for deferred taxes and restated the prior-period financial statements, the auditor issued an unqualified report for both the current and prior years. The reader may ask why an explanatory paragraph

---

Comparative Report When the Prior Year Was Disclaimed for a Scope Limitation and the Current Year Received an Unqualified Opinion

Independent Auditor's Report

[*Standard wording for the introductory paragraph*]

Except as explained in the following paragraph, we conducted our audits in accordance with generally accepted auditing standards . . . [*same wording as for the remainder of the standard scope paragraph*].

We did not observe the taking of the physical inventory as of December 31, 1998, since that date was prior to our appointment as auditors for the Company, and we were unable to satisfy ourselves regarding inventory quantities by means of other auditing procedures. Inventory amounts as of December 31, 1998, enter into the determination of net income and cash flows for the year ended December 31, 1999.

Because of the matter discussed in the preceding paragraph, the scope of our work was not sufficient to enable us to express, and we do not express, an opinion on the results of operations and cash flows for the year ended December 31, 1999.

In our opinion, the balance sheets of RUUD Rubber Company as of December 31, 2000 and 1999, and the related statements of income, retained earnings, and cash flows for the year ended December 31, 2000, present fairly, in all material respects, the financial position of RUUD Rubber Company as of December 31, 2000 and 1999, and the results of its operations and its cash flows for the year ended December 31, 2000, in conformity with generally accepted accounting principles.

Change in the Report on the Prior-Period Financial Statements

Independent Auditor's Report

[*Standard wording for the introductory and scope paragraphs*]

In our report dated March 1, 2000, we expressed an opinion that the 1999 financial statements did not fairly present financial position, results of operations, and cash flows in conformity with generally accepted accounting principles because of two departures from such principles: (1) the Company carried its property, plant, and equipment at appraisal values and provided for depreciation on the basis of such values, and (2) the Company did not provide for deferred income taxes with respect to differences between income for financial reporting purposes and taxable income. As described in Note 8, the Company has changed its method of accounting for these items and restated its 1999 financial statements to conform with generally accepted accounting principles. Accordingly, our present opinion on the 1999 financial statements, as presented herein, is different from that expressed in our previous report.

[*Standard wording for the opinion paragraph*]

---

is not added after the opinion paragraph to reflect the facts (1) that a change from an accounting principle that is not generally accepted to one that is generally accepted is a correction of an error and (2) that such a change requires recognition in the auditor's report as to consistency. Since the paragraph included in Exhibit 18–12 contains all the information required by the explanatory paragraph on consistency, a separate explanatory paragraph is not necessary.

EXHIBIT 18–13

Example of an Unqualified Report on Comparative Financial Statements When the Predecessor's Report Is Not Included

Independent Auditor's Report

We have audited the balance sheet of Kinserdal Copper Company as of December 31, 2000, and the related statements of income, retained earnings, and cash flows for the year then ended. These financial statements are the responsibility of the Company's management. Our responsibility is to express an opinion on these financial statements based on our audit. The financial statements of Kinserdal Copper Company as of December 31, 1999, were audited by other auditors, whose report dated March 31, 2000, expressed an unqualified opinion on those statements.

[Standard wording for the scope paragraph]

In our opinion, the 2000 financial statements referred to above present fairly, in all material respects, the financial position of Kinserdal Copper Company as of December 31, 2000, and the results of its operations and its cash flows for the year ended in conformity with generally accepted accounting principles.

Report by a Predecessor Auditor

When an entity has changed auditors, the predecessor auditor can reissue, at the request of the client, his or her report on the financial statements of the prior period, when those statements are presented on a comparative basis. In such a situation, the predecessor auditor must determine if the previously issued report is still appropriate, given the current circumstances. The predecessor auditor should do the following before reissuing the report:

1. Read the financial statements of the current period.
2. Compare the prior-period financial statements reported on with the current-year financial statements.
3. Obtain a letter of representations from the current-year or successor auditor.

The letter of representations should indicate whether the successor auditor discovered any material items that might affect, or require disclosure in, the financial statements reported on by the predecessor auditor. If the predecessor auditor is satisfied that the financial statements reported on should not be revised, the audit report should be reissued using the date of the previous report.

In the event that the predecessor auditor becomes aware of circumstances or events that may affect the previously issued financial statements, he or she should make inquiries and perform any procedures considered necessary. For example, the successor auditor may discover errors indicating that the prior year's financial statements were materially misstated. If the financial statements are restated, the predecessor auditor should revise the report and dual date the reissued report.

If the prior-period financial statements have been audited but the predecessor auditor's report will not be included, the successor auditor should indicate in the introductory paragraph that the financial statements for the prior period were audited by other auditors and mention the date and the type of report issued by the predecessor auditor. Exhibit 18–13 is an example of a report issued when the predecessor's report was unqualified.

If the predecessor's report was not standard, the successor auditor should describe the nature of and reasons for the explanatory paragraph added to the predecessor's report. For example, the introductory paragraph of the successor's report might include the following wording:

> The financial statements of Kinserdal Copper Company as of December 31, 1999, were audited by other auditors, whose report dated March 31, 2000, on those statements included an explanatory paragraph that described a change in the depreciation method discussed in Note 10 to those financial statements.

Other Information in Documents Containing Audited Financial Statements

[LO 7] A client may publish documents such as annual reports and registration statements that contain other information in addition to the audited financial statements and the audit report. SAS No. 8, "Other Information in Documents Containing Audited Financial Statements" (AU 550), provides guidance for the auditor's consideration of other information contained in (1) annual reports of entities and (2) other documents to which the auditor devotes attention at the client's request.

The auditor has no responsibility beyond the financial information contained in the report, and he or she has no obligation to perform any audit procedures to corroborate the other information. However, SAS No. 8 requires that the auditor read the other information and consider whether such information is consistent with the information contained in the audited financial statements. For example, the audited financial statements may show a 10 percent increase in sales and a 5 percent increase in net income. If the president's letter that is included in the annual report states that sales were up 15 percent and net income increased by 12 percent, a material inconsistency would exist. The auditor would then have to determine whether the financial statements or the president's letter required revision. If the financial statements were correct, the auditor would request that the president change the other information. If the other information were not revised, the auditor should include an explanatory paragraph in the audit report, withhold the report, or withdraw from the engagement.

Going-Concern Evaluation

[LO 8] This section discusses how the auditor evaluates whether a client will be a going concern and the auditor's required reporting responsibilities.

Steps in the Going-Concern Evaluation

The auditor should follow three overall steps in making the going-concern evaluation:

1. Consider whether the results of audit procedures performed during the planning, performance, and completion of the audit indicate whether there is substantial doubt about the entity's ability to continue as a going concern for a reasonable period of time (one year).
2. If there is substantial doubt, the auditor should obtain information about management's plans to mitigate the going-concern problem and assess the likelihood that such plans can be implemented.

TABLE 18–2	Normal Audit Procedures That May Identify Conditions and Events Indicating Going-Concern Problems

- Analytical procedures.
- Review of subsequent events.
- Tests for compliance with debt agreements.
- Reading of board of directors and other committee minutes.
- Inquiry of legal counsel.
- Confirmations with parties on arrangements to provide or maintain financial support.

3. If the auditor concludes, after evaluating management's plans, that there is substantial doubt about the ability of the entity to continue as a going concern, he or she should consider the adequacy of the disclosures about the entity's ability to continue and include an explanatory paragraph in the audit report.

These steps are discussed next.

Identifying and Assessing Going-Concern Problems

Audit procedures are normally sufficient to identify conditions and events that indicate going-concern problems. Table 18–2 provides examples of audit procedures that may identify such conditions or events. SAS No. 59 identifies four major categories of such conditions or events: *negative financial trends, other financial difficulties, internal problems,* and *external matters.*

Negative financial trends consist of poor results from operations and adverse financial ratios. Analytical procedures during the planning phase of the audit may be particularly helpful in identifying negative financial trends. Table 18–3 lists a number of important financial conditions and ratios that prior audit research[1] has shown to be good indicators of financial distress that can lead to a going-concern report. If the entity being evaluated meets a number of these financial conditions and also has adverse ratios, the auditor may conclude that the entity is not a going concern.

Conditions or events that may occur in the other three categories identified by SAS No. 59 are shown in Table 18–4. Other financial difficulties are particularly important for the going-concern assessment. For example, if an entity has violated certain debt covenants or is in default on its debt, the debtholders may call for immediate payment. In such circumstances, the entity may be unable to meet its cash requirements and may have to seek bankruptcy protection or liquidation. Similarly, internal matters such as work stoppages may have severe consequences on the entity. In numerous recent instances strikes have caused entities to seek bankruptcy protection.

---

[1]J. Mutchler, "Auditors' Perceptions of the Going-Concern Opinion Decision," *Auditing: A Journal of Practice and Theory* (Spring 1984), pp. 17–30; J. Mutchler, "Empirical Evidence Regarding the Auditor's Going-Concern Opinion Decision," *Auditing: A Journal of Practice and Theory* (Fall 1986), pp. 148–63.

TABLE 18–3   Financial Conditions and Ratios That Indicate Financial Distress

Financial Conditions
- Recurring operating losses.
- Current-year deficit.
- Accumulated deficits.
- Negative net worth.
- Negative working capital.
- Negative cash flow.
- Negative income from operations.
- Inability to meet interest payments.

Ratios
- Net worth/total liabilities.
- Working capital from operations/total liabilities.
- Current assets/current liabilities.
- Total long-term liabilities/total assets.
- Total liabilities/total assets.
- Net income before taxes/net sales.

TABLE 18–4   Other Conditions and Events Indicating a Problem with the Going-Concern Assumption

Other Financial Difficulties
- Default on loans.
- Dividends in arrears.
- Restructuring of debt.
- Denial of trade credit by suppliers.
- No additional sources of financing.

Internal Matters
- Work stoppages.
- Uneconomic long-term commitments.
- Dependence on the success of one particular project.

External Matters
- Legal proceedings.
- Loss of a major customer or supplier.
- Loss of a key franchise, license, or patent.

Finally, external matters may cause an entity to cease being a going concern. For example, the loss of a single major customer has been known to cause a high-technology entity to face severe financial difficulties.

Consideration of Management's Plans

Once conditions have been identified that indicate substantial doubt about the ability of the entity to continue, the auditor should consider management's plans for dealing with the adverse effects of the conditions or events. The auditor should consider the following actions by management:

- Plans to dispose of assets.
- Plans to borrow money or restructure debt.
- Plans to reduce or delay expenditures.
- Plans to increase ownership equity.

For example, management may attempt to sell assets to pay off debt or dispose of operations that are losing money. Management may negotiate with creditors in order to restructure debt or seek additional financing. Frequently, management will develop a plan to reduce wages or cut back the workforce. When evaluating management's plans, the auditor should perform audit procedures to obtain evidence about the elements of the plans and their likelihood of success. This will require examining the assumptions used by management in developing such plans.

Reporting on Going-Concern Problems

If the auditor concludes, after considering management's plans, that there is substantial doubt about the entity's ability to continue as a going concern for a reasonable period, the auditor should consider the possible effects on the financial statements and the related disclosures. Additionally, the audit report should include an explanatory paragraph such as the one shown in Exhibit 18–14. The auditor may also disclaim an opinion on the entity. Exhibit 18–15 is an example of the types of footnote disclosures that are normally included with the financial statements and referenced in the auditor's report. If the entity's disclosures with respect to the entity's ability to continue as a going concern are inadequate, a departure from GAAP exists. If a client received a going-concern report in the prior period and the doubt

---

EXHIBIT 18–14

Unqualified Audit Report with an Explanatory Paragraph for Going-Concern Problems

Independent Auditor's Report

[Standard introductory, scope, and opinion paragraphs]

The accompanying financial statements have been prepared assuming that the Company will continue as a going concern. As discussed in Note 6 to the financial statements, the Company has suffered recurring losses from operations and has a net capital deficiency that raises substantial doubt about its ability to continue as a going concern. Management's plans in regard to these matters are also described in Note 6. The financial statements do not include any adjustments that might result from the outcome of this uncertainty.

EXHIBIT 18–15

Example of Footnote Disclosures for an Entity with Going-Concern Problems

The Company's financial position raises substantial doubt about its ability to continue as a going concern. As of September 30, 2000, the Company believes that cash on hand, cash generated by operations, and available bank borrowings will be sufficient to pay trade creditors and operating expenses in the ordinary course of business but will not be sufficient to meet all of its bank and subordinate debt obligations for the next 12 to 24 months. On July 25, 2000, the Company filed a registration statement with the Securities and Exchange Commission outlining a comprehensive debt restructuring designed to reduce the Company's debt and debt-service requirements by the exchange of existing subordinate debt for new senior subordinated debt and shares of Class A common stock. Pending completion of the comprehensive debt restructuring, the Company decided to suspend payment of interest on its subordinated debt, including the approximately $4.5 million of interest which was due on May 16, 2000, to holders of its 12.5% subordinated notes due 2005, the approximately $15.8 million of interest which was due on June 15, 2000, to holders of its 13.5% subordinated notes due 2007, and the approximately $9.9 million of interest which was due on August 15, 2000, to holders of its 12.75% subordinated debentures due 2008. The Company intends to continue to pay the monthly interest due on its bank debt and the interest and principal due on its other senior debt obligations as well as to pay operating expenses and trade creditors in the ordinary course of business.

The suspension of interest payments on the subordinated notes resulted in an event of default under the bank credit agreement and under the indentures relating to the subordinated notes. As a result, the Company is prohibited from making interest or principal payments on any of its subordinated debt.

concerning going concern is removed in the current period, the explanatory paragraph included with the prior year's audit report is not included with the auditor's report covering the comparative financial statements.

Special Reports

The first standard of reporting requires the auditor to report on whether the financial statements conform to GAAP. Auditors, however, are sometimes engaged to report on financial statements not prepared on the basis of GAAP. Auditors may also be engaged to report on parts of the financial statements or on a client's compliance with contractual agreements or regulatory requirements. SAS No. 62, "Special Reports" (AU 623), provides the auditor with specific guidance for such engagements and covers the auditor's reporting responsibilities for the following situations:

- Financial statements prepared on a comprehensive basis of accounting other than GAAP.
- Specified elements, accounts, or items of a financial statement.
- Compliance with aspects of contractual agreements or regulatory requirements related to audited financial statements.
- Financial presentations to comply with contractual agreements or regulatory provisions.
- Financial information presented in prescribed forms or schedules that require a prescribed form of auditor's report.

EXHIBIT 18–16

	Financial Statements Prepared on the Entity's Income Tax Basis

Independent Auditor's Report

We have audited the accompanying statements of assets, liabilities, and capital—income tax basis of Patroon Partnership as of December 31, 2000 and 1999, and the related statements of revenue and expenses—income tax basis and of changes in partners' capital accounts—income tax basis for the years then ended. These financial statements are the responsibility of the Partnership's management. Our responsibility is to express an opinion on these financial statements based on our audits.

We conducted our audits in accordance with generally accepted auditing standards. Those standards require that we plan and perform the audit to obtain reasonable assurance about whether the financial statements are free of material misstatement. An audit includes examining, on a test basis, evidence supporting the amounts and disclosures in the financial statements. An audit also includes assessing the accounting principles used and significant estimates made by management, as well as evaluating the overall financial statement presentation. We believe that our audits provide a reasonable basis for our opinion.

As described in Note 2, these financial statements were prepared on the basis of accounting the Partnership uses for income tax purposes, which is a comprehensive basis of accounting other than generally accepted accounting principles.

In our opinion, the financial statements referred to above present fairly, in all material respects, the assets, liabilities, and capital of Patroon Partnership as of December 31, 2000 and 1999, and its revenue and expenses and changes in partners' capital accounts for the years then ended, on the basis of accounting described in Note 2.

Financial Statements Prepared on a Comprehensive Basis of Accounting Other Than GAAP

[LO 9]

A widely used type of special report is employed when an entity has prepared its financial statements on a comprehensive basis other than GAAP ("other comprehensive basis of accounting" or OCBOA). SAS No. 62 defines OCBOA financial statements as including those prepared under the following bases:

- ***Regulatory basis.*** The basis used to comply with the requirements or financial reporting provisions of a governmental regulatory agency. An example would be when an insurance company reports in compliance with the rules of a state insurance commission.
- ***Tax basis.*** The basis the entity uses to file its income tax return. Real estate partnerships frequently use this basis for reporting to partners.
- ***Cash (or modified cash) basis.*** When the entity reports on revenues received and expenses paid. This may be modified to record depreciation or to accrue income taxes.
- ***A definite set of criteria having substantial support.*** Financial statements prepared on a price level–adjusted basis are an example of such a set of criteria.

Exhibit 18–16 is an example of a report on a set of financial statements prepared on a tax basis. Note that the introductory paragraph identifies the financial statements on which a report is being issued. It is important that these financial statements be titled so that they are not confused with financial statements prepared on a GAAP basis. In this case, the report covers a *statement of assets, liabilities, and capital—income tax basis* instead of a balance sheet and a *statement of revenues and expenses—income tax basis* instead of a statement of income or operations.

The scope paragraph is identical to that included in the standard unqualified audit report. The third paragraph discloses the basis used to prepare the financial statements and refers to a note in the financial statements that describes the basis in more detail. The opinion paragraph is a positive statement about the fairness of presentation in conformity with the OCBOA.

If the financial statements are prepared on a regulatory basis, the following paragraph is added (see SAS No. 87) to restrict the distribution of the report to those parties within the entity and those involved with filing with the regulatory agency:

> This report is intended solely for the information and use of the board of directors and management of Great Atlantic Insurance Company and for filing with the Excelsior State Insurance Agency and should not be used by anyone other than these specified parties.

Specified Elements, Accounts, or Items of a Financial Statement

[LO 10]

In some situations an auditor may be engaged to audit only part (specified elements, accounts, or items) of the financial statements. Examples include a report on rentals, royalties, or profit participation or on the provision for income taxes. The basis of accounting for the elements, accounts, or items may be GAAP, OCBOA, or a basis of accounting prescribed by a contract or agreement.

An engagement to express an opinion on one or more specified elements, accounts, or items of a financial statement may be performed as a separate engagement or as part of an audit of financial statements. The only exception is when the auditor is engaged to report on the entity's net income or stockholders' equity. In this case, the auditor must have audited the financial statements.

Generally, an audit of an element, account, or item is more extensive than if the same information were considered as part of an audit of the overall financial statements. Thus, materiality needs to be set in relation to the individual element, account, or item, and the auditor should consider how the item relates to other parts of the financial statements. For example, if the auditor was engaged to audit the entity's accounts receivable, other accounts such as sales and allowance for bad debts should also be considered.

Exhibit 18–17 is an example of a special report on gross sales for the calculation of rent. The introductory paragraph states that this specific account was audited. Similarly to the standard unqualified audit report, this paragraph states management's and the auditor's responsibilities. The second paragraph is the scope paragraph, which differs from the standard report only in that it references the account being audited. The third paragraph expresses the auditor's opinion on the account. Finally, in the case when the specified element, account, or item is audited in compliance with the provisions of a contract or agreement, the auditor includes a paragraph limiting distribution of the report to the parties who are part of the contract.

In addition to the audit of specified elements, accounts, or items, an auditor may be engaged to apply only *agreed-upon procedures*. SAS No. 75, "Engagements to Apply Agreed-Upon Procedures to Specified Elements, Accounts, or Items of Financial Statements" (AU 622), provides the auditor with the necessary guidance for such engagements. An engagement to apply agreed-upon procedures is one in which the auditor is engaged by a client to issue a report of findings based on specific procedures performed

EXHIBIT 18-17	**Report Relating to Sales Figures for the Purpose of Computing Rent**

Independent Auditor's Report

We have audited the accompanying schedule of gross sales (as defined in the lease agreement dated March 4, 1999, between McGill Company, as lessor, and Asare Stores Corporation, as lessee) of Asare Stores Corporation at its Main Street store, Dunwoody, Georgia, for the year ended December 31, 2000. This schedule is the responsibility of Asare Stores Corporation's management. Our responsibility is to express an opinion on this schedule based on our audit.

We conducted our audit in accordance with generally accepted auditing standards. Those standards require that we plan and perform the audit to obtain reasonable assurance about whether the schedule of gross sales is free of material misstatement. An audit includes examining, on a test basis, evidence supporting the amounts and disclosures in the schedule of gross sales. An audit also includes assessing the accounting principles used and significant estimates made by management, as well as evaluating the overall schedule presentation. We believe that our audit provides a reasonable basis for our opinion.

In our opinion, the schedule of gross sales referred to above presents fairly, in all material respects, the gross sales of Asare Stores Corporation at its Main Street store, Dunwoody, Georgia, for the year ended December 31, 2000, as defined in the lease agreement referred to in the first paragraph.

This report is intended solely for the information and use of the boards of directors and management of Asare Stores Corporation and McGill Company and should not be used by anyone other than these specified parties.

on the specific subject matter of specified elements, accounts, or items of a financial statement. On such engagements, auditing standards require that the specified users take responsibility for the sufficiency of the agreed-upon procedures. The auditor can satisfy this requirement by performing one of the following or similar procedures:

1. Compare the procedures to be applied to the written requirements of the specified users.
2. Discuss the procedures to be applied with appropriate representatives of the users involved.
3. Review relevant contracts or correspondence from the specified users.

Exhibit 18–18 is an example of an agreed-upon procedures report. The report (1) identifies the specified users, (2) references the specified elements, accounts, or items of a financial statement and the character of the engagement, (3) lists the procedures performed and related findings, (4) disclaims an opinion, and (5) states restrictions on the use of the report.

Compliance Reports Related to Audited Financial Statements

[LO 11]

An auditor may be asked to report on an entity's compliance with certain contractual agreements or regulatory requirements related to audited financial statements. For example, loan agreements may include covenants such as restrictions on dividends or maintenance of certain levels for selected financial ratios. Exhibit 18–19 is an example of a special report related to compliance with contractual provisions. Note that the auditor provides *negative assurance* as to compliance with the provisions of the loan agreement. Negative assurance consists of a statement that, as a result of specified procedures, nothing came to the auditor's attention that indicated that the provisions of the loan agreement had not been complied with.

Agreed-Upon Procedures Report in Connection with Claims of Creditors

Independent Auditor's Report on Applying Agreed-Upon Procedures

To the Trustee of Maxiscript Corporation:

We have performed the procedures described below, which were agreed to by the Trustee of Maxiscript Corporation, with respect to the claims of creditors to determine the validity of claims of Maxiscript Corporation as of May 31, 2000, as set forth in the accompanying Schedule A. This engagement to apply agreed-upon procedures was performed in accordance with standards established by the American Institute of Certified Public Accountants. The sufficiency of these procedures is solely the responsibility of the Trustee of Maxiscript Corporation. Consequently, we make no representation regarding the sufficiency of the procedures described below either for the purpose for which this report has been requested or for any other purpose.

The procedures and associated findings are as follows:

a. Compare the total of the trial balance of accounts payable at May 31, 2000, prepared by the company, to the balance in the Company's related general ledger account.

   The total of the accounts payable trial balance agreed with the balance in the related general ledger account.

b. Compare the amounts for claims received from creditors as shown in claims documents provided by Maxiscript Corporation to the respective amounts shown in the trial balance of accounts payable. Using the data included in the claims documents and in Maxiscript's accounts payable detail records, reconcile any differences to the accounts payable trial balance.

   All differences noted are presented in column 3 of Schedule A. Except for those amounts shown in column 4 of Schedule A, all such differences were reconciled.

c. Examine the documentation submitted by the creditors in support of their claims and compare it to the following documentation in Maxiscript Corporation's files: invoices, receiving reports, and other evidence of receipt of goods or services.

   No exceptions were found as a result of these comparisons.

We were not engaged to, and did not, perform an audit, the objective of which would be the expression of an opinion on the specified elements, accounts, or items. Accordingly, we do not express such an opinion. Had we performed additional procedures, other matters might have come to our attention that would have been reported to you.

This report is intended solely for the use of the Trustee of Maxiscript Corporation and should not be used by those who have not agreed to the procedures and taken responsibility for the sufficiency of the procedures for their purposes.

Special-Purpose Financial Presentations

[LO 12]

There are two basic types of special-purpose financial presentations: (1) incomplete presentations and (2) non-GAAP, non-OCBOA presentations. Incomplete presentations include statements that do not completely present the entity's assets, liabilities, revenues, and expenses but conform to GAAP or OCBOA. Non-GAAP or non-OCBOA presentations may include a complete set of financial statements or a single financial statement but are prepared on a basis of accounting other than GAAP or OCBOA. Exhibit 18–20 is an example of a report on an incomplete presentation.

EXHIBIT 18–19

Report on Compliance with Contractual Provisions Given in a Separate Report

Independent Auditor's Report

We have audited, in accordance with generally accepted auditing standards, the balance sheet of Lynch Lumber Company as of December 31, 2000, and the related statement of income, retained earnings, and cash flows for the year then ended, and have issued our report thereon dated February 16, 2001.

In connection with our audit, nothing came to our attention that caused us to believe that the Company failed to comply with the terms, covenants, provisions, or conditions of sections 6.1 to 6.14, inclusive, of the indenture dated July 21, 1998, with First State Bank insofar as they relate to accounting matters. However, our audit was not directed primarily toward obtaining knowledge of such noncompliance.

This report is intended solely for the information and use of the board of directors and management of Lynch Lumber Company and First State Bank and should not be used by anyone other than these specified parties.

EXHIBIT 18–20

Report on a Schedule of Gross Income and Certain Expenses to Meet a Regulatory Requirement and to Be Included in a Document Distributed to the General Public

Independent Auditor's Report

We have audited the accompanying Historical Summaries of Gross Income and Direct Operating Expenses of Gatorbait Apartments, Tallahassee, Florida ("Historical Summaries"), for each of the three years in the period ended December 31, 2000. These Historical Summaries are the responsibility of Gatorbait's management. Our responsibility is to express an opinion on the Historical Summaries based on our audits.

We conducted our audits in accordance with generally accepted auditing standards. Those standards require that we plan and perform the audit to obtain reasonable assurance about whether the Historical Summaries are free of material misstatement. An audit includes examining, on a test basis, evidence supporting the amounts and disclosures in the Historical Summaries. An audit also includes assessing the accounting principles used and significant estimates made by management, as well as evaluating the overall presentation of the Historical Summaries. We believe that our audit provides a reasonable basis for our opinion.

The accompanying Historical Summaries were prepared for the purpose of complying with the rules and regulations of the Securities and Exchange Commission for inclusion in the registration statement on Form S-11 of DEF Corporation as described in Note 10 and are not intended to be a complete presentation of Gatorbait's revenues and expenses.

In our opinion, the Historical Summaries referred to above present fairly, in all material respects, the gross income and direct operating expenses of Gatorbait Apartments described in Note 10 for each of the three years in the period ended December 31, 2000, in conformity with generally accepted accounting principles.

Financial Information Presented in Prescribed Forms or Schedules

🖋 [LO 13]

Sometimes an entity has to file with an agency on a preprinted form or schedule and the auditor is asked to report using the prescribed form. Many of these forms are not acceptable for auditors because they do not conform to professional reporting standards. In such instances, the auditor should reword the form or attach a separate form.

REVIEW QUESTIONS

[LO 1] 18-1   Describe what is meant when an auditor is associated with a set of financial statements.

[2] 18-2   Under what circumstances would the principal auditor refer to the other auditor in the audit report?

[2] 18-3   Distinguish between accounting changes that affect consistency and changes that do not.

[5] 18-4   How does the materiality of a condition that might lead to a departure affect the auditor's choice of audit reports?

[3] 18-5   Give examples of a client-imposed and a condition-imposed scope limitation. Why is a client-imposed limitation generally considered more serious?

[3] 18-6   How does a client's refusal to disclose information that is required by GAAP affect the auditor's report?

[6] 18-7   In 1999 your firm issued an unqualified report on Tosi Corporation. During 2000 Tosi entered its first lease transaction, which you have determined is material and meets the criteria for a capitalized lease. Tosi Corporation's management chooses to treat the transaction as an operating lease. What types of reports would you issue on the corporation's comparative financial statements for 1999 and 2000?

[6] 18-8   What procedures should a predecessor auditor conduct before reissuing his or her report?

[6] 18-9   When a predecessor auditor allows his or her audit report to be issued with a former client's comparative financial statements, what date is used for the reissued report? How would the reissued report be dated if the predecessor's report were revised or if the financial statements were restated?

[7] 18-10   What are the auditor's responsibilities for other information included in an entity's annual report?

[7] 18-11   If the auditor determines that other information contained with the audited financial statements is incorrect and the client refuses to correct the other information, what actions can the auditor take?

[8]   18-12   List the three overall steps in the going-concern evaluation process.

[8]   18-13   What four major categories of events or conditions may indicate going-concern problems? Give two examples for each category.

[8]   18-14   List actions that management can take to mitigate potential going-concern problems.

[8]   18-15   If the auditor concludes that an entity will not continue as a going concern, what type of audit report should be issued?

[9,10,11]   18-16   List three examples of special reports.

[9]   18-17   List four bases for OCBOA financial statements. Why is it important that these financial statements be properly titled in the audit report?

[11]   18-18   What type of special report does the auditor issue when reporting on an entity's compliance with contractual agreements?

MULTIPLE–CHOICE QUESTIONS FROM CPA EXAMINATIONS

[2]   18-19   An entity changed from the straight-line method to the declining balance method of depreciation for all newly acquired assets. This change has no material effect on the current year's financial statements but is reasonably certain to have a substantial effect in later years. If the change is disclosed in the notes to the financial statements, the auditor should issue a report with a(n)
a. "Except for" qualified opinion.
b. Explanatory paragraph.
c. Unqualified opinion.
d. Consistency modification.

[3,4]   18-20   In which of the following situations would an auditor ordinarily choose between expressing an "except for" qualified opinion and expressing an adverse opinion?
a. The auditor did *not* observe the entity's physical inventory and is unable to become satisfied as to its balance by other auditing procedures.
b. The financial statements fail to disclose information that is required by generally accepted accounting principles.
c. The auditor is asked to report only on the entity's balance sheet and not on the other basic financial statements.
d. Events disclosed in the financial statements cause the auditor to have substantial doubt about the entity's ability to continue as a going concern.

[3,4]   18-21   An auditor may reasonably issue an "except for" qualified opinion for a(n)

	Scope Limitation	Unjustified Accounting Change
a.	Yes	No
b.	No	Yes
c.	Yes	Yes
d.	No	No

[1,2]   18-22   An auditor includes a separate paragraph in an otherwise unmodi-fied report to emphasize that the entity being reported upon had significant transactions with related parties. The inclusion of this separate paragraph

    a. Is appropriate and would *not* negate the unqualified opinion.

    b. Is considered an "except for" qualification of the opinion.

    c. Violates generally accepted auditing standards if this informa-tion is already disclosed in footnotes to the financial statements.

    d. Necessitates a revision of the opinion paragraph to include the phrase "with the foregoing explanation."

[3,4]   18-23   Eagle Company's financial statements contain a departure from generally accepted accounting principles because, due to unusual circumstances, the statements would otherwise be misleading. The auditor should express an opinion that is

    a. Unqualified but *not* mention the departure in the auditor's report.

    b. Unqualified and describe the departure in a separate paragraph.

    c. Qualified and describe the departure in a separate paragraph.

    d. Qualified or adverse, depending on materiality, and describe the departure in a separate paragraph.

[3,4]   18-24   Tech Company has disclosed an uncertainty due to pending litiga-tion. The auditor's decision to issue a qualified opinion would most likely be determined by the

    a. Lack of sufficient evidence.

    b. Inability to estimate the amount of loss.

    c. Entity's lack of experience with such litigation.

    d. Lack of insurance coverage for possible losses from such litigation.

[3,4]   18-25   An auditor would issue an adverse opinion if

    a. The audit was begun by other independent auditors who with-drew from the engagement.

    b. A qualified opinion can *not* be given because the auditor lacks independence.

    c. The restriction on the scope of the audit was significant.

    d. The statements taken as a whole do *not* fairly present the finan-cial condition and results of operations of the company.

[3,4]   18-26   In which of the following circumstances would an auditor usually choose between issuing a qualified opinion and issuing a dis-claimer of opinion?

    a. Departure from generally accepted accounting principles.

    b. Inadequate disclosure of accounting policies.

    c. Inability to obtain sufficient competent evidential matter.

    d. Unreasonable justification for a change in accounting principle.

[3,4]   18-27   King, CPA, was engaged to audit the financial statements of Newton Company after its fiscal year had ended. King neither observed the in-ventory count nor confirmed the receivables by direct communication with debtors but was satisfied concerning both after applying alterna-tive procedures. King's auditor's report most likely contained a(n)

    a. Qualified opinion.

    b. Disclaimer of opinion.

    c. Unqualified opinion.

    d. Unqualified opinion with an explanatory paragraph.

[1,2]   18-28   In which of the following situations would an auditor ordinarily issue an unqualified audit opinion without an explanatory paragraph?

a. The auditor wishes to emphasize that the entity had significant related-party transactions.

b. The auditor decides to refer to the report of another auditor as a basis, in part, for the auditor's opinion.

c. The entity issues financial statements that present financial position and results of operations but omits the statement of cash flows.

d. The auditor has substantial doubt about the entity's ability to continue as a going concern, but the circumstances are fully disclosed in the financial statements.

[2,6]   18-29   When there has been a change in accounting principle that materially affects the comparability of the comparative financial statements presented and the auditor concurs with the change, the auditor should

	Concur Explicitly in the Change	Issue an "Except for" Qualified Opinion	Refer to the Change in an Explanatory Paragraph
a.	No	No	Yes
b.	Yes	No	Yes
c.	Yes	Yes	No
d.	No	Yes	No

[7]   18-30   Which of the following best describes the auditor's responsibility for "other information" included in the annual report to stockholders that contains financial statements and the auditor's report?

a. The auditor has *no* obligation to read the "other information."

b. The auditor has *no* obligation to corroborate the "other information" but should read the "other information" to determine whether it is materially inconsistent with the financial statements.

c. The auditor should extend the examination to the extent necessary to verify the "other information."

d. The auditor must modify the auditor's report to state that the other information "is unaudited" or "is not covered by the auditor's report."

[6]   18-31   Comparative financial statements include the prior year's statements that were audited by a predecessor auditor whose report is not presented. If the predecessor's report was unqualified, the successor should

a. Express an opinion on the current year's statements alone and make no reference to the prior year's statements.

b. Indicate in the auditor's report that the predecessor auditor expressed an unqualified opinion.

c. Obtain a letter of representations from the predecessor concerning any matters that might affect the successor's opinion.

d. Request the predecessor auditor to reissue the prior year's report.

[3,4] 18-32 An auditor decides to issue a qualified opinion on an entity's financial statements because a major inadequacy in the entity's computerized accounting records prevents the auditor from applying necessary procedures. The opinion paragraph of the auditor's report should state that the qualification pertains to
a. A client-imposed scope limitation.
b. A departure from generally accepted auditing standards.
c. The possible effects on the financial statements.
d. Inadequate disclosure of necessary information.

[6] 18-33 When reporting on comparative financial statements, which of the following circumstances should ordinarily cause the auditor to change the previously issued opinion on the prior year's financial statements?
a. The prior year's financial statements are restated following a pooling of interests in the current year.
b. A departure from generally accepted accounting principles caused an adverse opinion on the prior year's financial statements, and those statements have been properly restated.
c. A change in accounting principle causes the auditor to make a consistency modification in the current year's audit report.
d. A scope limitation caused a qualified opinion on the prior year's financial statements, but the current year's opinion is properly unqualified.

[6] 18-34 An auditor has previously expressed a qualified opinion on the financial statements of a prior period because of a departure from generally accepted accounting principles. The prior-period financial statements are restated in the current period to conform with generally accepted accounting principles. The auditor's updated report on the prior-period financial statements should
a. Express an unqualified opinion concerning the restated financial statements.
b. Be accompanied by the original auditor's report on the prior period.
c. Bear the same date as the original auditor's report on the prior period.
d. Qualify the opinion concerning the restated financial statements because of a change in accounting principle.

[10] 18-35 When an auditor is asked to express an opinion on the rental and royalty income of an entity, he or she may
a. Not accept the engagement because to do so would be tantamount to agreeing to issue a piecemeal opinion.
b. Not accept the engagement unless also engaged to audit the full financial statements of the entity.
c. Accept the engagement provided the auditor's opinion is expressed in a special report.
d. Accept the engagement provided distribution of the auditor's report is limited to the entity's management.

[9] 18-36 When reporting on financial statements prepared on the basis of accounting used for income tax purposes, the auditor should include in the report a paragraph that

a. Emphasizes that the financial statements are *not* intended to have been examined in accordance with generally accepted auditing standards.

b. Refers to the authoritative pronouncements that explain the income tax basis of accounting being used.

c. States that the income tax basis of accounting is a comprehensive basis of accounting other than generally accepted accounting principles.

d. Justifies the use of the income tax basis of accounting.

[8]   18-37   Which of the following audit procedures is most likely to assist an auditor in identifying conditions and events that may indicate substantial doubt about an entity's ability to continue as a going concern?

a. Review compliance with the terms of debt agreements.

b. Confirm accounts receivable from principal customers.

c. Reconcile interest expense with outstanding debt.

d. Confirm bank balances.

PROBLEMS

[1,2,3,4,8]   18-38   For each of the following independent situations, indicate the reason for and the type of audit report that you would issue. Assume that each item is significant.

a. Barfield Corporation, a wholly owned subsidiary of Sandy, Inc., is audited by another CPA firm. As the auditor of Sandy, Inc., you have assured yourself of the other CPA firm's independence and professional reputation. However, you are unwilling to take complete responsibility for their audit work.

b. The management of Gough Corporation has decided to exclude the statement of cash flows from their financial statements because they believe that their bankers do not find the statement to be very useful.

c. You are auditing Diverse Carbon, a manufacturer of nerve gas for the military, for the year ended September 30, 2000. On September 1, 2000, one of their manufacturing plants caught fire, releasing nerve gas into the surrounding area. Two thousand people were killed and numerous others paralyzed. The company's legal counsel indicates that the company is liable, but the company does not want to disclose this information in the financial statements.

d. During your audit of Cuccia Coal Company, the controller, Tracy Tricks, refuses to allow you to confirm accounts receivable because she is concerned about complaints from her customers. You are unable to satisfy yourself about accounts receivable by other audit procedures.

e. On January 31, 2001, Takeda Toy Manufacturing hired your firm to audit the company's financial statements for the year 2000. You were unable to observe the client's inventory on December 31, 2000. However, you were able to satisfy yourself about the inventory balance using other auditing procedures.

f. Gelato Bros., Inc., leases its manufacturing facility from a partnership controlled by the chief executive officer and major shareholder of Gelato. Your review of the lease indicates that the rental terms are in excess of rental terms for similar buildings in the area. The company refuses to disclose this relationship in the footnotes.

g. Mitchell Manufacturing Company has used the double-declining balance method to depreciate its machinery. During the current year, management switched to the straight-line method because they felt that it better represented the utilization of the assets. You concur with their decision. All information is adequately disclosed in the financial statements.

[1,2,3,4,8] 18-39 For each of the following independent situations, indicate the reason for and the type of audit report that you would issue. Assume that each item is significant.

a. International Mines, Inc., uses LIFO for valuing inventories held in the United States and FIFO for inventories produced and held in their foreign operations.

b. HiTech Computers is suing your client, Super Software, for royalties over patent infringement. Super Software's outside legal counsel assures you that HiTech's case is without merit.

c. In previous years, your client, Merc International, has consolidated its Panamanian subsidiary. Because of restrictions n repatriation of earnings placed on all foreign-owned corporations in Panama, Merc International has decided to account for the subsidiary on the equity basis in the current year.

d. In prior years Worcester Wool Mills has used replacement cost to value its inventory of raw wool. During the current year Worcester changed to FIFO for valuing raw wool.

e. Upon review of the recent history of the lives of their specialized automobiles, Gas Leak Technology changed the service lives for depreciation purposes on their autos from five years to three years. This change resulted in a material amount of additional depreciation expense.

f. During the 2000 audit of Brannon Bakery Equipment, you found that a material amount of inventory had been excluded from the inventory amount shown in the 1999 financial statements. After discussing this problem with management, you become convinced that it was an unintentional oversight.

g. Jay Johnson, CPA, holds 10 percent of the stock in Koenig Construction Company. The board of directors of Koenig asks Johnson to conduct their audit. Johnson completes the audit and determines that the financial statements present fairly in accordance with generally accepted accounting principles.

h. Palatka Savings and Loan's financial condition has been deteriorating for the last five years. Most of their problems result from loans made to real estate developers in Saint Johns County. Your review of the loan portfolio indicates that there should be a major increase in the loan-loss reserve. Based on your calculations, the proposed write-down of the loans will put Palatka into violation of the state's capital requirements.

[2]   18-40   The CPA firm of May & Marty has audited the consolidated financial statements of BGI Corporation. May & Marty examined the parent company and all subsidiaries except for BGI-Western Corporation, which was audited by the CPA firm of Dey & Dee. BGI-Western constituted approximately 10 percent of the consolidated assets and 6 percent of the consolidated revenue.

Dey & Dee issued an unqualified opinion on the financial statements of BGI-Western. May & Marty will be issuing an unqualified opinion on the consolidated financial statements of BGI.

Required:
a. What procedures should May & Marty consider performing with respect to Dey & Dee's examination of BGI-Western's financial statements that will be appropriate whether or not reference is to be made to the other auditors?
b. Describe the various circumstances under which May & Marty could take responsibility for the work of Dey & Dee and make no reference to Dey & Dee's examination of BGI-Western in their own report on the consolidated financial statements of BGI.

(AICPA, adapted)

[2,3,4,6]   18-41   Devon, Inc., engaged Rao to examine its financial statements for the year ended December 31, 2000. The financial statements of Devon, Inc., for the year ended December 31, 1999, were examined by Jones, whose March 31, 2000, auditor's report expressed an unqualified opinion. The report of Jones is not presented with the 2000–1999 comparative financial statements.

Rao's working papers contain the following information that does not appear in footnotes to the 2000 financial statements as prepared by Devon, Inc.:

- One director appointed in 2000 was formerly a partner in Jones's accounting firm. Jones's firm provided financial consulting services to Devon during 1998 and 1997, for which Devon paid approximately $1,600 and $9,000, respectively.

- The company refused to capitalize certain lease obligations for equipment acquired in 2000. Capitalization of the leases in conformity with generally accepted accounting principles would have increased assets and liabilities by $312,000 and $387,000, respectively, decreased retained earnings as of December 31, 2000, by $75,000, and decreased net income and earnings per share by $75,000 and $.75, respectively, for the year then ended. Rao has concluded that the leases should have been capitalized.

- During the year, Devon changed its method of valuing inventory from the first-in, first-out method to the last-in, first-out method. This change was made because management believes LIFO more clearly reflects net income by providing a closer matching of current costs and current revenues. The change had the effect of reducing inventory at December 31, 2000, by $65,000 and net income and earnings per share by $38,000 and $.38, respectively, for the year then ended. The effect of the change on prior years was immaterial; accordingly, the change had no cumulative effect. Rao supports the company's position.

After completing the field work on February 29, 2001, Rao concludes that the expression of an adverse opinion is not warranted.

Required:
Prepare the body of Rao's report dated February 29, 2001, and addressed to the board of directors to accompany the 2000–1999 comparative financial statements.

(AICPA, adapted)

[9]   18-42   On March 12, 2001, Brown & Brown, CPAs, completed the audit of the financial statements of Modern Museum, Inc., for the year ended December 31, 2000. Modern Museum presents comparative financial statements on a modified cash basis. Assets, liabilities, fund balances, support, revenues, and expenses are recognized when cash is received or disbursed, except that Modern includes a provision for depreciation of buildings and equipment. Brown & Brown believes that Modern's three financial statements, prepared in accordance with a comprehensive basis of accounting other than generally accepted accounting principles, are adequate for Modern's needs and wishes to issue a special report on the financial statements. Brown & Brown has gathered sufficient competent evidential matter to be satisfied that the financial statements are fairly presented according to the modified cash basis. Brown & Brown audited Modern's 1999 financial statements and issued an auditor's special report expressing an unqualified opinion.

Required:
Draft the audit report to accompany Modern's comparative financial statements.

(AICPA, adapted)

[1,2,3,4]   18-43   The audit report below was drafted by a staff accountant of Espinoza & Turner, CPAs, at the completion of the audit of the financial statements of Lyon Computers, Inc., for the year ended March 31, 2000. It was submitted to the engagement partner, who reviewed matters thoroughly and properly concluded that Lyon's disclosures concerning its ability to continue as a going concern for a reasonable period of time were adequate.

Auditor's Report

To the Board of Directors of Lyon Computers, Inc.:

We have audited the accompanying balance sheet of Lyon Computers, Inc., as of March 31, 2000, and the other related financial statements for the year then ended. Our responsibility is to express an opinion on these financial statements based on our audit.

We conducted our audit in accordance with standards that require that we plan and perform the audit to obtain reasonable assurance about whether the financial statements are in conformity with generally accepted accounting principles. An audit includes examining, on a test basis, evidence supporting the amounts and disclosures in the financial statements. An audit also includes assessing the accounting principles used and significant estimates made by management.

The accompanying financial statements have been prepared assuming that the Company will continue as a going concern. As discussed in Note 7 to the financial statements, the Company has suffered recurring losses from operations and has a net capital deficiency that raises substantial doubt about its ability to continue as a going concern. We believe that management's plans in regard to these matters, which are also described in Note 7, will permit the Company to continue as a going concern beyond a reasonable period of time. The financial statements do not include any adjustments that might result from the outcome of this uncertainty.

In our opinion, subject to the effects on the financial statements of such adjustments, if any, as might have been required had the outcome of the uncertainty referred to in the preceding paragraph been known, the financial statements referred to above present fairly, in all material respects, the financial position of Lyon Computers, Inc., and the results of its operations and its cash flows in conformity with generally accepted accounting principles applied on a basis consistent with that of the preceding year.

Espinoza & Turner, CPAs
April 28, 2000

Required:
Identify the deficiencies contained in the auditor's report as drafted by the staff accountant. Group the deficiencies by paragraph. Do *not* redraft the report.

(AICPA, adapted)

[1,3,4,6]   18-44   For the year ended December 31, 1999, Friday & Co., CPAs ("Friday"), audited the financial statements of Kim Company and expressed an unqualified opinion on the balance sheet only. Friday did not observe the taking of the physical inventory as of December 31, 1998, because that date was prior to its appointment as auditor. Friday was unable to satisfy itself regarding inventory by means of other auditing procedures, so it did not express an opinion on the other basic financial statements that year.

For the year ended December 31, 2000, Friday expressed an unqualified opinion on all the basic financial statements and satisfied itself as to the consistent application of generally accepted accounting principles. The field work was completed on March 11, 2001; the partner-in-charge reviewed the working papers and signed the auditor's report on March 18, 2001. The report on the comparative financial statements for 2000 and 1999 was delivered to Kim on March 21, 2001.

Required:
Prepare Friday's audit report that was submitted to Kim's board of directors on the 2000 and 1999 comparative financial statements.

(AICPA, adapted)

[1,9] 18-45 The following auditors' report was drafted by a staff accountant of Baker and Baker, CPAs, at the completion of the audit of the comparative financial statements of Ocean Shore Partnership for the years ended December 31, 2000 and 1999. Ocean Shore prepares its financial statements on the income tax basis of accounting. The report was submitted to the engagement partner, who reviewed matters thoroughly and properly concluded that an unqualified opinion should be expressed.

Auditors' Report

We have audited the accompanying statements of assets, liabilities, and capital—income tax basis of Ocean Shore Partnership as of December 31, 2000 and 1999, and the related statements of revenue and expenses—income tax basis and changes in partners' capital accounts—income tax basis for the years then ended.

We conducted our audits in accordance with standards established by the American Institute of Certified Public Accountants. Those standards require that we plan and perform the audit to obtain reasonable assurance about whether the financial statements are free of material misstatement. An audit includes examining, on a test basis, evidence supporting the amounts and disclosures in the financial statements. An audit also includes assessing the accounting principles used as well as evaluating the overall financial statement presentation.

As described in Note A, these financial statements were prepared on the basis of accounting the Partnership uses for income tax purposes. Accordingly, these financial statements are not designed for those who do not have access to the Partnership's tax returns.

In our opinion, the financial statements referred to above present fairly, in all material respects, the assets, liabilities, and capital of Ocean Shore Partnership as of December 31, 2000 and 1999, and its revenue and expenses and changes in partners' capital accounts for the years then ended, in conformity with generally accepted accounting principles applied on a consistent basis.

Baker and Baker, CPAs
April 3, 2001

Required:

Identify the deficiencies contained in the auditors' report as drafted by the staff accountant. Group the deficiencies by paragraph, where applicable. Do *not* redraft the report.

(AICPA, adapted)

DISCUSSION CASES

[1,2,3,4] 18-46 Your client, Texter, Inc., a publicly held shoe distributor, acquired 100 percent of Shoe-Rite in 1996. As a result, Texter owns approximately 30 percent of Armundi, S.A., an Italian shoe manufacturer, which is audited by an internationally recognized firm, Lafrance, Dematasco & Associates. Texter uses the equity method of accounting for its investment in Armundi.

Over the years, Texter's investment in Armundi has become a more substantial portion of its balance sheet. It originally accounted for 2 to 3 percent of Texter's total assets between 1996 and 1998 and for more than 5 percent during 1999. However, that investment has increased from about 8 percent of Texter's stockholders' equity in 1996 to approximately 39 percent of stockholders' equity in 2000. Further, Texter's share of Armundi's earnings has ranged from more than 5 percent of pretax earnings in 1996 to approximately 20 percent in 2000 and represents an average of approximately 14 percent of pretax earnings over the last five years except for one loss year. A weak US dollar has magnified Armundi's contribution to earnings. Currently there are no business transactions (sales/purchases) between Texter and Armundi.

From an audit risk and reporting standpoint, Texter's increasing investment in Armundi and Armundi's increasing contribution to Texter's earnings raise the question of whether you will have to state reliance on Armundi's auditors. Lafrance, Dematasco & Associates currently performs a full-scope audit of Armundi under GAAP/GAAS requirements in its country of domicile. This audit forms the basis for the US GAAP compilation that Lafrance, Dematasco & Associates prepares for your purposes. Your discussions with Lafrance, Dematasco & Associates over the last several years have provided you with a level of assurance necessary to opine on Texter's consolidated financial statements. In prior years, you have also received letters from Lafrance, Dematasco & Associates about their independence of Texter and its affiliates.

Because Armundi's stock is not publicly traded, Texter is bound by restrictions on the sale of the stock that are set forth in Armundi's Articles of Association, which also give existing stockholders a right of first refusal on any shares offered for sale.

Texter has been receiving cash dividends from Armundi continuously since owning the stock. The cash is remitted to Texter without any problems. There are no significant exchange restrictions involving repatriation of earnings or proceeds from the sale of the stock.

During the past several years, Texter has attempted to increase its ownership percentage of Armundi through various means. Texter has worked closely with its counsel and Italian counsel and with Armundi's auditors, Lafrance, Dematasco & Associates, to structure a transaction that would give Texter a controlling interest in Armundi.

Required:
a. With respect to Texter's investment in Armundi, can you assume responsibility for the work performed by Lafrance, Dematasco & Associates, or should you state reliance on their work in your report?
b. What procedures should you perform in either circumstance?
c. Draft Texter, Inc.'s, audit report for the year ended 2000, assuming that you have decided to state your reliance on Lafrance, Dematasco & Associates in the audit report. Assume that the audit report will cover only one year, 2000.

[2,8]   18-47   You are auditing the financial statements for your new client, Paper Packaging Corporation, a manufacturer of paper containers, for the year ended March 31, 2000. Paper Packaging's previous auditors had issued a going-concern opinion on the March 31, 1999, financial statements for the following reasons:

- Paper Packaging had defaulted on $10 million of unregistered debentures sold to three insurance companies, which were due in 1999, and the default constituted a possible violation of other debt agreements.
- The interest and principal payments due on the remainder of a 10-year credit agreement, which began in 1995, would exceed the cash flows generated from operations in recent years.
- The company had disposed of certain operating units. The proceeds from the sale were subject to possible adjustment through arbitration proceedings, the outcome of which was uncertain at year-end.
- Various lawsuits were pending against the company.
- The company was in the midst of tax proceedings as a result of an examination of the company's federal income tax returns for a period of 12 years.

You find that the status of the above matters is as follows at year-end, March 31, 2000:

- The company is still in default on $4.6 million of the debentures due in 1999 but is trying to negotiate a settlement with remaining bondholders. A large number of bondholders have settled their claims at significantly less than par.
- The company has renegotiated the 1995 credit agreement, which provides for a two-year moratorium on principal payments and interest at 8 percent. It also limits net losses ($2.25 million for 2000) and requires a certain level of defined cumulative quarterly operating income to be maintained.
- The arbitration proceedings were resolved in 2000.
- The legal actions were settled in 2000.
- Most of the tax issues have been resolved, and, according to the company's legal counsel, those remaining will result in a net cash inflow to the company.

At year-end Paper Packaging had a cash balance of $5.5 million and expects to generate a net cash flow of $3.2 million in the upcoming fiscal year.

The following information about Paper Packaging's plans for its operations in fiscal year 2001 may also be useful in arriving at a decision.

	Fiscal Year 2001 Budget	Fiscal Year 2000 Actual	Fiscal Year 2000 Budget
Net revenues	$66.2	$60.9	$79.8
Gross margin	34.7	33.6	45.6
Operating expenses	27.9	34.7	31.4
Interest—net	5.1	6.0	5.7
Other income (expenses)—net	(.8)	2.1	—
Earnings before income taxes and extraordinary items	1.5	(5.1)	(.2)
Cash flows:			
Receipts	69.9	79.7	
Disbursements	66.7	96.9	
Excess/deficit	3.2	(22.8)	

Required:

a. What should you consider in deciding whether to discuss a going-concern uncertainty in your report?

b. How much influence should the report on the March 31, 1999, financial statements have on your decision?

c. Should your report for the year ended March 31, 2000, include a discussion of a going-concern uncertainty?

PROFESSIONAL RESPONSIBILITIES

Chapter 19

The Code of Professional Conduct and Quality Control Standards

LEARNING OBJECTIVES

Upon completion of this chapter you will

[1] Know the definitions of ethics and professionalism.

[2] Understand the three theories of ethical behavior.

[3] Begin to understand how to deal with ethical dilemmas through an example situation.

[4] Understand how moral judgment develops in an individual.

[5] Understand the framework for the Code of Professional Conduct.

[6] Learn the principles of professional conduct.

[7] Understand the framework for the rules of conduct.

[8] Learn and understand the rules of conduct that apply to independence, integrity, and objectivity.

[9] Learn and understand the rules of conduct that apply to general standards and accounting principles.

[10] Learn and understand the rules of conduct that apply to responsibilities to clients.

[11] Learn and understand the rules of conduct that apply to other responsibilities and practices.

[12] Know the definition of a system of quality control.

[13] Learn the elements of quality control.

[14] Learn how a firm monitors its quality control system.

RELEVANT ACCOUNTING AND AUDITING PRONOUNCEMENTS

AICPA, Code of Professional Conduct (ET 50-500)

SAS No. 25, "The Relationship of Generally Accepted Auditing Standards to Quality Control Standards" (AU 161)

Statement on Quality Control Standards No. 2, "System of Quality Control for a CPA Firm's Accounting and Auditing Practice" (QC 10)

Statement on Quality Control Standards No. 3, "Monitoring a CPA Firm's Accounting and Auditing Practice" (QC 20)

AICPA, Standards for Performing and Reporting on Quality Reviews (PR 100)

The focus of this chapter is the AICPA Code of Professional Conduct and Quality Control Standards. Any professional organization must indicate to its members what acceptable professional behavior is and must also be able to demonstrate to the public that it is willing to monitor the actions of its members. Such actions by professional organizations are necessary because society, through federal and state legislation, grants professions monopoly rights to practice; in return, professions self-regulate their members and are expected to adhere to the public interest.

The AICPA has established such a set of policies. The Code of Professional Conduct deals mainly with the behavior and actions of the *individual* CPA. The Quality Control Standards, on the other hand, are concerned with a *firm's* monitoring of its own practice. The Bylaws provide a means by which the Institute can discipline individual members and member firms that do not comply with professional standards.

The chapter begins by providing a framework for studying ethics or professional conduct. This is followed by an overview of the Code of Professional Conduct. The last part of the chapter discusses a system of quality control for a CPA firm. 🌐

An Ethical Framework

Ethics and Professionalism

🖊️ **[LO 1]**

Ethics refers to a system or code of conduct based on moral duties and obligations that indicates how an individual should behave. *Professionalism* refers to the conduct, aims, or qualities that characterize or mark a profession or professional person.[1] All professions establish rules or codes of conduct that define what is ethical (professional) behavior for members of the profession. These rules are promulgated so that (1) users of the professional services know what to expect when they purchase such services, (2) members of the profession know what is acceptable behavior, and (3) the profession can use the rules to monitor the actions of its members. The accounting profession has a *Code of Professional Conduct* that guides the behavior of accounting professionals, and the AICPA monitors the actions of its professional members to ensure that they are in compliance with the Code.[2]

Theories of Ethical Behavior

🖊️ **[LO 2]**

When individuals are confronted with situations that have moral and ethical implications, they do not always agree on the issue at hand, which individuals or groups will be affected and how, or what solutions or courses of actions are available or appropriate for dealing with the situation. Such differences may be caused by differences in the individuals' concepts of fairness and different opinions about the right action to take in a particular situation.

S. M. Mintz has suggested that there are three methods or theories of ethical behavior that can guide the analyses of ethical issues in

---

[1]S. M. Mintz, *Cases in Accounting Ethics and Professionalism,* 3d ed. (New York: Irwin/McGraw-Hill, 1997), p. 4.

[2]Note that other accounting organizations have similar codes of conduct. For example, the Institute of Internal Auditors has a Code of Ethics that applies to members of the Institute and Certified Internal Auditors.

accounting.[3] These theories are (1) *utilitarianism,* (2) a *rights*~~proach,~~ and (3) a *justice-based approach.* No one approach is bett~~er~~ another. Elements of each theory may be appropriate for resolving ~~ethi~~cal dilemmas.

Utilitarian theory recognizes that decision making involves trade-offs between the benefits and burdens of alternative actions, and it focuses on the consequences of an action on the individuals affected. The theory proposes that the interests of all parties affected, not just one's self-interest, should be considered. One form of utilitarianism holds that rules have a central position in moral judgment. This approach may have significance for auditors who are expected to follow the Code of Professional Conduct in carrying out their responsibilities. One disadvantage in applying the utilitarian theory to ethical dilemmas is that it is difficult to measure the potential costs and benefits of the actions to be taken. It may also be difficult to balance the interests of all parties involved when those interests conflict with one another.

The theory of rights assumes that individuals have certain rights and other individuals have a duty to respect those rights. Thus, a decision maker who follows a theory of rights should undertake an action only if it does not violate the rights of *any* individual. An obvious disadvantage of the theory of rights is that, as with utilitarianism, it may be difficult or impossible to satisfy all rights of all affected parties, especially when those rights conflict. The theory of rights is important to auditors because of their public-interest responsibility. In conflicting situations, the rights of some individuals may not be satisfied in order that the primacy of the public-interest obligation of auditors may be maintained. According to the concept known as the "moral point of view," auditors must be willing, at least sometimes, to put the interests of other stakeholders, such as investors and creditors, ahead of their own self-interests and those of the CPA firm. Thus, if a difference of opinion with top management exists over an accounting or reporting issue, the auditor should emphasize the interests of the investors and creditors in deciding what action to take, even if it means losing the client.

The theory of justice is concerned with issues such as equity, fairness, and impartiality. Mintz indicates that decisions made within this theory should fairly and equitably distribute resources among those individuals or groups affected. There may be difficulty in trying to apply this theory in practice because the rights of one or more individuals or groups may be affected when a better distribution of benefits is provided to others; affirmative action programs are one example of the difficulty in applying the theory of justice. While none of these theories by itself can provide a perfect ethical framework, each can be useful in helping an auditor to solve dilemmas by providing an ethical perspective for resolving the dilemma.

---

[3]See S. M. Mintz, *Cases in Accounting Ethics and Professionalism,* 3d ed. (New York: Irwin/McGraw-Hill, 1997), for a more detailed discussion of each of these models.

ısider how an auditor might act given the following simplified situation.

SUN CITY SAVINGS AND LOAN COMPANY

Pina, Johnson & Associates has recently been awarded the audit of Sun City Savings and Loan Company for the year ended December 31, 2000. Sun City Savings and Loan is now the largest client of Pina, Johnson & Associates, and the fees from this engagement represent a significant portion of the firm's revenues. Upon accepting the Sun City engagement, the firm incurred additional costs by hiring several new employees and a new manager from a larger firm. In bidding on the engagement, Sam Johnson knew that the first-year fees would be just enough to cover the actual cost of the first year's audit, but he hoped that future audit fee increases and fees for other services might lead to a long-term, profitable engagement. Based on his discussions with the predecessor auditors, Johnson knew that there were possible problems with Sun City's loans because of the collateral used for security. Johnson was also concerned that there might be problems with the loan-loss reserves due to the effects of the economic slowdown on the tourist industry in Sun City over the last two years. However, Johnson felt that these problems were manageable.

During the current year, the amount included in the loan-loss reserves account was $675,000, approximately the same as the figure for the prior year. The state's banking regulations require that an amount equal to 1.5 percent of the loans outstanding be included as a reserve against losses. The $675,000 was slightly above the statutory requirement. However, the audit staff identified two large loans, aggregating to $15 million, that appeared not to be collectible in full. The working papers disclosed that each loan had originated during the current year and that both had been in default for four months. Additionally, the collateral used to secure the loans was worth considerably less than the amount of the loans and was not in accordance with Sun City's loan policy procedures. Based on this information, the staff estimates that about 40 percent of the $15 million, or $6 million, will not be collected. The staff has also determined that these loans are to entities owned by Patricia Cabot, Sun City's CEO, and some of her business associates.

When Johnson met with Cabot to discuss the two delinquent loans, Cabot tried to convince Johnson that the loans would be paid in full. She told Johnson that the loans had been properly made and that as soon as the economy picked up, payments would be made on the loans. She indicated that no additional reserves were needed and that if Johnson requires such adjustments, his firm might be replaced.

What ethical and professional concerns should Johnson consider in deciding on a course of action?

If Johnson follows a utilitarian approach, he should consider the consequences (benefits and costs) of his actions on all affected parties and whether any rules exist that might require a particular action. The benefits of requiring the increase in the reserve may be full and accurate disclosure of the facts as assessed by the audit team. Another benefit may arise from the time-honored convention of conservatism. Costs need to be assessed in terms of Sun City's stockholders, Cabot's reputation, and the situation of the public accounting firm. For example, Johnson might consider that if he requires an additional reserve amount for the loans, the price of Sun City's stock might decline and the stockholders would suffer losses. By forcing Sun City to increase the reserves, he might also damage Cabot's reputation if the loans are eventually paid. On the other hand, if Cabot is inappropriately using Sun City's funds for personal gain, the stockholders are being harmed by her actions. Finally, Johnson might consider how the loss of Sun City as a client would affect his firm. If the client is lost, the newly hired personnel may need to be terminated. While Johnson knows that the reserve is in accordance with the state's statutory rule on loan losses, from a rules perspective he also knows that generally accepted accounting principles require that the loans be presented in the financial statements at net realizable value. Given the facts in this case and using a utilitarian approach, Johnson may conclude that the loan-loss reserves should be adjusted by the $6 million.

The theory of rights requires that Johnson consider whose rights would be violated if he does not require an increase in the loan-loss reserves because, based on the evidence, generally accepted accounting principles would require an adjustment. The stockholders' right to fair and accurate information for decision-making purposes is being violated. If Cabot has entered into loans at the expense of the stockholders, they will not have received accurate information about Sun City's profitability, liquidity, and so on. If Johnson does not require the adjustment and the loans eventually become uncollectible, the stockholders' rights will be violated and Johnson may be in violation of GAAP, GAAS, and other professional standards. Thus, under a rights approach, Johnson is likely to conclude that he has a duty to require the adjustment to the financial statements.

The theory of justice requires that Johnson's decisions impartially consider the interests of the stockholders, Cabot, the depositors in the S & L, and the government, which is insuring the deposits. Johnson should therefore avoid favoring the interest of any individual or group. The theory of justice might lead Johnson to consider all interests without being biased toward any one. However, auditors are supposed to represent the public interest. This would likely lead Johnson to the conclusion that an adjustment should be made for the $6 million. The potential loss of the client may severely test Johnson's impartiality in this case. But integrity and objectivity would require that Johnson not subordinate his judgment to that of the client or place his own self-interest ahead of the public interest.

If Johnson follows the moral point of view, he should first consider the interests of Sun City's shareholders. This would result in Johnson requiring the client to book the $6 million adjustment for the delinquent loans.

In this case, Johnson's professionalism is likely to be tested. While he realizes that the loan-loss reserves probably should be increased, he is also likely to be concerned about the possibility of losing this valuable client and the significant investment in new personnel that the firm has made. While it seems fairly clear what action should be taken (requiring the client to adjust the reserve), the question becomes—as it so often does—does the auditor (Johnson) have the moral fortitude to do what is right?

Auditors frequently face such ethical dilemmas in their practice. It is important that auditors develop sound moral character so that they can respond appropriately in such situations. Mintz points out that auditors who possess certain "virtues" or traits of character are more capable of adhering to the moral point of view.[4] Examples of such virtues include honesty, integrity, impartiality, faithfulness, and trustworthiness. These are similar to the Principles of Professional Conduct discussed later in the chapter. The next section presents a model of moral development which can be used to demonstrate how Johnson's moral judgment should have developed to the point where he should require the S & L to provide additional reserves for the loans.

Development of Moral Judgment

/ [LO 4]

Substantial research[5] indicates that moral judgment develops over time and is a function of age, education, and complexity of experience. Lawrence Kohlberg[6] has proposed that moral development has six stages that can be divided into three levels of moral reasoning. Table 19–1 shows the six stages of Kohlberg's model. A *stage* refers to a mode or pattern of behaviors that characterizes some definable point in an individual's life. This model is more complex than it appears. For example, it is unlikely that an individual is in only one stage of development at a time. An individual is more likely to be moving from one stage to another. At the preconventional level, an individual is concerned with his or her own self-interest. Rules are imposed by others, and the individual is judged in terms of how well he or she obeys. Young children are typically in this stage of moral development. At the conventional level, the individual is aware of others and the need to conform to group norms; he or she is concerned with order in society and relies on laws and rules for guidance. At the postconventional level, the individual recognizes society's laws and rules but resolves conflict situations impartially, using universal moral and ethical principles.

Referring back to the Sun City Savings and Loan case, if Johnson were at stage II in his moral development, he would go along with Cabot and would not increase the loan-loss reserves by $6 million. He would be concerned about losing the client and future revenues and therefore would most likely act in his own self-interest. However, current research indi-

---

[4]S. M. Mintz, "Virtue, Ethics, and Accounting Education," *Issues in Accounting Education* (Fall 1995), pp. 24–31.

[5]See J. R. Rest, *Moral Development: Advances in Research and Theory* (New York: Praeger, 1986), for a detailed summary of this research.

[6]See L. Kohlberg, "Moral Stages and Moralization: The Cognitive Developmental Approach," in T. Lickona (ed.), *Moral Development and Behavior: Theory, Research, and Social Issues* (New York: Holt, Rinehart and Winston, 1976), for a complete discussion of the stages discussed here. Also see J. R. Rest, *Development in Judging Moral Issues* (Minneapolis: University of Minnesota Press, 1979), for a revised view of the stages in moral development.

TABLE 19–1	The Six Stages of Ethical Development

Level 1: Preconventional

At the preconventional level, the individual is concerned with self. Rules are imposed externally on the individual.

Stage I: The individual's actions are judged in terms of their physical consequences, such as avoidance of punishment.

Stage II: The individual is aware of others' needs, but satisfaction of the individual's own needs is the basic motivation for action.

Level 2: Conventional

At the conventional level, the individual is able to see situations from others' (such as family, peer group, or nation) points of view.

Stage III: The individual attempts to conform to group norms. The other's view of the situation is considered, and conflicts are resolved through the use of these norms.

Stage IV: The individual is concerned about order in society and its rules. The individual uses the laws and rules for guidance in conflict situations.

Level 3: Postconventional

At the postconventional level, society's laws and rules are questioned and redefined in terms of universal moral principles.

Stage V: The individual views social contracts and mutual obligations as important. Differences in conflict situations are resolved impartially and with consideration of everyone's interests.

Stage VI: The individual bases actions on universal moral and ethical principles (such as justice, equality, and dignity) that apply to all individuals and groups.

Source: Adapted from S. M. Mintz, *Cases in Accounting Ethics and Professionalism*, 3d ed. (New York: Irwin/McGraw-Hill, 1997), pp. 28–29.

cates that CPAs reason at stages III and IV.[7] At stage III, Johnson would be influenced by group norms, so his reasoning would likely be affected by the views of the members of his firm. This might explain why, in difficult situations, auditors consult with other members of their firm for guidance. At stage IV, the auditor's actions would be guided by strict adherence to the profession's technical standards and rules of conduct. If Johnson were at this stage, his reasoning would lead him to follow professional standards and increase the loan-loss reserve.

Code of Professional Conduct

[LO 5]   The AICPA Code of Professional Conduct has undergone substantial changes in the last 10 to 15 years. As a result of a consent agreement between the AICPA and the Federal Trade Commission, the Code was revised to allow direct solicitation, competitive bidding, and most forms of advertising. These changes, coupled with the increased complexity of business transactions and technical accounting standards, are major challenges that auditors must face in maintaining their professionalism. Concerns about the commercialization of the accounting profession have been raised by

---

[7]See, for example, L. A. Ponemon, "Ethical Reasoning and Selection Socialization in Accounting," *Accounting, Organizations and Society* 17 (1992), pp. 239–58; and M. K. Shaub, "An Analysis of the Association of Traditional Demographic Variables with the Moral Reasoning of Auditing Students and Auditors," *Journal of Accounting Education* (Winter 1994), pp. 1–26.

Congress and the Securities and Exchange Commission. Opponents of the profession have cited activities such as "lowballing" and "opinion shopping" as examples of practitioners' placing business interests above the interests of the public. The Code of Professional Conduct provides the principles and rules an auditor should follow in the practice of public accounting.

The AICPA Code of Professional Conduct consists of two sections:

- Principles of Professional Conduct.
- Rules of Conduct.

The Principles of Professional Conduct provide the framework for the Rules of Conduct. Additional guidance for applying the Rules of Conduct is provided by

- Interpretations of Rules of Conduct.
- Rulings by the Professional Ethics Division.

The Interpretations of Rules of Conduct consist of interpretations adopted by the AICPA Professional Ethics Division's executive committee to provide guidelines as to the scope and application of the Rules of Conduct. The Rulings by the Professional Ethics Division consist of formal rulings by the Professional Ethics Division's executive committee related to particular sets of factual circumstances. The interpretations and ethics rulings are enforceable, and an auditor who departs from such standards has the burden of justifying such departures.

The guidance provided by the Code of Professional Conduct starts at a conceptual level with the principles and progressively moves to general rules and their interpretations and then to specific rulings on individual cases. Figure 19–1 provides a pictorial representation of the four parts of the Code of Professional Conduct.

FIGURE 19–1

Code of Professional Conduct

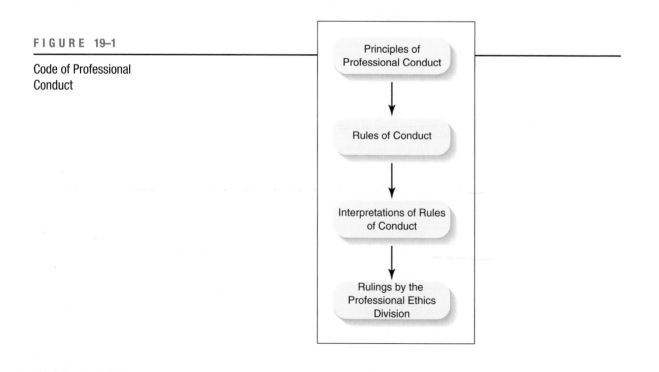

Principles of Professional Conduct

[LO 6]   Six ethical principles provide a framework for the Code of Professional Conduct. The preamble to the Principles of Professional Conduct states the following:

> They [the principles] guide members in the performance of their professional responsibilities and express the basic tenets of ethical and professional conduct. The principles call for an unswerving commitment to honorable behavior, even at the sacrifice of personal advantage. (ET 51.02)

Table 19–2 presents the definition of each principle. Note that the principles are stated at a conceptual level. These principles of ethical behavior are not enforceable.

The first two principles address a CPA's responsibilities to exercise professional and moral judgment in a manner that serves the public interest. These principles reinforce the conviction that the CPA's role in society is to serve the public (remember, the "P" in CPA stands for "public"). The profession's public includes clients, creditors, employers, employees, governments, investors, and other members of the business and financial community—all the groups discussed in Chapter 1.

These groups rely on CPAs' integrity, objectivity, and independence when providing high-quality services. Integrity requires that a CPA be honest and candid and honor both the form and the spirit of ethical standards. Thus, a CPA should make judgments that are consistent with the theories of rights and justice. When faced with an ethical dilemma, the CPA should ask, "What actions would an individual with integrity take, given these facts and circumstances?" Objectivity and independence are hallmarks of the public accounting profession. The principle of objectivity requires the CPA to be impartial and free of conflicts of interest. Independence requires that the CPA avoid relationships that would impair his or her objectivity. When a CPA provides auditing- or attestation-related services, independence in both fact and appearance must be maintained. If a CPA is perceived not to

---

TABLE 19–2   Principles of Professional Conduct

- *Responsibilities:* In carrying out their responsibilities as professionals, members should exercise sensitive professional and moral judgments in all their activities.
- *The public interest:* Members should accept the obligation to act in a way that will serve the public interest, honor the public trust, and demonstrate commitment to professionalism.
- *Integrity:* To maintain and broaden public confidence, members should perform all professional responsibilities with the highest sense of integrity.
- *Objectivity and independence:* A member should maintain objectivity and be free of conflicts of interest in discharging professional responsibilities. A member in public practice should be independent in fact and appearance when providing auditing and other attestation services.
- *Due care:* A member should observe the profession's technical and ethical standards, strive continually to improve competence and the quality of services, and discharge professional responsibility to the best of the member's ability.
- *Scope and nature of services:* A member in public practice should observe the Principles of the Code of Professional Conduct in determining the scope and nature of services to be provided.

be independent, the various groups mentioned will not place much value on the services provided. The fifth principle, due care, requires that the CPA perform his or her professional responsibilities with competence and diligence. While the performance of professional services must take into account the interests of the client, the public's interest is more important when the two interests conflict. The last principle requires that the CPA determine that the services to be rendered are consistent with acceptable professional behavior for CPAs. This principle also requires that the CPA have internal quality control procedures to ensure that services are delivered competently and that no conflict of interest exists.

Rules of Conduct

[LO 7] The Bylaws of the AICPA require that members adhere to the Rules of Conduct of the Code of Professional Conduct and that members must be prepared to justify any departures from the rules. Table 19–3 provides an overview of the existing Rules of Conduct and their related interpretations. But before proceeding to a discussion of the rules, here are a number of important definitions.

> *Client*—Any person or entity that engages a member or member's firm to perform professional services or a person or entity with respect to which professional services are performed.
>
> *Council*—The Council of the American Institute of Certified Public Accountants.
>
> *Enterprise*—Synonymous with the term *client* for purposes of the Code.
>
> *Financial statements*—Statements and footnotes related thereto that purport to show financial position that relates to a point of time or changes in financial position that relate to a period of time, and statements that use cash or another incomplete basis of accounting.
>
> *Firm*—A form of organization permitted by state law or regulation whose characteristics conform to the resolutions of the Council and that is engaged in the practice of public accounting, including the individual owners thereof.
>
> *Holding out*—In general, any action initiated by a member that informs others of his or her status as a CPA or AICPA-accredited specialist.
>
> *Member*—A member, associate member, or international associate of the AICPA.
>
> *Practice of public accounting*—The performance for a client, by a member or a member's firm, while holding out as CPA(s), of the professional services of accounting, tax, personal financial planning, litigation support services, and those professional services for which standards are promulgated by bodies designated by the Council.
>
> *Professional services*—All services performed by a member while holding out as a CPA.

The Rules of Conduct are organized in the professional standards under five headings with the numbers of the rules corresponding to the five sections:

- Independence, Integrity, and Objectivity (Section 100).
- General Standards and Accounting Principles (Section 200).

Rules of Conduct	*Interpretations*
101 Independence	• Interpretation of Rule 101 (101-1).
	• Former practitioners and firm independence (101-2).
	• Provision for other services to clients (101-3).
	• Honorary directorships and trusteeships of not-for-profit organization (101-4).
	• Loans from financial institution clients and related terminology (101-5).
	• The effect of actual or threatened litigation on independence (101-6).
	• Effect of independence of financial interests in nonclients having investor or investee relationships with a member's client (101-8).
	• The meaning of certain independence terminology and the effect of family relationships on independence (101-9).
	• The effect on independence of relationships with entities included in the governmental financial statements (101-10).
	• Independence and attest engagements (101-11).
	• Independence and cooperative arrangements with clients (101-12).
	• Extended audit services (101-13).
	• The effect of alternative practice structures on the applicability of independence rules (101-14).
102 Integrity and objectivity	• Knowing misrepresentations in the preparation of financial statements or records (102-1).
	• Conflicts of interest (102-2).
	• Obligations of a member to his or her employer's external accountant (102-3).
	• Subordination of judgment by a member (102-4).
	• Applicability of Rule 102 to members performing educational services (102-5).
	• Professional services involving client advocacy (102-6)
201 General standards	• Competence (201-1).
202 Compliance with standards	• None.
203 Accounting principles	• Departures from established accounting principles (203-1).
	• Status of FASB interpretations (203-2).
	• Responsibility of employees for the preparation of financial statements in conformity with GAAP (203-4).
301 Confidential client information	• Confidential information and the purchase, sale, or merger of a practice (301-3).
302 Contingent fees	• Contingent fees in tax matters (302-1).
501 Acts discreditable	• Retention of client records (501-1).
	• Discrimination and harassment in employment practices (501-2).
	• Failure to follow standards and/or procedures or other requirements in governmental audits (501-3).
	• Negligence in the preparation of financial statements or records (501-4).
	• Failure to follow requirements of governmental bodies, commissions, or other regulatory agencies in performing attest or similar services (501-5).
	• Solicitation or disclosure of CPA examination questions and answers (501-6).
502 Advertising and other forms of solicitation	• False, misleading, or deceptive acts in advertising or solicitation (502-2).
	• Engagements obtained through efforts of third parties (502-5).
503 Commissions and referral fees	• None.
505 Form of organization and name	• Application of rules of conduct to members who operate a separate business (505-2).

- Responsibilities to Clients (Section 300).
- Responsibilities to Colleagues (no rules currently exist).
- Other Responsibilities and Practices (Section 500).

Note that no rules currently exist for the section entitled "Responsibilities to Colleagues." The rules that were contained in this section were repealed by the members as part of the consent agreement with the Federal Trade Commission. Rules formerly included in that section dealt with encroachment and competitive bidding.

Independence, Integrity, and Objectivity

[LO 8] This section of the Rules of Conduct currently contains two rules related to these issues.

Independence

If an auditor is not independent of his or her client, it is unlikely that a user of financial statements will place much reliance on the CPA's work (see Exhibit 19–1). Rule 101 is a very general statement concerning auditor independence and relates only to attestation-related services.

> **Rule 101:** A member in public practice shall be independent in the performance of professional services as required by standards promulgated by bodies designated by Council.

Because of the difficulty that sometimes arises in defining independent relationships, numerous interpretations of Rule 101 have been issued. Table 19–4 presents Interpretation 101-1, a major interpretation related to independence. Interpretation 101-9 defines the term "member" as identified in Interpretation 101-1 and includes

- The member's firm and its proprietors, partners, or shareholders.
- All individuals participating in the engagement.
- All individuals with a managerial position located in an office participating in a significant portion of the engagement.
- Any entity whose operating, financial, or accounting policies can be controlled by persons defined as members of the firm.

EXHIBIT 19–1

The Securities and Exchange Commission (SEC) and the Independence Standards Board (ISB)

Chapter 1 discussed the SEC and ISB as organizations that impact the public accounting profession. In February 1998 the SEC gave authority to the ISB to develop independence standards for *public* companies and to provide guidance on specific auditor independence issues. This means that the SEC will no longer promulgate separate independence rules and that the ISB will provide auditor independence standards, interpretations, and practices. The relationship between the SEC and the ISB will be similar to the one that currently exists with the FASB; the SEC will provide oversight of the ISB and take enforcement action when appropriate. Auditors of *private* companies will comply with the AICPA's independence rules. For more information on the activities of the ISB, visit their home page at www.cpaindependence.org.

While titles (such as managers, directors, principals, and partners) and responsibilities may differ from firm to firm, an individual in a managerial position would normally have the following responsibilities:

- Overall planning and supervision of engagements.
- Authority to determine when the engagement is complete, subject to final partner approval.
- Responsibility for client relationships, including negotiating and collecting fees for engagements and marketing the firm's services.
- Existence of profit sharing as a significant feature of total compensation.
- Responsibility for overall management of the firm.

Note that Interpretation 101-1 examines independence along two dimensions: *financial interests* and *managerial interests*. A number of other interpretations provide further explanations on such financial and managerial interests.

Financial Interests   Interpretation 101-1 prohibits auditors from any financial relationship with a client that may impair or give the appearance of impairing independence. This includes any direct or material indirect financial interest in the client. In a number of situations additional interpretations have been issued to clarify or provide exceptions to such financial interests.

TABLE 19–4	Interpretation 101-1 (Interpretation of Rule 101)

Independence shall be considered to be impaired if, for example, a member had any of the following transactions, interests, or relationships:

A. During the period of a professional engagement or at the time of expressing an opinion, a member or member's firm

1. Had or was committed to acquire any direct or material indirect financial interest in the enterprise.
2. Was a trustee of any trust or executor or administrator of any estate if such trust or estate had or was committed to acquire any direct or material direct financial interest in the enterprise.
3. Had any joint, closely held business investment with the enterprise or with any officer, director, or principal stockholders thereof that was material in relation to the member's net worth or the net worth of the member's firm.
4. Had any loan to or from the enterprise or any officer, director, or principal stockholder of the enterprise except as specifically permitted in interpretation 101-5.

B. During the period covered by the financial statements, during the period of the professional engagement, or at the time of expressing an opinion, a member or a member's firm

1. Was connected with the enterprise as a promoter, underwriter, or voting trustee, as a director or officer, or in any capacity equivalent to that of a member of management or of an employee.
2. Was a trustee for any pension or profit-sharing trust of the enterprise.

The above examples are not intended to be all-inclusive. The period of professional engagement starts when the member begins to perform any professional services requiring independence for an enterprise, lasts for the entire duration of the professional relationship, which could cover many periods, and ends with the formal or informal notification of the professional relationship either by the member, by the enterprise, or by the issuance of a report, whichever is later. Accordingly, the professional engagement does not end with the issuance of a report and recommence with the signing of the following year's engagement.

EXHIBIT 19–2

> ### ESM Government Securities, Inc.'s, Audit Partner Had "Loan" from Client
>
> ESM Government Securities, Inc., was a Fort Lauderdale brokerage firm that specialized in buying and selling debt securities issued by the federal government and its various agencies. Its main customers were small to moderate-size banks and municipalities. The major type of transaction engaged in by ESM was known as a "repo," in which a securities dealer sells a customer a large block of federal securities and simultaneously agrees to repurchase the securities at a later date at an agreed-upon price. A massive fraud was conducted at ESM by Ronnie Ewton and Alan Novick, who hid trading losses and other misappropriations from ESM's auditor, Alexander Grant. The trading losses incurred by ESM were transferred to an affiliated company. When the thefts and trading losses were finally tallied, there was a net deficit of $300 million for ESM.
>
> The sad part of this case was that the audit partner, Jose Gomez, was aware of the fraud. Gomez was admitted as a partner to Alexander Grant in 1979. His major client was ESM Securities. Shortly after making partner, Gomez was informed by Novick that the company's 1977 and 1978 financial statements had been misstated. Novick was able to convince Gomez not to withdraw Alexander Grant's audit report on the assumption that ESM would recoup its losses. Novick was aware that Gomez was experiencing financial problems in spite of his salary as a partner. Over the course of the fraud (1977–1984), Gomez received approximately $200,000 in payments from Novick to relieve his financial problems.
>
> See the Chapter 20 appendix for more information on ESM Government Securities, Inc. *In re Alexander Grant & Co. Litigation.*

Generally a loan to or from a client is considered to impair the member's independence (see Exhibit 19–2). However, there are situations in which a CPA is permitted to obtain loans from a financial institution that is a client. Interpretation 101-5 permits the following types of personal loans from a financial institution:

- Automobile loans and leases collateralized by the automobile.
- Loans fully collateralized by the surrender value of an insurance policy.
- Loans fully collateralized by cash deposits at the same financial institution.
- Credit cards and cash advances where the aggregate outstanding balance is reduced to $5,000 or less by the payment due date.

Such a loan must be made in accordance with the financial institution's *normal* lending procedures, terms, and requirements and must, at all times, be kept current as to all terms. *Normal lending procedures, terms, and requirements* are defined as lending procedures, terms, and requirements that are reasonably comparable to those relating to loans of a similar character given to other borrowers during the period in which the loan to the member is given, including (1) the amount of the loan in relationship to the value of the collateral pledged as security and the credit of the member or member's firm, (2) repayment terms, (3) the interest rate, including points, (4) closing costs, and (5) the general availability of such loans to the public.

There may also be situations when financial interests of nonclients that are related in various ways to a client may affect a CPA's independence with respect to the client. Interpretation 101-8 specifically discusses two of these situations:

1. When a nonclient investee is material to a client investor, any direct or material indirect financial interest by a CPA in the nonclient investee impairs independence. If the nonclient investee is immaterial to the client investor, a CPA's material investment in the nonclient investee causes an impairment of independence.

2. When a client investee is material to a nonclient investor, any direct or material indirect financial interest of a CPA in the nonclient impairs independence. If the client investee is immaterial to the nonclient investor, and if a CPA's financial interest in the nonclient investor allows the CPA to exercise significant influence over the actions of the nonclient investor, the CPA's independence would be considered impaired.

For example, suppose a CPA has a direct financial interest in a partnership that invests in a client. If the CPA serves, or acts, as a general partner in the partnership, independence is deemed to be impaired because he or she is considered to have a *direct* financial interest. If the CPA is a limited partner in the partnership, the CPA is considered to have an *indirect* financial interest in the client and independence is impaired only if the indirect financial interest is material to the CPA's net worth.

Managerial Interests   Rule 101 essentially forbids a CPA from performing a managerial role within a client's organization. Interpretations of this rule, however, provide for certain exceptions. One situation that falls under Interpretation 101-2 can occur when a CPA goes to work for a client of his or her former firm. The firm's independence from the client is not impaired as long as the following conditions are met:

- The payments to the former practitioner for his or her interest in the CPA firm and for unfunded, vested retirement payments are not contingent on the fees received from the client. Such amounts for his or her share of the CPA firm and retirement benefits should be fixed in terms of both amount and dates.

- The former practitioner does not participate in the CPA firm's business or professional activities, whether or not he or she is compensated for such activities. For example, this would prohibit a long-term consultancy arrangement between the CPA firm and the individual.

- The former practitioner does not appear to participate in the activities of or be associated with his or her former firm. For example, the inclusion of the individual's name under the firm's name in an office building directory would give the appearance of participation by the former practitioner.

- A former practitioner in a position of significant influence with the client must no longer be provided with office space or other amenities by the CPA firm.

If the former practitioner meets these conditions, the CPA firm's independence is not impaired by his or her managerial position with the client.

Another situation can arise when a CPA is asked to serve as an *honorary* director or trustee for a not-for-profit organization. It is not unusual for members of a CPA firm to be asked to lend the prestige of their names to a charitable, religious, civic, or similar organization and for their firm to provide accounting and auditing services to the not-for-profit organization. Interpretation 101-4 allows a member to serve as a director or trustee for a not-for-profit client "so long as his or her position is clearly honorary, and he or she cannot vote or otherwise participate in board or management functions." Any of the organization's documents that contain the member's name must identify the member's position as honorary.

A third situation in which a member's independence may be impaired occurs when the client asks the member to provide manual or automated bookkeeping or data processing services. A member can provide such services and still remain independent if the following conditions are met:

- The client accepts responsibility for the financial statements. This means that the client must have sufficient knowledge of the enterprise's activities, financial condition, and accounting principles to accept such responsibility. In many cases, it may be necessary for the CPA to discuss accounting matters with the client to ensure that an appropriate level of understanding is attained.
- The CPA must not assume the role of an employee or management. For example, the CPA cannot consummate transactions for the client or maintain custody of the client's assets.
- When financial statements are prepared from books and records the CPA has maintained, the CPA must comply with applicable standards for audits, reviews, or compilations.

The last situation deals with the recent trend by companies to outsource various corporate activities, such as the internal audit function and audit services beyond the requirements of GAAS (referred to as *extended audit services*). Interpretation 101-13 allows a CPA firm to perform extended audit services for a client for which the member performs a professional service that requires independence. These extended audit services would not be considered to impair independence provided the member or his or her firm does not act or appear to act in the capacity of an employee or client management. For example, if a member provides assistance in the performance of an audit client's internal audit function, the member and client must understand that the client is responsible for

- Designating a competent individual or individuals, preferably within senior management, to be responsible for the internal audit function.
- Determining the scope, risk, and frequency of internal audit activities, including those to be performed by the member providing the extended audit services.
- Evaluating the findings and results arising from the internal audit activities, including those performed by the member providing the extended audit services.
- Evaluating the adequacy of the audit procedures performed and the findings resulting from the performance of those procedures by, among other things, obtaining reports from the member.

While the Code permits CPAs to provide bookkeeping services to clients (101-3), the Securities and Exchange Commission does not allow a CPA to provide such services to entities that report to the SEC. The SEC has concluded that performing such services and issuing an opinion on the entity's financial statements results in a lack of independence. However, the reader should realize that many CPA firms provide such services to their clients, which are not required to file reports with the SEC.

Effect of Family Relationships   The issues related to a CPA's financial or managerial interest in a client may extend to members of the CPA's family. Certain relationships between members of a CPA's family and a client are considered to affect the CPA's independence. The term *member,* as used in Rule 101, includes spouses and dependent persons. Therefore, if a spouse or dependent person has a financial or managerial position with a client, as discussed in the previous sections, the CPA would not be independent. An exception occurs when the spouse is employed by the client and he or she does not exert significant influence over the client's operating, financial, or accounting policies. If the spouse is in an audit-sensitive position, such as cashier, internal auditor, or general accounting clerk, the CPA should not participate in the engagement. However, the firm may continue to perform the engagement.

Generally, financial or managerial interests by close relatives such as nondependent children, brothers, sisters, parents, grandparents, parents-in-law, and their respective spouses do not normally impair independence. The independence of the member's firm may, however, be impaired if

- A close relative had a financial interest in the client that was material to the close relative and the CPA participating in the engagement was aware of the interest.
- An individual participating in the engagement has a close relative who could exercise significant influence over the operating, financial, or accounting policies of the client or who is employed in an audit-sensitive position.
- A proprietor, partner, or shareholder located in an office participating in a significant portion of the engagement has a close relative who could exercise significant influence over the operating, financial, or accounting policies of the enterprise.

For example, suppose a senior accountant's brother works as a plant manager for a client of the CPA firm. Because the accountant's brother exercises significant influence over the operating policies of the client, the accountant would not be allowed to participate in the audit of this client. Figure 19–2 summarizes the effect of family relationships on independence.

Effect of Actual or Threatened Litigation   Sometimes threatened or actual litigation between the client and the auditor may impair the auditor's independence. Such situations affect the CPA's independence when a possible adversarial relationship exists between the client and the CPA. Interpretation 101-6 cites three categories of litigation: (1) litigation between the client and the CPA, (2) litigation by shareholders, and (3) other third-party litigation where the CPA's independence may be impaired.

FIGURE 19–2

The Effect of Family Relationships on Independence

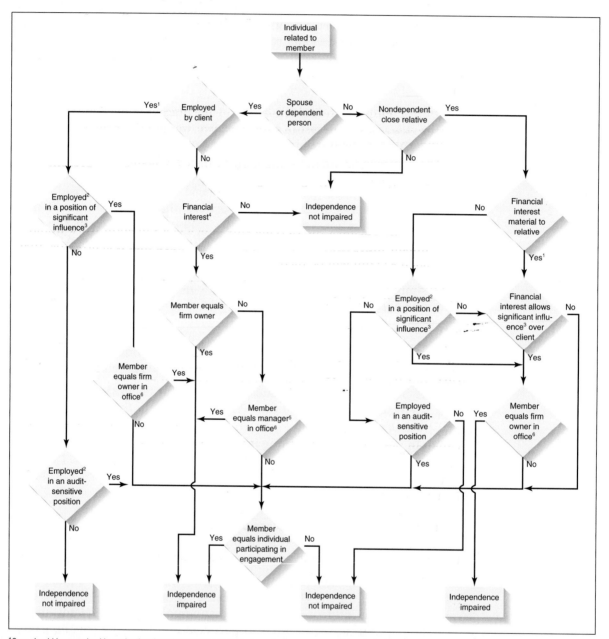

[1]Care should be exercised in evaluating the relationships a spouse, dependent person, or nondependent close relative has with a client.

[2]During the period covered by the financial statements, during the period of the professional engagement, or at the time of expressing an opinion.

[3]A person or entity able to exercise significant influence over the operating, financial, or accounting policies of another entity.

[4]During the period of the professional engagement, or at the time of expressing an opinion.

[5]An individual in a managerial position.

[6]An office participating in a significant portion of the engagement that is determined based on several factors, such as materiality of the office's engagement hours and fees related to the total engagement, office reporting responsibility, and so on.

Source: S. S. Coffey, ed., "Test Your Knowledge of Professional Ethics," *Journal of Accountancy* (December 1993), pp. 90–91. (Adapted; used with permission.)

In order for a CPA to provide an opinion on a client's financial statements, the relationship between the client's management and the CPA must be one of "complete candor and full disclosure regarding all aspects of the client's business operations." When actual or threatened litigation exists between management and the CPA, complete candor may not be possible. The following criteria are offered as guidelines for assessing independence when actual or threatened litigation exists between the client and the CPA:

- The commencement of litigation by the present management alleging deficiencies in audit work for the client would be considered to impair independence.
- The commencement of litigation by the CPA against the present management alleging management fraud or deceit would be considered to impair independence.
- An expressed intention by the present management to commence litigation against the CPA alleging deficiencies in audit work would impair independence if the auditor concluded that it is probable that such a claim will be filed.

Litigation by client security holders or other third parties also may impair the auditor's independence. For example, litigation may arise from a class action lawsuit by stockholders alleging that the client, its management, its officers, its directors, its underwriters, and its auditors were involved in the issuance of "false or misleading financial statements." Generally, such lawsuits do not alter the fundamental relationship between the CPA and the client. However, independence may be impaired if material client–auditor cross-claims are filed. For example, suppose that a class action suit is filed and the current client management intends to testify against the CPA, alleging that an improper audit was conducted. In such a situation, an adversarial relationship would exist and the CPA would no longer be independent. When this occurs, the CPA should either (1) withdraw from the engagement or (2) disclaim an opinion because of a lack of independence.

Other third-party litigation against the CPA may be commenced by lending institutions or by other creditors who rely on the client's financial statements that were opined on by the CPA. Normally, such lawsuits do not impair the CPA's independence unless the relationship between the CPA and the client is affected.

Integrity and Objectivity

Rule 102: In the performance of any professional service, a member shall maintain objectivity and integrity, shall be free of conflicts of interest, and shall not knowingly misrepresent facts or subordinate his or her judgment to others.

This rule expands on the principle from which it was developed and requires that a member maintain integrity and objectivity. There are a number of important interpretations of this rule. One interpretation (102-1) indicates that a member who knowingly makes or permits false and misleading entries in financial statements or records violates Rule 102. A second interpretation (102-2) states that a conflict of interest may occur if a member performs a professional service for a client or employer and the member of his or her firm has a relationship with another person, entity, product, or service that could be viewed as impairing the CPA's objectivity. Two other interpretations relate mainly to members in industry and were issued in response to matters related to the savings-and-loan scandal. One interpretation (102-3) states that, in dealing with his or her employer's external accountants, a member must be candid and not knowingly misrepresent facts or knowingly fail to disclose material facts. In a related interpretation (102-4), if a member and his or her supervisor have a disagreement or dispute relating to the preparation of financial statements or the recording of transactions, the member must take steps to ensure that the situation does not result in a subordination of judgment. If the member concludes that the financial statements or records could be materially misstated, he or she should communicate those concerns to a higher level of management within the organization. If appropriate action is not taken, the member should consider whether to continue the relationship with the employer. The member should also consider whether any responsibility exists to communicate the problem to third parties, such as regulatory agencies or the employer's external accountants.

Educational services are professional services and therefore are subject to Rule 102 (interpretation 102-5). Thus a member must maintain objectivity and integrity when performing such services. Finally, a member may be asked by a client to act as an advocate in performing tax or consulting services or in support of a client's position on an accounting or auditing issue (interpretation 102-6). While a member may accept such an engagement, he or she must be sure that the requested service does not go beyond the bounds of sound professional practice and impair independence, integrity, and objectivity.

General Standards and Accounting Principles

[LO 9]   This section of the Rules of Conduct contains two rules related to general standards and one rule related to accounting principles.

General Standards and Compliance with Standards

Rule 201: A member shall comply with the following standards and with any interpretations thereof by bodies designated by Council.

A. *Professional Competence.* Undertake only those professional services that the member or the member's firm can reasonably expect to be completed with professional competence.

B. *Due Professional Care.* Exercise due professional care in the performance of professional services.

C. *Planning and Supervision.* Adequately plan and supervise the performance of professional services.

D. *Sufficient Relevant Data.* Obtain sufficient relevant data to afford a reasonable basis for conclusions or recommendations in relation to any professional services performed.

Rule 201 captures much of what is contained in the 10 generally accepted auditing standards and codifies it as part of the Code. Interpretation 201-1 provides some additional clarification of "professional competence." In particular, when a CPA agrees to perform professional services, he or she is expected to have the necessary competence to complete those services according to professional standards. However, it is not necessary for the CPA to have all of the technical knowledge required to perform the engagement at the time the engagement commences. The CPA may conduct additional research or consult with other professionals during the conduct of the engagement. This need for additional information does not indicate a lack of competence on the part of the CPA.

> **Rule 202:** A member who performs auditing, review, compilation, management consulting, tax, or other professional services shall comply with standards promulgated by bodies designated by Council.

This rule is straightforward yet important because it requires that members of the AICPA comply with professional standards when performing professional services.

Accounting Principles

While Rule 202 addresses compliance with standards for professional services, Rule 203 relates to compliance with accounting principles.

> **Rule 203:** A member shall not (1) express an opinion or state affirmatively that the financial statements or other financial data of any entity are presented in conformity with generally accepted accounting principles or (2) state that he or she is not aware of any material modifications that should be made to such statements or data in order for them to be in conformity with generally accepted accounting principles, if such statements or data contain any departure from an accounting principle promulgated by bodies designated by Council to establish such principles that has a material effect on the statements or data taken as a whole. If, however, the statements or data contain such a departure and the member can demonstrate that due to unusual circumstances the financial statements or data would otherwise have been misleading, the member can comply with the rule by describing the departure, its approximate effects, if practicable, and the reasons why compliance with the principle would result in a misleading statement.

This rule was adopted to require compliance by CPAs with GAAP. Rule 203 and Interpretation 203-1 recognize that there may be unusual circumstances when applying GAAP may produce misleading financial statements. Some examples of circumstances that might require departure from GAAP are new legislation and the evolution of a new form of business transaction. An unusual degree of materiality and conflicting industry practices are examples of circumstances that would ordinarily not be considered unusual under Rule 203.

Interpretation 203-2 reiterates that the AICPA Council has designated the Financial Accounting Standards Board (FASB) as the body authorized to establish accounting principles. This interpretation defines GAAP to include FASB Statements of Financial Accounting Standards, together with those Accounting Research Bulletins and Accounting Principles Board Opinions issued by predecessors of the FASB that have not been superseded. Interpretations by the FASB are recognized as authoritative when determining the existence of a departure from GAAP. Interpretation 203-4, which relates mainly to members in industry, states that any representation regarding conformity with GAAP in a letter or other communication from a client to its auditor or others related to that entity's financial statements is subject to Rule 203. Thus, for example, if a member signs a representation letter indicating that the financial statements were in conformity with GAAP when they were not, he or she has violated Rule 203.

Responsibilities To Clients

[LO 10] This section of the Rules of Conduct contains two rules related to a CPA's responsibilities to his or her clients.

Confidential Client Information

Rule 301: A member in public practice shall not disclose any confidential client information without the specific consent of the client.

This rule shall not be construed (1) to relieve a member of his or her professional obligations under rules 202 and 203, (2) to affect in any way the member's obligation to comply with a validly issued and enforceable subpoena or summons, or to prohibit a member's compliance with applicable laws and governmental regulations, (3) to prohibit review of a member's professional practice under AICPA or state CPA society or Board of Accountancy authorization, or (4) to preclude a member from initiating a complaint with, or responding to any inquiry made by, the professional ethics division or trial board of the Institute or a duly constituted investigative or disciplinary body of a state CPA society or Board of Accountancy.

Members of any of the bodies identified in (4) above and members involved with professional practice reviews identified in (3) above shall not use to their own advantage or disclose any member's confidential client information that comes to their attention in carrying out those activities. This prohibition shall not restrict members' exchange of information in connection with the investigative or disciplinary proceedings described in (4) above or the professional practice reviews described in (3) above.

Rule 301 specifies four situations in which a CPA can disclose confidential information without the client's consent: (1) to meet disclosure requirements for GAAP and GAAS, (2) to comply with a valid and enforceable subpoena, (3) as required by an authorized peer review board or body, and (4) as part of an investigative or disciplinary proceeding.

Interpretation 301-3 specifically allows a review of a CPA's professional practice in conjunction with the purchase, sale, or merger of the practice. The CPA should take precautions that the prospective buyer does not disclose any confidential client information. This can generally be accomplished through the use of a confidentiality agreement. Members who review a CPA's practice in connection with a prospective purchase or merger should not use that information to their advantage, nor should they disclose any confidential client information that comes to their attention.

Contingent Fees

Rule 302: A member in public practice shall not

(1) Perform for a contingent fee any professional services for, or receive such a fee from a client for whom the member or the member's firm performs

   (a) an audit or review of financial statements; or

> (b) a compilation of a financial statement when the member expects, or reasonably might expect, that a third party will use the financial statement and the member's compilation report does not disclose a lack of independence; or
>
> (c) an examination of prospective financial information; or
>
> (2) Prepare an original or amended tax return or claim for a tax refund for a contingent fee for any client.
>
> The prohibition in (1) above applies during the period in which the member or member's firm is engaged to perform any of the services listed above and the period covered by any historical financial statements involved in any such listed services.
>
> Except as stated in the next sentence, a contingent fee is a fee established for the performance of any service pursuant to an arrangement in which no fee will be charged unless a specific finding or result is attained, or in which the amount of the fee is otherwise dependent upon the finding or result of such service. Solely for purposes of this rule, fees are not regarded as being contingent if fixed by courts or other public authorities, or, in tax matters, if determined based on the results of judicial proceedings or the findings of governmental agencies.
>
> A member's fees may vary depending, for example, on the complexity of the services rendered. 🖋

In negotiating with the Federal Trade Commission, the AICPA was able to maintain the prohibition on contingent fees for the attestation-related services listed under (1) above. If contingent fees were allowed for attestation-related services, users of those services might question the CPA's independence.

Interpretation 302-1 allows contingent fees for certain types of tax engagements. For example, a contingent fee would be permitted if a CPA represented a client in connection with obtaining a private letter ruling from the Internal Revenue Service. On the other hand, a contingent fee would not be appropriate if a CPA prepared an amended federal income tax return for a client claiming a refund of taxes because a deduction was inadvertently omitted from the return originally filed.

Other Responsibilities and Practices

🖋 **[LO 11]**   This section contains four rules of conduct that relate to other aspects of the profession.

Acts Discreditable

Rule 501: A member shall not commit an act discreditable to the profession. 🖋

This rule allows the AICPA to remove a member for committing acts that may affect the profession's reputation. So, for example, a CPA who is convicted of a serious crime could lose his or her membership in the AICPA. Five interpretations have been issued that identify acts considered discreditable under Rule 501:

- Retention of client records (501-1).
- Discrimination and harassment in employment practices (501-2).
- Failure to follow standards and/or procedures or other requirements in government audits (501-3).

- Negligence in the preparation of financial statements or records (501-4).
- Failure to follow the requirements of government bodies, commissions, or other regulatory agencies in performing attest or similar services (501-5).

For example, a CPA may not retain a client's accounting or other records that were provided by the client as part of conducting the engagement even if there are fees still unpaid. If the CPA retains certain client records such as journals or ledgers, the client may be unable to continue operations. The CPA's working papers, on the other hand, are the property of the CPA and are not covered by this interpretation. If a CPA did not return a client's accounting records, that member would have committed a discreditable act under Rule 501. Similarly, a CPA commits a discreditable act if he or she discriminates in hiring, promotion, or salary practices on the basis of race, color, religion, sex, age, or national origin. A third example of a discreditable act would be when a CPA, in auditing government activities, fails to follow any government standard procedure. Last, a CPA who, by virtue of his or her negligence, makes or permits or directs another to make false or misleading entries in the financial statements or records of an entity shall be considered to have committed a discreditable act.

Advertising and Other Forms of Solicitation

Rule 502: A member in public practice shall not seek to obtain clients by advertising or other forms of solicitation in a manner that is false, misleading, or deceptive. Solicitation by the use of coercion, over-reaching, or harassing conduct is prohibited. 🖋

Interpretation 502-2 provides specific examples of activities that are prohibited by this rule. These include

- Creating false or unjustifiable expectations of favorable results.
- Implying an ability to influence any court, tribunal, regulatory agency, or similar body or official.
- Claiming that specific professional services in current or future periods will be performed for a stated fee, estimated fee, or fee range when it is likely at the time of representation that such fees will be substantially increased and the prospective client is not advised of that likelihood.
- Making any other representations that would be likely to cause a reasonable person to misunderstand or be deceived.

Since the prohibition against advertising was lifted, many CPA firms have advertised their services to the public. CPAs are often asked to provide professional services to clients or customers of third parties when those clients or customers have been obtained through advertising and/or solicitation. Interpretation 502-5 allows CPAs to render such services to clients or customers of third parties as long as all promotional efforts used to obtain such clients were conducted within the Code.

Commissions and Referral Fees

Rule 503:

A. *Prohibited commissions*

A member in public practice shall not for a commission recommend or refer to a client any product or service, or for a commission recommend or refer any product or service to be supplied by a client, or receive a commission, when a member or the member's firm also performs for that client

- an audit or review of financial statements; or
- a compilation of a financial statement when the member expects, or reasonably might expect, that a third party will use the financial statement and the member's compilation report does not disclose a lack of independence; or
- an examination of prospective financial information.

This prohibition applies during the period in which the member is engaged to perform any of the services listed above and the period covered by any historical financial statements involved in the listed services.

B. *Disclosure of permitted commissions*

A member in public practice who is not prohibited by this rule from performing services for or receiving a commission and who is paid or expects to be paid a commission shall disclose that fact to any person or entity to whom the member recommends or refers a product or service to which the commission relates.

C. *Referral fees*

Any member who expects a referral fee for recommending or referring any service of a CPA to any person or entity or who pays a referral fee to obtain a client shall disclose such acceptance or payment to the client. ✍

Rule 503 also resulted from the negotiations between the Federal Trade Commission and the AICPA. Many professions, including doctors and lawyers, have been permitted to use referral fees. Prior to the consent decree, commissions and referral fees were prohibited for CPAs. The current rule does not allow commissions or referral fees in situations where the CPA's independence and objectivity are a focal point of the attestation-related services.

Form of Organization and Name

Rule 505: A member may practice public accounting only in the form of organization permitted by state law or regulation whose characteristics conform to resolutions of Council.

A member shall not practice public accounting under a firm name that is misleading. Names of one or more past partners or shareholders may be included in the firm name of a successor organization. Also, an owner surviving the death or withdrawal of all other owners may continue to practice under such name which includes the names of past owners for up to two years after becoming a sole practitioner.

A firm may not designate itself as "Members of the American Institute of Certified Public Accountants" unless all of its owners are members of the Institute. ✍

This rule requires that the form of a CPA's public accounting practice conform to state law or regulations whose characteristics conform to AICPA resolutions. In recent years, virtually all states have passed laws

Holding Out as a CPA

Since the early 1990s, American Express (and some other entities) have purchased a number of CPA firms. Stephen Miller, a Florida CPA working for American Express, prepared financial statements and compiled tax returns. American Express, a non-CPA firm, began to advertise the fact that Miller was providing accounting services to the public as a CPA. However, this violated the Florida statute that regulated the practice of public accounting and led to a lawsuit between American Express and the state of Florida over who can practice as a CPA. The US Supreme Court (*George Stuart, Secretary, as Head of the Florida Department of Business and Professional Regulation, et al. v. American Express Tax and Business Services, Inc., et al.*) let stand a lower court ruling that invalidated Florida's definition of the practice of public accounting. Florida responded to the court's ruling by passing legislation that regulates what CPAs do, and not when and where they call themselves CPAs. Basically, firms and individuals are licensed, and services are regulated. Therefore, American Express would not be licensed, but its employees could perform nonattest services as CPAs. This trend is likely to continue and will affect all states.

Sources: "An Agenda of Change: Important Legislative Victories for Public Accounting" *Florida CPA Today* (June 1998) and "We've Seen the Future, and It's Florida" *Journal of Accountancy* (September 1998), pp. 13–16.

that allow CPAs to practice as limited liability partnerships. Rule 505 also prohibits firms from operating under names that may mislead the public.

Interpretation 505-2 states that a CPA in the practice of public accounting may participate in the operation of a separate business that performs for clients any of the professional services of accounting, tax, personal financial planning, litigation support services, and those services for which standards have been promulgated by the Council. Such a member must observe all of the Rules of Conduct (see Exhibit 19–3).

Disciplinary Actions

The AICPA has a number of avenues by which members can be disciplined for violating the Code of Professional Conduct. For violations that are not sufficient to warrant formal actions, the Professional Ethics Division's executive committee can direct a member to take remedial or corrective actions. If the member rejects the committee's recommendation, the committee can refer the case to a hearing panel of the Trial Board. Membership in the AICPA can be suspended or terminated without a hearing if the member has been convicted of certain criminal offenses (such as a crime punishable by imprisonment for more than one year or filing a false income tax return on a client's behalf) or if the member's CPA certificate is suspended or revoked by a government agency. A member may also be expelled or suspended for up to two years by the Trial Board for violating any rule of the Code of Professional Conduct. For more information on the AICPA's disciplinary processes, the reader should refer to the AICPA Bylaws.

Quality Control Standards[8]

While the Code of Professional Conduct is mainly concerned with the ethical behavior of individuals, a CPA firm should have policies and procedures that monitor the firm's practice. Such a system of quality control helps the firm ensure that professional standards are being followed in its practice. In 1977 the AICPA started a voluntary peer review program,[9] and in January 1988 the AICPA approved mandatory quality review. The AICPA Division for CPA Firms SEC Practice Section Peer Review Committee and Private Companies Practice Section Peer Review Committee and the AICPA Peer Review Board (collectively, the AICPA practice-monitoring committees) conduct peer reviews for CPA firms.

Statement on Quality Control Standards (SQCS) No. 2, "System of Quality Control for a CPA Firm's Accounting and Auditing Practice" (QC 10), gives CPA firms professional guidance in establishing a system of quality control. SQCS No. 2 applies only to auditing and accounting practice (audit, attest, and review services). While not required, it is recommended that the guidance in this statement be applied to other services such as tax services and consulting services.

System of Quality Control

[LO 12]

A firm's system of quality control encompasses its organizational structure and the policies adopted and procedures established to provide the firm with reasonable assurance of conforming with professional standards (QC 10.03). A firm's system of quality control, however, has to be tailored to its size, the nature of its practice, its organization, and cost–benefit considerations. For a sole practitioner or small firm, a system of quality control is likely to be much less formal than one for a national or international firm. For example, a sole practitioner with three professional staff members may use a simple checklist to monitor his or her firm's compliance with professional standards. On the other hand, a large international CPA firm may develop very specific in-house procedures and assign full- or part-time staff to ensure compliance with the firm's quality control system.

Elements of Quality Control

[LO 13]

SQCS No. 1 identifies the following five elements of quality control:

- Independence, integrity, and objectivity.
- Personnel management.
- Acceptance and continuance of clients and engagements.
- Engagement performance.
- Monitoring.

---

[8]See R. K. McCabe, *The Accountant's Guide to Peer and Quality Review* (Westport, CT: Quorum Books, 1993), for a detailed discussion of quality and peer review.

[9]The Securities and Exchange Commission has also played a role in the establishment of peer review by using such reviews to settle disciplinary actions against CPA firms. The reader is referred to W. A. Wallace, "A Historical View of the SEC's Reports to Congress on Oversight of the Profession's Self-Regulatory Process," *Accounting Horizons* (December 1989), pp. 24–39, for a historical perspective of the SEC's involvement in peer review.

TABLE 19–5	Elements of Quality Control

- *Independence, Integrity, and Objectivity:* Policies and procedures should be established to provide the firm with reasonable assurance that personnel maintain independence (in fact and in appearance) in all required circumstances, perform all professional responsibilities with integrity, and maintain objectivity in discharging professional responsibilities.

- *Personnel Management:* Policies and procedures should be established for hiring, assigning personnel to engagements, professional development, and advancement activities that provide reasonable assurance that

  a. Those hired possess the appropriate characteristics to enable them to perform competently.

  b. Work is assigned to personnel having the degree of technical training and proficiency required in the circumstances.

  c. Personnel participate in general and engagement-specific continuing professional education and participate in professional development activities that enable them to fulfill responsibilities assigned, and fulfill applicable continuing professional education requirements of the AICPA and regulatory agencies.

- *Acceptance and Continuance of Clients and Engagements:* Policies and procedures should be established for deciding whether to accept or continue a client relationship and whether to perform a specific engagement for that client. Such procedures should provide the firm with reasonable assurance that the likelihood of association with a client whose management lacks integrity is minimized.

- *Engagement Performance:* Policies and procedures should be established to provide the firm with reasonable assurance that the work performed by engagement personnel meets applicable professional standards, regulatory requirements, and the firm's standards of quality.

- *Monitoring:* Policies and procedures should be established to provide the firm with reasonable assurance that the policies and procedures established by the firm for each of the other elements of quality control are suitably designed and are being applied effectively.

Table 19–5 defines each of the elements. It should be apparent from the definitions that these elements are interrelated. For example, personnel management encompasses criteria for professional development, hiring, advancement, and assignment of the firm's personnel to engagements, which affect policies and procedures developed to meet quality control objectives. It is important for a firm to develop a system of quality control that takes each of these elements into account and to ensure that members of the firm understand the firm's quality control policies and procedures. While not required, communication of the firm's quality control system should be in writing, with the extent of documentation varying with the size of the firm.

Table 19–6 provides some selected examples of the types of policies or procedures a firm can implement to comply with a sound system of quality control.

Monitoring Quality Control

[LO 14]

SQCS No. 3, "Monitoring a CPA Firm's Accounting and Auditing Practice," indicates that monitoring involves the ongoing consideration and evaluation of the effects of the firm's management philosophy and the environment in which the firm practices and its clients operate on (1) the relevance of and compliance with the firm's policies and procedures, (2) the adequacy of the firm's guidance materials and practice aids, and (3) the effectiveness of professional development programs. Procedures that let the firm identify and communicate circumstances that may necessitate changes and improvements to the firm's policies and procedures contribute to the monitoring function. Procedures for monitoring include:

- Inspection procedures.
- Pre-issuance and post-issuance review of selected engagements.

TABLE 19–6	Selected Quality Control Policies and Procedures

Independence, Integrity, and Objectivity
- Inform personnel of the firm's independence policies and procedures and advise them that they are expected to be familiar with these policies and procedures.
- Obtain from personnel annual, written representations stating that they are familiar with the policies and procedures and that prohibited investments are not held and were not held during the period.

Personnel Management
- Plan for the firm's personnel needs at all levels and establish quantified hiring objectives based on current clientele, anticipated growth, personnel turnover, individual advancement, and retirement.
- Identify the attributes to be sought in hirees, such as intelligence, integrity, honesty, motivation, and aptitude for the profession.

Acceptance and Continuance of Clients
- Establish procedures for evaluating prospective clients such as (1) obtaining and review of available financial information regarding the prospective clients and (2) inquiry of third parties about any information regarding the prospective client and its management.
- Designate an individual or group, at appropriate management levels, to evaluate the information obtained and to make the acceptance decision.

Engagement Performance
- Provide adequate supervision at all organizational levels, considering the training, ability, and experience of the personnel assigned.
- Develop guidelines for review of working papers and for documentation of the review process.

Monitoring
- Determine the inspection procedures necessary to provide reasonable assurance that the firm's other quality control policies and procedures are operating effectively.
- Inspect practice units, functions, or departments.

- Analysis and assessment of
  - New professional pronouncements.
  - Results of independence confirmations.
  - Continuing professional education and other professional development activities undertaken by firm personnel.
  - Decisions related to acceptance and continuance of client relationships and engagements.
  - Interviews of firm personnel.
- Determination of any corrective actions to be taken and improvements to be made in the quality control system.
- Communication to appropriate firm personnel of any weaknesses identified in the quality control system or in the level of understanding or compliance therewith.
- Follow-up by appropriate firm personnel to ensure that any necessary modifications are promptly made to the quality control policies and procedures.

The AICPA requires members to have their practices reviewed by peers every three years. Such peer reviews may substitute for some or all of a firm's inspection procedures for the period covered by the peer review.

REVIEW QUESTIONS

[LO 2]   19-1   Briefly describe the three theories of ethical behavior that can be used to analyze ethical issues in accounting.

[4]   19-2   Identify the six stages of ethical development. What level of development would typically be attained by a professional such as an auditor?

[5]   19-3   What are the two major sections of the Code of Professional Conduct? What additional guidance is provided for applying the Rules of Conduct?

[6]   19-4   Describe the six Principles of Professional Conduct.

[7]   19-5   What are the five major sections of the Rules of Conduct? Define the practice of public accounting as used in the Rules of Conduct.

[8]   19-6   Why are there so many interpretations of Rule 101, which deals with the auditor's independence?

[8]   19-7   What types of personal loans from a financial institution are allowed by the Rules of Conduct? What is meant by *normal lending procedures, terms, and requirements* within this context?

[8]   19-8   Describe how actual or threatened litigation may affect independence.

[9]   19-9   A CPA is allowed to issue an unqualified report when financial statements contain a departure from GAAP that is due to unusual circumstances. List two examples.

[10]   19-10   Generally a CPA is not allowed to disclose confidential client information without the consent of the client. Identify four circumstances in which confidential client information can be disclosed under the Rules of Conduct without the client's permission.

[11]   19-11   Give three examples of acts that are considered discreditable under the Rules of Conduct.

[11]   19-12   A CPA is allowed to advertise as long as the advertising is not false, misleading, or deceptive. Provide three examples of advertising that are forbidden by the Rules of Conduct.

[11]   19-13   A CPA is prohibited from accepting a commission for recommending or referring to a client any product or service when the CPA's firm conducts which types of engagements?

[12,13]   19-14   What is the purpose of a CPA firm's establishing a system of quality control? List the five elements of quality control and provide one policy or procedure that can be used to fulfill each element.

[12]   19-15   Why would a CPA firm join either the SEC or Private Companies Practices Section?

MULTIPLE-CHOICE QUESTIONS FROM CPA EXAMINATIONS

[8]   19-16   In which of the following situations would a CPA's independence be considered impaired?
1. The CPA maintains a checking account that is fully insured by a government deposit insurance agency at an audit-client financial institution.

2. The CPA has a direct <u>financial interest in an audit client</u>, but the interest is maintained in a blind trust. *doesn't matter* ~~no~~

3. The CPA owns a commercial building and leases it to an audit client. The rental income is <u>material to the CPA.</u> *no*
   a. 1 and 2.
   b. 2 and 3.
   c. 1 and 3.
   d. 1, 2, and 3.

[8]   19-17   The profession's ethical standards are <u>most likely</u> to be considered to have been violated when a CPA
   a. Continues an audit engagement after the commencement of litigation <u>against the CPA that alleges excessive fees were filed in</u> a stockholders' derivative action.   *no*
   b. Represents to a potential client that the CPA's fees are substantially lower than the fees charged by other CPAs for comparable services. *unless false*
   c. Issues a report on a financial forecast that omits a <u>caution regarding achievability.</u>
   d. Accepts an <u>MAS consultation engagement</u> concerning data processing services for which the <u>CPA lacks independence.</u>   *OK*

[8]   19-18   A violation of the profession's ethical standards is most likely to occur when a CPA
   a. <u>Compiles the</u> financial statements of a client that employs the CPA's spouse as a bookkeeper.   *OK*
   b. Receives a fee for <u>referring</u> audit clients to a company that sells limited partnership interests.   *NO*
   c. Purchases the portion of an insurance company that performs actuarial services for employee benefit plans.
   d. Arranges with a financial institution to collect notes issued by a client in payment of fees due.

[8]   19-19   A violation of the profession's ethical standards is *least* likely to occur when a CPA
   a. Purchases another CPA's accounting practice and bases the price on a <u>percentage of the fees accruing from clients over</u> a three-year period.
   b. Receives a <u>percentage of the amounts invested by the CPA's audit clients in a tax shelter</u> with the clients' knowledge and approval.
   c. Has a public accounting practice and also is president and sole stockholder of a corporation that engages in data processing services for the public.
   d. <u>Forms an association—*not* a partnership—with two other sole practitioners and calls the association "Adams, Betts & Associates."</u>

[8]   19-20   After beginning an audit of a new client, Larkin, CPA, discovers that the professional competence necessary for the engagement is lacking. Larkin informs management of the situation and recommends another CPA, and management engages the other CPA. Under these circumstances,
   a. Larkin's lack of competence should be construed to be a violation of generally accepted auditing standards.

    b. Larkin may request compensation from the client for any professional services rendered to it in connection with the audit.

    c. Larkin's request for a commission from the other CPA is permitted because a more competent audit can now be performed.

    d. Larkin may be indebted to the other CPA because the other CPA can collect from the client only the amount the client originally agreed to pay Larkin.

[8,9]   **19-21**   Green, CPA, is asked to render an opinion on the application of accounting principles by an entity that is audited by another CPA. Green may

    a. Not accept such an engagement because to do so would be considered unethical.

    b. Not accept such an engagement because Green would lack the necessary information on which to base an opinion without conducting an audit.

    c. Accept the engagement but should form an independent opinion without consulting with the continuing CPA.

    d. Accept the engagement but should consult with the continuing CPA to ascertain all the available facts relevant to forming a professional judgment.

[1,2,5]   **19-22**   Which of the following statements best explains why the CPA profession has found it essential to promulgate ethical standards and to establish means for ensuring their observance?

    a. Vigorous enforcement of an established code of ethics is the best way to prevent unscrupulous acts.

    b. Ethical standards that emphasize excellence in performance over material rewards establish a reputation for competence and character.

    c. A distinguishing mark of a profession is its acceptance of responsibility to the public.

    d. A requirement for a profession is to establish ethical standards that primarily stress responsibility to clients and colleagues.

[7]   **19-23**   The AICPA Code of Professional Conduct contains both general ethical principles that are aspirational in character and also a

    a. List of violations that would cause the automatic suspension of a CPA's license.

    b. Set of specific, mandatory rules describing minimum levels of conduct a CPA must maintain.

    c. Description of a CPA's procedures for responding to an inquiry from a trial board.

    d. List of specific crimes that would be considered as acts discreditable to the profession.

[10]   **19-24**   Without the consent of the client, a CPA should *not* disclose confidential client information contained in working papers to a

    a. Voluntary quality control review board.

    b. CPA firm that has purchased the CPA's accounting practice.

    c. Federal court that has issued a valid subpoena.

    d. Disciplinary body created under state statute.

[8]   19-25   Which of the following legal situations would be considered to impair the auditor's independence?

a. An expressed intention by the present management to commence litigation against the auditor, alleging deficiencies in audit work for the client, although the auditor considers that there is only a remote possibility that such a claim will be filed.

b. Actual litigation by the auditor against the client for an amount *not* material to the auditor or to the financial statements of the client arising out of disputes as to billings for management advisory services.

c. Actual litigation by the auditor against the present management, alleging management fraud or deceit.

d. Actual litigation by the client against the auditor for an amount *not* material to the auditor or to the financial statements of the client arising out of a dispute as to billings for tax services.

[8]   19-26   A client company has not paid its 2000 audit fees. According to the AICPA Code of Professional Conduct, for the auditor to be considered independent with respect to the 2001 audit, the 2000 audit fees must be paid before the

a. 2000 report is issued.

b. 2001 field work is started.

c. 2001 report is issued.

d. 2002 field work is started.

[12]   19-27   One of a CPA firm's basic objectives is to provide professional services that conform with professional standards. Reasonable assurance of achieving this basic objective is provided through

a. A system of quality control.

b. A system of peer review.

c. Continuing professional education.

d. Compliance with generally accepted reporting standards.

[13]   19-28   In connection with the element of personnel management, a CPA firm's system of quality control should ordinarily provide that all personnel

a. Have the knowledge required to enable them to fulfill the responsibilities assigned to them.

b. Meet the profession's independence rules.

c. Seek assistance from persons having appropriate levels of knowledge, judgment, and authority.

d. Demonstrate compliance with peer review directives.

[13,14]   19-29   A CPA firm's quality control procedures pertaining to the acceptance of a prospective audit client would most likely include

a. Inquiry of management as to whether disagreements between the predecessor auditor and the prospective client were resolved satisfactorily.

b. Consideration of whether sufficient competent evidential matter may be obtained to afford a reasonable basis for an opinion.

c. Inquiry of third parties, such as the prospective client's bankers and attorneys, about the prospective client and its management.

d. Consideration of whether the internal control system is sufficiently effective to permit a reduction in the extent of required substantive tests.

[13,14]   19-30   A CPA firm should establish procedures for conducting and supervising work at all organizational levels to provide reasonable assurance that the work performed meets the firm's standards of quality. To achieve this goal, the firm would most likely establish procedures for
a. Evaluating prospective and continuing client relationships.
b. Reviewing engagement working papers and reports.
c. Requiring personnel to adhere to the applicable independence rules.
d. Maintaining personnel files containing documentation related to the evaluation of personnel.

PROBLEMS

[8]   19-31   Each of the following situations involves a possible violation of the AICPA's Code of Professional Conduct. Indicate whether each situation violates the Code. If it violates the Code, indicate which rule is violated and explain why.
a. Mink & Darvis was recently awarded the audit of Hilly Farms Foods for the year ended August 31, 2000. Bill Fox, senior-in-charge, and an assistant observed the inventory on August 31. Upon completion of the inventory observation, Wally Warp, Hilly Farms' controller, informed Fox that the shipping supervisor had a small gift for him and the assistant. Fox asked Warp what the gift was for, and Warp responded that they had always given small gifts of food items to their previous auditors upon completion of the inventory observation. Fox estimates that the value of the food is less than $200.
b. Julia Roberto, a sole practitioner, has provided extensive advisory services for her audit client, Leather and Chains, Ltd. She has interpreted financial statements, provided forecasts and other analyses, counseled on potential expansion plans, and counseled on banking relationships.
c. Steve Rackwill, CPA, has been asked by his audit client, Petry Plumbing Supply, to help implement a new control system. Rackwill will arrange interviews for Petry's hiring of new personnel and instruct and oversee the training of current client personnel.
d. Bob Lanzotti is the partner-in-charge of the audit of Fleet Mobile Homes, Inc. Over the years, he has become a golfing buddy of Fleet's CEO, Jim Harris. During the current year Lanzotti and Harris jointly purchased an exclusive vacation home in North Carolina. The vacation home represents more than 10 percent of Lanzotti's personal wealth.
e. Kraemeer & Kraemeer recently won the audit of Garvin Clothiers, a large manufacturer of women's clothing. Jock Kraemeer had a substantial investment in Garvin prior to bidding on the engagement. In anticipation of winning the engagement, Kraemeer placed his shares of Garvin stock in a blind trust.

[8]   19-32   The questions on the next page are based on Rule 101 as it relates to independence and family relationships. Check "yes" if the situation violates the rule, "no" if it does not.

c. If Savage adds to his staff an individual who specializes in developing computer systems, what degree of knowledge must Savage possess in order to supervise the specialist's activities?

(AICPA, adapted)

[8,10,11]   19-39   Goodwin, a CPA, and Jensen, a banker, were the trustees of the Moore Family Trust. The trust, which was created as a spendthrift trust, provided for distribution of income annually to the four Moore adult children for life, with the principal to be distributed to their issue after the death of the last income beneficiary. The trust was funded with commercial and residential real estate and a stock portfolio.

Goodwin, in addition to being a trustee, was lawfully employed as the trust's accountant. As the trust's accountant, Goodwin prepared and signed all trust tax returns, kept the trust's accounting records, and supervised distributions to the income beneficiaries.

In 2000 Goodwin and Jensen, as trustees, sold a building owned by the trust for $400,000, its fair market value. The building had been valued at $250,000 when acquired by the trust. The $150,000 gain was allocated to income. In addition, the trust had rental, interest, and dividend income of $1,500,000 in 2000. Expenses for taxes, replacement of plumbing fixtures, roof repairs, utilities, salaries, and fees and commissions totaled $1,050,000.

On December 31, 2000, Goodwin and Jensen prepared and signed four $150,000 trust account checks and sent three of them to three of the income beneficiaries and the fourth one to a creditor of the fourth beneficiary. This beneficiary had acknowledged that the creditor was owed $200,000.

In February 2001 Goodwin discovered that Jensen had embezzled $200,000 by secretly selling part of the trust's stock portfolio. Goodwin agreed not to reveal Jensen's embezzlement if Jensen would pay Goodwin $25,000.

In April 2001 Goodwin prepared the 2000 trust income tax return. The return was signed by Goodwin as preparer and by Jensen and Goodwin as trustees and was filed with the IRS. Goodwin also prepared the 2000 income tax returns for the income beneficiaries. In an attempt to hide the embezzlement, Goodwin, in preparing the trust's tax return, claimed nonexistent losses and improper credits. The beneficiaries' returns reflected the same nonexistent losses and improper credits. Consequently, the beneficiaries' taxes were underpaid. As a result of an IRS audit, the nonexistent losses and improper credits were disallowed and the beneficiaries were assessed additional taxes, penalties, and interest.

Required:
Discuss each of the possible violations of the Code of Professional Conduct by Goodwin.

(AICPA, adapted)

DISCUSSION CASES

[3,8,10,11]   19-40   Refer back to the Sun City Savings and Loan case presented on page 664 and consider each of the following independent situations:

a. Suppose that Pina, Johnson & Associates also audited one of the entities who had received one of the large loans that are in dispute. Sam Johnson is not involved with auditing that entity. Is it ethical for Johnson to seek information on the financial condition of that entity from the auditors in his firm? What are the rights of the affected parties in this instance, and what are the costs and benefits of using such information?

b. Suppose that Johnson has determined that one of the entities that owes a disputed loan is being investigated for violating environmental laws and may be sued by the Environmental Protection Agency. Can Johnson use this information in deciding on the proper loan-loss reserve? What are the ethical considerations?

[3,8,9,10]   19-41   Wall Precision Tool Company is a large, publicly held manufacturer of precision-tooled parts with five subsidiaries located throughout the United States. On January 15, 2000, the company entered into negotiations to sell one of its subsidiaries to Tough-Nut Tool Corporation. The sale was contingent on numerous events, including a complete physical inventory that was to be taken on January 31, 2000. The physical inventory, which was observed by Tough-Nut's auditors, indicated that the inventory of the subsidiary at January 31, 2000, had been overstated by 25 percent, or $10.5 million. When the inventory shortage was discovered, Tough-Nut withdrew from the negotiations.

Surprisingly, Wall's independent auditors, Arte & Sensor (A&S), had just observed the taking of the physical inventory at that location on December 31, 1999, as part of Wall's annual audit. Inquiries by Wall's management and its internal auditors disclosed that A&S's audit procedures for the inventory observation at the subsidiary had been deficient. In particular, A&S personnel had not obtained adequate control of the inventory tags, and they had not investigated certain inventory items that represented material amounts of inventory.

The following year, Wall and A&S agreed that an extensive study of Wall's inventory controls and management information system would be conducted. A&S offered to perform the study at 50 percent of normal billing rates. Wall demanded that A&S perform the work for free because the firm had failed to detect the inventory shortage. A&S eventually agreed to perform the work free of charge.

Late in 2000, Wall retained legal counsel to determine if it had grounds for a lawsuit against A&S. The board of directors met on February 1, 2001, and voted to initiate a lawsuit against A&S. This decision was not recorded in the board's minutes. On February 7, 2001, A&S issued an unqualified report on Wall's financial statements. A week later, Wall notified A&S of its intention to file a $10 million lawsuit for damages due to the inventory shortage.

On February 28, 2001, Wall's management and A&S met to negotiate a settlement. A&S agreed to pay Wall $2.5 million and to provide an additional $2 million in professional services at no cost. The $2.5 million payment was disclosed to the public when the suit was settled. No mention of the free professional services was announced.

When the agreement was reached, Wall requested that the two parties meet with the Securities and Exchange Commission (SEC) to discuss the arrangement. Wall was concerned about whether the agreement with A&S would be viewed by the SEC as affecting A&S's independence.

Required:
a. Did A&S act ethically when agreeing to study Wall's inventory control and management information system for free? If not, what actions should A&S have taken at that time?
b. When A&S learned of Wall's lawsuit, should A&S have withdrawn from the engagement? Justify your answer.

[8,11]   19-42   Schoeck, CPA, is considering leaving a position at a major public accounting firm to join the staff of a local financial institution that does write-up work, tax preparation and planning, and financial planning.

Required:
a. What are the ethical issues for Schoeck in deciding whether to make this career change?
b. Are the Rules of Conduct applied differently to CPAs that work for a local financial institution that is not CPA-owned, as compared to a major public accounting firm?
c. Do you think the rules should be applied differently to CPAs depending on the type of entity they work for?

Chapter 20

Legal Liability

LEARNING OBJECTIVES

Upon completion of this chapter you will

[1] Understand the current legal environment for auditors.

[2] Know the definitions of key legal terms.

[3] Know the auditor's liability to clients under common law.

[4] Understand the auditor's liability to third parties under common law.

[5] Understand the auditor's legal liability under the Securities Act of 1933.

[6] Understand the auditor's legal liability under the Securities Exchange Act of 1934.

[7] Know how the Private Securities Litigation Reform Act of 1995 relieves some of the auditor's legal liability.

[8] Know how the SEC can sanction an auditor or audit firm.

[9] Understand how the Foreign Corrupt Practices Act can result in legal liability for auditors.

[10] Understand how the Racketeer Influenced and Corrupt Organizations Act can affect the auditor's legal liability.

[11] Know how an auditor can be held criminally liable for various federal and state laws.

[12] Know and understand the various approaches that the public accounting profession and firms can take to minimize legal liability.

RELEVANT ACCOUNTING AND AUDITING PRONOUNCEMENTS

AICPA, Code of Professional Conduct (ET 50-500)

SAS No. 54, "Illegal Acts" (AU 317)

SAS No. 60, "Communication of Internal Control–Related Matters Noted in an Audit" (AU 325)

SAS No. 61, "Communications with Audit Committees" (AU 380)

SAS No. 82, "Consideration of Fraud in a Financial Statement Audit" (AU 316)

Chapter 1 presented an economic view of auditing. The auditor adds value to the principal–agent relationship by providing an objective, independent opinion on the quality of the information reported. However, what prevents the auditor from cooperating with management and issuing an unqualified report on a set of financial statements that are materially misstated? The main deterrent is the threat of legal liability to the client and certain third parties. If a client or certain third parties suffer a loss from such fraudulent behavior, the auditor's personal wealth and professional reputation may be affected by litigation.

This chapter discusses auditors' legal liability. The current legal environment is presented first because in recent years auditors have been subjected to increased liability for their work product. This is followed by a brief overview of the types of legal liability an auditor may encounter. Auditors' liability under common law to clients and third parties is discussed first. Statutory liability for both civil and criminal complaints is presented next. The last section discusses a number of actions that auditors can undertake to minimize their exposure to legal liability. The appendix discusses some significant legal cases. 🌐

The Legal Environment

🖋 **[LO 1]**   The public accounting profession is very concerned about the effect of litigation on the profession. In 1992, the major accounting firms issued a Statement of Position entitled "The Liability Crisis in the United States: Impact on the Accounting Profession."[1] The position paper stated that

> The present liability system has produced an epidemic of litigation that is spreading throughout the accounting profession and business community. It is threatening the independent audit function and the financial reporting system, the strength of the U.S. capital markets, and the competitiveness of the U.S. economy.
>
> The principal causes of the accounting profession's liability problems are unwarranted litigation and coerced settlements. (p. 1)

Some of the facts revealed in this document indicate the effect of litigation on the profession. For example, Big 6 (now Big 5) expenditures for settling and defending lawsuits from 1991 to 1993 were between 9 and 12 percent of their auditing and accounting revenues in the United States.[2] The profession received some relief with passage of the Private Securities Litigation Reform Act of 1995 (discussed in this chapter), but this statute provides relief only for litigation under the federal securities laws. Significant litigation costs continues for the public accounting profession.

Overview[3]

🖋 **[LO 2]**   In the current legal environment, auditors can be held liable for a number of types of actions. Table 20–1 defines key legal terms, and Table 20–2 summarizes the auditor's liability by type of liability and actions resulting in liability.

Under common law, an auditor can be held liable to clients for breach of contract, negligence or gross negligence, and fraud. The auditor's liability to third parties under common law represents one of the more perplexing

---

[1]Arthur Andersen & Co., Coopers & Lybrand, Deloitte & Touche, Ernst & Young, KPMG Peat Marwick, and Price Waterhouse, "The Liability Crisis in the United States: Impact on the Accounting Profession, A Statement of Position" (August 6, 1992).

[2]*Accounting Today* (January 24, 1994).

[3]A number of excellent sources provide more detailed coverage of issues related to legal liability. The reader is referred to M. J. Epstein and A. D. Spalding, *The Accountant's Guide to Legal Liability and Ethics* (Homewood, IL: Business One Irwin, 1993), and R. S. Kay and D. G. Searfoss, *Deloitte & Touche Professor's Handbook,* chap. 34 (Boston: Warren, Gorham & Lamont, 1992 update). See also P. J. Ostling, "Accountants' Legal Liability—A Historical Perspective," *Auditing Symposium VIII: Proceedings of the 1986 Touche Ross/University of Kansas Symposium on Auditing Problems* (Lawrence: University of Kansas, 1986), for an excellent historical overview of auditors' legal liability.

TABLE 20–1	Definition of Key Legal Terms

• *Privity*	Absent a contractual or fiduciary relationship, the accountant does not owe a duty of care to an injured party.
• *Breach of contract*	Occurs when the client or auditor fails to meet the terms and obligations established in the contract, which is normally finalized in the engagement letter. Third parties may have privity or near privity of contract.
• *Tort*	A wrongful act other than a breach of contract for which civil action may be taken.
• *Ordinary negligence*	An absence of reasonable or due care in the conduct of an engagement. Due care is evaluated in terms of what other professional accountants would have done under similar circumstances.
• *Gross negligence*	An extreme, flagrant, or reckless departure from professional standards of due care. This is also referred to as *constructive fraud.*
• *Fraud*	Actions taken with the knowledge and intent to deceive.

TABLE 20–2	Summary of Types of Liability and Auditors' Actions Resulting in Liability

Type of Liability	Auditors' Actions Resulting in Liability
Common law—clients	Breach of contract Negligence Gross negligence/constructive fraud Fraud
Common law—third parties	Negligence Gross negligence/constructive fraud Fraud
Civil liability under federal statutes*	Negligence Gross negligence/constructive fraud Fraud
Criminal liability under federal statutes*	Willful violation of federal statutes

*Auditors may also be civilly and criminally liable under state statutes. Coverage of liability under specific state statutes is beyond the scope of this book.

areas of litigation. While the overall trend in this area has been to hold auditors liable to an expanded group of third parties, the problem is complicated by the fact that the outcomes of many cases have been determined by the location in which the case is tried. Some state courts follow a strict privity rule on lawsuits by third parties against auditors, while others allow a liberal interpretation of auditors' liability to third parties under common law.

Statutes such as the Securities Act of 1933 and the Securities Exchange Act of 1934 represent major sources of legal actions against auditors. Auditors are liable mainly for gross negligence and fraud under these statutes; however, some parts of the acts have been determined to hold auditors liable for ordinary negligence. More recent statutes, such as the Foreign Corrupt Practices Act and the Racketeer Influenced and Corrupt Organizations Act, represent potential areas for liability against auditors. Finally, under certain circumstances an auditor can be held criminally liable under federal and state statutes. There have been few instances of major criminal actions against auditors.

Common Law—Clients

[LO 3]   Common law does not require that the CPA guarantee his or her work product. It does, however, require that the auditor perform professional services with due care. This requires that the auditor perform his or her professional services with the same degree of skill, knowledge, and judgment possessed by other members of the profession. When an auditor fails to carry out contractual arrangements with the client, he or she may be held liable for breach of contract or negligence. Under common law, the auditor is also liable to the client for gross negligence and fraud.

Breach of Contract

Breach-of-contract liability is based on the auditor's failing to complete the services agreed to in the contract with the client. As discussed in Chapter 5, an engagement letter should establish the responsibilities for both the CPA and the client. In performing an audit, the CPA's obligation is to examine the client's financial statements and issue the appropriate opinion in accordance with professional standards. The contract between the client and the CPA stipulates the amount of fees to be charged for the designated professional services, and deadlines for completing the services are normally indicated or implied in the contract. If the client breaches its obligations under the engagement letter, the auditor is excused from his or her contractual obligations. If the CPA discontinues an audit without adequate cause, he or she may be liable for economic injury suffered by the client (see Exhibit 20–1). Similarly, other issues (such as timely delivery of the audit report or failure to detect a material defalcation) can lead to litigation by the client against the auditor.

Negligence

A tort is a wrongful act other than a breach of contract for which civil action may be taken. If an engagement is performed without due care, the CPA may be held liable for an actionable tort in negligence. Liability for negligence represents a deviation from a standard of behavior that is consistent with that of a "reasonable person." When an individual such as a CPA possesses special skills and knowledge, ordinary reasonable care is not sufficient. An oft-cited quote from Cooley's *Torts** indicates the responsibility of those offering special skills:

> In all those employments where particular skill is requisite, if one offers his services, he is understood as holding himself out to the public as possessing the degree of skill commonly possessed by others in the same employment, and if his pretensions are unfounded, he commits a species of fraud upon every man who employs him in reliance on his public profession. But no man, whether skilled or unskilled, undertakes that the task he assumes shall be performed successfully,

---

*D. Haggard, *Cooley on Torts*, 4th ed., p. 472.

EXHIBIT 20–1

Deloitte & Touche's Withdrawal from Medtrans Audit Upheld

Medtrans, an ambulance service provider, retained Deloitte & Touche to audit its financial statements. Medtrans needed capital and sought $10 million in financing from an outside investor. Medtrans gave the potential investor *unaudited* financial statements showing profits of $1.9 million. Deloitte & Touche was in the process of completing its audit during Medtrans negotiations with the outside investor. Deloitte & Touche proposed adjustments that resulted in Medtrans's financial statements showing a $500,000 loss. Prior to Deloitte & Touche proposing the adjustments, the company's CFO resigned after indicating that he could not sign the management representation letter. When presented with the proposed adjustments, Medtrans's CEO threatened to get a court order forcing Deloitte & Touche to complete the audit. Deloitte withdrew from the engagement. Medtrans retained two other CPA firms, both of which were either discharged or withdrew. A third firm issued an unqualified audit report that contained the adjustments proposed by Deloitte & Touche.

Medtrans alleged that Deloitte & Touche's wrongful withdrawal resulted in the company's failure to complete the financing, and that the subsequent sale of the company was for significantly less than its true value. At trial Medtrans asserted that, under California law, a CPA firm could not, under any circumstances, withdraw from an engagement if it unduly jeopardized the interest of the client. Deloitte & Touche argued that the approved California jury instructions on the duration of a professional's duty were contrary to professional standards, which authorize the auditor to resign. The jury in this case ruled in favor of Medtrans and awarded the company nearly $10 million.

In March 1998 the California Court of Appeals reversed the decision, holding that judges should instruct juries about the profession's standards. The court held that an auditor, by auditing financial statements, assumes a public responsibility that transcends any employment relationship with the client. This decision is significant because it held that an accountant's duty of care can be based on professional standards rather than rules of law that are contrary to professional standards. It also upheld the auditor's right to withdraw from an engagement when the client requests conduct that is not consistent with GAAP or GAAS.

Sources: National Medical Transportation Network v. Deloitte & Touche, 98 D.A.R., 2850, March 23, 1998, and "Court Rules on Importance of GAAP and GAAS," Journal of Accountancy (June 1998), p. 24.

and without fault or error; he undertakes for good faith and integrity, but not for infallibility, and he is liable to his employer for negligence, bad faith, or dishonesty, but not for losses consequent upon mere errors of judgment.

Thus, a CPA has the duty to conduct an engagement using the same degree of care that would be used by an ordinary, prudent member of the public accounting profession. The requisite elements required for establishing an auditor's liability for negligence are (1) the duty to conform to a required standard of care, (2) failure to act in accordance with that duty, (3) a causal connection between the auditor's negligence and the client's damage, and (4) actual loss or damage to the client.

Suits by clients against auditors often allege that the auditors did not detect some type of fraud or defalcation. The client can generally prove the existence of a duty of care based on the engagement contract. However, the auditor may be able to argue successfully that the client's loss was due not to any negligence on his or her part but rather to fraudulent actions committed by an employee or manager of the client. In such circumstances, there is contributory negligence by the client, and cross-claims may arise between the auditor and client. *Cenco, Inc.* v. *Seidman & Seidman* was a case that involved such circumstances. Exhibit 20–2 presents a summary of

EXHIBIT 20–2

Cenco, Inc. v. *Seidman & Seidman* (1982)

Between 1970 and 1975, managerial employees of Cenco, Inc., engaged in a massive fraud. The fraud began in the company's Medical/Health Division and eventually spread to Cenco's top management. By the time the fraud was made public, the chairman and president, plus a number of other top managers, were involved in the fraud. A number of the board of directors were not involved in the fraud, but there was evidence that they had been negligent in allowing the fraud to continue. Seidman & Seidman was Cenco's auditor throughout the period of the fraud.

The fraud involved primarily the inflating of inventories in the Medical/Health Division above their fair market value. This increased the apparent value of Cenco as well as its stock price. This allowed Cenco to purchase other companies cheaply, using its overvalued stock, and to borrow money at lower interest rates.

Cenco's new management and Seidman & Seidman filed cross-claims against each other, and a trial date was set. One day before the start of the cross-claims trial, Seidman & Seidman agreed to pay $3.5 million to settle the class action suit. Prior to submitting the case to the jury, the trial judge granted a directed verdict in favor of Cenco, dismissing Seidman's cross-claim, and a directed verdict in favor of Seidman & Seidman on those counts of Cenco's cross-claim that the CPA firm had aided and abetted the fraud. The case went to the jury on the three remaining counts of breach of contract, negligence, and fraud. The jury found that Seidman & Seidman was innocent on all counts. The verdict was appealed by Cenco to the US Court of Appeals for the Seventh Circuit. The court of appeals upheld the lower court and found that Seidman & Seidman had not been responsible for any liability for breach of contract, negligence, or fraud. The wrongdoing of Cenco's old management was deemed to be part of an adequate defense.

the case. In this instance, the client (new management) alleged that Seidman & Seidman was negligent for not having uncovered the prior management's fraudulent actions. The court ruled that, considering management's involvement in the fraud, the CPA firm had not been negligent.

Another well-known case that alleged negligence by an accountant is the *1136 Tenants' Corp.* v. *Max Rothenberg & Co.,* which relates to unaudited financial statements and the CPA's failure to communicate suspicious circumstances to the client. Exhibit 20–3 presents a summary of the case. The *1136 Tenants'* case established a duty on the part of a CPA doing work on unaudited financial statements to communicate to the client any circumstances that give reason to believe that fraud may exist. One outcome of this case was the establishment of Statements on Standards for Accounting and Review Services, which prescribe procedures that CPAs should follow when performing engagements such as compilations and reviews (discussed in Chapter 21). However, the outcome of legal cases that have resulted from actions taken for compilation and review services has not removed CPAs from potential liability. For example, in *Robert Woller & Co.* v. *Fidelity Bank,* the court held the firm liable for problems in a company resulting from internal control weaknesses, even though SSARS No. 1 states that a review engagement does not contemplate a study and evaluation of internal control.

Fraud

An auditor can be held liable for fraud when he or she acted with knowledge and intent to deceive. Generally, however, actions alleging fraud result from lawsuits by third parties and thus are discussed in more detail in the next section.

EXHIBIT 20–3

1136 Tenants' Corp. v. Max Rothenberg & Co. (1967)

Jerome Riker was a powerful New York City businessman with extensive business interests in the real estate industry. During the early 1960s, Riker diverted money from a number of trust funds of cooperatives that he managed for use in a personal real estate investment.

One of the cooperatives that was involved in the embezzlement was the 1136 Tenants' Corporation. Riker had misappropriated approximately $130,000 of the cooperative's funds. When the cooperative was unable to recover the funds from Riker, it filed a civil suit against the public accounting firm, Max Rothenberg & Company, which had prepared the annual financial statements and tax return. The plaintiffs alleged that the accounting firm should have discovered the embezzlement of funds by Riker.

One issue that arose during the trial was the contractual agreement between the public accounting firm and the 1136 Tenants' Corporation. There was no written engagement letter, only an oral agreement between one of the firm's partners and Riker. The cooperative alleged that the firm had been retained to do an audit, while the firm alleged that it had been retained only to prepare the tax return and perform "write-up" services. Another issue was the fact that the firm had identified some missing invoices and had not investigated these items further. The working papers detailed $44,000 of expenses for which no supporting documentation could be located. These were fictitious expenses used by Riker to extract funds from the cooperative.

The court ruled that even if the firm had agreed to provide only write-up services, it had an obligation to notify the tenants about the suspicious nature of the missing invoices. Damaging to the firm's defense was the admission by one of its partners that the engagement had been more extensive than that called for by a normal write-up engagement. The income statement also included a line item labeled "audit." The court ruled in favor of the tenants and awarded them damages of more than $230,000. The decision was upheld upon appeal by the New York appellate court. The size of the judgment was far in excess of the fee of $600 paid to the firm.

This court decision resulted in two significant changes in the profession:

- It reinforced the need by firms to have *written* engagement letters.
- It led to the issuance by the AICPA of Statements on Standards for Accounting and Review Services.

Common Law—Third Parties

[LO 4]   Under common law, auditors can be held liable to third parties for negligence and fraud. However, this area of liability is very complex, and court rulings are not always consistent across federal and state judicial jurisdictions.

Negligence

When an auditor fails to conduct an engagement with due care, he or she can be held liable for negligence to third parties (plaintiffs). To prevail in a suit alleging negligence, the third party must prove that (1) the auditor had a duty to the plaintiff to exercise due care, (2) the auditor breached that duty by not following professional standards, (3) the auditor's breach of due care was the proximate cause of the third party's injury, and (4) the third party suffered an actual loss as a result. The main difficulty faced by third parties in proving negligence against an auditor is showing that the auditor's duty to exercise due care extended to them. Three standards have evolved for defining the extent of the auditor's liability to third parties: *privity, foreseen persons or classes,* and *reasonably foreseeable third parties.*

EXHIBIT 20–4

Ultramares v. *Touche, et al.* (1931)

Fred Stern & Company imported and sold rubber during the 1920s. This industry required extensive working capital, and the company used borrowings from banks for its financing activities. In 1924 Stern requested a $100,000 loan from Ultramares Corporation. Before deciding to make the loan, Ultramares requested that Stern provide an audited balance sheet. Touche, Niven & Company had just issued an unqualified audit report on the December 31, 1923, balance sheet.

Stern's management asked Touche to provide 32 serially numbered copies of the audit report. Touche had audited Stern for three years and knew that the audit reports were being used by Stern to obtain external debt financing. Touche, however, did not know which specific banks or finance companies would be given the reports. The balance sheet showed assets of $2.5 million. Ultramares provided the $100,000 loan and two additional loans totaling $65,000. In addition, Stern obtained bank loans of approximately $300,000 by providing the December 31, 1923, balance sheet audited by Touche.

In 1925 the company declared bankruptcy. It came to light during the trial that Stern had already been bankrupt in 1923 and that false accounting record entries had concealed the company's problems. Ultramares alleged that Touche had been both negligent and fraudulent in its audit of Stern. This case was viewed as a test case for third parties seeking damages from auditors. At that time, legal doctrine required that a contractual relationship exist between the auditor and a third party before losses could be recovered.

The jury in the case dismissed the fraud charges against Touche but ruled that Touche had been negligent and awarded approximately $186,000 in damages. The trial judge overturned the jury's verdict on the grounds that Ultramares had not been in privity with Touche. The appellate division of the New York Supreme Court voted 3 to 2 in favor of Ultramares, ruling that the judge had inappropriately overruled the jury verdict. Touche's attorneys appealed the decision to the court of appeals, which ruled unanimously in favor of Touche, therefore upholding the privity doctrine. The quote included in the text by Judge Cardozo, the chief justice of the court, summarizes the court's decision.

Privity   The traditional view held that, under common law, auditors had no liability to third parties who did not have a privity relationship with the auditor. *Privity* means that the obligations that exist under a contract are between the original parties to the contract, and failure to perform with due care results in a breach of that duty only to those parties. The landmark decision in this area, *Ultramares* v. *Touche, et al.*, held that the auditor was not liable to third parties who relied on a negligently prepared audit report. Exhibit 20–4 provides a summary of the *Ultramares* case. The rationale for this finding by the New York Court of Appeals is summarized in a famous quote by Judge Cardozo:

> If a liability for negligence exists, a thoughtless slip or blunder, the failure to detect a theft or forgery beneath the cover of deceptive entries, may expose accountants to a liability in an indeterminate amount for an indeterminate time to an indeterminate class. The hazards of a business on these terms are so extreme as to enkindle doubt whether a flaw may not exist in the implication of a duty that exposes to these circumstances.

While the *Ultramares* decision held to a strict privity standard, a number of subsequent court decisions in other states have eroded this precedent. In 1985, however, the New York Court of Appeals reaffirmed the privity rule in the case of *Credit Alliance* v. *Arthur Andersen & Co.* In this lawsuit, Credit Alliance alleged that the auditor had known that the plaintiff was the client's principal lender and had frequently communicated with the plaintiff regarding the audited financial statements. The court upheld the lender's claim that Arthur Andersen had known that Credit Alliance was relying on the financial statements prior to extending credit. The court also ruled that there had been direct communication between the lender and the auditor regarding the client. The *Credit Alliance* case lists the following tests that must be satisfied for holding auditors liable for negligence to third parties: (1) the accountant must be aware that the financial statements are to be used for a particular purpose or purposes, (2) in the furtherance of which a known party or parties was intended to rely, and (3) there must have been some conduct on the part of the accountants linking them to that party or parties, which evinces the accountants' understanding of that party or parties' reliance.

In a 1992 case, *Security Pacific Business Credit, Inc. v. Peat Marwick Main & Co.,* the New York Court of Appeals ruled in favor of Peat Marwick because the plaintiff's reliance was based on one telephone call to the firm's audit partner. Based on this case, it appears that a critical test established in the *Credit Alliance* case is element 3, the requirement that the third party be known to the auditor and that the auditor has directly conveyed the audit report or acted to induce reliance on the audit report.

Foreseen Persons or Classes   Many courts have reexamined the notion of *caveat emptor* ("buyer beware") and substituted the concept of public responsibility. Among the reasons that have been advanced by the courts for extending the privity standard are (1) the increased liability of other professionals to nonprivity users of their services, (2) the lack of fairness of imposing the burden of economic loss on innocent financial statement users, (3) the assumption that expanded liability will cause auditors to improve their auditing procedures, (4) the ability of auditors to obtain insurance against the increased risks, and (5) the ability of the auditors to pass the increased audit costs and insurance premiums on to their clients.

In 1968 a federal district court decision, *Rusch Factors, Inc. v. Levin,* applied Section 552 of the Restatement (Second) of the Law of Torts to an accountant's third-party liability suit. The case is described in Exhibit 20–5.

E X H I B I T   20–5

Rusch Factors, Inc. v. Levin (1968)

In this case, the plaintiff, Rusch Factors, Inc., had requested audited financial statements as a prerequisite for providing a loan to a Rhode Island corporation. Levin audited the financial statements, which showed the company to be solvent when it was actually insolvent. Rusch Factors loaned the corporation $337,000 based on the audited financial statements. When the company went into receivership, Rusch Factors sued Levin for a loss of $121,000.

The federal district court, sitting in Rhode Island, denied Levin's motion to dismiss for a lack of privity. In finding Levin liable for negligence, the court concluded that the *Ultramares* doctrine was inappropriate and relied heavily on the Restatement (Second) of the Law of Torts. The court stated that the auditor had known that his certification was to be used and relied upon by Rusch Factors, and therefore he could be held liable for financial misrepresentations relied upon by *foreseen and limited classes of persons.*

Basically, a company engaged Levin to audit the financial statements for the purpose of obtaining financing from Rusch Factors. The statements portrayed the company as solvent. The plaintiff made a large loan to the company, which subsequently went bankrupt. The federal district court found the public accounting firm negligent, relying on Section 552 of the Restatement in reaching its decision.

The Restatement is a compendium of common law prepared by legal scholars and presents an alternative view to the traditional *Ultramares* rule. Section 552 states the following:

1. One who, in the course of his business, profession, or employment, or in a transaction in which he has a pecuniary interest, supplies false information for the guidance of others in their business transactions, is subject to liability for pecuniary loss caused to them by their justifiable reliance upon the information, if he fails to exercise reasonable care or competence in obtaining or communicating the information.

2. Except as stated in subsection (3), the liability stated in subsection (1) is limited to loss suffered (a) by the person or one of the persons for whose benefit and guidance he intends to supply the information, or knows that the recipient intends to supply it; and (b) through reliance upon it in a transaction which he intends the information to influence, or knows that the recipient so intends, or in a substantially similar transaction.

3. The liability of one who is under a public duty to give the information extends to loss suffered by any of the class of persons for whose benefit the duty is created, in any of the transactions in which it is intended to protect them.

The Restatement narrows the auditor's liability to a small group of persons and classes who are or should be foreseen by the auditor as relying on the financial information. However, because the language of the Restatement is general, it is subject to different interpretations. The following examples abstracted from the Restatement help to illustrate the possibilities for auditor liability.

Example 1

Cornelius Manufacturing Co. is negotiating for a $1,000,000 loan from the First National Bank of Sun City. The bank requires that Cornelius Manufacturing provide audited financial statements. Cornelius engages the public accounting firm of Cantbe & Mustbe (C&M) to conduct the audit, informing them that the audit is for the express purpose of obtaining credit from the First National Bank of Sun City. C&M accepts the engagement with the understanding that the financial statements are for the bank's use. The First National Bank of Sun City goes into bankruptcy, and Cornelius submits the audited financial statements to Waldo National Bank without communicating with C&M. Waldo National Bank lends Cornelius the $1,000,000. The financial statements materially overstate the financial resources of Cornelius, and Waldo National Bank suffers a loss on the loan. In this example, the Restatement indicates that C&M is not liable to Waldo National Bank because Waldo was *not* a foreseen third party.

Example 2

> The same facts apply as in Example 1, except that Cornelius says nothing to C&M about supplying the financial statements to the First National Bank of Sun City; Cornelius merely tells C&M that the company expects to negotiate a bank loan and is considering going to the First National Bank of Sun City. In this instance, the Restatement indicates that C&M would be liable to Waldo National Bank because Waldo was a foreseen third party.

Example 3

> The same facts apply as in Example 2, except that Cornelius informs C&M that the company is planning on negotiating a bank loan without mentioning a specific bank. Again, under the Restatement, C&M would be liable to Waldo National Bank because Waldo was a foreseen third party.

Subsequent to *Rusch Factors,* a number of federal and state courts have followed the approach outlined in the Restatement. In fact, Epstein and Spalding state, "The *Restatement (Second)* approach is quickly replacing the *Ultramares* approach in many states, both by statute and case law, and is now considered the majority view."[4]

Reasonably Foreseeable Third Parties   A few states have adopted a more expansive view of auditors' liability to third parties: the "reasonably foreseeable third parties" approach. In the first case in this area, *H. Rosenblum, Inc.* v. *Adler,* the New Jersey Supreme Court ruled that Touche Ross & Co. was responsible for damages incurred by all reasonably foreseeable third parties who had relied on the financial statements. Exhibit 20–6 provides more details on this case.

Another important case that followed this approach was *Citizens State Bank* v. *Timm, Schmidt & Company* (1983). In this case, the bank sued the public accounting firm after relying on financial statements for one of its debtors that had been audited by Timm, Schmidt & Company. The Wisconsin court extended the scope of third parties to include all reasonably foreseeable users. The court used a number of the reasons just cited for extending auditors' liability beyond privity. The following quote from this case demonstrates the court's thoughts.

> If relying third parties, such as creditors, are not allowed to recover, the cost of credit to the general public will increase because creditors will either have to absorb the cost of bad loans made in reliance on faulty information or hire independent accountants to verify the information received. Accountants may spread the risk through the use of liability insurance.

---

[4]Epstein and Spalding, *The Accountant's Guide to Legal Liability and Ethics,* p. 52.

EXHIBIT 20–6

H. Rosenblum, Inc. v. *Adler* (1983)

The Rosenblum family agreed to sell its retail catalog showroom business, H. Rosenblum, Inc., to Giant Stores in exchange for Giant common stock. The Rosenblums relied on Giant's 1971 and 1972 financial statements, which had been audited by Touche Ross & Co. A year later, it was revealed that Giant Stores's financial statements contained material misstatements. Giant Stores filed for bankruptcy, and the company's stock became worthless. The Rosenblums sued Touche, alleging negligence. Touche did not know the Rosenblums and had not known that the financial statements would be relied on during merger negotiations.

The lower courts in this case did not allow the Rosenblums' claims against Touche, on the grounds that the Rosenblums did not meet either the *Ultramares* privity test or the Restatement (Second) of the Law of Torts' "foreseen third parties" test. The New Jersey Supreme Court overturned the lower courts' decisions. The court held that the auditor had "a duty to all those whom the auditor should reasonably foresee as recipient from the company of the statements for its proper business purposes, provided that the recipients rely on the statements." Thus the court concluded that auditors should be liable to all reasonably foreseeable third parties who rely on the financial statements. The court indicated that the auditor's function had expanded from one of a watchdog for management to that of an independent evaluator of the adequacy and fairness of the financial statements presented by management to third parties. The court also cited the accountant's ability to obtain insurance against third-party claims.

One difficulty with this approach is that, in the current legal environment, public accounting firms may no longer be able to secure sufficient liability insurance, or the cost of such insurance may be exorbitant.

Fraud

If an auditor has acted with knowledge and intent to deceive a third party, he or she can be held liable for fraud. The plaintiff (third party) must prove (1) a false representation by the accountant, (2) knowledge or belief by the accountant that the representation was false, (3) that the accountant intended to induce the third party to rely on the false representation, (4) that the third party relied on the false representation, and (5) that the third party suffered damages. Courts have held that fraudulent intent may be established by proof that the accountant acted with knowledge of the false representation or with reckless disregard for its truth (referred to as *scienter*).

Some courts have interpreted gross negligence as an instance of fraud (also referred to as *constructive fraud*). *Gross negligence* is defined to be an extreme, flagrant, or reckless deviation from professional standards of due care. An important case in this area is *State Street Trust Co.* v. *Ernst* (1938). In this case, the auditors issued an unqualified opinion on their client's financial statements, knowing that State Street Trust Company was making a loan based on those financial statements. A month later, the auditors sent a letter to the client indicating that receivables had been overstated. The auditors, however, did not communicate this information to State Street Trust Company, and the client subsequently went bankrupt. The New York court ruled that the auditor's actions appeared to be gross negligence and that "heedless and reckless disregard of consequences may take the place of deliberate intention."

Statutory Liability

Various statutes have been passed at both the federal and state levels that are intended to protect the public from malfeasance in the marketplace. While not aimed directly at auditors, these statutes do raise the potential for legal liability. The discussion in this section is limited to the major federal statutes.

The Securities Act of 1933 and the Securities Exchange Act of 1934 are the two major statutes that create liability for auditors when financial statements contain material misstatements. On the other hand, the Private Securities Litigation Reform Act of 1995 provides some protection for auditors, and others, from securities litigation. The Foreign Corrupt Practices Act and the Racketeer Influenced and Corrupt Organizations Act (RICO) are two other statutes that have the potential of imposing liability on auditors. The reader should also note that most states have securities laws and RICO statutes.

Securities Act of 1933

🖋 **[LO 5]**

This statute generally regulates the disclosure of material facts in a registration statement for a new public offering of securities. While a number of sections of the Securities Act of 1933 may subject auditors to liability, Section 11 imposes a liability on issuers and others, including auditors, for losses suffered by third parties when false or misleading information is included in a registration statement. Section 11 states:

> (a) *Persons possessing cause of action; persons liable.* In case any part of the registration statement, when such part became effective, contained an untrue statement of a material fact or omitted to state a material fact required to be stated therein or necessary to make the statements therein not misleading, any person acquiring such security (unless it is proved that at the time of such acquisition he knew of such untruth or omission) may, either at law or in equity, in any court of competent jurisdiction, sue—
>
> (4) every accountant . . . who has with his consent been named as having prepared or certified any part of the registration statement. . . .

In contrast to the situation under common law, the plaintiff does not have to prove negligence or fraud, reliance on the auditor's opinion, a causal relationship, or a contractual relationship; the plaintiff need only prove that a loss was suffered by investing in the registered security and that the audited financial statements contained a material omission or misstatement. The misstatement can be the result of mere ordinary negligence. Section 11 is more favorable for plaintiffs than is common law because the *auditor* must prove that he or she was not negligent.

One defense available to the auditor is that of "due diligence." That is, the auditor must have made a reasonable investigation of the facts supporting or contradicting the information included in the registration statement. Such an investigation should be similar to one that a prudent person would make under similar circumstances. A leading case under Section 11 is *Escott* v. *BarChris Construction Corp.*, in which the court held that the auditor's actions for events subsequent to the audited balance sheet had not been conducted with due diligence. In this instance, the senior auditor re-

EXHIBIT 20–7

Escott v. *BarChris Construction Corp.* (1968)

The primary business activity of BarChris Corporation was constructing bowling alleys. BarChris had two types of sales agreements. Under the first type, the bowling alleys were constructed for small investment syndicates, which would make a small down payment and give BarChris a note for the remaining amount, which was due over several years. Under the second type of sales transaction, the company entered into sale and leaseback arrangements with finance companies. Both of these types of transactions resulted in a constant need for external financing. In 1961 the company filed a registration statement to issue debentures. Shortly thereafter, the market for bowling alley construction dried up, and in October 1962 BarChris filed for bankruptcy protection.

The purchasers of the debentures filed suit against BarChris's auditors, Peat Marwick Mitchell & Company, who had audited the BarChris financial statements for 1958 through 1960 that were contained in the S-1 registration statement. Peat Marwick had also conducted an S-1 review on the unaudited financial statements for the first quarter of 1961. In finding the auditor liable, the court commented that the auditor can avoid liability under Section 11 if he or she can prove "due diligence," that is, that a reasonable investigation was performed such that there is reasonable ground to believe that the registration statement was true and there were no omissions of material facts. The judge criticized the firm's assignment of the senior auditor, who was not a CPA at the time, had had no previous bowling industry experience, and had just been promoted to senior. The judge ruled that the audit program used for the S-1 due diligence review had been in conformity with GAAS but that the senior's performance of the auditing procedures had not been satisfactory. The senior had devoted about 20 hours to the S-1 review, and he had accepted management's answers to questions without verifying them.

As a result of this case, the profession issued more definitive standards on reviewing subsequent events.

viewing subsequent events had not spent sufficient time on this important task and had accepted glib answers to key questions. The court determined that there had been sufficient danger signals that further investigation was necessary. The *Escott* v. *BarChris Construction Corp.* case is also of interest because of the court's ruling on certain accounting matters and its determination of materiality. Exhibit 20–7 presents a detailed summary of this case.

A more recent and significant case under Section 11 and other sections of the 1933 act was *Bernstein* v. *Crazy Eddie, Inc.* Crazy Eddie, Inc., made a number of public offerings of securities. Then the founder and president of the company resigned, and the successor management team discovered that the financial statements issued by the company during the public offering were fraudulent. The company's financial statements had been misstated through inflated inventory and improper transactions by the founder and his family. The court ruled against the auditors, indicating that the plaintiffs did not have to prove fraud or gross negligence. They had to prove only that the misstated information was material. Exhibit 20–8 describes the case.

Other important cases tried under the Securities Act of 1933 are Continental Vending (*United States* v. *Simon*) and National Student Marketing (*United States* v. *Natelli*). Both of these cases, which also resulted in criminal proceedings against the auditor, are described in the appendix to this chapter.

Bernstein v. Crazy Eddie, Inc. (1989)

Eddie Antar was the founder of and major shareholder in Crazy Eddie. The company made several public offerings of securities, including the sale of shares held by Eddie Antar and his family. The prospectuses and financial statements from 1984 through 1987 erroneously gave the impression that Crazy Eddie was a rapidly growing firm. When Mr. Antar resigned his position as president, the successor management discovered that the financial statements issued prior to and included in the public offerings had been materially misstated. In particular, there was an estimated inventory shortage of $65 million, and the company's net worth was now only $7 million.

The financial statements had been misstated by a number of schemes. Net income and inventory had been inflated through improper financial reporting practices. First, inventory marked for return to manufacturers had been included as inventory merchandise. Second, certain consignments had been treated as sales. Last, there had been related inventory sales to the founder and members of his family that were later resold to others. The company had also overstated per store sales figures. All of these actions appear to have been taken to support the price of Crazy Eddie stock and to directly benefit Mr. Antar and his family. The discovery of the extent of the problems was complicated by the fact that certain documents had been altered or destroyed prior to the new management's assuming control.

The plaintiffs in this case were purchasers of the company's stock prior to the disclosure of the fraudulent financial statements. They sued the public accounting firm, the board of directors, and others, alleging that the accounting firm had violated GAAS and GAAP by failing to uncover the company's fraudulent and fictitious activities. The plaintiffs were able to show that the certified financial statements in the registration statements and prospectuses had been false and misleading in violation of Sections 11 and 12 of the Securities Act of 1933.

The court ruled against the public accounting firm and upheld the plaintiffs' Section 11 and 12 claims. The court held that the plaintiffs did not have to prove fraud or gross negligence, only that any material misstatement in the registration statements was misleading.

Securities Exchange Act of 1934

[LO 6]

This statute is concerned primarily with ongoing reporting by companies whose securities are listed and traded on a stock exchange or that meet certain other statutory requirements. Typical reporting requirements under the 1934 act include the quarterly filing of a 10Q Form, the annual filing of a 10K Form, and the filing of an 8K Form whenever a significant event takes place that affects the entity. While a number of sections of this statute may have liability consequences for the auditor, two sections are particularly important: Section 18 and Section 10(b), including Rule 10b-5.

Section 18 imposes liability on any person who makes a material false or misleading statement in documents filed with the Securities and Exchange Commission (SEC). The auditor's liability can be limited if the auditor can show that he or she "acted in good faith and had no knowledge that such statement was false or misleading." However, a number of cases have limited the auditor's good-faith defense when the auditor's action has been judged to be grossly negligent.

Perhaps the greatest source of liability for auditors under the 1934 act is Section 10(b) and the related Rule 10b-5. Section 10(b) provides for a wide scope of liability. Rule 10b-5 amplifies Section 10(b) and states that it is

> unlawful for any person, directly or indirectly, by the use of any means or instrumentality of interstate commerce, or of the mails, or of any facility of any national securities exchange,

a. To employ any device, scheme, or artifice to defraud,
b. To make any untrue statement of a material fact or to omit to state a material fact necessary in order to make the statement made, in the light of the circumstances under which they were made, not misleading, or
c. To engage in any act, practice, or course of business which operates or would operate as a fraud or deceit upon any person, in connection with the purchase or sale of any security.

Once a plaintiff has established that he or she can sue under Rule 10b-5, the following elements must be proved: (1) a material, factual misrepresentation or omission, (2) reliance by the plaintiff on the financial statements, (3) damages suffered as a result of reliance on the financial statements, and (4) scienter. The first element can include material misleading information or the omission of material information. The fourth element, *scienter,* can be defined as an intent to deceive, manipulate, or defraud.

A number of important cases have used Section 10(b) and Rule 10b-5 as a basis for actions against auditors. In *Herzfeld* v. *Laventhol, Krekstein, Horwath & Horwath* (1974), the US District Court allowed recovery by an investor. The investor had purchased securities from the client prior to an audit conducted by Laventhol. After the audit, the client offered to refund all investments made prior to the audit. The plaintiff declined the refund based on the audited financial statements and lost his investment when the company went bankrupt a year later. The plaintiff sued, claiming that the financial statements had been false and misleading because profits from the sale of properties were reported in the income statement even though there was some uncertainty about the collectibility of the related receivables. Laventhol's opinion was qualified "subject to" the collectibility of the receivables. The court held that the disclosure of the qualification footnote had been inadequate and that Laventhol was liable "because of their active participation in the preparation and issuance of false and materially misleading accounting reports upon which Herzfeld relied to his damage."

In *Ernst & Ernst* v. *Hochfelder*, which is described in more detail in Exhibit 20–9, the president of a brokerage firm, Leston Nay, induced brokerage customers to invest in high-yield accounts that he personally managed. The accounts were fictitious, and he used the funds for his own purposes. Nay was able to conceal this scheme by having a rule that only he was to open mail addressed to him. The defrauded customers sued Ernst & Ernst, arguing that they, as auditors, should have been aware of the mail rule and that such knowledge would have led to discovery of the fraud. Ernst & Ernst argued that Rule 10b-5 did not encompass negligent behavior. The US Supreme Court ruled that an action under Rule 10b-5 may not be maintained by showing that the defendant was negligent; the rule requires that scienter, or intent to deceive, be present. Unfortunately, the Supreme Court did not decide whether reckless behavior was sufficient for liability under Section 10(b) or Rule 10b-5. A number of subsequent decisions by lower courts have recognized that reckless behavior or conduct by the auditor satisfies the scienter requirement of Rule 10b-5. Reckless conduct is behavior that represents an extreme departure from standards of ordinary care, that is, failure to see the obvious or a disregard for the truth.

EXHIBIT 20–9

Ernst & Ernst v. *Hochfelder et al.* (1976)

Leston Nay was the president and principal owner of First Securities Company of Chicago, a small brokerage firm. Nay induced brokerage customers to invest in a high-yield escrow syndicate that loaned money to companies experiencing working capital shortages. The investors were promised above-average returns on their investments. Nay converted his investors' money to his personal use. The fraud became public when Nay committed suicide after concluding that he could no longer conceal the scheme from some of his investors.

The investors eventually sued Ernst & Ernst, the public accounting firm that had audited First Securities Company, alleging that the firm had aided and abetted Nay's fraud by failing to detect Nay's "mail rule." Nay had forbidden anyone to open mail addressed directly to him. He had used this tactic to conceal the existence of the escrow syndicate from First Securities and the auditors. The investors charged Ernst & Ernst with negligence.

The civil lawsuit against Ernst & Ernst charged violation of Section 10(b) and Rule 10b-5 of the Securities Exchange Act of 1934. The federal district court dismissed the lawsuit, contending that there was no substantive evidence that the firm had been negligent in auditing First Securities. The court of appeals reversed the lower court's decision and ordered a trial. Ernst & Ernst appealed the court of appeals' decision to the U.S. Supreme Court. The Court held that an action under Rule 10b-5 could not be maintained by simply showing that the defendant had been negligent. The plaintiff had to prove that the defendant had acted with *scienter,* a manipulative intent to deceive. The Court, however, did not decide whether "reckless behavior" would be considered equivalent to scienter and thus violate Rule 10b-5. Lower-court decisions have found that reckless behavior can be used to maintain an action against an auditor under Section 10(b).

The appendix to this chapter contains a discussion of two recent significant legal cases that fall under the Securities Exchange Act of 1934: Mini-Scribe and Phar-Mor.

Private Securities Litigation Reform Act of 1995[5]

🖊 [LO 7]

Prior to the passage of the Private Securities Litigation Reform Act of 1995, auditors were held to the legal doctrine of *joint and several liability,* which holds each defendant fully liable for all assessed damages, regardless of the extent to which he or she contributed to the injury. The new legislation provides, in general, for *proportionate liability,* where each defendant is liable solely for the portion of the damages that corresponds to the percentage of responsibility of that defendant. The legislation still provides for joint and several liability when the defendant knowingly violates the securities laws. The act also raises the standard that investors must allege at the beginning of a case. This may discourage "deep-pockets" lawsuits where plaintiffs hope to pressure defendants to settle out of court because the legal costs to fight the lawsuit may be greater than the costs to settle. The reader should note that auditors' liability at the state level depends on state laws. Some states follow proportionate liability, while others follow a joint and several liability standard.

---

[5]See King, R. R. and R. Schwartz, "The Private Securities Litigation Reform Act of 1995: A Discussion of Three Provisions," *Accounting Horizons* (March 1997), pp. 92–106, for a detailed discussion of this statute.

SEC Sanctions

[LO 8]

Rule 2(e) of the Rules of Practice empowers the SEC to suspend for any person the privilege of appearing and practicing before it if that person

1. Has been convicted of a misdemeanor involving moral turpitude.
2. Has been convicted of a felony.
3. Has had his or her license to practice as an accountant suspended or revoked.
4. Has been permanently enjoined from violating provisions of the federal securities laws.
5. Has been found by the commission in an administrative proceeding or by a court of competent jurisdiction to have violated provisions of the federal securities laws.

This sanction can be applied not only to an individual auditor but also to an entire accounting firm. If a firm is suspended or barred from practice before the SEC, the impact on the firm's clients can be severe. For example, if a firm is suspended, its clients may not be able to file their reports with the SEC on a timely basis. Typically, if a firm is faced with suspension, it will work out some type of consent agreement in which the firm does not admit guilt but agrees to lesser sanctions. These sanctions may include not taking on new SEC clients for a specified period and subjecting the firm to special reviews to ensure that the alleged problems have been corrected. For example, one Big 6 firm agreed to a settlement arising out of its examinations of the financial statements of several companies, including National Student Marketing (see the chapter appendix). The settlement required a review of the firm's auditing and accounting procedures and a six-month prohibition on accepting new audit clients that were expected to file with the SEC.

Foreign Corrupt Practices Act

[LO 9]

The Foreign Corrupt Practices Act (FCPA) was passed by Congress in 1977 in response to the discovery of bribery and other misconduct on the part of more than 300 American companies. The act was codified in 1988 as an amendment to the Securities Exchange Act of 1934. As a result, an auditor may be subject to administrative proceedings, civil liability, and civil penalties under the FCPA. The FCPA prohibits corporate officers from knowingly participating in bribing foreign officials to obtain or retain business. The FCPA also imposes record-keeping and internal control requirements on public companies. Basically, corporations must keep their books, records, and accounts in sufficient detail to accurately reflect transactions. Companies are also required to develop and maintain adequate systems of internal control. To comply with the provisions of the FCPA, many corporations have established codes of conduct that prohibit bribery. Compliance with corporate codes of conduct should be checked by the audit committee and the internal auditors. The external auditor may detect activities that violate the FCPA; such violations should be communicated to management immediately. Guidance for such reporting can be found in SAS No. 60, "Communication of Internal Control–Related Matters in an Audit" (AU 325), and SAS No. 61, "Communications with Audit Committees" (AU 380). SAS Nos. 60 and 61 were covered in Chapters 6 and 17, respectively.

EXHIBIT 20–10

> ### *Reves* v. *Ernst & Young* (1993)
>
> This case arose from Ernst & Young's audit of Farmers' Cooperative of Arkansas and Oklahoma. The co-op raised funds for its operations by selling collateralized demand depository notes to investors. The money was used to fund a company that made gasohol. When the co-op subsequently went bankrupt, the noteholders sued Ernst & Young, alleging that the firm had misvalued the company and assisted the co-op's management in a scheme to defraud investors and violated RICO by engaging in a pattern of racketeering activity.
>
> The trial court and the US Court of Appeals excluded the RICO claim, basing their decisions on the reasoning that the auditors must be directly involved in managing the corrupt business to be within the scope of RICO. The US Supreme Court agreed that accountants supplying only audit, review, or compilation services to a client without participating in the management or direction of the business are outside the scope of RICO. Thus, the Supreme Court's ruling established an "operation and management test" for auditors.

Racketeer Influenced and Corrupt Organizations Act

🖉 **[LO 10]**

Although the Racketeer Influenced and Corrupt Organizations Act (RICO) was enacted by Congress in 1970 to combat the infiltration of legitimate businesses by organized crime, it has been used against auditors. RICO provides civil and criminal sanctions for certain types of illegal acts. A major factor in bringing an action under RICO is that the law provides for treble damages in civil RICO cases. Racketeering activity includes a long list of federal and state crimes, with mail fraud and wire fraud the most common acts alleged against auditors. For example, the federal mail fraud statute provides that

> Whoever, having devised or intending to devise any scheme or artifice to defraud, or for obtaining money or property by means of false or fraudulent pretenses, representations, or promises . . . for the purpose of executing such scheme or artifice or attempting do to so, places in any post office or authorized depository for mail matter, any matter or thing whatever to be sent or delivered by the Postal Service, or takes or receives therefrom, any such matter or thing, or knowingly causes to be delivered by mail according to the direction thereon, or at the place at which it is directed to be delivered by the person to whom it is addressed, any such matter or thing, shall be fined not more than $1,000 or imprisoned not more than five years, or both.

The wire fraud statute is similar, except that it relates to the use of wire, radio, or television communication to perpetrate the fraud.

Generally, a single instance of racketeering activity is not sufficient to establish a pattern of racketeering. In a recent case, *Reves* v. *Ernst & Young* (1993), the Supreme Court established an "operations and management test" for auditors that requires that the plaintiff prove that the accounting firm participated in the operation or management of the client's business. A number of lower courts have followed the Supreme Court and dismissed similar RICO claims against auditors.[6] The significance of the *Reves* v. *Ernst & Young* case is that auditors are less likely to settle out of court in RICO cases merely to avoid the possibility of treble damages. Exhibit 20–10 presents a description of this case.

---

[6]*Journal of Accountancy* (May 1993), p. 24; *Journal of Accountancy* (October 1994), pp. 119–22.

Criminal Liability

[LO 11] Auditors can also be held criminally liable under the laws discussed in the previous sections. In addition, auditors can be held criminally liable for various federal and state laws, such as banking and insurance regulations. Criminal prosecutions require that some form of criminal intent be present. However, many of the laws described in this chapter contain provisions for criminal penalties to be levied if an auditor's actions reflect gross negligence. In a famous quote from *United States* v. *Benjamin*, the Court stated that an auditor would be held criminally liable if he "deliberately closed his eyes to facts he had a duty to see . . . or recklessly stated as facts things of which he was ignorant."

A number of significant cases against auditors have resulted in criminal prosecution, with auditors being given large fines and serving time in prison. Included among these cases are Continental Vending (*United States* v. *Simon*), National Student Marketing (*United States* v. *Natelli*), Equity Funding (*United States* v. *Weiner*), and ESM Government Securities, Inc. (*In re Alexander Grant & Co. Litigation*). Note that, in addition to criminal prosecution of the auditors, the auditors' firms were civilly liable for violating various statutes and paid large sums to settle the cases. These cases are described in the appendix to this chapter.

Approaches to Minimizing Legal Liability

[LO 12] Everyone involved with the public accounting profession has an interest in minimizing auditors' exposure to legal liability. Lawsuits against CPAs not only result in direct financial effects such as large settlement costs but also impact the profession and society in other ways. For example, many CPA firms have seen their costs of defending such lawsuits, including management time and their insurance premiums, increase dramatically in recent years. The firms have also suffered significant blows to their reputations through the negative publicity arising from litigation. In addition, many public accounting firms now practice risk reduction. This includes avoiding clients that operate in certain industries or that are considered high risk. Some small to medium-size public accounting firms are limiting or abandoning their audit practices. A number of steps can be taken by the profession and by individual firms to minimize legal liability.

At the Profession Level

The public accounting profession, through the AICPA, state boards of accountancy, and state societies, can do a number of things to reduce its exposure to legal liability. These include

- ***Pushing for tort reform.*** As discussed earlier in this chapter, auditors received some relief from litigation from the Private Securities Litigation Reform Act of 1995. This, however, provides relief only for lawsuits under federal securities regulations. At the state level, the profession is lobbying to have joint and several liability replaced by a proportionate liability standard. This would restore balance and equity to the liability system.

- ***Establishing stronger auditing and attestation standards.*** While adherence to GAAS (and GAAP) is a minimum defense against lawsuits, the profession should strive to issue standards that require the best form of practice. This includes revising standards to address practice problems that are revealed through litigation.

- ***Continually updating the Code of Professional Conduct and sanctioning members who do not comply with it.*** The profession should continually revise the Code of Professional Conduct to reflect acceptable practices that meet users' needs. Members who do not comply with the Code should be sanctioned. Such sanctions will demonstrate to the profession's constituency that the profession is willing to discipline members who act unprofessionally.

- ***Educating users.*** In recent years, the profession has undertaken a number of actions to close the "expectation gap," including revision of a number of important auditing standards. These revisions clarified auditors' responsibilities for issues such as errors and fraud, illegal acts, and going-concern evaluation. The wording in the auditor's report was also revised so as to better communicate to users what an audit entails. The profession needs an ongoing program to educate the public about auditors' activities.

At the Firm Level

Individual public accounting firms can also take steps to avoid litigation. These include

- ***Instituting sound quality control and review procedures.*** A system of quality control and review can give the firm reasonable assurance of conforming with professional standards. Chapter 19 provided detailed coverage of quality control and review.

- ***Ensuring that members of the firm are independent.*** Members of the firm must be independent in both fact and appearance. A review of legal cases indicates that on numerous occasions auditors did not maintain a sufficiently high level of "professional skepticism" and accepted a client's responses without investigating the facts adequately.

- ***Following sound client acceptance and retention procedures.*** Auditors need to be very careful in accepting new clients. If a client is known to lack integrity, the likelihood increases that its management will take actions that are detrimental to user groups, including management fraud.

- ***Being alert to risk factors that may result in lawsuits.*** A number of important risk factors seem to lead to litigation. These include the presence of management fraud, the commission of illegal acts, insolvency, disagreements between auditors and management, first-year audits, and acquisition audits. For example, when management fraud occurs, auditors are usually subject to litigation, and such cases are more costly to resolve.[7] Some audit deficiencies have also been noted in the litigation against public accounting firms. These include incomplete client acceptance or retention procedures, unrealistic risk assessments given the client's circumstances, staff that is inadequately trained to audit specialized industries, inadequate documentation of difficult decisions, insufficient partner and manager participation in resolving key issues, and excessive reliance on management representations.

- ***Performing and documenting work diligently.*** A quality audit involves following relevant professional standards and includes (1) planning properly, (2) understanding the client's internal control adequately, (3) obtaining sufficient competent evidence as to financial assertions, (4) having experienced personnel review the work done, and (5) issuing an appropriate audit report.

The threat of legal liability serves to prevent or limit inappropriate behavior on the part of auditors. However, auditors cannot be expected to ensure the accuracy of either financial statements or the financial health of a business entity. The auditor's responsibility is to provide reasonable assurance that there are no material misstatements in the financial statements.

Appendix:

Summary of Significant Legal Cases

Continental Vending (United States v. Simon, 1970)[8]

The controversy in this case arose over the disclosure of a loan from Continental Vending Machine Corporation to Valley Commercial Corporation. Harold Roth, the president of Continental Vending, supervised the operations of Valley. He owned approximately 25 percent of the stock in each company. Continental made loans to Valley, and Roth borrowed money from Valley to finance his stock market transactions. When Valley was unable to repay its loans from Continental, Roth put up security for the loan. However, 80 percent of the security was composed of stock and debentures of Continental. When a Continental check to the Internal Revenue Service bounced, the company's plant was padlocked and it entered bankruptcy.

The main issue in the case against the auditors revolved around the disclosures of the loan to Valley and the collateral supplied by Roth. The auditors contended that they had complied with GAAP. However, the indictments against the auditors charged that the financial statement disclosures had been misleading. In particular, the government contended that the Continental footnote should have disclosed (1) that Roth had received the money, (2) the nature of the collateral, and (3) the netting of

---

[7]A review of lawsuits by Z. V. Palmrose, *Empirical Research on Auditor Litigation: Considerations and the Data* (Sarasota, FL: American Accounting Association, forthcoming), provides detailed data on the incidence and resolution of litigation against auditors.

[8]See D. B. Isbell, "The Continental Vending Case: Lessons for the Profession," *Journal of Accountancy* (August 1970), pp. 33–40.

the liability with the receivable from Valley. The court rejected the auditor's arguments and held that the critical test was whether the financial statements, taken as a whole, fairly present financial position and results of operations.

A senior partner, a junior partner, and a senior associate of the accounting firm of Lybrand, Ross Bros., & Montgomery were convicted of violating the Securities and Exchange Act of 1934 and the Federal Mail Fraud Statute. The auditors were fined but did not receive a prison sentence. In addition, the public accounting firm paid approximately $2.1 million to settle the related civil suit.

Two important concepts were established by this case with respect to criminal liability:

- The auditor must disclose improper activities of the client or the client's officers when such activities are known to the auditor and may reasonably affect the audited financial statements.
- Compliance with GAAP is not a conclusive defense against criminal liability.

National Student Marketing
(United States v. Natelli, 1975)

National Student Marketing provided its clients with fixed-fee advertising, promotional, and marketing programs. The company recognized the income from the contract at the time its clients committed to the company's services. The auditor's conviction for fraud was based on two items. First, the financial statements for the year ended August 31, 1968, contained approximately $1.7 million in purported commitments. Anthony Natelli, the partner-in-charge of the engagement, had ordered Joseph Scansaroli, the audit supervisor, to verify these commitments. Instead of obtaining written representations for the company's clients, Scansaroli verified the commitments by telephone. Second, the unaudited results that were included in a proxy statement dated September 30, 1969, included the results for the nine months ended May 31, 1969. These statements were misstated in a couple of ways. By May 1969, $1 million of the $1.7 million booked in 1968 was written off. The auditors were asked to write off approximately $678,000 of the $1 million against prior years' sales. However, this amount was netted against a newly discovered 1968 tax credit of approximately the same amount. The sales were not written off against National Student Marketing's results but were written off, at the direction of Natelli, against the results of companies acquired after 1968 and consolidated using pooling of interest. The unaudited statements also included a purported commitment of $280,000 and failed to write off an additional $177,000 of bad contracts identified by one of the firm's auditors. Natelli made the decision not to write off the contracts.

In this case, the two Peat, Marwick, Mitchell & Company auditors were convicted of willingly and knowingly making false and misleading statements in the 1969 proxy statements of National Student Marketing Corporation. Natelli received a one-year prison sentence and a $10,000 fine. The sentence was later reduced to 60 days. Scansaroli received a one-year sentence and a $2,500 fine. His sentence was later reduced to 10 days. On appeal, the conviction of Natelli was upheld while the conviction of Scansaroli was reversed.

Equity Funding
(United States v. Weiner, 1978)[9]

Equity Funding Corporation of America's principal line of business was creative financial investments, which included the sale of life insurance and programs that combined life insurance policies with mutual fund investment. Equity Funding derived its income from the commissions on such sales. One program consisted of selling mutual funds to program participants. The mutual fund shares were then used by the participants to secure a one-year note for a loan made by Equity Funding equal to the amount of the premium on the insurance policy. Each year, for a 10-year term, this type of arrangement was entered into by the participants. If the income and appreciation from the mutual funds exceeded the interest on the loan, a portion of the insurance premiums would be paid by the program.

The company went public in 1964 and by 1972 became one of the 10 largest insurance companies in the United States. During that same period the company's revenues and earnings increased dramatically, along with the price of Equity Funding common stock. As a result, the chairman of the board, Stanley Goldblum, and Fred Levin, vice president for insurance operations, became very wealthy. Maintaining a high price level for the company's stock appears to have been one of the key motives in masterminding the fraud.

The fraud apparently started just prior to the company's going public. Equity Funding inflated its earnings by recording fictitious commissions from the sale of its programs. The company also borrowed funds without recording them as liabilities on their books. These funds were used to show increased cash flow by being recorded as payments on the loan receivables from the participants. By reducing the loan receivables, Equity Funding could record more fictitious commissions. The last part of the fraud involved creating fictitious insurance policies, which were then reinsured with other insurance companies. (Reinsurance consists of reselling insurance policies to other insurance companies and splitting the premiums using some agreed-upon formula.) The use of the reinsurance scheme allowed Equity Funding to obtain additional cash to pay premiums on policies, which in turn required that more fictitious policies be created.

Equity Funding collapsed in 1973 when a former employee disclosed the existence of the massive fraud. During the period of the fraud, Equity Funding was audited first by Wolfson Weiner, which in 1968 merged with Ratoff & Lapin. Ratoff & Lapin was purchased by Seidman & Seidman just prior to the fraud's being uncovered. Many of the facts in this case suggest that the auditors, at best, closed their eyes to the fraud and, at worst, may have suspected the fraud and helped to conceal it. Three independent auditors (the partner-in-charge of the engagement and two audit managers) were convicted for criminal offenses related to securities fraud and filing false documents. The various public accounting firms that were involved with the audit paid $44 million to settle the civil lawsuits.

---

[9]See L. J. Seidler, F. Andrews, and M. J. Epstein, *The Equity Funding Papers: The Anatomy of a Fraud* (New York: McGraw-Hill, 1974), for a detailed discussion of the Equity Funding case. Also see American Institute of Certified Public Accountants, *Report of the Special Committee on Equity Funding* (New York: AICPA, 1975), for the profession's view of whether auditing standards required changing based on this massive fraud.

ESM Government Securities, Inc.

(In re Alexander Grant & Co. Litigation, 1986)

ESM Government Securities, Inc., was a Fort Lauderdale brokerage firm that specialized in buying and selling debt securities issued by the federal government and its various agencies. Its main customers were small to moderate-size banks and municipalities. The major type of transaction engaged in by ESM was known as a "repo," in which the securities dealer sells a customer a large block of federal government securities and simultaneously agrees to repurchase the securities at a later date at an agreed-upon price. ESM also entered into "reverse repos," in which the securities firm purchased the federal government securities from the customer, who simultaneously agreed to repurchase the securities later at a predetermined price. A critical part of a repo transaction is that the purchaser takes physical possession of the securities. If the purchaser does not take physical control, an unscrupulous securities dealer can sell the same securities to another customer. ESM's customers relied on ESM to maintain the securities. However, ESM's management used these securities for their own purposes. In addition, the officers of ESM engaged in speculative transactions for their own behalf. This led to large trading losses for ESM, which management concealed from its customers, investors, and auditors.

The main architects of the fraud were Ronnie Ewton and Alan Novick. Novick devised a way of hiding the trading losses from ESM's auditors, Alexander Grant & Co., by transferring trading losses incurred by ESM to an affiliated company. Novick would record a mirror transaction (a repo or reverse repo) on the affiliate's books. The losing side of the transaction was closed out to the unaudited affiliate and the profitable side to ESM. Over the course of years, these types of transactions resulted in a large receivable on ESM's books from the unaudited affiliates. Novick and his colleagues also used the unaudited affiliates to steal funds from ESM for their personal use. The fraud started to unravel when Novick died of a massive heart attack in November 1984. When the thefts and trading losses were finally tallied, there was a net deficit of $300 million for ESM.

In this case the audit partner, Jose Gomez, had been aware of the fraud. Gomez had been admitted as a partner to Alexander Grant in 1979, and his major client had been ESM Securities. Shortly after making partner, Gomez had been informed by Novick that the company's 1977 and 1978 financial statements were misstated. Novick had been able to convince Gomez not to withdraw Alexander Grant's audit report on the assumption that ESM would recoup its losses. Over the course of the fraud (1977–1984), Gomez received approximately $200,000 from ESM. Gomez was sentenced to a 12-year prison term, and Alexander Grant and its insurance companies paid approximately $175 million in civil payments.

MiniScribe

In 1986 MiniScribe was a high-flying maker of computer disk drives. It had hired Q. T. Wiles, a "turnaround expert," as chief executive officer in 1985. Subsequently, MiniScribe announced seven consecutive record-breaking quarters, and its stock quintupled in 18 months. The company's superlative record, however, was fabricated. MiniScribe actually had financial, operating, and marketing problems, and management manipulated sales and reserves to exaggerate the company's performance. There were charges that the company had shipped bricks to distributors and recorded them as sales and had broken into locked trunks to change auditors' working papers. The Securities and Exchange Commission also charged that MiniScribe had used a computer program called "Cook Book" to inflate inventory figures.

After MiniScribe went bankrupt, a number of items were noted. First, while MiniScribe's fiscal 1986 year ended on December 28, the company had supposedly booked $16 million of next-day sales as of December 28. Second, MiniScribe had improperly booked sales on disk drives that customers had not ordered, had returned, or had never received. Third, the company had understated its allowance for doubtful accounts. In 1985 MiniScribe had provided an allowance of $752,000 against $15.6 million of accounts receivable. However, in 1986 MiniScribe had reduced the allowance to $736,000 even though accounts receivable grew to almost $40 million. Finally, MiniScribe's 1985 financial statements had shown a reserve of $4.85 million for revaluing computer parts for its inventory that were obsolete. In 1986 revenues had increased from $114 million to $185 million, but a reserve of only $2.78 million had been established for inventory obsolescence. An accounting expert testified that MiniScribe should have reserved $5.27 million for obsolete inventory in 1986.

This case resulted in Coopers & Lybrand's making payments of at least $140 million to stockholders and bondholders.

Phar-Mor

Phar-Mor was formed in 1982 by combining businesses owned by two families. The concept behind the company was that a drugstore would attract more customers by offering low prices made possible by bulk purchases. Phar-Mor's initial marketing strategy was to set low prices by marking up merchandise 20 percent from "dead net cost," thus producing a gross profit margin of 16.67 percent. Phar-Mor lowered prices on some items to price them lower than competitors did and also lowered them at new locations to attract customers.

Phar-Mor grew rapidly. In 1985 it had 15 stores and began to expand nationally. By 1990 Phar-Mor was opening 60 to 75 stores a year. On August 3, 1992, Phar-Mor issued a press release stating that a scheme had been uncovered and the financial results had been overstated by $350 million (subsequently increased to more than $500 million). At that time Phar-Mor had more than 300 stores and $3 billion in annual sales. The fraudulent activities spanned six years and involved most of the senior management of the company. There were also significant related-party transactions.

It appears that a number of factors had led the officers and employees of Phar-Mor to participate in the fraud:

- Phar-Mor was a fast-growing, privately-held company whose financial statements were being used to obtain credit and capital from large investors.

- The president of the company had pledged his Phar-Mor stock as collateral for a number of personal loans, and a decline in the value of the stock could have led to personal bankruptcy.
- The officers and employees received generous salaries, bonuses, and stock options that were tied to Phar-Mor's financial results.
- The president was an autocratic leader who surrounded himself with people whom he could influence.

The officers and employees had used various schemes to conceal the fact that Phar-Mor's financial results had deteriorated significantly. Some of the major means of effecting the fraud were improper recognition of income on multiyear contracts with vendors, inventory manipulation, and manipulation of rebates from vendors.

Income Recognition from Multiyear Contracts   Phar-Mor received significant onetime payments from vendors in exchange for exclusive supply agreements. Phar-Mor treated the payments received under such multiyear contracts as current income rather than as deferred income to be amortized over the life of the contract. For example, Phar-Mor reported approximately $25 million in pretax income in 1990, and income recognized from multiyear contracts may have increased reported income by as much as $33 million.

Inventory Manipulations   Phar-Mor did not have a perpetual inventory system or a reliable information system to track inventory values. This allowed the company to manipulate recorded inventory values using a number of methods. For example, the chief financial officer altered the calculation of inventory cost by using a gross margin percentage that was close to the budgeted level, instead of the actual gross margin percentage. Additionally, the physical inventory was performed by outside inventory specialists. The company used fraudulent adjusting entries to misstate the amounts provided by the outside specialists.

Rebates from Vendors   Phar-Mor negotiated chargebacks to vendors in return for carrying out promotional events for certain products and meeting established purchase requirements. When Phar-Mor did not meet the required purchase levels, the chief financial officer directed the accounting department to adjust the amounts due to reflect the budgeted level of purchases. This led to an overstatement of income.

The plaintiffs in this case charged that the company's public accounting firm, Coopers & Lybrand, had not properly planned and conducted the audits of Phar-Mor in accordance with GAAS. Some of the issues raised were that Coopers & Lybrand (1) had failed to observe physical inventory at a sufficient number of stores, (2) had advised Phar-Mor, in advance, of the stores that would be observed, (3) had conducted a detailed review only of adjustments to physical inventory for stores chosen for physical inventory observation, and (4) had failed to adjust inventory for Phar-Mor's improper gross profit costing procedure. Coopers & Lybrand subsequently sued the officers of Phar-Mor.

REVIEW QUESTIONS

[LO 1]   20-1   Describe the current legal environment for auditors.

[2]   20-2   What is meant by *proportionate liability?* Contrast this legal doctrine with the doctrine of *joint and several liability.*

[3]   20-3   For what types of actions are auditors liable to a client under common law? Why would the client prefer to sue the auditor for a tort action rather than for a breach of contract?

[3]   20-4   Liability for negligence represents a deviation from a standard of behavior that is consistent with that of a "reasonable person." What behaviors constitute a "reasonable person" in this context?

[3]   20-5   What elements must a client prove to maintain an action against an auditor for negligence?

[3]   20-6   What significant changes occurred for the public accounting profession as a result of the *1136 Tenants'* case?

[4]   20-7   Distinguish among the three standards that have evolved for defining auditors' liability to third parties under common law. Why is this area of auditors' liability so complex?

[4]   20-8   When an auditor is accused of fraud, what must the third party plaintiff prove?

[5,6]   20-9   Distinguish between the Securities Act of 1933 and the Securities Exchange Act of 1934. Why is it easier for a plaintiff to sue an auditor under the Securities Act of 1933?

[6]   20-10   What elements must a plaintiff prove in order to win action under Rule 10b-5 of the Securities Exchange Act of 1934? What was the significance of the outcome of the *Ernst & Ernst* v. *Hochfelder* case for auditors' liability?

[8]   20-11   What types of sanctions can the SEC impose on auditors under Rule 2(e)?

[9]   20-12   Briefly describe the Foreign Corrupt Practices Act and how it can affect an auditor's liability.

[10]   20-13   Briefly describe the Racketeer Influenced and Corrupt Organizations Act and why plaintiffs seek to sue auditors under this statute.

[11]   20-14   What actions can result in an auditor being held criminally liable under statutes and regulations?

[12]   20-15   Identify steps that can be taken at the profession level and individual level to minimize legal liability against auditors.

MULTIPLE-CHOICE QUESTIONS FROM CPA EXAMINATIONS

[2,3,4]   20-16   Cable Corporation orally engaged Drake & Company, CPAs, to audit its financial statements. Cable's management informed Drake that it suspected the accounts receivable were materially overstated. Though the financial statements Drake audited included a materially overstated accounts receivable balance, Drake issued an unqualified opinion. Cable used the financial statements to obtain a loan to expand its operations. Cable defaulted on the loan and incurred a substantial loss.

If Cable sues Drake for negligence in failing to discover the overstatement, Drake's best defense would be that Drake did *not*

a. Have privity of contract with Cable.

b. Sign an engagement letter.

c. Perform the audit recklessly or with an intent to deceive.

d. Violate generally accepted auditing standards in performing the audit.

[3]   20-17   Which of the following best describes whether a CPA has met the required standard of care in auditing a client's financial statements?

a. Whether the client's expectations are met with regard to the accuracy of audited financial statements.

b. Whether the statements conform to generally accepted accounting principles.

c. Whether the CPA conducted the audit with the same skill and care expected of an ordinarily prudent CPA under the circumstances.

d. Whether the audit was conducted to investigate and discover all acts of fraud.

[3,4]   20-18   Sun Corporation approved a merger plan with Cord Corporation. One of the determining factors in approving the merger was the financial statements of Cord, which had been audited by Frank & Company, CPAs. Sun had engaged Frank to audit Cord's financial statements. While performing the audit, Frank failed to discover fraud that later caused Sun to suffer substantial losses. For Frank to be liable under common-law negligence, Sun at a *minimum* must prove that Frank

a. Knew of the fraud.

b. Failed to exercise due care.

c. Was grossly negligent.

d. Acted with scienter.

[4]   20-19   Brown & Company, CPAs, issued an unqualified opinion on the financial statements of its client King Corporation. Based on the strength of King's financial statements, Safe Bank loaned King $500,000. Brown was unaware that Safe would receive a copy of the financial statements or that they would be used by King in obtaining a loan. King defaulted on the loan.

If Safe commences an action for negligence against Brown and Brown is able to prove that it conducted the audit in conformity with GAAS, Brown will

a. Be liable to Safe, because Safe relied on the financial statements.

b. Be liable to Safe, because the Statute of Frauds has been satisfied.

c. Not be liable to Safe, because there is a conclusive presumption that following GAAS is the equivalent of acting reasonably and with due care.

d. Not be liable to Safe, because there was a lack of privity of contract.

[2,3,4]   20-20   In general, the third-party (primary) beneficiary rule as applied to a CPA's legal liability in conducting an audit is relevant to which of the following causes of action against a CPA?

	Fraud	Constructive Fraud	Negligence
a.	Yes	Yes	No
b.	Yes	No	No
c.	No	Yes	Yes
d.	No	No	Yes

Question 20-21 and 20-22 are based on the following information:

While conducting an audit, Larson Associates, CPAs, failed to detect material misstatements included in its client's financial statements. Larson's unqualified opinion was included with the financial statements in a registration statement and prospectus for a public offering of securities made by the client. Larson knew that its opinion and the financial statements would be used for this purpose.

[3,4]   20-21   In a suit by a purchaser against Larson for common-law negligence, Larson's best defense would be that the
   a. Audit was conducted in accordance with generally accepted auditing standards.
   b. Client was aware of the misstatements.
   c. Purchaser was *not* in privity of contract with Larson.
   d. Identity of the purchaser was *not* known to Larson at the time of the audit.

[3,4]   20-22   In a suit by a purchaser against Larson for common-law fraud, Larson's best defense would be that
   a. Larson did *not* have actual or constructive knowledge of the misstatements.
   b. Larson's client knew or should have known of the misstatements.
   c. Larson did *not* have actual knowledge that the purchaser was an intended beneficiary of the audit.
   d. Larson was *not* in privity of contract with its client.

[3]   20-23   Which of the following is the best defense a CPA firm can assert to a suit for common-law fraud based on its unqualified opinion on materially false financial statements?
   a. Lack of privity.
   b. Lack of scienter.
   c. Contributory negligence on the part of the client.
   d. A disclaimer contained in the engagement letter.

[5]   20-24   How does the Securities Act of 1933, which imposes civil liability on auditors for misrepresentations or omissions of material facts in a registration statement, expand auditors' liability to purchasers of securities beyond that of common law?
   a. Purchasers have to prove only that a loss was caused by reliance on audited financial statements.
   b. Privity with purchasers is *not* a necessary element of proof.
   c. Purchasers have to prove either fraud or gross negligence as a basis for recovery.
   d. Auditors are held to a standard of care described as "professional skepticism."

[5] 20-25 To be successful in a civil action under Section 11 of the Securities Act of 1933 concerning liability for a misleading registration statement, the plaintiff must prove

	Defendant's Intent to Deceive	Plaintiff's Reliance on the Registration Statement
a.	Yes	Yes
b.	Yes	No
c.	No	Yes
d.	No	No

Question 20-26 and 20-27 are based on the following information:

Dart Corporation engaged Jay Associates, CPAs, to assist in a public stock offering. Jay audited Dart's financial statements and gave an unqualified opinion, despite knowing that the financial statements contained misstatements. Jay's opinion was included in Dart's registration statement. Hansen purchased shares in the offering and suffered a loss when the stock declined in value after the misstatements became known.

[5] 20-26 In a suit against Jay and Dart under the Section 11 liability provisions of the Securities Act of 1933, Hansen must prove that
a. Jay knew of the misstatements.
b. Jay was negligent.
c. The misstatements contained in Dart's financial statements were material.
d. The unqualified opinion contained in the registration statement was relied on by Hansen.

[5] 20-27 If Hansen succeeds in the Section 11 suit against Dart, Hansen will be entitled to
a. Damages of three times the original public offering price.
b. Rescind the transaction.
c. Monetary damages only.
d. Damages, but only if the shares were resold before the suit was started.

[5,6] 20-28 Ivor and Associates, CPAs, audited the financial statements of Jaymo Corporation. As a result of Ivor's negligence in conducting the audit, the financial statements included material misstatements. Ivor was unaware of this fact. The financial statements and Ivor's unqualified opinion were included in a registration statement and prospectus for an original public offering of stock by Jaymo. Thorp purchased shares in the offering. Thorp received a copy of the prospectus prior to the purchase but did not read it. The shares declined in value because the misstatements in Jaymo's financial statements became known. Under which of the following acts is Thorp most likely to prevail in a lawsuit against Ivor?

	Securities Act of 1933, Section 11	Securities Exchange Act of 1934, Section 10(b), Rule 10b-5
a.	Yes	Yes
b.	Yes	No
c.	No	Yes
d.	No	No

[6] 20-29 Fritz Corporation engaged Hay Associates, CPAs, to assist in a public stock offering. Hay audited Fritz's financial statements and gave an unqualified opinion, despite knowing that the financial statements contained misstatements. Hay's opinion was included in Fritz's registration statement. Samson purchased shares in the offering and suffered a loss when the stock declined in value after the misstatements became known.

In a suit against Hay under the antifraud provisions of Section 10(b) and Rule 10b-5 of the Securities Exchange Act of 1934, Samson must prove all of the following *except* that
a. Samson was an intended user of the false registration statement.
b. Samson relied on the false registration statement.
c. The transaction involved some form of interstate commerce.
d. Hay acted with intentional disregard of the truth.

[4] 20-30 If a CPA recklessly departs from the standards of due care when conducting an audit, the CPA will be liable to third parties who are unknown to the CPA based on
a. Negligence.
b. Gross negligence.
c. Strict liability.
d. Criminal deceit.

[5,6] 20-31 The most significant aspect of the Continental Vending case was that it
a. Created a more general awareness of the auditor's exposure to criminal prosecution.
b. Extended the auditor's responsibility for financial statements of subsidiaries.
c. Extended the auditor's responsibilities for events after the end of the audit period.
d. Defined the auditor's common-law responsibilities to third parties.

[9] 20-32 Which of the following is a provision of the Foreign Corrupt Practices Act?
a. It is a criminal offense for an auditor to fail to detect and report a bribe paid by an American business entity to a foreign official for the purpose of obtaining business.
b. The auditor's detection of illegal acts committed by officials of the auditor's publicly held client in conjunction with foreign officials should be reported to the Enforcement Division of the Securities and Exchange Commission.
c. If the auditor of a publicly held company concludes that the effects on the financial statements of a bribe given to a foreign

official are *not* susceptible of reasonable estimation, the auditor's report should be modified.

d. Every publicly held company must devise, document, and maintain a system of internal accounting controls sufficient to provide reasonable assurance that internal control objectives are met.

PROBLEMS

[5,6]   20-33   Butler Manufacturing Corporation planned to raise capital for a plant expansion by borrowing from banks and making several stock offerings. Butler engaged Meng, CPA, to audit its December 31, 2000, financial statements. Butler told Meng that the financial statements would be given to certain named banks and included in the prospectuses for the stock offerings.

In performing the audit, Meng did not confirm accounts receivable and, as a result, failed to discover a material overstatement of accounts receivable. Also, Meng was aware of a pending class action product liability lawsuit that was not disclosed in Butler's financial statements. Despite being advised by Butler's legal counsel that Butler's potential liability under the lawsuit would result in material losses, Meng issued an unqualified opinion on Butler's financial statements.

In May 2001 Union Bank, one of the named banks, relied on the financial statements and Meng's opinion in giving Butler a $500,000 loan.

Butler raised an additional $16,450,000 through the following stock offerings, which were sold completely:

- *June 2001:* Butler made a $450,000 unregistered offering of Class B nonvoting common stock under Rule 504 of Regulation D of the Securities Act of 1933. This offering was sold over two years to 30 nonaccredited investors and 20 accredited investors by general solicitation. The SEC was notified eight days after the first sale of this offering.

- *September 2001:* Butler made a $10,000,000 unregistered offering of Class A voting common stock under Rule 506 of Regulation D of the Securities Act of 1933. This offering was sold over two years to 200 accredited investors and 30 nonaccredited investors through a private placement. The SEC was notified 14 days after the first sale of this offering.

- *November 2001:* Butler made a $6,000,000 unregistered offering of preferred stock under Rule 505 of Regulation D of the Securities Act of 1933. This offering was sold during a one-year period to 40 nonaccredited investors by private placement. The SEC was notified 18 days after the first sale of this offering.

Shortly after obtaining the Union loan, Butler began experiencing financial problems but was able to stay in business because of the money raised by the offerings. Then Butler was found liable in the product liability suit. This resulted in a judgment Butler could not pay. Butler also defaulted on the Union loan and was involuntarily petitioned into bankruptcy. This caused Union to sustain a loss and Butler's stockholders to lose their investments. As a result,

- The SEC claimed that all three of Butler's offerings had been made improperly and had not been exempt from registration.
- Union sued Meng for negligence and common-law fraud.
- The stockholders who purchased Butler's stock through the offerings sued Meng, alleging fraud under Section 10(b) and Rule 10b-5 of the Securities Exchange Act of 1934.

These transactions took place in a jurisdiction providing for accountants' liability for negligence to known and intended users of financial statements.

Required:
Answer the following questions and give the reasons for your conclusions:

a. Will Union be successful in its suit against Meng for
   1. Negligence?
   2. Common-law fraud?
b. Will the stockholders who purchased Butler's stock through the 2001 offerings succeed against Meng under the antifraud provisions of Section 10(b) and Rule 10b-5 of the Securities Exchange Act of 1934?

(AICPA, adapted)

[5,6] 20-34 Sleek Corporation is a public corporation whose stock is traded on a national securities exchange. Sleek hired Garson Associates, CPAs, to audit Sleek's financial statements. Sleek needed the audit to obtain bank loans and to offer public stock so that it could expand.

Before the engagement, Fred Hedge, Sleek's president, told Garson's managing partner that the audited financial statements would be submitted to Sleek's banks to obtain the necessary loans.

During the course of the audit, Garson's managing partner found that Hedge and other Sleek officers had embezzled substantial amounts of money from the corporation. These embezzlements threatened Sleek's financial stability. When these findings were brought to Hedge's attention, Hedge promised that the money would be repaid and begged that the audit not disclose the embezzlements.

Hedge also told Garson's managing partner that several friends and relatives of Sleek's officers had been advised about the projected business expansion and proposed stock offering and had purchased significant amounts of Sleek's stock based on this information.

Garson submitted an unqualified opinion on Sleek's financial statements, which did not include adjustments for or disclosures about the embezzlements and insider stock transactions. The financial statements and audit report were submitted to Sleek's regular banks, including Knox Bank. Knox, relying on the financial statements and Garson's report, gave Sleek a $2 million loan.

Sleek's audited financial statements were also incorporated into a registration statement prepared under the provisions of the Securities Act of 1933. The registration statement was filed with the SEC in conjunction with Sleek's public offering of 100,000 shares of its common stock at $100 per share.

An SEC investigation of Sleek disclosed the embezzlements and the insider trading. Trading in Sleek's stock was suspended, and Sleek defaulted on the Knox loan.

As a result, the following legal actions were taken:

- Knox sued Garson.
- The general-public purchasers of Sleek's stock offering sued Garson.

Required:
Answer the following questions and give the reasons for your conclusions.
a. Would Knox recover from Garson for fraud?
b. Would the general-public purchasers of Sleek's stock offerings recover from Garson
  1. Under the liability provisions of Section 11 of the Securities Act of 1933?
  2. Under the antifraud provisions of Rule 10b-5 of the Securities Exchange Act of 1934?

(AICPA, adapted)

[2,3,4]   20-35   Becker, Inc., purchased the assets of Bell Corporation. A condition of the purchase agreement was that Bell retain a CPA to audit its financial statements. The purpose of the audit was to determine whether the unaudited financial statements furnished to Becker fairly presented Bell's financial position. Bell retained Salam & Company, CPAs, to perform the audit.

While performing the audit, Salam discovered that Bell's bookkeeper had embezzled $500. Salam had some evidence of other embezzlements by the bookkeeper. However, Salam decided that the $500 was immaterial and that the other suspected embezzlements did not require further investigation. Salam did not discuss the matter with Bell's management. Unknown to Salam, the bookkeeper had, in fact, embezzled large sums of cash from Bell. In addition, the accounts receivable were significantly overstated. Salam did not detect the overstatement because of Salam's failure to follow its audit program.

Despite the foregoing, Salam issued an unqualified opinion on Bell's financial statements and furnished a copy of the audited financial statements to Becker. Unknown to Salam, Becker required financing to purchase Bell's assets and furnished a copy of Bell's audited financial statements to City Bank to obtain approval of the loan. Based on Bell's audited financial statements, City loaned Becker $600,000.

Becker paid Bell $750,000 to purchase Bell's assets. Within six months, Becker began experiencing financial difficulties resulting from the undiscovered embezzlements and overstated accounts receivable. Becker later defaulted on the City loan.

City has commenced a lawsuit against Salam based on the following causes of action:

- Constructive fraud
- Negligence

Required:
In separate paragraphs, discuss whether City is likely to prevail on the causes of action it has raised. Set forth reasons for each conclusion.

(AICPA, adapted)

[3,4,5] 20-36 Astor Electronics, Inc., markets a wide variety of computer-related products throughout the United States. Astor's officers decided to raise $1 million by selling shares of Astor's common stock in an exempt offering under Regulation D of the Securities Act of 1933. In connection with the offering, Astor engaged Apple & Company, CPAs, to audit Astor's financial statements. The audited financial statements, including Apple's unqualified opinion, were included in the offering memorandum given to prospective purchasers of Astor's stock. Apple was aware that Astor intended to include the statements in the offering materials.

Astor's financial statements reported certain inventory items at a cost of $930,000 when in fact they had a fair market value of less than $100,000 because of technological obsolescence. Apple accepted the assurances of Astor's controller that cost was the appropriate valuation, despite the fact that Apple was aware of ongoing sales of the products at prices substantially less than cost. All of this was thoroughly documented in Apple's working papers.

Musk purchased 10,000 shares of Astor's common stock in the Regulation D offering at a total price of $300,000. In deciding to make the purchase, Musk had reviewed the audited financial statements of Astor that accompanied the other offering materials and had been impressed by Astor's apparent financial strength.

Shortly after the stock offering was completed, Astor's management discovered that the audited financial statements reflected the materially overstated valuation of the company's inventory. Astor advised its shareholders of the problem.

Upon receiving notice from Astor of the overstated inventory amount, Musk became very upset because the stock value was now substantially less than what it would have been had the financial statements been accurate. In fact, the stock was worth only about $200,000.

Musk has commenced an action against Apple, alleging that Apple is liable to Musk based on the following causes of action:

- Common-law fraud.
- Negligence.
- A violation of Section 10(b) and Rule 10b-5 of the Securities Exchange Act of 1934.

During the litigation Apple has refused to give to Musk its working papers pertaining to the Astor audit, claiming that these constitute privileged communications. The state in which the actions have been commenced has no accountants' privileged communication statute.

The state law applicable to this action follows the *Ultramares* decision with respect to accountants' liability to third parties for negligence or fraud. Apple has also asserted that the actions should be dismissed because of the absence of any contractual relationship between Apple and Musk, that is, a lack of privity.

Required:
Answer the following, setting forth your reasons for any conclusions stated.
a. Will Apple be required to give Musk its working papers?
b. What elements must be established by Musk to support a cause of action based on negligence?
c. What elements must be established by Musk to support a cause of action based on a Rule 10b-5 violation?
d. Is Apple's assertion regarding lack of privity correct with regard to Musk's causes of action for negligence and fraud?

(AICPA, adapted)

DISCUSSION CASE

[4,5,6] 20-37 Conan Doyle & Associates (CD&A), CPAs, served as the auditors for Lestrad Corporation and Watson Corporation, publicly held companies traded on NASDAQ. Watson recently acquired Lestrad Corporation in a merger that involved swapping 1.75 shares of Watson for 1 share of Lestrad. In connection with that merger, CD&A issued an unqualified report on the financial statements and participated in the preparation of the pro forma unaudited financial statements contained in the combined prospectus and proxy statement circulated to obtain shareholder approval of the merger and to register the shares to be issued in connection with the merger. Watson prepared a Form 8K and Form 10K in connection with the merger. Shortly thereafter, financial disaster beset the merged company, resulting in large losses to the shareholders and creditors. A class action suit on behalf of shareholders and creditors has been filed against Watson and its management. In addition, it names CD&A as codefendants, challenging the fairness, accuracy, and truthfulness of the financial statements.

Required:
Discuss the various bases of CD&A's potential civil liability to the shareholders and creditors of Watson as a result of issuing an unqualified report on the audited financial statements of Watson and Lestrad and having participated in preparing the unaudited financial statements required in connection with the merger under
(a) State common law.
(b) The federal securities acts.

(AICPA, adapted)

Part VIII

ASSURANCE, ATTESTATION, AND OTHER FORMS OF SERVICES

21
Assurance, Attestation, and Other Forms of Services

Assurance, Attestation, and Other Forms of Services

LEARNING OBJECTIVES

Upon completion of this chapter you will

[1] Learn the definition of assurance services.

[2] Understand why there is a demand for assurance services.

[3] Know the types of assurance services.

[4] Understand CPA *WebTrust*[SM] assurance service.

[5] Know the *WebTrust*[SM] Principles and Criteria.

[6] Understand the assurance process for *WebTrust*[SM].

[7] Understand CPA ElderCare assurance service.

[8] Know the types of ElderCare services.

[9] Understand the assurance process for ElderCare.

[10] Learn the definition for an attestation engagement.

[11] Know the types of attestation engagements.

[12] Learn the 11 attestation standards and how they compare to the 10 GAAS.

[13] Understand an attestation engagement that reports on an entity's internal control over financial reporting.

[14] Understand an attestation engagement that reports on an entity's financial forecasts and projections.

[15] Learn about accounting and review services.

RELEVANT ACCOUNTING AND AUDITING PRONOUNCEMENTS

Committee of Sponsoring Organizations of the Treadway Commission, *Internal Control—Integrated Framework* (New York: AICPA, 1992)

SAS No. 55, "Consideration of Internal Control in a Financial Statement Audit" (AU 319)

SAS No. 60, "Communication of Internal Control–Related Matters Noted in an Audit" (AU 325)

SSAE No. 1, "Codification of Statements on Standards for Attestation Engagements" (AT 100–300)

SSAE No. 2, "Reporting on an Entity's Internal Control over Financial Reporting" (AT 400)

SSAE No. 3, "Compliance Attestation" (AT 500)

SSAE No. 4, "Agreed-Upon Procedures Engagements" (AT 600)

SSAE No. 6, "Reporting on an Entity's Internal Control over Financial Reporting: An Amendment to SSAE No. 2" (AT 400)

SSAE No. 7, "Establishing an Understanding with the Client" (AT 100)

SSAE No. 8, "Management's Discussion and Analysis" (AT 700)

Statements on Standards for Accounting and Review Services (AR 100–400)

In recent years, auditors have been asked to perform a variety of services beyond the audit of historical financial statements.

However, auditors found it difficult to provide such services within the bounds of GAAS. In 1986 the AICPA, through its various rule-making bodies, developed *attestation standards*. The attestation standards are broader in scope than GAAS so that they can be applied to the vast array of services being requested of the accounting profession by society.

More recently, the profession recognized a need to expand the opportunities for auditor services even further. In May 1993 the AICPA held the Sante Fe Audit/Assurance Conference to develop recommendations for the profession. As a result of the conference, the AICPA Special Committee on Assurance Services ("the Elliott Committee") was established to "analyze and report on the current state and future of the audit/assurance function and trends shaping the audit/assurance environment." In late 1996 the committee completed its work and issued its report.[1] Based on the Elliott Committee's report, the AICPA established a program to promote assurance services.

This chapter first discusses assurance services, including a detailed presentation of two types of services. Attestation services and standards are presented next, with emphasis on two types of attestation engagements that are specifically covered by attestation standards. The reader should note that many of the proposed assurance services will be conducted as attestation engagements. The last part of the chapter covers other types of accounting services offered by CPAs. 🐾

Assurance Services

[LO 1]   Figure 21–1 reproduces Figure 1–2 which presents the relationship of assurance services to attestation and auditing. As discussed in Chapter 1, assurance services include attestation and auditing services. The AICPA Special Committee on Assurance Services has defined assurance services as follows:

> **Assurance services** are independent professional services that improve the quality of information, or its context, for decision makers.

This definition captures a number of important concepts. First, the definition focuses on decision making. Making good decisions requires quality information, which can be financial or nonfinancial. Figure 21–2, adapted from the Elliott Committee's report, presents a model for decision making and the role of information in decision-making activities. Information is critical in this decision model. For example, the Elliott Committee points out that three types of information enter into the problem definition stage of the decision model: (1) environmental information, (2) process monitoring and diagnostic information, and (3) outcome feedback information. An assurance service engagement can help the decision maker search through this information in order to identify which pieces of information are relevant for the required decision. The second concept relates to improving the quality of information or its context. In the decision model shown in Figure 21–2, an assurance service engagement can improve quality through increasing confidence in the information's reliability and relevance. Context can be improved by the format in which information is presented.

The third important concept in the definition of assurance services is independence. As with the earlier discussions of financial statement auditing, independence is the hallmark of the profession. However, with assurance services, the practitioner needs to be independent only with respect to the quality or context of the information.[2] The last concept is professional services, which encompasses the application of professional judgment. The practitioner applies professional judgment to the information that is the subject of the assurance service. In summary, assurance services can capture information, improve its quality, and enhance its usefulness for decision makers.

---

[1]See the AICPA's home page www.aicpa.org for more information about the Committee's charge and its various reports.

[2]For a more detailed discussion of assurance independence the reader is referred to the committee's report on the subject (http://aicpa.org/assurance/scas/comstud/assind/index.htm).

FIGURE 21–1

The Relationship between Assurance Services, Attestation, and Auditing

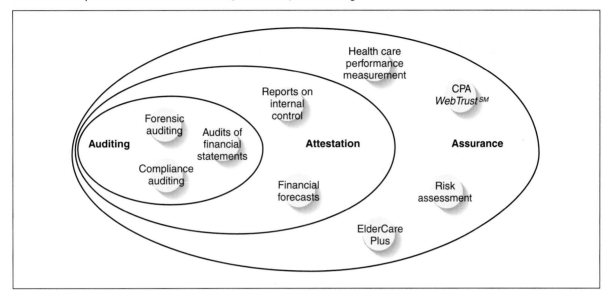

FIGURE 21–2

A Model for Decision Making and the Role of Information

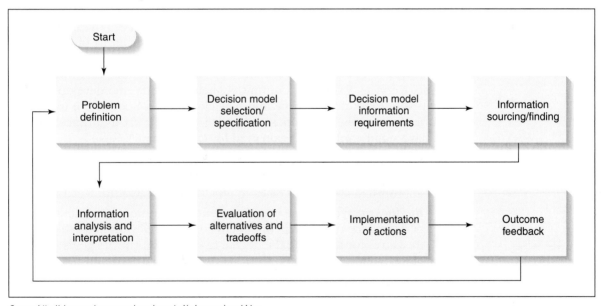

Source: http://aicpa.org/assurance/scas/comstud/relevance/pract.htm.

The Demand for Assurance Services

🖋 [LO 2]

Economic, social, and regulatory trends are changing the context in which CPAs provide services. These trends include the explosion of information technology, increased competition for entities and CPA firms, globalization of business, accountability of corporate managers, and aging of the population. For example, information technologies continue to advance at a tremendous pace and, generally, at a lower cost. The new technologies change the way entities and people work, and they increase the amount of information and the speed at which this information is available to users. While these changes may potentially threaten the traditional audit, they offer an enormous opportunity for CPAs to provide additional services. The generation of information will require assurance about its reliability, credibility, relevance, and timeliness. Another example is the aging of the population. The U.S. Census Bureau reported that persons over 65 and those 45–64 years old represented 17 percent and 26 percent of the population in 1985, respectively. By 2005 these percentages are expected to increase to 18 percent and 33 percent, respectively. This increased number of older adults gives CPAs opportunities to provide additional services related to health care performance, personal financial planning, estate planning, pension plan audits, and fraud protection services.

Thus the demand for assurance services can be traced to two sources. First, clients and others have asked auditors to provide services that rely on the auditor's traditional competencies of independence, objectivity, and concern for the public interest. Second, in the face of flat revenue growth from traditional audits, the profession has sought to identify new services that can be delivered to existing and new clients.

Types of Assurance Services

🖋 [LO 3]

There are numerous opportunities for assurance services. The Elliott Committee surveyed 21 large and medium-sized CPA firms to identify what types of services these firms were currently offering. The firms enumerated over 250 different services. The AICPA, through the formation of the Assurance Services Executive Committee, helps identify and develop services for firms to market to existing and new clients. The Special Committee on Assurance Services has proposed detailed plans for six assurance services that have significant market potential for CPA firms:

- *Risk assessment*—assurance that an entity's profile of business risks is comprehensive and evaluation of whether the entity has appropriate systems in place to effectively manage those risks.
- *Business performance measurement*—assurance that an entity's performance measurement system contains relevant and reliable measures for assessing the degree to which the entity's goals and objectives are achieved or how its performance compares to competitors.
- *Information system reliability*—assurance that an entity's internal information systems provide reliable information for operating and financial decisions.
- *Electronic commerce*—assurance that systems and tools used in electronic commerce provide appropriate data integrity, security, privacy, and reliability.

- **Health care performance measurement**—assurance about the effectiveness of health care services provided by HMOs, hospitals, doctors, and other providers.
- **ElderCare**—assurance that specified goals regarding the elderly are being met by various caregivers.

The AICPA has established a task force for each of these services, charged with developing and communicating guidance for providing the service. The Elliott Committee also identified seven other areas where assurance services might be appropriate: corporate policy compliance, internal auditing services, trading partner accountability, mergers and acquisitions, ISO 9000 certification, investment managers' compliance with Association of Investment Management and Research Performance Presentation Standards, and World Wide Web assertions. These proposed services should give the reader a sense of the tremendous opportunities that exist for practitioners to provide assurance services to their existing and new clients. The following two sections present detailed coverage of two assurance services that have great potential for CPAs: CPA *WebTrust*^{SM} and CPA ElderCare.

CPA *WebTrust*^{SM} Assurance

[LO 4]   Electronic commerce involves individuals and organizations conducting business transactions, without paper documents, using computer and telecommunications networks. This includes transactions under electronic data interchange (EDI), where formal contracts exist between the parties, and business over the Internet (World Wide Web), where the parties do not have a preexisting contractual relationship. In recent years electronic commerce over the Internet has grown tremendously. However, this growth has been inhibited by consumer concern over the confidentiality of customer information (such as credit card numbers). To respond to these concerns, the AICPA and the Canadian Institute of Chartered Accountants (CICA) developed a set of principles and criteria for electronic commerce with consumers, referred to as *WebTrust*^{SM} Principles and Criteria.[3] The *WebTrust*^{SM} seal of assurance symbolizes to potential customers that a CPA has evaluated the Web site's business practices and controls to determine whether they conform to the principles and criteria for business-to-consumer electronic commerce.

The Risks of Electronic Commerce

Three broad risks are associated with electronic commerce: business practices, transaction integrity, and information protection. Because commerce over the Internet may involve transactions between parties who do not know each other, how can a consumer know that the entity behind the Web page is "real"? In other words, how can the consumer be sure that the entity follows good business practices and that consumers will not be defrauded? Similarly, how can the consumer have assurance that electronic transactions will not be changed, lost, duplicated, or processed incorrectly?

---

[3]In Canada, it is referred to as CA *WebTrust*^{SM}.

TABLE 21–1	***WebTrust*^SM Principles**

Business Practices Disclosure
The entity discloses its business practices for electronic commerce transactions and executes transactions in accordance with its disclosed business practices.

Transaction Integrity
The entity maintains effective controls to ensure that customers' orders placed using electronic commerce are completed and billed as agreed.

Information Protection
The entity maintains effective controls to provide reasonable assurance that private customer information obtained as a result of electronic commerce is protected from uses not related to the entity's business.

And how can the consumer be sure that private information will be protected? While setting up a Web page on the Internet is relatively easy, establishing strong security controls can be complex and costly. As a result of these risks, consumers have legitimate concerns about transaction integrity and confidentiality. An objective third party, such as a CPA, can provide assurance to customers about these risks.

WebTrust^SM Principles and Criteria[4]

[LO 5]

Table 21–1 presents the *WebTrust*^SM Principles. These are broad principles that are nontechnical and easy to understand. They address each of the risks of electronic commerce discussed previously. The *WebTrust*^SM Criteria provide more specific guidance on how to meet the principles. These criteria can help an entity assess its conformity with the criteria and provide a consistent set of criteria for practitioners to use in testing and evaluating Web sites.[5] Table 21–2 presents one *WebTrust*^SM criterion for each principle and illustrative disclosures for EarthWear Clothiers.

The Assurance Process for *WebTrust*^SM

[LO 6]

In order to obtain the *WebTrust*^SM seal of assurance, an entity must meet all the *WebTrust*^SM Principles as measured by the *WebTrust*^SM Criteria and engage a CPA who is licensed by the AICPA to provide *WebTrust*^SM service. Generally, this service will cover a period of three months or more. Once the seal is obtained, the entity can display it on its Web site provided the assurance examination is updated regularly and the entity informs the practitioner of any significant changes in its business policies, practices, processes, or controls. The entity's *WebTrust*^SM seal will be managed by a trusted third-party service organization (the "seal manager"). If the entity receives an unqualified report, the practitioner notifies the seal manager that the seal can be displayed on the entity's Web site and provides an expiration

---

[4]The discussion presented here is based in the AICPA/CICA *WebTrust*^SM Principles and Criteria for Business-to-Consumer Electronic Commerce, Version 1.0, December 23, 1997.

[5]See www.aicpa.org for a complete listing and discussion of the principles and criteria.

TABLE 21–2	**Selected *WebTrust*^{SM} Criteria for EarthWear Clothiers**

Business Practices Disclosures

Criterion	Disclosure
1. The entity discloses the terms and conditions by which it conducts its electronic commerce transactions, including, but not limited to, the following: • Time frame for shipment of orders for goods. • Time frame and process for informing customers of backorders. • Normal method of delivery, including customer options. • Payment terms, including customer options. • Product return policies.	• EarthWear's policy is to ship in-stock orders on the following day. Approximately 95% of orders are shipped within one day. • At the time of ordering, customers know the availability of the goods. If the goods are on backorder, the customer is informed of the approximate availability date. • Orders are generally shipped utilizing two-day UPS service at standard rates. Expedited delivery service is available at additional charges. • The customer's credit card is charged at the time of shipment for the goods available. • EarthWear offers an unconditional guarantee on all its products.

Transaction Integrity

Criterion	Controls
1. The entity maintains controls to provide reasonable assurance that • Each order is checked for accuracy and completeness. • Positive acknowledgment is received from the customer before the order is processed.	• EarthWear's order entry system automatically checks each order for accuracy and completeness. • All customer order information is stored in a "shopping basket." When the customer has finished shopping, the contents of the shopping basket are displayed. The customer clicks "yes" to accept the order.

Information Protection

Criterion	Controls
1. The entity maintains controls to protect transmissions of private customer information over the Internet from unintended recipients.	• Private customer information is protected during transmission by encryption technology. • EarthWear has registered its domain name and Internet IP address. The address is unique. • The company's Web page has a digital certificate that can be checked using features in a standard Web browser. • EarthWear's Webmaster updates and reviews the site daily to ensure that no improper content or links have been added.

date. Unless update notification is received, the authorization to display the seal expires on the expiration date, and the seal manager will remove the seal's display authorization. The seal displayed at the Web site can be verified by clicking on the seal, which displays a special *WebTrust*^{SM} digital certificate. Verisign, Inc., serves as the designated seal manager for the AICPA.

A *WebTrust*^{SM} assurance engagement is performed as an examination under the attestation standards described in this chapter. In examining an

EXHIBIT 21–1

Management's Assertions for EarthWear's Web Site

EarthWear Clothiers, on its Web site for electronic commerce (at www.mhhe.com/earthwear), asserts the following:

- We have disclosed our business practices for electronic commerce and executed transactions in accordance with these disclosed business practices;
- We have maintained effective controls to provide reasonable assurance that customers' orders placed using electronic commerce were completed and billed as agreed; and
- We have maintained effective controls to provide reasonable assurance that private customer information obtained as a result of electronic commerce was protected from uses not related to our business

during the period from January 1, 2000, through March 31, 2000, in conformity with the AICPA *WebTrust^SM* Principles and Criteria.

Calvin J. Rogers	James C. Watts
President & CEO	Chief Financial Officer

---

entity's Web site, the practitioner would use guidance provided in SSAE No. 1, SSAE No. 2, and the Committee of Sponsoring Organizations of the Treadway Commission's *Internal Control—Integrated Framework.* In such an examination, the practitioner expresses a positive opinion that the presentation of assertions conforms to the AICPA's *WebTrust^SM* Principles and Criteria.

 Exhibit 21–1 presents EarthWear's management's assertions about its Web site. Note that management's assertions address the three categories of principles. The report of management's assertions is signed by the president and CEO and the chief financial officer. Exhibit 21–2 contains Willis & Adams's unqualified report on those assertions. The first paragraph of the Willis & Adams report states that the assertions have been examined and that management is responsible for the assertions. The second paragraph states the four steps that were undertaken to complete the examination of management's assertions. In particular, Willis & Adams (1) obtained an understanding of EarthWear's electronic commerce business practices and its controls over the processing of electronic commerce transactions and the protection of related private customer information, (2) selectively tested transactions executed in accordance with the disclosed practices, (3) tested and evaluated the operating effectiveness of the controls, and (4) performed other procedures that they considered necessary. The opinion paragraph provides an unqualified opinion on Earth-Wear's management's assertions.

EXHIBIT 21–2

Willis & Adams's Unqualified Examination Report on EarthWear's Web Site

To the Management of EarthWear Clothiers:

We have examined the assertion by the management of EarthWear Clothiers that on its Web site for electronic commerce (at www.mhhe.com/earthwear) during the period from January 1, 2000, through March 31, 2000, EarthWear:

- Disclosed its business practices for electronic commerce transactions and executed transactions in accordance with its disclosed business practices,
- Maintained effective controls to provide reasonable assurance that customers' orders placed using electronic commerce were completed and billed as agreed, and
- Maintained effective controls to provide reasonable assurance that private customer information obtained as a result of electronic commerce was protected from uses not related to EarthWear's business

in conformity with the AICPA *WebTrust^SM* Principles and Criteria. EarthWear's management is responsible for its assertion. Our responsibility is to express an opinion on management's assertion based on our examination.

Our examination was made in accordance with standards established by the American Institute of Certified Public Accountants. Those standards require that we plan and perform our examination to obtain reasonable assurance that management's assertions are not materially misstated. Our examination included (1) obtaining an understanding of EarthWear's electronic commerce business practices and its controls over the processing of electronic commerce transactions and the protection of related private customer information, (2) selectively testing transactions executed in accordance with the disclosed practices, (3) testing and evaluating the operating effectiveness of the controls, and (4) performing such other procedures as we considered necessary in the circumstances.

Because of the inherent limitations in controls, errors or fraud may occur and not be detected. Also, projections of any evaluation of controls to future periods are subject to the risks that controls may become inadequate because of changes in conditions or that the degree of compliance with the policies or procedures may deteriorate.

In our opinion, the assertion by the management of EarthWear Clothiers for the period January 1, 2000, through March 31, 2000, is fairly stated, in all material respects, based on the AICPA/CICA *WebTrust^SM* Principles and Criteria.

The CPA *WebTrust^SM* seal of assurance on EarthWear's Web site for electronic commerce constitutes a symbolic representation of the contents of this report and it is not intended, nor should it be construed, to update this report or provide any additional assurance.

This report does not include any representation as to the quality of EarthWear's goods nor their suitability for any customer's intended purpose.

Willis & Adams
Boise, Idaho
April 3, 2000

CPA ElderCare

[LO 7]   The population in the United States and Canada is aging, and many of these people have accumulated significant wealth. Additionally, individuals are living to ages where they require some form of assisted living. In the past these individuals relied on family members to provide some level of care. However, changing demographics show a more mobile younger generation. Many of these younger families have both spouses working outside the home, and they do not have time to care for elderly relatives. The CPA can bring another level of assurance or comfort to the elderly person and his or her family members. ElderCare services build on the CPA's reputation for independence, objectivity, and integrity to provide a service that is in the public interest. More specifically, ElderCare service is designed to assure family members that proper care is provided to elderly family members who are no longer totally independent. The role of the practitioner is one of oversight. The practitioner acts in the place of the absent family members and relies on qualified specialists, employed by the client or the responsible family member, to provide the services outside the scope of the practitioner's expertise. The practitioner's role is to observe and report on how those service providers are meeting the needs of the client and the criteria for care established by the family members. It is likely that this service will be combined with traditional financial services, and the practitioner will establish strategic alliances with other professionals (such as elder law attorneys, geriatric care managers, and social workers or medical personnel). Based on research conducted by the AICPA, it appears that there is a demand for this type of service.[6]

Types of ElderCare Services

[LO 8]   Practitioners can offer three types of ElderCare services: (1) consulting/facilitating services, (2) direct services, and (3) assurance services.

Consulting/Facilitating Services   This type of service includes the practitioner consulting with the client or third party (the responsible individual) to establish the standards of care expected. This might include giving the third party a list of services that are available in the community. Consulting services might also include assisting the client or third party in selecting the care provider and level of care for each type of care required.

Direct Services   Direct services include practitioner services such as receiving, depositing, and accounting for the individual's income; paying bills and conducting routine financial transactions for the client; and supervising investments and accounting for the estate. These services might also include arranging for proper care, paying for it, and periodically ensuring that the care is being received at the appropriate level; arranging for transportation for the client; and supervising household items such as home maintenance and repairs.

---

[6]The reader should examine the market research conducted by Hill & Knowlton and Yankelovich Partners, Inc., in the United States, and Hazelton Group in Canada, at the AICPA's home page (www.aicpa.org).

Assurance Services   In this type of service the practitioner issues periodic reports about the quality of care provided to the elderly person. It is likely that ElderCare assurance services will be conducted as agreed-upon procedures in attestation engagements as described in this chapter. This type of assurance service may involve the practitioner visiting the elderly person and inspecting documentation such as logs, diaries, or other evidence to support that the contracted services have been provided at the appropriate level of care.

The Assurance Process for ElderCare

✒ [LO 9]

Most CPAs do not have experience with ElderCare-type services, except for tax and financial planning. The AICPA has developed a number of continuing education courses, and additional guidance is available from commercial vendors (such as Practitioners Publishing Company) to help CPAs acquire the necessary knowledge. Unlike *WebTrust*^SM, which has a set of well-defined criteria for measuring performance, the criteria for an ElderCare engagement will vary significantly depending upon the client's needs.

The first step for a practitioner is to create an inventory of services available in his or her community for older clients and identify other professionals, such as doctors and geriatric care managers, who can help the practitioner provide services for older clients. The practitioner may want to establish a strategic alliance with qualified specialists to provide services outside the scope of the practitioner's expertise. For example, the practitioner may partner with a social worker to periodically assess the level of health care provided to the client. The practitioner then observes and reports how the service providers are meeting the needs of the client.

The second step that is critical for ElderCare services is an engagement letter that is specifically tailored to the elderly individual. It should clearly identify the practitioner's responsibilities and duties on the engagement. While the elderly person is normally considered the client, a family member or a third party who has power of attorney for the elderly person may be the client. Once the engagement is initiated, it must be properly staffed. While the practitioner will rely on other professionals to deliver services not in the practitioner's area of expertise, the practitioner or members of the practitioner's staff should be assigned tasks commensurate with their abilities.

The type of work that the practitioner will perform on an ElderCare engagement will vary depending upon the circumstances of the engagement. A typical ElderCare engagement would include consulting services involving assisting the client or third party in selecting the care provider, and level of care, for each type of care required. The typical engagement would also include direct services such as depositing income and paying bills. The more difficult work would involve assurance-related procedures such as visiting the client and inspecting logs, diaries, or other evidence to support that the services contracted have been provided appropriately.

ElderCare engagement reporting will depend on the level of service provided. For direct services, such as depositing income and paying bills, the practitioner may perform a compilation service. For assurance services,

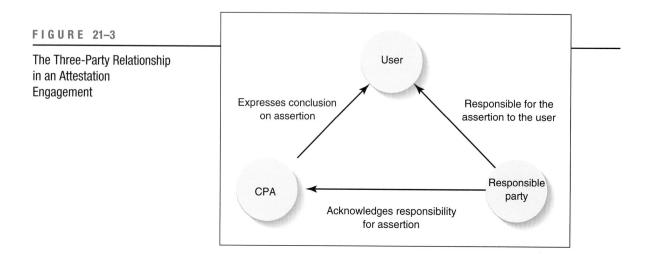

FIGURE 21–3

The Three-Party Relationship in an Attestation Engagement

the practitioner will likely prepare an agreed-upon procedures report. The engagement may require that the practitioner periodically report to family members less formally.

Attestation Engagements

[LO 10]   SSAE No. 1 defines an attestation engagement as follows:

> **Attestation** is when a practitioner is engaged to issue or does issue a written communication that expresses a conclusion about the reliability of a written assertion that is the responsibility of another party.

In this definition, *practitioner* refers to a certified public accountant in the practice of public accounting. Because attestation engagements are not audits as defined in GAAS, the attestation standards use *practitioner* instead of *auditor*. The term *assertion* here refers to any declaration, or set of related declarations, taken as a whole by a party responsible for it. An example of an assertion by management would be "EarthWear Clothiers maintains an effective internal control over financial reporting."

Typically, an attestation engagement involves three parties: a user or users; a party responsible for making the assertion, such as management; and a CPA. Figure 21–3 depicts the relationship among the three parties to an attestation engagement. Note the direction of the arrows in this figure. The responsible party is responsible for the assertion to the user and acknowledges that responsibility to the CPA. The CPA expresses a conclusion to the user on management's assertion. In some cases, the engagement may involve only two parties because the user and the responsible party are the same.

The practitioner should use an attestation risk model to meet the standards of field work in an attestation engagement. Attestation risk is defined in a manner similar to audit risk and is composed of the same three components (inherent risk, control risk, and detection risk) as the audit risk model discussed in Chapter 3. The attestation risk should be set consistent with the type of engagement being performed.

TABLE 21–3	Overview of Attestation Engagements			
Type of Engagement	*Level of Assurance*	*Attestation Risk*	*Type of Report*	*Report Distribution*
Examination	High	Low	Opinion	General or limited
Review	Moderate	Moderate	Negative assurance	General or limited
Agreed-upon procedures	Variable	Variable	Summary of findings	Limited

Types of Attestation Engagements

[LO 11]

Attestation standards[7] generally provide for three types of engagements: *examination, review,* and *agreed-upon procedures.* However, an individual SSAE may prohibit one or more of these types of engagements. SSAE No. 1 allows a practitioner to conduct a compilation engagement on financial forecasts and projections.

Examination   The practitioner can examine the responsible party's assertions. In an examination, the practitioner expresses an opinion that the assertion is presented, in all material respects, in conformity with the established or stated criteria. Such an opinion may be for general or limited distribution. If distribution is limited, the opinion must state the limitations on the use of the report. Because an examination engagement provides the highest level of assurance on an assertion, the practitioner must gather sufficient evidence to limit the attestation risk to a low level.

Review   The practitioner may also perform a review engagement on the responsible party's assertions. In a review engagement, the practitioner expresses *negative* assurance—that is, that no information came to the practitioner's attention that indicates that the assertions are not presented in conformity with established or stated criteria. Distribution of a review report can also be either general or limited. A review engagement should provide sufficient evidence to limit the attestation risk to a moderate level.

Agreed-Upon Procedures   An agreed-upon procedures engagement is one in which a practitioner is engaged by a client to issue a report of findings based on specific procedures performed on the subject matter of an assertion (SSAE No. 4). The level of assurance provided by such an engagement depends on the nature and scope of the procedures agreed upon with the specified parties. Thus, the attestation risk is a function of the intended level of assurance. Distribution of the report based on such an engagement is limited to the specified users. The report on an agreed-upon procedures engagement summarizes findings about the application of the agreed-upon procedures.

Table 21–3 provides an overview of the types of attestation engagements.

---

[7]Statements on Standards for Attestation Engagements (SSAEs) can be issued by the Auditing Standards Board, the Accounting and Review Services Committee, and the Management Advisory Services Executive Committee.

Attestation Standards

✏️ **[LO 12]**   Table 21–4 lists the 11 attestation standards and the 10 GAAS for comparative purposes.

TABLE 21–4   Attestation Standards Compared with Generally Accepted Auditing Standards

Attestation Standards	Generally Accepted Auditing Standards
General Standards	
1. The engagement shall be performed by a practitioner or practitioners having adequate technical training and proficiency in the attest function.	1. The examination is to be performed by a person or persons having adequate technical training and proficiency as an auditor.
2. The engagement shall be performed by a practitioner or practitioners having adequate knowledge in the subject matter of the assertion.	
3. The practitioner shall perform an engagement only if he or she has reason to believe that the following two conditions exist: • The assertion is capable of evaluation against reasonable criteria that either have been established by a recognized body or are stated in the assertion in a sufficiently clear and comprehensive manner for a knowledgeable reader to be able to understand them. • The assertion is capable of reasonably consistent estimation or measurement using such criteria.	
4. In all matters relating to the engagement, an independence in mental attitude shall be maintained by the practitioner or practitioners.	2. In all matters relating to the assignment, an independence in mental attitude is to be maintained by the auditor or auditors.
5. Due professional care shall be exercised in the performance of the engagement.	3. Due professional care is to be exercised in the planning and performance of the examination and the preparation of the report
Standards of Field Work	
1. The work shall be adequately planned and assistants, if any, shall be properly supervised.	1. The work is to be adequately planned and assistants, if any, are to be properly supervised.
	2. There is to be a proper study and evaluation of the existing internal control as a basis for reliance thereon and for the determination of the resultant extent of the tests to which auditing procedures are to be restricted.
2. Sufficient evidence shall be obtained to provide a reasonable basis for the conclusion that is expressed in the report.	3. Sufficient competent evidential matter is to be obtained through inspection, observation, inquiries, and confirmations to afford a reasonable basis for an opinion regarding the financial statements under examination.

(continued)

TABLE 21–4 (*concluded*)

Attestation Standards	Generally Accepted Auditing Standards
Standards of Reporting	
1. The report shall identify the assertion being reported on and state the character of the engagement.	
2. The report shall state the practitioner's conclusion about the reliability of the assertion based on the established or stated criteria against which it was measured.	1. The report shall state whether the financial statements are presented in accordance with generally accepted accounting principles.
	2. The report shall state whether such principles have been consistently observed in the current period in relation to the preceding period.
	3. Informative disclosures in the financial statements are to be regarded as reasonably adequate unless otherwise stated in the report.
3. The report shall state all of the practitioner's significant reservations about the engagement and the assertion. 4. The report on an engagement to evaluate an assertion that has been prepared in conformity with agreed-upon criteria or on an engagement to apply agreed-upon procedures should contain a statement limiting its use to the parties who have agreed upon such criteria or procedures.	4. The report shall either contain an expression of opinion regarding the financial statements, taken as a whole, or an assertion to the effect that an opinion cannot be expressed. When an overall opinion cannot be expressed, the reasons therefore should be stated. In all cases where an auditor's name is associated with financial statements, the report should contain a clear-cut indication of the character of the auditor's examination, if any, and the degree of responsibility he is taking.

General Standards

There are five general standards for attestation engagements. All but the second and third general standards have counterparts in GAAS. The second standard requires that the practitioner have adequate knowledge of the subject matter of the assertion. Such a requirement can be met by the CPA through education and practical experience. The CPA may also use a specialist to help meet this knowledge requirement. The third standard is particularly important because it stipulates the two conditions that must exist in order for the practitioner to perform the engagement:

- The assertion is capable of evaluation against reasonable criteria that either have been established by a recognized body or are stated in the assertion in a sufficiently clear and comprehensive manner for a knowledgeable reader to be able to understand them.
- The assertion is capable of reasonably consistent estimation or measurement using such criteria.

The first condition requires that the assertion be capable of measurement against reasonable criteria. Such criteria can be issued by bodies designated under the AICPA's Code of Professional Conduct. For example, when we discuss attestation engagements for reporting on internal control, the practitioner can use criteria from SAS No. 55, which are based on the

Committee of Sponsoring Organizations of the Treadway Commission's document *Internal Control—Integrated Framework* (the COSO Report). Criteria issued by regulatory agencies or by bodies of experts that follow due process procedures also qualify. The second condition requires that the assertion be subject to reasonably consistent estimation or measurement. Basically, this condition can be met if competent individuals using the same estimation or measurement criteria would reach materially similar results.

Standards of Field Work

The only difference in field work between the attestation standards and GAAS is that the attestation standards do not require a study and evaluation of internal control. Given the varied nature of services that can be performed under the attestation standards, such a requirement would be prohibitively restrictive. The approach to field work for an attestation engagement should involve proper planning and supervision, and sufficient evidence must be gathered to provide a reasonable basis for the practitioner's conclusion about the assertion.

Standards of Reporting

Reporting standards for attestation engagements differ in a number of respects from those of GAAS. First, the attestation standards do not contain anything about consistent application of GAAP or informative disclosures. However, they do require that the report identify the assertion and the type of engagement being performed. The reporting standards also require that the practitioner state any significant reservation about the engagement or presentation of the assertion. The fourth standard of reporting also results in what are referred to as *general-distribution* and *limited-distribution* reports. If the engagement involves evaluating an assertion using agreed-upon criteria or agreed-upon procedures are applied, the report should contain a statement limiting the use of the report to the parties that agreed to the criteria or procedures.

Reporting on an Entity's Internal Control over Financial Reporting

[LO 13]   In recent years, accountants have been asked to provide reports on management's assertion about the effectiveness of an entity's internal control. Additional impetus for such reporting occurred when Congress passed the Federal Deposit Insurance Corporation Act of 1991, which requires that the management of large financial institutions issue a report on the effectiveness of the institution's internal control. The act also requires that accountants attest to management's report. The AICPA responded to the demands for such services by issuing SSAE No. 2, "Reporting on an Entity's Internal Control over Financial Reporting" (AT 400). The standard defines an entity's internal control over financial reporting as including those policies and procedures that pertain to an entity's ability to record, process, summarize, and report financial data consistent with the assertions embodied in either the annual financial statements or interim financial statements or both.

Management may present its written assertion about internal control in either of two forms: (1) a separate report that will accompany the practitioner's report or (2) a representation letter to the practitioner. When management's assertion does not accompany the practitioner's report, the first paragraph of the report should also contain a statement of management's assertion.

Conditions for Conducting an Engagement

In order for the practitioner to examine management's assertions about the effectiveness of internal control, the following conditions are necessary:

- Management accepts responsibility for the effectiveness of the entity's internal control.
- Management must evaluate the effectiveness of the entity's internal control using reasonable criteria (referred to as *control criteria*) for the effectiveness of internal control established by a recognized body.
- Sufficient competent evidence must exist or be able to be developed to support management's evaluation.
- Management provides to the practitioner its written assertion based on control criteria referred to in its report.

Criteria issued by the AICPA, regulatory agencies, and other bodies of experts that follow due process qualify as control criteria. For example, management may use the criteria provided in SAS No. 55, "Consideration of Internal Control in a Financial Statement Audit" (AU 319), which is based on the control criteria included in the COSO Report for reporting under SSAE No. 2.

A practitioner is allowed to perform either of two types of attestation engagements for reporting on internal control: (1) examination or (2) agreed-upon procedures. The standard specifically prohibits the practitioner from accepting an engagement to *review* and report on management's assertion.

Examination Engagement

The practitioner's objective in an engagement to examine management's assertion about the effectiveness of the entity's internal control is to express an opinion on (1) the effectiveness of the entity's internal control, in all material respects, based on the control criteria or (2) whether management's assertion about the effectiveness of internal control is fairly stated, in all material respects, based on the control criteria. An examination engagement involves five steps:

1. Planning the engagement.
2. Obtaining an understanding of the company's internal control.
3. Evaluating the *design* effectiveness of the controls.
4. Testing and evaluating the *operating* effectiveness of the controls.
5. Forming an opinion on the effectiveness of the entity's internal control or management's assertion.

The process followed by the practitioner to complete these five steps is virtually identical to the process for conducting an audit. Therefore, the techniques discussed in Chapter 6 are applicable to an examination engagement.

While examining the entity's internal control, the practitioner may encounter control deficiencies. SSAE No. 2 relies on auditing standards (SAS No. 60, "Communication of Internal Control–Related Matters Noted in an Audit") to distinguish between reportable conditions and material weaknesses. In general, a material weakness will preclude the practitioner from concluding that the entity has effective internal control. If the practitioner identifies any reportable conditions, they should be communicated to the audit committee.

Finally, the practitioner should obtain written representations from management

- Acknowledging management's responsibility for establishing and maintaining the internal control.
- Stating that management has evaluated the effectiveness of the entity's internal control and specifying the control criteria used.
- Stating management's assertion about the effectiveness of the internal control based upon the control criteria and identifying the point in time or period covered.
- Stating that management (1) has disclosed to the practitioner all significant deficiencies in the design or operation of the internal control system that could adversely affect the entity's ability to record, process, summarize, and report financial data consistent with the assertions of management in the financial statements and (2) has identified those that it believes to be material weaknesses in internal control.
- Describing any material fraud and any other fraud that, although not material, involve management or other employees who have a significant role in the entity's internal control.
- Stating whether there were, subsequent to the date being reported on, any changes in the internal control system or other factors that might significantly affect the internal control system, including any corrective actions taken by management with regard to significant deficiencies and material weaknesses.

If management refuses to provide written representations, a scope limitation exists.

Reporting on Management's Assertion about Internal Control

The practitioner's report should include (1) a title that includes the word *independent*, (2) an identification of management's assertion about the effectiveness of the entity's internal control over financial reporting as of a specified point in time, (3) a statement that the assertion is the responsibility of management, (4) a statement that the practitioner's responsibility is to express an opinion based on his or her examination, (5) a statement that the examination was conducted in accordance with standards established by the AICPA, (6) a statement that the practitioner believes the examination provides a reasonable basis for his or her opinion, and (7) a paragraph stating that, because of the inherent limitations of any internal control system, errors or fraud may occur and not be detected. The practitioner's report should contain an opinion on whether (1) the entity has maintained, in all material respects, effective internal control over financial reporting as of the specified date or for the specified period based on control criteria or (2) management's assertion about the effectiveness of the entity's internal control over financial reporting as of the specified date or for the specified period is fairly stated, in all material respects, based on the control criteria. When the report is subject to limited distribution, the practitioner's report should contain a statement limiting the use of the report. Again, these reporting requirements are similar

EXHIBIT 21–3

Example of an Examination Report Expressing an Opinion Directly on the Effectiveness of the Entity's Internal Control

Independent Accountant's Report

We have examined management's assertion included in the accompanying management's report on internal control that Smith International maintained effective internal control over financial reporting as of December 31, 2000, in conformity with control criteria included in SAS No. 55, "Consideration of Internal Control in a Financial Statement Audit." Management has represented to us that it is responsible for maintaining effective internal control over financial reporting in conformity with control criteria included in SAS No. 55, "Consideration of Internal Control in a Financial Statement Audit." Our responsibility is to express an opinion on the effectiveness of the internal control based on our examination.

Our examination was conducted in accordance with attestation standards established by the American Institute of Certified Public Accountants and accordingly included obtaining an understanding of the internal control over financial reporting, testing and evaluating the design and operating effectiveness of internal control, and performing such other procedures as we considered necessary in the circumstances. We believe that our examination provides a reasonable basis for our opinion.

Because of inherent limitations in internal control, errors or fraud may occur and not be detected. Also, projections of any evaluation of internal control over financial reporting to future periods are subject to the risk that internal control may become inadequate because of changes in conditions or that the degree of compliance with the policies or procedures may deteriorate.

In our opinion, Smith International maintained, in all material respects, effective internal control over financial reporting as of December 31, 2000, based on control criteria included in SAS No. 55, "Consideration of Internal Control in a Financial Statement Audit."

to those of audit reporting on financial statements with the exception of the paragraph describing the inherent limitations of internal control.

Exhibit 21–3 is an example of an examination report issued when the practitioner expresses an opinion directly on the effectiveness of an entity's internal contract as of a specified date.

Exhibit 21–4 presents an example of an examination report where the practitioner expresses an opinion on management's assertion about the effectiveness of the entity's internal control.

Report Modifications   The practitioner should modify the standard report if any of the following conditions is present:

- A material weakness exists.
- There is a restriction on the scope of the engagement.
- The practitioner refers to the report of another practitioner.
- A significant subsequent event has occurred since the date being reported on.
- Management's assertion relates only to part of the entity's internal control.
- Management's assertion relates only to the suitability of the design of the entity's internal control.
- Management's assertion is based on criteria established by a regulatory agency without following due process.

EXHIBIT 21–4

Example of a Practitioner's Examination Report On Management's Assertion about the Effectiveness on Internal Control

Independent Accountant's Report

We have examined management's assertion, included in the accompanying management report on internal control, that Harrison Corporation maintained effective internal control over financial reporting as of December 31, 2000, in conformity with control criteria included in SAS No. 55, "Consideration of Internal Control in a Financial Statement Audit." Management has represented to us that it is responsible for maintaining effective internal control over financial reporting in conformity with control criteria included in SAS No. 55, "Consideration of Internal Control in a Financial Statement Audit." Our responsibility is to express an opinion on management's assertion based on our examination.

[*Standard wording for the scope and inherent limitations paragraphs*]

In our opinion, management's assertion that Harrison Corporation maintained effective internal control over financial reporting as of December 31, 2000, is fairly stated, in all material respects, based upon control criteria included in SAS No. 55, "Consideration of Internal Control in a Financial Statement Audit."

EXHIBIT 21–5

Example of an Examination Report Regarding a Material Weakness

Independent Accountant's Report

[*Standard wording for the introductory, scope, and inherent limitations paragraphs*]

As discussed in management's assertion, the following material weakness exists in the design or operation of the internal control system of Conrad Company in effect at December 31, 2000: the company does not use adequate shipping documents to ensure that all goods shipped to customers are billed. This results in the company failing to meet the control criteria for proper recording. A material weakness is a condition that precludes the entity's internal control system from providing reasonable assurance that material misstatements will be prevented or detected on a timely basis.

In our opinion, management's assertion that, except for the effect of the material weakness described in the preceding paragraph on the achievement of the objectives of the control criteria, Conrad Company has maintained, in all material respects, effective internal control over financial reporting as of December 31, 2000, based upon control criteria included in SAS No. 55, "Consideration of Internal Control in a Financial Statement Audit."

Exhibit 21–5 is an example of an examination report issued when a material weakness has been identified in the entity's internal control system.

Financial Forecasts and Projections

[LO 14] Auditors have been asked to provide some type of assurance for entities that want to issue prospective financial statements. To respond to this market need, the AICPA issued an attestation standard that provides guidance for practitioners providing such services. The practitioner's involvement may include (1) assembling or assisting the client in assembling prospective financial statements or (2) reporting on client-prepared prospective financial statements. In either of these situations, the practitioner should examine, apply agreed-upon procedures, or compile the prospective financial statements if such statements are expected to be used by a third party.

Types of Prospective Financial Statements

Prospective financial statements contain financial information made up of either financial forecasts or financial projections. *Financial forecasts* are prospective financial statements that present an entity's *expected* financial position, results of operations, and cash flows. They are based on assumptions reflecting conditions the responsible party *expects to exist* and the course of action it *expects to take*. *Financial projections* are prospective financial statements that present, *given one or more hypothetical assumptions*, an entity's expected financial position, results of operations, and cash flows. The primary difference between the two is that the financial projection is based on hypothetical assumptions and is intended to respond to a question such as "What would happen if . . . ?" A financial projection is sometimes prepared to present one or more hypothetical courses of action for evaluation.

Prospective financial statements are for either general use or limited use. *General use* of prospective financial statements refers to the use of the statements by persons with whom the responsible party is not negotiating directly. An example would be an offering statement containing prospective financial statements for an entity's debt or equity securities. Because the intended users cannot question the responsible party, the best form of presentation is the *expected results*. Therefore, only a financial forecast is appropriate for general use.

Limited use of prospective financial statements refers to use of the statements by the responsible party alone or by the responsible party and third parties with whom the responsible party is negotiating directly. Examples include use in negotiations for a bank loan, submission to a regulatory agency, or use solely within the entity. In such cases, the third parties can question the responsible party about the prospective financial information. Any type of prospective financial statement is appropriate for limited use.

While the responsible party is responsible for presentation of prospective financial statements, other parties, such as accountants, may assist in meeting the presentation guidelines specified in the attestation standards. Prospective financial statements should preferably be in the format of the historical financial statements; however, they may be limited to the items shown in Table 21–5. A presentation that omits any item in Table 21–5 is referred to as a *partial* presentation.

A number of important items must be presented or disclosed in the prospective financial statements.

- The title of the prospective financial statements should describe the nature of the presentation and should include the word *forecast* or *projection*.
- Each page of the financial forecast should contain a statement that directs the reader to the summaries of significant assumptions and accounting policies.

TABLE 21–5	**Minimum Presentation Guidelines for Prospective Financial Information**

- Sales or gross revenues.
- Gross profit or cost of sales.
- Unusual or infrequently occurring items.
- Provision for income taxes.
- Discontinued operations or extraordinary items.
- Income from continuing operations.
- Net income.
- Primary and fully diluted earnings per share.
- Significant changes in financial position.
- A description of what management intends the prospective financial statements to present, a statement that the assumptions are based on information about circumstances and conditions existing at the time the prospective information was prepared, and a caveat that the prospective results may not be achieved.
- Summary of significant assumptions.
- Summary of significant accounting policies.

- The completion date of the preparation of the prospective financial information should be disclosed.
- A summary of significant accounting policies used in preparing the prospective financial information should be disclosed along with assumptions deemed to be significant to the statements.
- The basis of or rationale for the assumptions should be disclosed to assist the user in making an informed judgment about the presentation.
- The presentation should indicate which assumptions are particularly sensitive at the time of preparation—that is, which assumptions have a relatively high probability of variation that would materially affect the financial forecast.

Examination Engagement

An examination of prospective financial statements involves four steps: (1) evaluation of the preparation of the prospective financial statements, (2) evaluation of the support underlying the assumptions, (3) evaluation of the presentation of the prospective financial statements for conformity with the AICPA's presentation guidelines, and (4) issuance of an examination report. The accountant should be independent, have adequate technical training and proficiency to examine prospective financial statements, and obtain sufficient evidence to issue an examination report. Exhibits 21–6 and 21–7 present examples of the standard examination report for a forecast and projection, respectively. The only major difference between the two reports is the paragraph limiting distribution to specified users.

The following circumstances may require a departure from the standard examination report:

EXHIBIT 21–6

Example of a Standard Examination Report on a Forecast

Independent Accountant's Report

We have examined the accompanying forecasted balance sheet, statements of income, retained earnings, and cash flows of Panatta Company as of December 31, 2000, and for the year then ending. Our examination was made in accordance with standards for an examination of a forecast established by the American Institute of Certified Public Accountants and, accordingly, included such procedures as we considered necessary to evaluate both the assumptions used by management and the preparation and presentation of the forecast.

In our opinion, the accompanying forecast is presented in conformity with guidelines for presentation of a forecast established by the American Institute of Certified Public Accountants, and the underlying assumptions provide a reasonable basis for management's forecast. However, there will usually be differences between the forecasted and actual results, because events and circumstances frequently do not occur as expected, and those differences may be material. We have no responsibility to update this report for events and circumstances occurring after the date of this report.

EXHIBIT 21–7

Example of a Standard Examination Report on a Projection

Independent Accountant's Report

We have examined the accompanying projected balance sheet, statements of income, retained earnings, and cash flows of Hansen Company as of December 31, 2000, and for the year then ending. Our examination was made in accordance with standards for an examination of a forecast established by the American Institute of Certified Public Accountants and, accordingly, included such procedures as we considered necessary to evaluate both the assumptions used by management and the preparation and presentation of the projection.

The accompanying projection and this report were prepared for the Panama City National Bank for the purpose of negotiating a loan to expand Hansen Company's plant and should not be used by anyone other than these specified parties.

In our opinion, the accompanying projection is presented in conformity with guidelines for presentation of a projection established by the American Institute of Certified Public Accountants, and the underlying assumptions provide a reasonable basis for management's projection, assuming the granting of the requested loan for the purpose of expanding Hansen Company's plant as described in the summary of significant assumptions. However, even if the loan is granted and the plant is expanded, there will usually be differences between the projected and actual results, because events and circumstances frequently do not occur as expected, and those differences may be material. We have no responsibility to update this report for events and circumstances occurring after the date of this report.

- Departure from AICPA presentation guidelines.
- Unreasonable assumptions.
- Scope limitation.

The presence of such events can result in a report that is either qualified or adverse. A disclaimer may also be issued. Exhibit 21–8 provides an example of a qualified report on a forecast.

Example of a Qualified Examination Report

Independent Accountant's Report

We have examined the accompanying forecasted balance sheet, statements of income, retained earnings, and cash flows of Colaco Company as of December 31, 2000, and for the year then ending. Our examination was made in accordance with standards for an examination of a forecast established by the American Institute of Certified Public Accountants and, accordingly, included such procedures as we considered necessary to evaluate both the assumptions used by management and the preparation and presentation of the forecast.

The forecast does not disclose reasons for the significant variation in the relationship between income tax expense and pretax accounting income as required by generally accepted accounting principles.

In our opinion, except for the omission of the disclosure of the reasons for the significant variation in the relationship between income tax expense and pretax accounting income as discussed in the preceding paragraph, the accompanying forecast is presented in conformity with guidelines for presentation of a forecast established by the American Institute of Certified Public Accountants, and the underlying assumptions provide a reasonable basis for management's forecast. However, there will usually be differences between the forecasted and actual results, because events and circumstances frequently do not occur as expected, and those differences may be material. We have no responsibility to update this report for events and circumstances occurring after the date of this report.

Agreed-Upon Procedures

An accountant may perform an agreed-upon procedures attestation engagement for prospective financial statements provided that

1. The accountant is independent.
2. The accountant and the specified users agree upon the procedures performed or to be performed by the accountant.
3. The specified users take responsibility for the sufficiency of the agreed-upon procedures for their purposes.
4. The prospective financial statements include a summary of significant assumptions.
5. The prospective financial statements to which the procedures are to be applied are subject to reasonably consistent estimation or measurement.
6. Criteria to be used in determining findings are agreed upon between the accountant and the specified users.
7. The procedures to be applied to the prospective financial statements are expected to result in reasonably consistent findings using the criteria.
8. Evidential matter related to the prospective financial statements to which the procedures are applied is expected to exist and to provide a reasonable basis for expressing the findings in the accountant's report.
9. Where applicable, there is a description of any agreed-upon materiality limits for reporting purposes.
10. Use of the report is to be restricted to the specified users.

EXHIBIT 21–9

Example of an Agreed-Upon Procedures Report for a Forecast

Independent Accountant's Report on Applying Agreed-Upon Procedures

Board of Directors—Donnay Corporation
Board of Directors—Clinkton Company

At your request, we have performed certain agreed-upon procedures, as enumerated below, with respect to the forecasted balance sheet, and the related forecasted statements of income, retained earnings, and cash flows of Matlin Company, a subsidiary of Clinkton Company, as of December 31, 2000, and for the year then ending. These procedures, which were agreed to by the boards of directors of Donnay Corporation and Clinkton Company, were performed solely to assist you in evaluating the forecast in connection with the sale of Matlin Company to Clinkton Company. This agreed-upon procedures engagement was performed in accordance with standards established by the American Institute of Certified Public Accountants. The sufficiency of these procedures is solely the responsibility of the specified users of the report. Consequently, we make no representation regarding the sufficiency of the procedures described below either for the purpose for which this report has been requested or for any other purpose.

The procedures and associated findings are as follows:

a. With respect to forecasted rental income, we compared the assumptions about expected demand for rental of the housing units to demand for similar housing units at similar rental prices in the city area in which Matlin Company's housing units are located.

No exceptions were found as a result of this comparison.

b. We tested the forecast for mathematical accuracy.

The forecast was mathematically accurate.

We were not engaged to, and did not, perform an examination, the objective of which would be the expression of an opinion on the accompanying prospective financial statements. Accordingly, we do not express an opinion on whether the prospective financial statements are presented in conformity with AICPA presentation guidelines or on whether the underlying assumptions provide a reasonable basis for the presentation. Had we performed additional procedures, other matters might have come to our attention that would have been reported to you. Furthermore, there will usually be differences between the forecasted and actual results, because events and circumstances frequently do not occur as expected, and those differences may be material. We have no responsibility to update this report for events and circumstances occurring after the date of this report.

This report is intended solely for the use of the boards of directors of Donnay Corporation and Clinkton Company and should not be used by anyone other than these parties.

The accountant must satisfy the requirement that the specified users take responsibility for the sufficiency of the procedures to be performed by doing one of the following:

- Comparing the procedures to be applied to the written requirements of the specified users.
- Discussing the procedures to be applied with an appropriate representative of the specified users.
- Reviewing relevant contracts with or correspondence from the specified users.

Exhibit 21–9 presents an example of a report on the use of agreed-upon procedures.

EXHIBIT 21–10

Example of Standard Compilation Report for a Forecast

Independent Accountant's Report

We have compiled the accompanying forecasted balance sheet, statements of income, retained earnings, and cash flows of Lumatta Company as of December 31, 2000, and for the year then ending, in accordance with standards established by the American Institute of Certified Public Accountants.

A compilation is limited to presenting, in the form of a forecast, information that is the representation of management and does not include evaluation of the support for the assumptions underlying the forecast. We have not examined the forecast and accordingly do not express an opinion or any other form of assurance on the accompanying statements or assumptions. Furthermore, there will usually be differences between the forecasted and actual results, because events and circumstances frequently do not occur as expected, and those differences may be material. We have no responsibility to update this report for events and circumstances occurring after the date of this report.

Compilation

Under SSAE No. 1, a practitioner is allowed to perform a compilation of prospective financial information. A compilation of prospective financial statements involves

- Assembling, to the extent necessary, the prospective financial statements based on the responsible party's assumptions.
- Performing the required compilation procedures, which include reading the prospective financial statements with their summaries of significant assumptions and accounting policies and considering whether they appear to be (1) presented in conformity with the guidelines shown in Table 21–5 and (2) not obviously inappropriate.
- Issuing a compilation report.

A practitioner should *not* issue a compilation report on prospective financial statements that excludes disclosure of the *summary of significant assumptions.* The accountant may issue a compilation report in which the *summary of significant accounting policies* has been omitted; however, an extra paragraph should be added to the report. Exhibit 21–10 provides an example of a compilation report for a forecast. Exhibit 21–11 presents an example of a compilation report for a financial projection. The major difference is the middle paragraph in the report on the projection, which limits the distribution of the report to specified users.

Accounting and Review Services

[LO 15]   Many nonpublic businesses do not need an audit of their financial statements. This typically occurs because the entity is small and the owner is involved in the day-to-day operations, there are no debts or regulations requiring an audit, or an audit may be too costly for the entity. However, these same entities may employ a CPA to assist with preparing their financial statements, tax returns, or other financial documents.

EXHIBIT 21–11

Example of a Standard Compilation Report for a Projection

Independent Accountant's Report

We have compiled the accompanying projected balance sheet, statements of income, retained earnings, and cash flows of Conroy Company as of December 31, 2000, and for the year then ending, in accordance with standards established by the American Institute of Certified Public Accountants.

The accompanying projection and this report were prepared for the Palatka National Bank for the purpose of negotiating a loan to expand Conroy Company's plant and should not be used by anyone other than these parties.

A compilation is limited to presenting, in the form of a projection, information that is the representation of management and does not include evaluation of the support for the assumptions underlying the projection. We have not examined the projection and accordingly do not express an opinion or any other form of assurance on the accompanying statements or assumptions. Furthermore, even if the loan is granted and the plant is expanded, there will usually be differences between the projected and actual results, because events and circumstances frequently do not occur as expected, and those differences may be material. We have no responsibility to update this report for events and circumstances occurring after the date of this report.

FIGURE 21–4

Assurance Levels for a Compilation, a Review, and an Audit

Until 1977 there was relatively little guidance on how to perform or report on engagements involving *unaudited* financial statements. As discussed in Chapter 20, the *1136 Tenants'* case involved auditors' liability for unaudited financial statements. One outcome of this case was the establishment of the Accounting and Review Services Committee by the AICPA. This committee was designated by the AICPA to issue Statements on Standards for Accounting and Review Services (SSARS) in connection with unaudited financial statements.

SSARS provide for two types of services: *compilation* of financial statements and *review* of financial statements. A compilation differs significantly from a review. The work done on compilation provides no assurance about the fair presentation of the financial statements. A review, on the other hand, provides the accountant with a reasonable basis for expressing limited assurance that no material modifications should be made to the financial statements. This can be compared to an audit, in which the auditor provides an opinion about whether the financial statements present fairly the financial position and results of operations of the entity. Figure 21–4 compares the assurance provided by an audit with the assurances provided by a review and a compilation.

These forms of service specifically apply to engagements for which the output of the service is a set of financial statements. An accountant may provide other types of services, such as preparing a working trial balance, assisting in adjusting the account books, consulting on accounting, tax, and similar matters, preparing tax returns, and providing various manual or automated bookkeeping or data processing services, without having to comply with the standards for compilations and reviews.

Compilation of Financial Statements

A *compilation* is defined as presenting, in the form of financial statements, information that is the representation of management or owners without undertaking to express any assurance on the statements. In conducting a compilation, the accountant must have the following knowledge about the entity:

- The accounting principles and practices of the industry in which the entity operates.
- A general understanding of the nature of the entity's business transactions, the form of its accounting records, the stated qualifications of its accounting personnel, the accounting basis on which the financial statements are to be presented, and the form and content of the financial statements.

Note that the accountant is not required to conduct any inquiries or to perform any procedures to verify or corroborate any information supplied by the client. In addition, the accountant should read the compiled financial statements to determine whether they are in appropriate form and free from obvious errors, such as mathematical or clerical mistakes or mistakes in the application of accounting principles. Because this service is usually provided to small companies that have few accounting personnel, the accountant is normally heavily involved with preparing the financial statements.

There are three forms of compilation reports:

- Compilation with full disclosure.
- Compilation that omits substantially all disclosures.
- Compilation when the accountant is not independent.

The report should be dated as of the completion of the compilation. Additionally, each page of the financial statements should be marked with a notation such as "See Accountant's Compilation Report."

Compilation with Full Disclosure

When the entity presents a set of financial statements that contain all necessary financial disclosures required by generally accepted accounting principles or another comprehensive basis of accounting, the accountant can issue what might be referred to as a standard compilation report. Exhibit 21–12 is an example of such a report.

E X H I B I T 21–12

Example of a Compilation Report with Full Disclosure

We have compiled the accompanying balance sheet of Learn Medical Services as of December 31, 2000, and the related statements of income, retained earnings, and cash flows for the year then ended, in accordance with Statements on Standards for Accounting and Review Services issued by the American Institute of Certified Public Accountants.

A compilation is limited to presenting in the form of financial statements information that is the representation of management. We have not audited or reviewed the accompanying financial statements and accordingly do not express an opinion or any other form of assurance on them.

E X H I B I T 21–13

Example of a Compilation Report That Omits Substantially All Disclosures

We have compiled the accompanying balance sheet of Loisel Company as of December 31, 2000, and the related statements of income and retained earnings for the year then ended, in accordance with Statements on Standards for Accounting and Review Services issued by the American Institute of Certified Public Accountants.

A compilation is limited to presenting, in the form of financial statements, information that is the representation of management. We have not audited or reviewed the accompanying financial statements and accordingly do not express an opinion or any other form of assurance on them.

Management has elected to omit substantially all of the disclosures and the statement of cash flows required by generally accepted accounting principles. If the omitted disclosures were included in the financial statements, they might influence the user's conclusions about the company's financial position, results of operations, and cash flows. Accordingly, these financial statements are not designed for those who are not informed about the matters.

Compilation That Omits Substantially All Disclosures

Sometimes an entity may request that the accountant compile financial statements without making all the necessary disclosures. Many times this request is made to minimize the cost of the engagement. The accountant can compile such financial statements so long as the omission is clearly indicated in the report and the client's intent is not to mislead the user. Exhibit 21–13 is an example of a compilation report in which financial disclosures have been omitted.

Compilation When the Accountant Is Not Independent

An accountant can perform a compilation engagement even though he or she is not independent of the entity. This is allowed by the Code of Professional Conduct. If the accountant is not independent, the lack of independence must be disclosed in the report. However, the reasons for the lack of independence should not be described. The following sentence is added as the last paragraph of the report when the accountant is not independent: "We are not independent with respect to Learn Medical Services."

Review of Financial Statements

A *review* is defined as the performance of inquiry and analytical procedures that provide the accountant with a reasonable basis for expressing *limited assurance* that *no material modifications* should be made to the statements in order for them to conform to generally accepted accounting principles or another comprehensive basis of accounting. In conducting a review, the accountant's work involves the following:

- Obtaining knowledge of the accounting principles and practices of the industry in which the entity operates and an understanding of the entity's business.
- Obtaining a general understanding of the entity's organization, its operating characteristics, and the nature of its assets, liabilities, revenues, and expenses (this would include general knowledge of the entity's production, distribution, and compensation methods, types of products and services, operating locations, and material transactions with related parties).
- Asking the entity's personnel about some of the items noted in Table 21–6.
- Performing analytical procedures to identify relationships and individual items that appear to be unusual (the process followed for conducting analytical procedures is similar to the one described for audits in Chapter 5).
- Reading the financial statements to determine if they conform to GAAP.
- Obtaining reports from other accountants, if any, who have audited or reviewed the financial statements or significant components thereof.
- Obtaining a representation letter from management (generally, the chief executive officer and chief financial officer should sign the representation letter).

Note that a review engagement does not require the accountant to obtain an understanding of internal control, test accounting records, or corroborate inquiries, as would normally be done on an audit. However, if the accountant becomes aware of information that is incorrect, incomplete, or misleading based on the work performed, he or she should perform any

TABLE 21–6	Examples of Inquiries Made during a Review Engagement

1. Inquiries concerning the client's accounting principles and practices.
2. Inquiries concerning the client's procedures for recording, classifying, and summarizing accounting transactions.
3. Inquiries concerning actions taken at stockholders', board of directors', and other committee meetings.
4. Inquiries of persons responsible for the financial statements concerning
   - Whether the statements are in accordance with GAAP.
   - Changes in the client's business activities or accounting principles.
   - Any exceptions concerning other analytical procedures.
   - Subsequent events having a material effect on the statements.

additional procedures necessary to provide limited assurance that no material modifications to the financial statements are required.

Review Report

A standard review report assumes that the financial statements are in accordance with generally accepted accounting principles or another comprehensive basis of accounting. This includes all necessary disclosures. The review report should be dated as of the completion of the accountant's inquiry and analytical procedures. Additionally, each page of the financial statements should contain a notation such as "See Accountant's Review Report." Exhibit 21–14 is an example of the standard review report.

Conditions That May Result in Modification of a Compilation or Review Report

When the accountant conducts a compilation or review, he or she may become aware of situations that require modification to the standard report. Two particular situations are (1) a departure from generally accepted accounting principles and (2) a going-concern uncertainty. If there is a departure from GAAP, the departure should be disclosed in a separate paragraph of the report. Exhibit 21–15 is an example of a review report modified for a departure from GAAP (italics indicate an added phrase).

EXHIBIT 21–14

Example of a Standard Review Report

We have reviewed the accompanying balance sheet of Sierra Company as of December 31, 2000, and the related statements of income, retained earnings, and cash flows for the year then ended, in accordance with Statements on Standards for Accounting and Review Services issued by the American Institute of Certified Public Accountants. All information included in these financial statements is the representation of the management of Sierra Company.

A review consists principally of inquiries of company personnel and analytical procedures applied to financial data. It is substantially less in scope than an audit in accordance with generally accepted auditing standards, the objective of which is the expression of an opinion regarding the financial statements taken as a whole. Accordingly, we do not express such an opinion.

Based on our review, we are not aware of any material modifications that should be made to the accompanying financial statements in order for them to be in conformity with generally accepted accounting principles.

EXHIBIT 21–15

Example of a Modified Review Report for a Departure from GAAP

[*Same wording as in the first and second paragraphs of the standard review report*]

Based on our review, *with the exception of the matter described in the following paragraph,* we are not aware of any material modifications that should be made to the accompanying financial statements in order for them to be in conformity with generally accepted accounting principles.

As disclosed in Note 4 to the financial statements, generally accepted accounting principles require that inventory cost consist of material, labor, and overhead. Management has informed us that the inventory of finished goods and work in process is stated in the accompanying financial statements at material and labor cost only, and that the effects of this departure from generally accepted accounting principles on financial position, results of operations, and cash flows have not been determined.

If the accountant believes that there are questions concerning the continuing existence of the entity, the accountant should add the following paragraph after the standard three paragraphs:

> The accompanying financial statements have been prepared assuming that the company will continue as a going concern. As discussed in Note 7 to the financial statements, the company has suffered recurring losses from operations and has a net capital deficiency that raises substantial doubt about its ability to continue as a going concern. Management's plans in regard to these matters are also described in Note 7. The financial statements do not include any adjustments that might result from the outcome of this uncertainty.

The process the accountant follows in determining whether the entity is a going concern is similar to the process used for an audit, discussed in Chapter 18.

REVIEW QUESTIONS

[LO 2] **21-1** Why did the public accounting profession issue attestation standards and, more recently, promote assurance services?

[1] **21-2** Define *assurance services*. Discuss why the definition focuses on decision making and information.

[2] **21-3** Identify and discuss the two sources for the demand for assurance services.

[3] **21-4** The Elliott Committee has developed six assurance services with significant market potential for CPA firms. What are these six services?

[4,5] **21-5** What are the risks of electronic commerce? What are the *WebTrust*[SM] Principles?

[7,8] **21-6** Why is ElderCare potentially a major service for CPA firms? What types of ElderCare services can a practitioner offer?

[12] **21-7** What are the major differences between attestation standards and generally accepted auditing standards?

[10,12] **21-8** Define an attestation engagement. List the two conditions that are necessary in order to perform an attestation engagement.

[11] **21-9** What types of engagements can be provided under the attestation standards? Give two examples of attestation engagements.

[13] **21-10** A practitioner can be engaged to examine management's assertion about the effectiveness of the entity's internal control and express an opinion either (1) directly on the effectiveness of the entity's internal control or (2) on management's assertion about the effectiveness of internal control. How does the practitioner's report differ in each case?

[13] **21-11** List two sets of criteria that can measure the effectiveness of internal control.

[14] **21-12** What are the two types of prospective financial statements? How do they differ from each other?

[14] **21-13** Prospective financial statements are for either general use or limited use. In what cases would prospective financial statements be for limited use?

[14]   21-14   What types of engagements are allowed for prospective financial statements?

[14]   21-15   List the four steps required in an examination of prospective financial statements. What circumstances might lead to a departure from a standard examination report?

[11]   21-16   How can the practitioner satisfy the requirement that specified users take responsibility for the adequacy of procedures performed on an agreed-upon procedures engagement?

[15]   21-17   Why were standards issued for engagements that involve unaudited financial statements?

[15]   21-18   What types of services can be performed under Statements on Standards for Accounting and Review Services?

[15]   21-19   What type of knowledge must an accountant possess about the entity in order to perform a compilation engagement? A review engagement?

[15]   21-20   What type of assurance is provided by the accountant when a review report is issued?

MULTIPLE–CHOICE QUESTIONS FROM CPA EXAMINATIONS

[2]   21–21*   An assurance report on information can provide assurance about the information's
   a. Reliability.
   b. Relevance.
   c. Timeliness.
   d. All of the above.

[5]   21–22*   Which of the following is not a *WebTrust*^SM Principle?
   a. Transaction integrity.
   b. Information protection.
   c. Digital certificate authorization.
   d. Business practices disclosure.

[9]   21–23*   Which of the following reasons best explains why a practitioner should obtain an engagement letter for an ElderCare engagement?
   a. Attestation standards require that the practitioner use an engagement letter.
   b. An engagement letter will specify the practitioner's responsibilities and duties on the engagement.
   c. It will provide absolute protection for the practitioner in the event of a lawsuit by the client.
   d. The practitioner will be able to shift the responsibility for non–assurance-related actions to others.

[8]   21–24*   Which of the following is not a type of ElderCare service?
   a. Assurance services.
   b. Consulting/facilitating services.
   c. Direct services.
   d. Systems design services.

---

*These questions were prepared by the author.

[10,11]   21-25   Which of the following professional services would be considered an attestation engagement?
  a. A management consulting engagement to provide IT advice to a client.
  b. An engagement to report on compliance with statutory requirements.
  c. An income tax engagement to prepare federal and state tax returns.
  d. Compilation of financial statements from a client's accounting records.

[14]   21-26   An accountant's compilation report on a financial forecast should include a statement that the
  a. Compilation does *not* include evaluation of the support of the assumptions underlying the forecast.
  b. Hypothetical assumptions used in the forecast are reasonable.
  c. Range of assumptions selected is one in which one end of the range is less likely to occur than the other.
  d. Prospective statements are limited to presenting, in the form of a forecast, information that is the accountant's representation.

[14]   21-27   An accountant may accept an engagement to apply agreed-upon procedures to prospective financial statements, provided that
  a. The prospective financial statements are also examined.
  b. Responsibility for the adequacy of the procedures performed is taken by the accountant.
  c. Negative assurance is expressed on the prospective financial statements taken as a whole.
  d. Distribution of the report is restricted to the specified users.

[14]   21-28   Which of the following statements concerning prospective financial statements is correct?
  a. Only a financial forecast would normally be appropriate for limited use.
  b. Only a financial projection would normally be appropriate for general use.
  c. Any type of prospective financial statement would normally be appropriate for limited use.
  d. Any type of prospective financial statement would normally be appropriate for general use.

[15]   21-29   Jones Retailing, a nonpublic entity, has asked Winters, CPA, to compile financial statements that omit substantially all disclosures required by generally accepted accounting principles. Winters may compile such financial statements, provided the
  a. Reason for omitting the disclosures is explained in the engagement letter and acknowledged in the management representation letter.
  b. Financial statements are prepared on a comprehensive basis of accounting other than generally accepted accounting principles.
  c. Distribution of the financial statements is restricted to internal use only.
  d. Omission is *not* undertaken to mislead the users of the financial statements and is properly disclosed in the accountant's report.

[15] 21-30 The standard report issued by an accountant after reviewing the financial statements of a nonpublic entity states that
a. A review includes assessing the accounting principles used and significant estimates made by management.
b. A review includes examining, on a test basis, evidence supporting the amounts and disclosures in the financial statements.
c. The accountant is *not* aware of any material modifications that should be made to the financial statements.
d. The accountant does *not* express an opinion or any other form of assurance on the financial statements.

[15] 21-31 When compiling the financial statements of a nonpublic entity, an accountant should
a. Review agreements with financial institutions for restrictions on cash balances.
b. Understand the accounting principles and practices of the entity's industry.
c. Inquire of key personnel concerning related parties and subsequent events.
d. Perform ratio analyses of the financial data of comparable prior periods.

[15] 21-32 Which of the following procedures is *not* usually performed by the accountant during a review engagement of a nonpublic entity?
a. Inquiry about actions taken at meetings of the board of directors that may affect the financial statements.
b. Issuance of a report stating that the review was performed in accordance with standards established in the AICPA.
c. Reading of the financial statements to determine if they conform with generally accepted accounting principles.
d. Communication of any material weaknesses discovered during the consideration of internal control.

[15] 21-33 Which of the following statements is correct concerning both an engagement to compile and an engagement to review a nonpublic entity's financial statements?
a. The accountant does *not* contemplate obtaining an understanding of internal control.
b. The accountant must be independent in fact and appearance.
c. The accountant expresses *no* assurance on the financial statements.
d. The accountant should obtain a written management representation letter.

[15] 21-34 Financial statements of a nonpublic entity that have been reviewed by an accountant should be accompanied by a report stating that
a. The scope of the inquiry and the analytical procedures performed by the accountant have *not* been restricted.
b. All information included in the financial statements is the representation of the management of the entity.
c. A review includes examining, on a test basis, evidence supporting the amounts and disclosures in the financial statements.
d. A review is greater in scope than a compilation, the objective of which is to present financial statements that are free of material misstatements.

[15]   **21-35**   During an engagement to review the financial statements of a non-public entity, an accountant becomes aware of a material departure from GAAP. If the accountant decides to modify the standard review report because management will *not* revise the financial statements, the accountant should

a. Express negative assurance on the accounting principles that do *not* conform with GAAP.

b. Disclose the departure from GAAP in a separate paragraph of the report.

c. Issue an adverse or an "except for" qualified opinion, depending on materiality.

d. Express positive assurance on the accounting principles that conform with GAAP.

PROBLEMS

[4,5,6]   **21-36**   Your client, Rhett Corporation, a local sporting goods company, has asked your firm for assistance in setting up its Web site. Eric Rhett, the CEO, is concerned that potential customers will be reluctant to place orders over the Internet to a relatively unknown entity. He recently heard about companies finding ways to provide assurance to customers about secure Web sites, and Rhett has asked to meet with you about this issue.

Required:
Prepare answers to each of the following questions that may be asked by Rhett.

a. Why are customers reluctant to engage in electronic commerce?

b. What type of assurance can your firm provide to his customers concerning the company's Web site?

c. What process will your firm follow in providing a *WebTrust*^{SM} assurance service for Rhett's Web site?

[7,8,9]   **27-37**   Mr. and Mrs. Greg Jun called your firm, Hillison & Reimer, in response to a brochure they received from Greg's elderly mother. The Juns reside in Ann Arbor, Michigan, while Greg's mother has retired to Tallahassee, Florida. In recent months, the Juns have become very concerned about Greg's mother and her ability to care for herself. On a number of occasions, Greg has received calls from his mother's friends expressing concern that she has not been eating properly and is not regularly taking her medicine for a heart condition.

Required:

a. Describe CPA ElderCare to the Juns, including the types of services that can be offered.

b. Because the Juns' concerns do not relate to areas of your expertise as a CPA, explain to them how you will be able to provide assurance on the care providers.

[13]   **21-38**   You have audited the financial statements of the Orange Grove Savings and Loan for the year ended December 31, 2000. Because this financial institution has assets greater than $200 million, its man-

agement is required to provide a report about the effectiveness of Orange Grove's internal control over financial reporting under the Federal Deposit Insurance Corporation Act of 1991. You have been engaged to examine management's report, which will be presented in a separate report. Management uses the definition of internal control based on the internal control framework set forth in SAS No. 55.

Required:

a. Prepare a draft of the examination report on management's report on the effectiveness of the S & L's internal control. Assume that there are no material weaknesses.
b. Draft the same report, except assume that the S & L has a material weakness in its loan application procedures for ensuring the adequacy of collateral for loans.

[14] 21-39 Your client, Cheaney Rental Properties, has engaged you to perform a compilation of its forecasted financial statements for a loan with the National Bank of Rockwood.

Required:

a. Describe the steps an accountant should complete when conducting a compilation of prospective financial statements.
b. Prepare a standard compilation report for Cheaney Rental Properties.

[14] 21-40 You are the manager of the examination engagement of the financial projection of Honey's Health Foods as of December 31, 2000, and for the year then ended. The audit senior, Currie, has prepared the following draft of the examination report:

> To the Board of Directors of Honey's Health Foods:
>
> We have examined the accompanying projected balance sheet and statements of income, retained earnings, and cash flows of Honey's Health Foods as of December 31, 2000, and for the year then ending. Our examination was made in accordance with standards for an examination of a projection and accordingly included such procedures as we considered necessary to evaluate the assumptions used by management.
>
> In our opinion, the accompanying forecast is presented in conformity with guidelines for presentation of a forecast established by the American Institute of Certified Public Accountants, and the underlying assumptions provide a reasonable basis for management's projection. However, there will usually be differences between the projected and actual results because events and circumstances frequently do not occur as expected, and those differences may be material.
>
> Waller & Felix, CPAs

Required:

Identify the deficiencies in Currie's draft of the examination report. Group the deficiencies by paragraph.

[15] 21-41 The following report was drafted on October 25, 2000, by Major, CPA, at the completion of an engagement to compile the financial statements of Ajax Company for the year ended September 30, 2000. Ajax is a nonpublic entity in which Major's child has a material direct financial interest. Ajax decided to omit substantially all

of the disclosures required by generally accepted accounting principles because the financial statements will be for management's use only. The statement of cash flows was also omitted because management does not believe it to be a useful financial statement.

> To the Board of Directors of Ajax Company:
>
> I have compiled the accompanying financial statements of Ajax Company as of September 30, 2000, and for the year then ended. I planned and performed the compilation to obtain limited assurance about whether the financial statements are free of material misstatements.
>
> A compilation is limited to presenting information in the form of financial statements. It is substantially less in scope than an audit in accordance with generally accepted auditing standards, the objective of which is the expression of an opinion regarding the financial statements taken as a whole. I have not audited the accompanying financial statements and accordingly do not express any opinion on them.
>
> Management has elected to omit substantially all of the disclosures required by generally accepted accounting principles. If the omitted disclosures were included in the financial statements, they might influence the user's conclusions about the company's financial position, results of operations, and changes in financial position.
>
> I am not independent with respect to Ajax Company. This lack of independence is due to my child's ownership of a material direct financial interest in Ajax Company.
>
> This report is intended solely for the information and use of the board of directors and management of Ajax Company and should not be used for any other purpose.
>
> Major, CPA

Required:
Identify the deficiencies contained in Major's report on the compiled financial statements. Group the deficiencies by paragraph where applicable. Do *not* redraft the report.

(AICPA, adapted)

[15]   21-42   This question consists of 13 items pertaining to possible deficiencies in an accountant's review report. Select the *best* answer for each item. Indicate your answers in the space provided.

Jordan & Stone, CPAs, audited the financial statements of Tech Company, a nonpublic entity, for the year ended December 31, 2000, and expressed an unqualified opinion. For the year ended December 31, 2001, Tech issued comparative financial statements. Jordan & Stone reviewed Tech's 2001 financial statements, and Kent, an assistant on the engagement, drafted the following accountant's review report. Land, the engagement supervisor, decided not to reissue the prior year's auditors' report but instructed Kent to include a separate paragraph in the current year's review report describing the responsibility assumed for the prior year's audited financial statements. This is an appropriate reporting procedure.

Land reviewed Kent's draft and indicated in the supervisor's review notes (shown following the accountant's review report) that there were several deficiencies in Kent's draft.

Accountant's Review Report

We have reviewed and audited the accompanying balance sheets of Tech Company as of December 31, 2001 and 2000, and the related statements of income, retained earnings, and cash flows for the years then ended, in accordance with Statements on Standards for Accounting and Review Services issued by the American Institute of Certified Public Accountants and generally accepted auditing standards. All information included in these financial statements is the representation of the management of Tech Company.

A review consists principally of inquiries of company personnel and analytical procedures applied to financial data. It is substantially less in scope than an audit in accordance with generally accepted auditing standards, the objective of which is the expression of an opinion regarding the financial statements taken as a whole.

Based on our review, we are not aware of any material modifications that should be made to the accompanying financial statements. Because of the inherent limitations of a review engagement, this report is intended for the information of management and should not be used for any other purpose.

The financial statements for the year ended December 31, 2000, were audited by us, and our report was dated March 2, 2001. We have no responsibility for updating that report for events and circumstances occurring after that date.

Jordan and Stone, CPAs
March 1, 2002

Required:
Items 1 through 13 represent deficiencies noted by Land. For each deficiency, indicate whether Land is correct (C) or incorrect (I) in the criticism of Kent's draft.

Supervisor's Review Notes	C or I
1. There should be *no* reference to the prior year's audited financial statements in the first (introductory) paragraph.	
2. All the current-year basic financial statements are *not* properly identified in the first (introductory) paragraph.	
3. There should be *no* reference to the American Institute of Certified Public Accountants in the first (introductory) paragraph.	
4. The accountant's review and audit responsibilities should follow management's responsibilities in the first (introductory) paragraph.	
5. There should be *no* comparison of the scope of a review to an audit in the second (scope) paragraph.	
6. Negative assurance should be expressed on the current year's reviewed financial statements in the second (scope) paragraph.	
7. There should be a statement that *no* opinion is expressed on the current year's financial statements in the second (scope) paragraph.	
8. There should be a reference to "conformity with generally accepted accounting principles" in the third paragraph.	
9. There should be *no* restriction on the distribution of the accountant's review report in the third paragraph.	
10. There should be *no* reference to "material modifications" in the third paragraph.	
11. There should be an indication of the type of opinion expressed on the prior year's audited financial statements in the fourth (separate) paragraph.	
12. There should be an indication that *no* auditing procedures were performed after the date of the report on the prior year's financial statements in the fourth (separate) paragraph.	
13. There should be *no* reference to "updating the prior year's auditor's report for events and circumstances occurring after that date" in the fourth (separate) paragraph.	

(AICPA, adapted)

DISCUSSION CASE

[11]   21-43   The accounting profession is concerned about whether companies are in compliance with various federal and state environmental laws and regulations and whether they have reported environmental liabilities in their financial statements. *Environmental auditing* typically refers to the process of assessing compliance with environmental laws and regulations, as well as compliance with company policies and procedures.* SSAE No. 3, "Compliance Attestation" (AT 500), al-

---

*Price Waterhouse LLP, *Progress on the Environmental Challenge: A Survey of Corporate America's Environmental Accounting and Management* (New York: Price Waterhouse LLP, 1994).

lows a practitioner to perform agreed-upon procedures to assist users in evaluating management's written assertions about (1) the entity's compliance with specified requirements, (2) the effectiveness of the entity's internal control over compliance, or (3) both.

Required:

a. Discuss how a practitioner would conduct an agreed-upon procedures engagement to evaluate an entity's written assertion that it was in compliance with its state's environmental laws and regulations.

b. Assume that this same entity maintained an internal control system that monitored the entity's compliance with its state's environmental laws and regulations. Discuss how a practitioner would evaluate the effectiveness of the entity's internal control over compliance.

INTERNET ASSIGNMENTS

[4,5,6]   **21–44**   The AICPA has developed an assurance service related to electronic commerce called CPA *WebTrust*^SM. Visit the AICPA's home page (www.aicpa.org) and examine their CPA *WebTrust*^SM seal.

Required:

a. List the assertions made by the management of the AICPA. Who "signed" the management report on assertions? What time period is covered by the report?

b. Examine the assurance report prepared by the AICPA's CPA firm. What is the name of the CPA firm?

   [4,5,6]   **21–45**   EarthWear has a number of competitors that sell goods over the Internet. Visit the home page for any two of EarthWear's competitors. For example, visit the home page for Timberland (www.timberland.com), L. L. Bean (www.llbean.com), or Land's End (www.landsend.com).

Required:

a. Determine if any of the sites selected provides any type of assurance on its electronic commerce. Note that you may have to prepare to order a product before any assurances are presented on the site.

b. If any of the sites provides assurance on electronic commerce, compare the assurances provided with the CPA *WebTrust*^SM Principles and Criteria.

[7,8,9]   **21–46**   ElderCare services may require that the practitioner prepare an inventory of services that are available in his or her community.

Required:

a. Search the Joint Commission on Accreditation of Healthcare Organizations' Web site (www.jcaho.org) to investigate the types of information that are available on health care organizations in your area.

b. Search the Internet to identify other resources and services that might be available in your area.

Glossary

A

accounting data The books of original entry, related accounting manuals, and records such as worksheets and spreadsheets that support amounts in the financial statements.

agreed-upon procedures Specific procedures performed on the subject matter of an assertion while a practitioner is engaged by a client to issue a report of findings.

allowance for sampling risk The uncertainty that results from sampling; the difference between the expected mean of the population and the tolerable deviation or misstatement.

analytical procedures Evaluations of financial information made by a study of plausible relationships among both financial and nonfinancial data.

analytical procedures risk The risk that analytical procedures and other relevant substantive tests will fail to detect material misstatements.

application controls Controls that apply to the processing of specific computer applications and are part of the computer programs used in the accounting system.

assertions Expressed or implied representations by management that are reflected in the financial statement components.

assurance services Independent professional services that improve the quality of information, or its context, for decision makers.

attestation A communication issued by a practitioner to express a conclusion about the reliability of an assertion that is the responsibility of another party.

attribute sampling Sampling used to estimate the proportion of a population that possesses a specified characteristic.

auditing A systematic process of (1) objectively obtaining and evaluating evidence regarding assertions about economic actions and events to ascertain the degree of correspondence between those assertions and established criteria and (2) communicating the results to interested users.

auditor business risk The auditor's exposure to financial loss or damage to his or her professional reputation.

audit procedures Specific acts performed as the auditor gathers evidence to determine if specific audit objectives are being met.

audit risk The risk that the auditor may unknowingly fail to appropriately modify his or her opinion on financial statements that are materially misstated.

audit sampling The application of an audit procedure to less than 100 percent of the items within an account or class of transactions for the purpose of evaluating some characteristic of the balance or class.

B

blank or zero balance confirmation A confirmation request on which the recipient fills in the amount or furnishes the information requested.

breach of contract Occurs when the client or auditor fails to meet the terms and obligations established in the contract (engagement letter).

C

classical variables sampling The use of normal distribution theory to estimate the dollar amount of misstatement for a class of transactions or an account balance.

client business risk The risk that an entity's business objectives will not be attained as a result of the external and internal factors, pressures, and forces brought to bear on the entity and, ultimately, the risk associated with the entity's survival and profitability.

compilation of financial statements The presentation, in the form of financial statements, of information that is the representation of management or owners without undertaking to express any assurance on the statements.

compliance audit An audit that determines the extent to which rules, policies, laws, covenants, or governmental regulations are being followed by the entity.

computer-assisted audit techniques Computer programs that allow auditors to test computer files and databases.

confirmation The process of obtaining and evaluating direct communication from a third party in response to a request for information about a particular item affecting financial statement assertions.

contingent liability An existing condition, situation, or set of circumstances involving uncertainty as to possible loss to an entity that will ultimately be resolved when some future event occurs or fails to occur.

control activities The policies and procedures ensuring that necessary actions are taken to address the risks involved in achieving the entity's objectives.

control environment The tone of an organization, which reflects the overall attitude and actions of the board of directors, management, and owners influencing the control consciousness of its people.

control risk The risk that material misstatements that could occur will not be prevented or detected by internal controls.

corroborating evidential matter Written and electronic information such as checks, records of electronic transfers, invoices, contracts, minutes, confirmations, and written representation; it also includes information obtained by the auditor through inquiry, observation, inspection, and physical examination.

D

detection risk The risk that the auditor will not detect a material misstatement that exists in the financial statements.

distributed data processing Data processing that includes decentralized computer functions and computer power.

dual dating The auditor's report is dual dated when a subsequent event occurs after completion of field work but before the financial statements are issued.

E

electronic (Internet) commerce Business transactions between individuals and organizations that occur without paper documents, using computers and telecommunications networks.

electronic data interchange The transmission of business transactions over telecommunications networks.

end-user computing User departments' development of their own computer applications and data files.

engagement letter A letter that formalizes the contract between the auditor and the client and outlines the responsibilities of both parties.

errors Unintentional misstatements or omissions of amounts or disclosures.

ethics A system or code of conduct based on moral duties and obligations that indicates how an individual should behave.

evidential matter Accounting data and all corroborating information that support the amounts included in the financial statements.

expected misstatement The amount of misstatement that the auditor believes exists in the population.

F

financial forecasts Prospective financial statements that present an entity's expected financial position, results of operations, and cash flows.

financial projections Prospective financial statements that present, given one or more hypothetical assumptions, an entity's expected financial position, results of operations, and cash flows.

forensic audit Auditing activities that focus on detecting or deterring a wide variety of fraudulent activities.

forensic auditors Auditors that are employed by corporations, government agencies, public accounting firms, and consulting and investigative services firms. They are trained in detecting, investigating, and deterring fraud and white-collar crime.

fraud Intentional misstatements that can be classified as fraudulent financial reporting and misappropriation of assets.

G

general controls Controls that relate to the overall information processing environment and have a pervasive effect on the entity's computer operations.

Generally Accepted Auditing Standards Measures of the quality of the auditor's performance.

gross negligence An extreme, flagrant, or reckless departure from professional standards of due care.

I

illegal acts   Violations of laws or government regulations.

imprest bank accounts   Bank accounts that contain a stipulated amount of money and are used for limited purposes.

information asymmetry   Refers to the fact that the manager generally has more information about the true financial position and results of operations of the entity than the absentee owner does.

inherent risk   The susceptibility of an assertion to material misstatement, assuming no related internal controls.

intelligent systems   Computer programs that contain the knowledge and decision processes of experts.

internal control   A process effected by an entity's board of directors, management, and other personnel that is designed to provide reasonable assurance regarding the achievement of objectives in the following categories: (1) effectiveness and efficiency of operations, (2) reliability of financial reporting, and (3) compliance with applicable laws and regulations.

K

kiting   The process of covering a cash shortage by transferring money from one bank account to another and recording the transactions improperly on the client's books.

L

lapping   The process of covering a cash shortage by applying cash from one customer's accounts receivable against another customer's accounts receivable.

legal letter   An audit inquiry sent to the client's attorneys in order to obtain or corroborate information about litigation, claims, and assessments.

low-balling   Intentional underbidding for an engagement intended to not only obtain the audit but also enter into lucrative management consulting services.

M

materiality   The magnitude of an omission or misstatement of accounting information that, in light of surrounding circumstances, makes it probable that the judgment of a reasonable person relying on the information would have been changed or influenced.

material weakness   A reportable condition in which the design or operation of one or more specific internal control components does not reduce to a relatively low level the risk that errors or fraud in amounts material to the financial statements being audited might occur and not be promptly detected by employees performing their normal assigned functions.

monetary-unit sampling   Attribute sampling techniques used to estimate the dollar amount of misstatement for a class of transactions or an account balance.

monitoring   The process that assesses the quality of internal control over time.

N

negative confirmation   A confirmation request to which the recipient responds only if the amount or information stated is incorrect.

nonsampling risk   The possibility that the auditor may use inappropriate audit procedures, fail to detect a misstatement when applying an audit procedure, or misinterpret an audit result.

nonstatistical sampling   Audit sampling that relies on the auditor's judgment to select the sample and evaluate the results for the purpose of reaching a conclusion about the population.

O

operational audit   The systematic review of an organization's activities, or a part of them, in relation to the efficient and effective use of resources.

ordinary negligence   An absence of reasonable or due care in the conduct of an engagement.

other comprehensive basis of accounting   Financial statements prepared under regulatory, tax, cash basis, or other definitive criteria having substantial support.

P

positive confirmation   A confirmation request to which the recipient responds whether or not he or she agrees with the amount or information stated.

privity   A party's contractual or fiduciary relationship with the accountant.

professionalism   The conduct, aims, or qualities that characterize or mark a profession or professional person.

professional skepticism An attitude that includes a questioning mind and a critical assessment of audit evidence. The auditor should not assume that management is either honest or dishonest.

projected misstatement The best estimate of the population mean based on the sample.

proof of cash A statement used to reconcile the cash receipts and disbursements recorded on the client's books with the cash deposited and disbursed from the client's bank account for a specified period.

Q

quality control A firm's organizational structure, policies, and procedures established to provide the firm with reasonable assurance of conforming to professional standards.

R

reasonable assurance A term that implies some risk that a material misstatement could be present in the financial statements without the auditor detecting it.

relevance of evidence Whether evidence relates to the specific audit objective being tested.

reliability of evidence The diagnosticity of evidence; that is, whether the type of evidence can be relied on to signal the true state of the assertion or audit objective.

reliance strategy The auditor's decision to rely on the entity's controls, test those controls, and reduce the direct tests of the financial statement accounts.

reportable conditions Significant deficiencies in the design or operation of internal control that could adversely affect the organization's ability to record, process, summarize, and report financial data consistent with management's assertions.

representation letter A letter that corroborates oral representations made to the auditor by management and documents the continued appropriateness of such representations.

review of financial statements The performance of inquiry and analytical procedures that give the accountant a reasonable basis for expressing limited assurance that no material modifications should be made to the statements in order for them to conform to GAAP.

risk assessment The identification, analysis, and management of risks relevant to the preparation of financial statements that are fairly presented in conformity with GAAP.

risk of assessing control risk too high The risk that the assessed level of control risk based on the sample is greater than the true operating effectiveness of the control structure policy or procedure.

risk of assessing control risk too low The risk that the assessed level of control risk based on the sample is less than the true operating effectiveness of the control structure policy or procedure.

risk of incorrect acceptance The risk that the sample supports the conclusion that the recorded account balance is not materially misstated when it is materially misstated.

risk of incorrect rejection The risk that the sample supports the conclusion that the recorded account balance is materially misstated when it is not materially misstated.

S

sampling risk The possibility that the sample drawn is not representative of the population and that, as a result, the auditor reaches an incorrect conclusion about the account balance or class of transactions based on the sample.

sampling unit The individual member of the population being sampled.

scope limitation A lack of evidence, such as an inability to conduct an audit procedure considered necessary.

Statements on Auditing Standards Interpretations of GAAS that are considered minimum standards of performance.

statistical sampling Sampling that uses the laws of probability to select and evaluate the results of an audit sample, thereby permitting the auditor to quantify the sampling risk for the purpose of reaching a conclusion about the population.

subsequent event An event or transaction that occurs after the balance sheet date but prior to the issuance of the financial statements and the auditor's report that may materially affect the financial statements.

substantive strategy The auditor's decision not to rely on the entity's controls and to directly audit the related financial statement accounts.

substantive tests Audit procedures performed to test material misstatements in an account balance, transaction class, or disclosure component of the financial statements.

substantive tests of transactions Tests to detect errors or fraud in individual transactions.

T

test of details risk   The allowable risk for failing to detect material misstatement that is not detected by internal controls, analytical procedures, or other relevant substantive tests.

tests of account balances   Tests that concentrate on the details of amounts contained in an account balance.

tests of controls   Procedures that evaluate the effectiveness of the design and operation of internal controls.

tolerable misstatement   The amount of the preliminary judgment about materiality that is allocated to a financial statement account.

tort   A wrongful act other than a breach of contract for which civil action may be taken.

U

upper limit on misstatement   The total of the projected misstatement plus the allowance for sampling risk.

W

working papers   The auditor's record of the work performed and the conclusions reached on the audit.

Index